Mastering

Modern European History

Palgrave Master Series

Accounting
Accounting Skills
Advanced English Language
Advanced Pure Mathematics
Arabic
Basic Management
Biology
British Politics
Business Communication
Business Environment
C Programming
C++ Programming
Chemistry
COBOL Programming
Communication
Computing
Counselling Skills
Counselling Theory
Customer Relations
Database Design
Delphi Programming
Desktop Publishing
e-Business
Economic and Social History
Economics
Electrical Engineering
Electronics
Employee Development
English Grammar
English Language
English Literature
Fashion Buying and Merchandising
  Management
Fashion Marketing
Fashion Styling
Financial Management
Geography
Global Information Systems
Globalization of Business

Human Resource Management
International Trade
Internet
Java
Language of Literature
Management Skills
Marketing Management
Mathematics
Microsoft Office
Microsoft Windows, Novell
  NetWare and UNIX
Modern British History
Modern European History
Modern German History
Modern United States History
Modern World History
The Novels of Jane Austen
Organisational Behaviour
Pascal and Delphi Programming
Personal Finance
Philosophy
Physics
Poetry
Practical Criticism
Psychology
Public Relations
Shakespeare
Social Welfare
Sociology
Statistics
Strategic Management
Systems Analysis and Design
Team Leadership
Theology
Twentieth-Century Russian History
Visual Basic
World Religions

www.palgravemasterseries.com

Palgrave Master Series

Series Standing Order ISBN 0–333–69343–4

(outside North America only)

You can receive future titles in this series as they are published by placing a standing order. Please contact your bookseller or, in case of difficulty, write to us at the address below with your name and address, the title of the series and the ISBN quoted above.

Customer Services Department, Macmillan Distribution Ltd
Houndmills, Basingstoke, Hampshire RG21 6XS, England

Mastering

Modern European History

Second edition

Stuart Miller

palgrave
macmillan

First edition 1988
Reprinted 8 times
Second edition 1997

First published 1988 by
PALGRAVE MACMILLAN

Palgrave Macmillan in the UK is an imprint of Macmillan Publishers Limited,
registered in England, company number 785998, of Houndmills, Basingstoke,
Hampshire RG21 6XS.

Palgrave Macmillan in the US is a division of St Martin's Press LLC,
175 Fifth Avenue, New York, NY 10010.

Palgrave Macmillan is the global academic imprint of the above companies
and has companies and representatives throughout the world.

Palgrave® and Macmillan® are registered trademarks in the United States,
the United Kingdom, Europe and other countries

ISBN-13: 978-0-333-64081-4
ISBN-10: 0-333-64081-0

This book is printed on paper suitable for recycling and made
from fully managed and sustained forest sources. Logging,
Pulping and manufacturing processes are expected to conform
to the environmental regulations of the country of origin.

A catalogue record for this book is available
from the British Library.

11
09

Printed in China

Contents

Illustrations

Maps

Figures

Preface to the second edition

Very few people could have predicted a chain of events since 1988 which resulted in the demise of the USSR and the fragmentation of eastern central Europe. Certainly there was a healthy note of anticipation in the original edition of this book but it has taken far more than routine tinkering to encompass the dramatic developments which have changed the political, social and economic structure of Europe and torn up the old map. This second edition is, however, revised and updated to late 1995. The book has been amended or developed in other respects as well while the opportunity allowed, but the essential structure and logic remain the same. Other areas of change are indicated in the revised preface.

There is very little originality of content in *Mastering Modern European History*. It is a textbook. There are no pretensions to it being anything other than that. The ideas and interpretations embodied in it have been carefully quarried from many of the books referred to in the Bibliography, which has been substantially extended. A general acknowledgement is owed to the various authors concerned. Any claim to originality on behalf of this book rests upon the fact that it displays three features:

1 *A logical synthesis* There is a middle way between the Marxist view that there are preordained patterns in historical development and Henry Ford's claim that 'History is just one damn thing after another' (a fraction more charitable than his dismissal of history as 'bunk'). I have avoided the 'There were 37 causes of the French Revolution' approach, although a system of enumeration is employed for the sake of convenience. Historical events are due usually to the interaction of several factors and do follow some sort of chronological pattern. I have used narrative accounts as a base where necessary, but in combination with considered analyses of the component factors contributing to events. A new chapter on 'European Decolonisation', which fills a glaring gap, is a good example of this balance.

2 *Coverage of controversy* The work of the historian is both the accumulation of data and its interpretation. History is a subject founded upon conflicts of interpretation and controversy. That is what makes it so intriguing. I have occasionally succumbed to the temptation to name-drop in addressing matters of interpretation, but it is important that attention should be drawn to the main issues of controversial interpretations. On many occasions I have deliberately taken time to review conflicting theories of causation and their interaction. This aspect of the book has been strengthened even more.

3 *Introduction to methodology* With most of the chapters there is associated a section including sample questions and documentary extracts and pictorial

material. That feature of the book has been considerably extended and would have been even more so if time and space had allowed. This reflects the increasing emphasis upon methodology and source material in school history teaching. The book has not been written as a series of answers to questions as is the way with some textbooks. However, that is simply because it would cause structural problems. In fact there is much to be said for encouraging students to regard History as a vast complex of questions as to what happened, why it happened and why it mattered. Most of the section and paragraph headings which I have used are easily equated with these fundamental questions.

The book is aimed at whoever finds it useful. It is intended primarily for people studying for a first examination in Modern European History. However, it also provides a valuable guide and synthesis for those people involved in study at a higher level. Within both of those categories I include the growing volume of mature and part-time students handicapped by their belated return to study and a pressing shortage of time. I would like to think that the book is also quite readable in its own right and should be attractive to the general reader.

My thanks are due to Suzannah Tipple of the publishers for her help and advice, and also to the various readers and advisers whose comments influenced the development of this new edition. I am always grateful to my wife Constance and children Gillian and David for their support and tolerance. The original edition was typed initially by Mrs Mary Milburn and the ordeal must have been so awful that I still acknowledge her invaluable contribution.

STUART MILLER

Acknowledgements

The author and publishers wish to thank the following who have kindly given permission for the use of copyright material:

Cardiff University Press for an extract from Etienne Dumont, *Souvenirs sur Mirabeau et sur les deux premières Assemblées Legislatives* (Paris, 1832). Translated by N. Temple and included in N. Temple, *The Road to 1789: From Reform to Revolution in France* (Cardiff, 1992).

Constable for an extract from *Isis* quoted in J.G. Legge, *Rhyme and Revolution in Germany* (Constable, 1918).

Curtis Brown Group Ltd on behalf of C.&T. Publications Ltd for a telegram to Harry Truman from Winston Churchill, 12 May 1945. Copyright C.&T. Publications.

David Campbell Publishers Ltd for an extract from Gustave Flaubert, *Sentimental Education* (1869), trans. Anthony Grossmith (Everyman's Library, 1941).

Edward Arnold for an extract from W.N. Medlicott and D.K. Caveney (eds), *Bismarck and Europe* (Edward Arnold, 1971).

Edward Arnold Ltd for an extract from *Nantes au XIXe Siècle* (Nantes, 1835) by Dr A. Guepin in S. Pollard and C. Holmes (eds), *Documents of European Economic History*, Vol. I *The Process of Industrialisation 1750–1870* (Edward Arnold, 1968).

Hamish Hamilton for an extract from J. Gunther, *Inside Europe* (Hamish Hamilton, 1936).

Harper for an extract from Metternich, *Memoirs III* (1881) quoted in Mack Walker, *Metternich's Europe 1813–1848* (Harper, 1968).

Harper Row for an extract from T.S. Hamerow (ed.), *The Age of Bismarck: Documents and Interpretations* (Harper Row, 1973).

Heinemann for an extract from Rear-Admiral P. Colomb *et al.*, *The Great War of 189-* (Heinemann, 1895).

Longman and Cassell for an extract from J. Hanoteau (ed.), *Memoirs of General de Caulaincourt, Duke of Vicenza 1812–1813* (Cassell, 1935) quoted in D.G. Wright, *Napoleon and Europe* (Longman, 1894).

Longman for an extract from *Correspondence de Napoleon 1er* quoted in D.G. Wright, *Napoleon and Europe* (Longman, 1986).

Longman for an extract from Marx, *Neue Rheinische Zeitung*, quoted in P. Jones, *The 1848 Revolutions* (Longman, 1981).

Longman for an extract from V. Russo, *Pensieri Politici* (1798), and an extract from C. Balbo, *Delle Speranze d'l'Italia* (1844), quoted in S.J. Woolf, *The Italian Risorgimento* (Longman, 1969).

Longman for extracts from D.G. Williamson, *Bismarck and Germany 1862–1890* (Longman, 1986).

Longman for extracts from J.W. Mason, *The Dissolution of the Austro-Hungarian Empire 1867–1918* (Longman, 1985).

Macmillan for an extract from N. Barber, *Seven Days of Freedom* (Macmillan, 1974).

Northern Examinations and Assessment Board, Oxford and Cambridge Schools Examination Board, University of Cambridge Local Examinations Syndicate and University of Oxford Delegacy of Local Examinations for questions from past examination papers.

Oxford University Press for an extract from E.R. Vincent (ed.), *G.C. Abba: The Diary of Garibaldi's Thousand* (OUP, 1962).

Oxford University Press for an extract from the Kaiser's speech, 15 February 1881, quoted in G.A. Kertesz (ed.), *Documents in the Political History of the European Continent 1815–1939* (OUP, 1968).

Oxford University Press for an extract from von Moltke, *Memoirs*, quoted in L. Albertini, *The Origins of the War of 1914* (OUP, 1957).

Pearson for an extract from H. Cadett, *The Boys' Book of Battles* (Pearson, 1903).

Penguin for an extract from R. Westall, *Children of the Blitz* (Penguin, 1985).

Princeton University Press for an extract from G.F. Kennan, *The Decline of Bismarck's European Order* (Princeton University Press, 1979).

Unwin Hyman Ltd for an extract from *'J'Accuse'* by Emile Zola, quoted in *The Dreyfus Case* by F.C. Conybeare (George Allen & Unwin, 1989).

A.P. Watt Ltd on behalf of The National Trust for Places of Historic Interest or Natural Beauty for an extract from Rudyard Kipling, 'The White Man's Burden' from *Rudyard Kipling's Verse: Definitive Edition* (Hodder & Stoughton, 1940).

Every effort has been made to trace all the copyright-holders, but if any have been inadvertently overlooked the publishers will be pleased to make the necessary arrangement at the first opportunity.

Note on names and distances

I have followed certain conventions in referring to some of the states of Europe. First of all, though, a point should be made about the title of the book. Britain played a vital role in European history in the nineteenth and twentieth centuries due to her economic leadership until 1914, her recurrent interventions into European international relations and her imperial activities. However, I have tended to treat her very much as 'the off-shore island' until the post-1945 period, when Britain became a member of various European organisations and especially the EEC. I have not attempted to deal with the internal affairs and development of Britain. For this latter, the reader is directed to the excellent volume *Mastering Modern British History* (Macmillan, 1989) by Norman Lowe. Also, after 1945 it becomes increasingly difficult – and of questionable value – to try to segregate European from World history. I hope that I have achieved a reason-able compromise.

Apart from this, I have faced the usual problems of nomenclature in dealing with a number of states, and I hope that the following explanation is adequate.

1 *The Habsburg Monarchy*   The problem arises because the Monarchy included provinces called Upper Austria and Lower Austria. Nevertheless, for convenience I have usually referred to 'Austria' or 'the Austrian Empire'. However, in a number of chapters where this policy could cause confusion I have used the titles 'Habsburg Monarchy' – and, after 1867, 'the Dual Monarchy' or 'Austria–Hungary: At least the First World War solved this problem!

2 *Germany*   Before 1871, I have occasionally employed the old-fashioned contemporary practice of talking of 'the Germanies'. The complexities of the membership of the German Confederation are explained in the relevant chapter.

3 *The Ottoman Empire*   Although I have used the proper title before 1914, I have often used the term 'Turkey' and spoken of 'the Turks', just as contemporaries did.

4 *Piedmont*   Technically, the correct title of the northernmost Italian kingdom was 'the Kingdom of Sardinia–Piedmont'. In keeping with usual practice, though, I have used the term 'Piedmont'.

5 *Russia*   In the period 1917–91, I have tended to employ a number of titles interchangeably. 'Russia', 'the Soviet Union', 'Soviet Russia' and the 'USSR' all refer to the same state. In fact, technically, 'the Russian Socialist Soviet Republic' was only one – albeit the greatest – of the units of the USSR. In 1991 the USSR ceased to exist and the Confederation of Independent States (CIS) came into being.

Any other confusion that might arise on this subject must be attributed entirely to my own carelessness.

6   *European Union*   I have used the name European Economic Community (EEC) until the 1980s. From then onwards the terms European Community (EC) and European Union (EU) became prevalent.

7   *Distances*   Finally I have standardised distances on the mile (1 kilometre = 0.62 miles or 8 kilometres = 5 miles).

Prologue: eighteenth-century Europe

Introduction

The French Revolution is usually seen as the start of an era and the chief event to which can be related the main threads of European history in the nineteenth century. In fact – like other 'turning points' in history – the 'Great Revolution' was as much the end of a period as the beginning. Equally, Napoleon Bonaparte – the heroic 'superman' of the new Romantics – was in many respects the last and greatest of the old-style enlightened despots and mercantilists. The eighteenth century was characterised by a number of features:

1 A stratified social system, with a rigid pattern of orders and groups surmounted by monarchy.
2 'Mercantilism' or the commitment of state power to intervention in the economy to promote growth.
3 The rise of manufacturing industries with a range of economic and social implications.
4 'Enlightened Despotism', especially in the twenty-five years before the Revolution, which involved a recognition that royal power should be exercised to some extent in the interest of the subjects.

The Ancien régime

Although there were very considerable variations between the states of western Europe, worthwhile generalisations can still be made:

(a) *The overwhelming predominance of peasant society*

Society was essentially rural, and peasants were by far the largest social group. However, the status and conditions of the peasantry varied considerably throughout the continent, and even within states. There was a great difference between the lives of the free peasantry and the *serfs*, who were virtually the property of the landowner. In general, serfdom was more prevalent in Russia despite the best intentions of Catherine II after her accession in 1762.

(b) *The influence of the aristocracy*

The aristocracy exercised very considerable local influence, officered the professional armies and monopolised the higher posts in the bureaucracies. They also had rights of jurisdiction and exemption from some types of taxation in every state other than Britain and the United Provinces. In addition, two other features are worth noting:

1 *Varying degrees of exclusiveness.*   In Britain, entry to the nobility was traditionally easier than elsewhere. Marriage and money could easily compensate for birth. As was once remarked in the sixteenth century: 'In England gentlemen be made good cheap'. The situation was very different as one moved eastwards. In France though, although the old military *'noblesse de l'epée'* was dominant this had been supplemented by a more recent *'noblesse de la robe'* drawn from prominent middle-class families. In general, there was a tendency in the eighteenth century for the nobility to respond to economic and social pressures by trying to assert its powers and privileges and restrict further creations.
2 *The range of status and wealth within the nobility.*   There could be a vast difference between the great magnates and the small squires of, say, Poland, Hungary and England. In France, there were 250,000 *'noblesse'* but only 4000 genuine courtiers with any access to the king. In Spain, there were 500,000 nobles but only a hundred or so real *'grandees'*, as opposed to the myriads of petty *'hidalgos'*.

(c) *The prevalence of monarchy*

There were vast differences between the size and structure of states. They ranged from large, centralised nation states like Britain and France, to the masses of very small principalities of Italy and 'the Germanies' – the 'swarm of gnats' as William Pitt the Younger called them – and the diverse collections of peoples and territories which made up states such as Prussia and Austria. The antique *Holy Roman Empire* ruled by the Habsburg dynasty and extending from northern Italy to the Netherlands and Prussia existed only in theory. All of these units were ruled, however, by some form of *hereditary monarchy*. No one seriously questioned this form of government. Only in the United Provinces was republicanism strong, and its decline as a state was a bad advertisement. It was also the lack of a strong monarchy which largely explained the ease with which Poland was partitioned between Prussia, Russia and Austria in the last quarter of the century. The strength of monarchy was further enhanced by the continuance of the traditional view of one's king as the 'father of his people', and the survival of the legend that monarchy was ordained by God and that kings, therefore, enjoyed a 'divine right'.

'Prosperity by compulsion'

Since the late seventeenth century at least, governments had displayed a tendency towards *'mercantilism'* – that is, towards the use of state power to build up economic wealth and, thereby, political and military might. The process was *cyclical*, because the acquired strength was in turn used to accumulate territory and colonies to expand the economy. The wars of the eighteenth century were *power struggles* between dynasties and rival empires rather than ideological disputes. In practice, mercantilism involved a welter of legislation and regulations designed to steer trade and production into definite channels by means of bounties, trade tariffs, prohibitions and monopolies. There was no clearly articulated theory of mercantilism, but in practice it suffered from two particular *weaknesses*.

(a) The sacrifice of the interests of the consumer

The main critic of the system was the Scottish economist *Adam Smith* who, in *The Wealth of Nations* (1776), insisted that 'consumption is the sole end and purpose of production'. Instead of countries specialising in their most efficient industries and trading freely in wider markets and at lower costs and prices, they were caught up in 'beggar-my-neighbour' policies of *protection* and *self-sufficiency*.

(b) The opposition of vested interests

Mercantilism – with its complex rules, and large bureaucracies – involved *corruption, mismanagement and conflicts of interest* between protected and preferred trades and those which were discriminated against. *Smuggling* – often on an enormous scale – was one response to tariffs and prohibitions. It was the attempts of the British government to tighten up the regulations against smuggling and evasion which stimulated the problems in the British North American colonies which led eventually to the *American War of Independence* in 1775. In general, it was the emerging middle classes (see below) which were most adversely affected by mercantilist restrictions.

Economic changes (see Fig. P.1)

The century saw considerable demographic growth. In Spain the population grew from 5 million in 1700 to 11 million in 1800. In Russia it grew from 18 million in 1725 to 27 million in 1780. In Europe as a whole it grew from 118 million in 1700 to 187 million in 1800. The reasons for this are not very clear. It was partly associated with a decline in the virulence of epidemic diseases. However, it was broadly related to a general increase in the *standard of living*.

(a) Improved food supplies

Better transport and some agricultural improvements reduced the recurrence of *shortage crises*. They did not totally disappear however. In the 1770s and 1780s there were serious shortages and price increases. The fact that agriculture was the biggest sector of employment as well meant that a bad harvest not only affected the prices and increases of the agricultural sector but also had dire effects on urban employment.

(b) Industrial development

The *Industrial Revolution* in Britain was not matched on the continent. There were some large-scale factories such as the Van Robais textile factory at Abbeville which employed 3000 workers. But the bulk of manufacturing production, even in Britain, was still by means of the *'domestic system'* and in small workshops although it was increasingly significantly.

(c) Urban growth

One aspect of this rising prosperity was the expansion of the towns. In fact, only in the

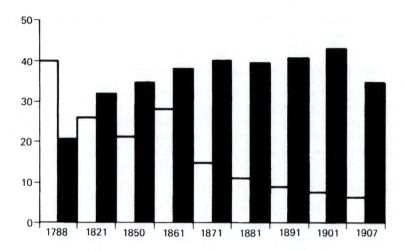

Fig. P.1 The relative contributions of agriculture and industry to the national product of the United Kingdom (1788–1907), percentages, the shaded columns represent industrial production

The changing proportions between the two sectors are typical of a developing economy. The pattern was most marked with the United Kingdom. What is also notable in this graph is the slackening off of growth in the *Edwardian* period. This reflects to some extent the tendency for the UK to derive more income from commercial and financial services.
Source: Based upon statistical information in C. Trebilcock, *The Industrialisation of the Continental Powers 1780–1914* (Longman, 1981).

United Provinces, England and part of Italy was it more than a fraction of the total. The population of Paris was only 2 per cent of the total French population. Even so, the towns were influential because of their – often considerable – municipal rights and privileges and the power of the class of great financiers, bankers and merchants. In fact, the middle class was largely made up not of manufacturers or merchants but of small property owners, office holders and professional people.

Enlightened despotism

Partly under the influence of the theories of intellectuals such as the Genevan, *Jean Jacques Rousseau* who, in his *Social Contract* (1762), argued that royal rule was a sort of two-way contract of duties, obligations and consultation between the monarchy and citizens, there was a tendency towards the use of monarchical power to improve the circumstances of the population. This was very marked in the last quarter of the century. Employing large bureaucracies and working to fairly coherent programmes a range of rulers such as Catherine II of Russia, Frederick the Great of Prussia and Joseph II of Austria pursued a range of social, legal, fiscal and administrative reforms. On the other hand, there were various threats and dangers associated with this.

(a) *The exaggeration of despotism*

Given populations made up largely of ignorant and superstitious peasants and in a situation where there were all sorts of obstacles arising from the existence of masses of local privileges and rights, bad communications and a diversity of dialects, the operation of enlightened government involved *centralisation* and the employment of a very strong hand which provoked resentment.

(b) *The resistance of conservative forces*

Joseph II's reign (1782–90) was an extreme example, but the *vested conservative interests* he antagonised existed all over Europe. His attempts to end their tax exemptions and abolish serfdom infuriated the aristocracy and the Magyar squires. Attempts to reduce the excessive influence and power of the Catholic Church provoked devout Catholics. Only the opportune death of Joseph II in 1790 removed the danger of a revolution in Hungary.

(c) *The theoretical implications*

The acceptance of the need to use power in the interests of the population also implied that it could be resisted rightfully if this 'contract' was broken. Revolutionaries could argue that they were acting in self-defence and as conservatives against misuse of royal power, and so attract support from moderates.

Conclusion: 'The world upside down'

When the defeated troops of General Cornwallis marched out of Yorktown in 1781 to the cynical strains of the most popular song of the day the situation was somewhat exaggerated. The American colonists – like the Magyar squires – were no social revolutionaries. Only on occasion in the eighteenth century – as in bread riots and the vicious Gordon Riots in London in 1780 – did the lower classes and the feared 'mob' emerge as a force to be reckoned with. However, once the ball of revolution has started to roll, it is not easy to control or stop. The *'Atlantic Revolution'* had started in North America in the prosperous British colonies. Thousands of European troops who had been involved in the war, including the young Marquis de Lafayette, returned to Europe after 1783. By the 1780s conditions were favourable to revolution in a number of European states. It was in France where all of the main ingredients were assembled at the ideal moment.

The French Revolution

Introduction

Whilst there were political disturbances elsewhere in Europe in the late eighteenth century the repercussions of a revolution in France upon the rest of the continent were bound to be immense. By the 1780s it was the most *populous* and *powerful state in Europe*, the most *centralised* and *culturally the most advanced*.

1.1   The causes of the French Revolution

The classic Marxist interpretation of the French Revolution sees it as a sharp break in history caused by the revolt of a developing bourgeois capitalist class against a reactionary and exclusive feudal nobility. More recent analyses emphasise the view that the Revolution was less to do with class conflict and more to do with a political struggle between groups within the same class and that social continuity was far more significant. This was 'blown off course' between 1792 and 1794 but equilibrium was restored and the élite was left in control.

(a)   'A tale of two economies'

The French economy saw considerable growth in the eighteenth century, and especially in the overseas trade sector which quadrupled in value. However, the mass of interior France was relatively unaffected by this and its development was handicapped by:

1   *The relatively primitive state of French financial institutions.* There was no central bank or stock exchange, and virtually no joint stock companies.
2   *The structural backwardness of manufacturing.* Thus, for instance, in 1789 when Britain had over 20,000 spinning jennies and over 200 Arkwright-type mills France had only a thousand and eight respectively.
3   *Low agricultural productivity.* Over 85 per cent of the population of 28 million in 1789 lived in the countryside. This population was sustained by a considerable expansion of output based on expanded acreage rather than productivity. The 'infernal circle of the fallow', the persistence of the *'servitudes collectives'* and inadequate communications blocked modernisation.
4   *Low levels of capital investment.* Unlike Britain there was not a flow of capital from land and trade into industry. The bourgeoisie invested in non-capitalist sectors,

and especially land. Ironically there were very good examples of enterprising noble capitalists, but they were exceptional.

(b) *Social division and cohesion*

The situation was not as clearcut as is traditionally portrayed:

1 *The aristocracy* was actually very extensive and open. There may have been up to 400,000 nobles. Far from being exclusive and a limited closed circle some 25 per cent of the nobility of 1789 were recently ennobled bourgeois. There were tensions within this class between the greater magnates, the provincial gentry and the new *'annoblis'* who had bought their way in. The main problem was that the poorer nobility had less access to employment in state office, the army or the church.
2 *The bourgeoisie* trebled in number between 1660 and 1789 but it was not a homogeneous class. The term could mean anything from a town dweller or any person of independent means up to an entrepreneur capitalist. In its higher reaches it was not easily distinguished from the nobility which it sought to join by purchase of land, government office or noble title. It is often more helpful to think in terms of *notables* rather than nobles.

(c) *'The language of liberty'*

The great *philosophes* who challenged the authority of the monarchy, aristocracy and church were equally ambiguous in terms of social origin and affiliation. Many of them were actually of noble birth. The greater proportion of the purchasers of *L'Encyclopédie* were nobles, officials, lawyers and clergymen. With the exception of Rousseau, who advocated the 'sovereignty of the people', they did not support the enlightenment of the masses. They had no clear programme of political change but they were hostile to Catholicism and to arbitrary absolutism. Their preference was for a society which gave far more recognition to ability, a *meritocracy*. The régime of Louis XVI represented an antique 'divine right' notion of monarchy, clericalism, censorship and despotism. In two directions the philosophes exercised more radical power than they might have wished:

1 *The scurrilous libelles* peddled by pamphleteers to an increasingly literate population were dominated by stories of sexual depravity in high places, especially of the Queen, but were loosely related to the ideas of the philosophes.
2 *The parlements used the 'language of liberty'* to attract popular support against the monarchy. Regional law courts dominated by the local provincial nobility claimed the right to block or delay the edicts of the monarchy. In 1788, for instance, the *parlement* of Rennes hypocritically dismissed royal power, 'man is born free . . . originally men are equal'.

1.2 The revolt of the nobility (February 1787–May 1789)

The French political scientist Alexis de Tocqueville observed: 'the most dangerous moment for a bad government is generally that in which it sets about reform'. The initial impetus came from the nobility.

(a) A *financial crisis*

The beginning of the end of the old régime came on 20 August 1786 when the comptroller general of finances, Calonne, told the King that the royal finances required radical reform. With a total revenue of 475 million livres there was an annual deficit of about 100 million livres. Some 50 per cent of total expenditure was devoted to servicing the existing debt. This situation had arisen because of:

1 *Defence costs.* A century of wars and recent involvement in the American War of Independence had raised defence costs to 25 per cent of the total. Despite attacks on the extravagance of court costs they amounted to only six per cent.
2 *Inadequate revenue.* The value of the land tax was reduced very much by aristocratic exemption and regional variations. The system of indirect taxation was cumbersome and regressive in its effects.

(b) A *socio-economic crisis*

The political crisis that resulted from the financial situation was unleashed in a country debilitated by deprivation and prey to brigandage and social disorder. The standard of living was deteriorating:

1 *The impact of a 30 per cent population growth* in an already densely populated state. Landholdings were more and more fragmented and pauperisation accelerated.
2 *Prices increased three times faster than wages* between the 1730s and 1789 as a result of the pressure of population on food supply.
3 *A recession* from the late 1770s intensified the secular trend. It was triggered by a collapse in wine prices in 1778, and falling agricultural incomes rapidly affected the local industries.
4 *Bad weather and the failed harvests* of the late 1780s aggravated these problems. In 1788 this culminated in the failure of the harvests in 27 of the 32 *généralités*. In 1787–9 unemployment rose by 50 per cent, wheat prices doubled and wage earners were devoting 80 per cent of their income to the purchase of bread. There was a common belief that this was the result of a speculative *'pacte de famine'* between the grain dealers and the government.

In the short term the lay and clerical aristocracy sought to meet falling rents and rising expenses by defending and reviving feudal rights, and by establishing a virtual monopoly of official posts to the detriment of the lesser notables and bourgeoisie.

(c) The *'defection of the army'*

At this critical moment morale in the army was at its lowest ebb:

1 *The catastrophic defeats of the Seven Years War* were followed by a whole series of embarrassing foreign policy setbacks associated with the alliance with Austria.
2 *The system of purchase of commissions* benefited the wealthy *annoblis* and worked against the old provincial gentry. In 1787 there was an attempt to enforce this system more rigorously.

The result was that many members of the poor provincial nobility were in the ranks of the revolutionaries. Half of the noble deputies at Versailles were army officers. Certainly the army was not to be relied upon in 1788–9.

(d) The revival of the Estates General

There had been half-hearted attempts to solve the problem of the royal finances since the 1760s. Clever accountancy by the Swiss financier Jacques Necker disguised its seriousness in 1781. Not until 1787 did Calonne produce a programme including a streamlined land tax without exemptions and collected by a new type of local assembly, a stamp duty on all official documents and measures to stimulate economic growth. However, for a well-organised and substantial group of nobles this was an opportunity not to reform absolutism but to dismantle it. Led by a *'Society of Thirty'*, portraying themselves as a 'patriot party' opposing royal extravagance and despotism and advocating the right of consent to taxation and the 'national interest', they worked through the *parlements* to force the modification of the proposals in 1788, and then a surrender by the King. He agreed to:

1   *The appointment of Necker* as finance minister. Although he was a charlatan he had a public image as the man who could solve the problem.
2   *The election of an Estates General.* This feudal institution had last met in 1614, and was seen by the aristocracy as a means of blocking royal power. Nation-wide every bailliage produced *cahiers de doleances*, or grievances, to go to the Estates General.

1.3   The revolution of the lawyers (5 May–27 June 1789)

The aristocracy would have been able to dominate the Estates General if it had had the same structure as in 1614. Then there were three separate assemblies – the clergy, the aristocracy and the commoners. Each had 300 representatives, but voting was by single agreed *corporate votes*, rather than by individuals. In fact a decision that the Estates General should meet in the form current in 1614 meant that many newly created nobles were relegated to the Third Estate so that a rift was created within the nobility.

(a) The 'doubling of the Third'

Before the elections took place the King and Necker gave way to demands that the commoners, who made up 97 per cent of the population, be given greater representation. In response to arguments such as those of the Abbé Sieyès in his *What is the Third Estate?* their delegates were doubled to 600.

(b) The creation of the National Assembly

In a bid for popularity and fear of rumours of '40,000 brigands' *en route* to Versailles, the King had virtually recognised the Third Estate as the real nation's voice. Its significance was recognised by Sieyès and reformist aristocrats like Mirabeau who got themselves elected to it. It was predominantly middle class, and 25 per cent of its members were lawyers. They were in favour not only of the reduction of royal power but also the elimination of privilege. Noble aspirations revealed in the *cahiers* show that a high proportion of them supported voting by head and peaceful transition towards a modernised constitutional monarchy. On 17 June the Third Estate adopted the title *'National Assembly'* and invited the other Estates to join them. On 20 June excluded from their normal hall, they met in a nearby tennis court (see Illus. 1.1) and swore not to dissolve until they had produced a constitution limiting the power of the government. The King gave way, and ordered the other delegates to join the National Assembly.

Illus. 1.1 The Tennis Court Oath, 20 June 1789 (Hulton Picture Library)

From a painting by Jacques Louis David

Source: The Life and Times of Robespierre (Hamlyn, 1968) p. 8.

a A number of people in this painting were not in reality at the oath-swearing ceremony. Why do you think this difference between art and reality might have occurred?

1.4 The revolt of the masses (14 July–5 October 1789)

Part of the background to this surrender was the mounting violence in Paris. Lower-class grievances had been reflected in the *'cahiers'* taken to the Estates General by the delegates. By summer though, Parisian *'sans-culottes'* – small workshop masters and workmen – were involved in destroying 40 of the 54 city customs barriers and in seizures of weapons. The situation was further aggravated by economic conditions and radical agitation developed. In early July, the breakdown of law and order was reflected in the establishment by the citizens of a city commune and a volunteer *National Guard* under Lafayette, the hero of the American War of Independence.

(a) *The spread of the revolution*

On 11 July, the replacement of Necker by one of the Queen's favourites seemed to confirm the rumour of an imminent royalist reaction with Swiss and German troops.

1 *The storming of the Bastille (14 July).* The assault on and capture of the old fortress prison by *sans-culottes* seeking gunpowder was a dramatic precedent for direct popular action. A symbol of royal power had been literally cast down. In most provincial towns now the lead of Paris was followed, and national guard units were established.
2 *The 'Great Fear'.* Necker was restored and the royal troops dispersed, but the fear of some sort of royal aristocratic counter-attack now set off a wave of peasant violence in late July and August. Food convoys were attacked, *châteaux* were burnt and records of leases and debts destroyed.

(b) *The end of the Ancien Régime*

Bloody anarchy seemed imminent. The royal army was not reliable. Drastic measures were needed to restore order.

1 *The 'Saint Bartholomew of privilege' (4 August).* This explains the astonishing scene at the National Assembly when a series of spokesmen ostentatiously discarded the dues and privileges of the aristocracy, clergy, town corporations and provinces.
2 *Declaration of the Rights of Man (26 August).* This was reinforced with a declaration of the *natural liberty and equality of all men* and a guarantee of individual rights. The abolition of privileges and restriction of royal power were confirmed. On the other hand, property was declared to be a 'sacred and inviolable right' and there was no talk of economic equality or 'one man, one vote'. The Assembly also provided for compensation for the privileges which had been surrendered.

(c) *The 'October Days'*

The ultimate subjugation of the monarchy took place on 5 October when a crowd of women (see Illus. 1.2) and 20,000 national guardsmen under Lafayette obliged the royal family to move from Versailles to Paris.

Illus. 1.2 Market women march on Versailles on 5 October 1789
Source: *Robespierre* (Paul Hamlyn, 1968).

Q In fact these very heavily armed and unshaven 'women' are very obviously men in disguise. Why do you think they chose to dress themselves in this way? Can you think of another significant revolutionary event accomplished by men in disguise?

1.5 Constitutional monarchy (October 1789–September 1792)

Now the self-styled *'Constituent Assembly'* set about devising a constitution. There were no republicans but there was a division between the so-called 'English Party' led by Mirabeau and the 'progressives' led by Sieyès over the powers to be given to the monarchy. The latter group succeeded in restricting the strength of the government.

(a) The Constitution of 1791

1 *The Legislative Assembly.* The idea of a two-chamber system was rejected. Deputies with a specified property qualification were to be elected by a limited electorate, the 'active' citizens, leaving a million and a half *passive' citizens* who did not meet the property qualification and possessed legal rights only.

2 *'The King of the French'.* The monarchy became a paid office of state. The King could appoint ministers but they would not have seats in the Assembly. He could only suspend legislation, and could not dissolve the Assembly.

(b) The measures of the Constituent Assembly

The old assembly continued until 1 October 1791, and in this reasonably peaceful interlude was active in reflecting the interests of its middle-class supporters.

1 *A new system of local government.* A new system of communes, with elected officials at every level, was established.

Illus. 1.3 The expropriation of the Church

From a contemporary broadsheet.

The idea of liquidating the national deficit by confiscating Church property came from Talleyrand. In this satire, fat ecclesiastics are being squashed in a press to squeeze out their wealth, and emerge, noticeably thinner, on the left.

2   *Legal tribunals.* The old *parlements* were abolished, and replaced with a new system of courts and elected judges.
3   *Free trade.* Weights and measures were standardised, and obstacles to trade like customs barriers, guild regulations and monopolies were abolished. Significantly, though, workers' unions were also prohibited (the *Le Chapelier* Law).
4   *The Civil Constitution of the Clergy* (see Illus. 1.3). In July 1790, the controversial step of making the clergy elected and paid officials of the state was taken. The Pope condemned this and the confiscation of church lands (from November 1789). In reality, steps such as these had become unavoidable in view of the fact that the Church was seen as a vital support of the monarchy and the ally of aristocratic privilege. On the other hand, these steps and the Pope's reaction were to have serious consequences in areas such as the ultra-Catholic La Vendée and placed all French clergymen in a terrible dilemma trapped between loyalty to their faith and loyalty to the state.
5   *The establishment of the assignat.* A new paper currency – the *assignat* – was introduced to try and stabilise the financial situation. In fact the consequences of this were to be catastrophic because the acceptability of paper money depends above all upon confidence in the stability of the state.

1.6 The overthrow of the monarchy (September 1792)

Chateaubriand remarked that 'The patricians began the Revolution, the plebeians completed it'. Between 1792 and 1794 a controlled revolution in the interests of the notables of France was blown wildly off course. The lull of 1790–1 was followed by the return of conditions favourable to extremism:

1 *Economic deterioration.* By January 1792, the *assignat* had fallen to 63 per cent of its face value. The price of sugar had trebled. Grain convoys were being attacked again. The *sans-culottes* and unemployed – the 'passive' citizens – looked to the Assembly for some sort of economic measures to control prices.

2 *The outbreak of war (April 1792).* The Legislative Assembly declared war on Russia and Austria in April with the approval of both revolutionary groups and the royalists. The King hoped that with defeat would come the collapse of the Revolution. The 'war party' in the Assembly – a group of deputies from the Bordeaux region known as the *Girondins* – believed war would rally patriotic support to the Revolution. In fact, a French invasion of Belgium was a fiasco and in August 1792 the Duke of Brunswick invaded France.

(a) The growth of republicanism

The Legislative Assembly was rather more extreme than its predecessor although the 'waverers' were still in a majority. The most radical group was the *Jacobins* (named after the old Paris monastery where they met), supporters of a centralised republic, extension of the vote to the 'passive' citizens and state economic controls. Led by Robespierre and Danton, they were prepared to ally with the *sans-culottes* to carry the revolution forward. The *Girondins*, led by Jacques Brissot, were a breakaway group from the Jacobins who were not prepared to go so far and were inclined towards a less centralised form of government. In fact republicanism was encouraged by:

1 *The 'flight to Varennes' (20–1 June 1791).* An attempted escape by the royal family, which simply put them on the same level as the growing tide of *émigrés* (130,000 in all) who rejected the Revolution.

2 *The Champs de Mars (July 1791).* Fuel was only added to the flames when national guardsmen fired on a pro-republican demonstration at the Champs de Mars, a meadow outside Paris.

3 *The Brunswick Manifesto (July 1792).* The King's cause was not helped at all by the Duke of Brunswick's threat to destroy Paris if the royal family was injured.

(b) 'The enemy is at the gates'

By August–September, the military situation was critical and the outcome of a mounting hysteria was:

1 *The Jacobin coup d'état (10 August 1792).* The Girondins' support lay in the provinces. The Jacobins controlled Paris through their links with the 48 Sectional Assemblies and their assumption of the leadership of the National Guard. On 10 August, they rallied their *sans-culotte* supporters to intimidate the Assembly into:

– The handing over of executive power to an emergency committee of six ministers under Danton.
– Agreeing to the *election of a National Convention* on a much wider franchise and its production of a new constitution.

2 *The September Massacres (2–4 September).* The imminent fall of Verdun triggered off the butchery – 'to frighten the enemy' – of over a thousand prisoners under the direction of a committee of a new revolutionary Commune, chaired by the Jacobin journalist Marat.

1.7 The popular revolution: democratic phase (September 1792–June 1793)

In the new National Convention which met on 21 September the old right was swept away. The Girondins now represented moderation and they were facing the 'Mountain' of Jacobins across a 'Plain' of uncommitted deputies.

(a) A revolutionary crusade

At Valmy on 20 September, a French army held its ground for the first time and now the offensive was taken. An Austrian defeat at *Jemappes* on 6 November was followed by the occupation of Belgium while other forces invaded Savoy and Nice and crossed the Rhine. The new tone of the war was represented by:

1 *The Edict of Fraternity (19 November 1792).* An appeal to the peoples of Europe to overthrow their rulers and an offer of French *'fraternity and assistance'*.
2 *A declaration of French 'natural frontiers'* on 31 January 1793 as extending to the Rhine, Alps and Pyrenees.
3 *Declaration of war* on Britain, Spain and the United Provinces on 1 February 1793.

British involvement was the result of the threat to commercial interests resulting from the opening of the Scheldt to trade by Dumouriez's invading forces. Then in March the Girondins' *protégé* general was defeated at Neerwinden, and defected to the Austrians.

(b) The concentration of power

Dumouriez's action gave the Jacobins a splendid advantage over the Girondins. The King had already been executed on 21 January on their insistence, and now they swept on towards a virtual wartime dictatorship:

1 *The concentration of the Convention's power* into the hands of the *Committees of Public Safety and General Security* in March. The Girondins reluctantly agreed to this emergency measure.
2 *The elimination of the Girondins (2 June 1793).* Identified with 'federalism' at a time when the military threat justified strong central control, they were very vulnerable. Backed by a 'revolutionary army' of *sans-culottes* on state pay of 40 *sous* a day, the Jacobins arrested the Girondins as 'disloyal deputies'.

Through their control of the committees of the Convention and with the Paris Commune under the extremist journalist Hébert, the Jacobins were now firmly in the saddle. On the other hand, how far they would ride depended upon their objectives, the circumstances and their allies. As for the latter Hébert and the so-called *Enragés* (or 'wild men') were far more radical in outlook than the Jacobins, and some sort of showdown was inevitable as soon as there was any attempt to slacken the pace of revolution. In the preceding events and in what was to follow the Jacobins had been pushed by radical forces as much as they had used them.

1.8 The popular revolution: dictatorship (June 1793–July 1794)

The transition towards dictatorship was accelerated by:

1 *'La Patrie en danger'*. France was threatened not only by foreign invasion but also by internal revolt. Especially in Brittany and La Vendée there were royalist- and clerical-led peasant uprisings. To these were added Girondin *'federalist'* revolts in the summer. At the peak, there were revolts in 60 out of 83 departments.
2 *Economic crisis.* By August 1793 the *assignat*'s value had fallen to 22 per cent. Shortages of food worsened by hoarding and speculation led to riots.
3 *Ideological commitment.* Although Robespierre has been portrayed as a bloodthirsty man of violence, in fact he was really an idealist strongly influenced by the theories of Jean Jacques Rousseau. He saw his role as the cleansing of the French community of its 'men of no virtue' before a true, equal democracy of small property owners could be established. This achievement of *'a single will'* required the temporary suspension of liberty and extreme executive action.

(a) *The Reign of Terror* (see Illus. 1.4)

There were really three aspects to the Terror:

1 *Economic controls.* To maintain the support of the *sans-culottes*, a degree of *social egalitarianism* was necessary:

   – The *Law of Maximum* (September 1793) fixed prices and wages.
   – A system of *food rationing* was introduced.

2 *Dechristianisation.* The Church was identifiable with counter-revolution and was a particular target of the atheist Hébertists. Clergy were persecuted, church property was seized and even a new *Republican calendar* was adopted. In fact Robespierre favoured the substitution of a new *'Cult of the Supreme Being'*, although his attempts to introduce this worsened a split with the Hébertists due to their support for even greater social equality.
3 *The purging of the 'enemies of the people'.* Altogether a total of some 18,000 people were executed in this period in a process accelerated by legislation which reduced the need for evidence or trial and the employment of roving Jacobin *'representatives en mission'* with wide powers. In fact, the death toll in this period is difficult to calculate. The figure given above depends upon official returns and refers to judicial executions. In Paris itself, even at the height of the bloodletting, the death rate was very modest compared to the horrors of Nazi Germany or Stalinist Russia in the twentieth century. Probably no more than 3000 victims mounted the steps of the guillotine in the very storm centre of the revolution. In addition, the death toll was bound to be exaggerated by ill-disposed enemies such as the British government and its agents and by French royalists in exile. On the other hand, the toll would be higher because it does not include the deaths in the virtual civil war in La Vendée or the tallies of overenthusiastic Jacobin agents like Fouché, Barras and the odious Carrier with his indiscriminate butcheries in Nantes.

Inevitably the pursuit of the 'single will' led the Jacobins to turn upon themselves. To the toll of royalists, Girondins, profiteers and others were added Hébert and the *Enragé* leaders in March 1794, because they wanted to go too far towards social revolution and the Dantonists in April because they wanted to end the Terror and the war.

Illus. 1.4 Robespierre's government (Hulton Picture Library)

From a popular print of 1794, 'Gouvernement de Robespierre', in the Bibliothèque Nationale.

Source: N. Hampson, *The First European Revolution 1775–1815* (Thames & Hudson, 1969), p. 116.

Q What is the message which the author of this cartoon wishes to convey? Who do you think would be likely to produce this sort of material?

(b) *The fall of Robespierre (27–8 July 1794)*

Robespierre was increasingly isolated. The execution of Hébert alienated the *sans-culottes*, fears of some sort of Hébertist social revolution still haunted the middle classes who looked for a restoration of order and stability and Robespierre's strange ideas about religion alienated good Catholics and atheists alike. These divisions were reflected in the Convention and in the two committees, with Robespierre trapped between the terrorists and the moderates. In fact, his end came when his colleagues began to fear that they would be next in line for 'purification' and when there was, in any case, less need for dictatorship and terrorism.

1 *The end of the immediate threat to security.* By the end of 1793, the back of the internal revolts had been broken and Rouen, Caen, Bordeaux and Toulon were all recaptured. Then in June 1794 a new revolutionary army built by Lazare Carnot opened up the route to Belgium and the United Provinces with a victory at Fleurus. France was fortunate in that Prussia and Austria were also preoccupied with the partition of Poland – between May 1792 and October 1795.

2 *An easing of the economic crisis.* By December 1793 the *assignat* was back up to 48 per cent of its face value and food supplies were eased. In fact by July 1794 it was proposed to cut workers' wages in Paris by 50 per cent.

The outcome was the *Coup de Thermidor* engineered by Fouché, Carnot and other Jacobins, and the execution of Robespierre and his supporters on 28 July.

1.9 The republic of the Thermidorians (July 1794–November 1799)

The Thermidorians were representative of the new class of republicans who had gained in wealth and property from the émigrés and the Church. They were opposed to the restoration of monarchy, but also the social republicanism of the Terror. A new constitution in 1795 reflected this. The electorate was reduced again by means of a property qualification. The legislature consisted of two chambers to balance each other. Executive power was in the hands of a five-man Directory. There were to be annual elections of a third of the legislature's members and one of the Directors. In fact, the period saw the development of a dangerous combination of the growing reputation of the military and the instability of the political system.

(a) *A war of annexations and conquest*

The new conscript armies of Carnot commanded by officers promoted on the basis of merit enjoyed considerable success.

1 *The end of the First Coalition (1795).* The Low Countries had been reoccupied by January 1795. At the same time there were French victories in the Rhineland, northern Italy and Spain. In March 1795 Prussia and Spain made peace by the Treaty of Basel which confirmed French possession of the left bank of the Rhine.

2 *The northern Italian campaign (Spring 1796–October 1797).* The young *General Bonaparte* enjoyed a string of remarkable victories over the Austrian and Sardinian forces. In October 1797 the Austrians agreed at Campo Formio to recognise the new Ligurian and Cisalpine Republics and French possession of Belgium and the left bank of the Rhine while receiving herself Venice and most of Venetia. In 1798 these puppet republics were joined by the Papal territories (the Roman Republic) and Switzerland (the Helvetian Republic).

3 *The War of the Second Coalition (1798–9).* In 1799 an alliance of Britain, Russia and Austria won a series of victories in northern Italy and the upper Rhine. However the coalition collapsed in October 1799 when Russia withdrew, turned against Britain over her insistence on the 'right of search' of ships at sea and joined Prussia, Sweden and Denmark in the anti-British *Armed Neutrality of the North*. The defeat of Austria by Bonaparte at Marengo and Moreau at Hohenlinden in 1800 was followed by the Treaty of Lunéville (1801), in which Austria recognised French puppet republics in Italy, Switzerland and the United Provinces and the annexation by France of all territory on the left bank of the Rhine.

(b) *Political instability*

By then there had been a dramatic change in the domestic régime in France. The Thermidorian republic had opened with the release of 80,000 suspects and a 'terror in reverse' against the Jacobins. From then on a deteriorating economic situation – the *assignat* finally collapsed in February 1796 and there were near famine conditions in some regions in 1795 – and the Directory's lack of any positive domestic policy led to recurrent Jacobin and royalist challenges to the régime:

1   *Prairial (May) 1795.* A second, and by far the most serious, *sans-culotte* insurrection of the year was suppressed by the army and followed by the purging and disarming of the *sans-culottes.*
2   *Vendémiaire (October) 1795.* A royalist revolt was broken by a 'whiff of grapeshot' aimed by the young Bonaparte.
3   The *'Conspiracy of the Equals' (May 1796).* A planned revolt by the socialist followers of Babeuf was nipped in the bud.
4   The *Coup de Fructidor (September 1797).* The rounding up and exiling of a group of generals and politicians – including *Carnot* – seeking a restoration of the monarchy.

1.10 The *coup de Brumaire* (1799)

There was a growing tendency to rely on the army to maintain order. When the elections of May 1799 indicated the possibility of another Jacobin revolt, a logical next step was to find a pliable military 'strong man' to keep order. Three members of the Directory – Sieyès, Roger-Ducos and Barras looked around for a *'sword'* to use. They selected Bonaparte, who had just returned in October 1799 from Egypt where he had abandoned an army which had been supposed to threaten the British territories in India. For a year he had been trapped after the destruction of his supporting fleet at Aboukir Bay by Nelson in August 1798. In November 1799 backed up by the plotters he used the threat of disorder as an excuse to disperse the two legislative councils with troops. Emergency powers were assumed by him, Sieyès and Roger-Ducos as consuls.

1.11 The consequences

The results of the Revolution were as paradoxical as many aspects of its origins and its course:

(a) *Serious economic decline*

Far from furthering the interests of capitalists the Revolution was a 'national catastrophe'. Instability caused by currency manipulation and war resulted in a sharp decline in manufacturing and commerce. The number of looms in Lyons fell from 12,000 in 1789 to 6,500 in 1802. The value of industrial production at Marseilles fell by 75 per cent after 1789. By 1797 only a tenth of the ocean going vessels of 1789 were available. By 1799 exports were down by 50 per cent. Associated with industrial decline was de-urbanisation. From 1789 to 1806 the population of Paris fell from 650,000 to 581,000. In the countryside the predominance of peasant subsistence agriculture was confirmed. Only the railway revolution of the mid-century would change all of this.

(b) *The continuity of the social order*

There was little change in the social élite:

1 *The nobility survived largely untouched.* The electoral lists compiled in 1802 suggest that most of the wealthiest landowners were still the nobility of the old régime. No more than 7 or 8 per cent had emigrated, and most of them returned.
2 *The bourgeoisie thrived* in the new meritocratic society and whatever their use of the language of universalism and the interests of all, it was the men of means and education who gained control in the communities of France. However, they were still as likely to invest in land and to buy their way into the nobility.
3 *The peasants had achieved their conservative objectives* by radical means. They had preserved themselves and their landholdings against the forces of feudalism and capitalism.

1.12 Conclusion

The consuls declared: 'The Revolution is established upon the principles which began it: it is ended.' In fact this was very premature. Bonaparte was an extremely ambitious man, described by Sieyès as 'a man who knows everything, wants everything and can do anything'. His drive towards power depended upon military success. The Peace of Amiens of 1802 with Britain could only be a temporary lull in the fighting. On the domestic front the Revolution had been more negative and destructive than positive in terms of the development of the institutions of France, these were now to be created in the image of the social order which had emerged from the Revolution.

Questions

1 Discuss the importance of: (a) the revolt of the privileged orders, and (b) popular discontent in bringing about the French Revolution of 1789. [OC]
2 How did Robespierre come to power, and why did he fall? [OC]
3 How far did economic difficulties affect the course of French politics 1789–99? [OX]
4 What part did each of the following play in the French Revolution?
   (a) the fall of the Bastille;
   (b) the abolition of feudal privilege;
   (c) the Declaration of the Rights of Man;
   (d) the March of the Women;
   (e) the Civil Constitution of the Clergy;
   (f) the flight to Varennes. [NEAB]
5 Give an account of events in France between the meeting of the States General in 1789 and the abolition of the monarchy in 1792. [NEAB]
6 Outline the grievances of the bourgeoisie and the peasantry in France in 1789. How, and with what success, were their grievances dealt with between May 1789 and September 1791? [NEAB]
7 Describe the part played during the French Revolution by:
   (a) Mirabeau, (b) Danton and (c) Robespierre. [CAM]
8 What impact did foreign wars have on the internal development of the Revolution in France between 1792 and 1799? [CAM]
9 Why did the French Revolution break out in 1789?
10 How effective was the Directory in dealing with the problems facing France between 1794 and 1799?
11 Study Sources A, B and C and then answer the questions which follow.

Source A: Economic growth and the French Revolution.

A study of comparative statistics makes it clear that in none of the decades immediately following the Revolution did our national prosperity make such rapid forward strides as in the two preceding it ...

At first sight it seems hard to account for this steady increase in the wealth of the country despite the as yet unremedied shortcomings of the administration and the obstacles with which industry still had to contend ... That France could prosper and grow rich, given the inequality of taxation, the vagaries of local laws, internal customs barriers, feudal rights, the trade corporations, the sales of offices, and all the rest, may well seem hardly credible. Yet the fact remains that the country did grow richer and living conditions improved throughout the land, and the reason was that though the machinery of government was ramshackle, ill regulated, inefficient, and though it tended to hinder rather than to further social progress, it had two redeeming features which sufficed to make it function and made for national prosperity. First, though the government was no longer despotic, it was still powerful and capable of maintaining order everywhere; and secondly, the nation possessed an upper class that was the freest, most enlightened of the day, and a social system under which every man could get rich if he set his mind to it, and keep intact the wealth he had acquired ...

In 1780 there could no longer be any talk of France's being on the downgrade; on the contrary, it seemed that no limit could be set to her advance. And it was now that theories of the perfectibility of man and continuous progress came into fashion. Dazzled by the prospect of a felicity undreamed of hitherto and now within their grasp, people were blind to the very real improvement that had taken place and were eager to precipitate events.

(a) According to this analysis, how is it possible to reconcile the growth of French national prosperity in the 1770s and 1780s with the outbreak of revolution in 1789 (lines 4–17)?
(b) In de Tocqueville's opinion how were the effects of a 'ramshackle, ill regulated and inefficient' machinery of government counteracted?
(c) To what extent would you agree with this explanation of the origins of the French Revolution?
(d) Why do you think that notions such as 'perfectibility' and 'continuous progress' should have such revolutionary implications?

Source: Alexis de Tocqueville, *The Old Régime and the French Revolution* (1856).

Source B: The renunciation of privileges.

But if the Assembly lost a lot of time in discussing the rights of man, it certainly made up for it during the night session of 4 August. Never was so much business accomplished in so short a time. What needed a year's care and attention was proposed, discussed, voted, decided by general acclamation. I do not know how many laws were decreed: the abolition of feudal dues, the abolition of the tithe, the abolition of provincial privileges, three matters which by themselves alone embraced a whole system of jurisprudence and policy, were decided, along with ten or twelve others, in less time than it takes in the English Parliament for the first reading of a bill of any importance. You could compare the assembly to a dying man who makes his will in haste, or to put it better, each liberally gave away that which did not belong to him, and took pride in being generous at the expense of others.

I witnessed this unexpected scene, which Sieyès and Mirabeau, and several other leading deputies, missed.

It began with a report on the unrest in the provinces, of châteaux in flames, gangs of bandits attacking the nobility and devastating the countryside. The duc d'Aiguillon, Noailles, and several others of the noble minority, after these accounts of disaster, declared that only a great act of generosity could calm the people, and that it was time to abandon odious privileges and let them feel the benefits of the revolution. I don't know what excitement got hold of the Assembly. There was no longer any calm or calculation. Each in turn proposed a sacrifice, brought a new offering to the altar of the fatherland, divested himself or divested others. There was no chance to reflect, object, ask for time; an emotional contagion seized their hearts. This renunciation of all privileges, this abandonment of so many rights that were a burden on the people, this multitude of sacrifices had an air of magnanimity which led one to forget the indecency of this impetuosity and haste so unsuitable in legislators. That night I saw good and brave deputies who cried for joy to see the work advanced so quickly, finding themselves swept along, minute by minute, on the wings of an enthusiasm which exceeded all their hopes. It is true that not everyone was carried along by the same sentiment. Many a one who felt ruined by a proposition which had just been carried unanimously, proposed another for revenge so as not to suffer alone; but the Assembly as a whole was not privy to the intentions of those who started the debate and they advanced their cause by profiting from this kind of general intoxication. The renunciation of provincial privileges was made by their respective deputies; those from Brittany were mandated to uphold theirs and were as a result more embarrassed than the rest; but they came forward as a group, and declared that they would use all their efforts with their constituents to get them to ratify the renunciation of privileges. This great and proud operation was necessary to make a political unit of a monarchy which was formed piecemeal by aggregating several states, each of which had preserved some ancient rights, some special privileges, a form of constitutional order which had to be destroyed to found a single body capable of receiving a single Constitution.

The next day people began to reflect on what had been done and there was discontent on all sides. Mirabeau and Sieyès, each for his own reasons, rightly condemned the follies of this enthusiasm. 'Just like the French', said the first, 'to spend an entire month arguing about syllables and in a night they overthrow all the ancient order of the monarchy.' The decree on tithes annoyed Sieyès more than all the rest. In the sessions which followed the deputies deluded themselves that they could amend and modify what had been most imprudent in these precipitate decrees; but it was not easy to retrace concessions which the people already regarded as indisputable rights. Sieyès made a speech that was vigorous and sound. He pointed out that to abolish the tithe without indemnity was to rob the clergy of their property and to enrich proprietors; because each having bought his property at a price which allowed for the tithe, found himself at a stroke enriched by a tenth as a free gift. It was this speech, which it was impossible to refute, that he ended with this phrase, so often quoted: 'They wish to be free, but they do not know how to be just.'

(a) According to Dumont what was the main stimulus to the renunciation of privileges (lines 13–18)?
(b) What factors accelerated the movement once it had started (lines 24–31)?
(c) What was the context of the remark by Sieyès that 'They wish to be free, but they do not know how to be just' (line 51)?
(d) In Dumont's view why was this process of renunciation necessary for the establishment of a unitary constitutional state (lines 46–49)?
(e) Judging from the contents of this extract what would you say where did the political sympathies of Dumont lie?

Source: Etienne Dumont, *Souvenirs sur Mirabeau et sur les deux premières Assemblées Législatives* (Paris, 1832). Translated by N. Temple and included in N. Temple, *The Road to 1789: From Reform to Revolution in France* (Cardiff, 1992). Dumont was a Genevan adviser to Mirabeau.

Source C: Saint-Just justifies the Terror.

Citizens, how could anyone delude himself that you are inhuman? Your Revolutionary Tribunal has condemned three hundred rogues to death within a year. Have the assizes in England slaughtered no one in that period? What about the kings of Europe, does anyone moan to them about pity? Oh, do not allow yourselves to become soft-hearted! Since the month of May last, our history is a lesson about the terrible extremities to which indulgence leads. In what period, Dumouriez had abandoned our conquests; patriots were being assassinated in Frankfurt; Custine had abandoned Mainz, the Palatinate and the banks of the Rhine; Calvados was in revolt; the Vendée was victorious; Lyon, Bordeaux, Marseilles and Toulon were in arms against the French people; Condé, Valenciennes and Le Quesnoy had capitulated; our armies were being beaten in the Pyrenees and around Mont Blanc, you were being betrayed by everyone and it seemed as if men headed the government and the armies only to destroy them and plunder the debris. The navy was bribed, the arsenals and ships were in ashes; the currency was undermined, our banks and industries were controlled by foreigners. Yet the greatest of our misfortunes was a certain fear of the concentration of authority necessary to save the state. Today there are still some who would like once again to break these weapons.

(a) Describe the functions and powers of the 'Revolutionary Tribunal' (lines 1–2).
(b) Who was Dumouriez (line 6)? What were the circumstances in which he 'had abandoned our conquests' (lines 6–15)?
(c) Explain 'the Vendée was victorious' (line 8).
(d) Why had 'Lyon, Bordeaux, Marseilles and Toulon [been] in arms against the French people' (lines 8–9)? What measures were taken to deal with these cities and with the other disasters outlined by Saint-Just?

Source: From a speech of 24 February 1794.

2 The Napoleonic era 1799–1815

Introduction

For the next fifteen years the fate of France and Europe was in the hands of the man described by Chateaubriand as the 'mightiest breath of life which ever animated human clay'. In his development and consolidation of the results of the Revolution there was much to justify Napoleon's claim to be its 'heir'. He also displayed many of the qualities of an old fashioned war lord. Louis Bergeron (*France under Napoleon*) states the paradox that 'Napoleon was both behind and ahead of his time, the last of the enlightened despots, and a prophet of the modern state'. Ironically his ultimate downfall was very much due to the very forces unleashed by the Revolution and accelerated by himself.

2.1 The 'man of destiny'

As a Corsican and an officer of artillery, an unfashionable branch of the army, Napoleon was somewhat handicapped. However he had qualities which compensated for his accent and calling.

(a) *The right connections*

During the Terror, his friendship with Robespierre's brother, together with his skilful use of artillery at Toulon in September 1793 helped him to the rank of brigadier. His cool head during the Vendémiaire revolt and friendship with Barras carried him to the next level. Marriage to Barras' ex-mistress Josephine de Beauharnais in October 1796 put him into the centre of fashionable circles, and got him the command of the 30,000 ragged men of the Army of Italy.

(b) *Image consciousness*

Napoleon had a great flair for publicity His published battle reports and *'ordres de jour'* attracted popular attention. He once remarked of propaganda that 'moral force wins more victories than mere numbers'. He was an excellent actor who could appeal to the deepest loyalties of his soldiers: 'The military are a free masonry and I am their grand master'.

(c) Military ability

He inherited from the Revolution a professional officer corps, a supply of veterans and systems of recruitment, tactics and formations. His main contribution to development was the self contained army corps. His ability consisted of an emphasis on logistical planning, brilliant improvisation when necessary and the most flexible use of the new conscript armies 'living off the land' as they moved. He was a consolidator rather than an innovator. He was also fortunate in having so many able subordinates, although the fact that he did not allow them to use their initiative enough would cost him dearly in the end.

(d) Ruthlessness

Napoleon was capable of humane gestures, but they never came between him and his ambition. He had little concern for the casualty rates of 30–40 per cent which resulted from the tactics of *toujours l'attaque*. After the carnage of one battle he once remarked 'one Paris night will replace them all'. He also deserted two armies in his life; one in Egypt in 1799 and one in Russia in 1812.

2.2 Napoleon's rise to power

Napoleon was also incredibly lucky. Not only did he slip past a couple of roving British frigates on his way back from his Egyptian disaster; he also happened to be the best man on hand when Sieyès was looking for some way of linking the army and the political system and, in particular, a popular military hero as a 'front' or a 'sword'. Not a man often given to making mistakes, Sieyès made one now. He chose Napoleon from a shortlist of three potentials.

Initially Sieyès produced a constitution in the cynical belief that 'authority must come from above and confidence from below'. A complex system of indirect elections would produce lists from which an unelected Senate would choose the legislators and two Consuls, one for foreign and one for internal affairs. From this basis Napoleon manipulated his way towards sole, unlimited executive power.

(a) First Consul (February 1800)

First of all he got Sieyès to agree to one of the Consuls being in office for four years and having considerable powers over appointment of officials and the initiation of legislation. He used these powers to restructure the police, departmental, local government and criminal courts systems so that he could control them in his own interests. The principle of election of officials was discarded even for local mayors.

(b) Consul for life (May 1802)

Napoleon's personal standing enhanced by the military victories of 1800 and the Treaty of Lunéville (see Section 1.9(a)) he conducted purges of the legislature, the army officer corps and surviving Jacobins. Then, with the rejoicing at the Peace of Amiens in the background, he converted his office into a life tenure and amended the constitution to give himself virtually dictatorial powers over the electoral and legislative systems. A plebiscite of $3\frac{1}{2}$ million votes to 8000 ratified the extension of his term of office.

(c) Emperor of the French (May 1804)

In 1803, war broke out with Britain again and a plot by the royalist Georges Cadoudal to kidnap Napoleon with the assistance of British agents was revealed. This was an excuse for another purge of royalists and Jacobins and the Senate also offered Napoleon the status of *hereditary emperor* in the interests of national stability. In December 1804 he crowned himself at Notre Dame in the presence of Pope Pius VII.

2.3 The civil foundations of the Empire

Largely with the advice of his Council of State, a non-political body of experts, Napoleon introduced significant reforms which built upon the Revolution to some extent. However, the emphasis was very much upon executive rule from above, management through an élite and the restoration of order rather than popular sovereignty.

(a) Central, departmental and local government

The key principles were uniformity, devolution of authority from above and a well-established hierarchy of status, command and reward.

1   *The Constitution of Year VIII* affirmed rights of property and individual liberty. However, in reality there was little scope for democratic accountability:

   – A system of indirect 'selection by tenths' filtered out real democracy and favoured an élite of Notables. The Constitution of Year X increased the 'filtering up' process and introduced a property qualification for public elections.
   – There was a separation of powers between an advisory Tribunate, a *Corps Legislatif* with legislative but not debating powers and a Senate with constitutional amendment powers. The membership of the first two bodies was selected by the Senate whose members were, in turn, largely chosen by a combination of nomination by the First Consul and cooption.

2   The *'little emperors'* governed at regional and local level.

   – *Prefects* governed 98 departments created in 1800. They had considerable powers but were appointed by the First Consul.
   – At local level there were 402 *arrondisements*, subdivided into *cantons*. All of the mayors, deputies and police commissioners were appointed by the First Consul.

(b) Financial and economic management

One of the worst features of the Revolutionary régimes was fiscal and monetary policy. In fact the Directory had already started to take this in hand, but Napoleon built upon their efforts to great effect.

1   *Reorganisation of taxation and tax collection.* The main direct taxes continued to be on land and income taxes but by 1813 71 per cent of state revenue came from indirect taxes and excise duties. These included a tax on salt from 1806 and a state monopoly of tobacco from 1810 and a whole range of consumer duties from 1804. The system of collection and accountability was considerably improved. However, even with the increases in taxation and improved collection military expenses

resulted in a permanent deficit which was balanced only by means of loot, levies and indemnities from conquered states (the *domaine extraordinaire*).

2   *Financial reforms* included:
   – the establishment of a sound bi-metallic currency from 1803, the so called *'franc de germinal'*.
   – the establishment of the *Bank of France* in 1800. It was given a monopoly of note issue in 1802.

3   *Labour and prices controls.* Napoleon's ideas on economics were rather old fashioned anyhow, but in the later war years he turned more and more to market restrictions. He once considered restoring the guilds. The ban on trade unions remained (see Section 1.5(b)(iii)) and passbooks were introduced to limit workers' freedom of movement. The export of corn was firmly restricted and maximum prices for bread and flour were introduced in 1812. By then, however, he was under serious military challenge, and his luck with the weather and harvests had come to an end in 1811. He was well aware that hunger was a greater threat than the desire for liberty.

(c)   *Legal and educational reforms*

1   *The Code Napoleon*, the Civil Code completed in 1804, was a recapitulation of 36 laws passed between 1801–3. It was followed by Criminal, Penal and Commercial Codes and Codes of Civil and Criminal Procedure. The Civil Code replaced the 360 local codes of the Ancien Régime.
   – It guaranteed equality, property rights and the rights of the citizen and also the Revolutionary principle of 'partage' or the subdivision of estates between male heirs. It gave legal title to the earlier sales of émigré and church property.
   – It reflected Napoleon's conservative and authoritarian views. The old paternal authority within the family was restored and women's rights were circumscribed (Napoleon once remarked that 'women should stick to knitting'). Published in a small compact edition in 1810 it became a model for legal rationalisation in many other states of Europe.

2   *The establishment of the system of lycées* also reflected the emphasis on élitism and support for authority. These selective secondary schools were designed to train the future military and civil leaders of France. A third of the scholarships were reserved for the sons of soldiers and civil servants. The curriculum in secondary education was standardised by the introduction of the *baccalaureate* in 1809. Equally the establishment of the regulatory *University of France* in 1808 represented control of post secondary education. Napoleon had little interest in the education of the poor or of women.

(d)   *The Concordat*

Napoleon was broad minded about religion: 'if I were governing Jews I would restore the Temple of Solomon'. However, he realised the value of organised religion in maintaining social order: 'The people must have a religion and that religion must be in the hands of the government.' The *Concordat* and *Organic Laws* were the result:

1   Roman Catholicism was recognised, but only as 'the religion of the vast majority of French citizens'.
2   Possession of former church lands was guaranteed to purchasers.
3   The state was to be responsible for the payment of clerical stipends.
4   Bishops were to take an oath of loyalty to the state before they could take up their posts.

In this way Napoleon managed to reconcile Catholics to the régime and seriously weaken the royalist cause. On the other hand, his attempt to control the Church through 'prefects in purple' and 'mayors in black' was not successful. The bishops sided with the Pope when Rome was annexed in 1809 and he became a French prisoner and they refused to agree to the possibility of investiture by French metropolitans. In the long term the hierarchy became strongly *ultramontanist*, looking towards the Vatican for leadership in matters of policy even though this could involve conflict with the views of the French civil authorities.

(e) *Rehierarchisation*

Underpinning this régime was an élite of Notables the vast bulk of whom were bourgeois beneficiaries of the French Revolution who rallied to Napoleon and who were blended with the older nobility to form a new hierarchy.

1   *Promotion by merit* was especially marked in the army. For instance, a study of the officers of company grade appointed in 1800 and still in service in 1814 demonstrated that 5.5 per cent were nobles, 22.1 per cent were the sons of commoner landowners and the rest were from bourgeois or rural family backgrounds. The vast bulk of imperial generals were from bourgeois families.
2   *The creation of titles and honours.* In 1802 Napoleon established the Order of the *Legion of Honour.* By 1814 it had 32,000 members, of whom 95 per cent were soldiers. In 1804 and 1806 he established princedoms and ducal grand fiefs but the full panoply of barons and chevaliers came in 1808. Titles were used to reward military and civilian service. Of the new nobility, only 22.5 per cent were from the old.
3   *Tenure of purchased émigré and church lands* was confirmed and to this were added donations of lands and rents from the conquered territories to support the newly ennobled groups.

It has been estimated that a total of 75,000 notables made up this new élite.

2.4   The renewal of war (1803–7)

Both Britain and Napoleon saw the Peace of Amiens as a mere truce. Napoleon remarked: 'In the existing situation every treaty of peace means no more to me than a brief armistice.' Both sides infringed the terms of the agreement, although Britain finally broke it by refusing to surrender Malta.

(a) *The war at sea*

Initially it was a war between France and Britain only. Napoleon planned an invasion with 100,000 troops and 800 barges assembled at Boulogne. However, his plan to decoy away the British fleet and use combined Franco-Spanish fleets to escort the invasion came to grief on 21 October 1805 when Nelson destroyed the joint force under Villeneuve in the 'pell mell battle' of Trafalgar.

(b) *The creation of the Third Coalition*

Britain alone could not follow up the victory with a land offensive, but a new coalition formed as grievances accumulated:

1   *The Anglo-Russian Convention (April 1803).* The young Tsar Alexander sought to restore Poland under Russian suzerainty and was disturbed by the growing French influence in central Europe and Napoleon's seizure of Hanover.
2   *Agreement with Austria (August 1805).* Austrian interests were directly challenged by Napoleon's new alliances with Bavaria, Baden and Würtemberg, his annexation of Genoa and acceptance of the crown of the new Kingdom of Italy in March. In September, Austrian forces invaded Bavaria.

(c)   The campaign of 1805

The Army of England, restyled the Grand Army, left Boulogne in August. It moved so quickly that in October the Austrian army was caught and defeated at Ulm in Bavaria before linking with the Russian forces. Having occupied Vienna, Napoleon then went on to inflict a crushing defeat on the Austro-Russian forces under Tsar Alexander at Austerlitz on the 1 December. By the Peace of Pressburg, Austria surrendered Venetia and the Tyrol and recognised Baden, Bavaria and Würtemberg as independent kingdoms.

(d)   The campaign of 1806–7

Russia had remained neutral although irritated by Napoleon's activities in Germany. However Frederick William III was driven to war by Napoleon's forced surrender of the Duchy of Cleves and rumours that he was about to restore Hanover to Britain, having just forced Prussia to exchange Neuchâtel and Ansbach for it:

1   *The collapse of Prussia.* Prussian forces were mobilised in August but they were slow moving, inefficient and hidebound by memories of a glorious past. They were defeated at Jena and Auerstadt. Prussia then virtually collapsed before the French invaders.
2   *The Pacification of Tilsit (July 1807).* The Russian army was defeated in February 1807 at Eylau then in June at Friedland. The Tsar, somewhat attracted by Napoleon's character, reached an agreement on the basis of the division of Europe into two rather vague spheres of influence between himself and Napoleon. Prussia lost a third of her territories and her Polish possessions were reconstituted as the Grand Duchy of Warsaw. Britain was to be forced to recognise the 'freedom of the seas', and indeed briefly Russia and Britain were technically at war over the issue.

2.5   The Grand Empire

By 1807, Napoleon was at his peak and could concentrate on consolidation of his conquests and mobilisation of his full resources against Britain.
There were two elements to this:

1   *The Continental System* or economic blockade of Britain.
2   The rationalisations of the *Grand Empire*.

2.6   The Continental System

Napoleon was an old-fashioned protectionist. However, his military dilemma was the key to the Continental System. His power was land based: 'Napoleon was master in

Europe, but he was also a prisoner there' (Bertrand de Jouvenel). The concept was based on old mercantilist economic theory and was just one more episode in the long process of maritime conflict and commercial rivalry between France and Britain. As early as 1793 the Jacobin Barère had suggested: 'Let us decree a solemn navigation act and the isle of shopkeepers will be ruined.'

(a) The nature of the Continental System

Albert Sorel once described it as a 'two-trigger machine'. It had two purposes:

1 A *'war machine'* designed to 'conquer Britain by excess'. By cutting the export trade of Britain to Europe, some 42 per cent of her total in 1807, Napoleon sought to drain her bullion reserves and produce inflation.
2 A *'market design'* to create a new system of markets for imperial and European merchants and manufacturers and to seek to replace Britain as 'the First Industrial Nation'.

The Berlin Decree (1806) and the Decrees of Fountainebleau and Milan (1807) closed the European coastline to British trade.

(b) Assessment of the Continental System

In effect this was a 'self blockade' or boycott. Between 1808–11 it was reasonably successful and Britain was reduced to the depths of an economic recession compounded by a bad harvest and, in 1812, a war with the USA over British interference with neutral shipping. However, the attempt failed:

1 *It was based on key assumptions.*

   – It required that France should maintain her superiority on land and over her satellite partners. Napoleon never had the naval means to direct the blockade against Britain on the high seas. Indeed Britain retaliated with the *Orders in Council* which required all neutral vessels to pay a duty to trade with the Continent, and the 1807 decrees by Napoleon were designed to threaten any neutrals who did pay with confiscation of vessels and cargo.
   – It envisaged imperial and European self sufficiency, but the dominance and protection of the interests of French producers meant that it was very much a 'one-way common market' which would never produce an integrated European economy.

2 *It was never fully enforced.*

   – There were not enough troops and customs officials to enforce it, and the latter were notoriously corrupt. The European coastline was never totally closed off. In the case of Spain, Portugal and Russia the attempt to enforce closure produced resentment against Napoleon's influence.
   – *Smuggling* was so significant and well organised that it was even possible to insure against seizure. France and her allies were put under pressure themselves, and there was considerable unemployment in 1811–13. The French army, in fact, was increasingly equipped with goods smuggled in from Britain.
   – *Licenses* to trade were being sold by Napoleon as early as 1809 in order to relieve glutted wine and grain stocks. This produced the ironic situation in 1810–11 that Napoleon passed over the chance to starve Britain and allowed grain shipments in return for bullion.
   – *Britain found new markets* in South America, the Near East and the Baltic.

In fact not until 1826 did French foreign trade regain the level of 1787. The blockade just undermined the maritime sector even more. On the other hand, there was a marked concentration of trade and industry in the Rhine corridor as a result of its distorting effects. Strasbourg, for instance, handled a third of the French import and export trade during the blockade period.

Fundamentally what Napoleon needed and never achieved was supremacy at sea.

2.7 The organisation of the Grand Empire

Napoleon had no master plan. David Thomson says of the Grand Empire that it was: 'the transient product of lightning war and diplomatic coups, hastily bound together by dynastic settlements of thrones upon members of his family and by the emergency devices of the Continental System ... Opportunism and expediency haunted it throughout.'

(a) *Territorial restructuring and frontier revision* (see Map 2.1)

By 1812, Europe was redesigned into three elements:

1 *The French Empire.* France extended well beyond her 'natural frontiers', reaching from Hamburg to Rome and to the Illyrian provinces of the Adriatic. A total of 130 departments covered an extent of 500,000 square miles and enclosed a population of 44 million.
2 *A cordon of client states.* France was surrounded by a protective cordon of dependent states, some of them ruled by Napoleon's relatives and marshals. Italy was rationalised by 1812 into the Kingdom of Naples and the Kingdom of Italy (see Section 6.2a). The fragmented Germany was drastically restructured into the German Confederation of the Rhine in 1806 and consisted of only sixteen states (see Section 7.3). Apart from this, there was the new Swiss Confederation, the Grand Duchy of Warsaw entrusted to the King of Saxony, Sweden ruled by the ex-Marshal Bernadotte from 1810 and Spain ruled by Joseph Bonaparte from 1808.
3 *Threatened states.* Then there were the free states like Prussia, Denmark and Austria which were very susceptible to French influence and whose independence could be revoked – as in Prussia in 1812. It should be noted that Napoleon paid little real account to any sort of popular nationalist feelings in this empire building. Many non-French territories were annexed. Alien dynasties were frequently imposed, as with Louis Bonaparte in Holland, Jerome Bonaparte in Westphalia and Joseph Bonaparte in Spain. Finally where plebiscites were used they were only to confirm decisions. In the Batavian Republic in 1801 Napoleon even counted the abstentions to give a majority.

(b) *'Enlightened despotism'*

Napoleon's main aim throughout was to maximise his resources. He remarked of his territorial restructuring: 'I desire only a federation of men and money.' Equally his application of administrative reforms in the client states of France may be seen as a trigger of nationalism in Italy and Germany by displaying the benefits of unity and modernised institutions, but the reality and the motives were rather different.

1 *The idea is weakened by elementary chronological facts.* Not all of Germany and Italy were brought under French rule at the same time. The period of rule differed

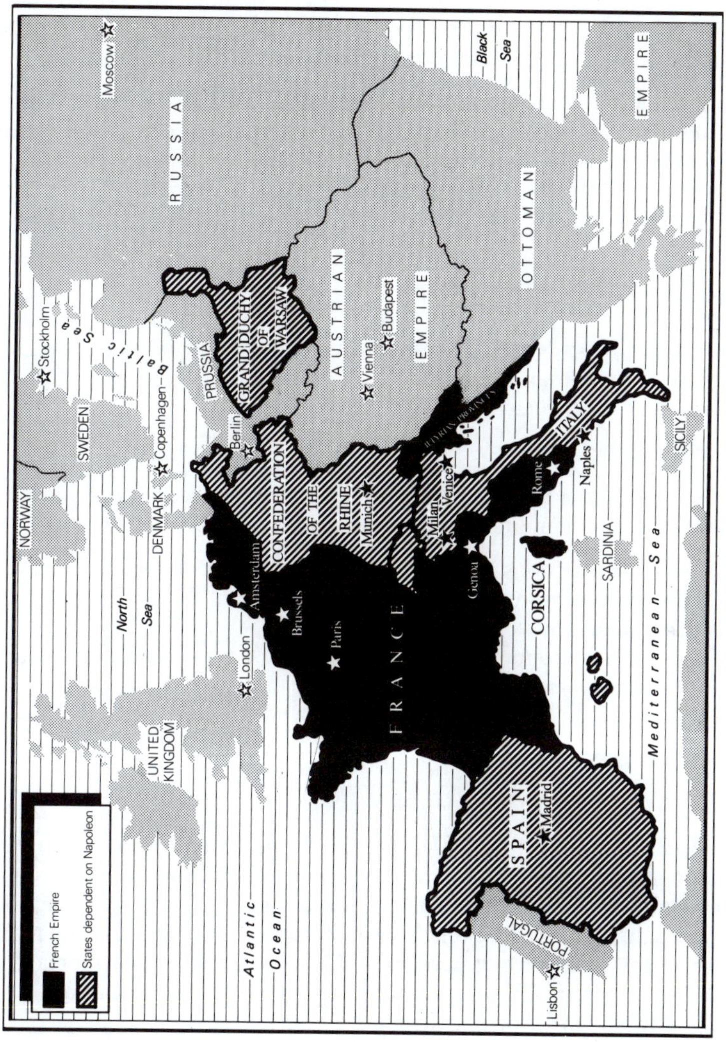

Map 2.1 Europe in 1810

considerably and different systems of government were adopted for different territories. Certainly though those areas long under French rule such as Piedmont-Liguria and the German left bank of the Rhine did feel the effects of assimilation considerably.

2   *The use of territory as a reward for his new nobility* worked against the principle of the redistribution of land and opportunity. In Westphalia and Warsaw especially it simply bolstered feudalism.

3   *The old landed élites were remarkably resilient.* In Naples, for instance, of a total population of 5 million there were only 2704 buyers of monastic, church and émigré lands when they came on the market after 1806. Of those 7 per cent took 65 per cent of the land. Most of them were members of the old nobility.

This meant that while the Napoleonic codes and impact of French rule are related to the growth of nationalism and liberalism, Napoleon's practical compromise with feudalism meant that the dynastic restoration of 1815 was made that much easier.

2.8   The fall of Napoleon

Only seven years after Tilsit Napoleon was forced to abdicate, and was exiled to Elba. This was the result of a complex of factors:

(a)   *British resistance*

Britain sought to maintain a balance of power in Europe and keep open her commercial connections. While not a military power, she made two vital contributions:

1   *Naval supremacy.* Britain was invulnerable after Trafalgar and would intervene wherever ships could be moved. As Napoleon grumbled: 'Wherever there is water to float a ship we shall find you in the way'.

2   *'Pitt's guineas'.* British economic power enabled her to buy coalitions of allies to fight her continental wars.

(b)   *The 'Spanish ulcer'* (see Illus. 2.1)

There were really two aspects to the Spanish War:

1   *A guerrilla war.* From May 1808 Napoleon faced a persistent guerrilla resistance in Spain resulting from his imprisonment of King Charles IV and Prince Ferdinand and his imposition of Joseph Bonaparte on the throne. In July 1808 Spanish troops and guerrillas actually forced a French army to surrender at Baylen. The main contribution of this resistance of peasants led by conservative noblemen and clergy against the French forces which represented atheism and revolution was that they helped to tie down an army of 30,000 men.

2   *The Peninsula War (1808–14).* It also provided a very favourable environment for the regular war by British forces led by the Duke of Wellington. With an established base in Portugal behind the fortified lines of Torres Vedras, the Duke fought a series of summer campaigns resulting in great victories at Talavera (1809), Salamanca (1812) and Vittoria (1813) and worsening the *'running sore'* which beset Napoleon. The Duke's view of his allies was somewhat limited though: he once remarked: 'I never knew the Spanish do anything – let alone do anything well'.

Illus. 2.1 The execution of the defenders of Madrid (1808): 'the good lesson just meted out to the city of Madrid must without question promptly decide matters' (Cooper–Bridgeman Library)

From a painting by Francisco Goya in the Museo del Prado, Madrid, showing a French firing squad executing Spanish rebels on 3 May 1808 in obedience in Napoleon's orders.

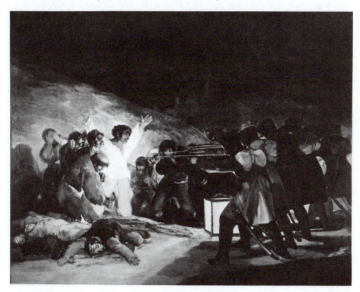

Source: C. Barnett, *Bonaparte* (Allen & Unwin, 1978) p. 147.

Q   After the event Napoleon wrote 'the good lesson just meted out to the city of Madrid must without question promptly decide matters'. In fact it was the start of the national uprising. Goya was a well-established court artist but he embarked upon the production of a series of sketches illustrating the horrors of the war in Spain. How does he heighten the horror of this event?

(c)   *The persistence of Austria and Prussia*

As well as British subsidies, Austrian and Prussian resistance was revived by an element of patriotic resentment, together with mounting fears as to their futures in Napoleon's Europe:

1   *The Prussian revival.* In the case of Prussia this resulted in a programme of French style reforms implemented by a group of reformers led by Stein and Hardenberg (see Section 7.4) designed to strengthen the state in readiness for the earliest opportunity to fight back.

2   *The Austro-French War (1809).* French setbacks in Spain allowed a 'war party' to lead Austria back to war with Napoleon with an improved army. In fact it was defeated again at Wagram in July 1809 and Vienna was occupied. Further territorial losses were inflicted by the Peace of Schönbrunn and a forced alliance was sealed with the marriage of Napoleon and the princess Marie Louise.

(d)   *The Russian 'Great Patriotic War'*

The growing rift between Napoleon and the Tsar was due to the impact of the Continental System, territorial disagreements over the future of Turkey, Poland and Sweden and Alexander's anger at Napoleon's failure to marry his sister Catherine as he had expected. Tension built up and in June 1812 Napoleon launched an invasion of

Illus. 2.2   The retreat from Moscow (Bildarchiv Preussicher Kulturbesitz, Berlin)

From a contemporary painting showing the last stages of the retreat, when the *Grande Armée* suffered more from Bonaparte's mismanagement than from the weather.

Source: C. Barnett, *Bonaparte* (Allen & Unwin, 1978) p. 180.

450,000 troops into Russia (including only one-third drawn from France itself) to win a quick victory (see Illus. 2.2). In the end he was defeated by:

1   *Space and time.* The Russian forces simply withdrew before Napoleon and his lines of communication became dangerously extended.
2   *'Scorched earth'.* The French armies were used to 'living off the land'. The Russian troops and peasants destroyed villages and crops as they fell back. By the time he reached Smolensk, Napoleon had only 160,000 men left. A victory at Borodino opened up Moscow to him, but it was set on fire by the Russians.
3   *'General Winter'.* In appalling conditions and harried by cossacks and peasants when the Grand Army recrossed the Niemen in December 1812 only 30,000 men were left.

(e)   The 'awakening of the peoples'

Napoleon was left with time to scrape together another army but throughout 1812–13 his former allies and client states took advantage of the situation to turn against him – Prussia in February 1813 and then Saxony, Bavaria, Sweden and Austria re-entered the war. Napoleon won remarkable victories at Lützen and Bautzen, but in October 1813 was decisively defeated at Leipzig, the *'Battle of the Nations'*. There were two factors behind this build up of opposition:

1   *Reaction against the burdens of war.* Jerome, King of Westphalia, wrote of the unrest arising from 'not only resentment at foreign domination, its deeper causes lie in the ruination of all classes, the crushing burden of taxation, war levies, the upkeep and quartering of troops and endless other vexations'.
2   *The self-interest of German rulers.* A. J. P. Taylor says: 'in fact Germany turned against Napoleon only in the sense that German princes sensed the coming storm and changed sides'.

(f) Napoleonic megalomania

Napoleon was not prepared to compromise at any stage as advocated by Fouché (minister of police) and Talleyrand (foreign minister) in 1807 and 1810. British persistence, the need for *'la gloire'* to strengthen his position at home and perhaps a degree of megalomania meant he would not cut back his ambitions: – 'I wanted to rule the world – who wouldn't have in my place. The world begged me to govern it.'

With unlimited ambitions, deteriorating health and limited resources he was bound to fail because in the end, as everyone knows, 'God is on the side of the big battalions'.

2.9 The final stage

In the end Napoleon's downfall resulted from:

1 *The creation of the Fourth Coalition (March 1814).* Resisting attempts by Napoleon to play them off against each other, Castlereagh, the British Foreign Secretary, persuaded Russia, Prussia and Austria to join with Britain in signing the Treaty of Chaumont and agreeing to a twenty-year alliance to defeat Napoleon and restore Europe.
2 *An internal coup (April 1814).* French resistance crumbled before the invaders. Chaumont, for instance, surrendered to a single horseman. Finally it was a conspiracy by Talleyrand seeking to restore the Bourbons and the refusal of Napoleon's marshals to serve him which led to his abdication on 6 April and exile five days later to the island of Elba.

2.10 The 'Hundred Days'

The first Treaty of Paris was reasonably moderate. French territories were cut back only to those of 1792, leaving France with Savoy and the Saar. There was to be no indemnity or army of occupation. Talleyrand even obtained the right for France to be represented at the conference in Vienna (see Section 3.3).

(a) The Waterloo Campaign (March–June 1815)

The arguments at Vienna were interrupted by Napoleon's return. An army fearful for its future with the return of the émigrés rallied to him. He needed a quick victory to help negotiate a restoration. Although he inflicted initial setbacks on the allied forces, he was finally defeated by Wellington at Waterloo (see Illus. 2.3) on 18 June when Prussian reinforcements arrived in the nick of time.

(b) The second Treaty of Paris (November 1815)

The French Chamber of Deputies accepted Louis XVIII again in July 1815, but the peace terms were much harsher:

1 *French frontiers* were set back to those of *1790*.
2 *An occupation* of 3–5 years and an *indemnity* of 700 million France was imposed.

Illus. 2.3 *Scotland for Ever!*

Source: Oil painting by Lady Elizabeth Butler, 1881 (Leeds City Art Galleries).

Lady Butler never witnessed war at first hand but was one of the most famous war artists of the nineteenth century. This, her most sensational picture, was based on an account by an eyewitness who was actually involved in the charge of the Scots Greys at Waterloo. The main technical criticism of the painting is that the riders are grouped together so closely that in reality they and their mounts would have been a tangle of fallen bodies and saddlery before they reached the French.

Q   In your view what is it that makes this so effective as an action painting?

2.11 Conclusion

Napoleon was exiled to the 47 square-mile St Helena in the Atlantic where he died in 1821 (see Illus. 2.4). His real impact on Europe was profound enough, but even greater impact was made by his rambling memoirs about his thwarted intentions for Europe, the bequeathed 'legend of Napoleon': 'Europe thus divided into nationalities freely formed and free internally, peace between states would have become easier. The United States of Europe would become a possibility.'

Questions

1   What did Napoleon Bonaparte achieve between 1799 and 1807 either as a commander or in the domestic affairs of France?   [OC]
2   How did Napoleon come to be involved in a war in Spain? Why did he regard this involvement as a 'running sore'?   [OX]
3   Explain Napoleon's rise to political power between 1795 and 1804.   [OX]
4   What problems faced Napoleon in France in 1799? How successfully did he deal with them between 1799 and 1815?   [NEAB]
5   To what extent may the defeat of Napoleon I be attributed to the forces of nationalism?   [NEAB]
6   Give an account of the events in Europe which led to the defeat and overthrow of Napoleon between 1812 and 1814. Why did the French people welcome him back as Emperor in 1815?
                                                                                            [CAM]

Source: C. Barnett, *Bonaparte* (Allen & Unwin, 1978) p. 213.

a Is there not something oddly religious about this picture? In what ways did Napoleon – even after his death – exercise an influence on the future of Europe?

7   What was the 'Continental system', and why did Napoleon try to enforce it after 1806? Why did he fail? [CAM]

8   Study Sources A, B, C and D and then answer the questions which follow.

Source A: The personality of Napoleon.

When he so wished, there could be a power of persuasion and fascination in his voice, his expression, his very manner, giving him an advantage over his interlocutor as great as the superiority and flexibility of his mind. Never was there a man more fascinating when he chose to be ... Woe to him who admitted a single modification, for the adroit interlocutor led him from concession to concession to the end he had in view, casting up a previous concession against you if you defended yourself, and assuming that it consequently implied the point you refused to concede. No woman was ever more artful than he in making you want, or agree to, his own desire when he thought it was to his interest to persuade you, or merely wanted to do so. These reflections call to my mind what he once said on a similar occasion, which explains better than any other phrase could have done the price he was ready to pay for success: 'When I need anyone,' he said, 'I don't make too fine a point about it; I would kiss his ...'.

The Emperor needed much sleep, but he could sleep when he wanted to, by day as well as by night ... On a campaign he was awakened for everything. Even the Prince of Neuchâtel [Berthier], who received and despatched and knew his Majesty's plans, decided nothing ... The Emperor occupied himself with the most minute details. He wanted everything to bear the imprint of his genius. He would send for me to receive his orders for headquarters, for the orderly officers, for his staff officers, for the letters, for the couriers, postal service etc. The commanding officers of the guard; the controller of the army commissariat; Larrey, the excellent surgeon-general; all were summoned at least once a day. Nothing escaped his solicitude. Indeed, his foresight might well be called by the name of solicitude, for no detail seemed too humble to receive his attention ... he had an astonishing memory for localities. The topography of a country seemed to be modelled in relief in his head. Never did any man combine such a memory with a more creative genius. He seemed to extract men, horses and guns from the very bowels of the earth. The distinctive numbers of his regiments, his army service companies, his baggage battalions, were all classified in his brain most marvellously. His memory sufficed for everything. He knew where each one was, when it started, when it should arrive at its destination ...

But his creative genius had no knowledge of conserving its forces. Always improvising, in a few days he would consume, exhaust and disorganize by the rapidity of his marches, the whole of what his genius had created. If a thirty-day's campaign did not produce the results of a year's fighting, the greater part of his calculations were upset by the losses he suffered, for everything was done so rapidly and unexpectedly, the chiefs under him had so little experience, showed so little care and were, in addition, so spoiled by former successes, that everything was disorganized, wasted and thrown away ... The prompt results of the Italian and Austrian campaigns and the resources those countries offered to the invader spoiled everyone, down to the less important commanders, for more rigorous warfare. The habit of victory cost us dear when we got to Russia and even dearer when we were in retreat; the glorious habit of marching ever forward made us veritable schoolboys when it came to retreating.

(a)   List the qualities of Napoleon which made him, according to this account, a great leader of men and a military genius.

(b)   What were the negative aspects of his character?

(c)   Given this assessment of Napoleon's personality, why were Russia and Spain likely to prove unsuitable for his approach to campaigning?

(d)   Do you regard this personality assessment as a balanced one? What sort of factors should a historian bear in mind in using such personal descriptions as evidence?

Source: J. Hanoteau (ed.), *Memoirs of General de Caulaincourt, Duke of Vicenza 1812–1813* (Cassell, 1935). Quoted in D. G. Wright *Napoleon and Europe* (Longman, 1984).

Source B: Napoleon as a Christian champion.

I *Letter to the Pope, 7 January 1806.*

I am in receipt of a letter from Your Holiness under date 13th November. I cannot but be keenly affected by that fact that, when all the powers in English pay have united to wage an unjust war against me, Your Holiness should listen to bad advice and write to me in such immoderate terms ... Your Holiness complains that since your return from Paris, you have nothing but disappointments. The reason is that all those who called themselves my friends, only because they feared my power, have since taken heart from the strength of the Coalition and changed their tune ... I have always considered myself the protector of the Holy See. I shall continue to protect it, whatever the mistakes, ingratitude and ill will of the men whom these last three months have unmasked. They thought I was done for; but by the success with which He favoured my arms, God has signally demonstrated His protection of my cause. So long as Your Holiness consults the true friends of religion, and your own heart, I shall be your friend. God knows, I have done more for religion than any other prince alive.

II *Napoleon to his minister in Rome, 7 January 1806.*

The Pope has written to me a quite ridiculous and lunatic letter ... For the Pope's purposes I am Charlemagne. Like Charlemagne, I join the crown of France with the crown of the Lombards. My Empire, like Charlemagne's, extends to the eastern borders. I therefore expect the Pope to accommodate himself to my requirements. If he behaves well, I shall make no outward changes; if not, I shall reduce him to the status of the Bishop of Rome.

(a) Name the Pope, and outline his relationship with Napoleon between 1800 and 1814. For what purpose had he visited Paris?
(b) How had God 'favoured my arms' (I, line 10), against 'the strength of the Coalition' (I, lines 6–7)? What great victory had the French achieved between the date of the Pope's letter and Napoleon's reply?
(c) With reference to I and II, discuss Napoleon's claim to be 'the protector of the Holy See' (I, lines 7–11), and to have 'done more for religion than any other prince alive' (I, lines 12–13).

Source C: Be a constitutional king.

Fontainebleau, 15 November 1807
To Jérôme Bonaparte, King of Westphalia

My Dear Brother, You will find enclosed the constitution of your kingdom. This constitution contains the conditions on which I renounce all my rights of conquest and all the claims I have acquired over your kingdom. You must observe it faithfully. The happiness of your people is important to me, not only because of the influence it can have on both your reputation and mine, but also from the point of view of the whole European system. Refuse to listen to those who tell you that your subjects, accustomed to servitude, will greet the benefits you offer to them with ingratitude. They are more enlightened in the Kingdom of Westphalia than some would have you believe; and your throne will only become truly established with the confidence and affection of the people. What the peoples of Germany impatiently desire is that men of talent, who lack noble rank, will have an equal claim to your favour and to government employment; they also demand that all kinds of servitude and intermediate links between the sovereign and the lowest class of the people be entirely abolished. The benefits of the *Code Napoléon*, public trials, the introduction of juries, will be the distinctive features of your rule ... It is necessary for your subjects to enjoy a degree of liberty, equality and prosperity hitherto unknown among the peoples of Germany; and that your liberal government produces, one way or another, changes which will be most salutary for the Confederation of the Rhine and for the strength of your monarchy. Such a method of government will prove a more powerful barrier separating you from Prussia than the Elbe, the fortresses and the protection of France. What people would wish to return to the arbitrary government of Prussia when they have tasted the benefits of wise and liberal administration? The peoples of Germany, as well as those of France, Italy and Spain, desire equality and demand liberal ideas. I have been managing the affairs of Europe long enough to be convinced that the burden imposed by the privileged classes is contrary to the wishes of general opinion. Be a constitutional king.

(a) Do you see anything contradictory in the insistence that Jerome should be 'a constitutional king' and Napoleon's own manner as revealed in this letter?
(b) According to Napoleon what did the people of Germany desire (lines 9–19)?
(c) In advising this light handed approach to the government of Westphalia what were the strategic considerations in the mind of Napoleon (lines 18–19)?

Source: *Correspondence de Napoléon 1er, publiée par ordre de l'Empereur Napoléon III*, Vol xvi (1864) no. 13361. Quoted in D. G. Wright, *Napoleon and Europe* (Longman, 1986).

Source D: France first!

To Eugene Napoleon, Viceroy of Italy, at Monza

My Dear Son, I have received your letter of 14 August. The silks of the kingdom of Italy seem to go entirely to England, since silks are not manufactured in Germany. Obviously I wish to modify this trade route to the profit of French manufacturers, for without it my silk products, which are a principal staple of French trade, will suffer considerable losses. I cannot accept the observations you make. My motto is: France first. You must never lose sight of the fact that, if English commerce triumphs on the seas, that is because the English dominate the oceans; it is therefore logical that, since France is superior on land, she should make her trade dominant there; otherwise all is lost. Would it not be better for Italy to come to the aid of France in such circumstances, rather than find herself covered with customs-posts? For it would be very unwise not to recognise that Italy is independent only with the goodwill of France; that the independence has been gained by French blood and French victories, and that Italy must clearly not abuse it; that it would therefore be very injudicious to try to decide whether or not France ought to obtain significant commercial advantages . . . Italy must not make calculations independent of the need to assure the prosperity of France, she must combine French interests with her own; above all, she must avoid giving France a motive for the annexation of Italy, for if France decided to do so, who could stop her? Therefore you should take for your motto: France first.

(a) What do you think Napoleon had in mind when he remarked: 'Obviously I wish to modify this trade route to the profit of French manufacturers' (lines 2–3)?
(b) What was the strategy which lay behind the 'Continental System' (lines 5–8)?
(c) According to Napoleon, what had Italy gained by French intervention (lines 10–14)?
(d) What threat lay behind Napoleon's demands (lines 15–17)?
(e) What part did the operation of the 'Continental System' play in the ultimate downfall of Napoleon?

Source: Napoleon, *Correspondence*, xxi (1867), no. 16284, pp. 60–1.

3 The concert of Europe 1815–30

Introduction

The defeat of France did not remove the threat of international revolution and war. To a large extent the Vienna Settlement at the end of the wars was intended to maintain peace and stability. More than this was needed though. To the Austrian chancellor Prince Metternich what was necessary was some sort of league between European rulers which would maintain the Settlement and police the continent. What makes the period after 1815 so noteworthy is the operation of the *'Metternich system'*. This is why it is often referred to as the 'Age of Metternich'. In fact, it was a very brief and passing phase, because it was impossible to maintain a minimum degree of agreement between the rulers.

3.1 The legacy of the French Revolution

To the ruling classes of Europe, the lesson which had been learned was that once change started, it got out of control. The French Revolution had produced chaos, a bloody reign of terror, military dictatorship and international war. It looked as if this was the pattern that would always be followed. To conservative politicians there were two possible responses to this situation:

(a) *'Riding the tiger'*

To many of the politicians of Europe it was impossible to dam the forces of revolution entirely. The Prussian statesman Prince Hardenberg wrote in 1807 about the French Revolution that: 'Those who stood in the path of the torrent ... have been swept away.' To the prince and his colleagues the answer was to attract support for the government and weaken the revolution by making moderate reforms. It was to be in Britain in the 1820s–40s where this policy was most successfully applied. A series of economic, social and political reforms enabled the aristocracy to maintain the real power and attract the support of the middle classes.

(b) *Stemming the torrent*

Of course the trouble with 'riding the tiger' is that it is not easy to steer, or to dismount. As a result the tiger tends to go further than intended. There was a danger that making reforms could actually trigger off revolution. To the ruling class of Europe advice to make compromises was not so easily taken, revolution and war were too recent. An obvious alternative was to stop the whole process of change before it had a chance to start. Metternich – the main spokesman of this theory – once remarked: 'All revolutions are lies. Never has a revolution truthfully declared its point of departure nor carried out its promises ... They destroy but do not create' and so 'The true merit of a statesman ... consists in governing so as to avoid the situation in which concessions become necessary.' History could not be reversed but at least could be brought to a 'full stop', as Metternich's friend Gentz remarked.

3.2 'A great European'

Metternich was the leading counter revolutionary of the period. As chancellor of the Austrian Empire his main concern was for its stability. However, he saw revolution as a problem to be tackled on a broad European front. There were three reasons for his European outlook:

1   *He was not really a native Austrian.* Metternich had been born and brought up in the Rhineland. He was very familiar with France and was ambassador there for some years. He tended to see himself as a European. If his real home had been Vienna, it is unlikely that he would have had such a broad view of European affairs.
2   *The conspiracy theory of revolution.* There are a number of theories as to why there were so many outbreaks of revolution in this period (see Section 4). Metternich believed that he faced a huge conspiracy, with close links between its leaders in different countries.
3   *The situation of the Austrian Empire.* The Empire was a ramshackle collection of diverse peoples and territories. There were eleven languages used by its citizens and many more dialects. It was threatened with disintegration more than any other state in Europe if revolution and international war broke out again. Keeping the Empire intact was very much linked to keeping peace in Europe. After all 'a man has an interest in putting out the flames when his neighbour's house is on fire'.

(a) *'The Doctor of Revolutions'*

Therefore Metternich had a professional concern for the stability of the states of Europe. He was a supporter of a particular cure and a method of treatment of the causes and symptoms of revolution:

1   *The principle of legitimacy.* Metternich believed that the best form of government was monarchy based upon a well-established claim to the throne. Hopefully the monarchs would be wise rulers with good advisers, although Metternich was well aware that many of them did not live up to his ideal. In the Vienna Settlement of 1815 this principle was a key feature.
2   *The principle of intervention.* Since revolution was a very contagious disease which easily spread across frontiers, states should have the right to intervene if they felt threatened. Where necessary this should be arranged by the European states acting together.

The reconstruction of the states system of Europe in the Vienna Settlement of 1815 was very much the work of Metternich. However, it did involve a range of deals and compromises between the Allies made before and during 1815. The negotiations at Vienna were further complicated by the fact that three different objectives had to be achieved:

1 *Restoration* of rulers and states on the basis of the principle of *legitimacy*.
2 *Reward the victors and punish the losers.*
3 Provide for the *maintenance of peace in Europe*.

Lord Byron described the purpose of the Settlement of 1815 more cuttingly as 'to repair legitimacy's crotch'!

(a) *Restoration*

Metternich and the French delegate, the 60-year-old 'survivor' Talleyrand, were the chief advocates of restoration. In fact, there was very little alternative to hereditary dynastic rulers. The few examples of republics were not very encouraging. The principle of legitimacy was applied in France, Spain, Piedmont, Tuscany, Modena and the Papal States. In Italy, Murat was allowed to remain King of Naples – it was only when he supported Napoleon's revolt that he was captured and shot and the Bourbons restored. However, it could not be applied in every circumstance because:

1 *It was not always practical.* It was quite impossible to re-establish the over 300 states of Germany. Instead, they were replaced by 39 states loosely linked as the *German Confederation* and represented by delegates to a Diet. The Austrian Empire dominated the Diet because its delegates were presidents of both chambers.
2 *It conflicted with other objectives* in some cases. The principle was not applied in the very many cases where international security or the self interest of the victorious powers were involved.

(b) *Reward and retribution*

There were two aspects to this:

1 *Penalties imposed upon France.* During the negotiations at Vienna Napoleon returned and the 'Hundred Days' campaign took place (see Section 2.10). Before this, the Allies had been prepared to follow the advice of the British delegate, Lord Castlereagh, and treat France with moderation. The Second Treaty of Paris (November 1815) was much more punitive (see Section 2.10(b)).
2 *Territorial adjustments.* Usually it was a question of the Allies and their friends being rewarded at the expense of Napoleon's allies:
   – Russia kept Finland which she had captured from Sweden in 1808 and Bessarabia which she had taken from Turkey. In return Sweden was given Norway, taken from Napoleon's ally Denmark. The Tsar, who wished to resurrect the Polish Kingdom, was also given the greater part of Poland. This new satellite state was ruled by the Tsar as King of Poland.
   – *Prussia lost much Polish territory* in this arrangement. However, she was compensated with 40 per cent of Saxony, the Duchy of Westphalia and Swedish Pomerania. She also received most of the new, consolidated Rhineland.

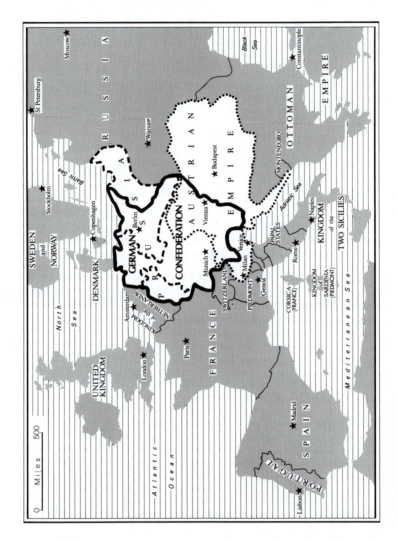

Map 3.1 Europe in 1815

– *Austria lost the Austrian Netherlands.* In exchange, she was given Lombardy and Venetia in northern Italy. She also received Illyria and Dalmatia on the east coast of the Adriatic and the Bavarian Tyrol.
– *Britain was not interested in mainland gains.* Instead she took a number of potential naval bases and staging posts for trade – Heligoland in the North Sea, Malta, the Ionian Islands, Ceylon and Cape Colony.

In some instances the victors had not got exactly what they wanted. Austria actually lost the Austrian Netherlands (recreated as Belgium). This was due to the existence of the third objective at Vienna, the maintenance of European peace.

(c) *Repose in Europe*

Again this was to be achieved in two ways:

1 *The creation of a barrier around France.* She was surrounded by a series of *buffer states.* Belgium and Holland in the north were combined to produce a stronger state. Piedmont was given Nice and Genoa to strengthen the north west border of Italy. As the Tsar remarked, 'republics are no longer fashionable'. On the western frontier, the Swiss Confederation was restored and strengthened by being increased to 22 cantons. The Rhineland was now held by Prussia.
2 *The preservation of a balance of power.* There was always the possibility that the threat to peace might come from another state. Russia was the most likely danger. She was militarily the strongest of the Allies and had been given considerable territorial advantages. As part of the deal with Prussia the Tsar had promised her the whole of Saxony for Poland. The problem was that this would considerably increase the size of Prussia. The Allies divided over this issue. Britain, Austria and France actually made a secret alliance as an insurance in case war was renewed. In the event, the European balance was retained by cutting back Prussian gains.

3.4   Assessment of the Vienna Settlement

In later years the Settlement came in for considerable criticism. However, this may not have been altogether deserved. There are two broad views of it which can be contrasted:

(a) *The 'Forty Years Peace'*

Not until 1854 did a general European war break out. It has been claimed that this period of peace was because the Vienna Settlement left no great grievance outstanding. On the other hand, there were other factors as well:

1 Much was due after 1815 to the work of 'internationalists' such as Metternich (see Section 7).
2 The powers were distracted from aggressive diplomacy by post-war economic exhaustion and internal revolutionary threats.

(b) *'Bartering the happiness of millions'*

The usual criticism is that the diplomats at Vienna were out of touch with the new ideas which were developing in Europe. In particular, it was claimed that they ignored the growing opposition to absolutist monarchy and the nationalist pressure towards the redrawing of the map of Europe on the basis of language and culture (see Section 4.3). On the other hand:

1 *Few people in 1815 actually understood these new forces.* The liberals and nationalists did not have any clearly expressed programmes. Anyhow they could be easily seen as terrorists and crazed fanatics.
2 *There was no alternative* for much of what the diplomats did. It was unlikely that an independent Belgium would have survived. In northern Italy, it seemed that the only alternative to Austrian rule was French rule.
3 *Some concessions were made to the new forces.* The new Germany was a good deal less divided than the old one. All of the German rulers were supposed to establish constitutions as well.
4 *The Settlement has been unfairly blamed for the revival of revolutions in the 1820s and 1830–1.* These seem to have been due more to the short-sighted repressive policies of European rulers like Charles X of France and the Spanish and Neapolitan monarchs.

3.5 Metternich's system

Metternich always denied that he had a 'system' of any sort. It is true that he dealt with revolutionary threats in different ways according to the circumstances. His activities can be divided into two strands, however:

1 *Direct intervention.* In some areas, action was easier than others. Even in the Austrian Empire he did not have a free hand (see Section 8.3). In Italy, he could intimidate the independent states because of the Austrian presence in Lombardy and Venetia. In Germany he could act directly through the Diet of the German Confederation.
2 *Indirect intervention* by employing the strength of other states acting under the authorisation of conference decisions. Clearly Austrian troops could not be used everywhere. In any case, the Empire was in financial difficulties. It had actually gone bankrupt in 1811 and between 1815–48 a third of its income was spent on paying interest on its debts. Through the *'Congress System'* Metternich could use less direct methods to safeguard Europe and the Austrian Empire.

3.6 The Congress system

The war had been won by co-operation. It was natural that the powers should consider keeping the peace by continuing that co-operation. From Metternich's point of view this could also be a means of combating revolution anywhere in Europe. The problem was that the idea of co-operation was expressed in two separate documents, and these were the source of disagreement:

1 *The Quadruple Alliance* and Article VI of the Treaty of Paris (November 1815).
2 *The Act of the Holy Alliance* produced by Tsar Alexander (May 1815).

(a) *Article VI and the Quadruple Alliance*

Napoleon's near success in the 'Hundred Days' proved the need to make some permanent arrangements to safeguard the Settlement. Largely as a result of the efforts of Lord Castlereagh, the British foreign secretary, it was agreed:

1 That the Quadruple Alliance of Austria, Russia, Britain and Prussia should continue for another twenty years to exclude the Bonaparte dynasty from France.
2 Article VI provided that Congresses would be held so that the Allies could discuss 'great common interest' and measures necessary 'for the repose and prosperity of the peoples and for the maintenance of the peace of Europe'.

(b) *The Holy Alliance*

Some time before this the Tsar (under the influence of the German religious mystic Baroness von Krudener) had produced another document. This was to be the basis of a *personal pact* between the European rulers. Its main signatories were Prussia, Austria and Russia. Indeed it was signed by all of the rulers except the Pope, the Sultan and the King of Britain. Its intention was very vague. The Tsar probably intended it as a renewal of the old Christian unity of Europe. The governments and peoples were to behave as 'members of one and the same Christian nation'. Rulers were urged to behave as 'fathers of families' towards their subjects. Castlereagh said it was nonsense. Even Metternich called it a 'loud sounding nothing'. However, he had a use for this vague link between the three great absolutist powers.

3.7 The Concert of Europe

Between 1815 and 1822 there were a series of conferences to discuss matters of common interest. The most important matters were the revolutions which broke out in some of the states of Europe in 1820 and continuing revolutions in South America. Very soon a rift grew between the European powers over the purpose of the congresses:

(a) *The Congress of Aix La Chapelle (1818)*

The first congress settled the issues of payment of the indemnity and withdrawal of the army of occupation from France. France was now admitted to the conferences on an equal basis. However, even at this early stage the Tsar was seeking to convert the system into a sort of alliance against revolution. He wanted troops to be sent to South America to crush revolution in the Spanish colonies. He even talked about raising an international army. Castlereagh bluntly warned his fellow diplomats against these proposals.

(b) *The Congress of Troppau, Silesia (1820)*

In 1820 revolts broke out in Spain, Portugal and the Kingdom of the Two Sicilies. It was over these events that the line was first clearly drawn between the attitudes of Castlereagh and Metternich towards intervention:

1 *The State Paper of 5 May 1820.* Even before the meeting Castlereagh made his position clear. He saw the congresses as designed to prevent the restoration of the

Bonaparte dynasty in France and to protect the Vienna Settlement. It was not that he sympathised with revolution. He once remarked 'we are always pleased to see evil germs destroyed'. His fear was that intervention could upset *the balance of power* in Europe. Revolutions were *internal matters*, to be dealt with by the governments of the states concerned.

2   *The Troppau Protocol.* Metternich's view was summed up by the agreement of Russia, Prussia and Austria that they would intervene in the affairs of any state in Europe where events seemed to threaten the interests of any other state. Clearly this was an alliance against revolution. Castlereagh sent only an observer to Troppau and after the agreement was made he protested at the misuse of the Congress for this purpose.

(c)   *The Congress of Laibach (1821)*

The meeting was adjourned to Laibach. By then the King of the Two Sicilies had asked for help. It was agreed that Austria should suppress the revolution there. The Holy Alliance powers again claimed the power to support any established government against internal revolt. Again the British spokesman objected. In fact the more moderate intentions of the Quadruple Alliance had been shattered by the Holy Alliance.

(d)   *The Congress of Verona (1822)*

By the time the next meeting took place, things had changed considerably:

1   *The Greek War of Independence* had developed from a small scale revolt against the Turks in 1819. The Tsar sympathised with this rebellion because Turkey was Russia's old enemy.
2   There was a new British foreign secretary, George Canning (Castlereagh had committed suicide in 1821). On the whole Canning followed Castlereagh's line in opposing general European agreements to intervene in the affairs of other states. However, Canning was very different in other ways:
   – He had a reputation for being *more liberal in outlook*. Castlereagh had been associated with repression in Britain, and Canning had long opposed him.
   – He had a greater understanding of the *needs of British trade*. He was the MP for Liverpool, which brought him into close contact with merchants and businessmen.
   – He was a *brilliant speaker*, whereas Castlereagh was very poor. Canning could stir public opinion much more easily, fully understood the power of the press and was cuttingly witty.

All he could do at this stage, though, was to send the Duke of Wellington to the Congress of Verona to object to the French intervention with 100,000 troops in Spain. Even so, that intervention took place in 1823 with the approval of the Congress.

3.8   'Back to a wholesome state'

Canning now took the initiative in three regions:

1   *In the Spanish American colonies*, he guaranteed the independence of the newly created states.
2   *In Portugal*, he actively supported the more liberal group against their opponents.
3   *In Greece*, he brought about a diplomatic agreement to achieve self government. In so doing he also split the Holy Alliance powers.

As a result of these events he could rejoice that he was restoring things to normality, 'back to a wholesome state'. In fact, what these three regions had in common was that the *Royal Navy* could be brought into action and that *British trade interests* were strong.

(a) *The Spanish American colonies*

Since 1830 large areas of South America were being progressively freed from Spanish rule under the leadership of Simon Bolivar and others. In 1823 it was rumoured that the European powers led by France and Russia were prepared to support the re-establishment of Spanish rule. Britain had a growing trade relationship with the new states. It was also feared that France had greater ambitions in the region than just to help Spain. Indeed, French naval and military forces were active in the West Indies and South America. In December 1824 Canning officially recognised the independence of the new states. Then, in a speech which suggested sympathy for the liberal cause, he declared: 'I called the New World into existence to redress the balance of the old.'

In fact, he exaggerated what he had done:

1 *The facts of geography* virtually guaranteed the independence of the new states anyway. As long as the Royal Navy patrolled the seaways of the South Atlantic, intervention was impossible.
2 *The Monroe Doctrine* declared by the then president of the United States in 1823 had already made it clear that any European intervention in South America would be opposed by the United States.

(b) *Portugal*

In 1824, King John of Portugal asked for British help to restore him to his throne. Here the situation was unusual. Instead of liberal revolutionaries forcing a constitution upon the ruler the King had already granted one and wished to maintain it. He was supported by the liberals and the threat came from his own wife and his brother Miguel. Britain had a long-established relationship and trade links with Portugal. It looked as if France would step in if no action was taken, and would support Miguel. So Canning contributed naval assistance and the king was restored to his throne. The persistent Miguel tried again at a later date, and in 1833 the Royal Navy was used again to restore the throne of the grand-daughter of King John, Maria.

(c) *Greece*

In Greece, the nationalist society *Philike Hetairia* established in Odessa had 200,000 members by 1820, mostly in the Greek commercial community. In 1821 in the hope of triggering off a revolt the Greek tsarist general Alexander Ypsilantis invaded Moldavia and Wallachia. He was defeated at Dragashan. However in 1821 while the Turks were occupied in dealing with the troublesome provincial governor Ali, Pasha of Yanina, they were faced with a widespread Greek revolt starting in Morea. By 1823, the rebels were so successful that the Sultan turned for help to his vassal, Mehemet Ali, Pasha of Egypt. Under his rule Egypt had been ruthlessly modernised and he had followed an expansionist policy. In 1824 he was given command in the Morea and his son Ibrahim Pasha began systematically to exterminate the population.

The Greek War of Independence had a considerable impact on European relationships. It produced a different set of attitudes entirely.

Source: Oil painting by Eugène Delacroix, 1827 (Musée de Beaux Arts, Bordeaux).

1   *Russia sympathised very strongly with the Greeks.* The Tsar had no hesitation in wanting to support rebels in this case.
2   *Austria was opposed to intervention.* Metternich had already been embarrassed by the Tsar's keenness to throw Russia's weight about all over Europe. Now he feared Russia would 'gobble Greece at one mouthful and Turkey at the next'.
3   *Britain faced a dilemma.* A Russian victory over Turkey could increase her power in the Near East and threaten India. On the other hand Canning was aware of tremendous enthusiasm in Britain for the Greek cause and at the prospect of considerable *trade opportunities*. A loan of £80,000 had been floated in London in 1824 to help the Greek cause.

By 1826 it looked as if the Greeks were about to be defeated by the Egyptian army acting on behalf of the Turkish government. The new Tsar Nicholas I and Canning were both under pressure to do something. In a very clever move to prevent Russia acting alone and getting out of control, Canning brought Britain, Russia and France together with the Treaty of London in 1827. They agreed to persuade Turkey to grant self government to Greece. Canning was jubilant. He had broken the link between Russia, Prussia and Austria. He rejoiced 'The Holy Alliance no longer marches *en corps*, I have dissolved them into individuality'. Canning's timing was excellent. Having become prime minister only in 1827 he died soon after the treaty was signed. He did not, therefore, witness the collapse of his arrangements and a chain of events which culminated in a Russo-Turkish war and full independence for Greece (see Section 11.3).

3.9 Conclusion

In 1830 there was another revolution in France (see Section 5.3(d)) which Metternich gloomily saw as 'the bursting of a dyke'. It was the trigger for a series of revolutions in Belgium (see Section 5.6(a)), Poland (see Section 10.4(c)) and Italy (see Section 6.3(c)). This time, with the exception of Belgium, they were unsuccessful. However, the events of 1815–30 left open the possibility of further revolutions:

1   *The continued division between the powers.* Austria, Prussia and Russia did come together to some extent in 1833 in the guaranteeing of each others' Polish possessions (the Treaty of Munchengrätz). Britain and France tended to side together.
2   *The connection between revolutionaries was being made international.* Metternich feared a conspiracy. In fact, the real links between the revolutionaries arose from the fact that their enemies were the same.

Metternich himself was too inflexible. He once remarked in 1851 'my principles ... have not changed and they never will change ... that which I wished in 1831 I wished in 1813 and in all the period in between and 1848'. More smugly, he once confessed 'error has never entered my spirit'.

Questions

1   What were the merits and defects of the peace settlement of 1814–15?   [OC]
2   What was the 'Metternich system', and what were the chief threats to it?   [OC]
3   'The Vienna Settlement of 1815 was dictated throughout by considerations of power politics.' Examine this view.   [OX]
4   State the terms of the Vienna Settlement of 1815. Describe the attempts to preserve peace in Europe between 1816 and the Congress of Troppau (1820).   [NEAB]
5   'A praiseworthy effort to maintain peace by international co-operation.' Discuss this view of the work of the Congress System in the period 1815 to 1827.   [NEAB]
6   Why, and with what results, did major European powers intervene to suppress revolutionary movements between 1815 and 1830?   [CAM]
7   How far did the Congress System between 1815 and 1822 demonstrate that the great powers shared common aims?   [CAM]
8   What international complications were produced in the 1820s by the Greek War of Independence?
9   Study Sources A, B and C and then answer the questions which follow.

Source A: The Old World and the New.

Canning's speech in the House of Commons on Spain, 12 December 1824, comparing recent events to a similar situation in Spain in the days of Queen Anne when Britain responded by military intervention.

It was not Spain they (our ancestors *temp.* Queen Anne) feared; India [the West Indies] was the cause of their apprehension; and I admit that if, when France made that attack, Spain had still been placed in possession of the same resources, there might have been ground for a more decisive interference. I will admit, for argument's sake, that the occupation of Spain by France was a disparagement to the character of this country; I will admit even that it was a blow to the policy which ought to be maintained in the regulation of the balance of power. What, then, was to be done? There were two means to be adopted in our resistance to it, one of them was to attack the French troops which entered Spain; the other was to render the Conquest harmless as far as regarded us, and valueless, or something worse, actually injurious, to the possessor. I say, then that if we have been for the present dispossessed of anything in our situation as forming part of the balance of power, we are fully compensated. Was it necessary to blockade Cadiz, I say, to restore the situation of England? No. I look at the possessions of Spain on the other side of the

Atlantic; **I LOOK AT THE INDIES AND I CALL IN THE NEW WORLD TO REDRESS THE BALANCE OF THE OLD.** *(Great cheering)*

(a) What were the main differences in style between Canning and Lord Castlereagh in dealing with foreign policy?
(b) Why had French forces been sent into Spain?
(c) What do you think Canning had in mind when he said that it was not actually the invasion of Spain that was the cause of British 'apprehension' (lines 1–2)?
(d) What were the two means of resisting the intervention and its effects which were offered by Canning?
(e) What were the factors which allowed Canning to guarantee the independence of the new states of South America and to 'call in the New World to redress the balance of the Old' (lines 13–15)

Source: *Hansard*, 12 December 1826.

Source B: The issue of intervention.

A secret memorandum to the Tsar Alexander from Metternich, 15 December 1820.

Kings have to calculate the chances of their very existence in the immediate future; passions are let loose, and league together to overthrow everything which society respects as the basis of its existence; religion, public morality, laws, customs, rights, and duties, all are attacked, confounded, overthrown, or called into question. The great mass of the people are tranquil spectators of these attacks and revolutions, and of the absolute want of all means of defence. A few are carried off by the torrent, but the wishes of the immense majority are to maintain a repose which exists no longer, and of which even the first elements seem to be lost ... We are convinced that society can no longer be saved without strong and vigorous resolutions on the part of the Governments still free in their opinions and actions ... The first principle to be followed by the monarchs, united as they are by the coincidence of their desires and opinions, should be that of maintaining the stability of political institutions against the disorganised excitement which has take possession of men's minds; the immutability of principles against the madness of their interpretation and respect for laws actually in force against a desire for their destruction ... In short, let the great monarchs strengthen their union, and prove to the world that if it exists, it is beneficent, and ensures the political peace of Europe; that it is powerful only for the maintenance of tranquillity at a time when so many attacks are directed against it; that the principles which they profess are paternal and protective, menacing only disturbers of public tranquillity.

(a) What were the 'passions' which disturbed Europe in 1820 (line 1)?
(b) What was Metternich's diagnosis of the events of 1820? How justified was his view that resistance by the monarchies was the only answer?
(c) Metternich remarked that Austria, Prussia and Russia were united 'by the coincidence of their desires and opinions' (lines 10–11). How true was this of the period 1815–30?
(d) Was there any alternative to resistance to the forces of change?

Source: K. Metternich, *Memoirs of Prince Metternich*, (iii) (1881). pp. 454ff.

Source C: Students, professors and the press.

THE STUDENT, taken in himself, is a child, and the *Burschenschaft* is an unpractical puppet-show. Then, I have never – and of this you are a witness – spoken of the students, but all my aim has been directed at the professors. Now, the professors, singly or united, are most unsuited to be conspirators. People only conspire profitably against things, not against theories. The last, indeed may grow to power, but this can never be the case if they leave the sphere of theology. Where they are political, they must be supported by deed, and the deed is the overthrow of existing institutions, and the *ôtez-vous de là que je m'y mette*.[1] This is what learned men and professors cannot manage, and the class of lawyers is better suited to carry it on. I know hardly one learned man who knows the value of property; while, on the contrary, the lawyer class is always rummaging about in the property of others. Besides, the professors are, nearly without exception, given up to theory; while no people are more practical than the lawyers.

Consequently, I have never feared that the revolution would be engendered by the universities; but that at them a whole generation of revolutionaries must be formed, unless the evil is restrained, seems to me certain. I hope that the most mischievous symptoms of the evil at the universities may be met, and that perhaps from its own peculiar sources, for the measures of the Government will contribute to this less than the weariness of the students, the weakness of the professors, and the different direction which the studies may take. But this feeling will never restrain me from taking steps from above; and, indeed, what seem to me the only possible measures are taken.

If we are together I can give you many satisfactory explanations of the course of the business, which at a distance I could not communicate to you without an enormous correspondence, and even then must remain futile and imperfect.

The greatest and consequently the most urgent evil now is the press. The measures referring to it which I intend to bring forward at the Carlsbad Congress I will tell you all the more gladly as I wish you to give me your opinion on my ideas without reserve, and put yourself in a position to help me effectually in Carlsbad, where the business must begin without delay.

[1] "Get out and make room for me." – Ed.

(a) What were the 'Burschenschaften' to which Metternich refers in this extract? (line 1)
(b) Why, according to Metternich, do lawyers make more effective revolutionaries than professors? (lines 9–12)
(c) In your opinion what would be the qualities which would make an effective revolutionary? Would they be different in the circumstances of the present day as contrasted to those prevailing in the early nineteenth century?
(d) What was the danger presented by the Universities if the 'student, taken in himself, is a child' and professors were 'unsuited to be conspirators' (lines 1–5)?

Source: Metternich, *Memoirs III* (1881). Quoted in Mack Walker, *Metternich's Europe 1813–1848* (Harper, 1968).

4 The age of revolutions 1815–48

Introduction

The absence of international wars in the period 1815–48 was compensated for, and partly explained by, the high level of domestic disturbances. There were almost decennial spasms of revolution culminating in the general European outbreak in 1848. Since then there have been very few instances of spontaneous revolutions in Europe.

4.1 Theories of revolution

Broadly there are two sets of factors which go to make a revolution and which may also explain the degree of interconnection between revolutions:

(a) *Opposition to the established authorities*

This may arise from:

1 *The impetus and pursuit of ideals.* In the 1820s–40s a variety of causes involved a challenge to authority:

   – *Romanticism*, the 'spirit of the age'.
   – *Nationalism*, which was undergoing a change of definition.
   – *Liberalism*, constitutionalism and democracy.
   – *Socialism* in its 'Utopian' or 'scientific' forms.

2 *The dissatisfaction of vested interests.* In the form of:

   – An organised and coordinated conspiracy by a group of agitators, or
   – A broader involvement resulting from *socio-economic changes* producing discontented groups seeking greater political recognition and social and economic reforms.

(b) *The vulnerability of the 'establishment'*

Mere disturbances may be converted to revolution by the actions of the authorities themselves. This depends upon:

1 The availability of *adequate forces* to abort revolution.
2 The readiness of the government to act decisively.

4.2 Romanticism

The 'Romantics' were never a political party, but 'romanticism' had political implications although initially associated with music and the Arts. It was a broad 'protest movement', which emphasised the importance of human passion and imagination to creativity rather than the cold reason and logic which had so dominated eighteenth century philosophy. Humanity was not bound always to behave according to 'iron laws'. This had several implications:

(a) The return of God

The Age of Reason had reached a peak of cynicism about faith and God. The Romantics believed there must be a God to breathe inspiration and imagination into man. So the century was to see a *revival in Catholicism* which was to have political repercussions.

(b) Glorification of individuality

Since passions were so important it was easy to see the wild, reckless, eccentric and even fanatical character as being admirable. Lord Byron, who died fighting in the Greek War of Independence (see Section 3.8(c)), was 'mad, bad and dangerous to know'. *Action* was valued more than thought and reason.

(c) An unfolding pattern of history

Far from history being just 'one damn thing after another', it was developing through God's will and the activities of 'supermen' like Napoleon in a certain direction and that was the creation of a series of tightly bound national states based on a close sense of *community*.

(d) The 'excellence of diversity'

What helped history to unfold was the contributions made at different times by particular groups of 'Chosen People' kept distinctive by their cultural quality – their language above all. These missions for humanity would be with different peoples at different times. To Mazzini, for instance, the Italians' pursuit of unification was only part of a general European movement against absolutist repression by multinational empires.

4.3 Nationalism

The words 'nation and nationalism' can mean different things at different times. Also, like romanticism, nationalism could be radical or conservative in different situations.

(a) Political definition of nationalism

Before 1789, the 'nation' was simply the *ruling political class*. With the writings of Rousseau and events of the French Revolution it came to mean the wider community sharing political rights. This did not mean, however, that the 'natural frontiers' of France could not include Italians and Germans and Belgians.

(b) Cultural definition of nationalism

As a result of the work of people like Johann Herder reviving old folk legends, languages and cultures there was a growing tendency to see nationalism in terms of *ethnic features*. This had explosive implications for the old multinational empires, but also had a very creative side to it.

(c) The significance of nationalism in 1848

The complex intermingling of ethnic groups which had developed for centuries before 1848 was to be of great significance. However the strength of nationalist feeling was exaggerated by nineteenth-century historians. Only a small minority of people were actually interested in achieving some sort of ethnic nationalist objectives. However, it did play a part in that there was resentment in provinces in the Habsburg Monarchy at the increasing German character of the Empire and the preferential position of German speakers. Also in Italy and Germany there was a developing argument that national unity was essential for the achievement of political and economic modernisation. Nationalism and Liberalism were thus linked.

4.4 Liberalism

The emphasis of liberalism is on the rights of the individual citizen to pursue and protect his own interests. There were different varieties and extremes.

(a) Constitutionalism

The essence of liberal constitutionalism was:

1 *A guarantee of individual liberties and rights* as a basic restriction on the government and other individuals.
2 *A constitution.* A series of rules and regulations distributing and controlling the use of political power. Of course there were several different 'models' with more or less restrictions on the electoral franchise, the legislature and the executive. Today the idea is moderate and readily acceptable but to early nineteenth-century conservatives it was very radical. Metternich remarked, 'There is ... scarcely any epoch which does not offer a rallying cry to some particular faction. This cry since 1815 has been "constitution"!'

(b) Democracy

A constitutional régime may not be democratic since it markedly reduces the proportion of citizens politically involved. Democracy is based on the principle of equal political rights for all citizens. However, there is also an element of state intervention to achieve equality of opportunity and defend the interests of the poor against the rich as with the more extreme Jacobins of the 1790s (see Section 1.8). With the drive to equality as a possible danger to individual liberty liberals could see a constitution as a check against 'plundering' democratic majorities as well as overpowerful monarchs.

From radical democracy to socialism is not a great step since it can be held that the great obstacle to true liberty and equality is social inequalities, property ownership and the accumulation of wealth. Against the grim background of developing industrialisation under unrestricted capitalism there inevitably developed proposals for a more rational organisation of society to cover areas such as the condition of the workers in Nantes, for whom 'living meant not dying' or the Flemish weavers in 1846 digging up dead horses and cats and dogs for food. In fact, there were several theories.

(a) *Saint-Simon and the maximisation of production*

Saint-Simon, ex-army officer reduced to clerical work, looked to a more equal society based on increased *productivity* by eliminating wasteful competition from credit and industry, the elimination of parasitic non-productive classes, abolition of inheritance to stimulate work and a greater valuation upon the status of labour. He is often held to have strongly influenced Louis Napoleon, 'Saint-Simon on horseback' (see Section 12.3).

(b) *Utopian Socialism*

1 *Cooperative self-sufficiency.* A group of socialist philosophers such as Charles Fourier (a shop assistant), Pierre Proudhon (a Lyons printer) and Robert Owen (a Welsh factory manager) looked towards the establishment of small-scale cooperative units of industrial and agricultural workers. Money would be replaced by barter and exchange if necessary. There would be no need for a central political authority. Nor in this *anarchic paradise* would there be private property; as Proudhon remarked 'Property is theft'.
2 *State-sponsored cooperatives.* Louis Blanc in his *Organisation du Travail* (1840) was rather different. State power should be taken and used to end capitalism by creating cooperative national workshops.

(c) *Scientific Socialism*

The *'utopians'* thought in obsolete terms of small units. *Karl Marx*, the son of a German Jewish lawyer, produced a theory of socialism more adapted to the circumstances of advanced industrialisation and with a logical historical analysis. The essentials were expressed in the *Communist Manifesto* (1848).

1 *Economic production* is the main determinant of the nature of society.
2 *The dominant economic class always controls the State* in its own interests.
3 *With economic development new classes emerge* and struggle with the old to win control of the State.
4 *The capitalist industrialist phase* was the last great change in economic development and the concentrating force of the factory workers would overthrow the bourgeois.
5 *Class conflict would cease.* The new society would be classless, egalitarian and democratic. The absence of the need for repression would mean 'the withering away of the State'.

(d) *The role of Socialism in the revolutions in 1820–48*

Socialism had a limited influence in France and Germany. It was handicapped by:

1 The distraction of republicanism in France (see Section 5.5(d)).

2 The absence of concentrated pockets of working-class solidarity.

The artisans and tradesmen in the small workshops, though, were susceptible to utopian socialism because of their comparable situations.

4.6 Communications

Of course, the influence of ideas upon revolution depends very much upon *communications*.

(a) *Increased circulation of pamphlets and newspapers*

The introduction of steam-powered machinery, the telegraph and railway meant that newspaper circulation in Paris rose from 60,000 in 1830 to 148,000 in 1845.

(b) *Limited literacy*

However, circulation was likely to be restricted to the middle classes and artisans. Even in Britain, France and Belgium in the 1840s the literacy rate was only 40–50 per cent. In Russia in 1840 it was 1 per cent. This did not make the lower classes likely to be revolutionary, but meant that they would be motivated more by economic and social factors.

4.7 'This great and dangerous plot'

Metternich rather exaggerated the role of the many secret societies drawn from fanatics, half-pay army officers and so on.

(a) *Internal divisions between conspirators*

The Italian *Carbonari*, for instance (see Section 6.3(a)), had up to 600,000 members but they were linked only by a vague belief in Italian unity and opposition to Austria. Secret societies of intellectuals and activists are in any case very prone to internal rivalries.

(b) *The absence of international unity*

Revolutionaries like Buonarotti and Mazzini (see Section 6) were bound to exaggerate the degree of international conspiracy to frighten the enemy.

4.8 Social theories

Europe was subject to *intense social and economic change*. It may be that the answer should be sought in the discontent arising from this. There are three possible culprits:

1 A peasantry trapped in the new capitalist economy.
2 A downtrodden and desperate working class.
3 An ambitious but frustrated middle class.

4.9   The peasantry

Rural interests were still predominant in central and western Europe. Only in Britain did industrial workers make up 25 per cent of the population. The further east one looked the more prevalent was feudal landlord power and serfdom. Semi-feudal tenures and serfdom still prevailed in eastern Germany, most of the Habsburg Monarchy, Russia and the Danube provinces of Moldavia and Wallachia. The peasantry were vulnerable to powerful long-term trends:

(a)   *Population pressure*

The European population grew from 187 million in 1800 to 266 million in 1850. Together with inefficient farming techniques the result was rural poverty and migration to the cities.

(b)   *The decline of rural manufacturing*

In the face of competition from the new factories the merchant clothiers increased pressure on their peasant 'out-workers'. Hence the strikes and riots of the French and Silesian weavers in the 1830s–40s.

(c)   *Commercialisation*

Peasants were increasingly at the mercy of world prices and grain speculators. The bigger farmer absorbing the holdings of weaker neighbours was likely to survive. Scattered, illiterate and conservative the peasants were not easily mobilised into more than old-fashioned bread riots, although they were always an underlying threat. Rural unrest was normal. The 1840s saw agrarian riots in East Prussia, Silesia and Posen. In 1846 hundreds of Polish noblemen and their families were slaughtered in Galicia in a peasant revolt.

4.10 The 'labouring and dangerous classes' (see Illus. 4.1)

The cities were the storm centres of the revolutions of 1848. Towns played a key role in this 'proto-industrial' phase of European economic history. However, with the exception of a handful of rapidly growing centres the majority of towns were still pre-industrial in structure and medieval in appearance. It is easy to see links between the pressure of population growth – Berlin, for instance, grew from 172,000 in 1800 to 419,000 in 1850 – deteriorating conditions and desperate workers driven to revolt. In fact, what evidence there is suggests that in France there was no clear relationship between the speed of urban growth and the frequency of disturbances between the 1830s–70s. Analyses of the killed and wounded in 1830 and 1848 also suggested that the barricades were manned by skilled workers and craftsmen.

In reality, there were at least three 'working classes':

1   *The factory proletariat.* Actual factory workers played only a limited part. There were relatively small numbers of them. In France in 1848, only a fourth of manufacturing workers were in factories and mines. Their susceptibility to

Illus. 4.1   Houndsditch, 1875 (Hulton Picture Library)

From an 1875 engraving by Gustav Doré, from a series showing life in the London slums.

revolution was also limited by relatively high wages compared to the craftsmen, relative newness to the towns and the illiteracy and dialects which made communication difficult.

2   *The 'lumpen proletariat'.* The absolutely destitute and criminal elements were growing in numbers, but too busy surviving to be revolutionary. On the other hand, their existence, concentrated in the city centres, was a constant spectral warning to the middle and working classes to seek to improve and maintain their status.

3   *The Artisans.* The traditional craftsmen such as weavers and metal workers from small workshops were the revolutionary muscle:

– The new factories and mechanisation threatened them with redundancy and the degradation of their crafts.
– Traditional defences could not be relied upon. The masters, under pressure, were trying to exploit their men even more. Guild regulations to restrict entry to

trades were becoming illegal. State and municipal government were more likely to repeal price regulations or prosecute trade unions in the new atmosphere of free trade.

These craftsmen might turn to machine breaking or mutual societies and friendly societies but they also had a tradition of self defence by political activity, were more likely to be literate and attracted by socialism.

4.11 The middle classes

Metternich blamed *'the presumptuous men'*, the ambitious new middle classes seeking to break the discrimination which deprived them of the vote – in France only 25 per cent of the adult middle class males had a vote in 1848, and the situation was worse elsewhere. European bureaucracies and officer corps were still dominated by the aristocracy. For instance, in Prussia in 1842 nobles had 9 out of 11 ministries and 20 of 28 provincial governorships, and there were twice as many noble as bourgeois members of diets throughout Prussia.

(a)   *The business and financial class*

These groups had too much to lose from disorder, and wanted to be accepted by the 'establishment' rather than overthrow it. On the other hand:

1   They wanted *specific reforms* such as free trade and an improved financial system.
2   The prospect of a breakdown in order might oblige them to take action in self defence if the régime proved unreliable.

(b)   *The intelligentsia*

The academics, doctors, lawyers and officials were very political and tended to speak for the middle classes:

1   *Education.* Unlike businessmen, they had been educated to a relatively high level and been exposed to radical ideas.
2   *Repression.* As students, they were far more likely to be subject to police restrictions, repression and censorship than anyone else.
3   *Frustration.* By the 1840s, the higher education system was turning out more professional people than there were jobs. Opportunities were limited by absolutist restrictions on journalism, education and the legal system. States without *habeas corpus* need few defence lawyers. In areas like Lombardy–Venetia, the situation was doubly worse, because what jobs there were would go to Habsburg nominees.
       These groups were not total revolutionaries. They wanted greater opportunities but to maintain order as well.
4   *Organisation.* Membership of clubs and professional organisations provided opportunities for debate and for training in political organisation.

4.12 Weakness at the top

The régimes lacked adequate police forces and proper anti-riot provision. Regular troops had been known to refuse to fire in the past, and their use could escalate a situation. The real problem, however, was a lack of will to use force in the right amount at the right time:

1 *Unpreparedness.* The outbreaks were often totally unexpected and started off as mere bread riots.
2 *'Mouldering buildings'.* Metternich despaired at the character of the monarchs he was 'propping up'. Louis Philippe was old, tired and inflexible. The Emperor Ferdinand was mentally defective. Frederick William of Prussia was a bogus liberal with great ambitions but lacking decisiveness or consistency.
3 *Pessimism.* The 'red skies of Paris' were a very recent memory and once revolution actually broke out the belief that an irreversible process had started made flight rather than resistance a sensible response.

4.13 The accelerator

In 1848 very few people actually wanted or expected revolution. In fact the memory of 1789 was still very vivid in the minds of most politically aware people. The key factor in 1848 was the coincidence between a severe economic and social crisis and political difficulties. Intensified social tension and aggravated differences of opinion within the élite set against unresponsive régimes which were unwilling or unable to maintain order or deal with the causes resulted in political mobilisation, which was triggered into revolution by specific incidents.

(a) *An economic crisis*

Between 1845 and 1847 poor cereal harvests and an outbreak of potato blight, together with communications problems and speculation produced an escalation in food prices of over 50 per cent in some localities for grain and 100 per cent for potatoes. This affected different groups in different ways:

1 *An increased cost of living* for the poorer classes in town and country, who already had very low living standards. The impact of the crisis varied between countries and regions. Britain, Russia and Poland were not so badly affected. Conditions were worst in Ireland, Flanders, Silesia and Galicia. In Ireland over half a million people died of starvation or famine related diseases.
2 *Reduced demand* for manufactured goods. As the price of food rose so people had less to spend on consumer goods and so the crisis was transmitted to urban and rural industry. Wages and employment fell and workers migrating back to the countryside increased the pressures there.
3 *The contraction of credit* and resultant liquidity crises. Credit was reduced by the use of bullion to pay for grain imports, rising interest rates and the withdrawal of British capital.

(b) *Social tension and disorder*

Deteriorating social conditions, rising death rates (in Paris from 24.4 per 1000 in 1842 to 29.3 per 1000 in 1847) increased crime, vagrancy and prostitution were the first symptoms. Then in 1846–7 food and anti-tax riots became prevalent. Typical of these was the 'potato revolt' in Berlin in April 1847. This sort of general sense of grievance and social malaise would not itself produce revolution, but the danger was that it would become politicised. Count Galen, the Prussian representative at Kassel, described graphically the state of things at the start of 1848: 'The old year ended in scarcity, the new one opens with starvation. Misery, spiritual and physical, traverses Europe in ghastly shapes – the one without God, the other without bread. Woe if they join hands!'

(c) Political mobilisation

In fact although the situation was beginning to improve slightly in 1848 more action was expected from governments than they were prepared to take, and the decisive factor now was the aggravation of discontent amongst middle-class groups who became involved partly to exploit the situation in their own interests, but largely because the governments seemed to have lost control. They were not advocates of revolutionary political change. Their main objective was 'modernisation' on the British model. This involved the elimination of arbitrary government and the establishment of some form of constitutional régime as well as the guarantee of individual freedoms and the rule of law. They usually opposed democracy because they feared that anarchy would result unless political power resided in the hands only of those who had a propertied stake in society. It was the widespread failure of ruling élites to respond to the pressure for change which resulted in political polarisation, the deepening loss of confidence in government and the breakdown of political systems.

4.14 Conclusion

In Britain in 1848 the disturbances amounted to the Chartist demonstration at Kennington Common. There was no revolution. A flexible constitution and a politically minded aristocracy had divided and bought off potential opposition with the Great Reform Act of 1832 which won over a section of the middle class and Sir Robert Peel's economic reforms in the 1840s which stimulated growth and retarded price increases. Reasonable concessions made in time could preserve the basic social order.

Questions

1   Which classes of society mainly supported liberal and national movements in the first half of the nineteenth century?   [OC]
2   'Economic considerations must predominate in any explanation of the revolution of 1848.' Discuss.
                                                                                              [OC]
3   Why were there so many outbreaks of revolution in Europe between 1815 and 1848?
4   How far should the Vienna Settlement of 1815 be held responsible for the revolutionary outbreaks which occurred in Europe during the next twenty years?
5   How justified was Metternich's belief in the existence of a 'great and dangerous plot' against European stability between 1815 and 1848?
6   What contribution was made by 'Romanticism' to the revolutions which broke out in Europe between 1815 and 1848?
7   Study Sources A, B, C and D then answer the questions which follow.

Source A: The emergence of the proletariat.

> Modern industry has converted the little workshop of the patriarchal master into the great factory of the industrial capitalist. Masses of labourers, crowded into the factory, are organised like soldiers. As privates of the industrial army they are placed under the command of a perfect hierarchy of officers and sergeants. Not only are they slaves of the bourgeois class, and of the bourgeois state; they are daily and hourly enslaved by the

machine, by the overlooker, and, above all, by the individual bourgeois manufacturer himself. The more openly this despotism proclaims gain to be its end and aim, the more petty, the more hateful and the more embittering it is . . .

The lower strata of the middle class – the small trades-people, shopkeepers and retired tradesmen generally, the handicraftsmen and peasants – all these sink gradually into the proletariat, partly because their diminutive capital does not suffice for the scale on which modern industry is carried on and is swamped in the competition with the large capitalists, partly because their specialised skill is rendered worthless by new methods of production. Thus the proletariat is recruited from all classes of the population . . .

But with the development of industry the proletariat not only increases in number; it becomes concentrated in greater masses, its strength grows, and it feels that strength more. The various interests and conditions of life within the ranks of the proletariat are more and more equalised, in proportion as machinery obliterates all distinctions of labour, and nearly everywhere reduces wages to the same low level. The growing competition among the bourgeois, and the resulting commercial crises, make the wages of the worker ever more fluctuating. The unceasing improvement of machinery, ever more rapidly developing, makes their livelihood more and more precarious, the collisions between individual workmen and individual bourgeois take more and more the character of collisions between two classes. Thereupon the workers begin to form combinations (trades unions) against the bourgeois, they club together in order to keep up the rate of wages, they found permanent associations in order to make provision before hand for these occasional revolts. Here and there the contest breaks out into riots.

(a) What did Marx and Engels mean by the term 'proletariat' and how were its ranks swelled (lines 1–14)?
(b) Do you see anything significant in the constant use of military terms and analogies in this extract?
(c) How did the process of industrialisation drive the proletariat towards resistance and riots? How did it help their organisation (lines 15–27)?
(d) According to this view, was the process of industrialisation one to be welcomed by all of the middle classes?

Source: K. Marx and F. Engels, *The Communist Manifesto* (1847–8).

Source B: Life in the Rue des Fumiers.

If you want to know how he lives, go – for example – to the Rue des Fumiers which is almost entirely inhabited by this class of worker. Pass through one of the drain-like openings, below street-level, that lead to these filthy dwellings, but remember to stoop as you enter. One must have gone down into these alleys where the atmosphere is as damp and cold as a cellar; one must have known what it is like to feel one's foot slip on the polluted ground and to fear a stumble into the filth; to realise the painful impression that one receives on entering the homes of these unfortunate workers.

Below street-level on each side of the passage there is a large gloomy cold room. Foul water oozes out of the walls. Air reaches the room through a sort of semi-circular window which is two feet high at its greatest elevation. Go in – if the fetid smell that assails you does not make you recoil. Take care, for the floor is uneven, unpaved and untiled – or if there are tiles, they are covered with so much dirt that they cannot be seen. And then you will see two or three rickety beds fitted to one side because the cords that bind them to the worm-eaten legs have themselves decayed. Look at the contents of the bed – a mattress; a tattered blanket of rags (seldom washed since there is only one); sheets sometimes; and a pillow sometimes. No wardrobes are needed in these homes. Often a weaver's loom and a spinning wheel complete the furniture. There is no fire in the winter. No sunlight penetrates [by day], while at night a tallow candle is lit. Here men work for fourteen hours [a day] for a daily wage of fifteen to twenty *sous*.

Particulars of the expenses of this miserable section of the community are better evidence than anything else [of their situation] – rent 25 francs [a year]; washing 12 francs; fuel – wood and peat – 35 francs; light 35 francs; repair of worn-out furniture 3 francs; removal expenses – at least once a year – 2 francs; footwear 12 francs; nothing for clothes since they wear cast-off garments given to them; nothing for medical expenses since nuns give them medicines on a doctor's note; total – 104 francs [a year]. This leaves 196 francs – out of an annual income of 300 francs – which has to feed four or five persons. They cannot afford more bread than 150 francs' worth – an amount which is quite insufficient and which entails much privation. So only 46 francs remain to buy salt, butter, vegetables and potatoes. And when we realise that something goes to the tavern ... we can appreciate ... how terrible are the conditions under which these families live.

As they chat between their coffee and liqueurs many philanthropists often declare that drunkenness is the main cause of the misfortunes of the common people whose miseries they are discussing. For our part we think that one can only destroy a bad habit by replacing it by a better habit. And we ask: What enjoyments are available to the worker when he is free on Sundays? In the summer he can go into the country and he does not deny himself this outing. But in the winter? A room in the Rue des Fumiers or elsewhere with children crying and with a wife embittered by poverty – or the tavern ...

(a) What do you think were the main health problems facing families living in such conditions?
(b) According to Guépin, given an average family size of four or five persons what was the average expenditure per head upon food (lines 20–30)? What was the main item of diet? What is wrong with the dietary pattern outlined by Guépin?
(c) How was medical care catered for (lines 24–25)?
(d) What was Guépin's attitude towards drunkenness and the critics of the working-class expenditure upon drink (lines 31–37)?

Source: Dr A. Guépin, *Nantes au xixe Siècle* (Nantes, 1835).

Source C: The June Days in Paris.

The Paris workers have been overwhelmed by superior forces; they have not succumbed to them. They have been beaten, but it is their enemies who have been vanquished. The momentary triumph of brutal violence has been purchased with the destruction of all the deceptions and illusions of the February revolution, with the dissolution of the whole of the old republican party, and with the fracturing of the French nation into two nations, the nation of the possessors and the nation of the workers. The tricolor republic now bears only one colour, the colour of the defeated, the colour of blood. It has become the red republic.

There was no republican group of repute on the side of the people. . . . Without leaders, without any means other than the insurrection itself, the people withstood the united bourgeoisie and soldiery longer than any French dynasty, with all its military apparatus, ever withstood a fraction of the bourgeoisie united with the people. In order that the people's last illusion should disappear, in order to allow a complete break with the past, it was necessary for the customary poetic accompaniment of a French rising, the enthusiastic youth of the bourgeoisie, the pupils of the école *polytechnique*, the three-cornered hats, to take the side of the oppressors. The pupils of the Faculty of Medicine had to deny the aid of science to the wounded plebeians, who have committed the unspeakable, infernal crime of hazarding their lives for their own existence for once, instead of for Louis Philippe or M. Marrast.

(a) On what grounds would you qualify or reject this argument by Marx that the June Days were the product of class divisions and antagonism?
(b) How, according to Marx, did this French uprising differ from those which had preceded it?
(c) In what sense could it be said that the Paris workers had actually triumphed?
(d) How would Marx symbolise this 'victory'?

Source: K. Marx, *Neue Rheinische Zeitung*. Quoted in P. Jones, *The 1848 Revolutions* (Longman, 1981).

Source D: The Magyar address to the Emperor.

Whilst the blood of Hungary is flowing in Italy in defence of the Austrian monarchy, one portion of her children is perfidiously excited against the other, and casts off the obedience due to the local Government of the country. Insurrection threatens our frontiers, and, under the pretence of upholding your authority, it is actually assailing the integrity of the kingdom, and our ancient and new liberties . . . It is in the name of the people we call on your Majesty to order the Hungarian regiments to obey the Hungarian Ministry, without reserve and notwithstanding all other orders. We desire that Croatia be freed from military despotism, in order that it may unite fraternally with Hungary. finally, we demand that your Majesty, discarding the reactionary counsels of those about you, give your immediate sanction to all the measures voted by the Diet, and come and reside in Pesth among you people, where your royal presence is necessary to save the country. Let your Majesty hasten. The least delay may occasion indescribable calamities.

(a) In this Address how is the Hungarian Diet seeking to avoid the implication that it is threatening revolt against the Emperor?
(b) What were the measures voted by the Diet which the Emperor was being called upon to sanction?
(c) How would you rewrite the Address to say what it really means?
Source: *Annual Register*, 1848, p. 408.

8   Study Illus. 4.1 (p. 56) again. How has Doré's picture heightened the drama (and so the impact) of this scene of London poverty?

5 Restoration France 1815–48

Introduction

With the 'universal tyrant' safely exiled to the mid-Atlantic the main priority was to restore stability to France. Unfortunately the political pattern of swings from one extreme to another which was so obvious between 1789–1815 was to continue. The confrontation of returning émigrés who had 'learnt nothing and forgotten nothing' and the new classes of bourgeois, propertied men and professional officials would prove to be too severe to establish a stable régime.

5.1 The restoration of the Bourbon Monarchy

The new King, Louis XVIII, was the brother of Louis XVI. The fiction that there had been a Louis XVII was maintained. He was a clever, cultivated man but fat, gout-ridden and a prematurely aged 59-year-old. This old, rather indolent man in a wheelchair was a complete contrast with the personal magnetism of Napoleon. Nevertheless he declared in 1817 that 'All the efforts of my government are directed into the effort to forge the two peoples who exist only too much in fact into a single one'. From the start, however, divisions were very apparent:

(a) The Constitutional Charter

During the brief First Restoration the King granted a constitution although clumsily it was dated in 'the nineteenth year of my reign' and was based on royal prerogative rather than coming from an elected assembly. Nor were matters helped by the replacement of the tricolor with the Bourbon white flag:

1   *A guarantee of individual rights.* The 'public rights of the French' were confirmed. The equality and freedom which were the great gains of the revolutionary period were guaranteed. The confirmation of property rights even extended to those who had gained from the confiscation of Church and émigré lands.
2   *A parliamentary system.* A Chamber of Deputies of substantial property holders was to be elected by voters restricted by age and property qualifications to about one in a hundred French males. In addition there was an hereditary Chamber of Peers. The monarchy was given considerable powers including a veto over legislation, the dissolution of the Chamber, appointment of the ministers and

control over foreign policy and the armed forces. There was also a royal power to issue emergency ordinances.

(b) *The 'Ultras'*

Paper schemes did not match the real divisions in France, which were made even worse by the 'Hundred Days'. Only one in twelve of the aristocracy had actually emigrated, but they or their descendants returned with a vengeance to lead an 'ultra' royalist back-lash:

1 *The White Terror.* The 'Hundred Days' was followed by the temporary suspension of some of the liberties of the Charter and a brief but vicious 'terror' in which at least 300 Protestants, republicans and Bonapartists died. Eighteen of the most prominent rebels were executed, including the famous 'Red Michael', Marshal Ney.
2 *'Chambre introuvable'.* The 'incomparable' Chamber elected in 1815, and which condoned this persecution, was dominated by the Ultras. They had no belief in constitutionalism but were after official posts, the return of émigré property, social dominance and the restoration of the political influence of the clergy. Headed by the Comte d'Artois, the brother of the King, who was also the commander of the National Guard, they were well disciplined and 'stood up, sat down, spoke and kept silent like a single man'.

5.2 The failure of conciliation (1815–24)

On the other hand, the Charter was supported by two other political groups:

1 *The Independents.* Drawn from the urban middle class, purchasers of émigré property and ex-imperial soldiers and led by Lafayette they were united in looking beyond the Charter to 'the will of the nation', although they included liberals, Bonapartists and republicans.
2 *The Doctrinaires.* The King depended heavily upon this moderate conservative group, which saw the Charter as the basis for stability. They included men of great talent such as the historian Guizot but had no well-established roots in the country.

(a) *The first Richelieu Ministry (1815–16)*

The first government headed by the former émigré but relatively moderate Duc de Richelieu was deadlocked when faced with an avalanche of demands by Ultra deputies for the repudiation of all government debts incurred before the Restoration, the return of confiscated lands, further limitations on the electoral system and abolition of Napoleon's University of France which supervised educational provision. In April 1816, under pressure from his ministers and the Allies, the King dissolved the Chamber.

(b) *The second Richelieu Ministry (1816–18)*

With a majority of Doctrinaires and a new harmony, there was a chance for some valuable legislation.

1 *The restoration of the national finances.* The war indemnity was even paid off before the deadline, and the army of occupation evacuated by November 1818.

2   *The rebuilding of the army.* The *Loi Gouvion St Cyr* restored conscription, which had been over-hastily abolished by the Charter. The result was the gradual recreation of a professional army (drawn largely from peasants because of the possibility for those with money to 'buy' a substitute).

3   *The electoral laws of February and March 1818.* The laws confirmed the provisions of the Charter, but also introduced a new voting system known as *'scrutin de liste'* which weakened the influence of rural interests.

4   *Relatively liberal press control.* The Charter had been rather vague about censorship. The legislation of 1819 did abolish it, but also introduced a system of licences and retained a stamp duty to limit the establishment and circulation of newspapers.

(c)   *The revival of the Ultras*

Changing circumstances forced the Duc de Richelieu to advocate an alliance with the Ultras. There was a new wave of right-wing pressure, based upon:

1   *The mounting threat from the Bonapartist–liberal group.* The Napoleonic legend and a system of annual elections of a fifth of the deputies allowed them to double their representatives to 90 from 1818–19.

2   *An outbreak of liberal revolts* throughout Europe in 1820.

3   *The murder of the Duc de Berry (February 1820).* The son of the Comte d'Artois was murdered by a crazed Bonapartist fanatic who was easily represented as a liberal puppet.

A brief attempt by the King to maintain a moderate government was ruined by the murder, and Richelieu returned again, this time with the Ultras.

(d)   *The Ultras (1820–4)*

Richelieu soon gave way to the more right-wing *Comte de Villèlle*. A large Ultra majority followed very right-wing policies:

1   *The re-establishment of censorship.* In addition, new newspapers would need government authorisation.

2   *A new electoral law in the interests of the Ultras.* Some 16,000 of the wealthiest citizens were given a double vote. A new *'scrutin d'Arrondissement'* restored the influence of small town and rural interests.

3   *A 'military promenade' in Spain in 1822.* With the backing of the Congress of Verona (see Section 3.7(d)). French troops were used to restore the authority of Ferdinand VII of Spain against the constitutionalists.

In the elections of 1824, government influence was used to its fullest extent. The new Ultra-dominated *'Chambre retrouvée'* at once extended its life to seven instead of five years and abolished the system of partial renewals. Then in September 1824 Louis XVIII died, and was succeeded by the Comte d'Artois, now Charles X.

5.3   The reign of Charles X

The new King was quite an attractive personality. France was at peace and was prospering, and at least there would be total harmony between the government and the Chamber. Charles X even started by abolishing censorship and releasing some political prisoners. But things worked out in a way which was not anticipated.

(a) The domestic policy of the Comte de Villèlle

A reactionary policy was inevitable:

1 *Compensation for the émigrés.* The 'Law of the *milliard émigrés*' angered the middle classes by providing compensation at the expense of interest rates on government securities.
2 *A clerical revival.* The very elaborate religious ceremonies at the coronation, the conspicuous return of the Jesuits, persecution of anti-clerical critics and re-establishment of clerical control over education were all very disturbing. However, fears of an imminent clerical coup were heightened by the introduction of the death penalty for sacrilege in 1826 and, in the same year, the revelations of the existence of a clerical-aristocratic secret society called the *Chevaliers de la Foi.* Even royalists were becoming alarmed.

(b) The fall of Villèlle

Villèlle was under mounting attack:

1 *A thriving opposition press challenged the domestic policies.* The ranks of journalists had been recently joined by the able Adolphe Thiers. By 1826, government newspapers had only 15,000 subscribers compared to the 40,000 of the opposition.
2 *Over-cautious foreign policy.* The Greek cause was popular in France, but Villèlle gave it little support.

Attempts to muzzle the press failed. Secret societies such as the constitutionalist anti-clerical *'aide-toi, le ciel t'aidera'* thrived. Then in November 1827 an opposition major-ity of 60 was returned in the elections and Villèlle resigned.

(c) The Ordinances of St Cloud, July 1830

The King was not obliged to choose ministers with a majority support but in August 1829 he selected the Prince Jules de Polignac and a very extremist cabinet. Bad har-vests, economic recession and a bad winter increased opposition. A new Chamber elected in July 1830 gave the opposition 274 members instead of 221. Polignac – the 'Ultra of Ultras' – could not govern. In the interests of the 'safety of the State' the King sought blatantly to achieve a political coup by his ordinances of the 26 July which pro-vided for:

1 Virtual suppression of the liberties of the press.
2 Reduction of the electorate to 25,000 from 100,000.
3 Fixing of a date for a new election.

Thiers and his fellow journalists invited the country to decide 'how far she ought to carry resistance against tyranny'.

(d) The July Revolution (1830) (Illus. 5.1)

The recent invasion of Algeria had removed the 40,000 best troops. The unpopular Marmont, betrayer of Napoleon, had only 11,000 men in Paris and they were not easily used in narrow streets. In the *'Trois Glorieuses'* of 29–31 July workers' and students' demonstrations were allowed to get out of hand. While Charles X hunted deer his sol-diers began to fraternise at the barricades. On 30 July a group of opposition deputies nominated Louis Philippe, Duke of Orleans, as Lieutenant General of the Kingdom.

Source: Oil painting by Eugène Delacroix, 1830 (Louvre, Paris).

He was supported by Lafayette and the National Guard. This was sealed by Louis Philippe's acceptance of the tricolor flag. On 2 August Charles abdicated in favour of his grandson the Duc de Bordeaux, but on 9 August the Chambers proclaimed Louis Philippe king.

5.4   The July Monarchy

The new régime was based upon:

(a)   *The qualities of the 'Citizen King'*

Louis Philippe was the son of the Duc d'Orleans, Philippe Egalité, who had flirted with the Revolution. He had also served as an officer in the revolutionary army. Having known poverty in exile he was now a wealthy man but deliberately cultivated a very humble exterior, symbolised by his top hat and umbrella.

(b)   *The support of the landed bourgeoisie*

A section of the royalists – the Legitimist supporters of the Bourbons – largely withdrew from politics (*'l'émigration intérieure'*). The new régime was backed by wealthy business and commercial interests, and above all the landed bourgeoisie.

(c)   *The revised Charter of Liberties*

The Chamber of Deputies produced a Charter which extended liberty:

1   The Chamber of Peers became an upper house of life members – mostly army officers and civil servants.

2   Extension of the franchise to an electorate of 170,000.
3   The abolition of censorship ('for ever').
4   Roman Catholicism was recognised as the religion of only 'the majority of
     Frenchmen'.
5   The King lost the power to veto legislation absolutely. In addition, a system of
     elected councils was introduced in 1831 for municipalities, although with a very
     limited franchise. Recruitment to the National Guard was made more selective to
     ensure that it would be another bulwark of the régime.

5.5   The early problems of the régime

The excitement of expectations was reflected in the swarms of place-hunting ex-
Napoleonic servants and literary propaganda in favour of further political and social
reform. In fact there were serious problems from the start.

(a)   Division of the supporters of the régime

1   The Party of Resistance including Guizot and the Duc de Broglie saw the
     revolution as complete, and opposed further change.
2   The Party of Movement including Lafayette saw this as just the start of further
     reforms.

The struggle between the two groups persisted throughout the reign, which became
symbolised by the rivalry.

(b)   Hostility of political extremists

A compromise solution always faces threats from two sides. There was a series of
Ultra-royalist and republican plots and attempts on the life of the King. In 1832 there
was an attempt to raise La Vendée in support of 'Henri V', grandson of Charles X. In
1836 and 1840 Louis Napoleon attempted to stimulate Bonapartist risings in Strasbourg
and Boulogne.

(c)   Social unrest

Industrialisation made the condition of industrial workers a political issue for the first
time:

1   *The deterioration of living standards.* By 1846 over a million workers were
     employed in large-scale industry. Very rapid urbanisation – Roubaix grew by 425
     per cent between 1831 to 1841 – was associated with very poor living conditions.
     By 1840 nine in ten of the men called up in the ten industrial departments were
     rejected as physically unfit.
2   *Irregular employment.* General standards of living were probably rising but
     industrial workers lived on the edge of crisis which would be triggered by
     recession, price rises or unemployment. Of course, the July Revolution did not
     produce higher wages and reduced hours. In fact, unemployment increased in
     1830–1, and there were a number of demonstrations – including the one in Lyons
     in November 1831 by silk workers which was supported by National Guardsmen
     and had to be suppressed by regular troops.

(d) *A policy of resistance (1831–4)*

Social reform to win the workers' support for the régime was out of the question in view of the dependence on the bourgeoisie and the socialist tone of the Lyons revolt. In fact the period 1831–4 saw an increasing tendency of workers towards republicanism, and mounting disturbances. Very much influenced by Thiers, the government of the day took very firm steps:

1 *Repression.* Risings in eastern Paris and Lyons in April 1834 were crushed savagely, and republicanism was driven underground.
2 *Restriction of liberty.* The right of association was restricted in April 1834, and the press was brought under tighter control in September 1835.

By 1836, when Thiers formed his own government, the situation was under control.

5.6 'France is bored'

The July Revolution triggered off disturbances throughout Europe and nationalists and liberals looked forward to a foreign policy supporting peoples struggling for freedom. Caution, opposition to expense and the need to maintain relations with France's only potential friend, Britain, led Louis Philippe to be far more realistic. The result was that his policies were easily seen as 'peace at any price', and the poet Lamartine reflected wide opinion when he described France as 'bored'.

(a) *Belgian independence*

A revolt in Belgium in 1830 developed into a move for separation from Holland with whom there were all sorts of economic, religious and cultural differences. The absolutists' proposals for intervention to deal with this first rupture of the 1815 settlement were resisted by Britain and France, who organised an international conference to ratify the situation, forced the Dutch King to give way and then arranged the general European guarantee of Belgian neutrality. In fact, France was better off with this small friendly state on her frontier. However, Louis Philippe was criticised for not accepting the invitation by the Belgian National Congress for his son the Duc de Nemours to become King of the Belgians, and because he did not incorporate Belgium despite support in both countries for this step.

(b) *Occupation of Ancona (1832–8)*

Again, France did not help the Italian rebels in 1830–1 (see Section 6.3(c)) although when Austrian troops entered the Papal States to crush a revolt French troops were sent to occupy Ancona, as a gesture against Austrian interference rather than support for unification or revolution.

(c) *The second Mehemet Ali crisis (1839–41)*

Anglo-French relations were seriously damaged over the Near Eastern Crisis of 1839–41 (see Section 11.5). Thiers supported Mehemet Ali as a sort of French protégé. In fact, Lord Palmerston, the British Foreign Secretary, largely isolated and humiliated France over this issue. In the resultant war fever Thiers fell from office, and for the rest of the régime Guizot was the dominant political leader.

(d) *The Spanish Marriages Question*

In the 1840s Anglo-French relations were largely restored. By 1846 Palmerston was back in office and he and Guizot fell out over an agreement that the Queen of Spain should marry and produce an heir before the Infanta was allowed to marry a French prince. In fact the Queen was married off to an impotent Spanish nobleman and the Infanta to the Duc de Montpensier, son of Louis Philippe. However much of a coup this might have been, it left France isolated at a dangerous moment. New colonies in Africa and the Pacific and the completion of the pacification of Algeria were no consolation. In Europe France had no prestigious foreign policy successes to counteract her internal problems.

5.7 Growing opposition

Over the period industry and commerce actually developed, and agricultural production grew. Between 1837–48 1287 miles of railway were built. However, the opposition mounted:

(a) *Alternatives*

1 *Socialism.* Pierre Proudhon, Louis Blanc and Charles Fourier all attacked the régime for its failure to deal with the social questions and looked to republicanism to produce an answer (see Section 4.5).
2 *Bonapartism.* The cult of Napoleon was fanned by the return of his ashes to Les Invalides in 1840, Prince Louis Napoleon's book *Idées Napoléonnes* (1839) and a whole range of new histories of the revolutionary and Napoleonic period. Nostalgia can be very dangerous.

(b) *The growth of literacy*

A primary education law of 1833 and development of a cheaper press extended the reading public. In 1825 there were only 60,000 subscribers to dailies in Paris, by 1846 there were 180,000. The new press also had a considerable left-wing, socialist and republican component.

(c) *Economic crisis (1846–7)*

France shared in the general European economic crisis (see Section 4.13), worsened because of relative economic backwardness – France had 1287 miles of railways in 1848 when Prussia had 2287 miles. She also experienced a serious financial crisis until 1848 arising from overspeculation in railway shares and a shortage of capital. By 1846, a third of Paris workers were destitute and starving.

5.8 Conclusion

In 1840, Guizot declared: 'Let us not talk about our country having to conquer territory, to wage great wars, to undertake bold deeds of vengeance. If France is prosperous, if she remains free, peaceful and wise we need not complain.'

By 1846–8 France was isolated, humiliated and in a state of economic depression. The opposition ranted in 1847 'What has been done during these last seven years? Nothing! Nothing! Nothing!'. The most critical issue, though, was the government's refusal to extend the franchise. Guizot bitterly opposed universal suffrage; the franchise was restricted to 240,000 men and excluded the majority of educated and professional people. The 'Bourgeois Monarchy' did not have enough bourgeois support. Then on 22 February 1848 the government's banning of one of a series of banquets sponsored by the opposition in support of parliamentary reform triggered off a chain of events which led to 'a revolution by accident'.

Questions

1 Why was the rule of the restored Bourbons in France 1814–30 so brief?   [OC]
2 Why did Louis Philippe gain the throne of France in 1830 and lose it in 1848?   [OC]
3 Did the French Revolutions of 1830 and 1848 have similar social, economic and political roots?
                                                                                       [OX]
4 'Eighteen years of neglect at home and obedience to Britain abroad.' Explain this comment on the reign of Louis Philippe.   [NEAB]
5 What were the successes and failures of the restored Bourbon monarchy in France between 1814 and 1830?   [NEAB]
6 Give an account of the main events of the reigns of Louis XVIII and Charles X of France.
7 Study Sources A and B and then answer the questions which follow.

Source A: Royal policy under Louis Philippe.

Whatever may have been King Louis Philippe's views immediately after the revolution of July I will not decide; perhaps he may for a moment have wished to do something for France. But two months of his reign were sufficient to show him that the great question was not to conquer territories or gain influence abroad but to save Monarchy. He saw clearly that although he might begin a war, necessarily it would soon degenerate into a war of internal propaganda, and that he and his family would be the first victims of it. His struggle has constantly been to strengthen his government, to hold together or create anew the elements indispensable for a monarchical government; and most probably the remainder of his life will be devoted to this important task ...

Therefore, knowing as I do all the proceedings of the King and his Cabinet, seeing constantly in the most unreserved manner the whole of the despatches, I must say that no one is more against acquiring influence in foreign states, or even getting burthened with family aggrandisement in them, than he ...

His fear of being drawn into a real intervention has been the cause of his having been so anxious not to have a French Legion in Spain. He may be right or wrong on this subject, but his fear of being drawn too far, like a man whose clothes get caught by a steam-engine, is natural enough.

(a) What was 'the revolution of July' (lines 1–2)?
(b) Who was King Leopold? Why might he have had the intimate knowledge of French policy that he claims in lines 10–11?
(c) Why does he say that Louis Philippe's principal task was 'to save Monarchy' (line 4) and 'strengthen his government' (line 7)? What efforts did Louis Philippe make to accomplish this, and why was he ultimately unsuccessful?
(d) Comment on Leopold's assessment of France's foreign policy during the reign (lines 10–17).
Source: Letter from King Leopold to Queen Victoria, October 1837.

Source B: The outbreak of the February revolution.

A sudden rattle of musketry made him wake with a start; and, in spite of Rosanette's entreaties, Frederic insisted on going to see what was happening. He followed the sound of the firing down the Champs-Elysées. At the corner of the rue Saint-Honoré he was met by a shout from some workmen in blouses:

'No! Not that way! To the Palais-Royal!'

Frederic followed them. The railings of the Church of the Assumption had been pulled down. Further on he noticed three paving stones torn up in the middle of the road, doubtless the foundation of a barricade – then bits of broken bottles, and bundles of wire, to hamper the cavalry. Suddenly, out of an alley, rushed a tall young man, with black hair hanging over his shoulders and wearing a sort of pea-green singlet. He carried a soldier's long musket; there were slippers on his feet and he was running on tiptoe, as lithe as a tiger, yet with the fixed stare of a sleep-walker. Now and then explosions could be heard.

The previous evening the public exhibition of a cart containing five bodies from the boulevard des Capucines had changed the temper of the people. At the Tuileries there was a continuous coming and going of equerries; M Molé, who was constructing a new Cabinet, did not reappear; M Thiers tried to form another; the king shuffled, hesitated, gave Bugeaud full authority, then prevented him from making use of it. Meanwhile, as though directed by a single hand, the insurrection grew even stronger and more menacing. Men addressed crowds at street corners with frantic eloquence; others, in the churches, were sounding the tocsin with all their might; lead was melted, cartridges rolled; trees from the boulevards, public urinals, benches, railing, gas jets were torn down or overturned; by morning Paris was filled with barricades. Resistance was not prolonged; everywhere the National Guard intervened; so that by eight o'clock, through force or by consent, the people were in possession of five barracks, nearly all the town halls, and the most important strategic points. No great exertion was necessary; through its own weakness the monarchy was swiftly tottering to its fall. And now the people were attacking the guard post known as the Château-d'Eau, in order to liberate fifty prisoners who were not there.

(a) What indications are there that this account of the February Revolution is drawn from a novel? Do you think there is any value in studying history through historical novels? What are the dangers in that approach?

(b) In this passage what is meant by 'tocsin' (line 20), 'equerries' (line 15) and 'boulevards' (line 16)?

(c) What was the point of melting lead (line 20), and where do you think the revolutionaries got it from?

(d) What event triggered off the revolution in the first place?

(e) Flaubert appears to suggest two possible versions as to the nature of the revolution. What are they (lines 5–13 and 14–17)?

(f) Explain the little touch of humour in the last line.

Source: Gustave Flaubert, *Sentimental Education* (1869) (Dent, 1941) pp. 267–8.

6 Italy 1796–1848

Introduction

By the mid-eighteenth century the heartland of the European Renaissance had degenerated into one of the most underdeveloped regions in the continent. Equally remarkable, though, was the revival or *'Risorgimento'* which it experienced from the early nineteenth century and which culminated eventually in its *political unification*. Yet the route followed to this creation was by no means preordained, or even the best one possible.

6.1 A 'geographical expression' (see Map 6.1)

Metternich sneered that Italy was no more than a *'geographical expression'*. He remarked that 'in Italy provinces are against provinces, towns against towns, families against families and men against men.' Italy suffered from two related handicaps:

(a) *Disunity*

1 *Political fragmentation.* Apart from a number of tiny principalities and enclaves, the Italy of 1815 consisted of nine states. Of these the Duchies of Lombardy and Venetia were subject to direct Habsburg rule from Vienna, while the Duchies of Parma, Modena, Tuscany and Lucca were ruled by branches of the dynasty. Effectively, the peninsula was dominated by Austria. Apart from the Papal States, the only state with a native Italian ruling family was Piedmont.
2 *Regional divisions.* Even within the states there were regional antagonisms. Differences in interests and outlook divided the cities of Rome and Venice from their associated rural territories. The old Republic of Genoa was to prove a difficult mouthful for Piedmont to swallow. Equally hostile were the islanders of Sicily to the mainland government.
3 *'Campanilismo'.* Ignorance, local rivalries and bad communications also sustained a very 'small town' parochial outlook.

(b) *Economic backwardness*

By the seventeenth century the Italian economy was in such decline that population was drifting from towns to the countryside. The only significant Italian exports were

Map 6.1   *The states of Italy in 1815*

raw materials such as wine and olive oil. Apart from the fragmentation which was associated with a multiplicity of customs barriers and systems of currency and weights and measures, this was due to:

1   *Historical factors.* Italy was one of the 'cockpits' of Europe, bedevilled by the wars of the early sixteenth and eighteenth centuries.
2   *Natural factors.* In particular the Italian terrain did not favour internal communications, and there was a lack of natural resources such as coal and iron ore.

Even so, there was still a north–south differential with the south far more backward and poverty stricken than the north, and the gap would only get worse with economic development. In 1860, when Garibaldi and his followers arrived in Sicily, they were astonished to find people still clad in animal skins.

6.2   The Napoleonic occupation

Even before the French Revolution the situation in Italy had been somewhat improved by the modernising reforms of several enlightened rulers – in Tuscany, Lombardy and

Naples especially. Then between 1796 and 1814 only in 1795–1800 was Italy not under French occupation to a greater or lesser extent. The French influence on the development of Italy was especially significant in the Napoleonic period.

(a) *Revelation of the benefits of unification*

By 1814 Italy was rationalised into three units. A third was annexed by France. A third became the Kingdom of Naples ruled by the flamboyant cavalry general Murat. The remainder, called the Kingdom of Italy, was ruled by Napoleon on behalf of his son the King of Rome. Associated with those developments were the elimination of barriers to internal commerce, the building of new roads and the application of a standardised system of law.

(b) *The emergence of a new class*

The selling off of church lands had drastic effects on landholding. In the plain of Bologna alone between 1789 and 1804 the church holdings fell from 19 per cent to 4 per cent, while middle-class holdings rose from 18 per cent to 34 per cent. Large numbers of Italians also held responsible posts in the army and administration. This new middle class would not take kindly to loss of rank and prestige after the wars.

(c) *Increased political participation*

Feudalism was abolished, and by 1814 all areas of Italy had experienced a degree of constitutional government for a reasonably lengthy period. There had been unprecedented opportunities for political discussion and participation.

(d) *Stimulus to a nationalist reaction*

Efficient French tax collection, economic restriction and levies of recruits also provoked the development of an anti-French reaction in the form of secret societies, and also occasionally mass risings by peasantry led by priests and noblemen such as the 'Army of the Holy Faith' in Naples in 1799, the mysterious 'Aretine Army' in Tuscany and the 'Christian Mass' in Piedmont.

6.3 The era of the Secret Societies (1814–32)

After 1814, Metternich set out to 'extinguish the spirit of Italian unity and ideas about constitutions'. The fate of Italy became linked to the international position of Austria. However it was useless to pretend, as Metternich did, that 'Italian affairs do not exist'. Too many Italians looked back to the 'good old days' before the restoration of the old states and rulers. The Piedmontese ambassador at London wrote of 'a new impetus, a new spirit [given] to our land' by the changes of the previous fifteen years.'

(a) *The Secret Societies*

The lead in the revolutionary outbreaks of 1820–1 and 1831–2 was taken by two secret societies in particular:

1   *The Adelfia.* This was the creation of the old Jacobin Filippo Buonarotti and was

especially strong in Piedmont amongst the army officers and one-time members of old republican freemason lodges. It was characterised by:
– Advocacy of a *single, indivisible and communist republic.*
– *Conspiracy and infiltration* to achieve power by coups rather than popular revolution. The revolution would then be carried through by a 'dictatorship of the virtuous'.
– *A disciplined and exclusive membership* in order that secrecy could be maintained.
– *Commitment to international European revolution* with that in Italy only as one component.

2   *The Carbonari.* Far more diversified and ambiguous than the Adelfia, this started as an anti-Murat movement in Naples. More moderate than the Adelfia, the *Carbonari* represented opposition to feudalism and support for constitutions and administrative decentralisation. There were vast divisions between regions, and even within regional branches. They were also far more prepared to try and work through sympathetic princes tempted by expansionist ambitions.

There were lots of other societies, such as the Spillo Nero (Black Pin), the Latinisti, and the Bersiaglieri.

(b)   *The revolutions of 1820–1*

There were two spasms of revolution:

1   *The Kingdom of the Two Sicilies, 1820–1.* A constitutionalist revolt in Naples led by General Pepe and a group of young Carbonari army officers obtained a constitution from Ferdinand IV. However the more moderate upper- and middle-class revolutionaries became alarmed at the radicalism of supporters drawn from the peasantry and craftsmen. In March 1821, Austrian forces defeated the revolutionaries at Rieti. A separate outbreak in Sicily in July 1820 arose not only from the grievances of peasantry and craftsmen but also the desire of Sicilian noblemen for independence from the mainland. Again the divisions between the two groups explained the success of the counter-revolution.
2   *The Piedmontese revolution (1821).* A group of constitutionalist army officers looked to the inscrutable Prince Charles Albert, who had a vague reputation for liberal beliefs, to lead Piedmont against Austria and free Lombardy. In fact, while acting as regent for his brother Charles Felix in his absence he rejected a constitution and betrayed the plotters. At Novara in May 1821 Austrian and loyalist forces easily defeated the revolutionaries.

(c)   *The revolution of 1831–2*

The next decade was marked by repression and economic recession. In Piedmont, there were considerable purges where Charles Felix summed up his attitude: 'In a word: the bad are all educated and the good are all ignorant.' The July Revolution of 1830 triggered off a new wave of revolutions in Italy. This time hopes were centred on a combination of the ambitions of Francis IV of Modena and of Charles Albert seeking to gain the throne of Piedmont together with an invasion by Italian exiles from France. Both princes betrayed promises to help, but even so the revolutionaries got as far as the proclamation of the United Provinces of Central Italy in February 1831 before Austrian troops restored order.

6.4 Routes to unification (1832–48)

Lack of popular support, internal divisions, the cowardice of princes and the strength of Austrian reaction meant that the secret societies were ineffective. Over the next few years though a range of options became defined. There were in fact four alternative routes to unification:

1 Mazzinian republicanism.
2 Liberal reformism.
3 Neo-Guelphism.
4 Piedmontese expansionism.

6.5 Mazzini and the Italian Republic

Born in Genoa in 1805, Guiseppe Mazzini became a *Carbonaro* in 1827 and was exiled from Piedmont in 1830. In 1831 he published *Young Italy* and founded a new society with a new outlook on the future of Italy.

(a) *Mazzini's programme, 'Thought and Action'*

His views had similarities to, but also contrasted with, those of the secret societies.

1 *An Italy 'independent united, free'*. While he was not egalitarian or socialist, Mazzini believed in undivided popular sovereignty rather than a federation of states.
2 *Education and propaganda.* Publicity would educate a revolutionary class which would be the basis for an insurrection and *'war by bands'*, to be followed by a popularly elected national assembly to carry through the revolutionary programme.
3 *'Young Italy'*. Mazzini looked to the educated young of the middle class and urban artisans for support. He rejected the peasantry and poorest classes, not only because 'the people cannot read' but also because their support could be the basis of a class division within the revolution.
4 *The 'Third Rome'*. Mazzini saw Italy as providing a vanguard and model for revolution throughout Europe and the eventual unity of humanity. Italy had a *mission*, 'each man and each people possesses a particular mission which ... necessarily plays its part in the fulfilment of the general mission of humanity'. He also helped in the formation of other movements such as Young Poland, Young Germany, and (in 1834) Young Europe.

(b) *The success of Mazzini*

In reality, Mazzinians were still driven towards conspiracies by circumstances. The result was a string of dismal failures throughout Italy in the 1830s and early 1840s. However, on the other hand:

1 *Radicalism was revitalised.* Mazzini's publications circulated widely and the movement largely replaced the old secret societies in Piedmont and the north.
2 *Fanaticism could play a vital role.* The threat of assassination and revolt was an ever-present influence on rulers and Mazzinian enthusiasts were to play vital roles

at several key moments – in Rome in 1848, in 1858 in seeking to assassinate Napoleon III, and in Sicily in 1860.

3   *The personal example of Mazzini was invaluable.* His dedication, self-sacrifice and romantic image added considerably to the cause he supported.

6.6   Liberal reformism

Influenced by a new international economic situation largely produced by the industrialisation of Britain, a number of governments and moderate intellectuals began to sponsor programmes of social and economic modernisation. Some of these reformist liberals began to see the true route of Italian unification to rest in practical integration by economic development.

(a)   *Tuscan liberalism*

Tuscany's reputation as one of the least oppressive régimes in Italy was maintained in the years before 1848 by programmes of agricultural improvement, free trade to encourage the export of produce, and popular education. On the other hand, industrialisation was feared as a cause of social disorder and in the last resort the régime was dependent upon Austrian bayonets.

(b)   *Carlo Cattaneo and the Lombard middle class*

The academic Cattaneo looked to an Italy based on the model set by the urban middle classes of Lombardy. For him modernisation meant industrialism and capitalism and growing wealth would also eliminate the danger of class conflict. However he recognised the vast differences in development between the different regions and especially between the north and south; thus he advocated a *federation of Italy* until all regions were at a comparable economic level so that the shock of unification was not too great.

(c)   *Cavour and 'the happy mean'*

Count Camillo di Cavour of Piedmont represented a compromise. The son of the Turin chief of police and member of a respected aristocratic family, his attitude to government was influenced by two factors:

1   *Familiarity with modern economic trends.* He served in the army of Piedmont for a few years only. On leaving it, he travelled and read widely and became very aware of the growing importance of industry, trade and communications. He gained practical experience as well through involvement in banking, agricultural improvement and railway development.

2   *The example of Britain.* Not only was Britain the model of economic progress but it was not threatened by revolution and the landed aristocracy still dominated the government. Cavour especially admired the policies of Sir Robert Peel. Trade and banking reforms had encouraged British prosperity, reduced working class discontent and brought together the old landed class and the new industrial and commercial middle classes.

The lesson learnt by Cavour was that moderation was the safest line, that 'the *"juste milieu"* is the only policy right in the circumstances capable of saving society from the two rocks which threaten to break it – anarchy and despotism'. In practice, this meant the encouragement of industrial and commercial development to reduce the danger from the growing population in Piedmont, to bring together the old rural aristocracy and the new middle classes as the basis for the development of the unity of northern Italy. Southern Italy could only be a handicap. From 1850 Cavour virtually dominated the Piedmontese government (see 13.3(b)).

(d) The liberal movement

The *liberals did not form any sort of united party*. However, there were factors which did produce a sort of consensus:

1 *A literary and historical revival.* The 1830s–40s saw the publication of many patriotic works which emphasised Italy's glorious past, especially Balbo's *Summary of the History of Italy* (1846).
2 *Growing co-operation.* Congresses of Italian scientists from 1839, debates about the creation of a customs league, and support for the construction of a national railway network all helped provide an alternative to the revolutionary option of Mazzini.

6.7 Gioberti and neo-Guelphism

Vincenzo Gioberti, a Piedmontese priest and ex-Mazzinian, looked towards Italy's Catholic faith and the Pope, as had the medieval Guelph supporters of politically-minded popes.

(a) Gioberti's programme

Gioberti's views contrasted very much with Mazzini's:

1 *A Papal led confederation.* In his *Of the Moral and Civil Primacy of Italians* (1843), Gioberti dismissed total unity as 'madness' and could see no alternative to the princes and states, albeit modified by the presidency of the Pope and provision for some sort of advisory councils.
2 *The military force of the 'warrior province'.* Gioberti dismissed the idea of a popular insurrection. Instead, he looked to the forces of Catholic Piedmont to eject the Austrians.
3 *The primacy of Italy.* Like Mazzini, Gioberti could see Italy as able to act independently of the rest of Europe. Partly this was because of his fear of extreme radicalism as revealed elsewhere in the continent, and his hope that Italy could offer a moderate example.

(b) The 'Neo-Guelph illusion'

This programme was bound to attract moderates, men of property and liberal aristo-crats. However, the wide support it achieved in the 1840s was partly because it was so vague:

1 *Social and political reforms were neglected.* The Papal States especially were one of the most misgoverned regions in Italy.
2 *Excessive optimism.* The dependence upon patriotic princes and a liberally minded papacy was tremendous.
3 *The Austrian presence.* Although Gioberti implied the need for force, he could not risk persecution by being more positive.

6.8 Charles Albert and Piedmont

There was an alternative. In works like Balbo's *Speranze d'Italia* and d'Azeglio's *I Casi de Romagna* Piedmont was looked to, to expel the Austrians and start the movement towards unity.

(a) Piedmont and Italy

There were several reasons why Piedmont should be looked to as the leader of a new Italian federation, especially in the north:

1   *'Artichoke policy'.* The Savoyard dynasty was traditionally expansionist anyhow, 'swallowing' territories like the leaves of an artichoke.
2   *Internal support for the dynasty.* A body of influential moderate-minded aristocrats like Cavour identified stability in Piedmont with a 'forward policy', with modernisation and economic integration.
3   *The problem of Genoa.* From Genoa and Sardinia there were pressures for constitutional reforms and even support for *separatism*. One way of diffusing these movements was to undertake a popular nationalist, expansionist policy.
4   *Austro-Piedmontese relations in the 1840s.* Charles Albert as king detested Metternich and relations were very bad in the late 1840s, with disputes over issues like Austrian customs duties on wine and railway construction.

(b) Charles Albert

On the other hand, Charles Albert was an unlikely revolutionary hero. A fanatical Catholic with a reputation for repression and the hobbies of cutting out paper saints and arranging toy soldiers, he had actually made an alliance with Austria in 1831 in contrast to his family's traditional avoidance of entanglements. However, he was a very deep, brooding man who talked about his 'mission'. Much could be read into him. Mazzini once described him as 'like Hamlet'.

6.9 Conclusion

In 1846, Pius IX was elected Pope. He started his reign with a series of mild concessions to his subjects and angry words with Austria over her occupation of Ferrara. This triggered off expectations in Rome and he was forced to concede reforms to the Papal government in 1847. This apparent breath of reality into the visions of Gioberti was one of the triggers of the revolutions of 1848 in Italy, but the outcome of the revolutions was to be a marked simplification of the options.

Questions

1   What did Italian nationalism owe to Napoleonic rule?   [OC]
2   Compare the impact of France on any *two* of the territories she occupied in the Revolutionary and Napoleonic period.   [OC]
3   How did governments in the Italian States deal with demands for reform between 1815 and 1848?
                                                                                                [NEAB]
4   Account for the failure of revolutionary movements in Italy before 1848.   [NEAB]
5   Describe the development of Italian nationalism during the years 1830–48.
6   Compare and contrast the alternative routes to Italian unification which were advocated between 1815 and 1848.

7   In what ways did the theories of Mazzini as to Italian unification differ from those prevalent before 1830?

8   Study Sources A, B, C and D and then answer the questions which follow.

Source A: The virtues of country living.

A small landowner, who raises sufficient animals and crops on his own land, does not need to trade; or, if society is not yet quite perfect, if the population has still not reached its maximum, he may need to trade only as much as he can easily manage by himself. . . .

It used to be thought that all industry and agriculture would decline without trade. This is true, given the present state of disorder and immense inequality. But in a different society, where everyone takes care of his own needs, the very desire to live would, I think, be sufficient stimulus to produce one's own needs. Idleness is impossible in man, once he has experienced the adventurous state of living in comfort and independence. . . .

Are large cities, enormous masses of men, compatible with democracy? The first care of politicians of old was to determine the number of individuals in a republic. . . . In a great mass of people it is more difficult to avoid oligarchy, because the common man is less able to understand and control excessively wide-ranging and complicated relations.

Look at the world: you will see that the more men are densely packed in cities, the more corrupt they become. You will see that, in general, the smaller the village, the more pure the morals . . .

In a large town it is impossible for the majority of the inhabitants to be peasants: most of them will be suppliers and instruments of vice and luxury. We have already observed that such men do not make for a good democracy.

The chains of dependence and intrigue are strong in large towns, imaginary desires are more stimulated. Consequently large towns are changeable, unstable and rebellious.

(a)   What is meant by 'oligarchy'? (line 11)
(b)   Writing in the 1790s Russo regarded towns as being more rebellious than country dwellers, but was he advocating that the towns should lead the move towards unification? (lines 9–15)
(c)   Judging from this extract what do you think was Russo's prescription for a free, democratic and equal Italy?
(d)   Would you apply the same distinctions today to town and country life which Russo did in the 1790s? In what ways have the circumstances changed to affect the difference?

Source: V. Russo, *Pensieri Politici* (1798). Quoted in S. J. Woolf, *The Italian Risorgimento* (Longman, 1969).

Source B: The hopes of Italy.

[The unitary solution] No nation has been less frequently united in a single body than the Italian. . . . The dreamers say that one can still achieve what hitherto has never been achieved. . . . But this is childish, no more than the fantasy of rhetorical schoolboys, two-a-penny poets, drawing-room politicians. . . . What would be the pope's position in a kingdom of Italy? That of king? But this is impossible, nobody even dreams of it. That of subject? But in that case he would be dependent. . . .

[Federation] Confederations are the type of constitution most suited to Italy's nature and history. . . . The only obstacle to an Italian confederation – a most serious obstacle – is foreign rule, which penetrates deep into the peninsula. . . . I maintain than an Italian confederation is neither desirable nor possible if a foreign power forms part of it; and that it would perhaps be desirable, but so difficult as to be impossible without a foreign power. . . .

[Princes] At the present time the fact is that all power is in the hands of the princes. But this does not mean that everybody else has only a minimal part to play. There is no such danger; it is not a minimal part for the following reason: the moment the actions of princes move from the plane of ideas to that of facts, they become the actions of the nation. If the peoples can do nothing without the princes, the princes can do nothing without the peoples, they are not princes except in so far as they make their peoples act. . . .

[Democracy] To tell the truth, although a democratic conflagration is much threatened and feared in our days, it seems to me improbable, given the progress of our present democracy.... In some cases democracy is tyrannical and so estranges every other class; in other cases it subjects itself to the aristocracy; in most cases it disappears within the great class of educated persons.... A democratic conflagration may continue for some time to be the fear of the police and the hope of secret societies. But it cannot enter into any assessment of the foreseeable future, it cannot be an element to be calculated as an important undertaking....

[Savoy] The peace of Utrecht in 1714 founded a new kingdom in Italy for that worthy house of Savoy which had upheld the sacred fire of Italian virtue for the last century and a half.... During the eighteenth century, up to '89, not a single state was eliminated, there were only exchanges of towns, amalgamations of provinces, at one state's expense in favour of another. But one should note that all these joining together of lands were in favour of the monarchy of Savoy, which in the course of the century increased by a third in population and almost doubled in territory. Equally notable is the method by which these additions were acquired, all at the expense of the house of Austria, and yet for the most part by fighting for them. Should such an example be imitated in similar natural conditions, or should it be avoided because the times have changed? One can only decide on each occasion....

(a) Why was the Pope a problem if the model of a unitary Italy was to be pursued (lines 4–6)?
(b) What were the limitations to the view that unification could be achieved by a democratic uprising (lines 18–25)?
(c) Was there any future for Austria in Italy as far as Balbo was concerned (lines 7–11)?
Source: C. Balbo, *Delle Speranze d'Italia* (Paris, 1844). Included in S. J. Woolf, *The Italian Risorgimento* (Longman, 1969).

Source C: An open letter from Mazzini to King Charles Albert in 1831.

If I believed you to be a common king, with a narrow tyrannical outlook, I would not address you in the language of a free man. But you, Sire, are not such a king. Nature, in creating you for the throne, has given you strength of mind and high principles. There is a crown more brilliant and sublime than that of Piedmont, a crown that awaits the man who dares to think of it, who dedicates his life to winning it.

All Italy waits for one word – one only – to make herself yours. Proffer this word to her. Place yourself at the head of the nation and write on your banner: 'Union, Liberty, Independence'. Proclaim the liberty of thought. Declare yourself the vindicator, the interpreter of popular rights, the regenerator of all Italy. Liberate her from the Barbarians. Select the way that accords with your time; you have the victory in your hands. Sire, on this condition we bind ourselves round you, we proffer you our lives, we will lead to your banner the little states of Italy. Unite us, Sire, and we shall conquer.

(a) Why should Mazzini have addressed his letter to Charles Albert?
(b) Explain 'There is a crown more brilliant and sublime than that of Piedmont' (lines 3–5).
(c) Who were 'the Barbarians' (line 9)? What parts of Italy did they influence or control?
(d) How did Charles Albert respond to Mazzini's appeal in 1831? What action did he take later, and with what results?
(e) What was the importance of Mazzini to the cause of Italian unity and independence?   [OC]

Source D: Railways in Italy.

Nevertheless, however great the material benefits to Italy from railways, they are much less important than the inevitable moral effects. A few brief considerations will suffice to justify this assertion to any who truly know our country.

Italy's troubles are of ancient origin. This is not the place to discuss them, and it would moreover be beyond our powers. But we are certain that the prime cause is the political influence which foreigners have exercised on us for centuries, and that the principal obstacles opposed to our throwing off this baleful influence are, first and foremost, the internal divisions, the rivalries, I might almost say, the antipathy that different parts of our great Italian family hold for each other; and, following that, the reciprocal distrust which divides our rulers from the most energetic section of those they rule. This latter group have an often exaggerated desire for progress, a keen sense of nationality and love for their country, which makes them the indispensable support, if not the principal instrument, of all attempts at emancipation.

If the action of the railways diminishes these obstacles and perhaps even abolishes them, it will give the greatest encouragement to the spirit of Italian nationality. Communications, which help the incessant movement of people in every direction, and which will force people into contact with those they do not know, should be a powerful help in destroying petty municipal passions born of ignorance and prejudice. These passions have already been undermined by men of intellect. The contribution of railways to this process will be denied by no one.

(a) Source D is an extract from a book review by Cavour. Who was he and what knowledge was he likely to have of railways?
(b) Who were the foreigners Cavour had in mind as the main cause of Italy's troubles in his own day?
(c) What were the internal problems of Italy which made it so vulnerable to foreign domination according to Cavour (lines 4–13)?
(d) What would be the benefits to Italian nationalism of a national railway system (lines 14–20)?
(e) Whom do you think Cavour means by 'the most energetic section of those whom they rule' (line 10)?

Source: Camillo di Cavour, 'Des chemins de fer en Italie, par la comte Petitti', *Revue Nouvelle*, 1 May 1846 (extract). Quoted in S. J. Woolf, *The Italian Risorgimento* (Longman, 1969).

7 Germany 1801–48

Introduction

As with 'Italy', the term 'Germany' (see Map 7.1) had no real political significance at the turn of the nineteenth century, although the multitude of states which made it up were loosely linked by their membership of the archaic Holy Roman Empire. The French Revolution and Napoleonic conquests laid the basis for the movement towards unification which was reinforced by economic and social pressures.

7.1 'The Germanies' in 1800

On the eve of the Treaty of Lunéville, the region was characterised by two features:

(a) Political fragmentation

Some 23 million people were divided into 314 independent territories ruled by secular and religious authorities. Another 1400 towns, cities and territories had a degree of autonomy. The states varied in size from the 115,533 square miles of the Habsburg monarchy to the 33 square miles of Schwartzburg-Sonderhausen. There was also a cultural difference between the Protestant and conservative north and the Catholic and more liberal states of the south.

(b) Economic underdevelopment

Over 90 per cent of the population earned their living from agriculture and lived in rural areas. Development was retarded by:

1 *The absence of a unified market.* A variety of factors limited horizons:

   – A high degree of *commercial disunity*. There were great varieties in currencies and weights and measures. In 1790 there were 1800 customs barriers and one Frenchman remarked that 'the Germans trade like prisoners behind iron bars'.
   – *Poor communication.* For instance in 1816 it took travellers five hours to cover the twelve miles from Weimar to Erfurt. One traveller was said to carry splints as a regular precaution!
   – *Parochialism.* A 'small town' mentality prevailed. In 1832 one observer mocked the tendency of villagers in the south to regard villages two or three miles away as 'abroad'.

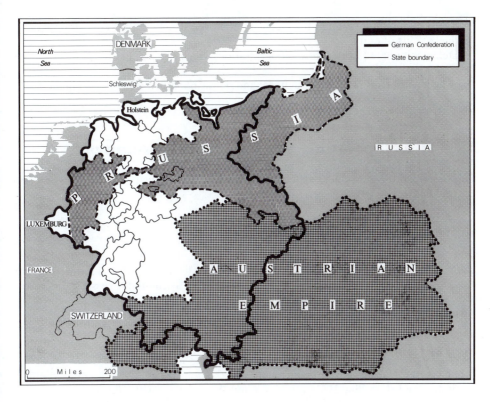

Map 7.1 The German Confederation

    – *Self-sufficiency.* For military reasons, there was a tendency for states to avoid dependence on their neighbours, so trade was retarded and high military budgets were common.

2   *An antique social structure.* Individuality was not encouraged:

    – *Feudal power prevailed.* East of the Elbe the peasants were still in a state of serfdom while west of the river although the peasantry were freer they were burdened by rent, tithes and labour dues.
    – *There was no mercantile class.* Except in towns like Hamburg and Leipzig, the princely court was the real focus rather than trade.
    – *Guild restrictions survived* in Germany longer than elsewhere and their effect was to restrict output by penalising 'illegal craftsmen'.

7.2 The impact of the French Revolution and Napoleon

Ironically although traditional French policy had been to keep Germany divided, it was the French who provided an initial stimulus to the movement towards national unification.

1 The Napoleonic revision of the German territorial structure allowed a glimpse of the benefits of unity.
2 Defeat stimulated Prussia into modernisation, which enabled her to become a leader in the movement.
3 A peculiarly German form of cultural and political nationalism was germinated.

7.3 The Napoleonic Settlement of Germany

Marx described this settlement as 'cleansing the German Augean stables'. The process occurred in three stages:

(a) The Treaty of Lunéville (1801)

France had been ceded the left bank of the Rhine. In exchange, the losers were enabled to compensate themselves from the ecclesiastical territories and ancient free cities. In 1803 a sixth of German territory was thus redistributed. Prussia gained five times as much as she had lost, while substantial gains were made by Baden, Bavaria, Würtemburg, Nassau and the Hesses.

(b) The Confederation of the Rhine (1806)

To balance the Habsburg Monarchy's influence, Napoleon began deliberately to build up middle-sized states like Baden, Bavaria and Würtemburg with Habsburg territories and small states. Then in 1806 sixteen states were formed into the *Confederation of the Rhine*, but Prussia and the Habsburg Monarchy were excluded. The process of *'mediatisation'* of the smaller states proceeded.

(c) The Peace of Tilsit (1807)

As a result of Tilsit (see Section 2.4(d)) Prussia lost all her territory west of the Elbe, which became the Kingdom of Westphalia under Jerome Bonaparte. Her Polish territories became the Grand Duchy of Warsaw. Her smaller allies' territories were confiscated.

7.4 The Prussian revival

Prussia's fragmented territories had been largely the product of war, and there was no true sense of community. Mirabeau remarked 'other states have an army, in Prussia the army has a state'. The shallowness of this 'great barracks' was revealed by its shattering defeat (see Section 2.4(d)) with an indemnity, a French army of occupation and reduction of the Prussian army to rub into the wound. The problem was that, as Queen Louise remarked, Prussia 'slumbered on the laurels of Frederick the Great'. Now, under the leadership of Baron Stein, a body of administrators set out to reform Prussian institutions and to try to win the support of the people in the state.

There were two influences on Stein:

1 *The Wealth of Nations* by Adam Smith, the Scottish economist. Smith remarked 'It

appears . . . that the work done by free men is cheaper in the end than done by slaves'.

2   *The French example.* Hardenberg advised King Frederick William III in 1807, 'we must do from above what the French have done from below'.

(a)   *The Prussian liberal era (1807–10)*

1   *The emancipation of the serfs* (1807–10). Peasant support was increased, but more land became available for the nobility and labour to the towns and estates as poorer peasants fell behind in their compensation payments.
2   *The relaxation of a rigid class system.* For instance, the nobility were now free to enter trade and industry and the bourgeois could own land.
3   *Municipal Ordinance (1808).* Towns were given elected municipal councils. In fact, Stein envisaged an elected national assembly, but the King would never accept such a radical move.
4   *Educational reforms.* Wilhelm von Humboldt was responsible for the establishment of general elementary education *lycée*-type secondary education and the founding of a University of Berlin in 1810.
5   *Military reforms.* Scharnhorst and Gneisenau overhauled the army.

   – The officer corps was purged and opened up to middle class men of merit.
   – Flogging and other degrading punishments were abolished.
   – Universal military service was introduced, with training in a professional army (limited to 42,000 by the Napoleonic agreement) then service in the *Landwehr*, a militia force.

The result was that if Prussia was not free, she was at least to become the most modernised state in Germany.

7.5   German nationalism

Before 1789 there was little obvious sign of German 'Patriotism'. Germans tended to ape the French in language and culture. German liberals welcomed the French Revolution, and even the French military successes. As late as 1806 the philosopher Hegel hoped Napoleon would defeat his German enemies: 'everyone prays for the success of the French army'. But by 1813–14, there were signs of German nationalism emerging:

(a)   *French impositions*

Napoleon's benefits had to be paid for in taxes, levies and freelance looting. It gradually became possible still to admire Napoleon and the ideals of the Revolution but to feel a national resentment against the French invaders.

(b)   *The influence of German intellectuals*

1   *The philosophers.* Herder, Fichte and Hegel especially developed the view that the German people were a unique *'volk'*, with a pure language who should be the basis of a tightly united *'Volkstadt'*.
2   *The popularisers.* More accessible to most Germans were the writings of Ernst Arndt, the poet and pamphleteer who urged the creation of a *German fatherland*.

The Prussian Friedrich Jahn propagated the new gospel in the students' unions *'Burscherschaften'* and his *'gymnasium'* movement for the instruction of pupils in drill, physical activities and the national spirit. This nationalism favoured the use of a rather coarse 'pure' German language and the maintenance of ethnic purity by discrimination against the Jews and even foreign language teachers.

(c) Myths

As many Germans fought on the side of Napoleon as against him. However there were two great 'myths' which would be powerful in the later history of Germany:

1 *'Lützow's wild hunt'* (see Illus. 7.1): A 'free corps' of German student volunteers, under the Prussian officer Adolf von Lützow was the nearest thing to a popular German army. Used as a shock force by the Prussians these black-clad enthusiasts with the death's head insignia and black, red and gold flag captured popular imagination. They were crushed by German Confederation troops in 1813.
2 *War of Liberation.* In December 1812 the withdrawal of Prussian contingents from Napoleon's retreating army by General von Yorck was the start of resistance to Napoleon in Germany. However, it never became the sort of popular uprising it was later portrayed as. King Frederick William and the German princes were not all prepared to appeal for popular support and risk an 'overheated people'. Even so at Lützen Napoleon admitted a change in the Prussian spirit: 'these beasts have learnt something!'

7.6 The German Confederation

After 1814 neither the restoration of pre-1801 Germany nor its total unification were practical propositions. There were too many rivalries and jealousies and vested interests. The Confederation (or *Bund*) of 39 states was an attempt by Metternich to establish a stable and controllable system in central Europe. As far as unification was concerned, it laboured under several handicaps:

(a) The looseness of the Confederation

The Confederation was really just a diplomatic congress representing the princes and not the peoples. Technically, Britain, Denmark and the Netherlands were also members because until 1837 the King of Britain ruled Hanover, the King of Denmark was the Duke of Holstein and the King of the Netherlands was also the Grand Duke of Luxembourg.

(b) Limited power

The *Diet* had limited powers:

1 *Its jurisdiction was circumscribed.* Member states could refuse to accept laws as binding on them, and a *two-thirds majority* was needed for major issues.
2 *There was no federal army.* In theory, such an army existed from 1821 with contingents from the member states. In reality, the states failed to meet their obligations.

Illus. 7.1   Blessing of the Lützow Free Corps, 1813 (Bildarchiv Preussicher Kulturbesitz)

From a painting by J. Martersteig in the Bildarchiv Preussicher Kulturbesitz, Berlin, showing the blessing ceremony on 27 March in the Hogan Church.

Source: E. Sagarra, *An Introduction to Nineteenth Century Germany* (Longman, 1980) p. 11.

Q   Lützow's troops wore uniforms of black with silver trimmings and sported a death's head badge. Do you see any connection between this and the Nazi state of Hitler?

(c)   *Non-implementation of constitutions*

The Vienna Settlement did require the member states to produce constitutions. The response varied:

1   *In southern and central Germany*, there was some compliance, Nassau introduced a constitution in 1814, Baden introduced a very liberal one.
2   *In northern Germany*, the movement was in the opposite direction. After the accession of Ernest Augustus to the throne of Hanover in 1837 he repealed a constitution granted by King William IV and the Diet approved this. In Prussia, partly because of the influence of the Habsburg Monarchy, repeated promises by Frederick William III to introduce a constitution were broken. In 1847 his successor Frederick William IV flatly refused to grant a constitution, despite his liberal pretensions.

7.7   The *Vormärz* (1815–48)

The years before 1848 (the *'Vormärz'* or *'pre-March'*) saw repression coordinated by Metternich but also the development of a liberal and nationalist opposition:

(a) The growth of intellectual opposition

Most of the ordinary Germans were apathetic within their limited local worlds, and were not easily mobilised. Complacency tended to be the rule, *'bei uns gehts hübsch ordentlich zu'* ('We're all right Jack'!). Discontent came from the intellectuals. University staff and students and some businessmen. Their organisations included the Young Germans, a league of writers and poets, the Burschenschaften and a few fanatical terrorist groups such as the 'Blacks'. In 1817, it was students who converted the *Wartburg Festival* from a celebration of the battle of Leipzig into a demonstration against the princes and militarism.

(b) The Metternich system

Metternich coordinated repression through the Confederation. The key elements were:

1   *The Carlsbad Decrees (1819).* Following the murder of the reactionary propagandist and secret agent Kotzebue in 1819, Metternich got the Diet to introduce:

  – Closer supervision of political activities at universities.
  – Censorship of the press, pamphlets and literature.
  – A central commission at Mainz to track down revolutionary secret societies.

2   *The Final Act of Vienna (1820).* The Diet agreed:

  – To limit the subjects which elected assemblies would discuss.
  – To confirm its right of intervention in individual states.

3   *The Six Acts (1832).* In the late 1820s, radicalism revived. Disturbances in 1830 produced new constitutions in Brunswick, Saxony and Hesse-Kassel. There was a crowd of 25,000 at the Hambach Festival in 1832 to denounce the Holy Alliance and support a united German republic. The Diet's new measures:

  – Banned public meetings.
  – Obliged German princes to resist any attempt to reduce their sovereignty.

(c) The Watch on the Rhine

Even so, nationalism still developed. In the 1840s when there were fears that French humiliation in the Near East (see Section 11.5) could lead to her seeking consolation in Germany there was a wave of nationalism expressed in a flurry of ballads, songs and poems such as *'Die Wacht am den Rhein'* and *'Deutschland über Alles'*.

7.8 Economic development

At the same time, economic developments were adding force to the movement for unification and political reforms.

(a) Integration

Germany was becoming more of a reality in an economic sense, due to:

1   *The Zollverein* (see Fig. 7.2). In 1818, Prussia standardised her own internal

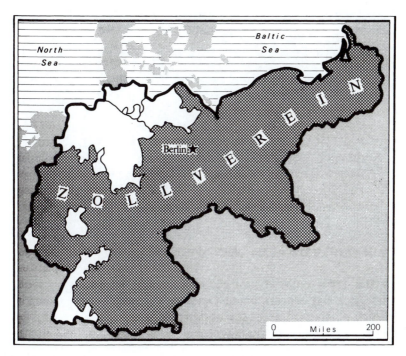

Map 7.2   *The Zollverein*

customs system. In 1819 she moved naturally into tariff agreements with states separating Prussian territories. Other states began to try and form similar unions but in 1834 the *Zollverein* was formed from all of these units. By 1844 only Hanover, Oldenburg, Mecklenburg, the Hanseatic towns and the Habsburg Monarchy were not members. The significance of the *Zollverein* was that:

– The cause of German unification was strengthened since the economic and financial prosperity of the members of the economic union were clearly revealed.
– Prussian economic growth was boosted – her road mileage grew from 24,000 miles in 1815 to 52,000 by 1829 – and her status amongst the other states was enhanced as a result.
– Conversely the influence of the Habsburg Monarchy was reduced. A Habsburg spokesman called the *Zollverein* in 1833 'one of the chief nails in the coffin of the Confederation'. In 1849 and 1857 the Habsburg Monarchy failed to join the *Zollverein* itself, and in the 1850s it failed to establish an alternative union. It was too protectionist, and just did not have Prussia's economic strength.

2   *The building of the railways.* Like Cavour (see Section 6.6(c)) the German economist Friedrich List saw railways as a vital element in power and unification (see Illus. 7.2). By 1840 Germany had a total of 343 miles but 3750 by 1850 and 6875 by 1860.

(b) *Social distress*

By 1870, largely as a result of a high birth rate, the population reached 40 million. Urban populations experienced vast increases – Berlin grew by 872 per cent over the

Source: Unknown.

The new communications systems in Italy and Germany weakened the conservative forces of regionalism and localism and paved the way for greater economic and political integration. The railways were quoted as the epitome of speed and technological achievement in the way that the Internet is today.

century. At the same time, there was a move from rural and agricultural employment to industrial employment. This had several implications which provoked radical responses:

1   *A growing rift in employer–worker relations* with *the rise of the factory* and *the decline of the workshop*, with its closer relationship between employers and workers. Socialism was emerging in the 1830s–1840s although it did not play a very great part in the events of 1848.

2   *'The social question'*. Working conditions deteriorated. Working days of up to 13 hours a day were common in the 1830s, wages were low, and female and child labour was grossly exploited. Living conditions matched this situation; housing was inadequate in terms of quantity and quality. Between 1820 and 1850 the cost of living was rising, while wages lagged and dropped from 1845. The dietary standard was poor; Silesian linen weavers got meat only at Easter, Whitsun and Christmas, and the diet of the workers of the north and east of Germany was described in the 1830s as 'Irish, that is, potatoes'.

7.9   Conclusion (see Illus. 7.3)

By the 1840s political aspirations, economic expectations, social grievances and concern about Germany's international standing in Europe all focused upon the obstacle to progress presented by the princes and their Habsburg protector. Two events in 1847 strengthened the demands of liberals and nationalists:

Illus. 7.3 German economic and political advances: 'while the political ambition of the citizen advances at snail's pace, the industrial development rushes by on wheels' (Bildarchiv Preussicher Kulturbesitz)

Source: E. Sagarra, *An Introduction to Nineteenth Century Germany* (Longman, 1980) p. 64.

1   Frederick William IV rejected liberal demands for regular meetings of the Prussian Landtag. The Landtag retaliated by refusing to vote a loan. This led to growing support for the meeting of a national parliament with elected representatives from all the German states.

2   The King of Denmark threatened to produce a constitution which would bind Schleswig tightly to Denmark. This was related to a succession dispute over the Duchy between the Duke of Augustenburg and Christian von Glücksburg, and German nationalists agitated for the independence of the largely German-speaking Schleswig and Holstein from Denmark.

Questions

1   What factors made for greater unity in Germany between 1815 and 1848? Why was more not achieved?   [OC]
2   Describe the constitution and membership of the German Confederation of 1815. What problems arose in Germany between 1815 and the outbreak of revolution in 1848?   [OC]
3   What were the principal factors in the recovery of Prussia after 1806?   [OC]
4   In what ways did the *Zollverein* contribute to the economic and political developments of Germany?   [OX]
5   Discuss the significance of the revival of Prussia in the period 1806 to 1815.   [NEAB]
6   Describe the attempts of Metternich to control the German Confederation between 1815 and 1848, and the events that occurred in the German Confederation (excluding Austria) in the year 1848. Why did the revolutionary outbreaks fail?   [CAM]
7   What were the greatest obstacles in the way of German unification between 1815 and 1848?
8   To what extent was the German Confederation dominated by Metternich in the first thirty years of its existence?
9   Study Sources A and B and then answer the questions which follow.

Source A: A British view of the *Zollverein*.

The objects proposed by the *Zollverein* were the removal of all restrictions to communication and transit, the abolition of all internal custom-houses, the establishment of a common tariff and system of collection, and the repartition of the receipts on all imports and exports according to the population among all the members of the League ... The intention of the tariff is to admit raw materials without any, or on merely a nominal duty ...

   The *Zollverein*, by directing capital to internal, in preference to external trade, has already had a great influence in improving the roads, the canals, the means of travelling, the transport of letters – in a word, in giving additional impulse to inland communications of every sort. The isolation of the several German states, with separate fiscal interests, and often hostile legislation, prevented those facilities from being given to intercourse which are alike the evidence and the means of civilisation. On every side beneficial changes are taking place. Railways are being constructed in many parts of the German territory – steam-boats are crowding the German ports and coasting along the German shores – everything is transported with greater cheapness and rapidity ...

On the whole Saxony is the portion of Germany which has profited most by its connection with the Commercial League, for in Saxony manufacturing industry was most developed, and in the competition with other states of the League Saxony had the vantage ground. To her especially it has opened a market of 26,000,000 of consumers, and closed the gates to a great extent against foreign rivals. Saxony being far more advanced in manufacturing aptitude than most of their states, was enabled at once to take up a predominant manufacturing position. A considerable rise in the cost of the necessaries of life followed the greater demand for labour, and of course pressed heavily on all that species of labour, for which the *Zollverein* created no demand. Much capital was suddenly disturbed and made less productive; much was misdirected to objects for which there was an artificial, but not a durable demand, or in which competition with other parts of the *Zollverein*, or with foreign countries, could not be profitably maintained.

(a)   What were the objectives of the *Zollverein* according to Bowring (lines 1–5)?
(b)   What was the connection between the *Zollverein* and the development of inland transport systems in Germany (lines 6–14)?
(c)   Why was Saxony particularly able to benefit from the *Zollverein* (lines 15–26)?
(d)   How do you think Britain was likely to be affected by the working of the *Zollverein*?
Source: John Bowring, *Report on the Prussian Commercial Union, Parliamentary Papers* (1840).

Source B: The Wartburg festival.

The students who thronged to the sacred festival were quartered in the town [of Eisenach] ... ; The Hall of the Knights in the Wartburg was bedecked with wreaths, and provided with tables and benches to seat seven hundred to eight hundred men. Such was the total number present at the midday meal on the day of victory, the rest of us included. Representatives had come from Berlin, Erlangen, Giessen, Göttingen, Halle, Heidelberg, Jena, Kiel, Leipzig, Marburg, Rostock, Tübingen and Würzburg.

On the 19th at 9 a.m. the students, who had assembled in the market-place, marched to the castle, banners and a band at their head. We accompanied them. Of the professors who had this festival at heart, who saw in it the germ of some great and fruitful tree, and had come designedly to judge, from the proceedings, the students' conduct, and events that passed, what might be expected of its blossoming, there were four of us ... When general silence was obtained a student delivered a speech on very much the following lines: he spoke of the aim of this assembly of educated young men from all circles and all races of the German fatherland; of the thwarted life of the past; of the rebound, and the ideal that now possessed the German people; of hopes that had failed and been deceived; of the vocation of the student and the legitimate expectations which the fatherland founded upon it; of the destitution and even persecution to which a youth devoting himself to learning had to submit; finally how they must themselves take thought to introduce among them order, rule, and custom.

(a)   The festival was held on 19 October 1817. Why was this a significant date in German history?
(b)   Why do you think it was university students in particular who took the lead in the Germans nationalist movement? What was it about their circumstances which gave them a greater awareness of a wider Germany and tendency to oppose authority?
(c)   What is meant by the term 'the germ of some great and fruitful tree' (lines 8–11)?
(d)   What were the greatest obstacles to German nationalism in this period?
Source: From the journal *Isis*, produced by Lorenz Oken, a professor at the University of Jena.
   Quoted in J. G. Legge, *Rhyme and Revolution in Germany* (Constable, 1918) pp. 22–5.

10   Study Illus. 7.1 (p. 89) again. The uniforms of Lützow's unit were black, with silver braid and a
'death's-head' skull and crossed bones badge:

(a)   When in later German history was such a uniform adopted?
(b)   How did Lützow's brigade meet its end?

8 The Habsburg Monarchy 1809–48

Introduction

A constructive force in Italy and Germany, nationalism was a potentially destructive force in the Habsburg Monarchy. Throughout the nineteenth century the story of the Monarchy was one of a struggle between forces threatening to shake it apart and forces holding it together.

8.1 The Habsburg Monarchy

The Habsburg Monarchy – an empire of some 30 million subjects by 1815 – was quite unique in its lack of any obviously dominant majority ethnic group. It was an accumulation of territories and peoples collected by the Habsburg family largely from the fifteenth century when they became the holders of the title of *Holy Roman Emperor*. This huge central European dynastic estate survived a series of threats:

1 *The religious wars of the seventeenth century.* The Protestant challenge to the Roman Catholic dynasty was ended with the defeat of Bohemia in 1620 at the start of the Thirty Years War.
2 *The threat from the Ottoman Empire.* The Turks had besieged Vienna unsuccessfully in 1529 and 1683. The Ottoman Empire was now in decline but the same forces which threatened it could be turned against the Habsburg Monarchy.
3 *Internal rebellion.* Especially the Magyar revolt in 1707 which resulted in Hungary retaining a privileged, autonomous status subject to the Emperors as Kings of Hungary (1711).
4 *European war.* Most recently the Napoleonic wars, which severely strained the Monarchy and posed a threat to the dynasty itself.

8.2 The pillars of the Habsburg Monarchy

The dynasty did not depend upon any sort of national patriotism for survival, because there was no logic to the ethnic make-up of the state. Instead it depended upon:

1 *Personal loyalty of subjects to Emperor.* Bismarck once described this feudal loyalty as 'a garnish of medievalism'. The most likely threat to this personal loyalty

would be if the dynasty overidentified too much with their German background. Joseph II, Emperor from 1780–90, was exceptional in doing this – 'I am the Emperor of the German Reich; therefore all the other states which I possess are provinces of it'.

2 *Aristocratic authority.* The provinces were dominated by the great nobility, a closed caste loyal to the Habsburgs. They resided at the court at Vienna, largely divorced from local feeling except in Italy and Polish Galicia.

3 *The institutions of state*

– *An extensive bureaucracy* largely divorced from local loyalties, although the central administration was dominated by Germans and German was the language of culture and administration.

– *A professional army* levied from all parts of the Monarchy. It was a sort of school of dynastic loyalty. The local languages were used within units, but the general language of command was *German.*

– *The Roman Catholic Church.* Over 60 per cent of the population was Catholic. The higher clergy were German, although the provincial clergy were usually drawn from the varied ethnic groups.

4 *Economic links.* The economy was predominantly agricultural and peasant-based. Joseph II had abolished serfdom, but the peasants were still not allowed to sell their land freely. The state was, however, strengthened by two aspects of the economy:

– *The Danube* was the main communications axis of the Empire. Rivers tend to be links rather than boundaries.

– The towns were islands of German loyalty in seas of peasantry. Germans dominated commerce and were usually in a majority in the towns. In Budapest in 1848 Magyars only made up a third of the population; in Prague in 1815 there were 50,000 Germans but only 15,000 Czechs.

8.3 Threats to the dynasty

There were two contradictory dangers to the integrity of the state.

(a) *Centralisation of government*

There was a tendency for administrative reformers and liberals to support more centralised control of the Monarchy, because the provincial divisions were seen as an obstacle to more efficient management. However, as Joseph II's actions displayed, this would involve:

1 *Provocation of the provincial nobility.* The risk of losing their local legal and administrative powers to imperial bureaucrats could weaken the loyalty of the aristocracy and gentry. Opposition to absolutist centralisation could be a good rallying call for popular support.

2 *Overidentification with the Germans.* German liberals and merchants were supporters of a unitary state with a more equal and rational administrative system. This could be seen by other national groups as being biased in the interest of one nationality. This was worsened in the 1830s–40s when there was a tendency for some Austrian Germans to see Germanisation as a vital step to modernisation and to inclusion of the Habsburg Monarchy in a united Germany.

(b) *Nationalist pressures towards decentralisation* (see Map 8.1)

The Empire contained eleven nationalities. However, before 1848 nationalism was rather limited in its support;

1 *Intellectual nationalism.* Academics and intellectuals were seeking to break through the German monopoly of employment in official posts. There were few of them in number. The Czech writer Franticek Palacky once remarked to his colleagues 'If the ceiling were to fall on us now that would be the end of the national revival'. They did not look to the illiterate peasantry for support but justified their demands on the basis of the revival of the traditional rights of the 'lands of St Stephen' or 'lands of St Wenceslas'.

2 *The traditional nationalism of the smaller nobility.* In Hungary there were 500,000 small, often very poor, country gentry out of a population of 10 million. These Magyar squires identified themselves with the *Hungarian 'nation'* which, historically, they had largely created. They were united especially by:

– Common privileges such as exemption from land tax and their election of representative to the Diet at Budapest.
– The occupation of official positions in local government and as magistrates rather like British justices of the peace.
– Their use of *Magyar* which was the language of only half of the Hungarian population. The official language in government and administration was Latin.
– Membership of a staunchly *Calvinist* church.

Their 'nationalism' in the past had amounted to resistance to Habsburg attempts to centralise and to reduce their powers which they associated with defence of the *'historic rights'* of the Kingdom of Hungary.

2 *Popular nationalism.* This third force would appear only after 1848 as literacy grew and peasants moved into the towns where tensions developed between Czech or Slovene labourers and German or Jewish employers, and national reassignments and rivalries were sharpened by social and economic divisions.

8.4 Metternich and the problems of the Habsburg Monarchy (1815–48)

The Emperor Francis I compared his empire to a 'worm-eaten house', and said: 'if one part is removed one can never tell how much will fall'. From 1809 as chancellor Metternich was responsible for holding together this ramshackle edifice. However, his power was limited, and he had several alternative policies facing him.

(a) *Limits to the power of Metternich*

1 *The quality of kingship.* Until 1835 Francis I insisted on playing a very active role in the detailed management of affairs. A mediocre man of limited views he expressed himself in favour of a situation where 'Every people watches its neighbour. The one does not understand the other and one hates the other ... From their antipathy will be born order and from the mutual hatred general peace.' In 1835 he was succeeded by the mental defective Ferdinand I, to whom he left the advice 'Govern and change nothing'.

2 *Court rivalries.* In 1826 the Czech Count Kolowrat became minister of the interior.

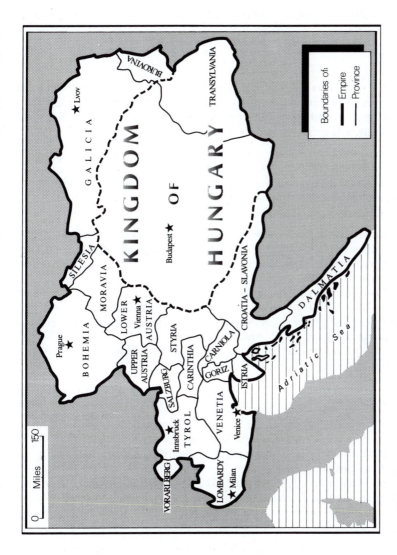

Map 8.1 The Habsburg Monarchy in 1848

He was an enemy of Metternich's from the start with the advantages of considerable financial ability and a readiness to pretend to liberal sympathies. After 1835 the Monarchy was ruled by a Council of State which Metternich could not always control, and within which Kolowrat intrigued for support.

3   *Administrative weaknesses.* For an absolutist régime it was remarkably inefficient. The bureaucracy was complex and over-cumbersome. In addition, the Monarchy had serious financial problems (see Section 3.5).

Not surprisingly, Metternich once remarked: 'I have sometimes held Europe in my hands but never Austria.'

(b) *Options*

There were several alternative defences against liberalism and nationalism. Partly because of the limits to power and partly because he had no long-term constructive visions – he was once described as 'an empiricist who dealt only in palliatives' – Metternich tended towards gimmicks and short-term solutions.

1   *Repression.* Metternich was never reluctant to use force as in Italy or to employ swarms of informers, secret policemen and censors.

2   *Economic amelioration.* A radical approach would have been to try and win popular support by means of economic improvement to buy off opposition. However, this approach was limited by:

   – A fear by conservatives that economic improvement would lead to greater independence of outlook. Metternich's friend Gentz remarked: 'We do not desire at all that the great masses shall become well off and independent . . . How could we otherwise rule over them?'
   – Distrust of modern innovations. Francis I said of the railway, 'No, no. I will have nothing to do with it lest the revolution might come into the country.'
   – The government had persistent budgetary problems already, and increased taxation to 'prime the pump' would arouse opposition.
   – Before the masses felt any benefit the middle classes would be further stimulated, and they were a centre of discontent.

3   *Constitutional concessions.* Conceivably concessions could be given without really reducing imperial power:

   – The restoration of the old provincial Diets was encouraged because Metternich saw the provinces as conservative. Symbolic gestures were also made in this direction, with Ferdinand crowned as King of Hungary in 1830, of Bohemia in 1836, and of Lombardy in 1838.
   – The creation of an *Imperial Reichsrat* of delegates from the provinces to discuss the budget and legislation. Resistant to this until the last, Francis I agreed only in 1834, the year before his death. This attempt to release pressures was never employed.

4   *Cultural nationalism.* As a diversion and to encourage nationalist divisions Metternich actually sponsored literary revivals and considered a reconstruction of the Empire on some sort of linguistic basis.

8.5 The growth of opposition

Metternich became caught in a trap:

(a) *Court resistance*

By the 1840s Metternich's proposals were increasingly blocked by his enemies led by Kolowrat and groups like the great magnates opposed to tariff changes to enable membership of the *Zollverein*, and especially the reduction of sugar duties which would hit the sugar beet industry.

(b) *'New wine in old bottles'*

The recreated Diets, far from being symbolic decorations became the weapons of liberals and nationalists turned against the imperial government.

8.6 Lower Austria

Here the opposition came from German nobility and bureaucrats. Their programme was presented by the Tyrolean aristocrat Baron Andrian in 1842 in his pamphlet *Austria and her Future*, in which he advocated the revival of feeling in the Empire by strengthening the power of the provincial Diets and calling a national Reichstag. The Diet of Lower Austria took up these calls, opened itself to middle-class deputies and began to demand publication of Treasury accounts.

8.7 Bohemia

In Bohemia, an alliance developed between the old nobility and academic intellectuals.

(a) *A Slavonic revival*

A Slav cultural revival was focused on the *University of Prague* and led by the Abbé Dobrowsky with his linguistic studies, the poet Jan Kollar and the famous scholar Safarik. It was the historian Palacky who took this a stage further, by seeking the revival of the historic rights of the Kingdom of Bohemia.

(b) *The Bohemian nobility*

Initially, the Czech and German aristocrats added their support to these demands as a means of self-protection against imperial centralisation. Not until the 1840s did the movement begin to attract the Prague middle class and lead to Czech demands for independence. Then the Germans became apprehensive.

8.8 The South Slavs

Agitation even developed in the south, where the Serbs and Croats were divided by historical tradition and religion and there was only a tiny educated class.

(a) *Illyrism*

There was a common language and there existed an independent Serbia (see Section 11.2). Ljudevit Gaj began to advocate a union of the Catholic Croats and Greek Orthodox Serbs of the Empire with Serbia to create an Illyrian state.

(b) *A Kingdom of Croatia*

More moderately, the anti-Magyar Croats advocated a separate Croat unit within the Empire and the government actually encouraged this because it embarrassed the Magyars. This was a dangerous game to play because there was Croat support for Illyria as well, and the one could easily develop into the other.

8.9 Hungary

Until 1825 the Kingdom of Hungary was administered by imperial officials, then the Diet was called for the first time since 1812 to try and deal with Magyar opposition. In fact, with a Magyar literary revival in the background and fear as to social stability in Hungary in an age of economic pressures and European revolutions two Magyar leaders especially represented conflicting views as to the future of Hungary:

(a) *Istvan Széchenyi*

A brooding aristocrat with a deep faith in the revitalisation of Hungary, Széchenyi was especially impressed by Britain and he sought to stimulate economic development as a basis for the rebirth of Hungary. His programme consisted largely of:

1   *Increased economic productivity* financed by the abolition of the nobility's exemption from taxation, increased borrowing and more commercialised agriculture based on hired labour rather than peasant services. He took a strong interest in improvements in communications such as railways, steam navigation and river improvement and the building of the suspension bridge between Buda and Pest.
2   *Social reform.* Especially the improvement of the conditions of the peasantry.
3   *Maintenance of the link with the Monarchy.* Széchenyi saw political demands as a weakening of Hungary's capacity to concentrate on economic improvement.
4   *The establishment of Magyar as the official language.* He saw this as a valuable step towards modernisation. He founded the Budapest Academy to assist in the purification of the language. This modern national state would be carried through by an alliance of the great landowners and the new urban middle classes. He looked down upon the rather backward and narrow minded country squires who opposed him.

(b) *Lajos Kossuth*

Kossuth came from a poor, minor noble family and was much nearer to the squires in origin and background. Various careers as a lawyer and estate manager led eventually to membership of the Diet where he leapt to fame as the reporter of the debates in the newspaper *Pesti Hirlap*. He shared some of Széchenyi's aims, but his programme was far more political and radical:

1 *Autonomy for Hungary.* The creation of a separate Magyar Ministry and parliamentary government together with a separate customs system. The Magyar squires were attracted to this because the Habsburg connection could be seen as a cause of their own economic problems.
2 *Radical reforms* to broaden the base of the nation:

   – Extension of the franchise.
   – Emancipation of the peasants from feudal obligations, but with full compensation to the landowners.
   – Abolition of exemption from taxation.
   – Freedom of the press and association and freedom of religion.

3 *Magyarisation.* Several motives could be seen in making Magyar the only official language:

   – A means of improving the lot of the 'inferior' cultures and more fully opening up the political system to them.
   – An obstruction to the literary revivals of the other peoples of Hungary and to the appeal of Russian Pan-Slavism (see Section 10.5(b)).
   – The guarantee to Magyar squires of a monopoly of official jobs to supplement their limited incomes by excluding the 'inferior' nationalities.

(c) *The triumph of the liberals*

Kossuth won the support of the Magyar squires. He had considerable advantages:

1 He was a brilliant orator and had a magnetic personality.
2 Széchenyi opposed the programme of magyarisation (he could barely speak Magyar himself).
3 The encouragement given to the Croats by the government in Vienna, which seemed a direct challenge to the Magyars.

By legislation in 1840 and 1843 the liberals won virtually all of their language demands. Then in 1847, in response to an attempted showdown brought about by Metternich, they spelt out their Oppositional Declaration which now included a demand for a totally separate Hungarian government responsible to the legislature. In March 1848, Kossuth carried these demands to Vienna. In April, they were enacted. The *'lawful revolution'* had been achieved.

8.10 Conclusion

By March 1848, the government in Vienna had too much to contend with to be able to resist Kossuth's demands. However his followers should have been aware of two dangers:

1 *A peasant reaction.* Conservative by nature when released from their feudal obligations, they were as likely to support as to oppose the dynasty. In 1846, for

instance, peasants in Polish Galicia had murdered 2000 nobles and intellectuals seeking to stir them into revolution and proudly displayed the bodies to Habsburg officials.

2   *The awakening of the subject nationalities.* The *April laws* included Croatia and Transylvania as part of Hungary even though they had hitherto enjoyed a favoured status. That, together with the application of Magyar language legislation, would provoke tremendous opposition.

By 1848, however, the most immediate threat to property and stability seemed to many citizens of the Monarchy to be the reactionary policies to which Metternich was more and more inclined. Support for internal reforms grew rapidly as the alternative to international crusades against revolution and the damage to trade and finance associated with war and upheaval.

Questions

1   How successful was Metternich in dealing with the internal problems of the Habsburg Monarchy from 1815 to 1848?
2   Why was the Magyar language so important in the story of the development of Hungarian nationalism between 1815 and 1848?
3   Why were revolutionary activities so prevalent in the Habsburg Monarchy in 1848?
4   Compare and contrast the contributions made to the development of Hungarian nationalism by Istvan Széchenyi and Lajos Kossuth.
5   'I have sometimes held Europe in my hands but never Austria.' Why was Metternich so pessimistic about his position within the Habsburg Monarchy?
6   To what extent was nationalism a threat to the Habsburg Monarchy between 1815 and 1848?

9 The revolutions of 1848

Introduction

In what Germans know as *'the crazy year'*, western Europe exploded spontaneously into a wave of revolutions. There were uprisings in fifteen capital cities. Despite all of the efforts of Metternich the forces of reaction were uncoordinated, and all of the revolutions were fought out internally. The coincidence is to be explained largely by the common underlying causes (see Section 4) and by a sort of 'domino theory'. However, the course of the revolutions also displays great similarities in pattern, again partly because of some interaction. There was bound to be some difference in 'colouring', though, because of variations in historical backgrounds, the extent of economic development and the depth of social and ethnic divisions. Broadly speaking, the nearer central and eastern Europe the state was, the greater was the role of nationalism and the less important the role of liberalism.

I 'THE SPRINGTIME OF THE PEOPLES'

9.1 Italy (January–March 1848)

Already in October 1847 Metternich observed 'I am an old doctor; I can distinguish a passing illness from a mortal ailment, [and] we are in the throes of the latter'. However, the first real outbreak of open revolt was in February, in Italy.

(a) *The achievement of Sicilian autonomy*

A revolt in Palermo forced Ferdinand II to grant Sicily a constitution which gave it virtual independence. Inevitably the disease radiated to Naples and he had to concede a constitution for the whole kingdom. Meanwhile Charles Albert was pressured by moderate liberals and nationalists into agreeing to a constitution and a bid for leadership in northern Italy. The Grand Duke of Tuscany also gave way.

(b) *The 'Five Days' of Milan*

Events were accelerated by the news of revolutions in Paris and Vienna. Pius IX granted a constitution to the Papal States on 15 March. In Venice a republic was proclaimed. It was in Milan, however, where the greatest shock occurred. Tension had developed since the *'tobacco riots'* of January (arising from a boycott by the citizens of tobacco, a good which was a government monopoly). Although there were differences between the upper-class constitutionalists and the radical republicans they were united in support of a massive demonstration on 17 March. It developed into street fighting. With only 100,000 men in the whole of Italy, a third of them Italians, scattered in small garrisons and with revolutionary threats all over the place Marshal Radetsky withdrew his forces from Milan to regroup. A liberal–radical provisional government was established under Cattaneo.

(c)   The first Austro-Piedmontese War

Radetsky was partly influenced by the threat from Piedmont. With pressure coming from both political extremes to declare war and floods of enthusiastic volunteers and contingents of regular troops from regions where revolutions had succeeded heading north to help, Charles Albert was forced to 'grasp the artichoke'! War was declared on Austria. Days later 60,000 Piedmontese troops had linked up with the Milanese rebels.

9.2   France (February–April 1848)

Events in France were equally unexpected.

(a)   The February Revolution

De Tocqueville remarked that 'No one overthrew the government, it just allowed itself to fall'. Barricades resulting from the banning of the reform banquet (see Section 5.8) were a good excuse for the King to dismiss Guizot, of whom he was already tired. The disturbances developed into near revolution after royal troops killed sixteen rioters. The King turned to Thiers, who gambled by calling off the troops. The rebels sensed a victory. Troops began to fraternise. The sound of the National Guard units called out to provide a counter demonstration shouting *'à-bas le système'* was the signal that the bourgeois had withdrawn their support. Old and sick, the King gave up and left for England.

(b)   The establishment of the Second Republic

There was no obvious claimant available to fill the throne and working-class radical republicanism was very strong. The Chamber was intimidated by a noisy mob into accepting a republic and established a provisional government. It was divided socially, personally and politically. It was dominated by wealthy nobles but included Louis Blanc and a token workman called Albert. The measures of the liberal–socialist régime reflected this odd marriage:

1   *Liberal measures* included the abolition of censorship (with the prompt appearance of 200 new journals by June) and extension of the electoration from 250,000 to all 8 million adult males.
2   *Social reforms* provoked more debate, especially the reduction of hours of work and the creation of national workshops to absorb the unemployed at 2 francs a day.

The problem was that revolution produced uncertainty for the future, and renewed economic crisis. The provisional government was mainly concerned to promote business confidence and restore prosperity. That meant establishing public order and avoiding the appearance of socialism.

(c) *The Constituent Assembly*

The key was held by the peasantry, who were conservative and affected by a 45 per cent increase in direct taxation to cover the growing deficit. Reacting against Paris and socialism they accounted for the high 84 per cent poll which produced a right-wing Assembly of middle-class moderates, 80 per cent of them were over 40 years of age. Of the 876 delegates, there were only 100 radical republicans and socialists. Only a minority expressed any concern for social reform. A clash with the Paris radicals and socialists was inevitable.

9.3 Germany (March–April 1848)

The shock waves reverberated in Belgium and Holland with less dramatic events but a similar outcome. In Germany the spasm was stronger.

(a) *The spread of revolution*

Revolts started in the more politically advanced southern states. In Bavaria the uprising against Louis I and his domineering mistress Lola Montez preceded that in Paris. Then disturbances spread through Saxony in northern Germany. On the whole, these were liberal constitutionalist revolts by the 'respectable' classes. However, in addition there were rather more radical and disturbing tendencies:

1 *Peasant and artisan attacks* on property, officials, landowners and money lenders.
2 *Socialist demands* in the Prussian Rhineland, in Hanover and above all in Baden where a communist-inspired insurrection in support of a German republic was crushed by constitutionalist forces at Kandern in April.

(b) *The* Vor *Parliament*

These were all local revolts. However, Heinrich von Gagern, minister of Hesse-Darmstadt, arranged a meeting of state representatives at Heidelberg in late March to arrange for an elected National Constituent Assembly to meet at Frankfurt. This meeting had no legal standing, and an unbalanced membership – Baden had 72 and the Metternich Monarchy only two delegates. The Federal Diet endorsed the arrangements nevertheless. The restoration of order and nationalist ambitions were two sides of the same coin.

(c) *The 'March Days'* (see Illus. 9.1 and 9.2)

Prussia was in no position to restore order. A revolt broke out in Cologne on 3 March. Anti-Prussian feelings, 30 per cent unemployment and a strong middle class were powerful factors in urging concessions. By 18 March, Berlin itself was beset. The killing of 250 demonstrators by overzealous troops added fuel to the flames. The dithering King Frederick William with a belief in his 'dear Berliners' and a dislike for the army and loud noises tried to restore order by saluting the dead rebels and ordering the troops to withdraw from the city where a middle-class Civic Guard was formed. Then he

Illus. 9.1 The King of Prussia salutes the dead (Hulton Picture Library)

From the *Illustrated London News* of March 1848, showing the dead carried before the king and queen.

Source: *Illustrierte Geschichte der Deutschen Revolution 1848–1849* (Dietz Verlag, Berlin, 1973) p. 92.

Q By saluting the bodies of the rebels killed by his troops, what effect would this be likely to have on the position of the King? Would it help him or weaken his authority?

embraced the black, red and gold flag of nationalism and announced that 'Prussia is henceforth merged in Germany'. He promised to summon a Constituent Assembly and in April it was determined that this should be elected by virtual manhood suffrage. To be fair to Frederick William, these could be seen as the actions of a man trying to gain time for the forces of counter-revolution.

9.4   The Habsburg Monarchy (March–May 1848)

The heart of reaction was in Vienna, and attention was focused on the meeting of the Diet of Lower Austria set for 13 March when a reform petition was to be debated.

(a)   *The fall of Metternich* (see Illus. 9.3)

On the 13 March the challenge to Metternich came from two directions:

Illus. 9.2 Frederick William IV (1848) (Archiv Gerstenberg)

From an anonymous caricature of 1848, in the Archiv Gerstenberg.

Source: Illustrierte Geschichte der Deutschen Revolution 1848–1849 (Dietz Verlag, Berlin, 1973) p. 95.

a The King is shouting, 'You, in front, listen, don't run away so quickly, I want to be at the front of the movement!' What does the cartoonist intend the reader to understand by this? How does this picture relate to the previous one? Do you think Frederick William was right to follow the policy which the cartoon suggests he was?

From a lithograph by A. Zampis in the Archiv Gerstenberg, caricaturing Metternich's flight from Vienna in 1848.

Jede Constitution erfordert Bewegung

Source: *Illustrierte Geschichte der Deutschen Revolution 1848–1849.*

Q According to this cartoonist the more constitutions that were granted in early 1848 the longer grew the nose of Metternich. Which children's story does this remind you of? What sort of power do you think cartoonists can have in politics?

1 *Popular disturbances* by some 5000 radical students and academic staff and several thousand manual workers. The use of troops under an inexperienced officer just worsened the situation.

2 *A court conspiracy* in contact with liberal constitutionalist groups, persuading the Emperor that Metternich's dismissal was more likely to save the situation than the resistance he was proposing. The Emperor gave way; Metternich was dismissed and later fled to England (see Illus. 9.4). A cabinet of moderate aristocratic officials was appointed. An armed National Guard and Academic Legion replaced

From a caricature of 1848, 'A Whist Party', showing Louis Philippe, Frederick William IV and Metternich in London exile.

Source: *Illustrierte Geschichte der Deutschen Revolution 1848–1849* (Dietz Verlag, Berlin, 1973) p. 92.

Q   'For the time being only one table with one dummy.' What is the warning for the other rulers of Europe which is contained in this cartoon? What 'trumps' did the forces of conservatism and reaction have which they could play?

the troops in the streets. A constitution was promised. Indeed the hapless Emperor said 'tell the people that I agree to everything'.

(b) *A victory for radicalism*

Initially, there was an alliance of moderate liberal constitutionalists and more radical elements. In fact this alliance now began to break up because:

1 *A radical constitution* was forced on the Imperial government on 15 May by popular demonstrations. A more moderate constitution acceptable to properties classes was rejected in favour of a single-chamber legislature and universal male suffrage. A Constituent Assembly met in Vienna.
2 *An abortive counter-attack* by the government relying on support from the alarmed properties classes. In the event Vienna was left in the hands of a Committee of Artisans, National Guards and students. On 17 May the Emperor and the court took refuge in Innsbruck.

(c) *The provinces*

Outside Lower Austria the main trouble spots were Hungary and Bohemia:

1 *The 'Lawful Revolution'.* With the reluctant approval of the Imperial government, the Kossuthite liberals enacted the sweeping *April Laws* against the opposition of the great aristocrats and higher clergy of the upper house. A National Guard was also established. The 'Lawful Revolution' was completed. However, the agreement reached remained dangerously ambiguous.

2   *Austroslavism.* Liberal minded Czech nationalists and German aristocrats could unite to support a form of autonomy in Bohemia with equality for the two languages, and the Imperial government did give concessions. However the Czechs and Germans were divided as to the administrative relationship between German Silesia and Czech Moravia, and above all over the relationship between Bohemia and a united Germany. Palacky rejected inclusion because he feared German domination of the Czechs. Indeed he advocated the survival of the Monarchy as a benefit to its Slav minorities: 'Assuredly if the Austrian state had not existed for ages it would have been necessary for us in the interests of Europe and indeed of humanity to endeavour to create it as soon as possible'. However, the Czech nationalists were a small group of militants. For most of the rural population of Bohemia freedom meant freedom from feudal obligations.

II 'A TROUBLESOME SUMMER'

9.5   Italy (March–July 1848)

From very early on, the vulnerability of the revolutions was revealed:

(a)   *The divisions of the revolutionaries*

Debates over the amalgamation of Lombardy, Venetia, Parma and Modena with Piedmont revealed the crucial divisions between three groups:

1   *Moderate liberals and constitutionalists*, who supported total fusion under the Piedmontese monarchy as a guarantee of property against social disorder with the Habsburgs gone and now that the working class radicals who had defeated the Austrian army were transformed into a 'mortal menace' as Cavour described them.
2   *Republican federalists* like Cattaneo, who were jealous of Piedmont and sought a federal Italy.
3   *Republican unitarians* led by Mazzini, who wanted victory first and discussions afterwards.

In June–July the *Kingdom of North Italy* came into being under Charles Albert.

(b)   *The rallying of counter-revolution*

1   *The Pope.* The Pope could hardly join a crusade against the devoutly Catholic Habsburg Monarchy. He condemned the war on the 29 April. Papal troops were recalled to the fury of Roman radicals.
2   *Reaction in Naples.* The 'rot' had started. Partly influenced by the Pope's action, by the growth of separatism in Sicily and radicalism everywhere, Ferdinand revoked the promises made in May, ignored the constitution and recalled Neapolitan troops from their northward journey. He had the support by then of moderate liberals who united with the landed classes in fear of social revolt.
3   *Custozza (July 1848).* In the central states, and in Tuscany especially, the story was the same – one of a restoration of order with the connivance of middle-class liberals and constitutionalists fearful of revolutions by peasants and artisans. The most decisive development was in the north. The French revolutionary régime sent no help, and Charles Albert boastfully set out to prove that *'Italia fara da se'* –

'Italy can manage by herself'. At Custozza, between 23 and 27 July the octagenarian Radetsky proved that Italy was not yet ready to 'manage by herself'. Bad generalship – Radetsky advised his gunners to 'spare the enemy generals – they are to valuable to our side', reinforcements from a more stable Habsburg Monarchy and inadequate assistance from the rest of revolutionary Italy led to a decisive defeat in Piedmont and the reoccupation of Milan.

9.6   France (April–June 1848)

De Tocqueville said of Paris in the spring of 1848: 'I saw society split in two; those who possessed nothing united in a common greed; those who possessed something united in a common fear'. The right-wing reaction against the swelling tide of radicalism and socialism was inevitable after the election. It came in two stages:

(a)   *The curbing of radical power*

A range of legal measures undercut radical power:

1   *An executive commission replaced the provisional government.* Of its five members only Ledru-Rollin was a radical.
2   *A purge of radical elements.* An attempt by the mob to intimidate the Assembly on 15 May was prevented by the National Guard and the socialist leader Blanqui was arrested. This was followed by:

   – Closure of the revolutionary clubs, 450 in Paris alone.
   – The rooting out of 'undesirables' from the National Guard.
   – Replacement of a radical prefect of police by a moderate.

3   *The national workshops were dissolved* on 21 June. The 100,000 workers – an expensive reservoir of mob ingredients – were offered the choice of army service or employment on provincial public works.

(b)   *The 'June Days'*

Next day, the barricades went up in the eastern districts of Paris. Most of the insurgents were drawn from the small scale artisan trades of the city. The Assembly called in the tough non-political general Eugéne Cavaignac and rushed in troops by train. Days of savage street fighting resulted in the crushing of the 50,000 armed rebels, the killing of at least 1500, the arrest of 19,000 and deporting of 4000. More political clubs were closed, censorship restored and the right to work became a dead letter. Apart from the long-lived legend about the suppression of the working class by the middle class, although in fact about a fifth of the National Guard used against the insurrection were workers, this 'Panic of property' produced the clear moral that order could be best pre-served by a 'strong man'.

9.7   Germany (April–October 1848)

In Germany, the divisions between the liberal moderates and radicals was also dis-played, albeit confused by a cross-current of nationalism:

(a) The failure of the Frankfurt Assembly

The Assembly met on 18 May. Restrictive state franchises and a high level of absten-tion contributed to making it very much an assembly of middle-class intellectuals. Of its 596 members, 81.6 per cent had had a university education, there were 223 lawyers, 106 professors, 118 senior officials, 80 businessmen, 60 landowners and 116 without profes-sion. There was only one peasant, four artisans and six clerks. The Austrian Archduke John was appointed to head a cabinet, but the debates revealed four areas of weakness:

1   *The definition of frontiers.* Moderate and anti-Prussian groups advocated a
    'Grossdeutschland' including the Habsburg Monarchy except for Hungary. A
    'Kleindeutschland' excluding the non-German Habsburg provinces was favoured
    by radical nationalists; this would give Prussia the paramount influence. By 28
    October it was finally agreed that the latter should be the case; the Habsburg
    Monarchy was then otherwise occupied, and in no position to respond.
2   *Divisions over the form of the constitution.* Not until October 1848 was a draft
    document produced and a bill of fundamental rights agreed. A system of
    representative and responsible state governments with a federal government
    responsible to a nationally elected legislature were proposed. However, an upper
    house would represent state interests and conservatism. The head of state would
    have no veto.
3   *The absence of lower-class support.* Although the Assembly advocated abolition of
    feudal privileges, it supported *compensation* to uphold respect for property rights.
    In general, with its fears of peasant and socialist disorders and belief in free trade,
    the Assembly could not attract popular support by giving way to demands for
    progressive income tax, protective tariffs, state employment schemes and so on.
4   *The inability to combine liberalism and nationalism.* The most disturbing feature
    was the way in which liberals were prepared to embrace a crudely illiberal
    nationalism on occasion. Hence the defeats of the Czechs and Italians were
    cheered while there was an aggressive unity in favour of the use of Prussian troops
    against Danish attempts to incorporate Schleswig and Holstein and in forcing the
    Polish liberals of the Grand Duchy of Posen to accept a two-thirds majority on the
    local assembly for a German minority of immigrants.

(b) Growing strains in Prussia

The Assembly depended to an embarrassing extent on Prussian force. This was espe-cially revealed by the Prussians making a separate truce with the Danes at Malmö on 26 August 1848 under pressure from Britain and Russia. However in Prussia the forces of counter-revolution were strengthening:

1   *The alienation of the moderates.* The liberal middle classes had got what they
    wanted – a Civic Guard and an upper-middle-class cabinet (the 'March Ministers')
    under Camphausen. However, a rift between them and the radical workers grew
    with the latter's more extreme political and social demands. In May, June and
    October outbreaks of disorder revealed the inadequacy of the Civic Guard and
    propertied people began to leave Berlin and support conservatism.
2   *'With God for King and Fatherland'.* With the King at Potsdam there developed a
    well-organised conservative group around him made up of Junkers such as Otto
    von Bismarck and army officers. Well-organised and financed, with court support
    and its own newspaper – the *'Kreuzzeitung'* – this anti-democratic, anti-liberal and
    deeply Prussian group was poised for a counter-attack under the leadership of
    Otto von Manteuffel.

3   *The Constituent Assembly.* The very radical Assembly elected in May on universal, male suffrage played into reactionary hands by its provocative display of extremist tendencies as it advocated the abolition of titles of nobility and even the removal of 'by the Grace of God' from the title of the King.

9.8   The Habsburg Monarchy (May–October 1848)

In the Habsburg Monarchy, there were also several levels of activity which all inter-acted to some extent.

(a)   *The Constituent Assembly*

The Assembly met on 22 July in Vienna. It was riddled with divisions, although basically there were two causes of debate:

1   *Federalism v. unitarianism.* The Slavs tended to be in favour of greater federal devolution, although rivalries between different Slav groups meant that the 190 Slavs of the total of 400 delegates did not vote as a bloc. The 140 Germans, on the other hand, were largely moderate liberals, who believed in the unity of the Monarchy as the route to liberalism and modernisation, although Hungary would be treated separately.
2   *The relationship with Germany.* The division in the Frankfurt Assembly was paralleled in the Monarchy. Moderate Germans preferred the *'Grossdeutschland'* solution because the Habsburg Monarchy would have a more powerful voice. Radicals wanted to lose the non-German provinces and preferred a *'Kleindeutschland'*. In fact, the most significant act of the Assembly was the abolition of all feudal dues on 7 September which effectively cancelled out the peasantry as a revolutionary force.

(b)   *The Habsburg recovery*

As elsewhere, the forces of reaction were able to exploit the divisions of the revolutionaries. By withdrawing to Innsbruck in May the pretence of legality had been weakened. Now, with the growing alarm of propertied groups, it was possible for more positive steps to be taken:

1   *The 'June Days' of Prague.* A *Slav Congress* had been meeting concurrently at Prague. On *12 June* it voted in favour of a federal structure. However, a group of some 1200 radical students and workers revolted in favour of an independent Czech republic. Divorced from any sympathy from the moderates they were bloodily crushed by Marshal Windischgrätz (whose wife was killed in the early hours of the revolt).
2   *The 'Battle of the Prater'.* By July the court was confident enough to return to Vienna. Then in August a revolt by workers resulting from cuts in wages and in public works schemes was crushed by police and the National Guard.
3   *The invasion of Hungary.* The Hungarian National Assembly under radical control was withholding tax revenue and troops and had incorporated Croatia and Transylvania. Attempts to impose linguistic and administrative uniformity on Croatians and Rumanians generated resistance, and a cycle of atrocity and counter-atrocity started. The Imperial government chose the rabid anti-Magyar

Josip Jellačić to be Governor of Croatia and Transylvania. In September, predictably, he invaded Hungary from Croatia. This had two effects:

– *Magyar extremism was encouraged.* Kossuth declared the 'country in danger', and assumed near-dictatorial powers. This reached a bloody climax when Magyars assassinated the Habsburg emissary Count Lamberg in Budapest.
– *Divisions between the Viennese revolutionaries* were increased, and in Vienna the Constituent Assembly radicals and Germans supported Hungary while moderates and Slavs were anti-Magyar.

On 3 October, Jellačić was appointed head of the government in Hungary and Latour, the minister of war, sent him reinforcements to make his claim good. The Hungarians rejected the decree with contempt and established a *National Defence Committee* under Kossuth and with an army of some 170,000 ex-imperial and newly raised troops at its disposal.

III 'A DISASTROUS WINTER'

9.9   Italy (July 1848–August 1849)

In Italy, the revolutions entered a new phase with the continued distraction of the Habsburg Monarchy and the defeat of Charles Albert.

(a)   *The radical revolution*

Since March 1848 there had been a radical régime in the Venetian Republic of St Mark under Manin. In Rome, the flight of the Pope to Naples in November 1848 and election of a radical Constituent Assembly in January 1849 was followed by the proclamation of a Roman Republic and the abolition of Papal temporal powers. Then in February Charles Albert – very much under pressure from ultra-nationalists and radicals – appointed a new cabinet under Rattazzi. On 12 March, war was again declared on the Habsburg Monarchy. Within days the Piedmontese army had been defeated at Novara, and Charles Albert abdicated in favour of his son the Duke of Savoy.

(b)   *The triumph of reaction*

The Habsburgs could now concentrate on the residual pockets of resistance, helped by the apathy of peasants and poorer classes – who could not expect any gains from the revolutions – and the desire of the propertied classes to see order restored. In April–May Tuscany, Modena, Parma and Lucca were all restabilised and occupied by Habsburg forces. With the loss of the help of the Piedmontese fleet the Republic of St Mark fell in August. In Rome despite the leadership of Mazzini and the enthusiasm of Garibaldi's 'red shirt' volunteers the city fell in June 1849 to the French forces sent by Louis Napoleon appealing for Catholic support in France. Garibaldi made a legendary escape. In April 1850, the Pope returned and took up his misgovernment where he had left off.

Illus. 9.5 Louis Napoleon takes the oath (Collection Viollet)

From a painting in the Musée de Montreuil, Paris, showing Louis Napoleon taking the oath to uphold the constitution in 1849.

LOUIS NAPOLÉON BONAPARTE,
PROCLAMÉ PRÉSIDENT DE LA RÉPUBLIQUE FRANÇAISE,
prête serment à la Constitution.

Source: G. Soria, *Grande Histoire de la Commune* (Livre Club Diderot, Paris, 1970) Part 1, p. 59.

Q   The irony of this is that Louis Napoleon was the only citizen of the Second Republic who was obliged to take an oath of loyalty as President. In view of later events how would this affect attitudes towards him?

9.10 France (June 1848–December 1851)

A constitution was produced in November 1848. It lasted until 2 December 1851.

(a) Louis Napoleon (see Illus. 9.5)

The most prominent feature of the new constitution was the direct election of the president by universal male suffrage. He would hold office for four years, not be re-elected and was not able to dissolve the single-chamber National Assembly which had a three-year term. In fact, the first president was a nephew of the great Napoleon, Louis Napoleon, who won an overwhelming 5½ million votes. He was rather unprepossessing. A long-time exile with a heavy German accent and a dull expression, a romantic who had been the leader of two rather preposterous 'revolts' in 1836 and 1840 he did, nevertheless, have qualities which attracted support:

1   A *'strong man'*. To the right-wing bourgeois, Louis Napoleon seemed a great substitute for a monarch. As the Spanish ambassador wrote, France was 'filled with monarchists who cannot establish a monarchy and who groan under the weight of a republic which has no republicans to defend it' – although, as Thiers snidely remarked, Louis Napoleon was 'a *cretin* whom we will manage'. The peasantry were less perceptive but wanted order.
2   *The nephew of his uncle.* His very name suggested *'la gloire'* of which romantic and nationalist Frenchmen had been starved for years.
3   *A prospect of social reform.* The author of *L'extinctien du paupérisme* (1844) offered a prospect of some reform to the workers.

(b) Coup d'état (2 December 1851)

Louis Napoleon was a stand-in for a monarch. Conservative strength grew, and this was reflected in the *Loi Falloux (1850)* re-establishing freedom for religious orders and an electoral law of May 1851 which disenfranchised 3 million of the poorest voters. Meanwhile negotiations went on with the representatives of the several claimants to the throne. Bonaparte built up a national following by extensive journeying, but in 1851 he failed to obtain an extension of his tenure of office. On 1 December 1851 he used troops to arrest all opposition leaders and the next day used the pretext of a conspiracy against the State to seize power with the Napoleonic appeal 'Soldiers! It is your mission to save the country'. This was followed by a massive wave of social protest, especially in central and south eastern France.

9.11 Germany (October 1848–September 1849)

The fate of Germany was determined by the interaction of events in Berlin, Frankfurt and Vienna.

(a) The end of the Frankfurt Assembly

By March 1849 the Assembly had achieved some sort of consensus and offered the crown to Frederick William IV of Prussia as hereditary German emperor with command of the military forces, a suspensive veto and ability to dissolve the lower house. This was accepted by 28 states. However, Frederick William rejected the offer partly because of concern about Habsburg reactions but also because he refused to collect a 'crown from the gutter' of popular acclaim. The Assembly now became rather purpose-less, and began to disintegrate. In June 1849 it was dispersed by troops, still debating to the bitter end.

(b) The restoration of order in Prussia

In October 1848, a virtual coup took place in Prussia as Berlin was flooded with troops and it was declared under 'military siege' and the King's uncle Count von Brandenburg became the leader of the government. In December 1848, the Assembly was dissolved. As the King had been advised, 'only soldiers can help against democrats'. However the King now made a clear bid for the leadership of liberal and national elements:

1   *The proclamation of a constitution (April 1849).* It was a very modest document, comparable to many others. However the executive retained extensive powers to suspend rights, to revise the constitution and to govern by emergency decrees. Above all, the complex three-class electoral system based on tax payment gave 5 per cent of the population the ability to elect a third of the deputies and another 20 per cent selected another third. Not only did this vastly increase the power of the Junker aristocracy, but there was also a hereditary upper house established, and ministers were made responsible only to the king.
2   *The Erfurt Union.* In May 1849 Frederick William embraced a scheme for 'Kleindeutschland' supported by Saxony, Hanover, some smaller states and some liberals. In June–July, as the Prussian army restored order in a series of states, especially in Baden, Saxony, Westphalia and the Rhineland Palatinate, more of them came to see the wisdom of agreeing. In March 28 states were represented at the parliament at Erfurt.

9.12 The Habsburg Monarchy (October 1848–August 1849)

By March 1849 the Habsburgs were very much back in power. In November the 'Humiliation of Olmütz' occurred, when Prussia was forced to abandon the Erfurt scheme and the old Confederation was restored.

(a) The October revolt in Vienna

As the economic situation deteriorated and popular misery increased the radical mili-tants became more forceful, establishing their own central Committee of the Democratic Clubs to coordinate their actions. The crisis came in early October when radicals tried to stop reinforcements en route to the Croats and murdered Latour in revenge. About 40,000 radical students and workers held the city briefly but on 31 October Windischgrätz and Jellačić captured it at the expense of the deaths of up to 5000 insurgents. A new government under Prince Schwartzenberg then took two steps to strengthen the imperial cause:

1   *The abdication of Ferdinand* in favour of Francis Joseph, December 1848). At least the Emperor's nephew had not accepted the April Laws.
2   *The Stadion Constitution (March 1848).* The Constituent Assembly was dissolved but a constitution was produced by Count Stadion, the minister of the interior, with a unitary state and an elected two-chamber assembly. This was a clear bid for moderate support. The façade was needed only until 1851.

(b) The crushing of Hungary

The Hungarian Diet had already behaved illegally and was officially dissolved. Now Hungary was included in the new unitary state without Croatia and Transylvania. In response in April 1849 independence was declared. Conscription and the military talents of Artur Görgey and a group of Polish émigré generals enabled a powerful resistance to be made. However in April 1849, by invitation, the Tsar – concerned about the new Polish dimension – sent in 80,000 troops to help the Habsburg forces. In August 1849 at Világos the Hungarian forces surrendered. Over 50,000 men had died in the fighting, and thousands of Russians died in a subsequent cholera epidemic.

9.13 Conclusion

About the 'Year in which history failed to turn' there are two concluding points of significance:

(a) The reasons for failure

In general, the revolutions were followed by a wave of restoration and repression (see Illus. 9.6). Herzen said of 1849 'everything ... has been sinful, gruesome and vile.' The causes of the failure had been fairly common:

1 *The natural conservatism of the peasantry*, and its harnessing in France and the Habsburg Monarchy especially.

Illus. 9.6 Reactionary victory in Europe

Source: Cartoon by F. Schroeder, 1849.

Prussian, French and Habsburg troops sweep the Continent clean of revolutionary elements while being observed by constitutional Britain. Refugees from persecution flee to Switzerland or take passage to the United States.

2   *Internal rivalries and antagonisms* between the revolutionary forces which were
    clearly displayed in all of the states examined. In the Habsburg Monarchy, these
    had been deliberately fomented, especially against Hungary.
3   *The rallying of the propertied classes* to the forces of order and authority as the
    prospect of social revolt developed.
4   *The decisive use of military force at key moments* could stop or turn the tide of
    revolution. On the whole, the regular armies had remained loyal, this was
    especially notable in the case of the multi-national Habsburg army.

(b)   *The lessons learnt*

The revolutions of 1848 marked the end of an age of revolutions. This was partly
because of the easier mobilisation of troops by means of the railway, and improved
armaments such as the breech-loading rifle. However, it was due mostly to:

1   *A developing alliance between the old authorities and the new forces of industry and
    commerce*, as in Britain. Cavour especially illustrated the value of this alliance (see
    Section 13).
2   *The movement of middle-class liberals and nationalists away from intellectual
    romanticism towards the realities of established state power* in the form of Piedmont
    and Prussia.
3   *Positive state policies to woo the masses.* By means of accelerating rural
    emancipation (in 1848 in east Elbe Prussia only 70,000 peasants were free, by 1865
    they were joined by another 640,000) and social legislation to curb the abuses of
    industrialism and urbanisation, the base of the state could be broadened. As
    important was the improvement of food supplies by improving communications
    and sponsoring industrial development to provide employment.

With hindsight the events of 1848 were the product of a chronologically limited period
of transition towards industrialisation in which the older strains of population pressure
and food shortage were compounded by the new ones of accelerating economic and
social change. This was the real end of the *Ancien Régime*.

Questions

1   Account for the risings in the Italian states in 1848. Why did they fail?   [OC]
2   Why were the revolutions of 1848 mostly unsuccessful?   [OC]
3   Why were the 1848 revolutions ultimately unsuccessful in *either* (a) Prussia, or (b) Austria–
    Hungary?   [OC]
4   Examine the influences working towards unification in Italy in the period 1815–48. [OX]
5   Why was 1848 a year of revolution? Describe events in 1848 and 1849, *either* (a) in Germany *or* in
    Italy, *or* (c) in the Austrian possessions, and state what the outcome was in the area you have
    selected.   [NEAB]
6   Describe the causes, events, and results of the revolutions with its non-German peoples between
    1815 and 1849?   [CAM]
7   How successful was the Austrian Empire in dealing with its non-German peoples between 1815
    and 1849?   [CAM]
8   How far, and for what reasons, did liberalism fail in Germany during 1848 and 1849? [CAM]
9   Why were there so many political upheavals in France in the period 1848–52?
10 To what extent was the failure of the revolutions of 1848–9 the result of common causes?
11 Study Sources A and B and then answer the questions which follow.

    Source A: Revolution in Italy.

        When I came into office, Europe was, so to speak, on fire, although by then the blaze had
        been put out in certain countries. Sicily had been conquered and subdued; the Neapolitans

had returned to their obedience or even slavery; the Battle of Novara had been fought and lost; the victorious Austrians were negotiating with the son of Charles Albert, King of Piedmont after his father's abdication; beyond the frontiers of Lombardy, Austrian armies occupied part of the Papal States, Parma, Aiancenza, and even Tuscany where they had come in uninvited and in spite of the fact that the Grand Duke had been restored by his own subjects, who were very ill-repaid later for their loyalty and zeal. But Venice still held out, and Rome, having repulsed our first attack, was calling all the demagogues in Italy to its aid and exciting the whole of Europe with its clamour.

(a) Explain what happened at 'the Battle of Novara' (line 3).
(b) Who was 'the son of Charles Albert, King of Piedmont' (line 4)?
(c) What happened in Rome (lines 5–10) in 1848 and 1849?
(d) Why were the uprisings in Italy eventually unsuccessful?
Source: Alexis de Tocqueville, *Recollections* (1893).

Source B: Why an Austrian state must exist

I am a Czech of Slav descent and with all the little I own and possess I have devoted myself wholly and for ever to the service of my nation ...

You know that in south-east Europe, along the frontiers of the Russian Empire, there live many nations widely different in origin, language, history and habits – Slavs, Rumanians, Magyars, and Germans, not to speak of Greeks, Turks and Albanians. None of whom is strong enough by itself to be able to resist successfully for all time the superior neighbour to the east; they could do it only if a close and firm tie bound them all together ... Certainly, if the Austrian state had not existed for ages, we would be obliged in the interests of Europe and even of mankind to endeavour to create it as fast as possible.

But why have we seen this state, which by nature and history is destined to be the bulwark and guardian of Europe against the Asiatic element of every kind – why have we seen it in a critical moment helpless and almost unadvised in the face of the advancing storm? It is because in an unhappy blindness which has lasted for very long. Austria has not recognised the real legal and moral foundation of its existence and has denied it: the fundamental rule that all the nationalities united under its sceptre should enjoy complete equality of rights and respect ... I am convinced that even now it is not too late for the Austrian Empire to proclaim openly and sincerely this fundamental rule of justice ...

When I look behind the Bohemian frontiers, then natural and historical reasons make me turn not to Frankfurt but to Vienna to seek there the centre which is fitted and destined to ensure and defend the peace, the liberty and the right of my nation. Your efforts, gentlemen, seem to me now to be directed as I have already stated, not only towards ruinously undermining, but even utterly destroying that centre from whose might and strength I expect the salvation not only of the Czech land.

(a) Who was Palacky, and why was a Czech invited to the Frankfurt Assembly?
(b) Why did Palacky believe that an Austrian state existed, and must continue to exist (lines 3–9)?
(c) What sort of internal reforms was Palacky implying ought to be implemented within the Habsburg Monarchy (lines 10–17)?
(d) Why do you think Palacky rejected the invitation?
Source: The reply of Frantisek Palacky to an invitation to attend the Frankfurt Assembly as a Czech delegate in April 1848.

Imperial Russia 1801–81

Introduction

The enduring problem of Russia throughout the nineteenth century was whether to look towards the western example, and seek to modernise an archaic society, economy and administration, or to turn away from these influences. Both of these policies shared the same danger; that in different ways they could provoke growing tensions within Russia. The dilemma of an eastward or westward-looking Russia is a recurrent theme in Russian history.

10.1 Russia in the early nineteenth century

With the additions made by the Vienna Settlement (see Section 3.3), the Russian Empire in 1815 had a population of 45 million. Regarded as the paramount military power, it was in fact one of the most underdeveloped states in Europe.

(a) *A feudal society*

Only 4 per cent of the population lived in towns. Half of the total population were *serfs* owned by hereditary nobles who were usually absentee landlords. The serfs worked so many days a week on their strips in the communal landholding, and for three days a week on the land of the landlord. Another 18 million state and crown serfs worked the land owned by the *Tsar*.

(b) *A backward economy*

1   *Low productivity.* In 1804, industry employed only 225,000 workers. It included textiles production around the leading towns and the mines and iron foundries of the Urals worked by unfree serf labour. Agriculture was predominant, but average grain yields were very low because of inefficient techniques, and the peasant market was very limited.

2   *Poor communications.* For instance, it took two years for grain from the lower Volga to reach St Petersburg. The first railway was built in 1838 but only to join St Petersburg to the Tsar's private residence at Tsarskaye Selo.

3   *Limited trade.* Exports were dominated by naval stores and raw materials to Britain. Badly affected by the Continental System (see Section 2.6), they were not encouraged by indecisive tariff policies after 1815.

4   *Financial weakness*

> – There was a persistent budget deficit, vastly increased by the campaign of 1812–14.
> – with the end of British subsidies, the Treasury was now dependent upon the heavy but irregular peasant taxation, reducing in total as the nobles tried to expand their holdings. Increased borrowing simply worsened the problem.

(c)   *An autocratic régime*

More so than in the Habsburg Monarchy or Prussia, or even in the Ottoman Empire, political and constitutional power was centralised in the person of the Tsar, divinely appointed to wield autocratic powers over the people of Russia. In this situation, not only was any suggestion of devolution of power easily seen as revolutionary, it could also be held to be against the will of God. Even so, despite its astonishing backwardness and stifling size, even Holy Russia could not remain immune to the political germs released by the French Revolution.

10.2 'The enigmatic Tsar' (1801–25)

Alexander I was influenced by the paradoxical currents of a liberal education under tutors employed by his grandmother Catherine the Great and the growing influence of advisers and mistresses who drew him more towards right-wing policies and a sort of mystical interdenominational Christianity. He was once described as 'too weak to rule and too strong to be ruled', a typical Romanov quality.

(a)   *Tentative liberalism (1801–15)*

Alexander's reign started off with promise with an amnesty for political prisoners and exiles, the abolition of torture and repeal of the prohibition of foreign books. However, his reforms never really met expectations.

1   *The condition of the serfs.* A law of *1803* gave landowners the discretion to free serfs with their land in return for a *redemption payment*. In fact by 1825 only a $\frac{1}{2}$ per cent of the serfs were affected.

2   *Constitutional reforms.* Vague promises and admiration of the British system of constitutional government by the Tsar's friends led only to slight administrative reforms. However Speransky's influence produced:

> – A State Council to assist the Tsar in the formulation of legislation.
> – Qualifying examinations for senior administrative posts.

3   *The nationalities.* Alexander's hesitant liberalism was displayed towards his non-Russian subjects:

> – A degree of autonomy was given to Finland after its annexation in 1809.
> – The Kingdom of Poland was given a constitution and the first Diet was opened in 1818 although Polish expectations were greatly disappointed.

4   *Educational provisions*

> – Three new universities were established. The number of students rose from 405 in 1809 to 1700 in 1825.

– A system of county and parish schools was projected but was only partly implemented due to lack of money and the lack of support of the nobility, which was all too obvious in all areas of reform.

(b) A period of reaction (1815–25)

Alexander's distraction by international events and mystical idealism after 1815 left his right-wing adviser Arakcheyev with virtually absolute powers. Represssion produced opposition which broke into outright rebellion in 1818–19 over the operation of the 'military settlements', an attempt to convert whole regions into reservoirs of military manpower with the serfs under military law. Then in 1820 the crack Semyonovsky guards mutinied over inhuman discipline.

10.3 The Decembrist revolt (1825)

There was no revolt in Russia in 1848. The equivalent was an abortive revolt in 1825.

(a) 'Constantine and Constitution'

The disappointment at Alexander's record against the background of patriotic expectation raised by the campaign of 1812 led to the formation of two secret societies by young noblemen and army officers who had received a fairly liberal, western education. The Society of the North in St Petersburg was more moderate than the Society of the South in the Ukraine, supporting constitutional monarchy as opposed to a republic and abolition of serfdom with compensation for the landlords rather than without. In 1825, the death of Alexander I bequeathed not only the mystery of an empty coffin and rumours of a wandering royal mystic but also a succession crisis. There was some doubt as to whether the throne should go to the more moderate Constantine or Alexander's younger brother Nicholas, who had a reputation as a military martinet. In a farcical situation the two brothers proclaimed each other as Tsar. In the confusion on 14 December 1825 3000 troops of the St Petersburg garrison took to the streets under *Decembrist* officers and milled around the Senate Square declaring support for 'Constantine and Constitution' (the latter believed by some of the soldiery to be his wife). Unsure as to what to do next, and afraid to risk an appeal to the masses, the rebels were easily crushed by loyal troops led by Nicholas I. Not surprisingly these amazing events left his wife Alexandra with a permanent facial twitch!

(b) The significance of the revolt

The revolt has an importance well beyond its small scale:

1   *A model and inspiration for future idealists.* 1825 was the start of the Russian revolutionary movement.
2   *Decimation of the intellectual élite.* A total of 579 people were arrested; while five were hanged, over 200 were sent into exile.
3   *Widening of the gap between the Tsar and nobility.* The new Tsar Nicholas became distrustful of any reforms which might produce a chink in the defences of absolutism.
4   *Conspiratorial tactics.* Partly because they had no choice given their small numbers and partly because of their degree of social unity the Decembrists adopted a

tightly-organised conspiratorial pattern, rejecting out of hand any idea of appeal to the people. To some extent future societies would imitate their model.

10.4 Nicholas I and reaction (1825–55)

For the next thirty years, Nicholas I ruled as a virtual military dictator.

(a) Reforms

The reforms produced by a series of secret committees were not very spectacular:

1 *Codification of the law.* Under Speransky's leadership codified laws were eventually published in 1832, although the laws were not modernised.
2 *Reform of serfdom.* Even Nicholas described the institution as evil and a close adviser saw it as 'a powder magazine in the foundations of the state'. However, the fear of social disorder led Nicholas to declare in 1840 'to tamper with it now would be ... an evil still more perilous'. The most he was able to do was prohibit the selling of land without its serfs (1827) and try to reduce some of the abuses which were prevalent. Legislation to encourage the freeing of serfs (1842 and 1847) was largely abortive, but the growing indebtedness of landowners did lead to a tendency to free serfs with their land in return for some payment. By 1855, there was an average of twenty outbreaks of peasant violence a year, with 54 in 1848.
3 *Economic reform.* Between 1839 and 1843 an important currency reform was coined, which based the currency on the silver rouble. However, economic growth still lagged. By 1854 Russia only had 660 miles of railway. Foreign trade grew slowly; textiles and metal goods led the growth in manufacturing but in 1860 only 800,000 people (or 1 per cent of the total population) were thus employed.

(b) Repression

Repression was far more positive.

1 *The notorious Third Section* was revived in 1826. This was a secret police section which had been abolished by Alexander.
2 *Restriction of entry to schools.* Quite progressive provincial Gymnasiums had developed on the basis of Alexander's reforms. However, the poorer classes were discouraged from sending their children to them while the nobles were encouraged to do so.
3 *Censorship.* Universities were subjected to strict controls. A rigid censorship was introduced and in 1848 a committee was even established to censor the censors.

(c) Russification

Nicholas's belief that liberalism did not work was confirmed by the Polish revolt in 1830. It failed because it lacked popular support which in any case would have been seen as an embarrassment by the upper class, intellectuals and young officers who made up the rebels. By August 1831 the revolt was defeated. The constitution was revoked, Poland was incorporated into the Empire and a process of *Russification* was commenced.

(d) 'Official nationalism'

Repression and Russification were in fact justified by the view in the 1830s that true patriotism and Russian nationalism should support autocracy and the Greek Orthodox faith against the decadent, atheist liberalism of the west. It was an attempt to establish an alliance between the Tsar and a superstitious conservative peasantry against the intellectuals.

10.5 The development of opposition (1836–54)

In 1836 Chaadayev published his *Philosophical Letter*, emphasising Russia's backwardness and stagnation. This was the basis for a series of responses.

(a) Westernisation

From the 1840s a group of intellectuals took up Chaadayev's message and began to urge the modernisation of Russia in terms of government, economy and society.

(b) Slavophilism

Alternatively, the west could be rejected entirely, in favour of:

1 *Pan-Slavism.* A faith in the purity of Russia uncontaminated by the west and with a mission to bring together the Slavs of Europe. At its most extreme, this became a political movement towards the freeing of the Slavs of the Ottoman Empire, Hungary and Austria and their unification with Russia. This movement was often an embarrassment to those directing Russian foreign policy.
2 *Agrarian socialism.* Alexander Herzen, an exile abroad after 1847, looked for freedom in Russia not to liberalism but to the establishment of a free and equal society based upon the peasant communes and with the elimination of the landlords and the tsarist system.

(c) 'The discipline of the camp'

Nevertheless in 1848–9 Russia was isolated and disciplined into immunity from revolution with intellectuals lingering in exile and prison. The historian Granovski wrote: 'Russia is nothing but a living pyramid of crimes, frauds and abuses, full of spies, policemen, rascally governors, drunken magistrates and cowardly aristocrats, all united in their desire for theft and pillage and supported by six hundred thousand automata with bayonets'. Then in 1854 war broke out between the progressive west and reactionary Russia (see Section 11.6).

10.6 'The Epoch of Great Reforms'

The successor of Nicholas I was his son Alexander II. Coming to the throne in 1855, he faced serious problems resulting from the Crimean War. These gave a practical impetus to the policies he adopted. Alexander was also, however, a more humanitarian character with a real concern for his subjects' well being, even though he was as firm a

Source: *The Russian Revolution* (CBS Legacy Books, 1967) p. 43.

believer in autocracy as his father. On the other hand, he was often rather naive. A British observer at his coronation described him as 'well intentioned, but weak as water'.

(a)   *The abolition of serfdom (1861)* (see Illus. 10.1)

In 1856, Alexander remarked that it was 'better to abolish serfdom from above than to await the time when its abolition would begin from below without action on our part'. A committee began to investigate the problem in 1857. The proposal of Lithuanian nobles that the serfs be freed without their land was unacceptable, but so was the radical idea of freeing the serfs with their land and without compensation for the landowners. The *Emancipation Act* of February 1861 gave the serfs their freedom, and made provision for them to be able to buy their land, repaying government assistance of up to 80 per cent of the total value over 49 years. However:

1   *The freedom had strings attached.* The 'free village dweller' was given only a qualified freedom.

   – It was not immediate. The privately owned serfs had to wait for two years, and the state serfs for five.
   – The peasants were subjected very much to the discipline and influence of the *commune* or unit of which they had to be members. The land was allocated through these units, which also paid taxes collectively and exercised powers over the peasantry through an elected council of elders.
   – Since the landowners also had to be compensated for the value of the services they lost, the serfs' freedom had in effect to be bought.

2   *Economically the peasants were worse off.* The peasants' incomes fell by up to 50 per cent, because:

- The average *redemption* charges tended to work out at a level higher than the market value of the land.
- In practice, the area of land worked by the peasants fell by between 18 per cent and 40 per cent of the total they worked before the reform.
- In most areas, the landowners had the option of retaining a third of the best land.
- Since the *commune* could repartition the holdings, the peasants' incentive to increase productivity by making improvements was lessened.

The result of this was that together with high taxation peasant impoverishment increased, redemption payments had to be extended in 1896, many peasants had to rent land from landowners at rising rents or hire themselves out as labourers to supplement their incomes, and peasant revolts continued in some provinces.

(b) *Local government reform (1864 and 1870)*

The resultant reduction in the power of the local landowners was partly compensated for by the creation of new elected provincial or county assemblies in the rural areas. In the election of these *zemstvas*, the nobility and wealthy classes were given very disproportionate power while the peasants had only an indirect share in the choice of delegates. Even so, the new assemblies had considerable responsibilities for local services, and were to be a training ground for liberal reformers. In 1870, provision was made for the election of municipal *dumas* or councils, although again the system was heavily biased towards the wealthiest citizens.

(c) *Reform of the judicial system (1864)*

The nobles had also lost their role as local law enforcers:

1 The establishment of a system of magistrates', district and regional courts.
2 Procedural reforms. Juries, open proceedings, defence by qualified lawyers and the independence of the judges were quite marked improvements over the previous system.

On the other hand, police powers were still very extensive, censorship was virtually unlimited and special courts were maintained for the trial of political prisoners.

(d) *Economic and financial reforms*

The exaggeration of financial problems by the war made reforms urgent:

1 *Improved financial control.* The State Bank was established in 1860, and a ministry of finances introduced.
2 *New sources of income were exploited.* An excise tax was imposed upon spirits, and foreign investment was encouraged, especially in railway building.

Even so, the problems persisted and the national debt and inflation were much worsened by the Russo-Turkish War of 1877–8 (see Section 16.3(c)).

(e) *Education reforms*

Desire to reform checked by fear of the consequences was equally obvious in the sphere of education.

1 *University reform (1863).* The freedom of the universities was somewhat increased, as was their accessibility to the less wealthy. In fact, though university

appointments were still vetted it remained very difficult for anyone but the well off to take places, and women were positively discriminated against.

2   *Secondary Gymnasiums were established (1864).* On the other hand, the curriculum was censored to remove 'dangerous' subjects like history. Primary schools were opened by the *zemstvas*, but they were supervised by an inspectorate. One of the first inspectors, Ilya Nikolayevich Ulyanov, was the father of Lenin (see Section 20.5(a)).

(f)   *Reform of the armed forces*

Universal conscription was introduced in 1874, replacing the old system of peasant recruitment for 25 years. All males over 20 years of age were liable to six years' service. The benefits were the creation of a body of reservists and the reduction of the cost of a large standing army. Even so, despite this and the best efforts of General Milyutin to reorganise, re-equip and modernise it, the army remained inferior to most others in quality.

(g)   *The nationalities*

Even here there was a paradox:

1   *Liberalism in Finland.* Considerable attempts were made to reconcile the Finns to Russian rule, including the calling of the first Diet since 1809 in 1863, the introduction of a virtual constitution in 1867, recognition of Finnish as the official language in 1872 and a range of economic and administrative reforms.
2   *Russification in Poland.* Similar mild attempts in Poland merely led to the great revolt of 1863. From then on, a policy of Russification was adopted, Russian became the official language and the Kingdom of Poland was reduced in status to the Vistula Region. A bid was also made to divide the potential revolutionaries from the peasantry by giving the latter complete emancipation with very much lower redemption payments.

10.7 The growth of opposition (1861–81)

The effect of the reforms was very limited by Russia's considerable backwardness, and because they were not wholehearted. The appetite for further reform was simply encouraged, especially with the peasantry. Bismarck pronounced upon the latter subject 'the Emperor would do even more for Russia who should free the peasants from communal proprietorship'. By the early 1870s, the railway network had increased twentyfold as compared to 1855 and between 1865–79 there was a 150 per cent increase in the number of factory workers – especially concentrated in large plants. However, the opposition of the 1860s–1870s was not founded upon the grievances of industrial workers, but on the grievances and a rather 'rosy' coloured view of the peasantry.

(a)   *Nihilism*

Some of the new intelligentsia of the 1860s were attracted to a sort of *anarchism* preached by Bakunin and Nechayev which rejected all authority and saw even liberalism as a trick by the ruling classes. They sought the establishment of a socialist federal republic and a planned reconstruction of society and the economy. Chaos was the first objective, and this was to be achieved by arson and assassination. However, one group did seek to mobilise peasant support through a movement called 'Land and Freedom' established in 1861 and appeals for an uprising in 1862. The later 1860s saw a government 'White Terror' following an attempt on the Tsar's life. In the 1870s many of the nihilists were attracted to an even more peculiarly Russian movement.

(b) *Populism*

The emphasis was on the achievement of a socialist society based upon the peasant units which were seen as a near-socialist organisation. The capitalist industrialist stage required by Marxism (see Section 4.5(c)) as part of the chain of events was unnecessary.

1   *The 'going to the people'*. Under the influence of the teachings of Lavrov, who emphasised the guilt of the privileged classes for the condition of the peasantry, in 1874 over 3000 young people went to live, dress and work as peasants in communes to try and absolve themselves and their ancestors of guilt and carry to the peasants the 'truth' of equality and their right to the land. The government arrested many of them and in any case the peasantry, reasonably enough, regarded them as cranks. A second attempt in 1877 led to the arrest of 250 populists who were given show trials although most were acquitted.

2   *Land and Freedom (1876)*. In 1876, a new organisation with 200 members was established in St Petersburg by George Plekhanov. It was far more tightly organised, secretive and conspiratorial. Its founders saw it as a propagandist movement, but even from the start there was a *nihilist* terrorist factor and in 1878 the organisation was split by the wounding of General Trepov, Governor of St Petersburg by Vera Zasulich, who was actually acquitted by a jury:

– The 'Black Partition', despite its sinister name, was the moderate propagandist wing.
– *Narodnaya Volnya* – the 'People's Will' – was the terrorist breakaway group.

(c) *Right-wing opposition*

Embarrassing to the government in other respects was the right-wing pressure from *Pan-Slavist* organisations to take the lead in the liberation and unification of the Slav peoples. It was supported by propagandists like Danilevsky and high-ranking officers and officials such as Ignatyev, the ambassador at Constantinople from 1864 to 1877. Their pressure was visible in the form of support for a 'hard line' with Turkey and in the building up of all sorts of contacts with other Slav peoples. The so-called 'War of Liberation' against Turkey in 1877–8 did not live up to expectations and the pressure continued.

10.8 Conclusion

Repression escalated from the 1860s. In 1879, most large cities were put under virtual military law. Then in 1880 Alexander's newly appointed adviser, the popular General Loris Melikov, proposed conciliation to blunt the opposition. Repression was markedly relaxed, and in March 1881 the Tsar called together a committee to prepare a constitution as Melikov had also recommended. The same afternoon the second of two bombs thrown by a terrorist killed Alexander. A constitution had no place in the subsequent wave of frantic repression.

Questions

1 Explain the aims of Alexander I and Nicholas I in the domestic affairs of Russia. How successful were they? [OC]
2 'The emancipation of the serfs and Alexander II's other reforms made little real difference to Russian politics and society.' Discuss. [OC]
3 'A long period of repression and gloom.' Discuss this view of the rule of Tsar Nicholas I. [OX]
4 Why were there demands for reform in Russia between 1825 and 1865? How and with what results did *either* Nicholas I, *or* Alexander II respond? [NEAB]
5 'The Tsar believed that God had given them the duty to rule Russia without challenge or oppositions.' How was this belief put into effect by Nicholas I and Alexander II? [NEAB]
6 'Thirty lost years.' Is this a fair assessment of the reign of Nicholas I of Russia (1825–55)?
7 Does Alexander II deserve the title 'Tsar Liberator'? [CAM]
8 Study Source A and then answer the questions which follow.

Source A: Alexander II.

Take a good look at this martyr. He was a great Tsar and deserves a kinder fate. Remember the reforms he introduced. Peter the Great was the author of none more deeply reaching. Think of all the resistance he had to overcome to abolish serfdom and to restore the foundations of rural economy. Think that thirty million men owe their franchisement to him. And his administrative reforms! He aimed at nothing less than the destruction of the arbitrary bureaucracy and social privilege. And this was done by the immediate successor of the despot Nicholas I. In foreign politics his work is on the same scale.
And the Nihilists have killed him.

(a) Why did Alexander II 'abolish serfdom' (line 3)? What was the 'resistance' (line 3)? How far did Alexander's work 'restore the foundations of rural economy' (line 4)?
(b) What other 'reforms' (line 2) did Alexander introduce?
(c) Who were the 'Nihilists' (line 8)? Why had they killed the Tsar?
(d) Give your opinion of the judgement 'he was a great Tsar' (line 1). [OC]
Source: M. Paléologue, *The Tragic Romance of Emperor Alexander II* (London, n.d.).
M. Paléologue was a French diplomat.

The Eastern Question 1804–56

Introduction

In fact, substantial changes in the problem of Europe were much more due to the impact of the Eastern Question than to the revolutions of 1848. The 'Eastern Question' dated back to the 1770s and was a factor of long-term influence upon the relationship of the powers. The 'answers' of the various powers to the question of how best to respond to the decay of Ottoman power and authority in the eastern Mediterranean were contradictory, inconsistent and varied in changing circumstances.

11.1 The nature of the Eastern Question

By the eighteenth century, the over-large and cumbersome Ottoman Empire was starting to crumble. According to B. Lewis in *The Emergence of Modern Turkey* (1961) it 'reverted to a medieval state with a medieval mentality and a medieval economy – but with the added burden of a bureaucracy and a standing army which no medieval state had to bear'. Symptoms of this decay were:

1 *Administrative fragmentation.* The tendency for local provincial officers such as Ali, Pasha of Yanina (see Section 3.8(c)) to try to establish themselves as independent rulers.
2 *Nationalist movements.* Vested interests such as native noblemen seeking to break the Turkish monopoly of jobs in the public service, or Greek merchants seeking a relaxation of trade restrictions, became the focus for more popular insurrections by the Christian subjects of the Empire. Religious discrimination, the harsh rule of the Ottoman representatives, the influence of the ideas of the French Revolution and sheer peasant desperation and brigandage accounted for this development.

The 'Question' arose because of the interests of the European states in these events, and especially in the European provinces of the Empire which covered 238,000 square miles and had about 8 million subjects in 1800.

(a) *Russia*

Russian interests arose from two sources:

1 *Strategic ambition.* As a landlocked state, Russia wanted a warm water port and access to the Black Sea and Mediterranean.

2   *Natural affinities.* In terms of ethnic origin and religion there were close links between Russia and the Ottoman Christian subjects.

In fact, how these interests should be best pursued was less obvious. Russian policy varied between support for the Ottoman Empire as a sort of protectorate or a neutral buffer state, or partition of the Empire by the European powers. Nor was it always clear which policy was being followed. From the 1760s a series of Russo-Turkish conflicts resulted in extensive gains for Russia in the Black Sea region. The treaty of Kutchuck Kainardji (1774) gave her key fortresses and other holdings and guarantees of freedom of navigation of the Black Sea and Bosphorus and Dardanelles. In 1783 Russia annexed the Crimea. Then another Russo-Turkish war between 1806–12 resulted in the Treaty of Bucharest (1812) which gave Bessarabia to Russia.

(b) *Britain*

British interests were also complex, but on the whole were based on a sensitivity to any extensive expansion by any power in the eastern Mediterranean which was likely to threaten her interests there or in India. In fact, as Professor Anderson points out, Britain tended to exaggerate the degree of the threat posed by Russia especially. Her naval power was overestimated and from the 1820s her essentially defensive policy was misread. Nevertheless, until the later nineteenth century it was British policy to exclude non-Turkish fleets from the Bosphorus and Dardanelles and to sustain the Ottoman Empire, although policy was confused by emotional urges to protect Greek Orthodox subjects of the Turks. In 1791 Britain had attempted to force Russia to disgorge the Black Sea fortress of Ochakov. In 1799, Britain guaranteed the integrity of the Empire. By the Peace of Dardanelles of 1809 it was agreed that the Straits should be closed in peacetime to non-Turkish warships but open to Turkey's friends in wartime.

(c) *France*

France was active in the region from the 1770s–80s, providing advisers for the Turkish armed forces. Then in 1797–8 there was the invasion of Egypt by Bonaparte to threaten British power in India, to 'stop that source of its corrupting wealth'. This had failed by 1801, but throughout the nineteenth century France had an interest in Asia Minor and in north Africa with her expanding territorial holdings to reinforce this.

(d) *Austria*

Although a traditional enemy of the Ottoman Empire, Austria found herself driven to support its integrity because of:

1   *Strategic concern.* The danger of the lower Danube falling into the hands of a strong power.
2   *The danger of infection.* Slav nationalism could be a double-edged sword. Metternich's secretary Gentz wrote in 1815, 'the end of the Turkish monarchy could be survived by the Austrian for but a short time'.

In fact, in 1788–91 Austria actually joined Russia in a war with the Ottoman Empire to partition the Balkans, and received some of northern Bosnia. This was an aberration. Additional Balkan territories were a nuisance to Austria, and she distrusted Russian interest in the region.

11.2 The main episodes (1821–56)

There was a kind of prologue in the story of Serbian independence. In 1804 the wealthy pig dealer Karageorge made a bid for power rallying support against the atrocities committed by Turkish Janissaries, and he set up his own dictatorial monarchy. By 1813, the Turks had recaptured the region but there was a revolt in 1815 led by Milosh Obrenovich, who was happy to rule as a 'Christian Pasha'. A long and bloody feud between the Karageorge and Obrenovich families followed. In 1817, Serbian independence was recognised; the new state's creation was owed to little more than recurring peasant grievances against any government, endemic brigandage and the self-interest of a couple of clan chieftains. The four main events between 1821–56 were:

1 The Greek War of Independence (1821–32)
2 The first Mehemet Ali crisis (1832–3)
3 The second Mehemet Ali crisis (1839–41)
4 The Crimean War (1854–6).

11.3 The Greek War of Independence (1821–32)

This is dealt with elsewhere (see Section 3.8(c)). The main difference between the struggle for independence in Greece and Serbia was that:

1 *The movement was led by a prosperous middle class.* Greek merchants dispersed throughout the Mediterranean were influenced by modern political ideas; they had the necessary ambitions and self-interest, the finance and the transport.
2 *The direct intervention of a European state.* The adventure led by Alexander Ypsilantis in 1821 was in reality a thinly disguised attempt at 'destabilisation' by the tsarist government. In April 1828 Russia invaded Ottoman territories.

(a) The Russo-Turkish War (1828–9)

The largely accidental destruction of the Egyptian fleet at *Navarino Bay* in October 1827 by Anglo-Russian Forces under Admiral Codrington made the position of the Greek rebels very strong. However, the attitude of the Ottoman government (the *Porte*) also hardened. Russo-Turkish relations deteriorated sharply, resulting in:

1 *Repudiation of the Convention of Ackerman of 1826.* This had dealt with Russo-Turkish differences over Moldavia and Wallachia, Serbia and the Caucasus.
2 *The closure of the Straits.* Since 1821 the Porte had obstructed movements of grain from Russia in Greek ships. Now the trade was stopped entirely. In April 1828, fighting broke out, and by September 1829 cossacks were 40 miles from Constantinople.

(b) The Treaty of Adrianople (1829)

Metternich had always seen the affair as 'a firebrand thrown by the radicals between the great powers and especially between Austria and Russia'. The latest event he saw as a 'disaster'. Russia had gained:

1 The territories of Georgia and eastern Armenia and territory at the mouth of the Danube.

2   A guarantee of free passage through the Straits for all merchant ships in peacetime.
3   A virtual protectorate over Moldavia and Wallachia.
4   An autonomous Greek state to be ruled by a hereditary prince.

(c)   Greek Independence (1832)

In fact, the powers came to prefer complete independence, because:

1   An independent Greece could be much more resistant to Russian interference.
2   A civil war between the rebels and the proclamation of a republic in 1827 suggested the need for a more stable government.

In 1832, agreement was reached by Britain, France and Russia on independence. The Sultan accepted the proposal. The first king of Greece was Crown Prince Otto of Bavaria.

11.4 The first Mehemet Ali crisis (1832–3)

By 1832, in any case, the Sultan's mind was otherwise occupied.

(a)   Syrian military expedition (1832–3)

Having failed to make the anticipated gains from his involvement in Greece (see Section 3.8(c)), Mehemet Ali now turned against his theoretical ruler and former paymaster and, in 1832, invaded Syria. Apart from blatant ambition, there were three factors behind this development:

1   *He had a claim to Syria.* It had been promised as a reward in 1827 if he sent troops to help the Ottoman Empire against attacks by Britain, France or Russia. In fact, he sent no troops; but that was beside the point.
2   *The French encouraged him.* The French had even discussed a so-called 'Drovetti Project', a Franco-Egyptian expedition to conquer Tripoli, Tunis and Algiers.
3   *The bad feeling between Egypt and Syria.* The Pasha of Syria had refused to return Egyptian refugees.

Confronted with the European-trained Egyptian army and navy, and the ability of Mehemet's son Ibrahim Pasha the weakness of the Turkish army was made very obvious. Acre fell in May 1832 and Damascus in June. Then in December a great victory at Konieh left the way open to Constantinople.

(b)   The Treaty of Unkiar Skelessi (1833)

In 1829, Nicholas I had been advised against too much pressure on Turkey by a secret committee which concluded that 'the advantages of the preservation of the Ottoman Empire outweigh its disadvantages'. The result was that when in desperation and unable to get help elsewhere, the Sultan turned to Russia, it was at a time when Russian policy was still to bolster up the Ottoman Empire. In response to the plea from Mahmud II, ships and 6000 troops were sent, although the Egyptians were bought off and were under Anglo-French pressure to make peace in any case. The price paid by the Ottoman Empire was the eight-year Treaty of Unkiar Skelessi.

1   The Treaty of Adrianople was confirmed.

2 Russia and Turkey would support each other in the event of an attack.
3 If Russia was attacked, Turkey would close the Straits to foreign warships.

The worst fears of Britain seemed to have materialised; Turkey had become a sort of Russian vassal and the Black Sea was a 'Russian lake'. Even more sinister was the coming together of Austria and Russia at Munchengrätz in 1833 to patch up their differences; this looked like a preparation for the partition of the Ottoman Empire. British popular opinion experienced a strong spasm of neurotic Russophobia.

11.5 The second Mehemet Ali crisis (1839–40)

Another crisis was almost inevitable, given the resentments of both Mahmud II and Mehemet Ali and Anglo-Russian distrust.

(a) The Egyptian-Turkish war (1839–40)

A tentative counter-attack by Turkish troops in April 1839 unleashed a renewed Egyptian onslaught and a great victory at Nizib. The situation became critical. The Sultan died and was replaced by a 16-year-old boy, Abdul Medjid. The whole Turkish fleet deserted to Mehemet Ali who now demanded hereditary possession of both Egypt and Syria.

(b) The attitude of the powers

The situation was complicated.

1 *French support for Mehemet Ali.* French interests in Egypt were longstanding, and the Pasha was urged on throughout the 1830s (but especially from 1839, when Thiers became prime minister).
2 *British support for the Ottoman Empire.* The British foreign secretary Lord Palmerston wanted the Pasha evicted because of their potential threat to routes to India and for fear that the Sultan would be permanently weakened.
3 *Russia sought to divide Britain and France.* There was an opportunity to split up a longstanding relationship in Europe.

The outcome was the London Convention of 1840, signed by Britain, Austria, Prussia and Russia and offering the Pasha only southern Syria for his lifetime and Egypt as a hereditary holding.

(c) The end of the crisis

France had been isolated and humiliated; after threats of war Thiers fell from office in October 1840, and was replaced by the more moderate Guizot. Mehemet Ali rejected the offer, but was under some pressure:

1 A revolt in the Lebanon against Egyptian rule in July 1840 became a guerrilla war.
2 In September–November 1840 Beirut and then Acre were bombarded and captured by British forces; with his lines of communication cut, Ibrahim Pasha withdrew.

(d) The results

The final outcome of these events was:

1 *A settlement between Egypt and the Ottoman Empire (November 1840)*. The Egyptians withdrew from Syria, and returned the Turkish fleet. Mehemet Ali gained the hereditary possession of Egypt. From then on, though, Egypt ceased to be a challenge. By 1854 it had declined into one of the weakest possessions in the Empire.

2 *The Straits Convention (1841)*. Russia lost her privileged position; now the Straits were to be closed to all warships while the Ottoman Empire was at peace.

11.6 The Crimean War

The first war between the European powers for forty years broke out in 1854. It was to be of considerable significance in the future of Europe.

(a) *The causes of the war*

1 *Napoleon III's pursuit of popularity*. The need for Catholic support in France led Napoleon III to emphasise a claim dating back to 1740 by which France had a position as the protector of Catholic monasteries and properties in Palestine.

2 *Russian overconfidence*. The issue was one over which there was considerable rivalry and an opportunity to exite popular support. Nicholas I took this up. In March 1853, Prince Menshikov on mission to Constantinople demanded far-reaching powers to protect Orthodox peoples in the Empire as well as reviving a claim to protect Orthodox Holy Places. Russian forcefulness was enhanced by:

– Belief that the collapse of the Ottoman Empire was imminent as its decline continued.
– The assumption that Austria would back Russia because of the help that had been given in 1849 in Hungary. Schwartzenburg the Russophobe had died in 1852 as well; there was even vague talk of Austria getting Constantinople and the Straits and Russia receiving Moldavia and Wallachia.

3 *Turkish resistance*. Turkey resisted threats that Moldavia and Wallachia would be occupied and rejected Russian demands in June 1853. The Turks were stiffened in their response by the influence of the anti-Russian British Ambassador Lord Stratford de Redcliffe and by the conspicuous movement of British ships from Malta to Besika Bay near the Dardanelles.

4 *British Russophobia*. Throughout the 1840s Britain distrusted Russian intentions. This arose from:

– Suspicion at the official level that Russia intended to partition Turkey. In 1844 and 1853, the Tsar had sought some sort of Anglo-Russian co-operation to this end, and had not been firmly rebuffed.
– Popular Russophobia. The British press had long been violently anti-Russian; public opinion now seized on the issue as another example of bullying by the Russian bear and resistance by a gallant underdog.

In July 1853, an attempted compromise, the *Vienna Note*, was rejected by the Ottoman Empire. In October 1853 Russian troops invaded Moldavia and Wallachia. In November, a Turkish squadron was destroyed at Sinope by a Russian fleet and there followed a wave of bitterness and demands for British intervention. In March 1854 Britain and France made an alliance with the Ottoman Empire and declared war on Russia.

(b) *The course of the war* (see Illus. 11.1 and 11.2)

There were really three stages:

1 *The war in the Danubian provinces (March–August 1854).* An Anglo-French naval expedition went to the Baltic in August but this was ineffectual and the area was in any case irrelevant to the causes of the war. Troops were also sent to Gallipoli to make a thrust into the Balkans. However in August the Russians withdrew from Moldavia and Wallachia because Austria threatened to intervene if she did not. Indeed, Austria was in the awkward position of being counted by both sides as a potential ally but never actually intervening; she was too weak internally to risk war.

2 *The war in the Crimea (September 1854–January 1855).* For political reasons, to challenge Russia in the Black Sea, 50,000 French and British were landed to capture the naval base at *Sebastopol*. In September, an initial victory at the Alma was wasted and the British and French generals Raglan and St Arnaud besieged Sebastopol. However a terrible stalemate resulted:

Illus. 11.1 Officers of the 68th Regiment in the Crimea (National Army Museum)

From a photograph by Roger Fenton in the National Army Museum, Chelsea.

Source: *Campaigns in Focus* (Standard Games & Publications, n.d.), 'The Crimean War'.

Q Cameras do not tell lies but photographers are sometimes very selective in their choice of subjects. Fenton was employed by a member of the British government to go to the Crimea to take photographs showing the improving conditions there which were resulting from the revelations of the journalists. If you had been Fenton, what would you not have wanted to take pictures of? Since the exposure time was quite lengthy and Fenton's photographic apparatus was very bulky, how would this affect the sort of pictures which Fenton could take? What sort of impression is conveyed by these officers of the 68th Regiment (later the Durham Light Infantry)?

Illus. 11.2 French infantry in the Crimea (National Army Museum)

From a photograph by Roger Fenton in the National Army Museum, Chelsea.

Source: *Campaigns in Focus* (Standard Games & Publications, n.d.), 'The Crimean War'.

– Sebastopol was very well fortified by the brilliant engineer Colonel Todleben, and it was never totally invested, so that supplies and men could get in.

– The Russians made frequent counter-attacks, especially in October and November. In October they were defeated at Balaclava (the occasion of the famous Charge of the Light Brigade) and in November at Inkerman.

– The terrible Crimean winter together with inadequacies of food, proper clothing and medical supplies led to the deaths of many thousands of soldiers as a result of sickness.

3   *The war in the Crimea (January–September 1855).* By January the situation of the Allies had improved. Press revelations and government changes of personnel led to British reforms in supply, transport organisation and medical facilities. Also in January Piedmont contributed 17,000 well-equipped troops to the Allied cause

(see Section 13.4(a)). In September, the fall of the key Malakhov Redoubt led to the Russians blowing up Sebastopol and evacuating it in good order.

(c) *The Treaty of Paris (1856)*

Both sides had been severely strained. The total losses amounted to 675,000 (only 190,000 men were lost in the Franco-Prussian war). Tsar Alexander II (see Section 10.6) was concerned about internal unrest, and Austria threatened again to intervene on the side of the Allies. In January 1856, Russia gave way:

1   *Reduction of Russian influence in the eastern Mediterranean*:

   – The Black Sea was to be totally demilitarised, and the Straits *closed* to all foreign warships while the Ottoman Empire was at peace.
   – *Russian territorial ambitions were checked.* The principalities of Moldavia and Wallachia were restored to the Ottoman Empire, and they were given southern Bessarabia. The great fortress of Kars was returned to Turkey.

2   *Guarantees of the independence and integrity of the Ottoman Empire*:

   – The Russian claim to a protectorate over Greek Orthodox subjects was specifically denied.
   – It was agreed that all conflicts between the Empire and other states should be dealt with by the mediation of the other powers.

3   *The Danube was placed under international control*, and free navigation was confirmed.

4   *Regulation of maritime warfare.* Long-standing controversial issues were settled here. Privateers were abolished; 'Contraband of war' or the goods which could be seized from a neutral ship were carefully defined.

11.7 Conclusion

Many of the provisions of the Treaty of Paris did not endure. In 1870, Russia renounced the Black Sea clauses (see Section 14.8(e)). In 1862, Wallachia and Moldavia united to become Rumania, independent of Turkey. The Ottoman Empire teetered on as unreformed as ever, and ill-treating Christian subjects. The map of the Balkans was rewritten in the Balkan crisis of 1875–9 (see Section 16.3) and the Balkan wars of 1911–12 and 1913 (see Section 22.9). However, the Crimean War did have a profound effect on Europe:

1   *The breakdown of the Concert of Europe.* After 1856, all of the continental powers except Austria were 'revisionists'. Russia wanted the Black Sea clauses revoked; Napoleon III wanted to embark upon a prestigious foreign policy (see Section 12). With Austria isolated, the cause of unification in Italy and Germany was considerably enhanced. Britain was not revisionist, but she did react away from war into isolationism.

2   *Balkan nationalism was stimulated.* With the denial to Russia and Austria of any extension of their influence, the neutralisation of the Black Sea and the freeing of the Danube from Russian influence by the Danube River Commission, the opportunities to Balkan states and nationalities were much expanded.

Questions

1 How were international relations affected by the decay of the Ottoman Empire in 1815–56? [OC]
2 Explain the principal causes and results of the Crimean War. [OC]
3 Why was Mehemet Ali of Egypt a figure of international importance? [OX]
4 Why did European powers go to war in the Crimea in 1854? Describe the main events of the war, and outline the terms of the Treaty of Paris (1856). [NEAB]
5 How seriously did the 'Eastern Question' threaten the peace of Europe between 1821 and 1841?
6 Outline the causes and main events of the Crimean War (1854–6). Did the results justify the fighting of such a war? [CAM]
7 Why did the various powers fight against Russia in the Crimean War? How far had they achieved their objectives by 1856?
8 Study Source A and then answer the questions which follow.

Source A: Life at the Crimean front.
From a report by W. H. Russell, correspondent of *The Times*, 4 December 1855.

Before Sebastopol, December 4.

The whole plateau on which stands 'the camp before Sebastopol' ... is a vast black dreary wilderness of mud, dotted with little lochs of foul water, and seamed by dirty brownish and tawny-coloured streams running down to and along the ravines. On its surface everywhere are strewed the carcasses of horses and miserable animals torn by dogs and smothered in mud. Vultures sweep over the mounds in flocks; carrion crows and 'birds of prey obscene' hover over their prey, menace the hideous dogs who are feasting below, or sit in gloomy dyspepsia, with dropped head and dropping wing, on the remnants of their banquet.

It is over this ground, gained at last by great toil and exhaustion and loss of life on the part of the starving beasts of burden, that man and horse have to struggle from Balaclava for some four or five miles with the hay and corn, the meat, the biscuit, the pork, which form the subsistence of our army. Every day this toil must be undergone ... Horses drop exhausted on the road, and their loads are removed and added to the burdens of the struggling survivors; then, after a few efforts to get out of their Slough of Despond, the poor brutes succumb and lie down to die in their graves. Men wade and plunge about, and stumble through the mud, with muttered imprecations, or sit down on a projecting stone, exhausted, pictures of dirt and woe unutterable. Sometimes on the route the overworked and sickly soldier is seized with illness, and the sad aspect of a fellow-countryman dying before his eyes shocks every passer-by – the more because aid is all but hopeless and impossible ... The painful recollection which ever occurs to one is, what necessity is there for all the suffering and privation created by this imperfect state of our communications? Why should not roads have been made when we sat down before the place? Their formation would have saved many lives, and have spared our men much sickness and pain. Had there been the least foresight – nay, had there existed among us the ordinary instincts of self-preservation – we would have set the Turks to work at once while the weather was fine, and have constructed the roads which we are now trying to make under most disadvantageous conditions. The siege operations have been sometimes completely – sometimes partially – suspended, and the attack on Sebastopol has languished and declined. Neither guns nor ammunition could be brought up to the batteries.

The mortality amongst the Turks has now assumed all the dimensions of a plague. Every sense was offended and shocked by the display, day after day, in the streets, of processions of men bearing half-covered corpses on litters at the busiest hour of the day.

(a) According to Russell, what was the root cause of the situation in which the army of the Allies found itself (lines 19–28)?
(b) Apart from the nature of the terrain, what other hazards faced the Allies (lines 29–31)?
(c) This is a report for the British public made by a newspaper reporter. Is there any reason, therefore, why we should be careful in regarding this sort of 'evidence'?
(d) Did the Crimean War have any real European significance? How did it affect international relations in the years that followed?

Source: *Russell's Despatches From the Crimea* (1854–6) (Geo. Routledge & Co., 1855) p. 192.

12 The Second French Empire 1852–70

Introduction

Louis Napoleon became the latest 'strong man' of France on 2 December 1851. His largely bloodless coup was ratified by 7,500,000 voters in a plebiscite three weeks later. His supporters included businessmen escaping from the spectre of the 'urban red mob', peasants expecting higher food prices, Roman Catholics looking to a new alliance of state and church, and many of the urban workers. He rode to power on a national mood rather than party support, and throughout his reign he had to rely on this general appeal: 'When one bears our name and when one is the head of the government there are two things one must do; satisfy the interests of the most numerous classes and attach to oneself the upper classes'. Unlike the dictators of the twentieth century, he was always dependent on public opinion at a time when the facilities to 'create' it were not present.

12.1 The new régime

The constitution was modelled on that of 1800 (see Section 2.2(a)).

(a) *The constitution's provisions*

1 *A bicameral legislature.* There was:

– *A Senate* of 150 presidential nominees which had the power to veto laws which violated the constitution. However, as life holders of office, they could be very independent.
– *A Corps Legislatif* of 260, elected by universal suffrage. However, it could vote on the budget and propose laws only, not discuss them. It did not choose its own president, and sat for only three months a year. Above all, the imperial government could exercise very strong influence on the elections in favour of the official candidates. Only six opposition candidates were returned in March 1852.

2 *The executive.* The title of 'prince president for ten years' was only temporary. In November 1852, a plebiscite ratified the assumption of the imperial title and on 2 December 1852 Louis Napoleon became Napoleon III, with the pretence that the son of Napoleon I (the Duc de Reichstadt) had reigned after his father's abdication. Louis's executive powers remained the same, however; control of the armed forces and foreign policy, initiation of legislation and the power to override

the legislature with a plebiscite and the appointment of all ministers and public officials who were responsible to him.

(b) *Repressive controls* (see Illus. 12.1)

In addition, there were the other less formal controls which supported the authoritarian system:

1 *The suppression of political clubs* and disbanding of the National Guard except in Paris.
2 *Censorship.* The 'decree law' of 1852 introduced a system whereby newspaper directors were allowed two warnings before a newspaper was liable to suspension.
3 *Control of state education.* The system was so regimented that it was said of it that it was a time 'in which every class in France did exercises at the same hour; the time when teachers were ordered to shave off their moustaches in order to remove the last vestiges of anarchy from their costumes as well as from their morals'.

Apart from this, as with all previous régimes, Napoleon III relied upon the prefectoral system and on a centralised administration of about 250,000 to execute his will. In fact, the actual repression was very limited. Censorship regulations could be easily evaded; of the 26,000 people arrested after the *coup d'état* 10,000 were acquitted or put under surveillance. Some 9000 people were sent to Algeria, but most were allowed to return by 1856. Napoleon III's success depended on more subtle factors.

12.2 The character of Napoleon III

Napoleon III was a man of contradictions.

(a) *The un-Napoleonic Napoleon*

He was reputedly the son of Louis Bonaparte, although there was some doubt about paternity. He was the heir to the legend of Napoleon but in many respect he was a victim of it. He was expected to have the qualities of the great Napoleon; he did not even look like a Bonaparte. He was brave, but no military genius. Nor was he as vigorous or ruthless as his uncle in the pursuit of his aims.

(b) *A crowned adventurer*

Napoleon III was brought up in a world of exiles, romantics and conspirators. He was involved in a series of conspiracies and adventures in the 1830s and 1840s. Even when he got the throne he was still very much the 'man on the make', a not-quite-respectable opportunist and the only man sworn to uphold the constitution which he had overthrown. Even his marriage to the Spanish Countess Eugénie de Montijo in 1853, the production of an heir in 1856 and the elaboration of a colourful court never overcame his rather 'flashy' image.

(c) *The 'gentle dictator'*

Napoleon III was actually a very humanitarian man and an idealist:

1 *L'extinction du paupérisme.* Napoleon III had a genuine feeling for the welfare of working people, and a loose belief in the need for state intervention to increase prosperity and promote the good of society along the lines proposed by the Comte de Saint-Simon (see Section 4.5(a)).

Illus. 12.1 Censorship under the Second Empire

From a contemporary lithograph.

Source: G. Soria, *Grande Histoire de la Commune* (Livre Club Diderot, Paris, 1970) Part 1, p. 66.

2 *Nationalism.* Again, Napoleon III had a vague idea of the principle of nationality, and of the desirability of applying it in Europe. However, he was also indecisive, and lacked ruthlessness. One contemporary dubbed him 'Napoleon the well-meaning'.

(d) *The sphinx*

His very contradictions of character, belief in his mission and apparent depth gave him the aura of a man of destiny, and it may be that as a result his significance has been exaggerated. Alexander Dumas dismissed his as '*Napoléon le petit*'; Bismark saw him as a great sham, a 'sphinx without a riddle'. Nevertheless, Napoleon III judged the feelings and desires of the majority of Frenchmen of the time, and this enabled him to hold power for as long as he did.

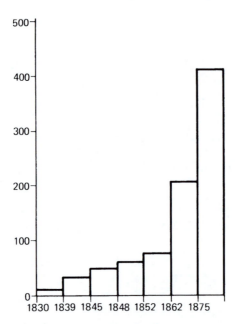

Fig. 12.1 The volume of horse power derived from steam engines in France (1830–75), 1000 horse power

The progress of industrialisation was slow in the first half of the century and 'took off' only during the period of the Second Empire. This relative slowness of France was due to the lack of coal and its high price, as opposed to the position in Britain and Germany. French coal mines were difficult to exploit because of their depth, thin seams and pockets of gas.

Source: Based upon statistics included in C. M. Cipolla (ed.), *The Fontana Economic History of Europe*: vol. 1, *The Emergence of Industrial Societies*, ch. 1, C. H. Fohen, 'France 1700–1914'.

12.3 'L'Empire, c'est la Paix' (see Fig. 12.1)

Peace, order and stability were more popular than revolutionary zeal and aggressive pursuit of '*la gloire*'. The new age of materialism was based on a wave of economic expansion after 1851, which contrasted with the leaner years of the July Monarchy and the Second Republic. Two factors especially underpinned this growth and improving standard of living:

(a) *Rising productivity*

Between 1851–70, coal consumption trebled, as did the volume of foreign trade. The price of steel was halved. This was aided very much by:

1 *Improved communications.* In 1848, France had 1200 miles of railway; by 1871 she had 11,500 miles – as much as Britain or Germany. The telegraph system expanded from 1350 to 46,000 miles.
2 *An improved credit system.* A whole range of new finance houses investing in industry emerged in this period, such as the *Crédit Lyonnais* and the *Crédit Mobilier*.
3 *Free trade.* Against considerable opposition, and using executive power, Napoleon reduced duties on imports in 1853, and after 1860 the Cobden–Chevalier commercial treaty with Britain was followed by a whole series of treaties with most European countries.

Symbolic of the broadening industrial base of France was the great Paris Exhibition of 1867.

(b) *Demographic changes*

1 *A falling rate of population growth.* The growing wealth of the country was not swallowed up by a 'swarming' population.
2 *Urbanisation.* As the poorer peasantry and labourers migrated from the countryside, the proportion of the population in the towns rose from 24 to 31 per cent; the population of Lyons, Lille and Toulon doubled, while Roubaix trebled in size.

(c) *The contribution of the government*

Most of this development was on the basis of private capital, rather than from a Saint-Simonian state leading economic growth with public expenditure, although Napoleon III was familiar with Saint-Simon's theories. As a result, capital was less readily available for the less profitable building of roads and canals, for port development and agriculture. However there were two particular contributions made by the state:

1 *Compulsory elementary education (1863).* The curriculum of secondary schools was also widened, and by 1866 there were 66,000 secondary school students.
2 *The rebuilding of Paris.* The Prefect of Paris, Baron Haussmann, built 85 miles of boulevardes and a range of great public buildings. Over 40,000 houses were built. This was very much a work 'à la Saint-Simon', and had a great propaganda value. Napoleon III himself played an active role in it. Ill-disposed cynics claimed, however, that the boulevardes were merely a device to prevent the building of barricades.

12.4 The Crimean War and the Congress of Paris

Prosperity at home coincided with success abroad. The contribution of Napoleon III to the causes of the Crimean War was very limited, and France entered it reluctantly, but the war and the Treaty of Paris were seen as triumphs for the Emperor who could now enjoy a re-established Anglo-French entente and international prestige. These were the 'fortunate years'.

12.5 The foundations of the Liberal Empire

By 1860, a turning point had been reached. From then on, there was a movement away from dictatorship. This was due to two factors:

(a) *The emergence of opposition*

1 *The Italian War of Liberation (1859).* Peace was the greatest asset of the Empire, but Napoleon III pursued an active foreign policy partly out of his own personal commitments and partly to try and compensate for the loss of liberty in France. However, his involvement in the unification of Italy (see Section 13.4(b)) had disastrous consequences. Traditionally it was in French interests to keep Italy divided; Napoleon risked involvement in 1858–9 to appeal to French nationalists

and Roman Catholics, and to produce a limited and grateful client Italy. The outcome of the events of 1859–61 was totally unexpected.

– The unification of Italy blocked French influence in the region.
– Franco-Italian relations were to be embarrassed for the next twenty years by the French guarantee of papal sovereignty in Rome.
– The cynical deal which gave France Nice and Savoy seriously damaged the valued entente with Britain.
– French Catholics were offended by Napoleon's agreement with Cavour, which allowed Piedmont to incorporate the Romagna in part exchange for Nice and Savoy.

2   *The rivalry of church and state.* Catholic support was also weakened with the extension of the state system of education and its rivalry with the church schools. In fact, the Catholic Church prospered under the Empire; the membership of the religious orders grew from 37,000 to 190,000. An increased state financial contribution also enabled clerical salaries and pensions to be increased.
3   *Free trade.* The progressive relaxation of trade (see Section 12.3(a)) helped improve the standard of living and relations with Britain. The Cobden–Chevalier treaty and other agreements stimulated the French economy, and exports continued to grow. On the other hand, there was bitter hostility from the big landowners and many industrialists – especially the textile manufacturers of Normandy and the north and the iron masters of the east.
4   *The emergence of republicanism.* A growing urban proletariat, more articulate and politically active, was attracted by republicanism. This was partly reinforced by the adverse impact of growing industrial concentration on small firms, which led to the reduction of wages in some cases.

(b)   *The need to strengthen the régime*

Even so, Napoleon III was under no real pressure to make concessions in 1860. A more positive influence was a genuine attempt to liberalise the Empire with the guidance of the Emperor's half-brother the Duc de Morny due to:

1   *The need for information.* A personal dictatorship without the facilities to manufacture opinion relied instead upon keeping in touch with public opinion. Napoleon realised this when he remarked: 'I am isolated, I no longer hear anything'.
2   *The need to attract greater talent to support the Empire.* The dominance of bureaucrats and unimaginative conservatives was increasingly a handicap. It would be far better to win the support of rising young stars like Emile Ollivier, the brilliant republican.

12.6 Liberal reforms (1860–1)

By 1859, all remaining exiles had been allowed to return. In 1860 the constitution itself was liberalised.

(a)   *Parliamentary changes*

1   *Freedom of debate in parliament.* Both chambers were now allowed to hold annual debates on the speech from the throne, which would be responded to by the imperial ministers. Reports of the debates were to be published.

2   *Voting of the budget by sections.* In 1861, the *Corps Legislatif* was given the power
    to vote the budget detail by detail instead of simply *en bloc.*

(b)   *A parliamentary opposition*

Political life began to revive. In 1863, a coalition of opposition groups, the *Union
Liberale*, gained 2 million votes and 35 seats. Of the 22 largest towns in France, 18 fell
to the opposition. Paris itself returned 8 republicans and Thiers. In the long term, the
Empire might have survived on the basis of this experiment with liberalism. In fact,
other events ran ahead of it.

12.7 Imperial and foreign policy (1859–66)

In the 1860s, Napoleon sought to appeal to nationalism to strengthen his position in
France.

(a)   *Imperial expansion*

Indeed some of Napoleon's greatest triumphs were not so obvious to the electorate:

1   *Africa.* By 1857, Algeria was conquered and by 1860 its European population was
    290,000 in number. In 1863 Napoleon described himself grandly as 'just as much
    the Emperor of the Arabs as the French'. On the other hand, Algeria was regarded
    by many Frenchmen as a drain on military resources and a potential economic
    rival. Other colonies were established in this period in Senegal, Guinea and
    Dahomey.
2   *The eastern Mediterranean.* French influence in this region was affirmed with an
    expedition to Syria in 1860 to protect the persecuted Christians. In Egypt, French
    capital was very active and in 1859 Ferdinand de Lesseps started to build the *Suez
    Canal.*
3   *The Far East.* In Indo-China French forces were very active. In 1862, Cochin China
    was annexed, and a protectorate established over Cambodia. In 1860, France and
    Britain joined forces in a punitive expedition to Peking which resulted in even
    greater trading concessions.

But these ventures did not win votes, and were overshadowed by failures elsewhere.

(b)   *The Mexican adventure (1861–7)*

In 1861 Napoleon became engaged in what was once called extravagantly the 'most
profound conception of the reign'. To try and win a foothold in the Americas and
attract support from Catholics, nationalists and commercial interests he embarked
upon an attempt to impose the Habsburg Archduke Maximilian upon the Mexican
throne in a sort of Catholic crusade against the anti-clerical forces of the ousted republican leader Juarez. The venture was an expensive fiasco. Juarez had far greater popular support than was anticipated, and with the end of the Civil War in 1865 the United
States objected to the French presence. French troops were withdrawn, although not
before 6000 had died. In 1867, Maximilian was executed by his republican opponents.

(c)   *The Austro-Prussian War (1866)*

In 1829 Polignac had warned of the danger of German unification – that it 'would confront us with rival forces which would be jealous and even hostile and our relative
power would be seriously affected. Napoleon III ignored this advice and did nothing to

try and block the Prussian drive for supremacy in Germany in the 1860s. Prussia's victory in the Austro-Prussian war (see Section 14.4) dramatically changed the balance of power in Europe. To make it worse:

1 *There were no territorial compensations.* The chance to seize the Rhineland was missed, and Bismarck rejected Napoleon's 'hotel-keeper's bill' of Belgium or the Bavarian Palatinate.
2 *French isolation was reinforced.* Bismarck could use the proposed deals by Napoleon to stir up British distrust of France, and Napoleon hardly helped by pretending loudly that he welcomed the smashing of the Vienna Settlement.

12.8 The Liberal Empire

From 1866, there was growing opposition from the moderate '*Third Party*' led by Thiers and from anti-clerical republicanism represented especially by Léon Gambetta and Jules Ferry. The late 1860s also saw an economic recession, with crises in the wine, silk and cotton industries and a severe financial crisis. Even so, Napoleon was in no danger of political defeat. His reforms of the late 1860s were an attempt to ride ahead of the tide.

(a) *Further liberalisation (1867–8)*

1 *The power of interpellation.* Both chambers were given the power to interrogate (or to 'interpellate') ministers.
2 *Relaxation of the press laws* and laws relating to public assembly. A flood of 150 new newspapers – mostly hostile – was the result. Prosecution of editors only created martyrs, and made the reputations of defence lawyers like Gambetta. By 1869–70 troops were being used against strikes and demonstrations.

(b) *The parliamentary Empire (1869–70)*

The elections of 1869 increased the Third Party to 116 deputies. Napoleon now took the step of conceding full parliamentary government with the Corps Legislatif having the power to initiate legislation and ministers drawn from either house. Emile Ollivier was chosen as the first prime minister under this régime. In May 1870, a plebiscite backed this development with an overwhelming vote of 7 million in favour and only 750,000 in favour of a republic. Understandably in 1870, Napoleon remarked 'more than ever before can we look forward to the future without fear'.

12.9 The Franco-Prussian war and the downfall of Napoleon III (see Illus. 12.2)

Napoleon's diplomacy meant that in 1870 France had no ally. However, over the origins and conduct of the war (see Section 14.6) he can be acquitted of two charges:

1 *The Hohenzollern candidature.* The issue was pushed not by him but by a group of hard liners in the entourage of the Empress, trying to counteract the insecurity they felt as a result of the liberal reforms of the Emperor.
2 *The inadequacy of the army.* In 1859, Napoleon had remarked 'we are never ready for war'. He managed to overcome military conservatism and get the quicker firing *chassepot* introduced. However, shortage of money due to expenditure on Paris

Illus. 12.2 A vision on the way: 'Beware!' (From *Punch*, 1870)

A VISION ON THE WAY. "BEWARE!"

Source: I. R. Mitchell, *Bismarck and the Development of Germany* (Holmes Macdougall, 1980) p. 40.

a Whose is the ghost and what do you think is the message of this cartoon? Was the cartoonist favourable towards or opposed to the ambitions of Napoleon III?

and public works schemes, the resistance of conservative deputies to any expenditure, and republican opposition to standing armies meant that conscription and other reforms were not introduced. Even so, in 1869 the war minister assured the cabinet that the army was ready 'to the last gaiter button'.

12.10 Conclusion

The military defeats of 1870 led to the bloodless revolution of 4 September 1870 and the proclamation in Paris of a republic. Napoleon fled to England, and died there in 1873. This 'first modern dictator' had displayed such a considerable flexibility and a limited use of force that it is unfair to compare him to the totalitarian dictators of the 1920s and 1930s. However, he had attempted to rule by working with the fundamental forces of the age. He once remarked 'Today the rule of classes is over and you can govern only with the masses'. He had attempted to break a vicious circle of revolution and restoration in France, and set it on the path of gradual evolution. However he never overcame the distrust which lingered from his *coup d'état* and his reign remained a 'tragedy of good intentions' (Theodore Zeldin).

Questions

1 What did Napoleon III achieve in France?   [OC]
2 What were the principal achievements of the Second French Empire?   [OC]
3 To what extent was the failure of Napoleon III's foreign policy the result of the Emperor's own blunders?   [OX]
4 'A charlatan in everything he did.' Is this a fair judgement on the Emperor Napoleon III?   [OX]
5 Outline the domestic policy of the Emperor Napoleon III between 1852 and 1870, and estimate its success.   [NEAB]
6 To what extent was Napoleon III responsible for his own downfall?   [NEAB]
7 Describe the policies followed by Napoleon III over: (a) the unification of Italy, (b) Mexico, and (c) the Austro-Russian War. Why was his foreign policy mainly unsuccessful after 1865?   [CAM]
8 To what extent, and for what reasons, did the rule of Napoleon III became more liberal after 1860?   [CAM]
9 Study Source A and then answer the questions which follow.

Source A: Napoleon the Little.

Though he has committed enormous crimes he will remain shoddy, the nocturnal garrotter of liberty who has glutted his soldiers, not with glory like the first Napoleon, but with wine, the pigmy tyrant of a great people. As Dictator he is a buffoon, as Emperor he will be grotesque, at once hideous and ridiculous. Once stripped of success, the pedestal removed, the sword detached, a poor little skeleton; can one imagine anything more paltry and pitiful? Tiberius, Nero, Timur and other murderers were tigers. M. Bonaparte is only a hyena, part brigand, part knave – Napoleon the Little, no more, no less. Think of it. At the head of the greatest people on earth, in the middle of the greatest century in history, this personage has made France his prey. *Grand Dieu!* You are a monkey, not a lion, a parrot, not an eagle, a comedian.

(a) What was the point behind Victor Hugo's jibe 'Napoleon the Little?
(b) What is meant by 'the nocturnal garrotter of liberty' (line 1)?
(c) How far do you agree with Hugo's claim that Napoleon had 'committed enormous crimes' (line 1)?
(d) What would you say was Napoleon's contribution to the development of France?
Source: Victor Hugo, *Napoleon le Petit* (1852).

10 What does Illus. 12.1 (p. 145)) tell us about the situation of political commentators under the Second Empire? How does the fact that this was a contemporary lithograph affect your view of the reality of that situation.

The unification of Italy 1850–71

Introduction

The events of 1848–9 in Italy (see Section 9) at least made the direction towards unification somewhat clearer. The failure of the revolutions and the defeat of Piedmont by Austria meant that Charles Albert's claim that *'Italia fara da se'* was nonsense. Success would require outside help to dislodge Austria from northern Italy. It also needed more positive leadership by a revived Piedmont. The man who was responsible for bringing about both of these was the Piedmontese chief minister, Count Camillo di Cavour. However, even Cavour could not totally control events, and the unification of Italy took some rather unexpected turns.

13.1 The effects of the revolutions of 1848

The bloodshed and failure of 1848-9 did at least have the after-effects of drawing together different groups of supporters of unification and of making it very clear who were the main enemies.

(a) *The removal of alternatives*

A number of ideas as to the future of Italy had been shattered or weakened:

1 *The idea of a Federation of Italy under the Presidency of the Pope* (see Section 6.7) which was advocated by Gioberti ended when Pius IX had shown himself clearly to be an enemy of liberalism and unification.
2 *A loose union of States* with links developing between reformist rulers had been preferred by moderates (see Section 6.6). Now the Grand Duke of Tuscany, the ruler they saw as the model for the rest, was shown up as a puppet, kept on his throne only by Austrian bayonets.
3 *Mazzinian unitary republicanism* still had a strong following (see Section 6.5) but support was weakened by a series of failed attempts at uprisings in the 1850s. Also Mazzini still refused to support the sort of social reforms which would attract the peasantry and town workers.

(b) *The Italian National Society*

By the 1850s, a lot of disappointed men were looking towards the only realistic alternative – the unification of Italy by the army of Piedmont. The Kingdom of Piedmont had three things in its favour:

1   Of all the states of Italy, only Piedmont still had a constitution. To liberals this was a great symbol.
2   Twice it had gone to war with Austria in 1848–9, and radical nationalists urged it to do so again.
3   To moderates and men of property, unification would be better under Piedmont's leadership because it could maintain order against the extremist revolutionaries.

In 1857, the National Society was formed to support unification by Piedmont. Led by the Sicilian republican Guiseppe la Farina it attracted both hardened revolutionaries like Garibaldi and men of property. No attempt was made to consider how to reform society in Italy, because this would lead to argument and division.

13.2 The obstacles to unification

What brought these groups together even more was the fact that their enemies, the obstacles to both liberalism and unification, were the same:

1   *Austrian repression* in northern Italy was far greater than before 1848. This, together with the high taxation necessary to pay for a strong military presence, increased resentment even amongst moderates. In addition the flow of exiles to Piedmont increased, while in Britain and France there was growing sympathy for the Italian case.
2   *The papacy was as great an obstacle.* The papal government was one of the most corrupt and repressive in the peninsula; it was also a bitter opponent of unification and, because of the position of the Papal States, could block it effectively.

Ironically it was Piedmont which attracted the hopes of liberals and patriots; yet Piedmont was one of the most backward, absolutist and Catholic states in Italy.

13.3 The transformation of Piedmont

Two factors gave Piedmont a very special position in the 1850s:

1   *The symbolic power of the constitution* and of King Victor Emmanuel, 'the man who saved the constitution'.
2   *The programme of reforms* implemented by Cavour, which modernised and strengthened Piedmont and made it even more attractive to liberals and nationalists throughout Italy (see Section 6.6(c)).

(a)   'Italy and Victor Emmanuel!'

The popular story about the survival of the Piedmontese constitution was that the new king Victor Emmanuel had resisted Austrian threats and offers of better peace terms if he would abolish it. So he became the hero of Italian patriots. However, the truth was very different; the King disliked the constitution, but was afraid that if he abolished it revolution would result. On the other hand, Field Marshal Radetsky, resisting pressure from Vienna to take a hard line, was careful to avoid putting the king into that position because a revolution in Piedmont would probably lead to war with Austria again. In any case, the constitution was very limited:

1   *The elected lower house had no direct control over the king's government.* It was more important for the ministers that they had the king's support than a majority in the Assembly.
2   *The electorate was very restricted.* Only $2\frac{1}{2}$ per cent of the population had a vote.

Nevertheless, legends are often more powerful than the truth. Victor Emmanuel enjoyed his popularity. Exiles from all over Italy made their way towards Piedmont, adding to the nationalist pressure on the government. In addition, Piedmont could always rely on the sympathy of Britain and France.

(b) 'Reforms, carried out in time . . .'

From 1850 onwards, Cavour dominated the Piedmontese government, becoming prime minister in 1852. The key to his policy was the belief that reforms could reduce revolutionary pressures and strengthen the government. This was a gamble, because there was a danger that he might go too far, and have the reverse effect:

1   *Political liberty.* Democracy was on the way, and Cavour believed that unless unreasonable privileges were given up there would be revolution.

   – Anti-ecclesiastical legislation removed the right of clergy to be tried by special church courts, suppressed 'useless' monasteries and gave the state control of education.
   – the landed aristocracy lost their monopoly of posts in the courts, the civil service and the army. The rising middle classes were not able to share these positions.

2   *A free economy.* In the long run, Cavour believed in as little government intervention in the economy as possible. However, there was a need for some government action to get growth started:

   – A series of trade treaties in 1850–1 and the reduction of customs duties in 1851 opened up new markets and cheapened raw materials. Abolition of the duty on imported grain benefited the lower classes.
   – Government expenditure on roads, railways and harbour improvement provided employment and boosted economic growth.

The combined effect of these reforms was to treble the volume of trade in the 1850s and stimulate industrialisation. Politically the effect was to draw together people of all classes into support for Cavour and weaken the support for more extremist politicians.

(c) The cost of reform

On the other hand, there were a number of problems associated with these reforms, and they would be carried over to the future Kingdom of Italy:

1   *The financial burden was high.* As customs revenue fell and government borrowing rose, the government debt rose from 120 million lire in 1847 to 725 million lire in 1859. Much of this was due to expenditure on the armed forces.
2   *The ecclesiastical reforms enraged devout catholics.* Cavour was portrayed by them as the agent of the devil; for many Italians, this raised the problem of whether they could remain good Catholics and still support the government.
3   *The parliamentary system was discredited* by the political activities of Cavour. He believed in parliamentary institutions, but not the predominance of parliament;

although he supported the constitution he often acted without parliamentary approval or consulting his cabinet colleagues. On some vital occasions, he governed through emergency powers and by-passed parliament completely. He rigged elections and bribed newspaper editors. Above all, he came to power in 1852 – and held on to it – by making some rather shady deals with the radicals. On the other hand, like a lot of people who are sure that they are right, he was determined to get through his programme by whatever means were necessary.

4   *Some vital reforms were neglected.* Piedmont's legal system and local government system were very backward, and it was these unreformed systems that would be extended to the whole of Italy after 1861.

In fact Cavour's declining interest in reforms and his growing use of dictatorial powers were related to his growing obsession with foreign policy.

13.4 Cavour and the unification of Italy

It is probable that Cavour's hopes for the future of Italy were rather limited. He certainly saw the Austrians as the great obstacle to Italian independence; he was a realist, however, and could not see beyond the possibility of the creation of a large Italian state in the north, together with some of the central states. He was also influenced by:

1   The pressure of pro-Piedmont nationalists in exile in Piedmont and especially the propaganda of the *National Society*.
2   The traditional policy of the royal house of Savoy of expansion and swallowing Italian territory piecemeal 'like the leaves of an artichoke'.

Certainly Cavour believed that only with foreign aid could change be brought about. By the late 1850s, the international situation was much more favourable to this.

(a)   *The Crimean War*

The old story that Cavour deliberately involved Piedmont in the Crimean War to win support for Italian independence is not true. Piedmont was asked by the Allies to send troops. This would weaken her as a threat to Austria, who would then be more likely to join the alliance against Russia. The Congress of Paris did no more than condemn the repressive government of the Kingdom of the Two Sicilies; however, the Crimean War did make the War of Italian Unification possible because:

1   *The Austrian Empire was left friendless in Europe.* Britain and France were angry because she had not helped them; Russia was angered because she had considered doing so.
2   *Britain's attitude was now more favourable to Italy.* The preservation of peace in the future was seen to lie in a better balance in Europe; in northern Italy a stronger Piedmont could block French ambitions, in eastern Europe Austria should balance Russia, but only if she lost her troublesome Italian territories.

(b)   *'We must do something for Italy'*

The other piece in this jigsaw was the attitude of the Emperor Napoleon III of France. He was a natural conspirator; he needed to strengthen his position in France, and foreign policy triumphs could do this. His great ancestor had been well known for his sympathy with Italy, and he himself had often remarked 'we must do something for Italy'.

And it could be very useful to have a grateful Kingdom of Northern Italy as a sort of puppet of France, although it was traditionally in French interests to keep Italy divided. Then in 1858 there was an attempt to assassinate the Emperor by the Mazzinian terrorist Orsini. The three Birmingham-made bombs killed 150 guards and bystanders and triggered Napoleon III into action because he now believed that Austria's involvement in Italy could lead only to more and more terrorism and tension in Europe. In July 1858, he met Cavour at Plombières on the frontier and an agreement was reached:

1 *Piedmont and France would ally themselves* in a war against the Austrian Empire in northern Italy.
2 *In the following territorial readjustment:*

– A state would be created in *northern Italy* under Victor Emmanuel.
– In *central Italy* a new state would be created from Tuscany and some of the Papal territories.
– Hopes were expressed that eventually an *Italian confederation* would be created under the presidency of the Pope.

3 The price paid to Napoleon III for his help would be the two French-speaking provinces of Piedmont, *Nice and Savoy.*

13.5 The process of Italian unification (1859–61)
(see Map 13.1)

The Pact of Plombières was an old-fashioned deal, with nothing too specific in writing, of course, between expansionist states. What followed was not at all what was expected to happen. The story can be divided into four stages:

1 *The War of Italian Unification* (April–July 1859)
2 *A crisis in central Italy* (July 1859–March 1860)
3 *Garibaldi's expedition* to the Kingdom of the Two Sicilies (April–November 1860)
4 *The occupation of the Papal States* by Piedmontese forces (September 1860).

(a) 'The Second War of Independence'

The Austrian Empire was provoked very reluctantly into war. Her armies were defeated by the Franco-Piedmontese forces, with difficulty, supported by units of irregular troops. The latter were raised from exiles and the 20,000 volunteers who flocked to Piedmont and were commanded by Garibaldi. The battles of Magenta and Solferino (see Illus. 13.1) led to the conquest of Lombardy. Austrian troops remained in Venetia. Then two unexpected events followed:

1 *Napoleon III made a separate peace at Villafranca.* Piedmont received Lombardy, but not Venetia. This betrayal of his agreement was probably because he was alarmed by the effects of the war in central Italy. It was also due to the high casualty rates. After Solferino Franz Joseph remarked that he would 'rather lose a province than undergo such a horrible experience again'. In addition as far as Austria was concerned there were other dangerous developments. Kossuth had arrived at Napoleon's headquarters – with obvious implications. Russia had also ostentatiously mobilised six army corps.
2 *Revolts and disturbances had broken out in Tuscany, Parma, Modena and the Papal States.* Austrian troops were no longer available to be called in. To maintain order

Map 13.1 The unification of Italy (1859–71)

and protect property, Piedmontese troops were invited in. National Society members undoubtedly saw a chance here to unite with Piedmont. Naturally Napoleon believed that Cavour had planned this from the start (see Illus. 13.2).

(b) *Crisis in Central Italy*

In later years, Cavour was to say 'How many times have I not exclaimed "Blessed be the peace of Villafranca".' Immediately, though, he resigned in fury. French pressure also forced him to recall his agents from central Italy; this left a vacuum in central Italy. Piedmont, France and Austria were each reluctant to intervene in case this produced opposition from the other European powers. In the end the deadlock was broken by:

1 *British pressure on France* to allow the creation of a stronger, more independent Italy than Napoleon III had wanted.
2 *Cavour's diplomatic activity* (see Illus. 13.3). Cavour came back as prime minister in January 1860. Napoleon III agreed to accept Piedmont's annexation of the central states, if he was given Savoy and Nice and if popular votes were held in all of the territories involved in the exchange.

Following this agreement, plebiscites were held in Tuscany, Parma, Modena and the Romagna. There was a lot of pressure on the voters by local landowners and notables

Illus. 13.1 Napoleon III at Magenta (Photographie Giraudon)

Source: G. Soria, *Grande Histoire de la Commune* (Livre Club Diderot, Paris, 1970) Part 1, p. 79.

Source: A cartoon of January 1860.

The signing of peace terms by Piedmont and the Habsburg Monarchy means that Cavour is 'released' and free to return to politics again, emerging upon the political scene like a veritable Jack in the Box.

and by the National Society members. The vote in favour of annexation was 97 per cent.

(c) *Garibaldi and 'the Thousand'* (see Illus. 13.4)

News of the events in the north now triggered off a revolt in Palermo in Sicily. There had been recurrent disorder in Sicily throughout the century. Poverty was severe amongst the peasantry and in the towns; banditry was a way of life. There was considerable opposition to the distant mainland government in Naples and its busy tax collectors. What made this revolt different though was that it spread very rapidly and local Mazzinian republicans saw a chance to produce a revolution. They invited Garibaldi to bring an expedition. He came to Sicily in early May and slipped past Neapolitan warships – late, as usual – with 1100 volunteers in two freighters. By early September, the whole of the Kingdom of the Two Sicilies was conquered and Garibaldi was at the northern frontier with 57,000 troops (see Illus. 13.5). This astonishing success was a result of:

BIZZARRIE

Cosa fate, buonomo?
Fo l' Italia.

Source: A contemporary cartoon.

Cavour is portrayed as stealing the dome of Florence Cathedral. In August 1860 Tuscany was incorporated into Italy. The caption reads 'What are you doing, my man?' 'I'm making Italy'.

1   *The presence at key moments of ships of the British navy*, which discouraged Neapolitan forces from attacking Garibaldi when he landed in Sicily and later when he crossed the Straits of Messina.
2   *The spread of disorder by peasantry and town workers* ahead of Garibaldi as he marched on Naples.
3   *The growing support for Garibaldi by men of property.* They saw him and annexation by Piedmont as the only hope of restoring order. Garibaldi encouraged these hopes when he suppressed the peasant revolts in Sicily.
4   *The quality of Garibaldi's leadership.* The king's troops were badly led, demoralised and bitterly unpopular. The Thousand were enthusiastic, wildly popular with the local people and led by a general skilled in guerrilla warfare.

(d)   *The occupation of the Papal States*

Cavour was in two minds as to how to respond to these events:

1   *There is no evidence that he arranged the expedition*, although Victor Emmanuel

Source: Unknown.

It was the revolt in Palermo which triggered off the most dramatic stage in the story of the Unification of Italy.

Q Why do you think that a very backward area like Sicily proved to be such a flashpoint in the story of the Unification of Italy?

certainly helped it. On the other hand, Cavour did not try to stop it. The British Ambassador was probably right in trying to guess Cavour's attitude: 'At the outset nobody believed in the possibility of Garibaldi's success; and Cavour ... thought the country well rid of him ... The argument was, if he fails we are rid of a troublesome fellow and if he succeeds Italy will derive some benefit.'

2 *There was a great danger in allowing the expedition to go.* Garibaldi and his men were old republicans. The result could be a republican government in Naples launching expeditions to the Papal States and Venetia and upsetting the whole situation again. By August, Cavour had decided that the advance must be stopped. Piedmontese troops were sent to protect the Papal States. In October these troops let by Victor Emmanuel met up with Garibaldi. Garibaldi then handed over his conquests to the king whom he saluted as 'the first King of Italy'. This apparently surprising move was partly because Garibaldi was increasingly afraid of the growing peasant disorder and also because he saw a united Italy as more important than a republican Italy. In 1859 a meeting between Garibaldi and the King in Turin established the basis for an alliance.

13.6 'A single, indivisible Italy'

The new territories were all annexed. Plebiscites were held but the only choice given to voters was for or against 'a single indivisible Italy, with Victor Emmanuel as constitutional king'. An Italian parliament was elected in January 1861 with a clear majority for Cavour. In March 1861, *the Kingdom of Italy* was proclaimed.

Illus. 13.5 The battle of the Volturno, October 1860 (Hulton Picture Library)

THE BATTLE ON THE VOLTURNO.—THE FINAL REPULSE OF THE NEAPOLITANS.—FROM A SKETCH BY OUR SPECIAL ARTIST, FRANK VIZETELLY.

It had all happened so quickly. In two years a new state of 22 million inhabitants had been created. The reasons for this can be summarised as follows:

1 *The defeat of the Austrians in 1859* made all the Italian states vulnerable because they could no longer rely on Austrian troops to support them.
2 *The reluctance of Napoleon III to intervene* because he feared that if he attempted to stop it he risked trouble with other European powers, especially Britain.
3 *Men of property wanted order to be re-established* as soon as possible before revolts by peasants and workers developed. The National Society played on these fears, and channelled support towards Piedmont.
4 *Mazzini and his followers were also taken by surprise.* They were put into a position where they had to choose between a united Kingdom and a divided Italy, half monarchy and half republican. For most of them, unity came first. Mazzini never considered appealing for the support of peasants and workers in a revolution because this would be a great threat to unity.
5 *Cavour was a great opportunist.* He had not planned the unification as it had occurred; what he did do brilliantly was to move with events and turn them to his advantage. He also had a knack of persuading people that he had actually arranged for things to happen in the way they had.

13.7 The completion of unification

In fact, Italy was still not unified. Venetia and Rome were missing. In the 1860s there was a series of unsuccessful attempts by Garibaldi and Mazzini to liberate both of them. In the end when they were acquired it was because the international situation changed again:

1 *The 'Seven Weeks War' (1866).* Before he went to war with Austria in 1866 (see Section 14.4), Bismarck made an alliance with Italy. Although the Italian forces were defeated nevertheless Italy was still given her payment, which was Venetia.
2 *The Franco-Prussian War (1870–1).* With the outbreak of war between France and Prussia (see Section 14.7), French troops were recalled from Rome. In September 1870, Italian troops entered Rome which now became the capital of Italy.

13.8 Conclusion

Even in 1870, unification was not total. In future years there was great resentment by Italians at the fact that Italy had not recovered the districts of Trent, Trieste and Istria. To some extent, this distracted them from the great problems which faced Italy internally. Gladstone called the unification of Italy 'one of the great marvels of our time'. but the problem was that unification had happened too quickly, and there were great differences between the attitudes of Italians throughout the country. As the Piedmontese politician Massimo d'Azeglio put it: 'We have created Italy. Let us now create Italians!' Lord Palmerston summed Cavour up as 'one of the greatest patriots that have ever adorned the history of any nation'. However, he died in 1861, and no Italian politician after him was really able to solve these problems.

Questions

1 'Italia fara da se' (Italy will make herself by herself) Did she? [OC]
2 'Italy was unified by improvisation rather than calculation.' Discuss. [OC]
3 Why was Italy eventually united as a monarchy, rather than as a republic or as a federation under the Papacy? [OX]
4 How was a united Kingdom of Italy established between 1852 and 1870? [NEAB]
5 Trace the careers of Garibaldi and Cavour, explaining the parts they played in the creation of a united kingdom of Italy. [NEAB]
6 'He was first a Piedmontese and only secondly an Italian.' How far does this explain Cavour's political career? [CAM]
7 How significant was the contribution of *either* Mazzini *or* Garibaldi to the unification of Italy? [CAM]
8 To what extent was the unification of Italy in 1859–61 the result of accident?
9 What contribution was made by Cavour to the modernisation of Piedmont before 1859?
10 Study Sources A and B and then answer the questions which follow.

Source A: Disillusionment.

The Italy which we represent today, like it or not, is a living lie. Foreigners won Italian territory on our frontiers with France and Germany. We still have only the material husk, the dead corpse of Italy. The life-giving touch of God, the true soul of the nation is lacking.

Italy was put together just as though it were a piece of lifeless mosaic, and the battles which made this mosaic were fought for reasons of calculating dynastic egoism by foreign rulers who should have been loathed as our natural enemies. The best of us once fought against France for possession of Rome; yet we remained the slaves of France so long as she was strong. Rome had to be occupied furtively when France lay prostrate at Germany's feet. Southern Italy was won by volunteers and a real movement of the people, but then it resigned its early promise.

Italians are now a vassal people, without a new constitution that could express their will. We can therefore have no real national existence or international policy of our own. In domestic politics we are ruled by an arbitrary violation of the law; administrative corruption has been elevated into a system; a narrow franchise means that we are governed by a few rich men who are powerless for good. Ordinary people are disillusioned. They had watched with astonished presentiment of great things to come as Italy, once ruler of the civilised world, began to rise again; but now they avert their gaze from what is happening and say to themselves; 'this is just the ghost of Italy'.

(a) What was the territory 'on our frontiers with France' (line 0) which was held by foreigners? How had it fallen into their hands?
(b) Explain how 'Rome had to be occupied furtively when France lay prostrate at Germany's feet' (lines 8–9).
(c) Describe how 'southern Italy was won by volunteers and a real movement of the people' (line 9). Why did Mazzini believe that 'it resigned its early promise' (line 10)?
(d) With close reference to the passage, explain in your own words why Mazzini believed Italy to be 'a living lie' (line 1). Is it surprising that these views should have been expressed by Mazzini? [OC]

Source: A letter from Mazzini, 25 August 1875.

Source B: The voice of our country in danger.
From the diary of one of Garibaldi's 'Thousand', describing the battle of Calatafimi (30 May 1860) between Garibaldi's forces and Neapolitan regular troops on the Neapolitan mainland.

At that moment one of our guns thundered from the road above. A cry of joy from all greeted the shot because it seemed as though we were getting the aid of a thousand strong arms. 'Forward! Forward! Forward!' was the cry heard on all sides and the trumpet that had continuously sounded the charge now pealed out with a kind of anguish as though it were the voice of our country in danger.

The first, second, and third terraces up the hillside were attacked at the point of the bayonet and passed, but it was terrible to see the dead and wounded. Little by little, as they yielded ground, the Royalist battalions retreated higher up. They concentrated and thus grew stronger. At last it seemed impossible that we could face them. They were all on the top of the hill and we were around the brow, tired, at the end of our tether, and reduced in numbers. There was a moment of pause; it was difficult to recognize the two opposing sides, they up there and we all flat on the ground. One could hear rifle fire and the Royalist troops started rolling down boulders, and hurling stones, and it was said that even Garibaldi was hit by one of these.

Already we had lost a great many of our men and I heard friends bewailing their comrades. Near by, among the prickly-pear bushes, I saw a fine young man fatally wounded, propped up by two of his comrades. He seemed to want to continue to charge, but I heard him ask his two friends to be merciful to the Royalist soldiers because they too were Italians. Tears came into my eyes.

(a) How had the 'Garibaldini' crossed the Straits of Messina with such ease?
(b) How was it that the resistance of the Royalist troops increased as the battle proceeded (lines 7–9)?
(c) What evidence is there in this extract of Italian nationalism (lines 16–19)?
(d) Why was it that the 'Garibaldini' proved so successful against forces far superior in number and professionalism?
(e) This is an extract from a diary. What sort of factors make diaries more (or less) valuable as sources for historians?

Source: From the diary of one of Garibaldi's 'Thousand', describing the battle of Calatafimi (30 May 1860) between Garibaldi's forces and the Neapolitan regular troops on the mainland. G. C. Abba, *The Diary of One of Garibaldi's Thousand*, transl. and introduction by E. R. Vincent (OUP, 1962).

The Unification of Germany 1862-71

Introduction

In 1859 Julius Froebel wrote: 'The German nation is sick of principles and doctrines, literary existence and theoretical greatness. What it wants is Power, Power, Power! In that year, Otto von Bismarck became the Prussian ambassador to St Petersburg and the mobilisation of Russian forces in response to a threat by Napoleon III to the Rhineland revealed weaknesses. The process of German unification had begun.

14.1 The rise of Bismarck

Bismarck had a typical *Junker* upbringing, with wild student days at Göttingen University, service in the Prussian army and civil service and management of extensive family estates in Pomerania and Brandenburg. In fact, he was a very complex character, very intelligent, highly strung and resentful towards authority although an authoritarian himself.

(a) *'Germany is too small for both of us'*

During the events of 1848–9 (see Section 9) he had scorned and opposed the liberal and nationalist revolutionaries of Frankfurt and Berlin. He represented the old belief in a German Confederation under Austro-Prussian dominance. Throughout the 1850s, as a representative at the Federal Diet, he became increasingly anti-Austrian. He remarked at this change of attitude: 'I was certainly no opponent of Austria on principle when I came here ... but I would have had to deny every drop of Prussian blood if I had wanted to retain even a moderate preference for Austria as she is conserved by her present rulers.' The fault for the growing rift was as much Austrian as Prussian. Before 1848 Metternich had followed a careful policy of co-operation. After 1848, Austria was claiming a preeminence in Germany which she no longer had in reality; by 1856 Bismarck was an outspoken advocate of a Prussian-dominated *'Kleindeutschland'*.

(b) *The constitutional crisis (1862–3)*

Following the war scare of 1859, reform of the Prussian army became a significant political issue culminating in a constitutional crisis:

1   The 'Moltkean Revolution'. In 1858 Frederick William IV had been declared insane and his brother William became the Prince Regent. A very practical military man whose first priority was army reform he worked with the minister of war von Roon and chief of the general staff von Moltke to produce proposals which would be the basis of the new Prussian army:

   – Each citizen would serve three years with the colours instead of two.
   – Expansion of the reserve, in which each citizen served two years at the expense of the militia *Landwehr*.

2   *The opposition of the Progressive Party*. In 1861 the middle-class Progressive Party was founded to fight the power of the Junkers and the army. It was liberal and nationalist, and in the *Landtag* elections it won a comfortable majority. It opposed the virtual doubling of the army and the reduction of the role of the *Landwehr* with its non-aristocratic officers. In 1862, it rejected the budget. The issue became that of parliamentary control over the executive. William I, who had succeeded his brother in 1861, rejected his earlier inclination to abdicate and selected Bismarck as minister president to try and break the deadlock.

(c) 'Iron and blood'

Bismarck was chosen because of his reputation for strength of character and ruthlessness. In fact, he failed to convince the *Landtag* by his insistence that 'it is not by speeches and majority resolutions that the great questions of our time are decided. That was the great mistake of 1848 and 1849. It is by iron and blood'. For the next four years Bismarck ignored the opposition majority and collected taxes illegally. It was to be his achievement of a Prussian solution to the German problem that enabled him to justify this action.

14.2 Diplomatic events (1863)

The scene was set by three developments in 1863.

(a) *Rejection of an Austrian proposal for reform of the Confederation*

In August 1863 Anton von Schmerling (see Section 21.4) proposed a 'Grossdeutschland' under Austrian presidency and with a federal assembly elected by the state assemblies. Bismarck took the line that there should be direct popular elections; his real objection was that Austria would be pre-eminent. Even more fearful of this outcome if Prussia withdrew, the princes outvoted the scheme. Apart from defeating the Austrian bid for the initiative Bismarck had won the sympathy of liberal nationalists and linked Prussian ambitions to popular German nationalism.

(b) *The Polish Rebellion*

During the Polish rising of 1863–4 Bismarck fully supported Russia, even agreeing to a military convention. Of course, Prussia also had Polish territories and could be threatened by rebellion but the most valuable effect of this support was to establish a bond between Prussia and Russia. At the same time, the issue drove a wedge between Russia and Austria and France, who both advocated concessions. By 1864, Austria was isolated.

(c) *Revival of the Schleswig-Holstein question*

The Treaty of London of 1852 between Denmark and the Confederation involved the German nationalist-supported Augustenburg family giving up its claim, while the Danes agreed that the two Duchies should be indivisible and that they would never attempt to incorporate Schleswig into Denmark. Then in 1863 the situation changed:

1   *The amendment of the Danish constitution.* The new king of Denmark (Christian IX) amended the constitution in such a way that the Treaty of London was broken.
2   *Revival of the Augustenburg claim.* Frederick von Augustenburg also broke the Treaty by reviving his family's claim to the Duchies.

14.3 The Danish War (1864)

Bismarck was careful to act in support of the legal technicalities of the Treaty, rather than seeming to be swept along by German nationalist anger and the Confederation's insistence on action. In January 1864 Prussia and Austria, independently of the Confederation, signed a military convention and invaded Schleswig. By August, Denmark was defeated and agreed to surrender the two Duchies to joint occupation by Prussia and Austria.

(a) *The implication of the war*

The conflict had considerable implications:

1   *Prussia was united with German nationalism.* By April–May 1864 Bismarck had started to ally with 'the spirit of 1848', by giving support to the idea of the independence of the Duchies under Frederick of Augustenburg. In fact, he was simply exploiting this factor against Austria. As he remarked 'I hitched the Prince to the plough as an ox to get it moving. Once the plough was in motion, I unhitched the ox'.
2   *The inability of the other powers to intervene* was revealed. Despite their sympathy for Denmark, neither Britain nor France intervened to help. Britain distrusted French intentions. Lord John Russell asked 'what will France require as the price of her alliance with England? And is it the interest of England to pay that price?' In any case, as Bismarck pointed out, the British fleet did not move 'on wheels'! Russia supported Prussia.
3   *A cause of Austro-Prussian antagonism.* As Bismarck assumed an increasingly provocative stance towards Austria, the joint occupation of the Duchies became a source of frequent disagreements. By May 1865 Bismarck was threatening to annex both Duchies and to reorganise the Confederation. The Convention of Gastein in August 1865 which divided the duchies – leaving Austria to govern Holstein and Prussia governing Schleswig – did not help improve relations, and left Austria looking as if she was a mere expansionist.

14.4 The Austro-Prussian War (1866)

In fact, it was Prussian expansionism which was the real motive force.

(a) The isolation of Austria

Bismarck effectively isolated Austria from potential support:

1 *The Biarritz discussions (October 1865).* Napoleon III, who had a loose commitment to assist foreign nationalism, accepted the vague bribe of Belgium as the price for inaction.
2 *The Prusso-Italian military alliance (April 1866).* Ironically it was Napoleon III who also encouraged the agreement between Italy and Prussia which offered Italy Venetia in return for her support against Austria. In fact, Napoleon III miscalculated the relative strengths of Prussia and Austria, and hoped that if they exhausted each other France would be able to exploit the situation.

(b) The course of the war

Bismarck provoked Austria by demanding in April 1866 that a German parliament should be elected by universal suffrage, and withdrawing from the Confederation. Prussian troops invaded Holstein in June but Austrian mobilisation was so inefficient that she had to start before Prussia to have any chance of matching her so she looked like the aggressor. The war was over by mid-July. Prussian armies – with the advantages of excellent staff work, a well-developed rail network and the Dreyse breech-loading needle gun – swept into the territories of Austria's allies Hanover, Hesse-Cassel and Saxony and invaded Bohemia. On 3 July at Königgratz the Austrians were defeated with the loss of 44,000 men, five times as many as those of Prussia. Meanwhile the Italians were defeated on 24 June at Custozza, and their fleet was annihilated on 20 July at Lissa.

(c) The Treaty of Prague (August 1866) (see Map 14.1)

In fact, Austria had been too decisively defeated. Bismarck remarked 'We need Austria's strength in future for ourselves'. There was also the danger that France might still intervene. Her internal troubles (see Section 21.6) also stimulated Austria into negotiations which were sealed in August:

1 *Prussian annexations.* Prussia absorbed Schleswig-Holstein, Hesse-Cassel, Hanover, Nassau and Frankfurt.
2 *The North German Confederation.* The states north of the plain were united in a new structure under Prussian leadership. The states south of the plain were left to create a form of union but through military alliances with Bavaria, Baden and Würtemburg Prussia could dominate the region.

Despite her poor showing, Italy was still rewarded with Venetia.

14.5 The triumph of Bismarck (see Illus. 14.1)

The policy of *'iron and blood'* was clearly successful; its success was to have very significant effects on the future of Germany.

(a) The Indemnity Bill (September 1866)

The conservatives made considerable gains in the Prussian Landtag elections of July 1866, but the Progressives themselves were also splitting. A new *National Liberty*

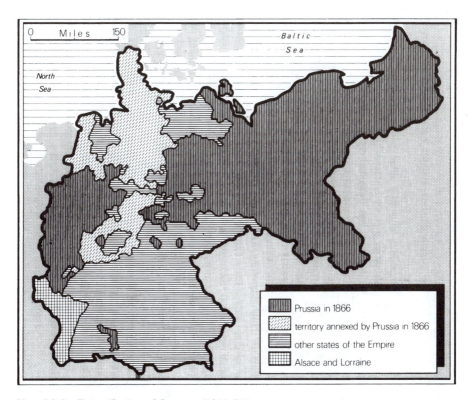

Map 14.1 The unification of Germany (1866–71)
Source: I. R. Mitchell, *Bismarck and the Development of Germany* (Holmes Macdougall, 1980) p. 53.

party emerged prepared to support Bismarck as the representative of German nationalism. In September 1866, the triumph of nationalist aspirations over liberalism was represented by the legalisation of the previous years of illegal tax collection and expenditure.

(b) *The constitution of the North German Confederation (July 1867)*

The triumph of Prussia was clearly reflected in the terms of the new law constitution:

1 *A strong executive.* The federal executive was the president who was the King of Prussia. He had the power to conclude treaties and declare war and was commander in chief of the armed forces. The only federal minister was the *chancellor* who was responsible only to the president.

2 *The legislature.* There were *two* chambers:

– The *Bundesrat* consisted of delegates from the states. However, Prussia had 17 votes, as opposed to the 26 votes of the other 21 states.
– The *Reichstag* was a representative chamber elected by direct universal male suffrage. It could veto legislation and the budget, but in many other respects its powers were limited.

Illus. 14.1 *Making omelettes*

From a cartoon: the cook is saying to the kitchen-maid: 'You can't make omelettes without breaking eggs.'

Source: I. R. Mitchell, *Bismarck and the Development of Germany* (Holmes Macdougall, 1980) p. 87.

Q   What sort of eggs was Bismarck obliged to break and what sort of omelettes was he involved in making? Is the cartoonist also suggesting something about the relationship between Bismarck and the King of Prussia?

14.6 The background to the Franco-Prussian War

The time had not been right to take in the southern states as well; Bismarck did not want Prussian influence to be swamped. Austria and France would also not accept such a sweeping rearrangement. However, the 'national question' was now paramount in Bismarck's mind.

(a) The isolation of France

Much of the isolation of France was due to Napoleon III:

1 *British distrust.* Napoleon's attempts to acquire Luxembourg by purchase, the Bavarian Palatinate by negotiation and Belgium by agreement with Bismarck all led to British distrust of France. On 25 July 1870, Bismarck deliberately published the details of the Belgian proposals, and so fomented this distrust.

2 *The failure to find an ally.* Austria had been exhausted and treated wisely by Bismarck, and the Magyars and Germans were anti-French. Russia made it clear in 1868 that her sympathies in any war would be with Prussia. As for Italy, the 'Rome Question' still separated her from France and Napoleon III dared not risk Roman Catholic support at home by withdrawing his protection from the Pope.

(b) The Hohenzollern candidature

In 1869 the Spanish Cortes chose Leopold of Hohenzollern, a relative of King William, to succeed Queen Isabella who had been expelled by a military coup. France was bitterly opposed to what was seen as an unacceptable linking of the two states. Bismarck firmly backed the candidature but King William responded to French approaches by withdrawing it on 12 July. However, when King William rejected a rather arrogant French demand that the issue should never be revived, Bismarck – in the *Ems Telegramme*, which was published in the press – made it appear that the King had snubbed the French ambassador. Against a background of growing Franco-German antagonism this was the last straw, and France declared war on 19 July 1870. Bismarck undoubtedly saw the issue as important in its own right, and valued the possibility of an ally to the south of France. On the other hand, as Heinrich von Holstein remarked: 'Bismarck handled the Hohenzollern candidature rather as one waves a lighted match over a gas tap to see if it is turned on.'

14.7 The Franco-Prussian War (1870–1)

Bismarck had already tried to attract the German states of the south into a closer link using the French threat to Luxembourg to alarm them, and then suggesting the extension of the *Zollverein* into a sort of German parliament. However, only a national war would achieve this link. All of the German states fought under Prussian leadership and the war assumed the level of a 'national crusade'.

(a) 'La Debâcle' (see Illus. 14.2)

Using six railway lines the Prussians could mobilise 380,000 men as opposed to the 200,000 of the French. In terms of weaponry, organisation and leadership the French army was inferior:

1 *Initial Prussian successes (July–August 1870).* A series of quick victories and the incompetence of the French commander Bazaine led to the trapping of 180,000 French troops in Metz.

2 *The failure to relieve Metz (August–September 1870).* On 1 September at Sedan, a relief army under Marshal MacMahon was defeated with the loss of 82,000 prisoners including Napoleon III who was later released to go into exile. In October, Bazaine surrendered Metz.

Illus. 14.2 Prussian troops trying to take the railway line between Nancy and Metz (1870)

Illus. 14.3 The Parisian diet during the first siege of Paris: the Marché St Germain (Collection Viollet)

From an engraving by Vierge Lorédan Larchey in a memorial volume to illustrate the two sieges of Paris, in the Bibliothèque de la Ville de Paris.

Source: G. Soria, *Grande Histoire de la Commune* (Livre Club Diderot, Paris, 1970) Part 1, p. 292.

a According to this cartoon, what sort of items had been added to the meals of Parisians?

3 *The 'peoples' war' (September 1870–January 1871).* The defeats were followed by the overthrow of the Second Empire and the establishment of a republic under a provisional Government of National Defence. The war now focused on the siege of Paris from 19 September (see Illus. 14.3) and attempts to relieve it by the Army of the Loire. On 28 January 1871, Paris finally surrendered and a newly elected constituent assembly with Thiers as 'Chief of the Executive Power' sued for peace.

(b) The Treaty of Frankfurt (February 1871)

Bismarck forced harsh terms on France, partly because of the strength of the German nationalist enthusiasm he had exploited but also to prevent any sort of 'comeback' attempt:

1 *The surrender of Alsace-Lorraine.* France lost valuable agricultural land and iron ore reserves, as well as territories of historic significance.
2 *National humiliation.* France was forced to accept an indemnity of 5000 million francs and a period of occupation of some of the departments. In addition, on 1 March 1871 there was a ceremonial entry to Paris by the German army.

14.8 The consequences of the Franco-Prussian War

There were wider implications beyond the actual Settlement provisions.

(a) The creation of the German Empire (January 1871) (see Illus. 14.4)

Given the wave of German nationalism, Bismarck was able to use the trump card of the threat of an appeal to the German people to persuade the princes of the southern states to agree to the proclamation of William I as the *German Emperor.* In addition, some special concessions were made to the kings of Bavaria and Würtemburg – such as the maintenance of their own postal service, and the maintenance of the Bavarian army as a self-contained unit. The invitation therefore came from the princes rather than from any popularly elected assembly. The proclamation was made by Bismarck in the Hall of Mirrors at the palace of Versailles on 18 January 1871.

(b) The Paris Commune (March–May 1871)

The indignity of the peace terms following the bitter four month's siege, the insistence that all bills outstanding due to the war should be paid, and the unwise cessation of payment of the National Guard before disarming them triggered the vicious civil war between the government of Thiers and the left-wing-led working class Paris Commune. Once again, there was a marked division between the provinces, where support for peace was strong, and Paris, which was still pro-war. After a climax of bitter street-to-street fighting, the revolt was crushed in May 1871 at a cost of 20,000 lives (see Illus. 14.5) while another 20,000 rebels were imprisoned or deported.

(c) Restoration of the monarchy in Spain (December 1874)

A brief unsuccessful reign by a son of Victor Emmanuel was followed by a briefer republican period, then a civil war. In 1874 the army overthrew the Cortes and put on the throne Alfonso the son of Queen Isabella. In February 1876 a limited constitution was adopted.

Illus. 14.4   The acclamation of the Emperor in the Hall of Mirrors at Versailles (Hulton Picture Library)

Source: I. R. Mitchell, *Bismarck and the Development of Germany* (Holmes Macdougall, 1980) p. 46.

Q   The painting is very notable for the total absence of civilians. What does this suggest to you about the birth of Germany? Nor does the picture illustrate – it could not – the bitter row which preceded this event. There was a dispute over whether the King of Prussia should be acclaimed as 'German Kaiser', 'Kaiser of Germany' or just 'Kaiser William'. The King of Bavaria preferred the first but William I preferred the second. Why do you think this mattered? In the end William was crowned simply as 'Kaiser William' when Bismarck broke his promise to use the words 'German Kaiser' as had been agreed as part of a compromise with the King of Bavaria and reduced him in the ranks another step! William walked past Bismarck and ignored him pointedly afterwards.

Illus. 14.5   Bodies of Communards in the morgue

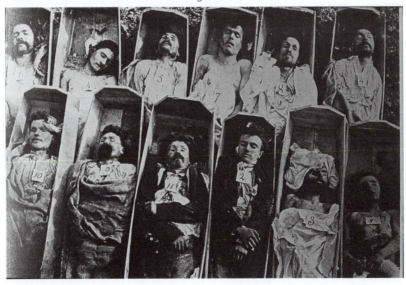

Source: *Illustrated London News*, tome LVIII, p. 564. Included in G. Soria, *Le Grand Histoire de la Commune*.

(d) The Italian occupation of Rome (September 1870)

With the withdrawal of French troops at the start of the war Rome was left open to occupation against all but token resistance. The new capital of Italy became the centre of further worsened relations between the Papacy and the Italian state.

(e) Abrogation of the Black Sea clauses of the Treaty of Paris (November 1870)

In fact, no one was in a position to stop Russia abrogating the clauses. To save face, a conference held in London in 1871 granted the Russian wish officially.

14.9 The process of unification

There are two views about the sequence of events from 1864 to 1871.

(a) A long-laid plan

The 'conspiracy' theory is based largely on the apparent interconnection of events, and a report by Disraeli of a meeting with Bismarck in 1862:

> What an extraordinary man Bismarck is! He meets me for the first time and tells me all his is going to do. He will attack Denmark in order to get possession of Schleswig-Holstein, he will put Austria out of the German confederation; and then he will attack France – an extraordinary man!

In fact, this is unlikely. Disraeli probably wanted to give the impression of having been 'in the know' during great events, and anyhow he was very old when he first told the story. On the other hand, there is no doubt that Bismarck was motivated by a developing animosity towards Austria. As early as 1856 he was expressing the view that war with Austria would be difficult to avoid.

(b) Opportunism

Bismarck confessed that 'By himself the individual can create nothing; he can wait [only] until he hears God's footsteps resounding through events and then spring forward to grasp the hem of his mantle', and he once remarked 'Many paths led to my goal. I had to try all of them one after the other, the most dangerous at the end'. In fact while the creation of a *Kleindeutschland* did become an objective, it seems to have grown from the success of Prussian dynastic expansion in alliance with German nationalism. Like Cavour, Bismarck's brilliance was his ability to exploit every opportunity to its utmost, to create an image as the controller of events and to reap the benefits of other factors such as the *Zollverein*, industrialisation and railway building (see Map 14.2) and the efficient military machine of Prussia.

14.10 Varieties of unification

In a decade, the Vienna Settlement of 1815 had been destroyed and the diplomatic map of Europe had been dramatically altered, and this in the same decade as the American Civil War which was also a form of war of unification. Naturally there is a tendency to compare Cavour and Bismarck, and their achievements.

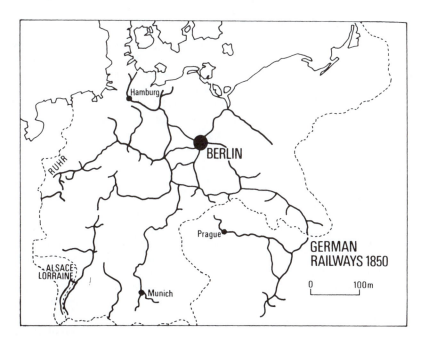

Map 14.2a   German railways (1850)

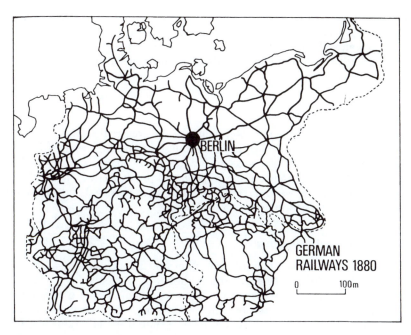

Map 14.2b   German railways (1880)
Source: I. R. Mitchell, *Bismarck and the Development of Germany* (Holmes Macdougall, 1980)
p. 54.

(a) A triumph for opportunism

Both were arch exponents of *Realpolitik*. Astute manipulators and extremely flexible in attitude, neither of them allowed their policies to be stifled by excessive adherence to principles. Bismarck once remarked that having to go through life with principles was like walking down a narrow forest path with a long pole in one's mouth. On the other hand, with relatively fewer resources at his disposal Cavour had been obliged to ride the tide of circumstances far more than Bismarck, and the result was that he was carried well beyond his original limited objectives.

(b) Unity imposed from above

In both cases, the key to unification had been the *expansionism of existing states*. This had several implications:

1   *Militarism.* The new Germany had been created by the success of the Prussian army. This meant that there was a strong identity between the two, which was a danger to the political and constitutional system. In Italy, the role of the army had been rather more limited and was rivalled by the success of the 'Garibaldini' volunteers, but the Neapolitan adventure was dangerous because it encouraged admiration for *direct action* outside the framework of constitutionalism and other legal restraints.
2   *Limited popular participation.* Although Bismarck had used the threat of popular radicalism, the German people had played very little part in unification. In Italy, a spirit of patriotism and democratic revolution had played a definite part and the expectations which had been thus excited would be disappointed by the failure of unification to match those expectations. In both states, the social system remained virtually untouched.
3   *The extension of existing institutions.* Since unification was really a process of Prussianisation and Piedmontisation, inevitably the institutions of the new states were Prussian and Piedmontese, although in some respects the process was even more marked in Italy where the institutions of the central and southern states were so much less developed.

(c) The economic substructure

The economic potential of the new Germany was far greater than that of Italy, and in the working of the *Zollverein* and the elaboration of the railway network German political unification was already matched by growing economic integration. In Italy, however, although Cavour had certainly appreciated the danger of a marked economic divide the vast contrast between the north and the south persisted and even intensified in the absence of similar economic integration.

(d) Irredentas and minorities

In the case of Germany, one result of unification was the inclusion of substantial non-German minorities who were to pose serious 'digestion problems' for the new state. In the case of Italy, the problem was reversed because even after 1871 unification was not complete and the surviving minorities, the 'irredenta', were the focus for a radical nationalist agitation which was to distract the new state from its serious internal problems.

14.11 Conclusion

What had been won by the wars of 1864–71 now had to be held. Moltke said 'What we have gained by arms in half a year we must protect by arms for half a century on'. Bismarck's diplomacy after 1871 (see Section 16) was to be directed at trying to avoid the need for force. On the other hand, Germany's ambitions were swollen by the successes of 1871, and she expanded in economic strength while the Europe of post-1871 was also much more insecure and prone to militarism.

Questions

1 In what circumstances did Bismarck come to office as minister president of Prussia? What had he achieved by 1871?   [OC]
2 What did the foundation of the German Empire owe to Bismarck?   [OC]
3 Why had Prussia rather than Austria achieved dominance in Germany by 1866?   [OC]
4 Estimate the part played by Bismarck's statesmanship in the rise of Prussia to the leadership of Germany between 1860 and 1870   [OX]
5 Write an account of the career of Bismarck between 1848 and 1870.   [NEAB]
6 How far was the unification of Germany, achieved between 1862 and 1871, due to Bismarck's diplomacy?   [NEAB]
7 How far did the German Empire of 1871 represent the 'Prussianisation', rather than the unification of German States?   [CAM]
8 Study Sources A, B, C and D and then answer the questions which follow.

Source A: Blood and Iron.

[He said] he would gladly agree to the budget for 1862, but without giving any prejudicial explanation. A misuse of constitutional powers could happen on any side, and would lead to a reaction from the other side. The crown, for example, could dissolve [parliament] a dozen times, and that would certainly be in accordance with the letter of the Constitution, but it would be a misuse. In the same way it can challenge the budget cancellations as much as it likes: but the limit is difficult to set; shall it be at 6 million, or 16 million, or 60 million? – There are members of the National Union, a party respected because of the justice of its demands, highly esteemed members, who considered all standing armies superfluous. Now what if a national assembly were of this opinion! Wouldn't the government have to reject it? – People speak of the 'sobriety' of the Prussian people. Certainly the great independence of the individual makes it difficult in Prussia to rule with the constitution; in France it is different, the independence of the individual is lacking there. A constitutional crisis is not shameful, but honourable. Furthermore we are perhaps too 'educated' to put up with a constitution; we are too critical; the ability to judge government measures and bills of the National Assembly is too widespread; there are in the country too many subversive elements who have an interest in revolutionary change. This may sound paradoxical, but it goes to show how difficult it is in Prussia to carry on a constitutional existence ... We are too ardent, we like to carry too heavy a weight of armour for our fragile bodies: but we should also make use of it. Germany doesn't look to Prussia's liberalism, but to its power: Bavaria, Wurttemberg, Baden can indulge in liberalism, but no one will expect them to undertake Prussia's role; Prussia must gather and consolidate her strength in readiness for the favourable moment, which has already been missed several times; Prussia's boundaries according to the Vienna treaties are not favourable to a healthy political life; not by means of speeches and majority verdicts will the great decisions of the time be made – that was the great mistake of 1848 and 1849 – but by iron and blood. . .

(a) What does this tell you about the attitude of Bismarck towards constitutionalism and governmental responsibility?
(b) What do you think he meant by the remark 'we like to carry too heavy a weight of armour for our fragile bodies' (line 18)?
(c) Why was constitutional crisis 'not shameful but honourable' when it took place in Prussia (lines 12–13)?

(d) In what sense were the boundaries of Prussia 'not favourable to a healthy political life'?

Source: Bismarck's speech to the budget commission of the Prussian Landtag on 29 September 1862. Included in D. G. Williamson, *Bismarck and Germany 1862–1890* (Longman, 1986).

Source B: The Gastein Convention.

Article I   The exercise of the Rights acquired in common by the High Contracting Parties, in virtue of Article III of the Vienna Treaty of Peace of 30th October, 1864, shall, without prejudice to the continuance of those rights of both Powers to the whole of both Duchies, pass to His Majesty the Emperor of Austria as regards the Duchy of Holstein, and to His Majesty the King of Prussia as regards the Duchy of Schleswig.

Article II   The High Contracting Parties will propose to the Diet the establishment of a German Fleet, and will fix upon the Harbour of Kiel as a Federal Harbour for the said Fleet.

Until the resolutions of the Diet with respect to this proposal have been carried into effect, the Ships of War of both Powers shall use this Harbour, and the Command and the Police Duties within it shall be exercised by Prussia ...

Article III   The High Contracting Parties will propose in Frankfurt the elevation of Rendsburg into a German Federal Fortress. Until the Diet shall have issued the regulations respecting Garrisoning the said Fortress, the Garrison shall consist of Imperial Austrian and Royal Prussian troops under a command annually alternating on the 1st July.

Article IV   While the division agreed upon in Article I of the present Convention continues, the Royal Prussian Government shall retain two Military Roads through Holstein; the one from Lubeck to Kiel, the other from Hamburg to Rendsburg.

Article VI   [Provision for the duchies eventually to enter the *Zollverein*.]

Article IX   His Majesty the Emperor of Austria cedes to His Majesty the King of Prussia the Rights acquired in the aforementioned Vienna Treaty of Peace with respect to the Duchy of Lauenburg; and in return the Royal Prussian Government binds itself to pay to the Austrian Government the sum of 2,500,000 Danish rix-dollars, payable at Berlin in Prussian silver, 4 weeks after confirmation of the present Convention by their Majesties the Emperor of Austria and the King of Prussia.

Article X   ... The joint Command-in-Chief, hitherto existing, shall be dissolved on the complete Evacuation of Holstein by the Prussian troops and of Schleswig by the Austrian troops, by the 15th September, at the latest ...

[L.S.] G. Blome
[L.S.] von Bismarck

(a) With which state had Austria and Prussia jointly fought a war over Schleswig-Holstein?
(b) What opportunities for discord between the two allies can you see in the wording of this document?
(c) What is the significance of the use of the word 'Federal' (lines 7 and 13)?

Source: Extracts from the agreement between Prussia and Austria signed on 14 August 1865. Included in W. N. Medlicott and D. K. Caveney (eds) *Bismarck and Europe* (Edward Arnold, 1971).

Source C: An edited telegram.
From Bismarck's memoirs.

In view of the attitude of France, our national sense of honour compelled us, in my opinion, to go to war; and if we did not act according to the demands of this feeling, we should lose the entire impetus towards our national development won in 1866.

These considerations strengthened my opinion that war could be avoided only at the cost of the honour of Prussia and of the national confidence in it. Under this conviction I made use of the royal authorisation to publish the contents of the telegram: and in the presence of my two guests reduced the telegram by striking out words, but without adding or altering, to the following form: 'After the news of the renunciation of the hereditary Prince of Hohenzollern had been officially communicated to the imperial government of France by the royal government of Spain, the French ambassador at Ems further demanded of his Majesty the King that he would authorise him to telegraph to Paris that his Majesty the King bound himself for all future time never again to give his consent if the Hohenzollerns should renew their candidature. His Majesty the King thereupon decided not to receive the French ambassador again, and sent to tell him through the aide-de-camp on duty that his Majesty had nothing further to communicate to the ambassador'. The difference in the effect of the abbreviated text of the Ems telegram, as compared with that produced by the original was not the result of stronger words but of the form, which made the announcement appear decisive.

(a) What was the original source of 'the telegram' (line 6), and what had been its purpose?
(b) Explain the reference to 'our national development won in 1866' (line 4).
(c) In what sense was Prussia 'compelled' to go to war with France at this time (line 2)?
(d) Who was the 'hereditary Prince of Hohenzollern' (lines 8–9)? Why was he the subject of the *Ems telegramme*?
(e) What does the passage tell us about Bismarck's political aims and methods?
Source: Otto von Bismarck, *Reflections and Reminiscences.*

Source D: The excessive power of Bismarck.

The *initiated* know that the emperor . . . has allowed Prince Bismarck to have his own way in *everything*; and the great chancellor revels in the absolute power he has acquired and does as he pleases. He lives in the country and governs the German Empire without even taking the trouble to consult the emperor about his plans, who only learns what is being done from the documents to which his signature is necessary, and which His Majesty signs without questions or hesitation. Never has a subject been granted so much irresponsible power from his sovereign, and never has a minister inspired a nation with more abject individual, as well as general, terror before. No wonder, then, that the crown prince should be worried at a state of things which he has not more personal power or influence to remedy than anyone else in Prussia, whilst Prince Bismarck lives and terrorises over Germany from Friedrichsruh with the emperor's tacit and cheerful consent.

Bismarck has gradually appointed a ministry of clerks out of the government offices, who do as they are told by him, and he has so terrified the *Bundesrat*, by threatening to resign whenever they disagreed with him, that they now vote entirely in obedience to his instructions. He now expects that at the next general election he will, by careful management, obtain the absolute majority he requires to carry through his new taxation and commercial policy.

If Bismarck should ever die suddenly from indigestion, which his doctors fear and predict, the difficulty of reforming the general abuses which his personal administration has created will be great, and will impose a hard and ungrateful task on the sovereign, who will have to find and appoint the ministers capable of reestablishing constitutionalism in Prussia.

(a) What does Lady Russell mean by the 'initiated' (line 1)?
(b) What are the abuses in government which she indicates in this account?
(c) What is meant by 'appointed a ministry of clerks out of the government offices' (line 12)?
(d) If you were Bismarck, how would you defend yourself against these allegations?
Source: An account of the relationship between Bismarck and the Emperor and his style of
        government written by Lady Emily Russell, the wife of the British ambassador in 1880.
        G. E. Buckle (ed.), *The Letters of Queen Victoria*, second series, 3 vols (Longman, Green,
        1926–30). Extract quoted in D. G. Williamson, *Bismarck and Germany 1862–1890*
        (Longman, 1986).

9 In Illus. 14.1 (p. 172), Bismarck is saying to the kitchen-maid: 'You can't make omelettes without
   breaking eggs':

(a) What does this imply about the relationship between Bismarck and William I?

(b) How successfully, and on what occasion, did Bismarck use his powers to 'break eggs'?

10 From Illus. 14.2 (p. 174):

(a) What can we tell about the new technology of warfare being used by the 1870s?

(b) Why were railways so significant, and what role would the telegraph network play?

(c) How would the new Prussian 'needle-gun' breech-loading rifles affect the conduct of the war?

The New Imperialism

Introduction

The last quarter of the nineteenth century saw a dramatic increase in imperial expansion. This contrasts with the earlier period when colonies had been regarded as an unjustified expense, and formal political control was seen as an irrelevance when the commercial benefits could be enjoyed anyway in an epoch of free trade. In 1852, Benjamin Disraeli had described colonies as 'millstones around our neck'. Twenty years later, he publicly endorsed a policy of imperial expansion in the Crystal Palace speech.

15.1 The course of the New Imperialism

The movement towards expansion was associated largely with the western European maritime nations, but the landward expansion of the USA and Russia was part of the general pattern. The British empire was increased in extent by 50 per cent to cover a fifth of the globe's surface and include 400 million subjects. The French empire grew from 700,000 to 6 million square miles and from 5 million to 52 million subjects. Germany had a million square miles and 14 million subjects by 1900. Italy collected 185,000 square miles – although the soil was 'very light' as Lord Salisbury wryly remarked. On the whole, the expansion was concentrated in two regions, both largely unsuitable for white settlement:

1   *Africa.* In 1870 a tenth of the continent – mostly coastal colonies – was under European control. By 1900, only a tenth was left independent.
2   *East and south-east Asia.* In particular in China and the region once known generally as Indo-China.

15.2 The 'Scramble for Africa' (see Map 15.1)

From 1879 onwards the *Congo basin* became a focus for the increasingly conflicting interests of three European states. Henry Morton Stanley, the famous explorer, was acting as the agent for the International Association for the Exploration and Civilisation of Africa chaired by King Leopold of the Belgians. From 1880 the French adventurer de Brazza was also making treaties with Congolese chieftains. From June 1884 Germany was making claims to the Cameroons and Togoland.

(a) The Berlin Conference (1884–5)

With the Congo becoming a matter of international rivalry, Bismarck called an international conference at Berlin. The outcome was:

1 *Recognition of the 'Independent State of the Congo'.* In effect until 1908 it was the private estate of King Leopold, who ruthlessly exploited it. There were also guarantees of free trade and navigation.
2 *Agreement on the doctrine of effective occupation.* It was this which did much to encourage the speculative scramble from 1885.

(b) The partition of Africa

In west Africa, Britain established colonies in Nigeria, the Gold Coast and a protectorate over the territories of the Ashanti. France concentrated her efforts in Senegal and Dahomey. It was the prospect of linking the latter with her territories to the north west and the Red Sea coast which led the two states into confrontations in Nigeria in 1897–8 and at Fashoda in 1898 (see Section 22.3(d)). Meanwhile from the late 1880s onwards the 'empire' of the Sultan of Zanzibar was carved up between Britain and Germany into the colonies of Kenya, Uganda, Tanganyika and Zanzibar. In the south, British speculators headed by the millionaire Cecil Rhodes and working through the British South Africa Company gained Rhodesia. By 1898, Rhodes's dream of a British controlled belt from 'Cape to Cairo' seemed very likely, as British troops reconquered the Sudan on behalf of Egypt which had been a virtual British protectorate since 1882. France had formally annexed Algeria in 1848 and moved on logically to establish a protectorate over Tunis in 1881 (see Section 16.4(c)) but found Morocco a far more problematic subject (see Section 22.5(c), 22.8). Italy had little choice but to concentrate on Abyssinia (see Section 17.5(c)) and Libya (see Section 17.7(c)).

15.3 East and South-East Asia

This area was dominated by two developments.

(a) Russian expansion eastwards

Partly in compensation for the defeat in the Crimea, Russian expansion in the Caucasus and Turkestan accelerated throughout the 1860s–80s and led to recurrent differences with Britain over the status of Afghanistan, Persia and then Tibet. Not until 1907 was a general agreement reached (see Section 22.6) which pacified British neuroses about the vulnerability of India.

(b) The decay of Manchu China

From the 1840s onwards the rapidly failing central authorities of China were forced to concede a range of diplomatic, commercial and territorial concessions to Britain, France, Russia, Germany and a rapidly westernising Japan. By the late 1890s, China was on the verge of partition as Japan established a virtual protectorate over Korea fol-

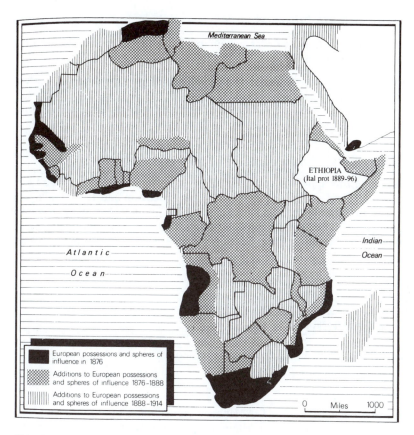

Map 15.1 The colonisation of Africa (1876–1914)

lowing the Sino-Japanese War of 1894–5 and as Russian influence grew in Manchuria. It was this predatory situation which resulted in the Anglo-Japanese Alliance of 1902 (see Section 22.3(f)) and the Russo-Japanese war of 1905 (see Section 22.5(c)) which had significant repercussions on international relations and on the Russian domestic situation (see Section 22.5(c)). The decline of imperial China was also largely responsible for the ability of France to win control over most of the old Annamese Empire.

15.4 The causes of the New Imperialism

The debate between historians about the motives behind this surge of European expansionism depends very much on how 'imperialism' is defined. Indeed the problem of definition led the eminent historian Keith Hancock to dismiss it in despair as 'no word for scholars'. It is traditionally interpreted to mean formal annexation and political rule; on the other hand, it could mean indirect 'control' by economic and cultural influences. This difference in terminology is the basis for two diametrically opposed theories, stressing 'discontinuity' and 'continuity' respectively.

(a) 'Discontinuity' theories

It could be argued that this was a genuinely new development based on changing European circumstances in the 1870s and 1880s:

1 *Industrial development.* The growing competition for new markets, sources of raw materials and outlets for investment.
2 *A changed European political situation.* A new tide of rivalries, tensions and ambitions following the unification of Italy and Germany.

(b) 'Continuity' theories

The essence of this approach is that the 1870s simply saw a change in the type of imperialism. An analysis of British motives by J. A. Robinson and R. E. Gallagher in their article 'The Imperialism of Free Trade' in 1953 suggested that an older, cheaper form of informal imperial exploitation was passing into a new form of direct control and formal intervention because of non-European nationalism and resistance and new strategic considerations.

15.5 Economic theories

There are, in addition, a range of economic theories.

(a) Surplus capital

The English radical economist J. A. Hobson argued in his book *Imperialism* (1902) that imperialism was a perversion of capitalism, the result of the endeavour of the great controllers of industry to broaden the channel for the flow of their surplus wealth by the exercise of illegitimate and undemocratic influences over governments and mass opinion as the level of industrialisation in western Europe became so developed that the rate of return on investment fell. As a supporter of the capitalist system Hobson argued that the real solution was to level out inequalities of wealth to increase domestic consumption. Lenin, the enemy of capitalism, followed a similar line in *Imperialism: the Highest Stage of Capitalism* (1916) when he argued that the First World War was the ultimate outcome of the world being eventually divided up by the capitalist powers, who were then forced to turn upon each other in their pursuit of opportunities for investment. His famous definition was:

> Imperialism is capitalism in the stage of development in which the domination of monopolies and finance capital has taken shape; in which the export of capital has acquired pronounced importance; in which the division of the world by the international trusts has begun; and in which the partition of all territory of the earth by the greatest capitalist countries has been completed.

In fact these ideas have serious flaws:

1 *The links between industry and imperialism* are difficult to establish. Only in Germany is there clear evidence of connections between banks, heavy industry and militarist and colonialist circles.
2 *The degrees of economic growth and imperial activity* do not match. France and Germany still had high rates of return on investment at home; Italy was virtually undeveloped and imported capital, Portugal was almost bankrupt.
3 *The relative unattractiveness of the new colonies.* The vast bulk of European

investment after the 1870s flowed in fact to independent European states or the Americas. There were few exceptions to the tendency for colonial trade to remain only an insignificant proportion of metropolitan commerce. Even in the case of Britain where it was 25 per cent this was largely accounted for by Canada, Australasia, India and South Africa.

(b) *Competition for markets and raw materials*

Certainly by the late nineteenth century there was an intensifying competition, which was associated with the revival of protectionism. Even in Britain, long identified with free trade, there were demands for 'Fair trade'. On the other hand, critics of this thesis have argued that the annexed territories were unlikely to provide lucrative markets or vital raw materials. This should be modified:

1   *The importance of specific trade links to particular industries.* Some raw materials were very important – for instance, the vegetable oil of the Niger was vital for lubricating machinery.
2   *The power of illusions.* In 1866 Bismarck remarked 'all the advantages claimed for the mother country are for the most part illusory', but it is also true that even exaggerated expectations about markets and colonial riches could be a stimulus to colonial ventures.

(c) *Outlets for emigration*

A lot was made of colonies as receptacles for surplus population in Germany and Italy. In fact by 1914 there were more Germans living in Paris than in all of the German colonies together. There was very little emigration to the new colonies; of the 60 million people who left Europe in this period 85 per cent went to the Americas.

15.6 An extension of European diplomacy

D. K. Fieldhouse says of the new imperialism that it was the extension into the periphery of the political struggle in Europe'. There are two main aspects to this.

(a) *A source of compensations and diplomatic advantage* (see Illus. 15.1)

Since the powers were deadlocked in Europe, colonialism was a means of affecting the balance:

1   *To exert influence on European alignments.* Bismarck, for instance, was involved in the Berlin Conference partly to distract France from European affairs. He also used imperial issues to help him find political allies in Germany, and once remarked 'all this colonial business is a sham but we need it for the elections'.
2   *A source of power and prestige in Europe.* Léon Gambetta was a very powerful supporter of imperial power as an indirect route to *revanche* (see Section 19.3(c)). In contrast were the views of anti-imperialists like Camille Pellatan – 'Alsace-Lorraine is still under the Prussian jackboot and our army is leaving for Tonkin'. The prestige factor was an important one, and especially in the case of France with its glorious imperial past, need for republican respectability and national grievance after 1870. It was also important in explaining the involvement of the self assertive new states. In the case of Portugal it had more to do with the reflection of

Illus. 15.1   On the swoop! (From *Punch*)

ON THE SWOOP!

Source: I. R. Mitchell, *Bismarck and the Development of Germany* (Holmes Macdougall, 1980) p. 114.

Q   Why does this cartoon give a rather unfavourable impression of German imperialism in Africa?

weakness and vulnerability. However, 'prestige' was not the real impetus. It merely raises the question of why prestige should be sought in imperialism rather than other outlets.

(b) 'International anarchy'

In *Europe since Napoleon* David Thomson sees the frantic nature of the imperial expansion as being caused by increasing concern at the direction being taken by international relations. Territories were seized sometimes simply to beat other powers to them. As Lord Rosebery described the process in 1893 'we are engaged ... in the language of mining, in "pegging out claims for the future". We have to consider not what we want now, but what we shall want in the future'. Thomson draws the conclusion 'To say, as it was often said after 1918, that imperialism had led to war, was only half the story; it was also true that the menace of war had led to imperialism'.

15.7 The peripheral explanation of Imperialism

According to Robinson and Gallagher, British imperial expansion had gone on uninterruptedly before the 1880s 'informally if possible and formally if necessary'. The result was an accumulation of £1000 million in overseas investment between 1815–80, of which only a sixth was in the formal empire. At the same time a growing list of territories was annexed to protect economic and strategic interests. Now in the 1880s the balance between two types of imperialism began to change, as a result of two factors.

(a) 'Protonationalisms' and local crises

The European tie tended to produce a gap between a westernised élite and the native population. The result was the stimulating of traditionalist reactions, with elements of nationalism also to be discerned. Typical were the revolts by Egyptian army officers in 1881–2, the Boxer Rebellion in China in 1899 and the Boer Wars of 1879–81 and 1899–1902. Such disturbances and challenges and local crises lay behind the need to formalise control of the regions concerned. Of course, the local crises could be as much the result of European 'sub-imperialists' seeking to pursue their own individual expansionist objectives as much as of the native population; hence the insubordinate expansion of French governors and commanders in Senegal and the Sudan in the 1860s and 1870s.

(b) Imperial security

Robinson and Gallagher deny the importance of economic motives. In 1882 Britain occupied Egypt to protect the *threatened routes to India* and defeat the nationalist uprisings. France was disturbed by this unilateral action because she had interests in Egypt as well. Compensations were sought in west Africa and Bismarck joined in for diplomatic reasons. A scramble had begun. All the Berlin Conference did was establish some *rules*; the accidental chain reaction was 'a remarkable freak'.

(c) Criticisms of the Gallagher–Robinson theory

This theory is a very complex one, and has been extremely influential. Nevertheless, there are weaknesses:

1 *Chronological inconsistency.* The theory depends upon a sequence of events, but it seems that the French forward policy started in West Africa before the summer of 1882 and the French government was keen to conciliate Britain in 1882 and reach agreement over Egypt.

2 *It is limited in application.* By definition 'peripheral' or 'excentric' explanations of imperialism do not easily lend themselves to global generalisations. Imperialism was a world-wide phenomenon, but only Britain and African partition are covered by the theory. It is doubtful whether it could be extended to other states and other areas of imperial expansion.

3 *Exaggeration of the peripheral pressures.* Certainly there were examples of imperial expansion unrelated to any prior nationalist resistance; the Congo Free state was the creation solely of King Leopold's economic and territorial greed; and Bismarck was responding entirely to internal domestic pressure.

4 *'The official mind'.* Only official archives were used, and the 'India in danger' argument was not related to economic motives. In fact it could well have been a mask for self-interested financiers and businessmen wanting intervention, provoking crises and putting pressure on the government.

5 *The anti-imperialism of free trade.* It is very difficult to establish any standards as to which territory before the 1870s qualified to be part of the substitute internal empire. In terms of economic commitment the USA might be included, but Canada should be excluded because of its economic relationship with the USA. There is also evidence that the strength of informal control was insufficient to prevent colonies acting with considerable independence – certainly in the case of Peru and Argentina.

15.8 Enabling factors

Apart from the range of motives attributed to the imperialist nations there are other factors which account for the actual *timing* of the expansion. Resources and attitudes which had not been present in the earlier century were now in existence. They made the hitherto more inaccessible tropical territories much more vulnerable to annexation and exploitation.

(a) *Technological and scientific advances*

Especially in the following spheres:

1 *Armaments.* With the development of the breech-loading rifle and the machine gun and advances in the sphere of field artillery, European troops had an overwhelming advantage over most native forces. The annihilation of a British force by Zulus at *Isandhlwana* in 1879 (see Illus. 15.2 and 15.3) and an Italian army in 1896 (see Section 17.5(c), were wholly exceptional events.

2 *Communications.* The railway, the steamship and the telegraph meant that troops, wealth and resources could be mobilised and deployed far more regularly and effectively. To some extent the desire to improve imperial communications became an actual end of imperial expansion – e.g., the establishment of coaling bases and cable posts, the vision of the Cape–Cairo railway.

3 *Tropical medicine.* Most of the major advances were made in this period. In 1897 Ross traced the connection between malaria and the female Anopheles mosquito. Robert Koch isolated the *cholera vibrio* in 1883 and in 1892 Haffkine introduced a

Ilus. 15.2   *The Battle of Isandhlwana* (1879)

Source: Oil painting by Charles Edwin Fripp, 1885 (The National Army Museum).

Fripp was a special artist for *The Graphic*. This painting shows the closing stages of the battle with the remainder of the British army reduced to a tiny square against the Zulu attack. All but 55 men of the force of 1700 were killed. In the background is the hill which closely resembled the Sphinx badge of the 24th Regiment which made up the bulk of the ill-fated column.

Q   What do you think is the theme of this picture? How does Fripp seek to influence the emotions of the viewer?

vaccine. The relationship between yellow fever and the Tiger mosquito was traced in 1881. Only after the Spanish American War did an American medical team investigating it in Havana unearth all of its secrets, and the Panama Canal was finally made possible.

(b)   *Mass politics and 'Social Imperialism'*

The term 'social imperialism' is used to refer to circumstances where political leaders resort to imperial expansion to unite the nation and defuse social tensions and conflicts at home, while avoiding significant domestic reform.

The concept was developed by Hans-Ulrich Wehler to explain the bid by Bismarck for colonies in Africa and the Pacific in 1884–5 and the *Weltpolitik* of pre-1914 Germany (see Section 18.8). Although the view of Bismarck as a social imperialist has been moderated, the motive does seem very attributable to radical conservatives like Joseph Chamberlain in Britain in the 1890s and Benjamin Disraeli in the 1870s, and to the conservative republican party of Gambetta, Ferry and the Méline in France in the 1880s and 1890s. The new slum-dwelling, semi-literate urban masses were increasingly susceptible to the imperialist appeals of popular literature and politicians, but so also were the middle classes who never fully lived up to the pacifist and rational ideals of free trade liberalism. Lord Derby wrote to Gladstone in 1884: 'This passion for annexation and consequent contempt of economy is not more to my taste than to yours – but it seems to be the dominant idea of the democracy ... and I think it will not be a mere passing fashion.' There were two attractions to exploit:

PUNCH, OR THE LONDON CHARIVARI.

A LESSON.

From Punch, *1 March 1879, drawn by Sir John Tenniel, alluding to the sharp lesson John Bull had been taught by the Zulus at Isandhlwana.*

1   *The escapism of foreign adventures.* Imperial expansion could be a means of distracting the attention of the masses from real grievances and proper demands for better conditions. The 'literature of action' proliferated with Rider Haggard's 'colonial butcheries' and G. A. Henty's popular adventure stories. This was also the period of the development of a jingoist popular press of which W. T. Stead remarked in 1898 'much of our modern journalism is the most potent weapon yet invented by the devil for banishing peace and goodwill from the earth'.

2   *'A bread and butter question'.* The economic aspects were attractive. Many prominent socialists and radicals supported imperialism. Karl Pearson assured working-class Germans: 'The day when we cease to hold our own among the nations

will be the day of catastrophe for our workers at home ... the daily bread of our millions of workers depends on their having somebody to work for ... our strength depends on our colonies.' Of course, in reverse, imperial expansion could be seen as strengthening 'national efficiency' at home and reinforcing the imperial drive.

(c) *'The tidal mood of mankind'*

By the late nineteenth century there was a very obvious tendency to regard all non-European societies as backward, and to see them as unable to assimilate and adapt to western ways. This was how incidents such as the Indian Mutiny (1857) and the Morant Bay Rebellion in Jamaica (1865) were interpreted. This view had several aspects:

1 *'The strongest tend to be the best'*. Darwin's theory of revolution could easily be perverted to apply to humanity as the basis for a sort of 'imperialism of inevitability':

– *'Justice in nature'* meant the ranking of the superior over the inferior, best over worst. J. Novicov in his *La Politique Internationale* (1886) remarked: 'If one animal is less perfect than another he must serve as prey. If one society is less perfect than another, the first must work for the second'.

– *'The path of progress'* must therefore be a rather bloody route of natural selection. Karl Pearson remarked in 1905: 'The path of progress is strewn with the wreck of nations ... these dead peoples are in very truth the stepping stones on which mankind has arisen to the higher intellectual and deeper emotional life of today.'

– *Militarism.* War and conflict were the mechanism for purification and the antidote to social and moral decay. Lord Wolseley saw a 'military spirit' as 'the purifier of civilisation, its defence against enemies from without and degeneracy from within'. Joseph Schumpeter defined imperialism as: '... the objectless disposition on the part of a state to unlimited forcible expansion'. He attributed it to the influence of old pre-capitalist social groups swayed by militarist values.

2 *Racialism.* The sensational reports of explorers such as Henry Morton Stanley who emphasised the more distasteful aspects of African society in books such as *Darkest Africa* reinforced a latent racialism. Karl Pearson said of this:

You may hope for a time ... when the white man and the dark shall share the soil between them ... But believe me, when that day comes mankind will no longer progress; there will be nothing to check the fertility of inferior stock and the relentless law of heredity will not be controlled and girded by selection.

3 *Imperial mission.* Humane and liberal thinkers could be brought to support the movement by seeing conquest and alien rule as necessary means to the extension of the benefits of civilisation. Lord Rosebery was not the only man to see God's hand at work in the British Empire: 'Do we not trace in this less the energy and fortune of a race than the supreme direction of the Almighty?' This view, of course, was popularised by Rudyard Kipling's poems *The White Man's Burden* and *Recessional*. The 'imperialism of benevolence' and of 'obligation' was an important factor from the 1860s, especially when religious and humanitarian groups began to exercise more and more influence upon government policy.

The processes of the evolution and propagation of such views are still unclear. Not only should popular and juvenile literature and the expansion of the periodical and newspaper press be looked to but also, in the case of Britain, the ethos of the boys' public schools.

15.9 Conclusion

The course of *European international relations* was also affected by imperialism. The influence could be seen as working in two directions:

1   *A cause of disagreement and conflict.* 'Colonial collisions' were numerous. They included the Fashoda Crisis (see Section 22.3(d), the Kruger *Telegramme* (see Section 22.3(c)) and the various Morocco Crises (see Sections 22.5(c) and 22.8). On the other hand, the division of Europe into alliance blocs does not seem to have been affected; priority was given to European affairs over colonial issues.

2   *The last frontier?* European tensions could be eased by using cheap, colonial compensations. By 1904 the 'elbow room' was limited and Europe was thrown back in upon itself.

Questions

1   What part did economic motives play in the colonial expansion of the European powers in this period?   [OC]
2   What do you understand by the term 'the scramble for Africa'? Why did the European powers take part?   [OC]
3   Should European imperial expansion be explained only in economic terms?   [OC]
4   Why did the major powers acquire new colonies between 1870 and 1890?   [OX]
5   What, if anything, was new in the 'New Imperialism'?   [NEAB]
6   'The product of political ambition and international rivalry'; 'the answer to overproduction and overpopulation'. Consider and explain these two theories of nineteenth-century imperialism in Africa.   [CAM, adapted]
7   Why were European countries engaged in a 'scramble for Africa' after 1880?   [CAM]
8   Study Sources A, B and C and then answer the questions which follow.

Source A: Kipling's imperialism.

> Take up the White Man's burden –
> Send forth the best ye breed –
> Go bind your sons to exile
> To serve your captives' need;
> To wait in heavy harness
> On fluttered folk and wild –
> Your new-caught, sullen peoples,
> Half devil and half child.

> Take up the White Man's Burden –
> In patience to abide,
> To veil the threat of terror
> And check the show of pride;
> By open speech and simple,
> An hundred times made plain,
> To seek another's profit,
> And work another's gain.

> Take up the White Man's burden –
> The savage wars of peace –
> Fill full the mouth of Famine
> And bid the sickness cease;
> And when your goal is nearest
> The end for others sought,
> Watch Sloth and heathen Folly
> Bring all your hope to nought.

(a) Source A is the first three verses of one of Kipling's most famous poems about imperialism. Apart from the popularity of the subjects he chose, what other factors were increasing the size of his readership by the late nineteenth century?

(b) Kipling is usually seen as the portrayer of a glamorous image of imperialism. According to this poem, what sort of pain and suffering did Kipling see as the real truth of imperialism?

(c) Is there any indication in his words that Kipling saw the native peoples of the Empire as 'inferior'?

(d) What is the irony involved in Kipling's use of the word 'captives' (line 4)?

Source: R. Kipling, *The White Man's Burden* (1899).

Source B: The battle of Omdurman.

On came the Dervishes, a magnificent army such as the world had not seen since the old, dead days of breastplate and shield and battle-axe. The Soudanese and Egyptian troops fired steady volleys that ripped great gaps in the advancing host. The Maxims swept down lines of men and narrowed the great living block just as one might reduce a sheet of paper by tearing off strips. The shrapnel bowled them over in forties and fifties at a time, but yet the Dervishes managed to come blade to blade with our men before they died.

But – miracle of miracles! – 'Gippy' was fighting coolly and steadily as though he wrote himself Briton. No flurry, no hurry; just a cartridge pushed home, a steady aim – and a dead man. And so on again and again.

The enemy were repulsed, but without a moment's breathing space. 'Fighting Mac' found himself menaced in flank by another force. Calmly as though he had been exercising his troops on parade he wheeled them round to meet the fresh attack. The Dervishes rushed on as though determined to die, since to conquer was impossible. They went down in hundreds; they came on in twos and threes, never halting and never faltering until they fell shattered with shell or riddled with shot.

But their cause was hopeless. British troops came up at the double and finished the work that 'Gippy' had done so well. The power of Mahdism was broken for ever, and 'Fighting Mac' had dealt the final blow. Through all that day his was the only force that was in reality in a critical position, and with troops that had a record of cowardice behind them he had accomplished heroes' work. No one will ever know how many Dervishes died on that day. Thousands of the wounded must have perished out in the waterless desert, but certainly the loss could not have been much under twenty thousand. It was a horrid necessity to kill all those gallant savages, yet it was for the best, since it relieved the Soudan from a grinding tyranny, and put a final end to the despotism that had wasted the land ever since Gordon had perished thirteen years before.

(a) Which other peoples were fighting alongside the British troops?

(b) What attitude is displayed in this passage towards the Dervishes (lines 1–2 and 12–15)?

(c) What did Cadett think about the qualities of the soldiers allied with Britain (lines 2–3, 7–9 and 16–20)? Would you say that Cadett was racialist in his attitudes?

(d) What degree of advantage did Kitchener's army have in terms of weaponry? What were 'Maxims' (line 3) and 'shrapnel' (line 5)?

(e) What was the vital contribution made to the victory by 'Fighting Mac' and his men (lines 10–12)?

(f) Why was it a 'horrid necessity to kill all those gallant savages' (lines 22–23)?

Source: From a children's book published in 1903. This is an account of the battle of Omdurman in 1898 where the Dervishes were defeated by General Kitchener. Since 1885, when the army of the Mahdi (or Christ) had captured Khartoum and killed General Gordon, the Soudan (Sudan) had been in the hands of the Dervishes and Omdurman was their capital city. H. Cadett, *The Boys Book of Battles* (Pearson, 1903).

Illus. 15.4   The Death of General Gordon at Khartoum (1885)

Source: Mansell Collection.

This is the classic depiction of the imagined fate of General Gordon on the morning of 26 January 1885. Standing on the veranda of his residency the great Victorian hero confronts his killers with supreme courage and self assurance. In fact, there are several different accounts of his death. They include at least one eyewitness from the Mahdist army who believed that the general died fighting in the streets of Khartoum with a revolver in his hand.

Q   The manner of the death of Gordon assumed considerable significance in the story of British imperial activity in Egypt and the Sudan. Why do you think this was so?

Source C: The Path of Progress

History shows me one way, and one way only, in which a state of civilisation has been produced, namely, the struggle of race with race, and the survival of the physically and mentally fitter race.

This dependence of progress on the survival of the fitter race, terribly black as it may seem to some of you, gives the struggle for existence its redeeming features; it is the fiery crucible out of which comes the finer metal. You may hope for a time when the sword shall be turned into the ploughshare, when American and German and English traders shall no longer compete in the markets of the world for raw materials, for their food supply, when the white man and the dark shall share the soil between then, and each till it as he lists. But believe me, when that day comes mankind will no longer progress; there will be nothing to check the fertility of inferior stock; and the relentless law of heredity will not be controlled and guided by natural selection. Man will stagnate ...

The path of progress is strewn with the wreck of nations; traces are everywhere to be seen of the hecatombs of inferior races, and of victims who found not the narrow way to the greater perfection. Yet these dead peoples are, in very truth, the stepping stones on which mankind has arisen to the higher intellectual and deeper emotional life of to-day.

(a) What are the assumptions underlying this 'analysis' of race relations?
(b) How could this view be compared to the natural biological world?
(c) Pearson argues not only that the stronger peoples and races will overpower the weaker, but that this is also a triumph for the 'better' peoples and races. In this passage, where can you detect that view?
(d) Can you express an alternative, more positive view of the role played by multiracial societies in the development of civilisation?

Source: Karl Pearson, *National Life from the Standpoint of Science* (London, 1905).

9 From Illus. 15.1 (p. 190):
(a) What is the significance of the German eagle 'swooping' into the colonial field?
(b) How does Illus. 15.1 convey a hostile attitude to the process of colonisation?
(c) Why is the cartoon by implication anti-German?

16 Bismarck and International Relations 1871–90

Introduction

In view of his activities between 1871 and 1890 it is not surprising that this period of diplomacy is frequently named after Bismarck. Through wars as an aspect of calculated diplomacy, he had built Germany; now he resorted to diplomacy to avoid international wars which would disturb the consolidation of the new state. He announced: 'We have no further demands to make ... We have enough annexed populations'.

16.1 The objectives of Bismarck's foreign policy

Fundamentally Bismarck sought to maintain peace and equilibrium in Europe. To do this involved:

1 *The isolation of France.* Since the desire for revenge made France the most likely threat, she had to be isolated from potential allies.
2 *The maintenance of good relations between Austria and Russia.* This was inspired by the need to:

– Avoid being entangled in a war between them which could be triggered off by their conflict of interest in the Balkans.
– Exorcise the spectre of a war on two fronts against a Franco-Russian alliance. In 1870 Bismarck had accepted the neutralisation of the Black Sea clauses to avert this danger (see Section 14.8(e)).
– Strengthen the forces of conservatism and anti-revolution in Europe against the challenges of socialism and republicanism. The best Bismarck could hope to achieve was an arrangement with both Russia and Austria to be '*à trois* in a world governed by five powers'.

(a) Changing circumstances

As in the 1860s Bismarck's real talent lay in pursuing these objectives amidst changing circumstances. In particular these included:

1 *The instability of French 'revanchisme'.* The right-wing politicians tended to be more aggressive and militarist than the republicans, although the latter were not necessarily less nationalist. Bismarck not only took advantage of such divisions, he also deliberately used the threat of 'revanchist' agitation to help his policies in

Germany; in 1875 and 1887 he skilfully used the 'Fatherland in danger' appeal.

2 *Slav nationalism.* This was a period of growing unrest among the Slav subjects of the Ottoman Empire and Austria. Together with the development of Pan-Slavism in Russia (see Section 10.5(b)), this was an explosive combination which could threaten Balkan stability and Russo-Austrian relations.

3 *Imperialism.* The new wave of imperialism (see Section 15) could be a source of deals and links as well as friction. Bismarck himself was not 'a colonies man', but did see advantages in imperial activities, including the distraction of France.

4 *Public opinion.* In general there was the growing influence of the opinion of more literate and more politically involved populations. Even of Russia the British politician Charles Dilke wrote: 'power . . . is the Emperor and the Moscow newspaper emperor, Katkov'. Bismarck could not afford to have German prestige suffer and lose popular support, which was a very fickle factor.

(b) *The alliance system*

The result of these objectives and variables was a series of formal alliances and treaties, deals and relationships.

16.2 The *Dreikaiserbund*

Initially Bismarck relied upon a less formal relationship.

(a) *Russian and Austrian friendship*

Capitalising upon his past relationship with Russia and the coming to power of the pro-German Magyar *Count Andrassy* as the Austrian foreign minister, he achieved a loose league of friendship in a series of meetings of the three men in 1872–3. There was no alliance, although there was an agreement to support each other in the event of an unprovoked attack. The flimsy nature of the arrangement was revealed by the events of the next four years.

(b) *The French war scare of 1875*

France recovered very quickly. In 1875 a reorganisation of the French army under a right-wing monarchist government (see Section 19.2) coincided with Bismarck being engaged in the *Kulturkampf* (see Section 18.5) and having difficulty in getting his Army Bill passed. To win support at home he deliberately used the fear of war. He was responsible in April for the publication in newspapers of the disturbing article 'Is war in sight?'. However, while Austria indicated her support for Germany, Russia displayed an alarming tendency to consider intervention which suggested that France might not be so isolated. Far more serious, though, were the events in the Balkans between 1875 and 1878.

16.3 The Bulgarian crisis (1875–8) (see Map 16.1)

Bismarck dismissed Balkan issues as not worth 'the bones of a Pomeranian musketeer'. But in 1875 the Balkans did become a vital interest when Russo-Austrian relations

Map 16.1 The Balkans according to the Treaties of San Stefano and Berlin (1878)

were seriously threatened by a crisis in the region. The problem arose from Slav nationalism being fed by a number of factors:

1   *The resentment of the Ausgleich of 1867* (see Section 21.5(c)) which was felt by Slavs who saw the Germans and Magyars given a preferred position.
2   *The existence of the independent Slav state of Serbia* which exerted a magnetic attraction is an example and focus of nationalism.
3   *Pan-Slavist propaganda* emanating from Russia which could be as dangerous to Austria as to the Ottoman Empire. The appointment of the extremist General Ignatyev as Russian ambassador at Constantinople reflected the influence of the 'hawks' at the Tsar's court.

Between 1875–8 a chain of events unfolded which threatened international security.

(a)   *The outbreak of rebellion in Bosnia and Herzegovina (1875)*

Initially the revolt of Greek Orthodox Slavs against the Ottoman Empire did not threaten Russo-Austrian relations. The Tsar joined in with Germany and Austria in urging reforms on the Ottoman Empire in the *Andrassy Note* of 1875, and the *Berlin Memorandum* of 1876. The British prime minister Disraeli suspected a new attempt to partition the Ottoman Empire, and refused to be involved. In fact, the situation grew worse. Revolts broke out in Bulgaria, there were anti-French riots in Constantinople and at this worst possible moment the weak-minded Murad IV became Sultan.

(b) *The Serbo-Turkish War (1876)*

In June, Serbia and Montenegro went to war with the Ottoman Empire. Nevertheless Russo-Austrian relations were still such that they could agree on considerable territorial changes in the Balkans if Serbia and Montenegro won. This *Reichstadt Agreement* was premature, because they were soundly thrashed. However, the Turkish suppression of the revolts in Bulgaria was so vicious that public opinion was outraged, especially in Britain where Gladstone used the 'Bulgarian Crisis' as an issue against Disraeli. A British attempt to get the Ottoman Empire to agree to reforms was also inconclusive.

(c) *The Russo-Turkish War (1877)*

With Pan-Slav hysteria at its peak Tsar Alexander decided to intervene. He made a preliminary agreement with Austria which would reward her neutrality with Bosnia and Herzegovina, and guaranteed that no large state would be created in the Balkans. In April 1877 Russian troops invaded Ottoman territory in the Balkans. The unexpected happened. At the town of *Plevna*, despite the presence of Todleben to coordinate the siege, Turkish troops held out for five months. By then British public opinion had swung round to see the Turks as the underdogs. When Russian troops finally broke through the British fleet was conspicuously moved to Besika Bay to warn them off the Straits.

(d) *The Treaty of San Stefano*

Russia then proceeded to make a sweeping rearrangement of the Balkans in the peace treaty with the Ottoman Empire. By its terms:

1   *Russia gained Black Sea territories* including the great fortress base at Kars and took southern Bessarabia from Rumania.
2   *Austria was given a protectorate over Bosnia and Herzegovina.*
3   Serbia and Montenegro were enlarged and *Rumania* was given the Dobrudja as compensation for her loss of Bessarabia.
4   *A large Bulgarian state* was created from the Black Sea through Macedonia to the Aegean at Salonika, it was to be occupied by Russia for two years.

(e) *The Treaty of Berlin*

Russia had overreached herself. However, it was Britain rather than Austria or Germany who made her reconsider. Troops and ships were moved to Malta in a clear warning. Disraeli made a series of agreements which underpinned a new structure in the Balkans. Russia agreed to abandon the 'big Bulgaria', Austria's rights over Bosnia and Herzegovina were confirmed and the Ottoman Empire agreed to give Cyprus to Britain as payment for her commitment to defend it against Russia. These agreements were the basis of the treaty produced at the *Congress of Berlin* in 1878 chaired by Bismarck as 'honest broker'. The fundamental change was that Bulgaria was divided into three elements. *Macedonia* remained under Turkish rule. In the south east Roumelia was given home rule under a Christian governor. Only the *residue* was to be an independent state. In fact the new treaty left several problems:

1   *The dissatisfaction of the Balkan states.* Rumania resented the loss of southern Bessarabia; Serbia, the Austrian occupation of Bosnia and Herzegovina; Macedonia, the loss of an outlet to the sea. Bulgaria resented strongly the retreat from the frontiers of San Stefano.
2   *The humiliation of the Ottoman Empire.* Not only had its territories been bartered around but it also had to agree to internal reforms and guarantee the safety of the Armenian Christians.
3   *The anger of Russia.* Russia's diplomatic defeat was felt acutely against the background of the events of 1877. Britain and Austria had both gained territories from Russian efforts, but had forced her to back down over Bulgaria. Nor had the backing of Germany been forthcoming.

16.4 Bismarck's alliance system (1879–82)

In these circumstances, Bismarck moved towards a more formal system of alliances.

(a)   *The Dual Alliance (1879)*

Bismarck's neutrality during the Bulgarian Crisis had suggested a preference for Austria in the last resort. The alliance of 1879 was intended to block any link between Austria and France; it gave a mutual guarantee of neutrality in the event of an attack by another state unless it was aided by Russia. It was secret, valid for five years and renewable. The danger with it was that Russia might be driven into alliance with France or Austria might be encouraged into Balkan adventures, but Bismarck in office was the greatest obstacle to either of these outcomes.

(b)   *The* Dreikaiserbund *(1881)*

Russian desires to escape isolation enabled Bismarck to revive the tripartite connection:

1   If one of the three states was at war with a fourth the other two would remain neutral.
2   No changes should take place in the Balkans without agreement and a division into spheres of influence at the Serbo-Bulgarian frontier was implied.
3   Austria reserved the right to annex Bosnia and Herzegovina in the future.
4   A British claim to free passage at all times through the Straits which had been made at the Congress of Berlin was declared to be not acceptable, and Turkey was warned not to agree to it.

The Dual Alliance was not replaced. A war between Russia and her two allies was not out of the question. On the other hand, an attempt was made to limit the likelihood of conflict in the Balkans. Austria followed this up by making alliances with Serbia in 1881 and Rumania in 1883.

(c)   The Triple Alliance (1882)

Although Italy's relations with Austria were poor, Bismarck hoped that an alliance might help to reduce this antagonism. Franco-Italian relations had deteriorated very sharply recently over the French establishment of a protectorate over Tunis (see Section 19.3(c)). The result was the treaty of May 1882, a five-year renewable agreement:

1   If Italy was attacked by France, Austria and Germany would go to her aid.
2   If one of the three powers was attacked by two or more powers, the others would support it. This covered the prospect of a war between Austria and France and Russia.
3   If one of the three allies made war upon a power which threatened it, the other two would maintain 'benevolent neutrality'.

Italy had been neutralised as a danger at the price of a guarantee against French attack which was unlikely to be collected. In fact while the alliance was supported by Italian conservative groups the left wing and radical elements were still more sympathetic to France and more markedly irredentist (see Section 17.5(a)).

16.5 The decline of the Bismarckian system (1882–90)

Berlin was at the centre of a web of alliances. Relations with Britain were friendly; after 1875 tension with France was much reduced by her distraction into colonial expansion, although the *Boulanger crisis* of 1885–9 (see section 19.5(a)) showed that *'revanche'* was not dead. However the real threat to peace lay in the Balkans.

(a)   The Bulgarian Crisis (1885–7)

Russo-Bulgarian relations remained good until 1879 when Prince Alexander of Battenberg, the Tsar's nephew, became ruler. Then relations began to deteriorate, largely because of the influence of the Bulgarian nationalist politician Stambulov. Two developments combined to cause the rift:

1   *A growing link with Austria.* Alexander forced his Russian ministers and advisers to resign in 1883 while his adoption of a more liberal constitution angered the Tsar. On the other hand, Alexander made arrangements with the Austrians for a Bulgarian link in the planned Orient railway.
2   *Union with eastern Roumelia* (see Illus. 16.1). A revolt in eastern Roumelia in 1885 led in 1886 to its union with Bulgaria following a brief war with Serbia who sought to resist this enlargement. Russia opposed this expansion of a very troublesome satellite while Austria was starting to see advantages in it.

At several points, Russia was on the verge of invasion which would have forced Bismarck to choose between allies. In August 1886 the Russians kidnapped Alexander, and although he returned he then abdicated. He was replaced by Ferdinand of Saxe Coburg, a one-time Austrian officer. The spheres of influence had clearly broken down.

(b)   The first Mediterranean Agreement (March 1887)

Bismarck was driven to try and strengthen Germany's position against a possible

From a contemporary lithograph, showing Serbian troops during the revolution in Roumelia.

Revolution in Roumelia (1885) showing Serbian troops on the march

Source: R. Parkinson, *The Origins of World War One* (Wayland Publishers, 1970) p. 85.

Franco-Russian combination. Britain would not commit herself to a positive alliance, but Bismarck did manage to engineer an agreement that Britain, Italy and Austria would cooperate to maintain the *status quo* in the Mediterranean. In effect, the British fleet would protect Italy against the French navy while Italy would support Britain in Egypt (see Section 15.7(b)).

(c)   *Renewal of the Triple Alliance (1887)*

When the alliance was renewed in February 1887, Bismarck's need for Italian support led to greater concessions which were potentially dangerous:

1   The original treaty of 1882 was renewed.
2   In addition Italy was now guaranteed German support in the event of war over French intervention in Tripoli or Morocco.
3   In a separate agreement Austria was encouraged to recognise Italian interests in the Balkans.

Bismarck relied upon the Mediterranean Agreement to check France.

(d)   *The Reinsurance Treaty (1887)*

The Bulgarian crises had smashed the *Dreikaiserbund*. However in 1887 Bismarck managed to 'restore the wire to St Petersburg'; it was agreed that if either Germany or

Russia went to war with a third great power, the other would maintain 'benevolent neutrality'. If Russia was an aggressor against Austria or Germany was the aggressor against France, the agreement would not apply. This was not incompatible with the Dual Alliance, which was simply defensive. Bismarck also revealed its existence to Russia and warned her that an attack on Austria would mean that she would have to face Germany as well. The problem was that Germany would have to decide whether Austria or Russia was the aggressor.

(e) The second Mediterranean Agreement (December 1887)

The Bulgarian selection of Ferdinand encouraged another Russian spasm of distrust of Austria. Bismarck warned Austria that he would not support her in the event of conflict over the issue. The most that Bismarck could do to reinforce Germany's position was to make a new agreement with Italy, now under the premiership of the anti-French Crispi (see Section 17.5), which linked her, Austria and Britain in resolving to support Turkey if necessary against Russia.

16.6 The 'dropping of the pilot'

This complex alliance system depended very much on Bismarck's skill to maintain it. In 1888 the Emperor William II succeeded to the throne. He was a very different character to his uncle (see Section 18.8) and not prepared to leave Bismarck to his own devices. From 1888 Russia and Germany began to drift apart again and Russian links with France began to be forged in the form of French loans and supplies of rifles. In 1890 a personality clash led to Bismarck's resignation, and in the same year the Reinsurance Treaty was not renewed.

16.7 Conclusion

Over the Bulgarian crisis of 1886 Bismarck remarked 'that little country ... is not by any means a matter of sufficient importance to justify an all European war ... [at] the end, after such a war nobody would know just what he had fought for'. In 1914 just such a war did break out, partly because of the absence of Bismarck's skills but partly because of them.

Questions

1 Why was the Congress of Berlin summoned in 1878? How far did it provide solutions to the problems of eastern Europe? [OC]
2 Was Bismarck's foreign policy after 1870 a success? [OC]
3 What difficulties did Bismarck encounter in his efforts to maintain the *Dreikaiserbund*? [OX]
4 Describe the events between 1875 and 1878 which led to the Congress of Berlin, and show why the Congress was an important factor in international relations. [OX, adapted]
5 What were the main causes of unrest in the Balkans between 1870 and 1885? How did the Great Powers become involved with the problems that arose between 1870 and 1888? [NEAB]
6 'In 1871 he sought security for the German Empire; by 1890 he had achieved domination in Europe.' How valid is this comment on Bismarck's foreign policy between 1871 and 1890? [NEAB]
7 Give an account of the foreign policy of Bismarck between 1871 and 1890. Why did Bismarck resign as Chancellor in 1890? [CAM]
8 Study Sources A and B and then answer the questions which follow.

Source A: The Austrian alliance (September 1879).

From the memoirs of a German diplomat.

The situation is as follows. The Chancellor, who does not trust Russia, has come here to conclude a defensive alliance with Austria within the League of the Three Emperors. Andrassy thought at first that it was not meant seriously; but when he saw that it was he jumped right up to the ceiling for joy. But when the Emperor received the Chancellor's proposition, the meeting with the Czar of Russia (on 3 and 4 September) had intervened, and now he will no longer consent to the project.

    The Chancellor, on the other hand, means to resign if the Emperor does not assent. Holstein has proposed that I should talk him over. To this Prince Bismarck has agreed. I have talked to Holstein this evening, and told him that so far I do not approve of the project.

    In the first place, I do not trust Austria, and, in the second, I do not regard Russia as seriously hostile. Lastly, I believe an alliance with Austria would result in one between Russia and France. And then there would be war, while Bismarck believes his treaty would ensure peace.

(a) Who was 'the Chancellor' (line 1)? Why had he 'come here to conclude a defensive alliance with Austria' (lines 2–3)?
(b) What was the 'League of the Three Emperors' (line 2)? How effective was it?
(c) Who was 'Andrassy' (line 3)? Explain why he 'jumped right up to the ceiling for joy' (line 4).
(d) 'In the first place, I do not trust Austria, and, in the second, I do not regard Russia as seriously hostile. Lastly, I believe an alliance with Austria would result in one between Russia and France' (lines 12–14). How correct was the author in making these judgements?
(e) What policies did Bismarck adopt to 'ensure peace' after 1879?   [OC]
Source: Prince Hohenlohe-Schillingsfurst, *Memoirs*.   [OC]

Source B: The atmosphere at St Petersburg.

Russia feels that she has disgraced herself without measure in Bulgaria. What has happened there in the last year – the Revolution in Philippopolis, Slivnica, Battenberg's return after the conspiracy of August 21, the manner in which he then abdicated, the behavior of the Regency, etc., – is viewed here as a series of humiliations. The sense of having produced this fiasco by one's own awkwardness only increases the touchiness. Vorontsov, on reading in the club an article about Kaulbars in the *Kölnische Zeitung*, remarked, with a bitter face: 'Nous sommes comme les chiens qu'on frotte avec le nez dans les ordures qu'ils ont faites.' The 'intelligentsia' is exasperated because the Panslav idea, which for twenty-five years has been regarded as an irreversible dogma, has turned out to be a great humbug ... The Emperor is embittered because even after the removal of his arch-enemy Battenberg, things are going contrary to his expectations and wishes. Russia and the Tsar, in this mood, ask themselves on whom they should vent their wrath. On Bulgaria? The Panslavs warn against an occupation of Bulgaria, in which they see a mouse trap. On England? They would like to settle their scores with England only after Austria has been disposed of. On us? To be sure, we are hated here, and the Russians are not to be trusted. But this hatred flows more from a vague antipathy to what Germany represents than from political calculation. 'C'est plutôt par sentiment que par raisons politiques qu'on est chez nous contre les Allemands,' is what they often say. On the other hand the Russians, thank God, fear us greatly. An early attack on us is unlikely. This of course does not exclude spurring the French on behind the scenes. I have already, in August, drawn attention to the intrigues of Zagulyayev[1], Katakazi[2], etc. These semi-official approaches will probably continue. The immediate object of Russian anger is Austria. I hear from every side: 'Il faut déplacer la question bulgare.' That means that Russia should extract herself from the Bulgarian swamp by a confrontation with Austria.

1 An *attaché* at the Russian embassy at Paris
2 Probably a Russian journalist in Paris

(a) What is meant by the remark that 'the Panslav idea ... turned out to be a great humbug' (lines 8–9)?
(b) In what sense could a Russian occupation of Bulgaria have become a 'mousetrap' (line 13)?
(c) Why were these circumstances likely to be so alarming for Bismarck?
(d) What policy towards Germany did von Bülow fear was being pursued by Russia?

Source: This is an extract from a letter written by Bernhard von Bülow the German *chargé d'affaires* in Russia, describing how the Russian government felt itself humiliated in Bulgaria. The letter is dated 15 November 1886. G. F. Kennan, *The Decline of Bismarck's European Order* (Princeton University Press, 1979). Included in D. G. Williamson, *Bismarck and Germany* (Longman, 1986).

17 The Kingdom of Italy 1870–1915

Introduction

The sudden and virtually unexpected unification of Italy posed the problem of matching its political unity with a proper level of social and economic development and national cohesion. As Massimo d'Azeglio, a Piedmontese politician, remarked, 'We have created Italy. Let us create Italians!'

17.1 'La Revolution manquee'

One of the fundamental problems facing Italy was that it had not been unified as a result of any spontaneous popular upsurge. Indeed its popular base was too narrow.

This could be explained by several factors.

(a) The absence of a social revolution

Popular involvement of the peasantry and urban workers had been discouraged because of the danger of social division and a radicalism which might attract international intervention. The unification of Italy was, on the whole, a struggle between the old ruling class and developing middle class in which the common people were largely irrelevant. Garibaldi himself suppressed the peasant revolt in Sicily which started off his adventure (see Section 13.5(c)).

(b) The use of the plebiscites

There had been no chance to discuss the best form of government for Italy, and especially the 'problem of the South'. A shortage of time, the threat of the breakdown of law and order or of international intervention meant that the voters were pressured. A vote against unification would be a vote to continue confusion. In addition many of the plebiscites were manipulated by local landowners and notables.

(c) 'Piedmontism'

The institutions of the new Kingdom were just the old ones of Piedmont. The extension of the literacy qualification to the south meant that the franchise was reduced to 3 per cent as opposed to 26.6 per cent in Germany. The administration was filled with

Piedmontese officials who tended to see the south as a conquered, backward colony. The strong departmental system of 59 provinces meant that the central government had too much power at the expense of the regions, when a good deal of flexibility might have been better.

17.2 The problems facing Italy (see Fig. 17.1)

If the process of unification had been any better it would have made no difference to the fundamental problems facing Italy.

(a) *The limited rate of economic growth*

This was the result of a range of factors, but especially:

1 *A limited internal market:*

    – *The poverty of communications.* There was no integrated railway system even in the north. In Naples in 1860 1621 villages out of 1848 had no roads at all.
    – *The low level of agricultural productivity.* 8 million of the population lived off the land. However labourers were poorly paid and the bulk of farming was on too small a scale.

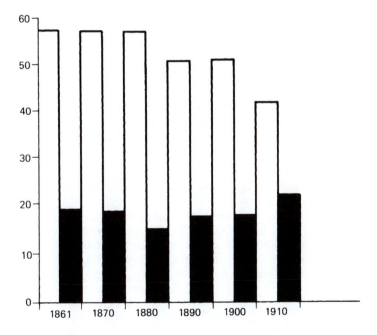

Fig. 17.1 The relative contributions of agriculture and industry to the Italian national product (1861–1910), percentages, the shaded columns represent industrial production

Note the relative *decline* of industry in the years after unification, but the high rate of growth in the years before the First World War.

Source: Based upon statistical information in C. Trebilcock, *The Industrialisation of the Continental Powers 1780–1914* (Longman, 1981).

2   *Inadequate investment:*

> – *A shortage of capital* existed because there was a tendency to prefer government stock or property mortgages rather than to invest in industrial or agricultural improvement.
> – *Psychological conservatism* prevailed in many ways. There was a very general tendency to look down on trade, on industry and speculation. In agriculture, the saints and the weather were relied on rather than improved techniques.

(b) The 'problem of the South'

The south was far more backward than the north in virtually every respect. The poverty was colossal; almost total illiteracy existed, as opposed to 78 per cent illiteracy in the whole of Italy. Diseases like pellagra and malaria were common. There were vast discrepancies of wealth between the peasantry and the overpowerful, almost feudal, landlords. Inevitably there was a tradition of violence, vendettas, banditry and peasant revolts easily confused with heroic resistance of the poor against tax collectors and oppressive landlords. The first half of the 1860s saw half of the national army fighting against a massive wave of brigandage.

(c) The public debt

Piedmont's debts, the debts of all of the other states and the cost of the war of unification meant that by 1866 60 per cent of the total state revenue was being paid to service the debt. To cover its deficit the governments turned to borrowing and inflation and to very high indirect taxation, as with the hated 'grist tax' on bread. Italy had the lowest wages in Europe but the highest indirect taxes.

(d) Church and state

Cavour did not live long enough to try to resolve this problem. The occupation of the Papal States and then Rome in 1870 resulted in a situation where the supporters of the new state were virtually excommunicated and patriotic Italian Catholics were in a terrible dilemma. This was worsened by:

1 *The state policy of secularisation.* The persecution of clergy, confiscation of church property, dissolution of religious orders and insistence upon civil marriage ceremonies were very provocative.
2 *The Ultramontanist policies of the Papacy.* In an encyclical in 1864 the Pope condemned liberalism. In the Declaration of Papal Infallibility of 1870 he emphasised papal authority against the states. In 1874, having rejected an attempted compromise on the Law of Guarantees of 1871, he forbade Catholics to vote in Italian general elections.

17.3 The 'parliamentary dictatorships' (1876–96)

The question was how well would the political system respond to these problems. In 1876 the old liberal–conservative coalition of Cavour fell from office, lacking any clear focus since unification and his death. From then on Italy was governed by radical–liberal politicians, and three of them dominated the period:

1   *Agostino Depretis* (1876–87). A one-time Mazzinian who had spent sixteen years in opposition.
2   *Francesco Crispi* (1887–96). A Sicilian of Albanian descent who had served with Garibaldi. He was a great patriot, although rather lacking in balance and extremely individualist. Once when asked if he was a Mazzinian or Garibaldian he replied, 'Neither, I am Crispi!'
3   *Giovanni Giolitti* (1903–15). A realist and skilful opportunist.

17.4 Depretis and the political system (1876–87)

There were gains made in this period, but at the expense of a pattern being stamped upon the political system which would have very unfortunate consequences.

(a)   *The achievements*

1   *Liberal reforms.* Typically liberal reforms were enacted:

– The introduction of free and compulsory education for all children aged 6–9 (the Coppino Law, 1877).
– A variety of legal and penal reforms, including abolition of imprisonment for debt (1877).
– A new electoral law in 1882 raised the electorate to 7 per cent of the total and revised electoral procedures to reduce corruption and influence and enable greater representation of minorities.

On the other hand, the administrative and local government systems were not reformed as promised, the financial resources were not always adequate – as with the educational reform – there was little social reform and the electoral reform disadvantaged the south even more while adding to the splintering of political life.

2   *Government-sponsored industrial development.* Largely on the basis of government contracts and subsidies, the period saw a great expansion of railway building, the establishment of the great Terni steel works at Breda in 1886, the opening of the Armstrong's naval shipyard and cannon foundry at Pozzuoli in 1885 and the expansion of the Italian shipping industry. Coal imports doubled to 3 million tons a year between 1879 and 1885.

(b)   'Transformisme'

On the other hand, Depretis set an example of political management which confirmed Cavour's precedents of the 1850s and considerably reduced the role of principle in Italian politics. The absorbing of new groups and reshuffling of old into new coalitions became a regular practise. Depretis once remarked 'we will accept the help of all honest and loyal men'; this meant that there were no clear parties or programmes, and that electorates had little control over the type of government or policy it followed. This had several implications:

1   *Instability.* Since there was no need to resign and have an election as a result of a defeat in parliament, there were frequent reshuffles and new cabinets. Between 1861 and 1896 there were 33 different cabinets.
2   *'Pork-barrel' politics.* Since major issues and principles were not the basis of the parties there was a tendency to rely on patronage, government contracts, and so on

to buy the support of individuals and personal followings. This was helped very much by the sectional nature of Italy and very parochial attitudes. For instance Depretis once persuaded parliament to vote 1200 miles of railroad which he parcelled out in exchange for votes.

3   *Electoral manipulation.* Elections tended not to be fought over principles. In fact, there was considerable scope for 'influence' in its various forms; all governments tended to seek to 'make' elections, which was done largely through the prefectoral system. The methods used varied tremendously. Mussolini's father once told of an election in which 50 cows were registered by name. It has been estimated that in the late nineteenth century three-quarters of the electoral districts never had a genuine contest. Only for a hundred or so seats was there a real fight.

4   *Corruption.* Inevitably, given a system in which principle counted so little and with mounting government economic activity, the scope for corruption was considerable. The worst example of this was the great *Tanlongo scandal* of the 1890s which involved the governor of the Banco Romana and a number of politicians including Crispi and Giolitti who had taken bribes in exchange for contracts and honours.

17.5 Crispi and radical nationalism (1887–96)

It was as a result of a periodic reshuffling that Crispi first came to power. All of the faults of the political system persisted under him, and in fact although he was a great believer in freedom and parliamentary government he became more and more authoritarian. It was by adopting a strong stance in imperial and diplomatic affairs that Crispi sought to compensate for the growing sterility of domestic policies.

(a)   Irredentism

In the 1880s a new aggressive nationalism, partly resulting from a sense of national inferiority, was developing. It tended to be rather right-wing and anti-democratic. One aspect of this was the growing demand for Trieste and Trent. Depretis treated this as nonsense, and was careful of Italy's relationship with Austria in the Triple Alliance (see Section 16.4(c)). Crispi, however, announced in 1888 'a man has appeared who considers Italy the equal of any other nation and intends to see that her voice shall be heard and respected'. One aspect of this was secret subsidies to the irredentists whose agitation became a considerable cause of friction between Italy and Austria in the early twentieth century.

(b)   *The Franco-Italian 'Commercial War' (1888–92)*

Franco-Italian relationships had been adversely affected by the French declaration of a protectorate over Tunisia, and this was a factor in causing Italy to ally with Germany and Austria (see Section 16.4(c)). Crispi was obsessively anti-French; he was responsible for the marked anti-French bias in Italian foreign policy in the late 1880s (see Section 16.5(b)–16.5(e)) and also for the repudiation of a commercial treaty in 1888. In fact it was Italy which was worst affected; some 40 per cent of her exports were dammed up. The producers of vegetable oil, wine, raw silk, fruit and vegetables were especially damaged. The wine industry was already badly hit by the outbreak of phylloxera and the wine industry in the south was especially vulnerable since it had overexpanded during the outbreak of vine disease in France. Italian industrialists and big grain producers did gain from protection, but Italian consumers were adversely affected in general.

(c) The Abyssinian adventure (1887–96)

Italy had been caught up in the imperial enthusiasm of the 1870s (see Section 15). However Denis Mack Smith says of this: 'Whereas elsewhere colonialism was a product of riches in Italy it grew out of poverty and from the illusion that here was a quick way to get rich'. The scope for Italian imperialism was rather limited but from 1887 interference in Abyssinia developed rapidly in the belief that the new emperor Menelik had agreed to a protectorate. In 1896, the affair ended in tragedy with the deaths of 6000 Italians at *Adowa* and a national embarrassment which produced the downfall of Crispi – one-time republican, Garibaldian and creator of Italy turned authoritarian and imperialist.

17.6 The threat to the parliamentary system (1896–1900)

In the late 1890s the conjunction of the weaknesses of the political system and a coincidence of serious challenges to it from radical and right-wing forces produced a major crisis.

(a) Peasant disorder

Industrial development had been largely at the expense of agriculture. Italian peasants and small farmers were trapped between:

1   *Low productivity.* Inadequate investment by landowners and the small scale of farming produced low yields; the Italian cereal yield was only a third of that in Britain.
2   *Falling incomes.* The improvement of world and European communications cut prices and adversely affected Italian producers of rice, silk and grain. The *'Commercial War'* with France exaggerated even further the vulnerability of Italian agriculturalists. Agrarian strikes became serious after 1890; in 1892–3 a near rebellion in Sicily eventually involved 50,000 troops in its suppression. By 1896 there were near-famine conditions in some regions, and peasant violence was endemic.

(b) Urban tensions

Italy was backward compared to other industrial nations in the 1890s. Her national income was only a quarter of that of Britain and a third of that of France. She exported less than Belgium. However, there had been very rapid urbanisation associated with all sorts of social problems. Milan's population grew from 200,000 in 1871 to 700,000 by 1921, while that of Rome grew from 220,000 to nearly 800,000. An Italian Socialist Party (PSI) had been established in 1892. There was a moderate wing grouped around the *Avanti!* newspaper, and by 1902 they were firmly in control. However in the 1890s the socialists were more extreme, and there were even more radical breakaway groups such as the anarchists. These new forces played a part in the outbreaks of violence and riots in 1897–8 in Rome, Parma, Florence and Milan.

(c) The anti-parliamentary right-wing

By 1898 civil government had to be suspended in 30 out of 59 provinces and 400,000 troops were under arms. Inevitably this reinforced the authoritarian tendencies in Italy. Crispi had used semi-dictatorial powers in 1892–3 during the Sicilian revolt, including the disenfranchisement of 100,000 people. One group led by the conservative Sonnino sought the restoration of royal prerogatives to make up for parliamentary weaknesses, for 'parliamentarism will kill liberty'. In fact in 1899 the king chose General Pelloux as prime minister and the general, with three of his colleagues in the cabinet, attempted to force through a law to enable him to rule by decree. This was defeated by a coalition of the extreme left, liberals, moderate conservatives and socialists. In 1900 Pelloux resigned and soon afterwards King Umberto was assassinated.

17.7 'Giolittisme' (1903–14)

The new King Victor Emmanuel III was a much more modest and retiring character than his father. By 1903 full parliamentary government was restored and in that year the very realistic reformist Giolitti became prime minister. A very wily politician, he was an astute deserter of 'sinking ships', leaving a replacement to take the brunt of opposition to unpopular policies then returning after an interlude. He was always ready to make deals, and was a master of the art of electoral management. Giolitti argued that 'if you wish to defend our present institutions you will have to persuade these new classes that they have more to gain from those institutions than from Utopian dreams of violent change'.

(a) The extension of the political base

Confronted by a wave of strikes in 1903 then a general strike in 1904 Giolitti was careful to use troops economically to avoid over-strengthening the hand of employers and landowners, and relied on socialist divisions and a well-timed appeal to the electorate in 1904 to blunt extremism. However he was prepared to go even further to stabilise the political system. He sought to apply *'transformism'* to the new political forces:

1   *The socialists.* By 1902 the moderates controlled the PSI and although supporting social revolution were prepared to collaborate within the parliamentary system. In 1903 Giolitti actually offered an alliance, but they rejected it (with some reluctance) because of the danger of exaggerating the division between the moderates and the 'syndicalist' advocates of general strikes and violence.
2   *The Catholics.* Since the 1890s there had been an increasing belief amongst churchmen that abstention from politics was dangerous. By the turn of the century, a new Christian Democracy was politically active, often in alliance with the radicals; in 1905, the Pope relaxed the prohibition against political involvement. The year before Giolitti had made overtures to the new movement against socialism, and from then on sporadically enjoyed its support.

(b) Liberal reforms

Giolitti's several terms of government resulted in a considerable spate of reform legislation:

1 *The nationalisation of the main railway system* in 1904–5 improved the service for exporters (and the scope for corruption).
2 *A range of laws were passed to regulate hours and conditions of work* in industry and agriculture.
3 *Stabilisation of the government's financial situation* by reducing the rate of interest paid on government debt in 1906. Food taxes were also reduced (there had been a tax on salt which increased its price by over 5000 per cent!).
4 *The Education Act (1911)* provided for a provincial system of elementary education and some national financial support.
5 *The 'Southern Problem'* was the subject of some agricultural reforms and expenditure on water supply and communications. But the main contribution to its solution though was *emigration*. By 1910 500,000 people were leaving Italy each year, largely for the Americas. Most of them came from the south.
6 *Extension of the franchise in 1911–12.* All males over 30, literate or not, were given the vote. The electorate rose from 3 to 8 million. In 1911, payment for deputies was introduced as well.

(c) The Libyan War (1911–12)

Altogether the period was one of relative financial stability and economic growth. Between 1901 and 1913, exports rose by 47 per cent and imports by 61 per cent. Wages rose and mortality rates fell although the gap between north and south actually grew and income per head was only 50 per cent of that in France in 1911–13. Yet by 1911 Giolitti faced renewed economic and political problems. One option was an imperial adventure to distract opinion and appeal to nationalism; the result was the invasion of Libya in 1911 (see Section 22.8(b)) where Italy already had slight economic interests. However:

1 The war, cost of the garrison and a struggle against rebels until 1916 reopened the *budget deficit*.
2 The forces of nationalism and the cult of violence were fanned.
3 By weakening Turkey, it contributed to the Balkan Wars (see Section 22.9) and the origins of the Great War.

By 1928 only 2800 Italians actually lived in 'Our Promised Land', and most of them had no choice.

17.8 Conclusion

Times were changing again. In 1912, Mussolini – the editor of *Avanti!* and, ironically, an opponent of the war – led the extremists to victory within the PSI congress and alliance with Giolitti was renounced. Giolitti had to turn to the conservatives led by Sonnino and the new Catholic party to fight the election of 1913. In addition the new constituency size made 'management' more difficult and Giolitti was also under attack for his zealous manipulation of the system. In fact, he was being tempted into the authoritarian trap which had captured Crispi. Then in 1914 his coalition finally fell apart and he resigned. The Great War which broke out in that year simply served to exaggerate all of the flaws and tensions in the Italian social and political system.

Questions

1   Examine the part played by Italy in international affairs between 1866 and 1915.   [OX]
2   Account for the weakness of parliamentary government in *either* **(a)** Germany *or* **(b)** Italy in the period 1870–1914.   [OX]
3   What weaknesses were there in Italy's position as a Great Power between 1870 and 1914?   [OX]
4   To what extent can Italy be regarded as a Great Power before 1914?   [OX]
5   How successfully did Italian statesmen solve the problems of a united Italy in the period 1871–1914?   [NEAB]
6   How successful was parliamentary government in Italy between 1861 and 1914?

18 | Imperial Germany 1871–1914

Introduction

As with Italy, the unification of Germany had not been achieved by a popular revolution but by the extension of the power of one of the states. The old social structure remained largely intact, and the constitutional system of the new Germany strongly reflected the old régime. The story of imperial Germany after 1871 was basically the failure to adapt its institutions to the newly developing economic and social conditions, a combination of material wealth and social tensions. Bismarck had orchestrated unification, but he and then William II could see no further than the maintenance of the existing power structure.

18.1 Economic growth (1871–1914) (see Fig. 18.1)

Growth was not unbroken in this period. In 1873 a long wave of expansion ended with a financial crisis, and was followed by some years of recession until in the 1890s a great wave of industrialisation occurred.

(a) *Industrialisation*

Coal production swept up by 8000 per cent between 1871 and 1914, while steel output increased tenfold in 1880–1900 alone. By 1912, Germany produced as much steel as Britain, France and Russia put together. In the chemical, electrical and precision engineering industries growth was even more spectacular. By 1914 Germany had become the second greatest trading nation in the world; about 75 per cent of her exports were manufactures and semi-manufactures to Europe, the Americas and Africa.

(b) *The implications*

There were several consequences associated with this growth:

1   *Urbanisation.* The total population grew from 41 million in 1871 to 67 million in 1913, but this was alongside a disproportionate growth of towns. Between 1875 and 1910, the number of cities with populations over 10,000 inhabitants grew from 271 to 576.
2   *Changes in occupational distribution.* In 1860 up to 70 per cent of Germans depended on agriculture for their living. By 1907 it was only 28.4 per cent, while

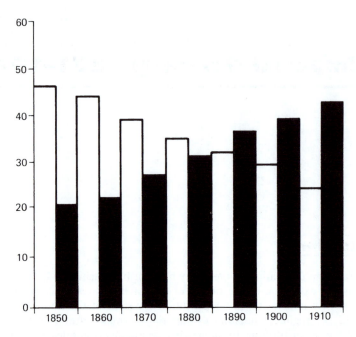

Fig. 18.1 The relative contributions of agriculture and industry to the German national product (1850–1910), percentages, the shaded columns represent industrial production

The industrial sector was clearly expanding, although the rural component and population remained comparatively high.

Source: Based upon statistical information in C. Trebilcock, *The Industrialisation of the Continental Powers 1780–1914* (Longman, 1981).

42.4 per cent worked in industry. By then the fastest-growing sector was the 'white-collar' administrative services.

3 The *emergence of cartels*. German industrialisation was associated especially with the concentration of production into a relatively small number of large firms or combines of firms (cartels) designed to keep up prices. This development was especially encouraged by the investing banks and finance houses.

4 *Regional variations.* There was a considerable difference between the rural, agricultural society east of the Elbe and the town and industries of western Germany. The average wage in east Prussia, for instance, was only 63.4 per cent of the national average. In industrialised Westphalia it was 117.4 per cent. There was an internal migration across the Elbe from east to west into the new towns.

18.2 The constitution of the Second *Reich*

On the whole, the constitution of the North German Confederation (see Section 14.5(b)) was simply adapted to the new circumstances. It suffered from all the weaknesses of the previous arrangements.

(a) Sham democracy

1 *The limited powers of the legislature.* There were two chambers, with theoretically equal legislative powers:

– The *Bundesrat* consisted of 58 members representing the states. It made policy recommendations to the lower house which gave it an advantage over the latter.
– The *Reichstag* was elected for five-yearly periods on the basis of manhood suffrage. There was no secret ballot, and the lack of payment of members until 1906 discriminated against lower class and more radical representatives. Ministers were not responsible to the Reichstag, and it was excluded from review of military expenditure and foreign treaties.

2 *An over-mighty executive.* The *Kaiser* had considerable potential power, which William I tended to delegate to Bismarck.

– As the war lord, the Kaiser controlled the armed forces and could declare a 'defensive' war.
– The chancellor was appointed by and only responsible to the Kaiser.
– The Kaiser could veto legislation and dissolve the *Reichstag*.

(b) The federal structure

Popular authority was further weakened by the persistence of state power. The state governments had considerable responsibility over matters such as direct taxation, education, transport, police and local government. On the other hand, the degree of popular control varied considerably. Alsace-Lorraine was governed by a military governor. The Mecklenburgs had no elected assemblies at all. In south Germany, the usual situation was that all direct taxpayers had the vote. In Prussia though – and Saxony from 1896 – the three-class franchise persisted (see Section 9.11(a)) in the interests of the rural aristocracy – and therefore the Prussian Conservative Party.

(c) Prussian dominance

Permeating the system at every level was Prussian power:

1 The imperial title passed by inheritance with the kingship of Prussia.
2 Prussia was preponderant in terms of population (three-fifths of the total) and territorial extent (two-thirds), so its state government was very powerful.
3 In the *Bundesrat* although there were 25 states represented their membership ranged from 1 to the 17 of Prussia. (Constitutional change could be blocked by 14 votes.)

18.3 The persistence of powerful privileged élites

The strength of two very conservative groups was not only preserved, it was increased.

(a) The nobility

The old nobility survived into the new Germany, and especially in Prussia. Its strength came from three sources:

1   *The persistence of natural deference.* The end of feudalism did not end the social dominance of the noble landowners, whose influence locally was reinforced by their employment of labourers and their power over tenant farmers and local tradesmen who relied on their business.
2   *A virtual monopoly of official positions.* In the army and the higher ranks of the government and administration the nobles still enjoyed a preferred status, which was all the more important now that the scale of the state was expanded.
3   *Political activism.* From the 1870s the challenge of cheap grain from Russia and America provoked the landowners to seek self-defence through the leadership of the Conservative Party in alliance with the new 'industrial barons' such as Krupp and Stumm who had pretensions to become accepted by the nobility and had similar attitudes to paternal control of the lower orders. However the Conservatives could also draw on support from a variety of groups who felt threatened by the new trends of urbanisation and industrialisation – the craftsmen, small shopkeepers, farmers and rural workers and some of the academic intellectual groups moving across from liberalism to an emphasis on nationalism.

(b)   The 'state within a state'

The status of the army was a potentially dangerous flaw. It was in theory a composite army of Prussian, Saxon, Bavarian and Würtemburger contingents. In fact, it was dominated by the Prussian staff. Apart from that its position was overstrengthened by:

1   *Constitutional irresponsibility.* The constitution originally specifically excluded parliamentary control, by nominating the size of the army as a percentage of the population and fixing the amount of expenditure per soldier. Only gradually did the *Reichstag* establish the right to review military expenditure every seven years in a special budget called the *Septennate*. Nor was there an imperial minister of war to be interrogated; even the powers of the Prussian minister of war were very limited, and the army general staff gradually freed itself from control.
2   *A special aura.* The army had a special place in the minds of many Germans:

   – As the creator of the unified Germany it was seen as somehow above criticism, and its opponents could be portrayed as disloyal.
   – It was widely seen as a vital 'school for citizenship'. The author of one military manual described army service as 'a school to inculcate blind obedience to those in authority as well as to foster monarchic sentiments in the citizen'.

3   *Social exclusiveness:*

   – The officer corps was drawn from the aristocracy. In 1913 80 per cent of the cavalry and 48 per cent of the infantry officers were noblemen. Between 1878 and 1910 there was not one Jewish officer appointed.
   – The army had traditionally been used to crush popular social disturbances, and this continued after 1871.

This militarism was opposed by many Germans – especially in the south where Prussia was unpopular. However, the Zabern Affair of 1913 was to illustrate the impregnable position of the army.

18.4 The 'Iron Chancellor'

Until 1890, Bismarck dominated the political system. Kaiser William I largely left political affairs to him. If he was thwarted, a threat of resignation was usually effective. The *Annual Register* remarked in 1880 'a resignation of Prince Bismarck must now be apparently accepted as a necessary incident of the year's history'. However the effect of his activities was to 'sterilise' the political system. His main objectives were to resist revolution and preserve the power of Prussia and the Junker nobility. The result was that he opposed the development of political parties and tended to treat any opposition as if it was a challenge to the state. His domestic political activities were characterised by:

1   The *Kulturkampf* (1871–9), a semi-ideological and semi-political struggle against the Roman Catholic Church.
2   The alignment with the 'Corn and Iron' conservatives, 1879–90.
3   Germanisation of the national minorities.

18.5 The Kulturkampf

The origins of the struggle were twofold:

1   *Potential identification of Catholicism with disloyalty to the state.* The 40 per cent Catholic minority tended to oppose the militarism, protestantism and liberalism associated with unification. The Roman Catholic Church was especially strong amongst the Poles and Alsatians; the Papal Decree of Infallibility of 1870 could easily be seen as an incentive to disloyalty. Bismarck was by no means alone in regretting this tendency; in 1874, the British prime minister Gladstone commented 'I cannot but say that the present doctrines of the Roman Church destroy the title of her obedient members to the enjoyment of civil rights'.
2   *The alliance with the National Liberals.* Bismarck's political allies were the National Liberals led by Rudolph von Bennigsen. In 1871 the newly founded Catholic Centre Party won 70 seats in the Reichstag, and could be seen as a new challenge politically. An attack on the Church, Bismarck hoped, would weaken it and tighten his political alliance.

(a)   *Anti-Catholic legislation*

1   *The Kanzel Paragraph* (November 1871). Throughout the Reich special penalties were imposed for 'political' sermons, civil marriage was made compulsory and a range of religious orders were expelled. In 1872, diplomatic relations with the Papacy were severed.
2   *The Falk Laws* (1873–5). In Prussia, state control of church discipline, appointments of office and clerical education was introduced. One effect of this was that by 1876 nine Prussian sees were unoccupied, and 1400 parishes had no priest.

(b)   *The failure of the* Kulturkampf

Of 10,000 priests in Prussia only 30 submitted; bishops and priests were turned into persecuted martyrs. The church was strengthened, and the Centre Party's representation rose to 100 by 1874. In 1879, Bismarck was forced to reopen relations with the newly-elected and more conciliatory Pope Leo XIII. Most of the legislation disappeared over the next decade; one factor which had shaken Bismarck was the danger of the Catholic Centre and the Socialists actually coming together.

18.6 A new alignment (1879–90)

The growing demands of landowners and industrialists for protection for the home markets in an age of increasing nationalist rejection of free trade, and the attractiveness of a source of Reich revenue independent from the states, led to the introduction of a tariff in 1879; the alliance with the Liberals was broken. This had several implications.

(a) *Alliance with the Conservatives*

Bismarck's new allies were the Conservatives, the Junkers and the 'Junkers of the chimney' who had little commitment to the constitution and a strong emphasis on the 'Prussian tradition' of discipline and social hierarchy.

(b) *Imperialism*

Protection and imperial expansion were linked in several respects. In fact, Bismarck had been opposed to imperialism – 'I do not wish to resemble the Polish nobility, whose fur coats conceal the fact that they cannot afford a shirt.' Pressures and propaganda increased, and in 1884 Bismarck gave way and Germany acquired its first colonies in Africa (see Section 15.2(b)). There is a view, however, best expressed by Hans Wehler in his *Bismarck and Imperialism* (1969), that Bismarck was positively attracted to imperial adventures. Wehler argues that it was in part a response to Germany's economic problems between 1873 and 1896, and partly intended to distract German workers from social problems. Broadly speaking, Wehler sees imperialism as having been adopted as an antidote to potential social revolution. However, the Wehler view has been strongly criticised. Bismarck's colonial initiatives seem to have been short term rather than part of a positive long term policy. He was well aware of the fact that formal empire could never be of economic value, and therefore of no political value. In 1890 when he fell from power it was to be partly because of his lack of enthusiasm for colonial commitment.

(c) *The* Kampfzeit

Until 1864 Bismarck had been able to cooperate with the socialist leader Lasalle, who shared his dislike of the urban middle class and liberalism. From 1864, socialism became more notably Marxist after Lasalle died in a duel. In 1875, the Socialist Party was formed at Gotha. In 1877, it won 10 per cent of the votes and 12 seats. Bismarck's decision to move against it (see Illus. 18.1a and 18.1b) was partly to strengthen his alliance with the Conservatives, but also because of his fear of the danger of the new forces to the state:

1 *Repression.* Newspapers were suppressed, the Exceptional Law of 1878 banned a range of supporting organisations and between 1878 and 1890 some 900 labour leaders were expelled and 1500 imprisoned.
2 *Social welfare legislation.* More subtly, Bismarck believed in attracting the workers from socialism: 'The poor must be made to look upon the state not as an agency

Illus. 18.1a Bismarck deals with the Liberals (18.1a) and Socialists (18.1b) (Archiv Gerstenberg)

From two lithographs in the *Archiv Gerstenberg*, Berlin; in 18.1a, a plague of 'Social-Colorado-beetles' is being exterminated.

devised solely for the protection of the better situated classes in society but also as one serving their needs and interests'. The result was a spate of legislative reforms which meant that by 1911 14 million Germans were insured against sickness, accidents and old age. Even so by 1893 the Socialists had 23.3 per cent of the votes and 11.1 per cent of the seats as compared to 1871 when they had only 3.2 per cent of the votes and 0.5 per cent of the seats.

18.7 Germanisation of the national minorities

The new Germany had French, Polish and Danish minorities. They posed a lasting problem. The fifteen representatives of Alsace-Lorraine in the Reichstag were a per-

Keeping It Down.

Source: H. Kurz, *The Second Reich* (Macdonald, 1970) p. 57.

manent opposition. In the Polish and Danish territories, a policy of Germanisation was followed with an insistence on German as the language of education and official business and encouragement of Germans to buy up Polish estates. The results were counter-productive. Polish resentment was considerably increased, and by 1914 a majority of the Danes of *Schleswig* wanted to join Denmark.

18.8 The Wilhelmine Era (1890–1914)

After the 99-day reign of his cancer-stricken father, the liberal Crown Prince Frederick, his son William II became Kaiser. In view of later events there has been a tendency to portray the new Kaiser as a Machiavellian plotter on a world scale, and the arch-agent of dark forces. In fact, the real problem was that he was too typical of the new state which he was now called upon to rule. A very complex personality with a rather stunted body and a withered arm, he was very insecure and unsure of himself and over-compensated for these inadequacies with bumptious aggressiveness and flamboyant posing. 'Psychological' versions of history can be very dangerous, but it is not difficult to see the problems and responses of the Kaiser and the state as being identical.

(a) *The German mirror image*

William II was significant not because he was mentally ill which was the view argued in several German psychiatric studies after 1918, when there was a need for the German people to distance themselves from the Kaiser. His importance lay in the fact that he was very much a product of his times who readily adapted himself to popular opinion and reflected it, and with whom his subjects could easily identify and around whom they could unite. He was a mirror image especially of those Germans who set the a tone of dynamism, enterprise and aggression; he was the symbol of the *nouveau riche*. The characteristics which defined the personality of William II and the new Germany alike were:

1   *'Personal Politik'*. He tended to take everything personally. So, for instance, he abandoned a policy of social welfare in 1894 and proposed to introduce anti-socialist legislation and suspend the constitution if it was not passed, largely because he saw labour unrest and socialist electoral successes as a personal rejection of him by his people. He saw politics in terms of personalities and personal issues rather than policies. In March 1907 he saw Edward VII as intriguing against him personally.

2   *Readiness to take offence.* The fundamental objective was that the Reich and the Kaiser should be treated with 'respect' and as 'equals', especially by Britain. Germany foreign policy was more a question of emotional reaction than calculation. During the Boxer Rebellion he demanded joint European action when his Peking envoy was killed in June 1900 and that 'Peking must be razed'. Then when order was restored without any great German victory he regarded that as a loss of honour and betrayal by Britain and Russia, and demanded an alliance with Japan whom he had previously regarded with contempt! Britain, on the other hand, acted far more on the basis of rational consideration of the interests of state and made little concession to issues such as national pride.

3   *Inconsistency and unpredictability.* Sir Edward Grey wrote of him: 'The German Emperor is ageing me; he is like a battleship with steam up and screws going, but with no rudder, and he will run into something one day and cause a catastrophe.' In 1907 Lord Fitzmaurice remarked that '. . . the Emperor is like a cat in a cupboard. He may jump out anywhere. The whole situation would be changed in a moment if this personal factor were changed.' The classic example of this was the crisis caused by remarks being printed in the *Daily Telegraph* in 1908 in which he claimed to be the Anglophile ruler of Anglophobe subjects. This produced national uproar, demands that he should be restrained, the contemplation of abdication and one of his periodic 'nervous breakdowns'.

(b) *The dropping of the pilot*

In 1890 the resignation of Bismarck was accepted by the Kaiser after a series of disagreements between them. It is probably untrue that Wilhelm had determined to get rid of Bismarck before his accession, a theory based on an alleged remark to Adolf Stoeker: 'I will let the old man snuffle on for six months and then I will rule myself.' There were two causes of division between the two men:

1   *The response to the threat of socialism.* At this point the Kaiser adopted a sympathetic stance towards social reform to try to stifle socialism, while Bismarck moved towards the belief that only military force and the destruction of the Reichstag would suffice. The disastrous election results of 1890 increased the seats of the Centre and left liberals and gave the Social Democrats 35 seats at the expense of the National Liberals and Conservatives.

2   *A personality clash.* The young Kaiser was keen to be seen as the director of
    German policy and not merely as a puppet of Bismarck, who, increasingly careless
    in his old age, played into the hands of his rivals by not keeping the Kaiser fully
    informed about political discussions with the Centre. For his part, the Kaiser
    consulted with Prussian ministers opposed to Bismarck, despite a cabinet order of
    1852 which required the presence and permission of the Chancellor in the case of
    any such discussions. This issue became the occasion for the dismissal of Bismarck
    when the Kaiser demanded its abrogation.

In March 1890 Bismarck was forced into a position where resignation was virtually
obligatory.

(c)   The dilemma of the régime

On his accession the Kaiser announced that 'the course remains the same, full steam
ahead!'. However, there was the growing problem of new social forces challenging the
prevailing constitutional structure. Before his resignation, Bismarck had considered
ending universal suffrage by an army *coup d'état.*

The new Kaiser initially saw himself as the *Volkskaiser* ('people's Kaiser'). In fact,
in the years before 1914 he sided with the ruling élite of landowners, industrialists, soldiers and bureaucrats. The Wilhelmine régime was trapped between two forces:

1   A *'red spectre'.* By 1912 the Socialists had 38.8 per cent of the votes and 27.7 per
    cent of the seats, even though the national and state electoral systems did not
    reflect their true appeal. As a threat to the state they were exaggerated. In fact a
    revisionist group supported the abandonment of Marxist dogma and a more
    respectable participation in public bodies at all levels.
2   A *financial crisis.* The government was caught between the growing expenditure on
    social welfare and the limitations on revenue from direct taxation, because of the
    resistance of the higher income groups and because it was under state control.
    Naval expenditure had to be based upon indirect taxation, which resulted in rises
    in the prices of food and goods consumed by the working class. By 1910 even this
    could not finance the fleet, and the cost of living was rising.

The Chancellors who succeeded Bismarck could not seek to match his talents and overcome the divisions within the Reichstag. Politics degenerated into a chaotic struggle
between the Chancellor, the Reichstag, the Prussian ministries, the state governments
and a range of cliques and interest groups. Following the failure of General von Caprivi
to pursue a policy of political non-alignment between 1890 and 1894, the tone was set
by Bernhard von Bülow (1900–9), a career diplomat who held office for a decade on
the basis of obsequious flattery of the Kaiser. He followed a social–political strategy
which combined an aggressive foreign policy with an attempt to build an alliance of
agrarian and industrial interests strong enough to dominate the parliamentary situation
in the Reichstag.

(d)   Weltpolitik and domestic policy

The key issue was the relationship between foreign and domestic policy, and the building of the imperial navy. There are two sets of theories:

1   *An attempt to preserve political authority* and social position by a threatened élite.
    From the 1960s the views of Fritz Fischer and Hans-Ulrich Wehler were
    predominant, and they identified two motives:

– *Sammlungspolitik* ('togetherness') to rally together the dominant social, economic and political élites, the Prussian aristocracy and the owners of heavy industry, in an alliance to protect their power and status. The method was to respond to agricultural distress and the fear of socialism with naval construction and colonial acquisition to benefit industry, in exchange for grain tariffs to protect East Elbian agriculture from foreign imports. Hence the *Navy Laws* of 1898 and 1900 and the grain tariffs of 1902 were linked. In practical terms the policy was underpinned by the following of the Conservative Party and a range of extremist interest groups. The Navy League founded in 1897 by Admiral Tirpitz had 100,000 members by 1913. It was ultra-nationalist, anti-Jewish and anti-Socialist. The industrialists (see Illus. 18.2) and East Elbian landowners were linked through the pro-tariff Economic Council. The Farmers' League, founded in 1893, was really a mass organisation of the Conservatives which had 118 sponsored candidates in the Reichstag by 1898. The very racialist Pan-German League was founded in 1893. The Colonial League dated back to 1882.

– *Social imperialism* to reconcile the mass of the population to the established order by means of naval construction and an active imperialist policy to appeal to nationalist sentiment, just as Bismarck had employed his colonial policy.

2   *A response to popular nationalist aspirations.* The alternative view, which was voiced especially by Geoffrey Eley in the 1980s, is that far from the manipulation of society the German leaders were merely responding to demands for an

Illus. 18.2   The Krupp cannon factory (Hulton Picture Library)

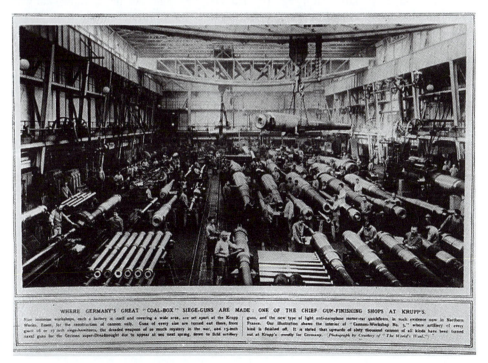

From a contemporary picture of the armaments works at Essen.
Source: H. Glaser and W. Putstuck, *Eine Deutsches Bilderbuch, 1870–1918* (Verlag C. H. Beck, Munich, 1982) p. 128.

imperialist policy and that some of the right-wing groups regarded it as a distraction from their goal. Indeed some of the leading advocates of Weltpolitik argued that the fundamental restructuring of the state and society were necessary to support an effective world policy, not the other way round. So, according to this view, the support of the Kaiser, Bülow and Tirpitz for naval and world policy was based on the belief that it was in the best interests of the nation and people because the mobilisation of national sentiment was an end in itself. Bismarck ruled by playing off one self interested group against another. Wilhelm II sought to cover over conflicts of interest by creating an emotional consensus.

Of course, these purposes and methods are not necessarily contradictory and could all be present at different times, to different degrees and supported by different groups and individuals.

18.9 The Zabern Affair

The opportunity to use the *Daily Telegraph* indiscretions of the Kaiser to reform the constitution was not seized by parliamentarians who in other national contexts would have used budgetary powers to force political reform. By then it was impossible to achieve any sort of unity within the Reichstag over any issues of great importance. In 1909 Bülow was dismissed and replaced by his nominee, the Prussian bureaucrat Theobald von Bethmann Hollweg, or 'Bülow's revenge' as he became known. Bethmann was handicapped by the chronic crisis in imperial finances which he inherited, and could resort only to temporary expedients to deal with it.

By then it was not only necessary to accommodate massive fleet increases but also the expansion of the army in 1912 and 1913 in the context of the increased international tension (see Chapter 22) and pressure from the propaganda organisation called the *Wehrverein*. However, militarism permeated the whole of German society. This was reflected above all in the case of the *Zabern Affair* in 1913 when a Prussian lieutenant grossly insulted the people of Alsace. In fact it was civilians who were arrested when they jeered at troops, and the local civilian authorities who were superseded. Throughout the resultant crisis the Kaiser insisted that the matter was one purely of military discipline, regardless of the repercussions of the attitude that the local population of Alsace could be regarded as potentially hostile. Bethmann supported the Kaiser's view and resisted successfully the idea that the Reichstag should have some say in the disciplining of the army.

18.10 Conclusion

In default of any internal reform programmes, the 'solutions' looked to were *outside the Reich*.

(a) 'Mitteleuropa'

A view popular with the middle classes in the 1890s was that a sort of German-dominated Central European trade area should be constructed through trade agreements with politically weak states like Serbia and Rumania, and even Russia.

(b) 'Mittelafrika'

Big landowners opposed any attempt to reduce tariffs with Russia. In fact in 1902 high tariffs on Russian grain were introduced. Industrialists and the big landowners favoured a colonial solution which would also appeal to nationalists. This was related to the need for sea power. As Tirpitz remarked, 'Without seapower Germany's influence in the world will be like that of a mollusc without any shell.' Without it, it would mean 'leaving the world to the Anglo-Saxons and the sons of Jehovah'.

(c) *A European war*

To attract support the Kaiser and his advisers sought to achieve a quick diplomatic *coup*. This had the effect of isolating Germany (see Section 22). The creation of the Triple Entente of 1907 seemed to fulfil all the fears of the encirclement of Germany. Pessimism about the future, an exaggerated fear of socialism and opposition to internal reform meant that a preventive war came to seem to be the solution which would pull the nation together. As Holstein, a senior diplomatic official, remarked 'success can . . . be expected [only] as a result of a European War'.

Questions

1 Give an account of the domestic problems of Germany between 1871 and 1890. How did Bismarck attempt to solve them? [OC]
2 Why did Bismarck find Germany difficult to govern after 1871? [OC]
3 Did economic growth transform German society between 1870 and 1914? [OC]
4 How successful was Bismarck in achieving his aims in domestic affairs in Germany after 1871?[OX]
5 How well did Bismarck deal with the constitution of the Empire, the Roman Catholic Church, the liberals and the socialists? [NEAB]
6 What problems faced Bismarck in Germany in the period 1871–90, and how successful was he in dealing with them? [NEAB]
7 Describe the domestic policies followed by Bismarck between 1870 and 1890. Why did he prove an unacceptable minister to the new *Kaiser*, Wilhelm II? [CAM]
8 Why was Bismarck able to maintain such personal power in Germany from 1871 to 1890? [CAM]
9 Study Sources A, B, C and D and then answer the questions which follow.

Source A: Remedying social ills

From the speech of the *Kaiser* at the opening of the *Reichstag*, 15 February 1881.

At the opening of the Reichstag in February 1879 His Majesty the Emperor with reference to the [anti-socialist] law of 21 October 1878 (No. 123) expressed the hope that the Reichstag would not refuse its continuing co-operation in remedying social ills by means of legislation. Such remedy shall be sought not only in the repression of socialistic excesses, but also in the promotion of the welfare of the workers. In this respect the care of such workers as are incapable of earning their livelihood is the first step. In their interest His Majesty the Emperor had a bill on the insurance of workers against the result of accidents presented to the Bundesrat – a bill which is intended to meet a need felt equally by workers and employers. His Majesty the Emperor hopes that the bill will receive the assent of the Governments of the States, and that it will be welcomed by the Reichstag as a complement of the legislation on protection against social-democratic activity (No. 123). The now existing provisions which should have protected the worker from becoming helpless through the loss of his earning capacity by accident or old age have proved inadequate, and their inadequacy has contributed no little to turning the members of this class to participation in social-democratic activity in order to seek help.

(a) Why were 'social ills' (and socialism) increasing in scale so rapidly in imperial Germany?
(b) What steps had been taken against socialism before 1881, and with what effect?

(c) How was the proposed legislation seen as being 'a complement of the legislation on protection against social-democratic activity' (lines 10–11)?

(d) Why do you think that the employers also supported such legislation (line 9)?

Source: translation in G. A. Kertesz (ed.), *Documents in the Political History of the European Continent, 1815–1939* (OUP, 1968) p. 267.

Source B: The flight from the land.

The general consensus of opinion in the country as a whole indicates a very great change for the better in the economic condition of the laborer during the last ten or twenty years. He is better fed and better clothed, better educated and better able to procure the means of recreation; nevertheless the migration statistics ... indicate a continuous movement of the population from the agricultural east to the industrial west. Except in a few southern districts, such as Bavaria, where peculiar conditions prevail, the agrarian question proper, interpreted in Germany to mean the difficulty of procuring a sufficient supply of labor, scarcely exists in the west. With regard to the east, on the contrary, Dr Weber points out ... that unless some means can be adopted for checking the outflow of the German population, there is every reason to fear that their places will be supplied by an inroad of Slavs, and that thus an element of disintegration already existing will be increased ... The inquiry instituted ... by the Economic Club (*Verein für Sozialpolitik*) has brought out clearly the predominant influence of the social over the economic factors in agrarian discontent. The gulf which separates the employer from the employed in the east, and the lack of opportunity for acquiring land are, in the opinion of the members of the Economic Club reporting on the subject, mainly responsible for its depopulation. Up to the present time it has appeared almost impossible to supply the remedy, though the great landowners are sufficiently ready to divide much of their land into small holdings, if this or any other measure would secure them a permanent supply of suitable labor.

(a) Why should a British Royal Commission have been interested in labour conditions in Central Europe in 1893?

(b) According to this analysis why was there a drift of population from the agricultural east to the industrial west (lines 12–16)?

(c) Why should it have been a cause for concern that this drift was occurring?

(d) What solution was being proposed, and why was it unlikely that it would be implemented (lines 16–19)?

Source: An extract from a report by a British Royal Commission on Labour conditions in Central Europe in 1893. T. S. Hamerow (ed.), *The Age of Bismarck: Documents and Interpretations* (Harper Row, 1973). Included in D. G. Williamson, *Bismarck and Germany* (Longman, 1986).

Source C: The condition of the urban working class in Germany.

The Weaver's Budget given by Dr. von Schulze-Gaevernitz is as follows:

Weekly Budget of North German Weaver and Wife and four Children

Income	M	Expenditure	M
Wages of father	15	42 lbs rye bread	
Amount paid by children		(second quality)	5.60
for board and lodging	7	30 pints potatoes	1.80
Total	22	2 lbs rolls	2.00
		2 lbs meal (second	
		quality)	0.40
		$\frac{3}{4}$ lbs meat (Sunday)	0.45
		$\frac{1}{2}$ suet	
		vegetables	3.40

coffee	0.20
$2\frac{1}{2}$ lbs butter	3.40
6 pints skimmed milk	0.60
rent	3.20
sick and old age insurance	0.65
school money	0.15
Total	21.85

In Berlin the conditions are specially bad, and the average number of persons inhabiting one tenement (*Grundstück*) has risen from 60.7 in 1880 to 66.0 in 1885. Subletting was shown by the census of 1880 to be exceedingly frequent, 7.1 per cent of the population took in persons who boarded and lodged with them, and 15.3 per cent took in persons to sleep (*Schlafleute*). One instance is given of a household taking 34 such night lodgers, in another case there were eleven, including two women. Thirty-eight per cent of the families taking night lodgers lived in a single room; one instance is mentioned in which a man and his wife with a family shared their one room with seven men and one woman. Though the worst kind of night shelters, known as 'Pennen', have now been suppressed by the police, it is still 'the opinion of experienced observers ... that the evils existing in the large towns of England are less crying than in Germany' ...

(a) How are the circumstances outlined in this section of the report related to the population drift referred to in Source A?
(b) What do you think are the dietary deficiencies of the expenditure pattern which is outlined?
(c) What items of expenditure are not budgeted for?
(d) Give some examples of the way in which this careful balance between income and expenditure could easily be disturbed?
(e) In view of the situation described in the extract, what do you think was likely to be happening to the level of rent in Berlin?
Source: As in Source B.

Source D: Either we export goods or we export people.

The working class is bound together with industry most intimately, and we would have neglected our duty if we had not, in concluding these treaties, kept the possibility of preserving our working class, preserving their ability to be productive, steadily before us. Two factors then came up for discussion: first, to procure cheaper foodstuffs. In so far as that could take place without endangering state interests ... the federated governments ... have effected the lowering of the tariff on foodstuffs which they considered permissible. For the preservation and prosperity of the working class, however, I regard it as far more essential that work should be found for them. (*Quite right! From the Right.*) If this were not the more essential question, then the rush of our rural labourers to the cities and to the West could hardly be explained ... Remunerative jobs will be found if these treaties are accepted. We will find them by means of export. We must export; either we export goods, or we export people. With this mounting population, and without a comparably growing industry, we are not in a position to survive any longer.

(a) Why do you think that the right-wing groups in the Reichstag were more likely to see the finding of work for the working class as more important than lowering the price of foodstuffs?
(b) What did Caprivi mean by 'either we export goods, or we export people'?
(c) What were the 'state interests' which might have been 'endangered' by seeking to lower the price of foodstuffs?
(d) To whom was Caprivi referring when he spoke of the 'federated governments'?
Source: Caprivi, speaking about his trade Treaties in the Reichstag, 1891.

19 The Third Republic 1871–1914

Introduction

The Franco-Prussian War, followed by the awful days of the Commune, produced an overwhelming desire for peace and stability, reflected in the swing to conservatism in the elections of February 1871. To many of the middle classes and monarchists, the Republic was a better option than the bloody anarchy which had preceded it. So out of the ruins of 1871 the Third Republic was born, largely by accident and as a 'second best'. Against all the odds, it was to survive until another '*débâcle*' in 1940.

19.1 Post-war reconstruction

Recovery was rapid. The war indemnity was paid off quickly, and by September 1873 the German troops had gone. Thiers, the 'Liberator of the Territory', proceeded with moderate administrative reconstruction.

(a) *Maintenance of administrative centralisation*

There was no attempt at devolution. Mayoral elections were introduced for towns with populations over 20,000 and council privileges were slightly extended. Prefectoral power was left untouched.

(b) *Financial orthodoxy*

It was of financial and commercial policy that Thiers announced 'The Republic will be conservative or it will not be at all'. A proposed income tax was rejected to reassure the middle class and investors, and there were steps to restore protection.

(c) *The Army Law (August 1872)*

Conscription was introduced for a service period of five years. However, it was qualified by exemptions, a system of drawing lots ('good numbers' served only for 6–12 months) and self-financed volunteers serving only for a year. By 1875 the army had been restored so quickly that it was the subject of a war scare (see Section 16.2(a)).

19.2 The constitution

Changing circumstances rather than any sort of theory determined the type of constitution which the National Assembly was empowered to produce by the *Rivet Law* of August 1871.

(a) *Failure of the restoration*

The royalist majority in the National Assembly had little time. The elections of February had been a freak; by July 1871 there was a swell of republicans into the Assembly resulting from the by-elections, and these included Gambetta. In November 1872, Thiers himself declared his support for a republic. So the royalists pressed ahead quickly:

1   *The powers of Thiers were reduced* in 1873 by the Assembly. Two months later he was replaced by Marshal MacMahon, devout Catholic, ultra-conservative and defeater of the Commune.
2   *The 'Republic of the Dukes'*. There followed a brief period of right-wing aristocratic government which confirmed Thiers's worst fears:

   – The administrative and judicial systems were purged of republicans.
   – Censorship was employed against the republican press.
   – There was a provocative display of support for the Catholic Church.

(b) *The question of the flag*

The main problem was the division between the Legitimist supporters of 'Henri V', the Comte de Chambord, and the Orleanists, who supported the Comte de Paris, the grandson of Louis Philippe. By the summer of 1873, this seemed to have been resolved and helped by the loss of some Orleanists to support for a moderate republic and the death of Napoleon III which freed the Bonapartist deputies to support 'Henri V'. In fact, he used his unacceptable insistence on the Bourbon white flag rather than the tricolor as the excuse to continue his quiet life. The restoration was impossible.

(c) *The 'Constitution of 1875'*

Since some form of organised government was vital, the Assembly enacted a series of laws seen as provisional and as equally applicable to a monarchy as to a republic:

1   *The Wallon Amendment.* The word 'republic' was slipped into the title of the President of the Republic who was to be appointed by the National Assembly for seven years. He had the power to dissolve the Chamber of Deputies.
2   *The Senate.* An upper house of 300 members was introduced. The National Assembly nominated 75 for life; the other 225 were to be elected at the rate of a third every three years but have a term of nine years. The Senate electorate was very restricted.

(d) *The 'Coup d'état de seize mai'* (see Illus. 19.1)

Elections in 1876 produced a Chamber of Deputies dominated by 363 republicans, and MacMahon was forced to accept the moderate republican Jules Simon as prime minister. The anti-clerical demands of Simon's allies led MacMahon to dismiss him in May 1877 and to dissolve the Chamber with its clear republican majority. The republicans

From a contemporary caricature, alluding to the fact that in the *coup d'état de seize mai* Jules Simon was dismissed by MacMahon.

Source: G. Soria, *Grande Histoire de la Commune* (Livre Club Diderot, Paris, 1970) Part 5, p. 314.

Q   What is meant by the symbols in the top left and right of the picture? What does the '363' refer to? Who do you think is the bearded 'jack in the box'?

won another majority and a period of deadlock led to MacMahon having to accept another republican administration in December 1877. The significance of these events was:

1   *The dominance of the legislature over the executive*:

  – The Presidential power of *dissolution* was never again used.
  – Selection of ministers was left entirely to the President of the Council, the prime minister.

2   *The dominance of the Chamber of Deputies.* With a guaranteed life of four years the Chamber could dictate the composition of the government. Unfortunately the Chamber itself was very rarely able to produce a clear majority, or maintain governments. In the first 40 years there were 50 changes of government.

19.3 The Republic of the Republicans (1879–85)

In 1879 the Senate fell to the republicans. The administration and judiciary were filled with republican nominees. In that year MacMahon resigned over attempts to purge the army command and was succeeded by the elderly republican lawyer Jules Grévy.

(a)   *The Opportunists*

Both Thiers and Gambetta, a one-time monarchist and one-time wild radical, had campaigned together against MacMahon. They had both moved in the same direction away from the extremes of ultra-royalism and social disorder to support a moderate republic and only limited social reform. This was in stark contrast to Gambetta's radical Belleville Programme of 1869. The new 'Opportunist' republicans' main electoral support came from the small propertied class, shopkeepers, clerks and draughtsmen and peasants. They were loaded with bourgeois members who distrusted social change and many of whom were ex-Orleanists.

(b)   *'Liberty, Equality and Fraternity'*

The republicans in office looked to the establishment of a true political – although not a social – democracy.

1   *Reconciliation.* Paris was symbolically restored as the capital in 1879. In 1880 the Fall of the Bastille was celebrated for the first time, but a great military review was an attempt to relate republicanism more closely to national patriotism. The next year the Communards were given an amnesty. Trade unions were legalised in 1884, and schemes of public works were set afoot to display concern for the well-being of the citizens.

2   *Removal of inequalities.* The provision for life senators was abandoned in 1884, and replaced by election. Competitive examinations were introduced into the recruitment of the diplomatic service, and this would be later extended to other branches.

3   *'Clericalism – there is the enemy'.* To Gambetta, the greatest obstacle to liberty was the power of the Church with its right-wing political bias, its great wealth – the religious orders had property worth at least £22 million – and, above all, its control of the education of the masses. The issue was one which could be used to draw republicans together; a whole string of anti-clerical measures resulted:

– The 'Godless school' was introduced in 1882 when Jules Ferry, minister of public instruction from 1879, enacted legislation which made primary education free and compulsory and excluded Church supervision from state schools.
– The dissolution and expulsion of religious orders. The Jesuits were disbanded in France in 1880; many orders did, however, obtain permission to continue.
– Clerical staff were ousted from hospitals, the administration of charities and from teaching in state primary schools.
– The re-establishment of civil divorce in 1884.

Clerical influence was undoubtedly reduced and religious practice declined. On the other hand, the split between church and state was deepened and characterised at local level by antagonism between the priest and schoolmaster.

(c) Imperialism and republicanism

Grévy's jealousy meant that Gambetta formed a cabinet himself only in November 1881; two months later he died, at the age of 44. The main issue now facing Ferry, the undisputed new leader, was imperialism. This split the republicans into two groups:

1 *'The blue line of the Vosges'*. Right-wing politicians and radical republicans both agreed that Alsace-Lorraine was the real issue, and that imperialism was a dangerous distraction and drain of resources. Hence the evacuation of Tonkin in 1874 when the monarchists were still powerful.
2 *'The last resource of our greatness'*. Ferry and Gambetta agreed with the writer Prévost-Paradol that French strength in Europe depended upon the resources of her empire. To some extent this was a view encouraged by Bismarck, as a distraction from *'revanche'*. Under Ferry, a 'forward' policy was resumed: Tunis became a French protectorate in 1881 by the Treaty of Bardo (see Section 16.4(c)), a firm foothold was established in Madagascar, the colony of the French Congo was recognised at the colonial conference in Berlin in 1884–5 (see Section 15.2(a)), Annam became a protectorate and Tonkin was reconquered.

(d) The Langson Affair

Indeed it was Tonkin which ended the political reign of Ferry. He had resigned on an earlier occasion when in 1881 there was a move to give up Tunis; in 1882 his associate Freycinet had been brought down for failing to share the initiative with Britain in restabilising a chaotic Egypt (see Section 15.7(b)). Then in 1885 a vastly exaggerated French defeat at Langson in Tonkin brought together all the enemies of 'Ferry-Massacre' (the man who had administered Paris in 1870–1) and forced his resignation. The great radical republican Clemenceau even accused the unfortunate 'Ferry-Tonkin' of treason.

19.4 Weaknesses of the parliamentary régime

The French political system had serious weaknesses, which became all too obvious in the 1880s when – against the background of an agricultural depression and general economic recession – extremist political groups challenged the system, and it was undermined by a series of crises.

(a) 'Immobilisme'

The French system of parliamentary government was carried to extremes. The main criticisms of it were as follows:

1 *Instability*. The combination of a Chamber which could not be dissolved and political parties which were very fragmented and ill-disciplined meant that governments were changed frequently. Very often they fell over an *'interpellation'*, a question to a minister which led on to a debate, then a vote. However, there was usually little change in policy because changes of government usually involved a simple 'replastering', as the French described it, of the old members into a new form.

2   *Mediocrity and parochialism.* The quality of the deputies was rather low, partly because the local committees of notables had too much say in their selection and they preferred men who would narrowly represent local interests.

The result was a lack of responsibility to real changes of opinion in the electorate and an inability to undertake consistent policies.

(b)   *The* 'tempéraments politiques'

The Opportunists survived the death of Gambetta and the fall of Ferry, but they were increasingly trapped in the middle between two extreme tendencies:

1   *Order.* There were those elements who feared democratic politics as a challenge to property and stability, and resisted further reform at all costs. The political right won 202 seats in 1885, largely due to Catholic discontent. The monarchists were in decline with the deaths of the Comte de Chambord and Napoleon the Prince Imperial and the weak image of the Comte de Paris. However, there was a focus for the right in clericalism, nationalism and resistance to social reform. It was represented by new movements such as Paul Déroulèdes's revanchist *'Ligue des Patriotes'* founded in 1882. This new right largely rejected the parliamentary system and tended to see the army as a sort of 'ark of national purity'.
2   *Movement.* On the other hand, there were groups who wanted to press the Republic forward into greater reforms. These included the Radicals led by Clemenceau, who urged an aggressive foreign policy, total separation of the church and state, abolition of the Senate and other extreme measures and a variety of socialist groups from 1880–1 supporting social changes, either by revolution or by reform.

19.5 Scandals and crises (1886–1906)

In 1886 the British ambassador wryly remarked, 'The Republic here has lasted sixteen years and that is about the time which it takes to make the French tired of a form of government.' From 1886 a series of crises and recriminations threatened the very survival of the Republic.

(a)   *The 'Saviour of all France' (1886–91)*

A war scare in 1887 resulting from the German 'kidnapping' of a French police official called Schnaebele made a hero of a dashing young image-conscious general called Georges Boulanger, whose bluster over the affair made him the darling of the 'hawks' and 'revanchists'. The centre of the new cult was originally chosen as minister of war in a Radical–Opportunist government of 1886, because he had displayed very progressive views for a soldier. In fact, he now came to represent a new Napoleon and a potential leader of an anti-parliamentary coup. His image was further enhanced by;

1   *The Wilson scandal* (1887). A revelation of the corrupt activities of the son-in-law of President Grévy, the deputy Daniel Wilson, and the possibility that Grévy might be replaced by the hated 'Ferry-Massacre' led to violent anti-Ferry and pro-Boulanger demonstrations.
2   *The electoral campaigns of the National Republican Party.* In alliance with the monarchist–Bonapartist right, Boulanger fought and won a series of by-elections

(one in Paris) on the basis of a rewriting of the constitution and in an atmosphere of great popular excitement.

The episode ended in anti-climax when the republicans drew together and threatened Boulanger with a trumped-up charge of treason. He fled to Belgium with his mistress, and on her death in 1891 he committed suicide over her grave. Even so, the division had been drawn between the new anti-parliamentary, ultra-nationalist and militarist right against the republicans, Radicals and socialists who were forced to take on the shade of pacific anti-militarism. It also meant that the old moderate republicans were increasingly seen as conservative, and it was the Radicals and new socialists who attracted the support of the workers and lower middle class as the parties of reform.

(b) *Panama (1892–3)*

There was a short interlude of reasonable moderation helped by the celebration of the Great Revolution in 1889, the reduction of military service to three years and the instruction of Pope Leo XIII in 1892–3 that French Catholics should recognise the Republic as exercising God-given authority. Then in September 1892 there were revelations that the Panama Canal Company, since starting work on the project in 1881, had become the centre of a web of corruption which involved a selection of deputies, ex-ministers and administrators. Few men were actually convicted, but the view that the régime was corrupt was strengthened. In addition, it was two Jewish financiers who had dispensed the bribes (about a third of the money raised by the company) so the strand of anti-Semitism in French right-wing nationalism was reinforced. Finally the growing gap between the moderate republicans and the Radicals and socialists was increased, although in fact Clemenceau was one of those who was accused of bribery. The movement of the republicans towards conservatism was reinforced by their concern at the wave of strikes and anarchist bombings of the early 1890s, and the assassination of President Sadi Carnot in 1894.

(c) L'Affaire Dreyfus (1894–1906)

In 1894, Alfred Dreyfus (a young Jewish staff officer) was court-martialled for espionage and exiled to Devil's Island for life. It was then discovered by another officer and the family of Dreyfus that it was a colleague of Dreyfus who was guilty, and that the army had fabricated evidence to cover up the injustice. The issue was taken up by Clemenceau and the novelist Emile Zola, who published an open letter to the president, *'J'accuse'*, in which he made a series of damaging allegations against the army. The case dragged on for a total of twelve years and produced two extreme positions:

1 *The Dreyfusards.* The supporters of Dreyfus identified justice for him with the basic principles of the Republic. To overlook his innocence for 'reasons of state' and to preserve the honour of the army would be a denial of these principles.
2 *The anti-Dreyfusards.* On the other hand, there were the extreme nationalists, anti-Semites, Catholics and others who saw the order and stability of the state as a priority above the Republic itself. This they identified with the army. To the extreme anti-Dreyfusards, the whole thing was seen as a plot to discredit the army despite the events of 1898 when Colonel Henry (the forger of the evidence) committed suicide and Esterhazy (the guilty officer) fled to Britain. In 1899, the election of President Emile Loubet, who had a reputation as a Dreyfusard, led to a farcical and abortive attempt at a *coup d'état* by fanatical anti-Dreyfusards led by Déroulède, and an outburst of rioting which threatened public order.

The new Radical–Socialist government led by Waldeck-Rousseau restored order with firmness, and was responsible for the pardoning of Dreyfus, although not until 1906 was the verdict actually reversed.

(d) *The significance of the Dreyfus Affair* (see Illus. 19.2)

Dreyfus had become a symbol, and the details of the case became secondary in importance to the tensions and the clash of principles for which the Affair acted as a catalyst. Trends which were already present in French attitudes were brought to a boil and would play a significant part in the future of the Third Republic.

1   *'La Patrie en danger!'*. The French Revolution had been revolutionary, republican

Illus. 19.2   *La dernière quille* (Collection Viollet)

From a cartoon by 'Caran d'Ache' in the anti-Dreyfusard magazine *Le Psstl*, February 1898; Baron Rothschild hurls a bowl against the Army.

Source: R. Kedward, *The Dreyfus Affair* (Longman, 1965) p. 53.

Q   The caption reads 'Go on Baron, another one like that and the country is ours.' Who is encouraging Rothschild and why should the great Jewish financier be chosen to appear rather than Dreyfus himself? What else, according to this, has fallen to the Jews? If you cannot guess who the other figure is just ask yourself who stood to gain the most from the destruction of the French army?

and nationalist and the army had represented this unity. Now the army itself had become the focus of a split between those who saw the nation as threatened by the anti-clerical and anti-militarist republicans and the republicans, who saw the army as identified with a counter-revolutionary Catholic authoritarianism. So the *Ligue de la Patrie Française* confronted the republican and anti-clerical *Ligue des Droits de l'Homme*. In the First World War, the Dreyfusard Clemenceau symbolised the defence of both the nation and the republic. In the Second World War, it would be the anti-Dreyfusard forces which overthrew the Third Republic and formed the fascist Vichy government (see Section 29.1).

2   *The Jewish question.* Some Dreyfusards behaved as if the Affair was part of a planned persecution of the Jews, while many anti-Dreyfusards saw Dreyfus as a traitor because he was a Jew. In fact anti-Semitism had been developing rapidly in France throughout the 1880s, fanned by:

– The urge to find a scapegoat to explain their own misfortunes amongst groups such as the *petit bourgeoisie*, the badly paid junior army officers and the Catholics and conservatives whose opportunities were restricted by anti-clerical legislation.
– Jewish identification with the republic and with the economy far beyond that of the Catholics and the monarchists and which was embarrassingly revealed in the *Panama Scandal* of 1892.
– A wave of anti-Semite fantasy stories in the 1890s which fed an ignorant public with images of ritual murder, infanticide, and so on. The rural population was all the more vulnerable to this rubbish because Jews were not very common in the countryside.

3   *Clericalism and anti-clericalism.* The Affair simply exaggerated this age-old conflict. Until then, it had been fought over issues such as education, but the army now became central because the Jesuits were suspected of having great influence in the selection of officers through the success of their college in the *Rue de Postes*. Certainly many of the clergy were anti-Semitic as well. On the other hand, there were Catholics who supported Dreyfus and a progressive France. In fact, after the high point of anti-clericalism with the Combes government (see Section 19.6) there was a tendency towards reconciliation between republicans and Catholics.

4   *'No enemies to the left!'.* Once it became evident that the very survival of the republic was threatened by the anti-Dreyfusard Catholics, the Radicals and even Socialists rallied in support of republican solidarity (the *Bloc des Gauches*), much as Gambetta had once done and as would happen repeatedly in the future. The trouble with this tendency was that it tended to distract the new reformist parties from their original purpose.

19.6 'The spring tide of Radicalism' (1899–1914)

Although they strengthened the diplomatic position of France (see Section 22), the Radicals did nothing to heal the divisions.

(a) *Reform of the army*

The army was subjected to a sort of revenge by the republicans:

1   *The officer corps was purged.* Indeed this process became so blatant that in 1904 General André, the minister of war, was obliged to resign when it was revealed

that he kept a card index of the political opinions of officers which had been collected using a system of spies within the army.

2   *The period of military service was reduced.* In 1905, the period was reduced from three to two years and all exemptions were removed. This had even more serious implications in view of the rising tide of anti-militarism; by 1907, of the conscripts due to serve some 36 per cent did not appear.

(b) Anti-clericalism

The 'Affair' ruined the truce which had prevailed. A policy of extreme anti-clericalism was adopted:

1   *The expulsion of monastic orders.* The Associations Law of 1901 was applied against many orders.
2   *State monopoly of education* (1904). It was ordained that all religious orders and congregations must give up teaching within ten years. Thousands of schools were shut as a result.
3   *Separation of church and state* (1905). The most fanatical anti-clerical was Emile Combes, an ex-professor of theology and prime minister from 1902. He was responsible for the abrogation of the Napoleonic Concordat of 1801 (see Section 2.3(d)) and the withdrawal of the Republic from any obligation to subsidise or support the Catholic Church or clergy. In fact Pope Pius X refused to recognise the new law, and with the French Church left in a state of limbo the army was actually subjected to the indignity of being used to confiscate church property.

19.7 The challenge from the extreme left (see Figs 19.1 and 19.2)

In the later nineteenth century France underwent a form of industrial revolution, despite the diversion of a quarter of French investment abroad by 1914 and the persistence – and after 1880 even the expansion – of peasant farming. Assisted by the Méline tariff of 1892 industrial production expanded. Coal production rose from 26 million tons in 1890 to 41 million tons by 1914, and iron production from 8 million tons in 1880 to 22 million tons in 1913. Associated with this growth were the problems of excessive hours, poor working and living conditions and insecurity of employment.

(a) Syndicalism

The radicals in alliance with moderate socialists were responsible for some limited reforms, such as the introduction of the ten-hour working day for factory workers in 1906 and old age pensions in 1910. However the church–state issue was too much of a distraction, and not enough was done. The result was that industrial workers were attracted by the idea of the overthrow of capitalism by general strikes which was propagated by the Syndicalist socialists who created the *Confédération Générale du Travail* (CGT) in 1895.

(b) Political instability

The result was a wave of strikes and violent demonstrations between 1906 and 1908. The Radicals responded by moving towards the right and the maintenance of order.

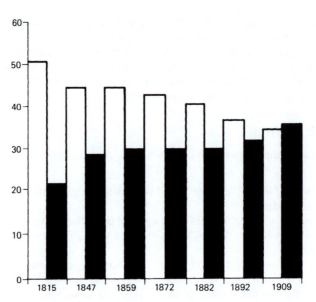

Fig. 19.1   The relative contributions of agriculture and industry to the French national product (1815–1909), percentages, the shaded columns represent industrial production

For a fairly early developer, the pace of industrial development was relatively slow, as was the decline in the agricultural sector which is normally associated with industrial expansion.
Source: Based upon statistical information in C. Trebilcock, *The Industrialisation of the Continental Powers 1780–1914* (Longman, 1981).

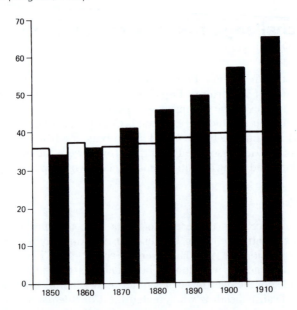

Fig. 19.2   Population growth in Germany and France (1850–1910), millions, the shaded columns represent the growth of the German population

The weakness of the long-term demographic trend in France is very marked, even given the notable effect of the territorial losses of 1871.
Source: Based upon statistical information in C. Trebilcock, *The Industrialisation of the Continental Powers 1780–1914* (Longman, 1981).

Clemenceau, prime minister between 1906 and 1909, used troops and arrested CGT leaders. Afraid of losing support, the moderate socialists ended their alliance with the Radicals and the resultant political instability led to seven ministries between 1911 and 1914.

19.8 Conclusion

The bitter divisions and instability continued to the eve of the outbreak of war. The election of August 1914 saw Radicals and socialists united in opposition to the restoration of three years' military service. Only a few weeks before the catastrophe the wife of the finance minister murdered a right-wing journalist because of his criticism of her husband. On 31 July, a nationalist fanatic murdered Jaurès, the popular leader of the moderate socialists. However with such violent extremism prevalent and an unstable deadlocked political system the French tendency to rally around a 'strong man' reappeared, and Raymond Poincaré was elected to the presidency in January 1913.

Questions

1. In what circumstances was the Third Republic established? What problems did it face before 1879? [OC]
2. What internal difficulties faced France between 1886 and 1914? [OC]
3. Why did the 'Dreyfus Case' have such an impact? [OC]
4. What evidence is there of anti-republican feeling in France in the period 1871–1914? [OX]
5. How was the Third Republic affected before 1914 by problems with (a) Boulanger; (b) Dreyfus; (c) the Church and education? [NEAB]
6. How far did the Third Republic provide France with a satisfactory system of government before 1914?
7. What domestic problems faced the Third French Republic between 1880 and 1914? How successfully did it cope with them? [NEAB]
8. Describe the domestic problems facing French governments from 1871 to 1902. Why did the Third Republic survive? [CAM]
9. Why was the Third Republic in France able to survive the problems which it faced between 1873 and 1906? [CAM]
10. Study Source A below and then answer the questions which follow.

Source A: I Accuse!

The final lines from Emile Zola's *J'Accuse*.

> I accuse Lieutenant-Colonel Du Paty de Clam of having been the diabolical contriver of the judicial error, unconscious I would fain believe; and of having afterwards defended his nefarious work for three years by machinations as ridiculous as they are guilty.
>
> I accuse General Mercier of having made himself the accomplice, through his mere weakness of character, in one of the greatest iniquities of the century.
>
> I accuse General Billot of having had in his hands the certain proofs of Dreyfus' innocence and of having stifled them; of having incurred the guilt of a betrayal of humanity, of a betrayal of justice, in order to serve political ends and to save a [General Staff] that was compromised.
>
> I accuse Generals de Boisdeffre and Gonse of having made themselves accomplices in the same crime – the one, no doubt, led on by clerical passion, the other perhaps by that *esprit de corps* which makes of the War Office Bureaux an ark holy and not to be touched.
>
> I accuse General de Pellieux and Commandant Ravary of having turned their inquiry into a

work of villainy, by which I mean that the inquiry was conducted with the most monstrous partiality; and that of this partiality the report of Ravary is an imperishable monument, brazen in its audacity.

I accuse the three handwriting experts – MM. Belhomme, Varinard, and Couard – of having drawn up lying and fraudulent reports; unless, indeed, a medical examination shows them to be the victims of a diseased eyesight and judgement.

I accuse the War Office of having carried on in the press . . . an abominable campaign intended to lead astray opinion and hide its misdoings.

Lastly, I accuse the first court-martial of having violated right by condemning an accused man on a document which was kept secret, and I accuse the second court-martial of having shielded this illegality to order, committing in its turn the judicial crime of acquitting a man they knew to be guilty.

   (a)   What was the initial issue at the root of the Dreyfus Affair?
   (b)   What do you think Zola meant by 'led on by clerical passion' (line 11)? What did this have to do with the case?
   (c)   According to Zola, why had the army become involved in this web of deceit (lines 20–21)?
   (d)   How did the very existence of the Third Republic become threatened by the Dreyfus Affair?
   Source: Emile Zola, *J'Accuse* (1898 – extract).
11   From Illus. 19.2 (p. 241):
   (a)   What was Emile Zola's contribution to the 'Dreyfus Affair'?
   (b)   State, and explain, what contribution the cartoon is trying to make to the 'Dreyfus debate'.
   (c)   Why was Baron Rothschild doing the bowling?

Imperial Russia 1881–1914

Introduction

Before 1917, the main pattern of history in imperial Russia was the movement towards a sort of alliance between a right-wing constitutional régime and the wealthy landed interest and industrial capitalist class. However the political base for this alliance was too narrow, and a rift developed between the new middle classes and the peasantry and proletariat. The race to strengthen the régime was lost and the outbreak of war in 1914 brought unacceptable pressure to bear on the social system.

20.1 An era of reaction (1881–1905)

Between 1881 and 1917, imperial Russia was unfortunate in the character of two of its autocrats. Alexander III was an upright man who over-identified the good of Russia and the maintenance of autocracy. He was also too easily influenced by extreme nationalist conservatives such as Pobedonostsev, the Chief Procurator of the Holy Synod and Katkov, the editor of the *Moscow Chronicle*. His son Nicholas II, who succeeded him in 1894, was subject to similar influences brought to bear by Princess Alexandra of Hesse and religious charlatans like the monk Gregory Rasputin (see Section 23.4(a)). He was an altogether weaker character, who would have been happier as an English country gentlemen. Trotsky said of him 'This "charmer", without will, without aim, without imagination, was more awful than all the tyrants of ancient and modern history'.

(a) *Repression*

Several lines were followed:

1 *The extension of police powers.* Measures in 1881 and 1885 considerably biased the judicial process against political prisoners and removed fines from cases of offences against state officials. The Third Section was fully restored after a suspension in 1880–1. By 1880, there were 8000 exiles in Siberia.
2 *Censorship.* In 1882, new 'temporary rules' introduced a more methodical censorship. Universities lost their autonomy in 1884 and were far more tightly subject to the control of the minister of education and inspectorate. Legislation in 1887 limited access to the gymnasia and universities to the wealthiest classes.

3 *Limitation of peasant freedom.* There was some attempt to aid the peasants with their redemption payments, but they were also vigorously subjected to the authority of the peasant commune and (from 1889) to the land captains, a species of magistrate drawn from the nobility. In fact peasant mobility was so hindered that they were being reduced to the level of serfs again.

4 *Modification of the freedom of the zemstvos and municipal dumas.* The power of the wealthier classes was increased and peasant membership of the zemstvos was reduced. Provincial governors' powers were considerably expanded.

(b) *Russification*

The internal reflection of the Great Russian nationalism which had produced Pan-Slavism was discrimination against minorities:

1 *The Jews.* A whole range of decrees barred Jews from official and professional posts, restricted their mobility and right to hold property or go to universities. Pogroms became far more prevalent and police-sponsored. From 1891, Jews were being driven to ghettos in the interior, but agreement to conversion would remove all of these disabilities. Jews, of course, had been involved in the assassination of Tsar Alexander II, and traditionally they made excellent scapegoats.

2 *The nationalities.* the 40 million non-Russian subjects were also subject to deliberate Russification from 1890. Poles, Finns, Ukrainians and Armenians were all excluded from holding government offices; the Finnish constitution was revoked in 1899 and the Baltic provinces of Estonia and Livonia also lost their traditional local liberties.

20.2 The economy (1881–1905)

Over the same period, economic changes were the basis for a groundswell of opposition:

1 *Agricultural stagnation and poverty* in a state where the overwhelming majority of the population were peasants.

2 *A high rate of industrial expansion*, with the associated urbanisation and emergence of an industrial proletariat which (although small in numbers) could be of extreme revolutionary significance.

20.3 Agricultural stagnation

There were two obvious developments.

(a) *Social stratification*

Peasant society was dividing into distinct classes, due to:

1 *The sale of the land of the nobility.* Between 1877 and 1905 a third of this went to the wealthy '*kulaks*', a third to the town dwellers or cooperative groups, and only a third to the vast majority of peasants.

2 *The emergence of an agricultural proletariat.* The poorer peasants were driven more and more to hire themselves out as labourers to the nobility or the kulaks.

(b) *Stagnation and decay* (see Fig. 20.1)

Poverty was immense. By 1900, the annual death rate was 31.2 per thousand (it was 16 per thousand in Britain). In 1899–1901 a fifth of potential conscripts were rejected on health grounds.

1   *A population explosion.* From 74 million in 1860 the population grew to 133 million in 1900; of these, over 97 million were peasants. This astounding growth put growing pressure on the land.
2   *Falling world prices.* The price of grain fell between the 1870s and 1890s, and with it fell peasant purchasing power, despite an increase in output of 70 per cent from 1880 to 1897.
3   *The burden of taxation.* Peasants were taxed twice as much as the nobility; they were also affected by indirect taxation on goods of common consumption.

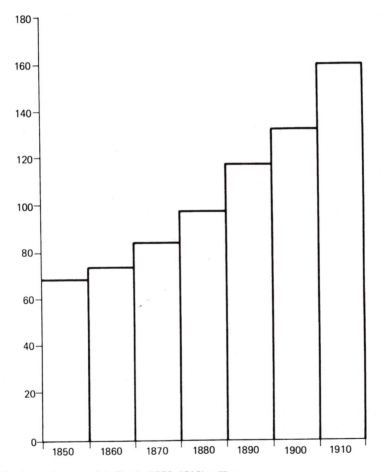

Fig. 20.1   Population growth in Russia (1850–1910), millions

One of the most outstanding characteristics of the demographic history of Europe in this period was the very high rate of population growth in Russia.

Source: Based upon statistical information in C. Trebilcock, *The Industrialisation of the Continental Powers 1780–1914* (Longman, 1981).

(c) Solutions

1 *Death.* Recurrent famines, as in 1890–2, exaggerated the already high death rates even further.
2 *Migration.* It was not easy for peasants to find work in industry because of the late development of industry and the communal restrictions on mobility; however some 100,000 a year turned in the 1890s to Siberia or to the Far East.
3 *Land redistribution.* Interest rates on loans to peasants were reduced in 1894, and the period for redemption payments was extended to 1896. Even so, while redistribution was a popular course with the peasantry it would not itself end poverty.

20.4 Industrial expansion

There was marked industrial development. The number of industrial workers in European Russia rose from 1.2 million in 1879 to 2.2 million in 1903. There were several aspects to this.

(a) *Growth* (see Fig. 20.2)

Between 1893 and 1900 industrial output doubled. By 1900 40 per cent of all industry had existed only since 1891. Coal production doubled in 1880–92, as did ferrous metal output. Oil production rose by fourteen times, and Russia was the world's leading oil producer. This process was based upon:

1 *Foreign investment.* Positive encouragement – in the form of high rates, a protectionist tariff from 1891 and the stablilisation policies of a series of excellent finance ministers – meant that by 1914 France held 80 per cent of Russian foreign debt securities and by 1900 foreigners owned a third of the private capital and industry in Russia.
2 *State intervention.* Especially noteworthy was the minister of finance from 1892 to 1903, Sergei Witte. He reversed the old distrust of industrial development and saw it as vital to achieve self-sufficiency and great power status – and 'a great power cannot wait'. His achievements – reflected in the increasing of government revenue by 250 per cent – were due to:

   – Sponsored railway expansion. In 1860, there were 1000 miles of line; there were 44,000 by 1914; Witte was responsible for increasing the mileage built by 250 per cent a year. In 1881, 95 per cent of the total had been privately owned; by 1902 only 33 per cent of it was.
   – Direct encouragement by means of protection and subsidies to promote specific leading industries.
   – Adoption of the gold standard in 1897 to integrate Russia fully into the European money markets.

(b) *Unrest*

Even so, the rising standard of living of industrial workers was matched by their vulnerability to agitators:

1 *Industrial instability.* In the recession of 1900–3, for instance 30 per cent of the labour force were put out of work.

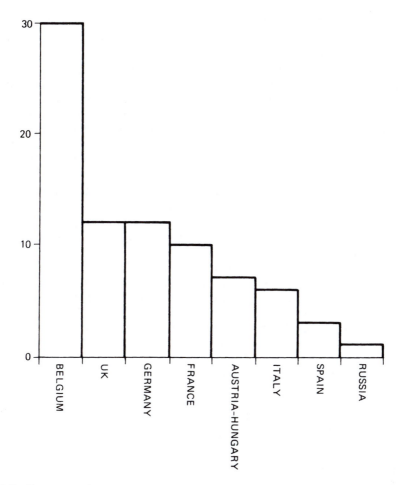

Fig. 20.2 The comparative densities of railway networks in Europe in 1913, length of open track in miles per each square mile of territory

Source: Based upon statistical information in C. Trebilcock, *The Industrialisation of the Continental Powers 1780–1914* (Longman, 1981).

2   *Labour concentration.* By 1914, 40 per cent of workers were in factories employing a thousand men or more. Such concentration could be far more easily mobilised on behalf of political disturbances.

3   *Frequency of strikes and disputes.* Working and living conditions and low, and irregularly paid wages led to disputes throughout the 1880s and 1890s. One result was a spate of factory legislation. However, troops were used against strikers, trade unions were made illegal, strikes were made punishable by fines and refusal to work could lead to arrest.

20.5 The development of opposition to Tsarism

A number of opposition groups emerged which reflected different aspects of this social and economic discontent, although they all tended to be drawn from the intellectual middle class.

(a) The Social Democratic Party

In the 1880s Plekhanov (see Section 10.7(b)) turned to Marxism and an emphasis on the industrial workers as well as the peasant communes. The true founder of the new Social Democratic Party, though, was *Lenin* (Vladimir Ilyich Ulyanov). He came from a respectable family of the bureaucratic nobility. The execution of his brother for attempting to assassinate the Tsar made 1887 a turning point. Even as a law student he was involved in Marxist student activities and later was sent to Siberia for five years for involvement with the Union of Struggle for the Liberation of the Working Class. In 1898 Marxist delegates founded the *Social Democratic Party* at Minsk, In 1900, freed from exile, Lenin began to capture this and convert it into a disciplined conspiratorial machine. Two controversies resulted:

1   *'Economic' revisionism.* The 'economists' opposed revolution as an objective and preferred to assist the industrial workers in their economic struggle. In the party newspaper *Iskra* (*The Spark*) and his pamphlet *'What is to be done?'* in 1902 Lenin argued that rather than await the 'inevitable' revolution, the Social Democrats would be the vanguard of the working class.
2   *The Bolshevik–Menshevik split.* It followed that the party should be very secret and tightly knit: Lenin said, 'Give us an organisation of revolutionaries and we will overturn the whole of Russia.' This was supported at congresses at Brussels and London by the Bolshevik faction ('those in the majority') while the Mensheviks ('those in the minority') urged a more loosely based open party. The split never healed, and the Mensheviks were by no means a permanent minority.

(b) The Social Revolutionary Party

The *Social Revolutionaries* were founded in 1901. They were very much descended from the older Populist movement with their emphasis on the land question and agrarian socialism and the terrorist methods of 'The Peoples' Will' (see Section 10.7(b)).

(c) The Union of Liberation Party

By the 1890s the moderate *zemstvo* liberals were actually meeting in congresses. In 1903 they, other moderates and even moderate socialists came together to form the Union of Liberation Party to urge the establishment of a liberal constitution.

20.6 The 'dress rehearsal' of 1905–6

The revolutionary events of 1905–6 are frequently seen as a sort of playing out of the scripts and parts of 1917.

(a) 'Bloody Sunday' (9 January 1905)

Witte wrote of the Russo-Japanese War (see Section 22.5(c)): 'Instead of enhancing the prestige and increasing the physical resources of the régime, the war with its endless misery and disgrace, completely sapped the system's vitality and laid bare its utter rottenness before the eyes of Russia and of the world generally'. A rising tide of peasant defaultings against conscription and workers strikes culminated in January 1905 in the mammoth procession of 150,000 workers led by *Father Gapon*, a part-time police agent, to present a petition of grievances to the Tsar at the Winter Palace. Troops fired

Illus. 20.1 Father Gapon and the Governor General of St Petersburg with members of the Russian Workers Assembly, January 1905

Source: F. Wyndham and D. King, *Trotsky* (1972).

and killed about 1000 people, wounding another 3000. Unnecessarily, the old image of the Tsar as the 'father of his peoples' had been destroyed.

(b) *General Strikes*

A general strike in St Petersburg and a wave of strikes in all industrial regions followed. By the summer, attempts at conciliation had failed and the strikes were more widespread and violent. *Peasant revolts* also added their ominous weight. In October there occurred a general strike in St Petersburg which included workers, students and the professional classes.

(c) *The demands of the opposition*

1 *The Social Democrats.* There was no disagreement about a revolution by workers and peasants to overthrow autocracy. However the time scale caused problems:

   – As orthodox Marxists, the Mensheviks believed in a bourgeois democratic revolution first, to be followed by a working-class revolution.
   – In 1905, Lenin announced 'We stand for the uninterrupted revolution. We shall not stop halfway'. This revision of the doctrines of Marx simply proposed a short cut to the dictatorship of the proletariat.

2 *The Constitutional Democratic Party.* In May 1905 the *zemstvo* liberals and professional intelligentsia created the Constitutional Democratic Party (the *Kadets*), which sought co-operation with a parliament or 'duma'.

3 *The Social Revolutionaries.* The Social Revolutionaries represented peasant demands for the nationalisation of land, and also the calling of a constituent assembly.

Very significant was the creation in October 1905 of the St Petersburg Soviet of Workers' Deputies, which acted as a sort of revolutionary government and linked together factory workers and intellectuals like the brilliant Jewish lawyer and Social Democrat Trotsky.

(d) The October Manifesto (17 October)

Revolution spread to the subject nationalities by winter 1905. The Tsar was forced to act by the lack of force at his disposal. The great mutiny in June 1905 on the battleship Potemkin was more the result of rotten food and 'sea lawyers', but there had been army mutinies and the very best units were at the wrong end of the Trans-Siberian railway. In October, the Tsar bought time by conceding:

1   Freedom of the press, opinion, assembly and association.
2   Provision for the election of a legislative *duma*.
3   Creation of a council of ministers under the presidency of Witte.

(e) Insurrection in Moscow (December 1905)

The Social Democrats went on with their agitation – now openly. They urged an armed uprising, and tried to influence the troops. But by December, the military situation was a good deal stronger, and the Tsar could rely on those moderates who accepted the *October Manifesto* and upon extremist gangs such as the 'black hundreds' who attacked revolutionaries and Jews. The Social Democrats rejected the Manifesto as a 'police whip wrapped in the parchment of the constitution' and in December the dissolution of the St Petersburg Soviet was followed by an armed revolt led by the Moscow Soviet. Two weeks fighting, 1000 dead and extensive destruction saw it crushed.

20.7 Stolypin and the *Dumas* (1906–7)

The manifesto was not revoked. Trade unions were openly organised; the press enjoyed considerable freedom. However, the Tsarist government almost at once began to undercut the concessions.

(a) The 'fundamental laws' (April 1906)

Witte's electoral system for the Duma was heavily biased towards the propertied classes and towards the peasantry who were seen as fundamentally conservative. It took 90,000 workers to elect a deputy. It took 30,000 peasants to elect one. In addition autocracy was virtually confirmed:

1   The State Council was to be half appointed by the Tsar, the rest were to be elected by wealthy and propertied classes.
2   The Tsar could choose and dismiss ministers to suit himself. He was in full control of the armed forces, the executive and foreign policy.
3   The Tsar could *veto* any legislation, and could govern by decree when the Duma was not in session, although legislation required the endorsement of the Duma and State Council.

Unfortunately Witte resigned at this point because of lack of support from the Tsar and his successor was the far more devious Peter Stolypin.

(b) Concessions to the peasantry (November 1906)

To try and attach the loyalty of peasant landowners to the state it was made possible for the peasants of the commune to *leave it*, and to divide the land between themselves or sell it. Redemption payments had already been abolished.

(c) Mobilisation of counter-revolutionary forces

The violence continued. In 1906 the Social Revolutionaries alone undertook 1500 assassinations and even made an attempt on Stolypin's life:

1 The establishment of military courts with wide powers over civilians. In six months they ordered 950 executions.
2 Counter-revolutionary propaganda was mobilised through the anti-revolutionary Council of the United Nobility established in May 1906.

(d) A strong hand with the Dumas

1 *The First Duma* (May–July 1906). The Social Revolutionaries and the Social Democrats, divided over their own policies, boycotted the elections to the first Duma. The Kadets had a majority, and the right-wing Octobrists dominated it. Even so, the opposition to the government was very clear. The Kadets urged the establishment of ministerial responsibility to the Duma, and (with peasant deputies) the distribution of the land to the peasantry.
2 *The Second Duma* (February–June 1907). In the new Duma government influence was not enough to prevent the Kadets' support falling while the Social Revolutionaries and Social Democrats were now represented. The main business of the Duma was legislation on peasant and land tenure, which was bitterly opposed by the socialists simply because it was likely to win peasant support for the government. Stolypin's response was to dissolve the Duma, arrest the Social Democrat leaders on trumped-up charges and bias the electoral system far more towards the nobility and bourgeoisie (about 50 per cent of the total) and against the peasants and workers (about 25 per cent).

20.8 A period of domestic peace (1907–12)

Stolypin sought to achieve a period of stability: 'Give the state twenty years of domestic and foreign peace and you will not recognise present day Russia.' Three factors underpinned this stability.

(a) A 'gamble on the strong'

Stolypin had made a clear bid for peasant support. By 1916 2 million peasant households (25 per cent of the total) left the communes and took legal title to their own land. In addition, the peasants were helped by the rise in food prices and the assistance of the new Peasant Bank.

(b) Expansion

1 *The growth of agricultural output.* Partly because of these reforms there was a 15 per cent expansion in land under cultivation between 1901 and 1913. Siberia was

becoming an important grain-producing area. Grain exports grew between 1920 and 1913; in addition, there was expansion of output in cotton-growing, flax, sugar beet, potatoes and livestock. However:

– Peasant farming was still profoundly *backward*. In 1913, there were only 166 tractors in the whole of Russia.
– The average standard of living of the peasants was still very low. By 1913, the average peasant income per head was £26 per year.
– Stolypin's gamble had been taken too late. It should have been taken in 1861.

2   *Industrial development.* By 1913 the total industrial labour force was 6 million. Between 1908 and 1913 there was a renewed wave of expansion, due to:

– Foreign investment, up to a third of the total capital investment in Russia by 1914.
– The stimulus of the need to replace equipment lost in the Russo-Japanese War and to build strategic railways. By 1914, 30 per cent of government expenditure was on these objectives.
– Growing foreign trade. Russia's main customers were Britain and Germany, although only 6 per cent of the total exports were manufactures.

On the other hand, Russia still produced fourteen times less than Britain in industrial terms. The government still depended for its revenue on the peasantry, whose wheat made up 55 per cent of total exports and whose indirect taxes made up half of the revenue.

(c)   *Some moderation of opposition*

The *third Duma* (November 1907–Autumn 1913) was very right-wing and concentrated on issues like the budget and educational reform. The Social Democrats were divided over whether the party should be a legal party operating openly, or a conspiratorial revolutionary party. In 1912, Lenin declared that the Bolshevik faction was the true Social Democratic Party.

20.9 Conclusion

After an interlude, the domestic peace began to recede:

1   *Extra-legal activities by the state.* Stolypin himself by-passed the Duma when necessary. The Duma displayed a reprehensible right-wing Great Russian bias in seeking to reduce the autonomy of Finland, supporting discrimination against the Jews and restoring Russification. Far more sinister was the assassination of Stolypin himself in 1911, which may have involved the security police and a steadily disenchanted Tsar. By then the Tsar and Tsarina were increasingly under the influence of the dissolute monk Rasputin, who had the apparent ability to stop the bleeding of the haemophilic Tsarevich.

2   *The revival of industrial unrest.* In April 1912 270 strikers in the Lena gold fields were shot. Waves of strikes followed. By 1914 they included $1\frac{1}{2}$ million workers, largely directed by the Bolshevik newspaper *Pravda (Truth)*. By July 1914 there was open unrest on the streets of St Petersburg.

3   *Growth of opposition in the Duma.* The Fourth Duma elected in 1912 had a sizeable liberal opposition, although the Octobrists still held the balance.

The race had been lost. The conditions of 1905 were duplicated between 1914 and 1917, but on a far greater scale and with the cracks in the autocratic edifice already obvious.

Questions

1 Were Tsarist reforms between 1890 and 1914 'too little, too late?' [OC]
2 How effectively did the Tsarist régime re-establish its position after 1905? [OC]
3 Assess the contribution of Count Witte and Stolypin to domestic reform in Russia [OX]
4 'The reign of Nicholas II was plagued by one disaster after another.' Explain this comment on the domestic affairs of Russia between 1894 and February 1917. [NEAB]
5 How successfully was Russia governed between 1906 and 1917? What brought about the abdication of the Tsar? [NEAB]
6 How far was Nicholas II responsible for the collapse of the Tsarist régime? [NEAB]
7 Describe the main events in Russia during the reign of Nicholas II from 1894 until 1914. Did Nicholas II deserve to lose his throne? [CAM]
8 Outline the problems facing Nicholas II inside Russia between 1894 and 1917. Why had he lost the support of the Russian people by 1917? [CAM]
9 How well were the lessons of the 1905 Revolution learned by the Tsarist régime and its opponents? [CAM]
10 Study Source A below and then answer the questions which follow.

Source A: The burdens of autocracy.
From the memoirs of a British diplomat.

> In that summer of 1912 I had the good fortune to see the Emperor twice – a rare opportunity in Moscow, for the Tsar of all the Russias seldom visited the ancient capital. The city had too many tragic memories for him. Moscow, too, was the centre of Radicalism and, as such, was anathema to the Empress. On the first occasion, the Tsar came to unveil the statue of his father, the Emperor Alexander III. It was a strictly official ceremony, attended only by the nobles, the military and civil heads of departments, and a selected number of the leading merchants. I remember the visit for two reasons: first, because for weeks before the Moscow police had pestered us and, indeed, all the Consular Corps with idiotic questions regarding the political reliability of our various nationals who lived anywhere near the route along which the Emperor was to pass, and secondly, because on his way to the Kremlin the Tsar stopped at the spot where the Grand Duke Serge had been murdered, and knelt down alone on the cobbled stones and prayed.
> The occasion of the Emperor's second visit was the centenary of Borodino and the liberation of Russia from the yoke of Napoleon. This time the celebration was a national one and strikingly impressive in the demonstration of loyalty it aroused. Never have I seem a finer body of men that the Cossack troops who formed the Emperor's bodyguard. Well may the pre-war foreign military attachés be forgiven for over-estimating the military strength of Russia. Yet the real symbol of Russia's strength was the frail bearded figure with the strange, wistful eyes, who rode at the head of his troops and whose feeble shoulders seemed incapable of supporting the mantle of autocracy which, like a shroud, hung over them.

(a) Who were the Emperor (line 1) and the Empress (line 4)? Why did Moscow hold 'tragic memories' (line 3) for them?
(b) Describe the aims and methods of the opposition groups which made Moscow 'the centre of Radicalism' (line 3).
(c) With reference to the events of his reign between 1894 and 1914, comment upon the description of the Emperor as 'the frail bearded figure ... whose feeble shoulders seemed incapable of supporting the mantle of autocracy' (lines 18–21).
(d) What does the passage tell us of the way in which the Russian Empire was governed, and of its strengths and weaknesses? [OC]
Source: R. H. Bruce-Lockhart, *Memoirs of a British Agent*.

21 The Habsburg Monarchy 1849–1914

Introduction

Between 1849 and 1914 there were recurrent attempts to discover some suitable structural form for the patchwork of Habsburg dynastic territories. To some extent, the objective of these efforts was the maintenance and enhancement of the resources of a huge family estate to continue to play its part in international affairs. However, there also evolved the claim that the Monarchy must fulfil some sort of 'historic mission', and that the 'Austrian idea' amounted to the persistence of a state in eastern central Europe which could protect and retain the loyalties of a diversity of nationalisms. A variety of organisational forms were tried, and they failed because of their own internal inadequacies and changes in external circumstances. By 1914 the forces of *centrifugalism* were overwhelming the *centripetal* pressures and a quick, pre-emptive local war was being urged in some circles as the only residual option. The Great War which was unleashed destroyed the Monarchy. As Metternich had realised, the greatest threat to an international state is an international war.

21.1 A broad perspective

Following the upheavals of 1848–9 there were various options available to the Habsburg Monarchy in planning the restructuring of the Empire. These can be conveniently grouped into two sets:

(a) *Centralisation*

It could be argued that the revolutions of 1848–9 had resulted from inadequate central authority, and that the modernisation and strengthening of the Empire required unity and standardisation. Conservatives and liberals could agree over this general diagnosis, but differ over the extent of governmental responsibility.

1 *Centralised absolutism* without any form of parliamentary control and reliant upon the bureaucracy and the army.
2 *Centralised constitutionalism* with a degree of restraint upon the executive and parliamentary responsibility. This, however, would require a definition of the extent of popular participation and the devising of some form of franchise. This, therefore, ran the risk of reopening the door to nationalist expectations and rivalries.

(b) *Decentralisation*

Again, there were two possible variants:

1 *Limited regional autonomy.* The restoration of the old pattern of provincial *Diets*,
   but combined with strong central institutions.
2 *Federalism.* This would involve the separation of nationality groups into self-
   governing units, but with key powers and responsibilities – such as defence, finance
   and foreign policy – reserved for the personal authority of the monarch.

The Emperor (see Illus. 21.1) was not the sort of man who was attracted by abstract
principles. He responded empirically to events and circumstances, trying to avoid
excessive commitment to any particular line of action and its advocates.

21.2 Centralised absolutism (1849–59)

The Stadion Constitution (see Section 9.12(a)) continued nominally until December
1851. By then, there was no longer a need to rally moderates against the Magyars or to
bid against Prussia for the leadership of a North German union. The Emperor then
assumed absolute control. For the next ten years the problem of nationalism was
ignored, and the Empire was governed directly, as a unit, from Vienna. The system,
known after Alexander von Bach, the Minister of the Interior, involved the elimination
of provincial and local governing institutions and the standardisation of all administra-

Illus. 21.1   The birthday of the Emperor in 1896

Carriages arriving at St Stephens for a service to celebrate the birthday of the Emperor

By 1896 Francis Joseph had reigned for nearly half a century. His total devotion to his duties at the
expense of personal comfort and sentiments meant that he had become a profoundly respected
institution in his own right. His sacrifices on behalf of his people could be counted to include his drug
addict son Rudolph who died in mysterious circumstances in 1889 at Mayerling, and his beautiful wife
Elizabeth of Bavaria, who was murdered in 1898.

tive procedures regardless of national or linguistic differences. It was applied by German and Czech bureaucrats. It was once described as comprising 'A standing army of soldiers, a sitting army of officials, a kneeling army of priests and a creeping army of denunciators'.

The *'Bach System'* endured until 1859, when it was replaced with a new structure. This was for two reasons.

(a) *Inherent inadequacies*

1 *Embittering of the national minorities.* At least there was an equality between the nationalities. They were all equally unprivileged and discontented. This was true of even the traditionally loyal Croats. As one Croat remarked cynically to a Magyar, 'What you are getting as punishment we are getting as reward.' The taste of national freedom in 1848–9 made the resentment at this famous 'gratitude of the Habsburgs' even greater. Since the bureaucracy was predominantly German and the official language was German, the system was easily portrayed as enforced *Germanisation*.

2 *The cost of absolutism.* There was some economic growth, some industrialisation and a fourfold increase in exports by 1854. This was helped by the effects of the freeing of the peasants (see Section 9.8(a)) and the abolition of the tariff wall between Hungary and the rest of the Empire. However, the rate of capital expansion was much inferior to the general European rate, and the government's inadequacy in financial affairs was highlighted by the 1857 economic crisis. Absolutism depended upon an expensive army and bureaucracy so taxation was high and rising rapidly. Direct taxation in Hungary increased tenfold between 1848 and 1857. The Germans, in particular, as the most productive and wealthiest group, were resentful at high taxation levels and the inequality of a single imperial taxation system.

(b) *A failed foreign policy*

The Emperor had expected foreign policy to be reinforced by domestic absolutism. In fact, the late 1850s saw two major reverses:

1 The Crimean War left the Monarchy isolated in Europe (see Section 11.6).
2 The War of Italian Unification in 1859 (see Section 13.5(a)) saw an embarrassing defeat by the forces of France and Piedmont.

21.3 A hiatus (1860)

Now the Emperor needed to conciliate one or more of the great *'historic nations'* to obtain the revenue and troops he needed. Initially he opted for a revitalisation of the old provincial Diets and the restoration of organs of local self-government in Hungary. The October Diploma of 1860 would have introduced a limited devolution of powers. The crown would co-operate with the provincial *Diets* in legislating on provincial matters and with an enlarged advisory Imperial Council in general matters. The proposals were drafted for the Emperor by the Hungarian Count Szeczen and were aimed especially at conciliating the Hungarian nationalists. In fact, they were acceptable to none of the interested groups. Criticism focused upon:

1 *Concessions made to the Hungarians.* Szeczen did not reflect the more prevalent

Magyar extremism. With the 'Bach Hussars' withdrawn they now wanted the restoration of the April laws of 1848 (see Section 8.8(c)) and refused to co-operate with the Imperial Council. Germans, on the other hand, resented the special preferential treatment given to the Hungarians.

2 *The revival of the provincial Diets.* German liberal middle classes saw this as a retrograde step. They identified the growth and success of the Empire with the Germans (the *'Staatsvolk'*) and preferred the unitary centralised system. On the other hand, the aristocratic advocates of provincialism were disappointed at the limited powers which were to be restored to the *Diets.*

3 *The status of the 'non-historic' peoples.* On the one hand the Slovaks, Serbs and Rumanians of Hungary opposed the restoration of Magyar powers which would lead to a renewal of Magyarisation. Yet the Diploma promised organs of local government in Croatia, Transylvania and other provinces and Germans and Magyars objected to these concessions to these culturally less-developed peoples.

As a result, the Emperor now turned to *alliance with the Germans* whose support he needed in the bid for Habsburg leadership of a 'Greater Germany'.

21.4 The 'Schmerling System' (1861–5)

Schmerling, the new minister of state, produced a constitutional programme that was a compromise between bureaucracy and liberalism, and disproportionately weighted towards the Germans.

1 *Centralisation.* The provincial Diets lost their legislative powers and the Imperial Council now became an imperial parliament, the Reichsrat. Its powers were limited; taxes could be raised without its consent, the Emperor kept control of the army, the executive and finance departments.

2 *Elected representation.* Nevertheless, the Reichsrat did have legislative powers and a degree of ministerial control. The electoral system which produced it was cynically weighted towards the German urban property owners. In Moravia, for instance, the towns (largely German 'islands') had 13 deputies representing a population of 430,000 while the 1,600,000 country dwellers (largely Slovak) had only 11 deputies.

The new system did not last as long as the old. Indeed it failed for similar reasons.

(a) *The persistence of Hungarian antagonism*

The new leader of the Magyars, Francis Deák, believed that in the long run the re-establishment of constitutionalism in Hungary could only be achieved by agreement with the other major 'historic' people, the Germans. However, at this point he put himself at the head of the Kossuthite hardliners who dominated the lower house of the Diet and insisted on the restoration of the March Laws of 1848, the Hungarian constitution as of right.

The Imperial government had two options:

1 *An appeal for the support of the 'non-historic' Slav peoples* in the Empire in general, and within Hungary against the Magyars. However, the Germans were already in dispute with the Czech nationalists over the future of Bohemia. In any case the German bureaucrats and liberals saw the claims of the backward Slav national groups as a threat to the integrity of the Empire, and as reactionary.

2   *Restoration of the 'Bach Hussars'.* Schmerling therefore rejected what could have been a turning point in imperial development, and simply restored German bureaucratic absolutism in Hungary.

(b) A failed foreign policy

It was changes in international relations which again dictated another internal reorganisation:

1   Rejection of the bid for membership of the *Zollverein* by the Monarchy (1863) brought the prospect of war with Prussia closer over the issue of German leadership. There was less urgency to play up the Germanness of the Empire, and a pressing need to reach an agreement with the Magyars.
2   *The Austro-Prussian War* (1866). Approaches had already been made to the Hungarians. The defeat at Königgratz encouraged the Magyar extremists who supported independence but Déak's argument was that Magyar dominance over the Slavs required the contrivance of an imperial connection.

The result was a sort of partnership between the 'peoples of state' – the Germans and the Magyars – and concessions by the Emperor to gain the time to preserve the rest of the Habsburg territories. In fact the Magyars virtually regained the lost March Laws. Déak could well rejoice 'We lost the war! We are now victorious!'

21.5 The *Ausgleich* (1867)

The *Ausgleich* was a compromise between federalism, centralisation and liberalism. The Dual Monarchy which resulted consisted of three elements.

(a) The 'Common Monarchy'

Austria and Hungary were to be linked only for the purposes of defence and foreign policy. There was no common executive or legislature. The essential links were maintained through:

1   *A common ruler.* The Emperor ruled as Emperor of Austria and King of Hungary.
2   *Joint ministries ('Kaiserlische and Königslische')* were responsible for foreign affairs, defence and finance.
3   *Annual delegations* of 60 members each from the two parliaments were to consider the demands of the common ministries and recommend appropriate levels of taxation and troop contingents.
4   *A decennial treaty* was to be negotiated which regulated tariffs and currency.

(b) Two separate states

The Monarchy was divided into two components:

1   *The Kingdom of Hungary*, which now included Croatia and Transylvania and was free to restore the March Laws of 1848 and the policy of Magyarisation. After 1867, it was in fact a criminal offence to call Francis Joseph 'Emperor' in Hungary.
2   *The vaguely named 'Cisleithania'*, which was not officially called Austria until 1915. Of the population 64 per cent were non-Germans although the old German-dominated constitution and franchise continued. Although there was still no real

parliamentary control over the executive, a genuine system of individual liberties was introduced.

The most immediate and obvious losers from the installation of the Ausgleich were the Slavs.

(c) 'The Slavs are not fit to govern'

Although the Slavs were theoretically protected by the Nationalities Law, both Germans and Magyars could agree with the remark by Count Andrassy, one of Déak's advisers, that the Slavs had been betrayed to the Magyars in Hungary. As Count Beust cynically remarked 'You take care of your barbarians and we will take care of ours!' In Austria, equal rights in linguistic matters were guaranteed, but there was great potential for conflict in areas of very mixed ethnic and linguistic nature, and the Germans enjoyed disproportionate political power. The *Ausgleich* was attacked by Slav leaders. Palacky warned that it would 'become the birthday of Pan-Slavism in its least desirable form'. In Bohemia, the Czech nationalists, allied with the Bohemian aristocracy, demanded the same rights as the Magyars and the introduction of a triple monarchy with Bohemia as the third kingdom. On the advice of the Germans and Magyars, the Emperor rejected this, and from then on the Czechs boycotted the imperial and provincial parliaments.

21.6 The Dual Monarchy (1867–1908): Austria (see Illus. 21.2)

The Germans could not provide a majority in the Reichsrat, even with the restricted franchise. In any case, the Emperor was reluctant to be excessively dependent upon one national grouping. However, he could not use the Czechs to balance the Germans until 1878. Politics in the Austrian half of the Monarchy can therefore be considered in two phases:

1 The political dominance of the German liberals (1867–79).
2 Coalition politics based upon alliances of interest groups (from 1879 onwards).

(a) The German liberals (1867–79)

The liberals were responsible for some progressive measures in this period, such as legal reforms and the establishing of compulsory elementary education. The fall of the liberals came as a result of two factors:

1 *The economic crisis of 1873*, which discredited *laissez-faire* and liberal capitalism. Since the capitalist class was (on the whole) German, the crisis had a nationalist dimension. The situation was worsened by the usual revelations of shady deals between officials and businessmen.
2 *The occupation of Bosnia and Herzegovina in 1878* (see Section 22.7) was opposed by the German liberals, because it was another Slav territory and it would be a burden on the taxpayer. Their voting against the establishment of a protectorate infuriated the Emperor.

In 1879 imperial influence was used against the liberals in the election, and they lost their majority. The Emperor now turned to the combination of a coalition of political groups drawn from the other nationalities. He entrusted the task to a great political manager, Count Edward Taaffe.

Illus. 21.2 Crowds at the Praterstein on a Sunday, 1905
Source: Unknown.

On the eve of a crisis in Austro-Hungarian relations, the next stage in the deepening nationalities problem of the Habsburg Monarchy, the Viennese displayed their characteristic lack of concern for these disturbing developments. After all the Monarchy had survived one crisis after another in one form or another for so many centuries that it was inconceivable that it was faced with a final mortal challenge.

(b) 'The resort of the men with a grievance'

By the 1870s changing circumstances were broadening the appeal of nationalism, which had been restricted to an intellectual élite earlier in the century. Nationalism was increasingly underpinned with self-interest, not just A. J. P. Taylor's 'men with a grievance' but people with rising expectations. Several factors contributed to this:

1   *The influx of Slavs to the growing towns* looking for work in the new industries as agricultural prices stagnated or fell. In the new towns social and working conditions were bad, and a developing class antagonism was inevitable. However, in Austria this was confused by the fact that the capitalists – the employers – were usually Germans or Jews over-emphasising their Germanness while the workers were Slavs.

2   *The growth of the educational system* not only made the lower social orders more susceptible to national literature, it also increased their expectation of a job in the bureaucracy in the professions which had in the past been identified with the culturally more advanced Germans. In universities, for instance, 50 per cent of students in the 1860s had been German; by the 1880s they made up only about 40 per cent.

3   *The expansion of the range and scale of the activities of the state* meant that there were so many more jobs available. By 1914 there were over 3 million civil servants alone. The expansion of the dealings of the state with ordinary people meant that there could be far greater opportunities for non-Germans if the way was opened.

So nationalism was becoming another factor in the every day life of jealousies, frustrations and ambitions. At its most basic, it was a matter of the language used in school teaching, in public services and in street names. Nationalist rivalry existed as a fact by the 1870s. Unfortunately Taaffe and his successors helped to make this rivalry a dominant feature in imperial politics. As Taaffe remarked: 'all the nationalities should be maintained in the same well tempered dissatisfaction.

(c) The politics of self-interest (1879–1908)

Taaffe built up a coalition (the 'Iron Ring') against the German liberals made up of the anti-liberal German Roman Catholic peasantry, the Poles, the Czechs and the Slovenes. He won the support of the nationalities by resorting to so-called 'pork-barrel' politics, the use of practical administrative concessions to buy votes. In particular, he bought the adherence of the newer, more aggressive young Czechs:

1 The electoral law of 1882 ensured a Czech majority in the Bohemian *Diet* and the Bohemian contingent in the *Reichsrat*.
2 The University of Prague was split into German and Czech divisions.
3 Czech and German were given equality as languages of the 'outer service' in Bohemia – the sections of public service which dealt directly with the public. The official language of the 'inner service' remained German. In fact by the 1890s 90 per cent of the Bohemian civil service were Czechs.

Taaffe also made notable concessions to the Poles in Galicia. The effect of this sort of government was that it further diminished political responsibility; it also built up German resentment and fears, especially on the 'racial frontiers' such as Bohemia. Although Taaffe's 'Iron Ring' broke in 1893, his methods were now entrenched, and crisis and confrontation became inevitable.

(d) Polarisation (see Map 21.1)

The Empire was very much a German institution. The Germans had been the most active and positive contributors to its development. The leading centripetal institutions – the dynasty itself, the church hierarchy, the bureaucracy, the army and capitalism – were German in character. Growing nationalist antagonism naturally weakened the force of these institutions because of that too easy identification. However, the Germans themselves felt increasingly threatened by the Slavs, who they felt were their cultural and social inferiors. There were several levels of response:

1 *Extreme German radicalism*, such as that exhibited by Georg von Schönerer and the *Linz Programme* of 1882. The creation of Germany in 1871 meant that the loyalty of some German radicals was torn between the Habsburg State and their German nationality. These could be reconciled by shedding from the Monarchy areas like Galicia, Dalmatia and Hungary and creating the 'Greater Germany'. The radicals and Pan-Germanists were also very racialist and anti-Semitic.
2 *The defence of the status of the German language*, which also protected the status of Germans themselves in areas like Bohemia, could attract wider support from moderates.

The German reaction was especially notable in Bohemia in confrontation with the Young Czechs and over issues minor in themselves. There were riots in the 1880s over the language to be used in town councils and in 1890 over the language used in Custom House receipts. There were recurrent struggles over the languages taught and used for instruction in schools. The Czechs always had the advantage that they had often learnt German as a practical necessity and a means of social advancement, while Germans

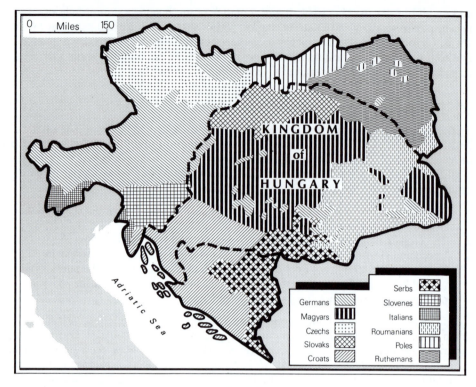

Map 21.1 *The nationalities of Austria–Hungary in 1914*

rarely learnt inferior languages like Czech. The greatest confrontation was over the *Badeni Ordinance* of 1897, which was to make Czech and German equal languages in the Bohemian 'inner service'. There were violent demonstrations throughout Austria and radical obstructionism in the Reichsrat. At a later date in 1899 the withdrawal of the Ordinance simply provoked Czech obstruction.

These national and linguistic rivalries were repeated all over the Empire – Poles v. Ruthenes, Italians v. Slovenes, Germans v. Slovenes. In Hungary, linguistic chauvinism was official policy.

21.7 The Dual Monarchy (1867–1908): Hungary

In Hungary, violent contrasts of wealth continued. A third of the Kingdom was owned by owner-cultivators with 20 acres or less and they worked as wage labourers to supplement their incomes. On the other hand there were 300 great estates of 40,000 acres or more. The largely rural population lived in wretched conditions, without the opportunity to escape to industrial employment. Indeed Hungary had higher rates of illiteracy and infantile mortality than even Spain. Hungarian domestic politics were dominated by the Magyar gentry. An electoral system with a 5 per cent franchise, riddled with anomalies and corruption, meant that the non-Magyar nationalities were virtually unrepresented. From the 1870s the leading Magyar party was the Liberals. In fact, they wished to retain a connection with Austria; one of the main reasons for this was that given the fall in agricultural prices and their own low productivity the gentry relied on income from official employment. The Habsburg connection also enabled Hungary to withstand the threat of Pan-Slavism and maintain the subjection of its Slav population. Led by Koloman Tisza, the Liberals followed two policies:

1   Magyarisation.
2   'External' chauvinism.

(a) *Magyarisation*

The Magyar language was the greatest tool in maintaining the monopolistic position of the Magyars against the other nationalities. By 1900, 80 per cent of all graduates, 95 per cent of all state officials and 89 per cent of doctors were Magyars. In fact Magyars made up barely half of the population. Linguistic standardisation could also be held to be a necessity for the modernisation of Hungary and an improvement in the prospects of the culturally backward Slavs:

1   *Discrimination against non-Magyar languages.* By 1905, for instance, the number of Slovak schools had been reduced from 2000 to 241. All Slovak cultural organisations had been dissolved in 1875.
2   *Promotion of the use of Magyar.* From the 1870s, a system of state primary schools was the main vehicle of Magyarisation. The teaching of the language was made compulsory in all schools. Place names, street names and station names were expressed in Magyar.

Not unnaturally the intensification of Magyarisation had the counter-productive effect of stimulating nationalism amongst the minorities – especially the Croats, who could look back to their traditionally privileged status as the guardians of the Military Frontier.

(b) *External chauvinism*

The Liberals also sought to exploit their built-in bargaining power in the *Ausgleich* to extort the maximum concessions short of dissolution of the connection. Some extremists wanted that connection reduced to 'personal union' only. Ironically, some of the greatest opponents of the connection were the magnates who had once been the allies of the Monarchy. This was because they did not hold offices and were adversely affected by the agrarian situation, which led them to support agricultural protection to keep up grain prices. There were really two main sources of contention:

1   *The tariff compromise.* Both Hungary and Austria wanted to retain the tariff between them, but while Hungary pressed for (and gained) more advantageous terms for agricultural exports to Austria, the Magyars resisted giving Austrian manufacturers an equivalent advantage in Hungary because of the protectionism of the Magyar industrialists. Every ten years the renewal of the tariff compromise was the occasion for intense nationalism, and an opportunity for the extortion of new concessions.
2   *The language of command.* One of the most vital supports of the Monarchy and integrating institutions in the Empire was the army. By 1914 78 per cent of the officers were German speakers, but they were encouraged to learn the languages of the troops they led. The situation was not unlike that of the Indian Army. There were three layers of language:

– *Kommandesprache* – i.e. a number of key words for the main commands, given in German.
– *Dienstsprache* – i.e. the basic common vocabulary for everyday service use, the names of the parts of a rifle for instance.
– *Regimentsprache* – i.e. the normal native language of the unit. In Magyar regiments this was obviously Magyar.

In 1903, Magyar nationalists were insisting that the *Kommandesprache* in Hungarian regiments should be Magyar, and the Hungarian parliament refused to vote the necessary contingents of troops. In 1905 the anti-German army radicals won a clear majority. The Emperor was adamant in resisting what he saw as a threat which would dissolve the army, and then the Monarchy. Only after a crisis which involved virtual martial law in Hungary was a compromise reached in 1906. The old alliance of the dynasty and the Magyars was saved, but by 1906 it looked as if the connection between the two units could not survive much longer.

21.8 Deadlock (1908–14)

(a) *Potential threats*

By 1908, the Monarchy faced two vital questions which threatened its integrity, and to which there seemed no answer:

1 *The national question in Austria*, which was blocking the political system.
2 *The South Slav question*, which was a threat to Hungary and to the loyalties of the Slavs of the Monarchy.

(b) *The National Question*

The *Reichsrat* and Bohemian *Diet* were deadlocked by the obstruction of the nationalities. There were two possible responses:

1 *Universal suffrage.* Taaffe fell in 1893 because he wanted to try the old idea of appealing beyond the nationalist intellectuals and middle class to the fundamentally loyal lower classes. Badeni had extended the franchise in 1896, and the threat had been used against the Magyar gentry in 1906: they would have been put in a minority against the other nationalities, the Magyar peasantry and the townspeople.
    The threat was dropped as part of the compromise, but in 1907 universal suffrage was introduced in Austria. However:

   – While the new mass parties like the Christian Socialists led by Karl Lueger (mayor of Vienna from 1897 to 1907) were broadly pro-Monarchy, its appeal to the masses was on the basis of anti-capitalism and anti-Semitism.
   – Even the new mass parties could be split by nationalism. By 1910 there was an independent Czech Social Democratic Party which had broken away from the Marxist, theoretically anti-nationalist, Austrian Social Democratic Party.

2 *Government by degree.* There was increasing reliance on Constitutional Article 14, which allowed the Emperor to rule by emergency decree, to enact budgets and legislation. Between 1897 and 1904 special decree legislation was used on 97 occasions, and no budget was voted in 1903, 1904 and 1905.

21.9 Conclusion

Magyarisation led to the development of Croat radicalism. As early as 1905 (the Fiume Resolutions) some of these Croats agreed with the Serbs across the border that 'Croats and Serbs are one people' even though the groups were traditionally hostile. The annexation of Bosnia and Herzegovina in 1908 frustrated the aspirations of Serbia to those territories, and converted it even more into the 'Piedmont of the South Slavs'. The result was growing Croat and Serb terrorism and nationalist propaganda. There were two possible responses:

1   *Triallism*, or the establishment of a third unit in the Monarchy based upon the Croats and other Slavs in the area. The majority of Croats were still fundamentally loyal to the Monarchy; however, the Emperor's compromise with the Magyars blocked this option and prevented an appeal to the Croats with universal suffrage. The plan was, however, supported by Franz Ferdinand, the heir to the throne, who detested the Magyars.
2   A *'preventive war' with Serbia*, to hit at the heart of the South Slav spectre and at the same time provide a rallying point for the Monarchy's squabbling nationalities.

In fact, it was the second option which was chosen in 1914. However, as A. J. P. Taylor remarked: 'war can only accelerate; it makes a dictatorial state more dictatorial, a democratic state more democratic, an industrial state more industrial and a rotten state more rotten'.

Questions

1   How did the Dual Monarchy attempt to deal with the problem of its nationalities between 1867 and 1914?   [OC]
2   What attempts were made by the Habsburg Monarchy to secure constitutional reform and internal reorganisation between 1850 and 1867?   [OC]
3   How far did the *Ausgleich* of 1867 solve the minority problems of the Austro-Hungarian Empire?
                                                                                                [OX]
4   Explain Austria-Hungary's problems between 1867 and 1914; (a) within the Empire, (b) with Italy, (c) with Serbia.   [NEAB]
5   Discuss the strengths and weaknesses of Austria-Hungary in the period from 1870 to 1914.[NEAB]
6   Was the collapse of the Austro-Hungarian Monarchy imminent in 1914?   [CAM]
7   Study Sources A, B and C and then answer the questions which follow.

Source A: An Imperial address.

> Franz Josef, Emperor of Austria, King of Bohemia and Apostolic King of Hungary, to the inhabitants of Bosnia and Herzegovina: When a generation ago our troops crossed the borders of your lands, you were assured that they came not as foes, but as friends, with the firm determination to remedy the evils from which your fatherland had suffered so grievously for so many years. This promise given at a serious moment has been honestly kept. It has been the constant endeavour of our government to guide the country by patient and systematic activity to a happier future. Remembering the ties that existed of yore between our glorious ancestors on the Hungarian throne and these lands, we extend our suzerainty over Bosnia and Herzegovina, and it is our will that the order of succession of our House be extended to these lands also. The inhabitants of the two lands thus share all the benefits which a lasting confirmation of the present relationship can offer.

> FRANZ JOSEF, 1908

(a) Explain the reference to 'a generation ago our troops crossed the borders of your lands' (lines 2–3). What arrangements had been made for Bosnia and Herzegovina at that time?
(b) Why did Austria-Hungary decide to extend its 'suzerainty over Bosnia and Herzegovina' (lines 8–9) in 1908?

(c) What were the immediate consequences of this decision? How did it affect relations between Austria-Hungary and her neighbours between 1908 and 1914?

(d) Comment upon the reasons given by Franz Josef for this extension of his authority. [OC]

Source: An address by Franz Josef to all the peoples of Bosnia and Herzegovina in 1908.

Source B: Parliamentary riots in Austria in 1897.

And now we see what history will be talking of five centuries hence: a uniformed and helmeted battalion of bronzed and stalwart men marching in double file down the floor of the House – a free parliament profaned by an invasion of brute force!

It was an odious spectacle – odious and aweful. For one moment it was an unbelievable thing – a thing beyond all credibility; it must be a delusion, a dream, a nightmare. But no, it was real – pitifully real, shamefully real, hideously real. These sixty policemen had been soldiers, and they went at their work with the cold unsentimentality of their trade. They ascended the steps of the tribune, laid their hands upon the inviolable persons of the representatives of a nation, and dragged and tugged them down the steps and out at the door: then ranged themselves in stately military array in front of the ministerial estrade and so stood.

Some of the results of this wild freak followed instantly. The Badeni government came down with a crash; there was a popular outbreak or two in Vienna: there were three or four days of furious rioting in Prague, followed by the establishing there of martial law; the Jews and Germans were harried and plundered and their houses destroyed; in other Bohemian towns there was rioting – in some cases the Germans being the rioters, in others the Czechs – and in all cases the Jew had to roast, no matter which side he was on. We are well along in December now; the new Minister–President has not been able to patch up a peace among the warring factions of the parliament, therefore there is no use in calling it together again for the present; public opinion believes that parliamentary government and the Constitution are actually threatened with extinction, and that the permanency of the monarchy itself is a not absolutely certain thing!

(a) The events described were triggered off by the Badeni language decrees of 1897. Why were they so explosive in their effects?

(b) Looking back on these events, the historian Joseph Redlich wrote in 1929: 'From this moment the Habsburg realm was doomed'. Why do you think that this should have been so?

(c) Why should the Jews have been 'harried and plundered' by both sides?

(d) What is the value to historians of accounts written by journalists of events which they witnessed?

Source: A description by Mark Twain of the riots which effectively ended parliamentary government Austria. M. Twain, 'Stirring Times in Austria', *Harpers New Monthly Magazine* (1897). Included in J. W. Mason, *The Dissolution of the Austro-Hungarian Empire 1867–1918* (Longman, 1985).

Source C: Adolf Hitler in Vienna.

In those days I followed both movements most attentively. One, by feeling the beat of its innermost heart, the other, carried away by admiration for the unusual man who even then seemed to me a bitter symbol of all Austrian Germanism.

When the mighty funeral procession bore the dead mayor from the City Hall towards the Ring, I was among the many hundred thousands looking on at the tragic spectacle. I was profoundly moved and my feelings told me that the work, even of this man, was bound to be in vain, owing to the fatal destiny which would inevitably lead this state to destruction. If Dr. Karl Lueger had lived in Germany, he would have been ranked among the great minds of our people; that he lived and worked in this impossible state was the misfortune of his work and of himself . . .

If, in addition to its enlightened knowledge of the broad masses, the Christian Social party had had a correct idea of the importance of the racial question, such as the Pan-German movement had achieved; and if, finally, it had itself been nationalistic, or if the Pan-German movement, in addition to its correct knowledge of the aim of the Jewish question, had adopted the practical shrewdness of the Christian Social Party, especially in its attitude towards socialism, there would have resulted a movement which even then in my opinion might have successfully intervened in German destiny ...

I was repelled by the conglomeration of races which the capital showed me, repelled by this whole mixture of Czechs, Poles, Hungarians, Ruthenians, Serbs, and Croats, and everywhere, the eternal mushroom of humanity – Jews and more Jews.

To me the giant city seemed the embodiment of racial desecration ... Yet Vienna was and remained for me the hardest, though most thorough, school of my life. I had set foot in this town while still a boy and I left it a man, grown quiet and grave. In it I obtained the foundations for a philosophy in general and a political view in particular which later I only needed to supplement in detail, but which never left me.

(a) Why do you think Hitler uses the term 'the eternal mushroom of humanity' when he refers to the Jews in Vienna (line 20)?
(b) At this time Hitler was living a very insecure life, little more than a tramp, in Vienna. Why do you think that someone living in those conditions might be vulnerable to strong racialist sentiments?
(c) What were the main themes of the political programme of the Christian Socialist party?
(d) This account was written in the 1920s. It was part of the manifesto of a mass political party. Why should those two factors affect its value for the historian as a record of life and events in Vienna?

Source: A. Hitler, *Mein Kampf* (English edition, Hutchinson, 1974). Included in J. W. Mason, *The Dissolution of the Austro-Hungarian Empire 1867–1918* (Longman, 1985).

22 The origins of the First World War 1890–1914

Introduction

None of Bismarck's successors could match him in ability. The new *Kaiser* William II, with his erratic personality, played a very active role in diplomatic affairs. His most influential adviser from 1890 to 1906 was Baron Fritz von Holstein, the so-called 'evil genius of Germany'. The change in the direction of policy did not follow any long-term plan, however; Bismarck's fall was followed by a restoration of fluidity. The outcome was the division of Europe into two reasonably balanced blocs, increasingly beset by rivalries and tensions which by 1914 focused upon one vital issue.

22.1 The Franco-Russian Alliance (1894)

One of the key assumptions of the Bismarckian System had been the separation of France and Russia. By 1894, they had been allowed to move together. This was not based on economic links although France was making loans to Russia regularly from 1888. Nor was it based upon any common territorial interests. Ideologically the two states could not be further apart. The basis of the rapprochement was simply the fear of isolation.

(a) *The changed emphasis of German diplomacy*

1   *The non-renewal of the Reinsurance Treaty (1890)*. Both the Kaiser and Russia were keen to renew the treaty. It was Holstein who argued that it could damage relations with Austria if it became known and that in any case if war broke out between France and Germany Russian neutrality was not guaranteed (see Section 16.5(d)).

2   *German pursuit of a relationship with Britain*. Both Russia and France were bound to be disturbed by the apparent movement together of Britain and the Triple Alliance:

– The Heligoland Agreement of 1890, which involved the exchange of Heligoland for Zanzibar, encouraged German hopes of an alliance.
– On the renewal of the Triple Alliance in 1890 Rudini, the Italian prime minister, deliberately gave the impression that Britain was somehow linked to the alliance to help strengthen the hand of Italy in her ambitions in North Africa.

Naturally France and Russia felt driven together. A visit by the French fleet to Kronstadt in 1891 was followed by a military convention in 1892 then a political agreement in 1894.

22.2 Terms of the Franco-Russian Alliance

It was a defensive agreement, responding to the Triple Alliance:

1   If France was attacked by Germany or Italy supported by Germany, Russia would provide up to 800,000 men against Germany. If Russia was attacked by Germany or Austria backed by Germany, France would come to her aid with 1.3 million men.
2   Mobilisation by any members of the Triple Alliance would lead both powers to mobilise without consultation.
3   Significantly the convention would expire when also did the Triple Alliance.

It was never a real alliance; it was never approved by the French parliament and was a secret until 1918. Even so, the link was obvious enough to be mocked in *Punch*:

> Beauty and the Beast *vis-à-vis* in the dance
> Were scarce funnier partners than Russia and France

It could also be seen largely as a challenge to British interests since she had colonial differences with both members.

22.3 The ending of British isolation (1893–1902)

Germany was now faced with the prospect of a war on two fronts, and began to make appropriate military plans for a quick 'knock-out' blow against France. Britain's involvement on either side could upset the new balance, but this would mean Britain departing from her traditional policy of isolation.

(a) *Naval insecurity*

Bismarck had described Britain in 1889 as 'the old traditional ally with whom we have no conflicting interests'. However, Germany did find just such a divisive issue:

1   *The Two-Power Standard.* Isolated and with no large conscript army, Britain depended on her navy. The new danger of a Franco-Russian combination was serious enough. Joseph Chamberlain said that if it occurred, 'The British navy would have to cut and run – if it could run.' In 1893 the Two-Power Standard was adopted – that is, the British fleet should be equal to the combination of the two next strongest navies in Europe.
2   *Anglo-German naval rivalry.* The irony is that Britain and Germany were driven towards war by a leader who admired Britain and sought an Anglo-German alliance. The Kaiser was very much influenced by Admiral Alfred Mahan's 'first class book', *The Influence of Sea Power upon History: 1660–1783* (1890) and came to see a large navy as a diplomatic tool to impress Britain. In his famous *Daily Telegraph* interview in 1908 he remarked:

> Only those powers which have vast navies will be listened to with respect when the future of the Pacific comes to be solved, and if for that reason only Germany must have a powerful fleet. It may even be that England herself will be glad that Germany has a fleet, when they speak together on the same side in the great debates of the future.

A series of navy laws were passed with the keen support of aggressive nationalists and industrialists linked in the German Navy League with the intention of creating a considerable battle-fleet based in Wilhelmshaven and Kiel. It would not only protect Germany from British attack but also pose a continual threat to Britain herself, hence the remark by Tirpitz, the minister of marine: 'The lever of our Weltpolitik was the North Sea; it influenced the entire globe without us needing to be directly engaged in any other place.' However, the Kaiser's strategy was bound to be counter-productive:

- He had to play on popular Anglophobia in Germany to achieve support, and this was bound to antagonise the British and increase their suspicions. Tirpitz hoped to be able to build up the fleet as quietly as possible, and feared the effects of diplomatic crises and naval scares which would produce a vigorous British response. It was not possible to have the one without the other.
- The desire to practise Weltpolitik was incompatible with his desire for an alliance because Weltpolitik meant a redistribution of world power while an alliance with Britain would mean alliance with the country which had the most to gain from maintaining the status quo.

In fact Paul Kennedy in his influential article, 'Strategic Aspects of the Anglo-German Naval Race' (included in *Strategy and Diplomacy, 1870–1945*, 1983) suggests that the longer term objective of Tirpitz and the Kaiser was actually to create a fleet more powerful than the British fleet because a second class fleet would never have been enough to match Britain on the world stage. The famous *'risk theory'* of Tirpitz assumed the possibility of a British Home Fleet, diminished by other commitments, taking the offensive and losing so many warships that the Royal Navy would become inferior to other rivals collectively; which prospect would mean that Britain could be blackmailed into concessions. However, the disadvantageous geographical position of Germany meant that Britain had merely to blockade the Baltic and the exits from the North Sea to neutralise the threat. Short of seizing bases in Norway or Belgium and north-west France the only real alternative for Germany was to build a fleet that would give her 'world-political freedom'. Of course, this would assume that Germany's great rate of industrial and commercial progress could sustain such building plans, and that control was wrested from the Reichstag.

Whatever the objectives of the Kaiser and von Tirpitz inevitably Britain was disturbed, and the naval rivalry of the next few years was to create a growing atmosphere of mistrust between Britain and Germany.

(b) *Revision of the Treaty of Shimonoseki (1895)*

The Sino-Japanese War of 1894 (see Section 15.3(b)) led to a treaty of 1895 which conceded to Japan Port Arthur and the Liaotung Peninsula. Korea became independent, albeit virtually a Japanese sphere. In fact France, Germany and Russia all had interests in the region which could be threatened by excessive Japanese influence. The result was that Japan was forced to disgorge her mainland gains in 1895. What was very disturbing as far as Britain was concerned was that despite her strong interests in the region, she was not consulted.

(c) *The Kruger Telegramme (1896)*

The significance of the Cape of Good Hope as an alternative route to India, the growing dream by the 1890s of Cecil Rhodes of a Cape–Cairo Railway spanning a trans-

African belt of British territory, and the discovery of gold in the 1880s in the Transvaal which produced an influx of *'uitlander'* miners all affected the relationship between Britain, her colonies in Natal and Cape Colony and the Boer republics of Transvaal and Orange Free State. In 1895, a raid was sponsored by Rhodes and led by Dr Jameson to trigger off an *uitlander* revolt against the Boer governments. The raid failed, and the British government was implicated. In January 1896, the Kaiser tried to emphasise British isolation and nudge her towards the Triple Alliance by congratulating President Kruger on having overcome the threat 'without appealing for the help of friendly powers'. In fact, when rebuked by Queen Victoria the Kaiser backed away. As Kruger remarked to the German consul: 'The old woman just sneezed and you ran away.' However, Anglo-German relationships were adversely affected.

(d) *Fashoda Crisis (1898)*

Partly justified by the need to avenge the death of General Gordon at Khartoum in 1885, but largely because of the prospect of French intervention in the upper Nile region, British forces under Kitchener reconquered the Sudan between 1896–8. With the victory at Omdurman over the Mahdist forces, then the reoccupation of Khartoum, the British were now only days away from an expedition led by Captain Marchand which had left Gabon in French West Africa in 1895 to establish a French territorial claim across Africa to the Red Sea. At Fashoda, Kitchener met Marchand and the issue was a potential cause of war. Anglo-French antagonism was increased and the Franco-Russian alliance was confirmed. However, agreement was reached on a dividing line between the Nile and Congo spheres and this removed one obstacle to an *entente* between the two powers.

(e) *The Anglo-Boer War (1899–1902)*

The war was significant because of two aspects:

1 *The revelation of British military weaknesses*, with a series of defeats in the field followed by a prolonged and very fluid guerrilla war.
2 *A display of anti-British feeling.* Volunteers from many states fought on the side of the Boers. *The Times* remarked of German attitudes 'the German people had displayed throughout the whole of that period more animosity, envy and hatred of England than the people of any other country'.

(f) *The British pursuit of allies*

British isolation could have been broken in several ways. In fact, it was Japan to whom Britain looked:

1 *Russian ambitions in the Far East.* In 1897–8 there were disturbances on Crete and in Macedonia. However, Russia wanted to keep her hands free to look after more pressing interests in the Far East. The result was in 1897 an Austro-Russian agreement 'putting the Balkans on ice'. The situation created by the Treaty of Berlin of 1878 (see Section 16.3(e)) was confirmed, as was Austria's right to annexe Bosnia and Herzegovina. This truce prevailed until 1905.
2 *Failure to achieve an Anglo-German alliance.* Attempts had already been sponsored by Joseph Chamberlain, the British Colonial Secretary, in 1898 and 1901 to achieve a limited defensive alliance. The second attempt was helped somewhat by co-operation between Britain, Germany and other European powers against the Boxer Rebellion in China. The attempts failed because Britain would

not join the Triple Alliance, and Germany would not join with Britain to block Russian expansion in Manchuria. However, Japan had a similar concern (especially after the conclusion of a Russo-Chinese defensive alliance in 1896 directed against Japan).

(g) The Anglo-Japanese Alliance (1902)

The main terms of the alliance were:

1 Recognition of the independence of China and Korea and mutual spheres of influence in China. Britain recognised the special interests of Japan in Korea.
2 Strict neutrality was to be observed if either of the two was involved in a war with a third power. If either was involved in a war with two powers the other would actively help.

A five-year agreement, it was renewed in 1905 and extended to include India and mutual support in the event of an attack by one other power. Britain had departed from her traditional peacetime isolation, although the main objective was to avoid a Russo-Japanese partition of China. On the other hand, Japanese confidence in dealing with Russia was strengthened.

22.4 The detaching of Italy from the Triple Alliance (1896–1902)

Meanwhile, the situation of Italy was changed. The fall of the anti-French Crispi in 1896 (see Section 17.5) and his replacement by the more pro-French Rudini opened the way to a changed relationship, reflected by the conclusion of a commercial treaty in 1898.

(a) The end of the anti-French Mediterranean alignment

In 1896, Italy effectively recognised the French protectorate over Tunisia. Then in 1900 France recognised Italian interests in Libya, and Italy recognised Morocco as a French sphere of interest.

(b) Franco-Italian Agreement (1902)

Only days after the renewal of the Triple Alliance Italy reached a vague agreement with France which guaranteed neutrality if either was attacked, but also meant that if either of them declared war in response to provocation the other had the option to remain neutral if the provocation could be interpreted as an attack. This was not entirely compatible with the terms of the Triple Alliance; Italy, the 'Jackal State', was left keeping her options open. Von Bülow, the German Chancellor, did try to make light of it: 'In a happy marriage a husband does not mind if his wife has a dance with another man. The main thing is that she should not elope.'

22.5 The Anglo-French rapprochement

Both Britain and France had motives for some sort of coming together.

(a) *European fears and colonial apprehensions*

1 *The strengthening of the international position.* An agreement with Britain was seen by the French Foreign Minister Delcassé as a means of strengthening France in Europe and avoiding the danger of embroilment in a Russo-Japanese War. Britain also wanted a limited European alliance, and had failed to reach one with Germany.

2 *Colonial interests.* There was room for some sort of colonial 'deal'; France wanted direct control over Morocco while Britain wanted French recognition of her position in Egypt after the years of resentment.

(b) *The* Entente Cordiale (1904)

An official visit to Paris in 1903 by King Edward VII helped clear the way; the following year saw a series of agreements which settled disputes over the frontier of Gambia, spheres of influence in Siam, recognised British interests in Egypt and French interests in Morocco (including the possibility of a partition of the latter between France and Spain). This was not an alliance, but the effect was undoubted. Lord Hardinge wrote of the *Entente* in 1904: 'What an effect it will have on Europe and how the Germans will hate it.'

(c) *The testing of the alignment*

1 *The Russo-Japanese War (1904–5).* War finally resulted over Manchuria and Korea in 1904 when the Japanese experimented with the new method of attacking before declaring war. The Russians were heavily defeated on land at Mukden and at sea at Tsushima Straits. Domestic problems in Russia (see Section 20.6) led her to make peace with Japan by the Treaty of Portsmouth. In fact, Germany hoped the war would ruin the Anglo-French relationship and that Russia would turn back to Germany. The Kaiser wrote to the Tsar: 'The naval battles fought by Togo are fought with Cardiff coal.' The accidental shredding of British fishing boats at Dogger Bank by a jumpy Russian Baltic fleet hardly helped. However, France and Britain valued the *Entente* too much to threaten it.

2 *The first Moroccan Crisis (1905–6).* With the annihilation of the Russian fleet, Britain now had 44 battleships against the 16 of Germany and 12 of France. She could have returned to isolation but for the Kaiser's 'sabre-rattling'. In 1905, the Kaiser visited the Moroccan Sultan at Tangier (see Illus. 22.1) and (possibly influenced by his anger at having to control a frisky horse) was very outspoken about French influence on Morocco. German demands for an international conference on the subject to try and isolate France were followed by the resignation of the uncompromising Delcassé. However, the outcome of the Algeçiras Conference of 1906 was totally the reverse of what Germany expected:

– The Act of Ageçiras recognised the special interest of France and Franco-Spanish responsibility for the preservation of order.
– Germany's bombastic attitude isolated her. Only Austria could be relied upon. The British attitude was hardened to such an extent that Britain and France reached an agreement in January 1906 which involved Britain sending 105,000 men to France within fifteen days of mobilisation. This was the real end of isolation.

3 *The Björko Agreement (1905).* The travelling Kaiser met the Tsar in the Baltic and tried to revive the old agreement for mutual defence. It was never ratified; Russia's defeat by Japan made her all the more reliant on France.

Source: R. Parkinson, *The Origins of World War One* (Wayland Publishers, 1970) p. 56.

22.6 The Anglo-Russian rapprochement

German foreign policy had always excluded the possibility of an Anglo-Russian agreement. In 1907, the impossible happened.

(a) The motives

1 *Russian weakness.* War and domestic tensions left Russia very vulnerable, and more conciliatory forces now prevailed at home. In 1907, there was even a secret agreement made with Japan as to the future partition of Manchuria.
2 *The German challenge.* The increasingly obvious German threat to peace was reinforced by another Navy Law in 1906, while the British launching of the Dreadnought revolutionised warship technology and revitalised naval competition. The German obstacle to agreement at the disarmament conferences sponsored at the Hague by the Tsar in 1899 and then 1907 pointed in the same unmistakable direction.

(b) The Anglo-Russian Agreement (1907)

Moderates on both sides wanted resolution of the worst colonial differences, although Britain would make no concession over the Straits. In both Russia and Britain there were fears that Russian conservatives would seek to restore the German link and upset the European balance. India was the key to the problem:

1 Britain and Russia agreed to keep out of Tibet – penetrated by the Younghusband expedition in 1905 – and acknowledged Chinese sovereignty.
2 Afghanistan was recognised as a British preserve, although not to be annexed.
3 Persia was divided. In the north the Russian sphere of influence was the larger area and included most of the towns. British influence was to prevail in the Gulf region. A neutral zone was recognised in the centre.

This was a largely negative agreement, and hardly directed against Germany. France and Russia still had no shared grievances in Europe or in the imperial world; Britain's real difference with Germany was over the naval threat. Rival camps were forming, and the violent German reaction hardened the new agreement, but the situation was still really quite fluid.

22.7 The Bosnian Annexation Crisis (1908)

It was a series of crises in Bosnia, Morocco and the Balkans which led to growing tension between the two blocs, and hardened the division.

(a) The origins of the Bosnian Crisis

The Bosnian Crisis not only split Russia and Austria, it was also a 'dress rehearsal' for 1914:

1 *A revival of Russian interest.* In 1897 and again in 1903 Austria and Russia had agreed to maintain the *status quo* in the Balkans. The murder of Stambulov (see Section 16.5(a)) helped considerably. Russia's defeat in the Far East meant that she was ready to turn back towards the Balkans, and the ambitious minister Izvolsky had a strong interest in opening the Straits.
2 *The South Slav problem.* Meanwhile, Austrian foreign policy passed into the hands of the expansionist Aehrenthal. Serbia was an obvious target; its relations with Austria had steadily deteriorated since the bloody overthrow of the pro-Austrian King Alexander Obrenovich and his replacement by the pro-Russian Peter Karageorgovich. This was followed by the 'Pig War' from 1905, in which Austria

closed her frontiers to Serb livestock exports. The Serbs simply established new links with France and Russia, but the prospect of antagonistic Serbs fomenting discontent amongst the South Slavs of the Dual Monarchy was appalling. There were two solutions:

– Concessions to the South Slavs to win them over. However the Magyars blocked any ideas of 'triallism' (see Section 21.9).
– A preventive war. 'Hawks' like the chief of staff Conrad von Hötzendorff favoured a quick, limited war to crush Serbia.

3 *The Young Turk Movement.* Since 1908 there had been a sort of nationalist revival in the Ottoman Empire, led by young army officers who favoured policies of reform and modernisation and were also in favour of the re-establishment of control over territories such as Bosnia and Herzegovina.

(b) *Annexation of Bosnia (1908)*

In 1908 Izvolsky and Aehrenthal agreed at Buchlau that the annexation could go ahead if Austria supported Russian attempts to open the Straits. In fact Austria jumped the gun and annexed the two states before Izvolsky could open his negotiations. The possibility of conflict did exist:

1 *Serbia was backed by Russia.* Serb troops were kept in preparation throughout 1908–9 and an eccentric Serb Crown Prince was 'ready to do a Garibaldi!' But Britain and France would not back Russia over this issue.
2 *Austria was assured of German support.* Germany saw this as a chance to force Russia to recognise her inability to resist Germany, and teach her the need for German friendship. So von Moltke, the German chief of staff, wrote to his opposite number in 1909: 'The moment Russia mobilises Germany also will mobilise and will unquestionably mobilise her whole army.'

By March 1909, Russia had ignominiously backed away while the Ottoman Empire was compensated with £2.4 million.

(c) *Significance of annexation*

This victory had been won at 'phyrric' costs.

1 *Encouragement to Austria.* Bismarck had written that 'Balkan questions can in no case be a motive for war'. In fact, the defensive Dual Alliance had been used to back aggression; the hand of the 'hawks' in Austria had been vastly strengthened. In January 1909 von Hötzendorff urged his Emperor against Serbia, that 'dangerous nest of vipers' with an emotive appeal: 'Full of the zest of battle the army awaits the tasks to which it is called ... our blood throbs in our veins, we strain at the leash!'
2 *Exaggeration of Serbian nationalism.* The new propagandist organisation *Narodna Obrana* was a front for the terrorist organisation the 'Black Hand'. These organisations had unofficial backing by members of the Serb government and army command; the Black Hand established links with Slav extremists in Austria, and embarked upon the assassination of Habsburg officials.
3 *Increased Italian discontent.* Italian interests in the Balkans had been ignored despite previous agreements (see Section 16.5). She was so disgruntled that she agreed with Russia to support her over the Straits if Russia supported her ambitions in Tripoli.

22.8 The second Moroccan Crisis (1911)

(a) French protectorate

In July 1911 Germany responded to the recent occupation of Fez by sending the gunboat *Panther* to Agadir. Franco-Russian relations at the time were not so strong, and Germany demanded the whole French Congo as compensation. In fact, Britain broke the dangerous deadlock. Naval preparations and a forceful Mansion House speech by Lloyd George led Germany to agree in November 1911 to recognise a French protectorate over Morocco, in return for a couple of slices of the French Congo. In 1912 the anti-Russian French prime minister Cailloux was replaced by the ultra anti-German Poincaré. Bülow said of this affair that it was 'like a damp squib – it startled, then amused the world, and ended by making us look ridiculous'.

(b) The consequences of 1911

In fact, the Moroccan crisis had far-reaching consequences:

1   *The Libyan War (1911–12)*. Nationalist pressures, the raising of expectations by previous agreements and the revelation of Turkish weakness led Italy to launch into an invasion of Libya. The timing was decided by the growing German interest in North Africa and in the Ottoman Empire. In the event the war – concluded with the Treaty of Lausanne in October 1912 – worsened Italian relations with Austria and Germany since Italy's occupation of the Dodecanese Islands in May 1912 threatened to extend the war to the Balkans.
2   *Anglo-French naval arrangements*. The German naval expansion had proceeded rapidly. In 1906 Sir John Fisher, the First Sea Lord, had actually proposed 'Copenhagening' the German fleet. In 1909 the naval issue produced the hysterical dreadnought campaign, 'We want eight and we won't wait'. A failure to achieve some sort of compromise with the Germans in 1912 and the Agadir crisis led Britain and France to make arrangements to concentrate the British fleets in home waters, while the French would cover the Mediterranean; British and French security were now interdependent.
3   *The Balkan League (March 1912)*. Revelations of Turkish weakness and Russian sponsorship with an eye to the Straits led to the league of Serbia, Bulgaria, Greece and Montenegro in 1912 to partition Macedonia. Ominously in August 1912 France and Russia also agreed on mutual military support if Russia had to go to war with Austria over the defence of Serbia, and Germany attacked Russia in keeping with the Dual Alliance. The chain was almost completed.

22.9 The Balkan Wars (1912–13) (see Map 22.1)

In 1912, the powers lost control in the Balkans.

(a) The first Balkan War (October 1912–May 1913)

League forces almost reached Constantinople and were forced by Russia and Austria to agree to the Treaty of London in which the Ottoman Empire – after a brief fightback in the so-called Second Balkan War – agreed to recognise its virtual expulsion from Europe. A new state of Albania was created to block Serbia's route to the sea; this latter was due to Austrian pressure. Russia again advised Serbia to hold back but the Tsar swore, 'For Serbia we shall do everything.'

Map 22.1 The impact of the Balkan wars (1912–13)

(b) *The Third Balkan War (June–August 1913)*

An outraged Serbia together with Greece and Rumania went to war with Bulgaria over the division of the spoils. The Ottoman Empire recaptured Adrianople. In 1913 the Treaty of Bucharest evicted Bulgaria from Macedonia and gave the southern Dobrudja to Rumania. Serbia was now much bigger. She could field a force of 400,000 men from a population that had increased by 50 per cent, and was a much more direct threat to Austria to whom the preventive war became so much more attractive – and William II swore that 'whatever comes from Vienna is to me a command'.

22.10 The outbreak of war

Tension increased in 1913 as Germany, Russia and France all made arrangements to *increase their military establishments*.

(a) *The assassination of Franz Ferdinand* (see Illus. 22.2)

With Austro-Serb antagonism at its peak in June 1914, Franz Ferdinand (heir to the Habsburg throne since the Mayerling tragedy) attended army manoeuvres in Bosnia. A Black Hand attempt on his life failed during a visit to Sarajevo on 28 June but shortly afterwards the young fanatic Gavrillo Princip managed to shoot the Archduke and his wife during a chance encounter.

(b) *The countdown to war*

1   *Austria's 'settlement of accounts'.* Berchtold, the Austrian Chancellor, had earlier remarked: 'Serbia must be eliminated as a power in the Balkans.' Strongly backed by Germany, an unacceptable ultimatum was presented to Serbia on 23 July, and on 28 July Austria declared war.

Illus. 22.2   The assassination of Franz Ferdinand

Source: D. Shermer, *World War I* (Octopus, 1973).

2 *Russian mobilisation.* Russia had assured Serbia of support. She now started to mobilise but her mobilisation plans assumed a war against Germany as well, and could not be easily modified. Germany warned Russia against such an action. France backed Russia who went ahead. On 1 August Germany declared war on Russia.

3 *The ignition of the Schlieffen Plan.* Germany was mobilising from 31 July on the basis of plans devised by General Alfred von Schlieffen, chief of the general staff from 1891 to 1905. A knockout blow against France was to be followed by turning against the slower Russians. Again this plan could not be modified and, since France refused to declare neutrality, on 3 August Germany declared war on France. Ironically the Franco-Russian alliance was never called upon.

4 *British declaration of war.* The Schlieffen Plan involved the violation of Belgian neutrality. The Britain was in any case virtually committed to support France by her agreement over the naval dispositions. In 1912 Churchill had written 'we have the obligations of an alliance without its advantages'. Nor could Britain stand and watch the European balance of power so grossly unbalanced. On 5 August, Britain declared war on Germany.

By 5 August, general war had broken out in Europe, although on 3 August Italy proclaimed her neutrality on the basis that the Austrian action violated the terms of the Triple Alliance (see Section 16.4(c)).

22.11 Conclusion

The search for the causes of the First World War dates back to the aftermath of the war in 1918, and the debate has passed through a number of phases since then. However, as with the debate about criminality, there are really only two major viewpoints – either the war was the result of calculated ambition, or it was the result of the international environment and personalities were only the victims of currents they did not understand.

(a) *Inherent criminal tendencies*

Given the heady emotionalism in the post-war period it was natural that the rather unprepossessing Kaiser should have been regarded as the culprit. However, even in the 1920s the pendulum swung away from trying to pin the blame upon Germany or the Kaiser. The Second World War revived attempts to find some sort of congenital criminality in Germany. The theories have taken two forms:

1 *The nature of German nationalism.* Elements in German nationalism such as racialism, aggressiveness and authoritarianism have been regarded as long-term trends in the Germanic outlook which make the Germans the most likely disturbers of European peace. This sort of 'dark nature' psychological theory is obviously impossible to prove.

2 *The 'drive towards the east'.* In 1961, Fritz Fischer in his *German Aims in the First World War* argued that Germany had deliberately sought territorial expansion, and used war to achieve it. Fischer argued that these aims did not just appear during the war as a result of military operations, but existed before 1914. He claimed that they grew from not only the Kaiser's ambitions but also from the socioeconomic structure and vested interests in Germany. According to Fischer, the objective of Germany in both wars was the creation of an empire in eastern central Europe.

(b) *A bad environment*

In fact, there were a number of influences at work:

1   *The 'old diplomacy'.* It became popular after the war to blame the alliance system. Designed by Bismarck for defensive purposes it had come to assume a more aggressive tone in the hands of other men. Even so the Balkan crisis of 1912–13 (see Section 22.9) showed that no blank cheques were being given by France or Germany to their allies. The alliances created an excessively rigid diplomatic framework, within which relatively small detonators could produce huge explosions:

– Fears and expectations were raised between two fixed points.
– The several general staffs made their strategic plans to fit the alliance pattern, and the danger was that soldiers and civilian ministers could be locked into an irreversible sequence if it was triggered off.

2   *Strategy, militarism and armaments.* Armies and weapons do not cause wars but they did contribute to attitudes in several ways:

– There was an inflated emphasis on military values. In Germany and Austria especially, too much freedom from political control tended to be given to the military leadership because of the special esteem in which the army was held. Britain, on the other hand, relied upon the 'blue water' theory of naval defence for herself and the empire. German naval expansion could thus be seen as a mortal threat, and meant that a choice had to be made between a mass conscript army or military agreements with France and Russia.
– Tension was heightened by the arms race (see Fig. 22.1). Increased armaments might have been justified in terms of defence and deterrence but had a cumulative

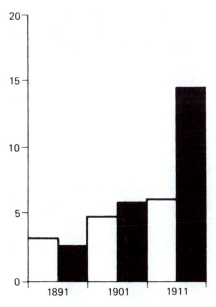

Fig. 22.1   Steel production in Great Britain and Germany (1891–1911), 1000 tons, the shaded columns represent Germany

Source: Based upon statistics in J. W. Mason, *The Dissolution of the Austro-Hungarian Empire 1867–1918* (Longman, 1985) p. 88.

effect. There is no doubt that the pace was set by Germany.

– Options were reduced by plans and technology. Mobilisation of forces had become so complex and speed was so critical that plans were not easily changed without producing chaos. However, the plans of Austria and Germany were the most dangerous because they expected to gain more from war than anyone else and believed in the 'short-war illusion'.

3   *Domestic crises.* All of the states suffered from serious internal problems and it could be argued that war was seen by some soldiers and politicians as a temporary diversion from these domestic dangers and as providing a national rallying cause. Austria above all, faced with the collapse of the parliamentary system and insoluble national divisions, most appreciated the value of a good, sharp, short war.

4   *The nature of capitalism.*

– The *'merchants of death'.* Armaments manufacturers were easily seen as a dangerous influence upon government decisions, and certainly they had a massive interest in defence contracts. On the other hand, there is no evidence of such influence and the dislocation of trade would damage the armaments trade.
– The bonds of finance capital. France and Russia and Austria and Germany had considerable investment links, which have been accused of leading to excessive diplomatic dependence. Yet international bankers depend on the uninterrupted flow of trade.
– Trade rivalry. Protectionist policies could also influence international relations. In particular, Britain was concerned about the threat of German competition and her declining share of world trade. Germany, for her part, was disturbed by the Russian introduction of a heavy duty on grain imports in June 1914 which would have serious effects upon Prussian landowners.

5   *Imperial rivalry.* Britain in particular identified her strength and future with the empire, which seemed to be threatened deliberately by Germany and her new fleet. Imperial rivalries, though, had more general effects:

– A hardening of alliances.
– Acclimatisation to war through frequent involvement in colonial 'small wars'.
– 'The last frontier' for capitalism, according to Lenin, was the exploitation of empires (see Section 15.5). With the end of this outlet, they would be obliged to confront each other.

(c)   *Accident and ignorance*

It may be that it is wrong to seek logical explanations since wars, like crime, are often the result of stupidity and illusions. Statesmen were blinded by fixed ideas like 'the short war' and were unable to grasp the likely consequences of a general European war. Too many small-minded men faced vast problems with little time for decision and so, as Lloyd George remarked, the nations 'slithered over the brink into the boiling cauldron of war'.

Questions

1   Why were the Balkans a source of international tension between 1908 and 1914?   [OC]
2   What part did imperial rivalries play in increasing international tension between 1880 and 1914?
                                                                                          [OC]

3　Should any one nation be held responsible for the outbreak of the First World War?　[OC]
4　Why was it impossible to localise the Austro-Serbian quarrel in 1914?　[OX]
5　What were the causes of the First World War?　[NEAB]
6　'Military rather than political factors were to blame for the outbreak of the First World War.'
　　Discuss this statement.　[NEAB, adapted]
7　Why did the assassination of the Archduke Franz Ferdinand plunge Europe into war in 1914?
8　Describe the following crises: (a) Tangier (1905); (b) Bosnia and Herzegovina (1908); (c) Agadir
　　(1911). Why did the First World War not break out before 1914?　[CAM]
9　Describe the main crises in the Balkans from 1908 to 1914. Why was there so much instability in
　　the Balkans during these years?　[CAM]
10　Study Sources A, B and C and then answer the questions which follow.

Source A: War against Russia only.

On 1 August, the Kaiser was under the impression that Germany would need to go to war against
Russia only, and that therefore the army had only to be marched eastwards.

> I assured His Majesty that this was not possible. The deployment of an army of a million
> men was not a matter of improvisation. It was the product of a whole year's work and, once
> worked out, could not be changed. If His Majesty insisted on leading the whole army
> eastwards, he would not have an army ready to strike, he would have a confused mass of
> disorderly armed men without commissariat. The Kaiser insisted on his demand and grew
> very angry, saying to me, amongst other things: 'Your uncle would have given me a
> different answer!' which hurt me very much. I have never claimed to be the equal of the
> Field-Marshal. Nobody seemed to reflect that it would bring disaster upon us if we were to
> invade Russia with our entire army, leaving a mobilised France in our rear. How, even with
> the best will, could England have prevented France from attacking us in the rear! In vain
> did I object that France was already mobilising and that a mobilised Germany and a
> mobilised France could not possibly come to an agreement to leave each other alone. The
> atmosphere grew more and more excited and I stood in a minority of one. I finally managed
> to persuade His Majesty that our concentration of strong forces against France and light
> defensive forces against Russia must be carried out as planned unless the most unholy
> muddle was to be created. I told the Kaiser that, once the concentration had been carried
> out, it would be possible to transfer forces at will to the eastern front, but that the
> concentration itself must proceed unchanged, or else I could not be responsible for
> things . . .
> 　　In the course of this scene I nearly fell into despair. I regarded these diplomatic
> moves, which threatened to interfere with the carrying out of our mobilisation, as the
> greatest disaster for the impending war . . . Years earlier the Foreign Ministry had told me
> that France might possibly remain neutral in a war between Germany and Russia. I had so
> little faith in this possibility that I said even then that, if Russia declared war on us, we
> should have to declare war on France at once were there the least doubt about her attitude.

(a)　What is meant by the term 'commissariat' (line 5)?
(b)　What evidence is there in this extract that by now the main consideration in von Moltke's
　　mind was not the need to prevent war, but simply the need to adhere to the mobilisation
　　timetable (lines 12–19)?
(c)　What impression do you get from this conversation about the relationship between the two
　　men, and about the character of the Kaiser?
Source: translation in S. Brooks, *Nineteenth Century Europe* (Macmillan, 1983).

Source B: The Kaiser's verdict on the outbreak of war.

> Frivolity and weakness are going to plunge the world into the most frightful war of which
> the ultimate object is the overthrow of Germany. For I no longer have any doubt that
> England, Russia and France have *agreed* among themselves – knowing that our treaty
> obligations compel us to support Austria – to use the Austro-Serb conflict as a *pretext* for
> waging a war of annihilation against us. That is the explanation of Grey's cynical remark . . .

that 'as long as the war is confined to Russia and Austria, England will sit still, and only when we and France get ourselves *mixed up* with it will he be forced to take active steps against us'. That means we are either basely to betray our ally and *leave her to the mercy of Russia* – thereby breaking up the Triple Alliance, or as a reward for keeping our *pledges* get set upon and *beaten* by the Triple Entente in a body, so that their longing to *ruin* us completely can be finally satisfied. That is in a nutshell the bare bones of the situation, slowly but surely brought about by Edward VII; carried forward systematically by the secret conversations in Paris and St Petersburg, the occurrence of which England has always denied; finally completed and put into operation by George V . . . So the celebrated *encirclement* of Germany has finally become an accomplished fact, in spite of all the efforts by our politicians to prevent it . . . We fell into the net and started to build only one capital ship a year in the pious hope that we would thereby reassure England! All requests and warnings on my part went unregarded. Now we get what the English consider to be gratitude. Our dilemma over keeping faith with the old and honourable Emperor has been exploited to create a situation which gives England the excuse she has been seeking to annihilate us with a spurious appearance of justice on the pretext that she is helping France and maintaining the well-known Balance of Power in Europe, i.e. playing off all European States for her own benefit against us.

(a) From the viewpoint of the allies of the Triple Entente what are the flaws in the self justifying remarks made by the Kaiser?
(b) How did the Kaiser view the doctrine of the Balance of Power (line 22–23)?
(c) Who was the 'old and honourable Emperor' (line 19) and under what obligations was Germany to him?

Source: Comments by Wilhelm II on a report in July 1914.

Source C: The Great War of 189–

ATTEMPTED ASSASSINATION OF PRINCE FERDINAND OF BULGARIA.

FULL ACCOUNT OF THE MURDEROUS ASSAULT; CRITICAL CONDITION OF THE WOUNDED PRINCE.

(By Telegraph from our Own Correspondent, Mr. Francis Scudamore.)

Constantinople, *Sunday, April 3 (viâ* Varna).

Noon.

A report has been current here since a late hour last evening, to the effect that an attempt has been made to assassinate Prince Ferdinand of Bulgaria, at a mining town named Samakoff, about forty miles south of Sofia. It is said that the Prince, who had been shooting in the Balabancha Balkans, was driving into Samakoff towards evening yesterday, when his carriage was stopped, and he was attacked by a number of men armed with knives and pistols. The Prince's attendants succeeded in saving their master's life and in beating off some and capturing others of his assailants, but not before His Highness had been severely wounded.

Prince Ferdinand was carried into the house of an American missionary resident in Samakoff, where he now lies. His Highness's condition is serious, and is rendered the more critical from the fact that there is no very adequate surgical aid obtainable in Samakoff, and it was necessary to telegraph for doctors to Sofia and Philippopolis.

The greatest excitement reigns in Constantinople since the receipt of this intelligence, and very grave anxiety is expressed in diplomatic circles as to the possible consequences of this terrible misfortune.

(a) How does this event parallel the actual cause of the First World War?
(b) Why is it feasible that the Russian government might conceivably have sponsored such an attempt in the 1890s?
(c) Assuming that this had actually occurred what do you think might have been the likely line-up of the European powers in a subsequent continental war in the 1890s?

(d)   In what way might this surge of war scare publications from the 1890s onwards have actually contributed to the eventual outbreak of war?

Source: Rear-Admiral P. Colomb *et al.*, *The Great War of 189–* (Heinemann, London, 1895). An extract from one of the many books and articles published before 1914 which envisaged the outbreak of a European war. The 'plot' in this war scare book is based on the premise that an attempt is made on the life of the ruler of Bulgaria by a Russian agent.

23 The First World War and its aftermath 1914–21

Introduction

Only the Anglo-Boer war of 1899–1902 and the American Civil War of 1861–5 had given any sort of idea as to the consequences for warfare of industrial developments and technological advances. In its scale and impact upon the economies and social structures of the combatants the First World War was unprecedented, the *first total war*.

23.1 Preparation for war

The plunge into war was supported and welcomed by a militaristic-minded European generation emotionally prepared for what was regarded as an inevitable clash. However, the war which occurred did not match expectations, and degenerated quickly into a colossal war of attrition on a scale without precedent and beyond imagination. The combination of psychological preparedness and logistical and material unpreparedness set the scene for Armageddon.

(a) *Psychological preparedness*

In all of the countries concerned the declarations of war were greeted with an outburst of popular enthusiasm. Colonel House reported to President Woodrow Wilson, 'The situation is extraordinary. It is militarism run mad.' There were several explanations for this phenomenon.

1 *'A plunge into the bath of steel'.* Numerous public figures were pro-war because they regarded war as a cure for social problems and moral decay. Lord Roberts, for instance, regarded it as the antidote for 'the mass of human rottenness that threads the thoroughfares of any of our large industrial cities'. Such views were powerfully supported by right-wing patriotic pressure groups such as the *Alldeutscher Verband* and the *Wehrverein* in Germany and the National Service League in Britain. The latter was founded in 1902 to counter the military and national weaknesses displayed in the Boer War and to agitate for compulsory military service in peacetime. Most of these movements were predominantly supported by right-wing parties and were anti-democratic. They were very active in seeking to 'militarise' youth through such movements as the Boy Scouts and the

Jungdeutschlandbund of General von der Goltz, and in generating all sorts of war propaganda.

2 *Jingoist and militarist literature.* The popular press fanned jingoism amongst semi-literate readerships. The years before the war were also notable for the proliferation of bellicose books such as Friedrich von Bernhardi's *Germany and the Next War* (1911) and the genre of British invasion and war-scare stories such as William Le Queux's *The Invasion of 1910* (1906) and *The Riddle of the Sands* (1903) by Erskine Childers.

3 *'An August Bank Holiday Lark'.* For very many of the young men who hastened to volunteer in August 1914 war was an escape from boredom and the problems of living in an urban industrial society into an open-air world and a comfortably anonymous and comradely community (see Illus. 23.1).

These circumstances explain why, against a leftward trend, France accepted so enthusiastically the increase in military service from two to three years in 1913; and why on mobilisation the polyglot peoples of the Habsburg Monarchy flocked to join the colours and abandoned the agitation for greater autonomy or independence. However, the war which they had been taught to expect and embrace was supplanted in reality by a dehumanising mechanised war which was a traumatic shock.

(b) *Logistical and technological unreadiness*

The key, mistaken, assumption was that a European war would be a short war. Only a few writers ventured to challenge this view. The most prominent of these was Ivan Bloch who argued that the strength of the tactical offensive would result in a long attritional struggle which would produce social convulsions. Even Bloch had no idea as to

Illus. 23.1 *Russian recruits mobilise in August 1914*

Source: Unknown.

Q In the early stages of the First World War men flocked to enlist in the armies of all the participants. Why do you think there was such enthusiasm for war amongst ordinary peasants and townspeople throughout Europe?

the scale of the economic mobilisation and state interference in the private sector which would be achieved. The French Lt.-Col. Henri Mordacq was one of the few soldiers who contradicted orthodoxy, but he thought that the war would last for no longer than a year. The necessary lessons were there to be learnt from the American Civil War, the Russo-Japanese War and the Boer War but they were not properly grasped. The long war of devastating attrition rather than the anticipated short, sharp and fast moving conflict was a result of four factors.

1   *Inadequate co-ordination of war plans.* In neither of the alliances was there adequate co-ordination of war plans. France and Russia acted at the outbreak of war to try to meet mutual needs, but they had not established proper institutional or geographical links. For instance, the only port available to deal with French supplies was Archangel, but it was not properly equipped to receive them. French generals had more faith in British support even though she was not treaty bound. Nor was there any more agreement between Germany and Austria–Hungary, and this had disastrous consequences when Moltke reneged on his promise that the Eighth Army in East Prussia would support the opening offensive against Russia and Conrad withdrew his forces from Serbia as a result. Mutual deceit resulted in the failure of offensives on all fronts.

2   *Disharmony of civil–military relations.* In no European country were defence and foreign policies properly co-ordinated because of the inadequate relationship between soldiers and diplomats, and frequently their mutual contempt for each other. In France this extended to the support of much of the officer class for the removal of parliamentary government. In Austria–Hungary Conrad bullied Berchtold into a preventive war in Serbia, but Berchtold's diplomacy delayed invasion and frustrated Conrad's plan. Above all the Schlieffen Plan, which governed German military strategy, committed Germany to an all-out attack on France regardless of when or how the war started and involved the blatant violation of neutral states.

3   *The cult of the offensive.* The emphasis in all European military thinking was on having the maximum number of trained soldiers available with the means to convey them to the site of the supposed decisive victory, to be achieved by moral qualities and weight of attack. The lessons of the wars of German Unification had been well learnt, but the experience of the American Civil War was ignored. The effectiveness of military management of the railways in mobilisation was demonstrated by the fact that within a month of the outbreak of war 62 French infantry divisions, 87 German, 49 Austrian and 114 Russian were delivered to the front along with millions of horses. However, the reverse of this was:

– A loss of mobility at the front where supply had to be by means of horse-drawn vehicles or by man-packing, but where the fire-zone created by artillery virtually blocked the movement of infantry. Horse fodder became the main item of military supply in the drive to deliver munitions the last few miles to the front. Defence was superior to offence. In 1899 Bloch had prophesied, 'Everyone will be entrenched in the next war. The spade will be as indispensable as the rifle.' At Waterloo it took 20,000 men to hold a mile front. By 1861 it took 12,000 men. By 1914 it could be held by a combination of barbed wire, a handful of machine guns and several hundred entrenched troops. Heavy bombardments simply broke up the ground and made offensives more difficult. Two-thirds of total casualties were caused by artillery fire. The *arme blanche* cavalry was obsolete in these circumstances despite the amazing strength of the cavalry doctrine.

– A lack of emphasis on building up reserves. Thus France allowed the critical Briey industrial area to fall to Germany without a fight, and with it 75 per cent of iron ore production, 75 per cent of coal resources and 70 per cent of steel producing facilities. No one had envisaged the region as being of strategic value in a short mobile war. In none of the states involved was there any practical pre-war preparation for the sort of control of manpower, industry, transport and commerce which was to be required for mass industrial conflict.

4   *The balance of military power.* Assessment of real military strength before 1914 is difficult but it certainly appeared as even at the time. Russia seemed to have been eliminated as a land and sea power in 1904–5 but had staged a remarkable recovery by 1914. The total inadequacy of Italy had been demonstrated by the Libyan War. France appeared to be at a peak of unity, confidence and military strength. On the other hand, the ability of Britain to mobilise and commit manpower on a large scale was underestimated. There was a rough military balance between the *Entente* and the Central Powers. The former had more divisions and unchallenged naval supremacy, but the forces of Russia and Austria were of unreliable quality. Germany had the finest army in Europe and the Central Powers had the great advantage of internal lines of communication and easy cross transfer of troops on an excellent railway system.

23.2 The conduct of the war (1914–18) (see Map 23.1)

There were three main phases to the war.

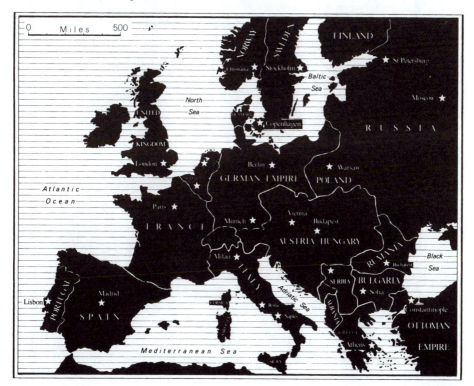

Map 23.1   Europe in 1914

(a) *The loss of fluidity (1914)*

Initially there was mobility. The Russian 'steamroller' moved to take pressure off France, but was crushed by General Hindenburg and his chief of staff Ludendorff at Tannenberg and the Masurian Lakes in late August–early September. Austrian invasions of Serbia and Russian Poland were driven back. By then the true future of the war had been decided, and von Moltke's prophecy that the next war would become 'a war between peoples which is not to be concluded with a single battle but which will be a long weary struggle' was confirmed (see Illus. 23.2, 23.3 and 23.4).

Illus. 23.2   *Wollt ihr dieses?*

From a war poster by an unknown artist, showing a peasant farming scene: 'Do you want this? . . . Defend our land'.
Source: P. Stanley (ed.), *What did you do in the war, Daddy?* (OUP, Melbourne, 1983) p. 68.

Daddy, what did YOU do in the Great War?

From a painting by F. Dadd (1914–18).
Source: P. Stanley (ed.), *What did you do in the war, Daddy?* (OUP, Melbourne, 1983) p. 45.

The *Schlieffen Plan* was intended to operate on the principle of a revolving door. The weight of the French army would be drawn into the Rhineland by deliberately weakening the German forces there while the main German thrust would come through Belgium to the west of Paris, then block the French army against the Swiss frontier. In fact in the Battle of the Frontiers the French did throw away 300,000 men in a month in a bid for Alsace-Lorraine. However, the Schlieffen Plan failed.

1   *Inadequate manpower.* A total of 1.5 million German troops were launched through Belgium and northern France but they failed to get to the west of Paris. Schlieffen's last death-bed words were 'make the right wing strong'. But Moltke weakened it initially and drained off more troops to the east during the advance.

From a poster by the American artist H. R. Hopps.
Source: P. Stanley (ed.), *What did you do in the war, Daddy?* (OUP, Melbourne, 1983) p. 55.

Q   In different ways this poster and the two which precede it influenced attitudes towards enlistment. How do they differ?

2   *Logistical miscalculation.* Schlieffen largely ignored logistical arrangements. Even if the manpower had been available for the plan to operate as intended it would have still been blocked by the shortage of supplies. By the time the German troops reached the Marne they were exhausted, their supply lines were desperately overstretched and there were acute shortages of ammunition and horse fodder.

By September the French army and depleted British Expeditionary Force had contained the advance and the result was the 'race to the sea', repeated outflanking attempts which just led to the development of lines of trenches. By then the war had extended also to the Near East because Turkey had become an ally of the Central Powers on the 2 August 1914 and the Straits were closed on the 26 September.

(b) Deadlock (1915–17)

1   *The Western Front.* The period was marked largely by a series of Anglo-French attempts to break through at the Ypres Salient. In 1916, however, the Germans attempted to 'bleed' the French army by concentrating their efforts on the historic fortress city of Verdun defended by General Pétain. A total of 600,000 casualties of both sides resulted between February and July. Sir Douglas Haig's Somme offensive from 1 July was an attempt to relieve the pressure, but lost 57,000 casualties on the first day alone. In 1917, the Nivelle Offensive of April at the infamous Chemin des Dames triggered off a wave of mutinies in the French army. In July–November 1917 the British again took the brunt, with Haig's Passchendaele offensive and its 240,000 casualties.

2   *The Eastern Front.* The war was not so static here. By December 1915, Austro-German forces had overrun Serbia and swept as far north as Warsaw and Lithuania, covering a distance of 300 miles in eight months. Then in June 1916 the great offensive of the Russians under General Brusilov swept into the Bukovina despite the loss of 3 million men in 1915 and the fact that only 30 per cent of Russian troops were armed. A second offensive in July 1917 was far less successful, and the Russian war effort was spent. The year ended with the panic rout of the Italians on October by an Austro-German army at Caporetto.

3   *The war at sea.* Allied sea power meant that all of the German colonies except Tanganyika were subdued, and the German South Atlantic Fleet was destroyed near the Falkland Islands. A British naval blockade was maintained from the start of the war. In response, Tirpitz had said in 1914: 'England wants to starve us. We can play the same game. We can bottle her up and destroy every ship that endeavours to break the blockade'. However unrestricted U-boat warfare introduced in February 1915 had to be called off when the *Lusitania* was sunk with the loss of 128 Americans among the total of 1200. There was never a 'Trafalgar of Dreadnoughts'; the confrontation between the Grand Fleet under Lord Jellicoe and von Scheer's German High Sea Fleet was inconclusive when they met at Jutland on 31 May 1916, but the German fleet never left its ports again.

(c) Attempts to break the deadlock

1   *'Sideshows'.* There was considerable support for schemes to outflank the Central Powers:

– The greatest of these was the Gallipoli expedition of 1915, designed to open the Straits to Russia, allow for a thrust up the Balkans and knock Turkey out of the war. The scheme, mainly inspired by Winston Churchill, failed and cost 250,000 casualties largely because Turkish resistance was underestimated.
– An advance on Baghdad by an Anglo-Indian army from 1915 culminated in its surrender after the siege of Kut el Amara in 1916.
– The 'Arab Revolt' started in June 1916, and was exploited by the British. Baghdad was taken in March 1917 and Jerusalem in December 1917. Set against the bloody drudgery of the Western Front the activities of heroes like T. E. Lawrence were bound to excite glamorisation.

2   *The involvement of new allies.* Turkey's entrance to the war had cut off supplies of Russian wheat from the Black Sea. Competitive bids were put in for other allies:

– Italy (April 1915). Italy's price was high, including Trieste, the Istrian Peninsula, northern Dalmatia and territory in Asia Minor. On 23 May she finally declared war on Austria.

- Bulgaria (September 1915). Promised Macedonia, parts of Greece and Rumania, Bulgaria joined the Central Powers in September and made the position of Serbia impossible.
- Rumania (August 1916). Drawn in by promises of Transylvania, the Bukovina and the Banat, she was easily crushed by a combined German–Bulgarian–Turkish invasion and a present made of her vast oil and grain resources.
- Greece (June 1917). With King Constantine at the head of a pro-German group and the leading politician Venizelos a pro-westerner the result was political turmoil until Constantine's abdication in June 1917; then Greece joined the Entente.

3   *The deployment of new weaponry:*

- Poisoned gas was used first by the Germans at the Second Battle of Ypres in April 1915, but it was always an unreliable weapon.
- Tanks were used successfully at the Somme in September 1916, but never in the concentrations or style necessary for a real breakthrough.
- Aircraft were used for reconnaissance from 1914, but not until 1915 was a method of synchronisation of machine gun firing with the turning of the propeller discovered. Even then, like tanks, their true role was yet to be understood.
- The submarine had been a rather neglected weapon before 1914; however by 1917 the Germans had 300 of them, and at one point had reduced Britain to six weeks' reserves of supplies.

(d)   *The restoration of fluidity (1917–18)*

Two unconnected events brought the war to a climax:

1   *The entry of the United States* (April 1917). President Woodrow Wilson was elected on the tide of isolationism in 1916. The reversal of attitudes was due to the revelation of German attempts to involve Mexico in an invasion of the USA (the Zimmermann Telegram of January 1917), but especially the return of unrestricted submarine warfare from February 1917. With the entry of the USA, the issue of war aims became more important. In their bid for support in January 1917, the Entente powers committed themselves to the restoration of the lost territories, reparations and the application of the principle of nationality in Europe. Wilson's *'Fourteen Points'* in January 1918, which included a pledge to open diplomacy and a general association of nations for the maintenance of peace, gave the war an element of an ideological crusade.
2   *The withdrawal of Russia from the war* (March 1918). At the stroke of a pen at Brest Litovsk in March 1918, the Eastern Front collapsed (see Section 23.4(d)) and a million men flooded to join the German army in the west.

The result of these twin factors of urgency and hope was the Ludendorff offensives of March–July 1918, which were so dangerous that the Allied armies agreed to a unified command by Marshal Foch. The Germans got to within 50 miles of Paris; Haig even gave the ultimate order to his men to 'fight on to the end'. The Allied counter-attack came on 8 August, the German army's 'black day'. The overstretched German forces were pushed right back. In September Bulgaria surrendered, and the Turks were routed north of Damascus. October saw the Austrian forces hurled back by the Italians at Vittoria Veneto. On 11 November, German delegates signed an armistice in Marshal Foch's railway train in the forest of Compiègne.

23.3 The domestic impact of the First World War

The consequences for each of the combatants varied with their circumstances. It is difficult to estimate costs because there is also the aspect of potential wasted, and it is also true that some developments might well have resulted without the war.

(a) *Physical damage*

There were a variety of 'costs':

1 *Casualties.* A total of 10 million men were killed, mostly under 40 years of age. In all the wars from 1802–1913 in Europe, only 4.5 million lives had been lost. The ratio of loss varied considerably. France's 1.75 million made up 10 per cent of her active male population. All combatants were left with the 'deficit of men' and erratic birth rate legacies. There were also 10 million refugees, 5 million widows and 9 million orphans.
2 *Destruction of resources.* By 1920, Europe's manufacturing production was 25 per cent below that of 1913. France and Belgium were particularly subject to war damage and severely reduced production. The total cost of the war was £45,000 million but this can take no account of 'opportunity costs'.
3 *Dislocation.* International trade in particular was interrupted. Britain more than anyone else was affected by:

– The growth of competition, from the USA and Japan especially.
– Loss of trade to the substitution of home-produced goods.

(b) *Extension of participation*

Total war meant that certain social groups came to enjoy a more valued position:

1 *Industrial workers.* Trade union membership expanded – in Britain from 4 million in 1914 to 8 million in 1920, and in France from 2 to 3 million. The greater power of the workers was seen in a growing number of days lost by strikes, and the great relative increase in family income.
2 *Emancipation of women.* The substitution of women in jobs previously held by men considerably boosted the cause of emancipation by giving an implicit recognition of equality, encouraging self-confidence and increasing economic independence.
3 *Middle-class leadership.* In Russia especially, the role of the middle classes was considerably enhanced through a variety of War Industries Committees and other organisations helping the war effort, but also able to press for constitutional reform.

(c) *State intervention*

There was a period of 'business as usual' in all of the states, but the war became a war between economic systems, and the old institutions and theories of government were challenged:

1 *Central planning.* In Britain, the process started with the creation of the Ministry of Munitions in 1915. In Germany, the War Raw Materials Department under the industrialist Walter Rathenau exercised vast powers. In France, the ultimate was reached in February 1918 when 'Tiger' Clemenceau was given the power to legislate by decree for the whole economic system.

2 *Controls of manpower and resources.* State control of the railway systems and
   systems of rationing and price controls were necessary to establish priorities;
   governments also assumed the power to requisition crops and raw materials.
   Control of labour was introduced in France in August 1915 and in Britain in 1916,
   while in Germany virtual conscription of all males between 17–60 years of age was
   introduced in December 1916.
3 *Modification of the political system.* By August 1916, Germany was subject to a
   semi-dictatorship by Hindenburg and Ludendorff. In Britain the 'shell shortage'
   crisis of December 1916 started the centralisation of policy-making by Lloyd
   George and a War Cabinet. France had a military dictatorship by Joffre and
   Nivelle before 1917, but after the mutinies Clemenceau established a strong
   civilian dictatorship. The Austrian parliament stopped meeting in 1917. However,
   the shock of defeat was to produce vast changes to the political systems of
   Germany, Austria and Russia.

23.4 The Russian Revolution (1917)

The outbreak of war was greeted in Russia, as elsewhere, with a spontaneous wave of
patriotic hysteria. In fact, with its chronic social problems, weak economy and narrow
base of political support Russia and the tsarist régime were deeply vulnerable to the
strains of a long, draining conflict.

(a) *The March Revolution*

1 *The impact of the war.* The effects were felt in two respects:

   – *A mounting casualty rate* at the front. Overwhelming defeats in 1914, then the
   tremendous offensives of 1915 and 1916 (see Section 23.2(b)) accounted for
   casualties of some 7 million dead, injured and wounded and the depletion of the
   officer corps. It also meant that the newly renamed Petrograd was left with a
   garrison of only 160,000 inferior troops.
   – *The breakdown of the economy.* By 1917, 15 million peasants had been
   conscripted and this together with the diversion of resources to the war,
   devastation of territory and the closing of the Straits led to food shortages in the
   countryside and the towns. Bread riots were a natural response, and in Petrograd
   in March these were followed by a general strike by many of the 400,000 workers.

2 *The fragility of autocracy.* The direct involvement of the Tsar in the conduct of the
   war identified him personally with the disasters. The Duma had been prorogued in
   September 1915, and policy-making fell increasingly into the hands of Alexandra
   and a group of right-wing advisers including Rasputin, until he was assassinated in
   a bizarre plot by a group of aristocrats. The Duma, recalled in November 1916,
   denounced the inefficiency and corruption of the government, but its next
   scheduled meeting in February 1917 was postponed. By then the crisis was
   breaking, and the failure of the government's power was clearly signalled by the
   fraternisation of troops with the Petrograd strikers.

On 11 March the Duma effectively assumed power, and three days later established a
provisional government under the liberal Prince Lvov. Nicholas abdicated on the following day, and his brother the Grand Duke Michael refused to succeed him in those
circumstances. As Trotsky sneered: 'The country had so radically vomited up the
monarchy that it could never crawl down the people's throat again.'

(b) The disintegration of authority

Throughout the spring and summer of 1917, a series of fragile coalitions faced mounting anarchy:

1   *A spontaneous popular revolution.* From March onwards there were growing seizures of land by the peasantry, with 17 incidents in that month rising to 545 in July 1917. They were partly associated with the continued collapse of authority in the army, where front-line conditions, Bolshevik agitators and the abolition of the death sentence led to mounting desertions. In Petrograd and other towns, the industrial workers established elected *soviets* which held weapons and were increasingly under *left-wing control.*
2   *The inadequacies of the provisional government.* By its own actions, the provisional government weakened its position. These included the abolition of the death sentence for soldiers, the decentralisation of local government and promises of the election of a constituent assembly and a decision about land ownership which raised peasant expectations. Above all, the government continued with the war and the inevitable strain.

The Bolsheviks had been taken by surprise by the events, but in between March and April their leaders returned from exile. As opposed to other Bolsheviks, Lenin and Trotsky realised the opportunity they had to jump the revolution forward – as Lenin remarked: 'History will not forgive us if we do not seize power'. On his return in April, in the 'April theses', he advocated the creation of a 'republic of Soviets of Workers, Poor Peasants and Peasants Deputies'. His cries for immediate peace and the rather un-Marxist slogan of 'land to the peasants' were bound to attract support. By September the Social Revolutionaries (SRs) and Mensheviks who supported co-operation with the government had been ousted from their positions in the soviets and Moscow and Petrograd especially were effectively in the hands of the Bolsheviks.

(c) The November Revolution

The base of the provisional government was too narrow. Its isolation was revealed by an abortive rising in mid-July 1917 by Petrograd sailors and workers, fomented by the Bolsheviks, then an attempted counter-revolution in early September by General Kornilov. The former led the new prime minister, the SR lawyer Kerensky, to arrest Bolshevik leaders and publish documents suggesting that Lenin was backed by the Germans. However against the latter he had to appeal to the Bolsheviks and their Red Guard militia and a strike by railwaymen. Lenin and Trotsky planned a *coup* to precede the meeting of the All-Russian Congress of Soviets, and the planned constituent Assembly. On the night of 6 November, key points in Petrograd were occupied. Kerensky fled the city the next day. At the Congress of Soviets the next day, where the Bolsheviks had a 60 per cent majority, Lenin announced that *peace negotiations* would be commenced and that land ownership was abolished without compensation. A government was formed with Lenin at the head and which excluded the SRs and Mensheviks who withdrew from the Congress, condemning themselves Trotsky remarked 'to the dust heap of history'. On 18 January, however, when the elected Constituent Assembly met, the Bolsheviks were in a minority. It was dispersed.

(d) The Treaty of Brest-Litovsk (February 1918)

Faced with the need to consolidate their power as soon as possible and to organise resistance to counter-revolutionary forces, Lenin was prepared to bid for peace at any price. The outcome was that although the German terms were colossal, and Trotsky briefly tried to stall with a claim of 'no peace, no war', terms were signed on 19 February:

1 Russia was to demobilise at once.
2 Territorial losses included the Polish territories, Courland, the Ukraine, Estonia, Latvia and Finland. A total of 34 per cent of the population, 32 per cent of the agricultural land and 54 per cent of the industry of the old Tsarist empire was lost. On the other hand, the Bolsheviks could now turn against the Tsarist White forces in the south and east (supported by the Allies from Murmansk from summer 1918), and the various anti-Bolshevik nationalist groups in the non-Russian territories.

23.5 The disintegration of the Dual Monarchy

Initially, there was little sign of nationalist disintegration, but following the accession of the Emperor Karl in November 1916 the process was fanned by three factors.

(a) *The need to conciliate the nationalities*

The Poles of Europe were fighting against each other in the armies of different states. In the Dual Monarchy Josef Pilsudski, a supporter of Polish independence, raised forces to fight for the Habsburgs. It was under German pressure that this support was more positively encouraged by the establishment of an autonomous Poland outside the Monarchy, an amalgam of Habsburg and former Russian territories. It was governed by a Polish Council of State and a German Governor General in Warsaw.

(b) *The stimulus of the Russian Revolution*

The Russian revolution in March 1917 led to mounting nationalist demands in the Dual Monarchy from Czechs, Ruthenes, Serbs, Croats and Slovenes. The Czechs advocated a federal division of the Monarchy, and their hopes were focused on a force of 45,000 former Czech prisoners-of-war led by Thomas Masaryk fighting their way back along the Trans-Siberian railway. Poles also deserted in mounting numbers because the promised new state did not include Polish territories taken from Russia.

(c) *Allied bids for support*

Committed to the principle of national self-determination, the Allies found in this a useful weapon against the Dual Monarchy. In April 1918 a congress of 'suppressed nationalities' was convened in Rome. In June, the Allies advocated the creation of an independent Polish state. In August the Czechs were recognised as a nation. With the virtual unification of the Dual Monarchy and Germany in May 1918, the residual nationalist loyalties were dispelled. In the week ending 3 November 1918 the Dual Monarchy collapsed, and new states of Czechoslovakia, Yugoslavia and Hungary emerged. The Emperor fled to Switzerland.

23.6 The fall of the Hohenzollerns

The 'war lords' and their industrialist allies held power in Germany until the last weeks, having dictated the increasingly extreme lines in diplomatic and military policy. The revolution in Germany was, in fact, a two-stage one.

(a) The 'revolution from above' (3 October 1918)

In an attempt to obtain more moderate peace terms and avert a social revolution, power was transferred to the Reichstag, a government of moderates was formed and the new chancellor Prince Max of Baden started negotiations with the Allies. Ludendorff was dismissed and the military leaders were to be subordinated to the civil authority. The whole façade of constitutionalism was to be sealed with the abdication of William II, who refused.

(b) Revolution from below (November 1918)

In the absence of an abdication, the moderate socialists refused to cooperate. At the same time there were *mutinies* in the armed forces and soviets were springing up; Socialist extremists actually declared a Bavarian Republic. William II did finally abdicate on 9 November. The next day the Socialists led by Friedrich Ebert proclaimed a German Republic. However the old military élite bought its survival; in a telephone conversation between Ebert and Ludendorff's successor General Gröner, the new régime was promised military support if it maintained military discipline and supplies. In January 1919 this alliance was tested when a revolt by the extreme Socialist *Spartacists* was suppressed by troops and units of para-military volunteer *'Frei Korps'*; the threat of communist revolution had been averted. An elected National Assembly met in Weimar in February 1919; Ebert was the first president, and the first chancellor was the moderate socialist Philip Scheidemann. However a threat as great as the communists was the nationalist reaction to the Allies' peace terms.

23.7 The Versailles Settlement

As in 1815, the post-war settlement consisted of a group of treaties and agreements, of which that with Germany was only the most important.

(a) The Paris Peace Conference

Deliberations started in January 1919. The main decisions were actually taken by an inner council of the USA, Britain, France, Italy and Japan (Japan and Italy both dropped out early). The final treaty was strongly influenced by a number of factors:

1   *The exclusion of the defeated states.* Only the victors were represented. The result was that the resultant treaty could be resentfully damned by Germans as a *'diktat'*.
2   *Idealism.* Especially with the entry of the USA into the war an idealism had been excited. This was very much represented by President Woodrow Wilson, a rather doctrinaire academic who reflected American distrust of Old World diplomacy and envisaged a new era of international peace based on the principles of national self-determination and a League of Nations to establish a legal framework within which states could deal openly.

3   *Public opinion.* The war had engendered considerable bitterness, very obvious in France and in the British general election of December 1918. With demands to 'hang the Kaiser' and 'squeeze the German lemon until the pips squeak' peace was bound to be made in a spirit of revenge against guilty states. Clemenceau especially represented the view that Germany should be so crushed that she could never again threaten France.

(b)   *The Treaty of Versailles (June 1919)*

In May 1919, the German delegates were presented with the terms:

1   *Territorial losses.* The main losses in Europe were:

  – Alsace and Lorraine to France.
  – Eupen and Malmèdy to Belgium.
  – Posen and West Prussia (the Polish Corridor) were to go to Poland to allow her access to the sea.
  Danzig was to be a free city.

  Altogether this involved a loss of 13 per cent of German territory, 10 per cent of her population, 14.6 per cent of her arable land and 74.5 per cent of her iron ore resources.

2   *Loss of the German colonies.* The German overseas empire was divided out between the Allies in the form of *mandated territories* governed on behalf of the League of Nations.

3   *Military limitations*

  – The army was not to exceed 100,000 men and have no tanks, heavy artillery or aircraft. The General Staff was to be dissolved.
  – The navy was to have no U-boats and only six battleships of no more than 10,000 tons.
  – The Rhineland was to be demilitarised on both banks, and to be occupied by Allied forces for 15 years.

4   *Reparations.* Article 231 held that Germany was guilty for the war, and liable for the payment of compensation for the destruction caused. The figures were not agreed and claims were left to later negotiation. For her part, France was to be paid in part by administration of the Saar district for 15 years to make up for the losses due to the fact that her own coal mines had been destroyed.

(c)   'Une belle Journée'

Since continued military resistance was out of the question, and the threat of social revolution was posed, the German Social Democrats and military leaders had no choice but to accept. Their resentment was all the more magnified because they were obliged to sign the document in the Hall of Mirrors at Versailles where the German Empire was first proclaimed.

23.8 Other treaties (1919–21) (see Map 23.2)

The other treaties were influenced not only by the 'Fourteen Points' but also by the struggles and diplomatic developments which continued beyond 1918.

(a) The Treaty of Saint Germain (September 1919)

Austria had been reduced to a barely viable rump by the birth of a number of small independent *'successor' states*. This treaty formally recognised the independence of Hungary and transfers of territory to Poland, Yugoslavia and Czechoslovakia. Italy was given Trieste, Istria and the South Tyrol.

(b) The Treaty of Neuilly (November 1919)

Bulgaria lost the Dobrudja to Rumania, western Thrace to Greece and also had to pay reparations.

(c) The Treaty of Trianon (June 1920)

Hungary was very seriously affected by the new territorial restructuring of eastern Central Europe. She lost about 75 per cent of her population. A range of settlements involved the loss of Slovakia to Czechoslovakia, Transylvania to Rumania and Croatia to Yugoslavia. For a few months in early 1919 the communist régime of Bela Kun fought Rumania and Czechoslovakia in an attempt to resist the loss of territory, but Bela Kun was overthrown in August and a stable government emerged under Admiral Horthy 'an admiral without a fleet and regent in a kingdom without a king'.

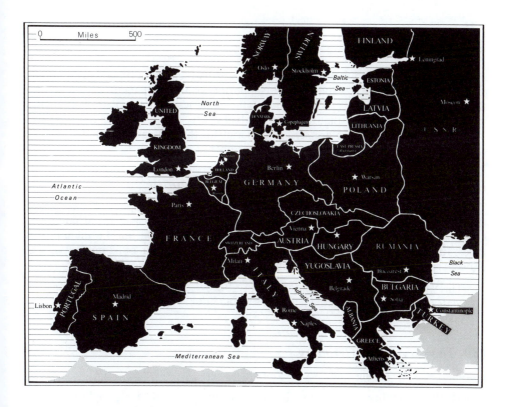

Map 23.2 Europe in 1923

(d) The Treaty of Riga (March 1921)

Following a period of struggle produced by attempts to establish soviet republics, the small states of Latvia, Estonia and Lithuania had their status and boundaries recognised by Russia. However, the region was even more extensively disturbed by a Polish war of expansion against Ukraine in 1919 then a war between Poland and Russia in 1920 in which Poland sought to restore the old frontier of 1772. The Allies had proposed a frontier, the *Curzon Line*, which would give Russia the Ukraine and White Russia, but as a result of the war Poland kept most of White Russia from March 1921.

(e) The Treaties of Sèvres (1920) and Lausanne (August 1923)

The first settlement with Turkey gave independence to Arabia, mandated Syria to France and TransJordania, Iraq and the Sheikhdoms of the Persian Gulf to Britain. This partition of the Middle East was based largely on the Sykes–Picot agreement of 1916. In the Balkans, Albania was to be given territory while Greece was to receive most of Thrace and much of Smyrna in Asia Minor. In fact, Turkish nationalists led by Mustapha Kemal were incensed at the loss of Smyrna and Greek forces were driven from Asia Minor by Autumn 1922. The support of the Allies for Greece had considerably weakened when the poisoned bite of a pet monkey removed the pro-Allies King Alexander and led to the restoration of Constantine. The Treaty of Lausanne rejected Greek claims in Asia Minor and restored half of Thrace to Turkey where Kemal Ataturk was to apply sweeping schemes of modernisation and westernisation in the next few years.

23.9 Conclusion

H. G. Wells said of the whole period that the war had 'ended nothing, begun nothing and settled nothing'. Even some of the supporters of the settlement were limited in their endorsement. Gilbert White, one of the Americans at the Paris Conference, wrote: 'It is not surprising that they made a bad peace: what is surprising is that they made a peace at all.' There are serious criticisms of the settlement, although the circumstances in which it was made must be remembered.

(a) The persistence of ethnic irredentas and minorities

The principle of national self-determination could not be fully applied. The result was that after 1919 nearly 30 million people were left as national and racial minorities. Czechoslovakia, for instance, had a population of 14.3 million but 4.6 million were Poles, Ruthenes, Magyars and Germans. Of Poland's population of 32 million, only 60 per cent spoke Polish. On the other hand:

1   This was still a better situation than before 1914.
2   States based entirely on ethnic grounds would not have been politically and economically viable.

(b) The survival of Germany

Germany was left strong, and very discontented over:

1   The large number of Germans who were left subject to 'inferior' peoples, and reflected the application of double standards in national self-determination.

2   A ban on union with Austria was resented for similar reasons.
3   The attribution of responsibility for the war to Germany and her allies.
4   The issue of reparations, which was to involve persistent interference with the internal affairs of Germany.

It was the failure to couple these insults with the physical crippling of Germany, which led Marshal Foch to remark: 'This is not a peace. It is an armistice for twenty one years'.

(c) *A general neglect of economic issues*

The Fourteen Points had sought the removal of economic barriers. In fact, with the fragmentation of eastern central Europe many new ones appeared – especially in the Danube valley. None of the new states had balanced economic systems, they lacked capital, were too dependent upon an unproductive agricultural sector and had limited and dislocated markets.

(d) *The absence of means for enforcement*

With the persistence of grievances and the 'revisionism' of Russia, Germany, Italy and other states some agreed means of enforcement was vital. In fact, the League of Nations was not able to meet this need. The US Senate rejected the Treaty of Versailles in March 1920, and with it the League of Nations because of an isolationist majority's refusal to become involved in European diplomacy. In any case, the League itself was to prove a flawed mechanism.

Questions

1   Account for the defeat of Germany and her allies in the First World War.   [OC]
2   On what grounds might the Treaty of Versailles be criticised?   [OC]
3   Show the effects of: (a) the treaties of St Germain and Trianon (1919) on the Austro-Hungarian Empire and (b) the treaties of Sèvres (1920) and Lausanne (1923) on Turkey.   [OX]
4   To what extent did the terms of the Treaty of Versailles, 1919, reflect the aims of the peacemakers?   [NEAB]
5   Why did the First World War last so long?   [NEAB]
6   'A harsh treaty for Germany and yet not harsh enough.' Discuss this comment on the Treaty of Versailles.   [NEAB]
7   Describe the part played by: (a) Italy, (b) Turkey, and (c) the USA during the First World War. Why did each of these countries become involved in the war?   [CAM]
8   In what ways did the nature of land warfare change between 1914 and 1918?   [CAM]
9   'Harsh and short sighted.' How justifiable is this criticism of the various peace settlements of 1919–20?   [CAM]
10 Why was the Bolshevik seizure of power in October 1917 so easy?
11 Study Sources A, B, C and D and then answer the questions which follow.

Source A: Stern but just?

From a speech by David Lloyd George, 1919.

The last time I had the opportunity of addressing the House upon this Treaty its main outlines had been settled. I ventured then to call it a 'stern but just Treaty'. I adhere to that description. The terms are in many respects, terrible terms to impose upon a country. Terrible were the deeds that it requites. Terrible were the consequences that were inflicted upon the world. Still more terrible would have been the consequences had they succeeded. What do these terms mean to Germany?
     Take the Territorial terms. In so far as territories have been taken away from Germany, it is a restoration. Alsace-Lorraine, forcibly taken from the land to which its

population were deeply attached. It is an injustice to restore them to their country? Schleswig-Holstein, the meanest of the Hohenzollern frauds; robbing a small, poor, helpless country, and then retaining that land against the wishes of the population for 50 to 60 years. I am glad the opportunity has come for restoring Schleswig-Holstein. Poland, torn to bits, to feed the carnivorous greed of Russian, Austrian and Prussian autocracy. This Treaty has re-knit the torn flag of Poland. The next question that is asked is, 'What are your guarantees for the execution of this stern Treaty?'

(a) Explain the reference to the restoration of Alsace-Lorraine (line 8). What arguments were used to justify this action?
(b) Who received Schleswig-Holstein (line 12) in 1919? How and why was the change of ownership carried out?
(c) How did the Treaty 're-knit the torn flag of Poland' (line 14)?
(d) What were the 'guarantees for the execution of this stern Treaty' (lines 14–15)? Did they prove effective?
(e) How far would you agree that the Treaty was 'just' (line 2)?   [OC]

Source B: 'We are on the eve of great events'.

The mass of the population is at present in a very troubled mood ... an exceptional heightening of opposition and bitterness of feeling became very obvious amongst wide sections of the population of Petrograd. There were more and more frequent complaints about the administration and fierce and relentless criticism of government policies ... Complaints were openly voiced about the venality of the government, the unbelievable burdens of the war, the unbearable conditions of everyday life. Calls from radical and left-wing elements on the need to 'first defeat the Germans here at home, and then deal with the enemy abroad' began to get a more and more sympathetic hearing ... a situation was created which was highly favourable to any sort of revolutionary propaganda and actions ... It is difficult to discount the possibility that German secret agents were operating in such a conducive atmosphere ...

Without doubt, rumours of this type are greatly exaggerated in comparison with the real situation, but all the same, the position is so serious that attention should be paid to it without delay ... the conviction has been expressed, without exception, that 'we are on the eve of great events' in comparison with which '1905 was but a toy' ...

Kadet delegates paint no less sorry a picture of food purchase in Russia. In the words of one of them, 'there is absolute ruin everywhere': the peasantry, cowed by requisitions, unhappy with interference in trading deals by provincial governors and the police, has no desire to sell its grain and other stocks, fearing that they will get only the statutory price ... As a result, prices are rising everywhere, and goods are disappearing ...

In the words of another delegate, 'the countryside is now passing through the most critical time, for the first time in Russian history demonstrating the antagonism of town and country' ... The attitude of the countryside to the war has, right from the outset, been extremely unfavourable, for conscription had a much greater effect there than in the towns. Now in the country there is no belief that the war will be successful ... The atmosphere in the country has become one of sharp opposition not only to the government, but to other classes of the population: workers, civil servants, the clergy, etc ...

In the words of other Kadets ... 'across the whole of Russia the same thing is seen: everyone understands that under the old order the Germans cannot be beaten ... that the nation itself must interfere in the war ... This movement, which was to begin with purely economic, has become political and in the future could turn into a serious movement with a definite programme.'

(a) What could have been meant by 'first defeat the Germans here at home' (line 7)?
(b) This is an analysis based on a series of police reports. What sort of factors would affect the value to this historian of this sort of evidence?
(c) Why, according to this analysis, were prices being forced up?
Source: Police reports on the situation in Russia, October 1916.

Source C: Lenin calls for a Second Revolution.

The Bolsheviks, having obtained a majority in the Soviets of Workers' and Soldiers' Deputies of both capitals, can and *must* take state power into their own hands.

They can do so because the active majority of revolutionary elements in the two chief cities is large enough to carry the people with it, to overcome our opponents' resistance to smash them, and to gain and retain power. For the Bolsheviks, by immediately proposing a democratic peace, by immediately giving the land to the peasants and be re-establishing the democratic institutions and liberties which have been distorted and shattered by Kerensky, will form a government which *nobody* will be able to overthrow.

The majority of the people are *on our side*. . . . A Bolshevik government *alone* will satisfy the peasants' demands.

Why must the Bolsheviks assume power at this *very moment*? Because the imminent surrender of Petrograd will reduce our chances a hundred times.

And it is *not in our power* to prevent the surrender of Petrograd while the army is headed by Kerensky and Co. Nor can we 'wait' for the Constituent Assembly, for by surrendering Petrograd Kerensky and Co. *can* always obstruct its convocation. Our Party alone, by seizing power, can secure the Constituent Assembly's convocation . . .

It would be naive to wait until the Bolsheviks achieve a 'formal' majority. No revolution ever waits for *that* . . . History will not forgive us if we do not assume power now.

There is no apparatus? There is an apparatus – the Soviets and the democratic organisations. The international situation *right* now, on *the eve* of the conclusion of a separate peace between the British and the Germans, is *in our favour* . . .

By seizing power both in Moscow and in Petrograd *at once* . . . we shall win *absolutely and unquestionably*.

(a) What does the phrase 'History will not forgive us' tell you about Lenin's view as to the nature of history (line 18)?
(b) Why would the conclusion of peace with Germany reduce Bolshevik chances 'a hundred times'?
(c) Why could this view be seen as a significant step away from democracy in Russia?
Source: Letter from Lenin to the Central Committee and the Petrograd and Moscow Committees of the Social Democratic Party.

Source D: The Kapp Putsch.

The Reich and nation are in grave danger. With terrible speed we are approaching the complete collapse of the State and of law and order. The people are only dimly aware of the approaching disaster. Prices are rising unchecked. Hardship is growing. Starvation threatens. Corruption, usury, nepotism and crime are cheekily raising their heads. The Government, lacking in authority, impotent, and in league with corruption, is incapable of overcoming the danger . . .

From the east we are threatened by destruction and violation by war-like Bolshevism. is this Government capable of resisting it? How are we to escape internal and external collapse?

Only by re-erecting a strong State . . . there is no other way but a government of action.

What are the tasks facing this new government? . . .

The Government will
ruthlessly suppress strikes and sabotage . . . striking is treason to the nation, the Fatherland and the future.

The Government will
. . . not be a one-sided capitalist one. It will rather save German work from the hard

fate of slavery to international big business and hopes by such measures to put an end to the hostility of the working classes to the State . . .

We shall govern not according to theories but according to the practical needs of the State and the nation as a whole. In the best German tradition the State must stand above the conflict of classes and parties. It is the objective arbiter in the present conflict between capital and labour. We reject the granting of class-advantage either to the Right or the Left. We recognise only German citizens . . .

Everyone must do his duty! The first duty of every man today is to work. Germany must be a moral working community!

The colours of the German Republic are

Black-White-Red!

The Reich Chancellor

Kapp

(a) Who was the self-styled Reich Chancellor Kapp?
(b) If you had to classify this proclamation as 'right wing' or 'left wing' which would you choose, and why?
(c) In devising this sort of proclamation what are the techniques employed to achieve the greatest impact on the reader?
(d) Why do you think Kapp chose to end with the reminder of the colours of the German Republic?

Source: Proclamation by Wolfgang Kapp, 13 March 1920.

24 The failure of Collective Security 1919–36

Introduction

The Versailles Settlement was followed by only twenty years of European peace. It left a series of grievances outstanding which stimulated nationalist resentments and rivalries. The inter-war economic situation exaggerated political reactions and condemned the democracy and constitutionalism necessary for a lasting settlement. In the last resort, the Settlement failed because it had no adequate guarantees.

24.1 The League of Nations (see Fig. 24.1)

(a) Work of the League

The League was an attempt to replace the 'international anarchy' of pre-war days with an organisation which would use economic and possibly military sanctions against aggressors to maintain *collective security* for both small and great states. A permanent assembly at Geneva and the international Court of Justice at the Hague were the main institutions for the preservation of peace. In addition the League was responsible for the:

1 Supervision of the protection of national minorities.
2 Government of the Saar and the free city of Danzig.
3 Development of organisations of international co-operation to deal with matters of health, working conditions, and so on.

(b) The weaknesses of the League

In fact the League was very successful in dealing with small disputes. Of the 66 international disputes it dealt with, 20 were transferred to other channels, 35 were successfully resolved, but the 11 most serious were not overcome. It also worked well in dealing with less dramatic affairs such as the repatriation of prisoners, the mandated territories and epidemic diseases. However, it suffered from two fundamental weaknesses:

1 *The absence of any independent power source.* The League depended upon the member states to provide any cooperative military or economic sanctions. Where a major state was involved, it could ignore the League with virtual impunity. As Frederick the Great once remarked of such schemes: 'The thing is most

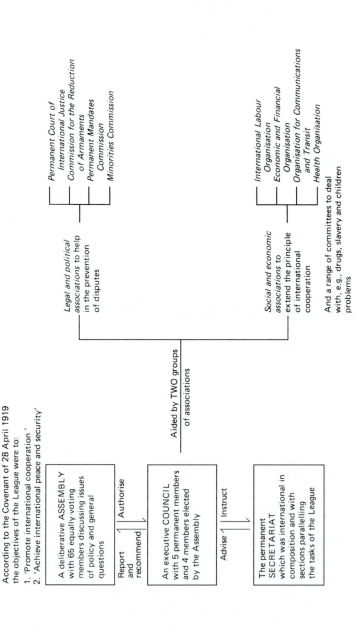

According to the Covenant of 28 April 1919
the objectives of the League were to:

1. 'Promote international cooperation '
2. 'Achieve international peace and security'

A deliberative ASSEMBLY
with 65 equally-voting
members discussing issues
of policy and general
questions

Report and recommend ⟍ ⟋ Authorise

An executive COUNCIL
with 5 permanent members
and 4 members elected
by the Assembly

Advise ⟍ ⟋ Instruct

The permanent
SECRETARIAT
which was international in
composition and with
sections parallelling
the tasks of the League

Aided by TWO groups
of associations

Legal and political
associations to help
in the prevention
of disputes

- Permanent Court of
  International Justice
- Commission for the Reduction
  of Armaments
- Permanent Mandates
  Commission
- Minorities Commission

Social and economic
associations to
extend the principle
of international
cooperation

- International Labour
  Organisation
- Economic and Financial
  Organisation
- Organisation for Communications
  and Transit
- Health Organisation

And a range of committees to deal
with, e.g., drugs, slavery and children
problems

Fig. 24.1   The structure of the League of Nations

practicable, for its success all that is necessary is the consent of Europe and a few similar trifles.'

2 *An incomplete membership.* It was easily seen as the tool of the victors, since it was written into the peace treaties. Initially Germany and Russia were excluded and, above all, in March 1920 the Senate of the USA rejected the scheme.

24.2 The German Question

(a) *The new balance of power*

There had been a dramatic change in the balance of power in Europe. The collapse of the Dual Monarchy, the virtual withdrawal of Bolshevik Russia from international affairs, and the growing view in Britain that Germany had been too harshly treated left France virtually alone to confront any renewed German challenge. Despite her losses of territory and resources, Germany still had a population of 65 million and massive economic potential. A French plan to carve off her territories to the west of the Rhine had been rejected by her allies and replaced with the idea of an Anglo-American guarantee of the frontier between France and Germany. The USA had then refused to ratify the Treaty of Versailles, and in 1922 Britain made it clear that only in the event of an actual invasion would she help France. France herself was exhausted by the war. She already had a declining population and in addition had lost 1.3 million of her best men while another 740,000 were maimed. The physical devastation and loss of resources had been considerable. The domestic debt had increased sixfold, and there was a huge foreign debt of 33,000 million francs.

(b) *The possible answers*

There were two possible responses to this situation:

1 *Restrict German power.* In the absence of a territorial amputation, it might be possible to use reparations as a way of 'bleeding' Germany.
2 *Accept the level of German power*, and compensate it with:

– A tightly organised European coalition to establish a *'cordon sanitaire'* around Germany.
– Strengthened international guarantees, expressed through a reformed League of Nations.

24.3 Reparations and war debts

The German liability to reparations had been linked with the war guilt clause; however, the sum had to be fixed and this caused international divisions and disagreements throughout the 1920s. There were two particular complications.

(a) *Inter-Allied war debts*

France and Britain owed considerable sums to the USA. France especially owed the USA three times as much as she herself was owed. A British proposal for the cancellation of all these debts and the payment of German reparations only to the USA was rejected. The USA was not prepared to overlook them, as President Coolidge remarked: 'They hired the money didn't they?' Conversely, a repudiation of the debts by the Allies would destroy international financial confidence.

(b) *Allied divisions over the purpose of reparations*

An interim payment of £1000 million had been required initially but Germany defaulted over this amount. An initial demand totalling £11,000 million was then reduced to £6000 million in 1921. This was to be paid in gold in annual instalments. However there was a growing split between Britain and France over the issue.

1 *A potential threat to the recovery of world trade.* British attitudes were very much influenced by the arguments of the economist John Maynard Keynes in the *Economic Consequences of the Peace* (1919) that the German market would be restricted by the drain of resources, and that only by greater German competition in world markets could she achieve the profits to pay the reparations. Either way, argued Keynes, Britain would suffer because of her especial dependence upon foreign trade.

2 *A method of retarding German recovery.* France had been particularly subjected to physical devastation, and was due 58 per cent of whatever was obtained. However, she was not so dependent upon foreign trade and in addition was induced to see reparations as an alternative to the territorial weakening of Germany. The general election of 1919 returned an ultra-nationalist Chamber of Deputies known as the 'Chambre bleu horizon' because of its high proportion of ex-servicemen. With the former president *'Poincaré la guerre'* as prime minister, the scene was set for a firm French international policy.

(c) *The occupation of the Ruhr (1923)*

The outcome was that when Germany again defaulted in 1923 French and Belgian forces were sent into the Ruhr to be able to collect reparations payments directly. Britain objected to the action, but France ignored this and the disapproval of the League of Nations. The German government responded by declaring non-co-operation, suspending reparations payments and encouraging strikes in the Ruhr. The crisis did contribute to the collapse of the German currency, however (see Section 27.2(a)), and weakened the basis of the Weimar Republic. In 1924 Poincaré's government fell, largely over its inadequate domestic policies, and was replaced by a Radical government. Between 1924 and 1932, French foreign policy was dominated by the far more conciliatory foreign minister Aristide Briand.

(d) *The Dawes Plan (1924)*

In August 1923 the more moderate Gustav Stresemann became German Chancellor (see Section 27.5). The payment of reparations was resumed in September 1924, and an Allied committee under the American General Dawes produced a settlement. It recommended:

1 *A German currency reform*, to set the mark at a value of £20 to the pound.

2 *A foreign loan of £40 million*, to be given to Germany to aid recovery.

3 *A more moderate system of reparations payment* was to be instituted. By November 1924 the troops had been withdrawn from the Ruhr, and from 1925 onwards the European economy was in a state of general recovery with international trade rising by 20 per cent by 1929.

24.4 The 'cordon sanitaire'

Without the option of an alliance with Russia, France now had to find allies elsewhere. The outcome was a series of military alliances in the 1920s with Belgium, Poland, Czechoslovakia, Rumania and Yugoslavia. But this 'coalition' could never be an adequate guarantee:

1 *The absence of unity.* In fact there were considerable divisions and distractions. The *'little entente'* of Czechoslovakia, Rumania and Yugoslavia was far more preoccupied with fear of a Hungarian revival, and Yugoslavia was locked in disagreement with Italy over Fiume (see Section 26.1(a)).
2 *The isolation of Russia.* Alliances with eastern central European states were not a great deal of value without Russian support, which was not only unachievable but would be very suspect to her smaller neighbour states.

24.5 The Geneva Protocol (1924–5)

France made two attempts to strengthen the machinery of the League of Nations.

(a) *The draft Treaty of Mutual Assistance (1923)*

This initial French proposal would have made military sanctions obligatory by member states against any aggressor nominated by the League. Britain would not accept this, because it would have been structured so that intervention would be only by states in the relevant continent, and this could mean that foreign states could intervene in the Commonwealth.

(b) *The Geneva Protocol (1924–5)*

In 1924 Britain and France neared agreement on the principle that where the lack of League unanimity prevented direct action, or where the domestic interests of a state were involved, arbitration should be sought. However, the new Conservative government in Britain led by Stanley Baldwin rejected the plan in March 1925 because of the fear that Japan might use it to force Australia, Canada and New Zealand to reopen their ports to Japanese immigration. The result was that the League was still without any effective power against aggressors. One of the basic reasons for this was the considerable difference in vulnerability of the member states. As one Canadian representative remarked about the Geneva Protocol: 'In this association of mutual insurance against fire, the risks assumed by the different states are not equal. We live in a fireproof house, far from inflammable materials.'

24.6 The 'Locarno Honeymoon' (1925–9)

The result was that after 1925 there was increasing reliance on regional agreements rather than the League of Nations to support international security. From the point of view of France, this was made all the more urgent by the Treaty of Rapallo of 1922 – the 'unholy alliance' between Russia and Germany which restored relations between the two states (see Section 27.5(a)).

(a) The Locarno treaties (1925)

The moderation which prevailed in relations between Germany and France from 1924 resulted in 1925 in treaty guarantees of the borders between Germany and France and Belgium by Britain, Italy, France, Belgium and Germany. However, these could not be a complete solution:

1 *The eastern frontiers of Germany were not guaranteed.* Germany did sign treaties with Poland and Czechoslovakia providing for arbitration for frontier disputes, but only France was prepared to underwrite these.
2 *Germany's ambitions in the east persisted.* The 'easterners' amongst German diplomatic circles produced the renewal of the Treaty of Rapallo in 1926, and in the same year while being admitted to League membership herself resisted successfully the conferral of any more than semi-permanent membership on Poland.

(b) The Kellog–Briand Pact (1928)

Originally a private agreement between the USA and France, this attracted eventually the signatures of 65 states. By it war was renounced by all of the subscribers as 'an instrument of national policy'. In fact, none of the states was committed to anything positive or subject to any sanctions. Furthermore, it was notable that this attitude was not reflected in any progress in disarmament discussions.

(c) The Young Committee (1929)

The annual payment of reparations was modified and transferred to German control. The Rhineland was evacuated by the western powers five years ahead of schedule. In fact in the same year Stresemann died, and changes of government in Britain and France removed the foreign ministers Austen Chamberlain and Aristide Briand who had contributed much personally to this period of conciliation.

(d) Successes of the League of Nations

The League did intervene in a whole series of frontier disputes with some success in the 1920s. Disagreements between Iraq and Turkey, Bulgaria and Greece, and Poland and Lithuania were all settled by League procedures. On the other hand, these were all relatively minor matters. A notable example of the potential weakness of the League was when it failed to secure Italian evacuation of Corfu, which had been occupied following the convenient killing of an Italian general in 1923, supposedly by Greek assassins. In the event, it was settled by an agreement between the Great Powers.

24.7 The Great Depression (1929–33)

In 1929 the world economy was stricken by a general depression which was to have serious diplomatic and political repercussions.

(a) The causes of the Great Depression

1 *Imbalance in the economy of the USA.* The 'trigger' came from the USA, where the situation was representative of a general world problem:

– *Relative overproduction* of raw materials and foodstuffs resulted in falling prices and a decline in the purchasing power of the farming population.
– *Optimistic industrial investment* in new areas, such as the production of automobiles and electrical goods.

In October 1929, the bubble burst when it was realised that industrial growth had outstripped the market and the 'Wall Street Crash' involved the loss of $40,000 million by investors. It was followed by a severe recession.

2 *The vulnerability of the international economy.* The world economy was already weakened by the impact of the war; German trade was down to 25 per cent and British trade to 50 per cent of pre-war levels. American protectionism and insistence on debt repayment worsened the problem even further. Austria and Germany were affected first because of their reliance on foreign loans which were now recalled, but a gathering financial panic drew in virtually the whole of Europe.

The associated tide of collapses of businesses and banks produced a *world recession* which at its lowest point resulted in 30 million unemployed.

(b) Responses

1 *Limited international co-operation.* There were regional agreements such as the Commonwealth Ottawa discussions in 1932 and the cancellation of reparations payments in July 1932 at the Lausanne Convention. On the other hand, attempts to coordinate a broader European or even world response failed.
2 *The pursuit of individual national interests.* There was a tendency instead to think within very limited national confines:

– *Manipulation of financial and trade relationships.* The general pattern of abandonment of the gold standard, currency devaluation and trade protection had a 'beggar my neighbour' effect on international trade.
– *Budget management.* The most common response was to try and balance state budgets by cutting expenditure, which tended if anything to worsen the problem. On the other hand, the 'New Deal' policies of President Franklin Roosevelt represented the view that governments should spend to reduce unemployment.

The most extreme situation was in the fascist economies of Italy and Germany, where policies of *self-sufficiency* were deliberately followed. However, these were as much associated with political and military objectives as to reduce unemployment, because the economic crisis had also had the effect of exaggerating an aggressive, nationalist extremism.

24.8 'Haves' and 'have nots'

The most threatening aspect of the recession was the tension which developed between those powers which possessed empires and those who aspired to gaining them. Economic recovery and growth became identified with colonial expansion.

(a) The advantage of empire

Imperialism did not disappear after 1918. It actually grew. Between a quarter and a third of the globe was now governed by Britain and France. There were two significant justifications for the maintenance of empire:

1   *Prestige* was a powerful if vague factor. Possession was justification enough in the eyes of the upper and upper middle classes who were its greatest advocates.
2   *The economic advantage* was genuine. French imperial investment grew from 9 per cent of her total overseas investment in 1914 to 45 per cent by 1940. Her imperial trade grew from 12 per cent of her total in 1929 to a third of the total in 1936. British investment grew to 59 per cent in 1936, and exports from a third of the total in 1910 to 50 per cent in 1938.

The result was that the preservation of empire and fear for its safety were major factors in appeasement. In fact the advantage of empire was illusory. It was a constant source of friction because of the rapid spread of nationalism (see Section 31.1), its possession did not excite widespread popular enthusiasm amongst the middle and lower classes and the costs of maintenance tended to outweigh the economic benefits.

(b)   *The ambition of the 'have nots'*

In the eyes of Japan, Italy and Germany long-term growth and survival and the possession of imperial territories were associated. Genuine shortages and vulnerability of the supply of industrial raw materials, such as iron ore in the case of Germany and Italy, limited access to foreign export markets and the restriction of emigration opportunities for Italians and Japanese by the USA and Australia were practical aspects of this problem, but it assumed much wider and less rational proportions.

1   *Japanese expansion was long term.* It had started in Korea in 1894. There had been a steady piecemeal expansion ever since. From 1936 the influence of the army led to an escalation of pressure to expand; and from 1938 onwards the focus was on the creation of the so-called Asian 'New Order' which was to be the basis for the wartime *'Co-Prosperity Sphere'*.
2   *Italian aspirations were more restricted* and were directed towards north and east Africa, the Dalmatian coast and the Mediterranean. Fascism 'lived on dreams of future prosperity' but also of racial superiority derived from the sense of succession to the Roman Empire. It is not clear to what extent Mussolini was a genuine imperialist and the extent to which he was just a victim of his own propaganda stimulated by the failure of Britain and France to challenge him.
3   *German aspirations were global* and governed by a much more coherent vision. Hitler thought in terms of a global struggle between Germans and Jews. In *Mein Kampf* (see Section 27.3) he envisaged a two-stage imperial expansion:

– *The construction of Mitteleuropa.* A central and eastern European area dominated by Germany and necessary for the provision of material resources.
– *The creation of lebensraum* by conquering western Russia. This would open up the possibility of threatening India and driving Britain and France from the Middle East. Eventually the final reckoning would be with the USA. Albert Speer was told to plan to complete the Berlin victory buildings by 1951.

All of this would require a massive military effort and commitment to war.

24.9 The reversal of the Treaty of Versailles (1933–7)

The first significant breach in collective security was made by the Japanese, who invaded Manchuria in September 1931 as part of a military and economic expansionary policy. The protectorate of Manchukuo was established. A League of Nations enquiry resulted in condemnation of Japan, who responded by simply leaving the League in 1933. However in Europe the most obvious challenge came from Hitler's drive to undo the Treaty of Versailles. It is unlikely that he worked to any sort of plan but was, as A. J. P. Taylor argues, a man who exploited the mistakes of his enemies. In addition, he preferred to achieve his objectives without violence and was an astute employer of appeals to peace, disarmament settlements based on 'justice and reason' and promises that every gain would be the last. But he made no secret of his desire to undo the treaty.

(a) Rearmament (October 1933)

In view of the absence of any international agreement about disarmament, Hitler argued that Germany could no longer accept that she alone should be disarmed. The result was that in 1933 Germany withdrew from the Disarmament Conference and the League of Nations.

(b) The German–Polish Pact (January 1934)

A ten-year pact with Poland allowed a display of peaceful intentions although only weeks later Hitler was telling his military commanders that Germany must be prepared to seize eastern 'Lebensraum'. It also damaged the French system of alliances in eastern central Europe. France responded in a number of ways:

1 *The Maginot Line.* The static defensive line between the Swiss–Belgian frontiers now assumed a greater urgency.
2 *Pursuit of an 'eastern Locarno'.* Attempts by the foreign minister Louis Barthou to achieve a satisfactory guarantee of Germany's eastern frontier foundered on the distrust of Russia by the smaller states. Then in October 1934 Barthou was killed during the assassination of King Alexander of Yugoslavia at Marseilles.
3 *A Franco-Italian Alliance.* Barthou's successor Pierre Laval achieved instead an alliance with Italy in January 1935. This was based partly on an agreement on colonial differences, and a guarantee of Austrian independence. This latter resulted from an abortive coup by Austrian Nazis in July 1944, in which the Chancellor Dr Dollfuss was killed. Italy backed the Austrian authorities and Hitler was obliged to disown German involvement.

(c) Introduction of conscription (March 1935)

The announcement of plans for an army of 600,000 men was censured by the League of Nations, provoked France, Britain and Italy to come together in the *Stresa Front* to continue the Locarno treaties, and even led Russia to conclude mutual assistance pacts with France and Czechoslovakia. However this apparently firm response was weakened by:

1 *The Anglo-German naval agreement of June 1935* limiting the German fleet to 35 per cent of the British tonnage, and giving her parity in submarines. Italy and France were not consulted, and *rearmament seemed to be condoned.*
2 *The Italian invasion of Abyssinia in October 1935* (see Section 24.10).

(d) Military reoccupation of the Rhineland (March 1936)

Hitler took advantage of the divisions of the Stresa Front to occupy the demilitarised zones with military forces and renounce the Locarno treaties. His excuse was the Franco-Soviet pact, which he claimed to be aggressive in intention. There is no doubt that the move could have been easily resisted; the number of troops involved was small, the German army was still distrustful of Hitler and France, Poland and Czechoslovakia could have mobilised 190 divisions quickly. On the other hand:

1   France was caught off guard, and was too preoccupied with the defensive Maginot strategy.
2   In Britain, there was sympathy with the German action in reoccupying what was hardly foreign territory. In addition, there was a growing view that a stronger Germany would be a barrier to communism.
3   Russia, Poland and the other French allies were well aware of the British and French hesitancy.

So at no cost Hitler increased his popular following, proved his generals wrong, and showed up the divisions in the opposition. In January 1937, he took the ultimate step in renouncing the German signature of the Treaty of Versailles.

24.10 The Abyssinian War (1935–6)

Since October 1935, attentions had been also somewhat distracted by the drama of Abyssinia (see Illus. 24.1).

(a)   *Italian colonial ambitions*

The existing Italian colonies were making a loss, but Mussolini had commercial ambitions towards Abyssinia, while a reversal of Adowa (see Section 17.5(c)) would be a great *coup*. From 1930, relations between the two countries deteriorated; in 1934 the contrived 'Wal-Wal incident' was an excuse to put pressure on Abyssinia, and in October 1935 Italian forces invaded.

(b)   *The international response*

1   *League of Nations condemnation* (October 1935). In response to the appeal by the Emperor Haile Selassie, Italy was 'named' as an aggressor and 52 nations voted for sanctions. In fact, coal and oil were excluded from the trade embargo imposed upon Italy, and it was ignored by the USA and by Germany as well as Russia (who had been a member of the League since October 1934). Britain was the most obvious state to take on additional sanctions in East Africa against the Italian invaders, but Britain did not have the resources to stand up to Italy and maintain commitments in the Far East and against Germany.
2   *Appeasement.* The result was that Britain and France, reluctant to risk the Stresa Front and apply military sanctions, had little choice but to look for ways of 'cutting losses'. In December 1935 the British and French foreign ministers Sir Samuel Hoare and Pierre Laval agreed to propose an 'exchange of territories' which would give Italy two-thirds of Abyssinia, leaving the Emperor with a rump state and a 'corridor for camels' to the sea. The offer was never made; the public outcry at the scheme was so great that Hoare had to resign.

(c)   *Consequences*

The Italian army did not make serious inroads until the able General Badoglio was

THE AWFUL WARNING.

FRANCE AND ENGLAND (*together !*).

"WE DON'T WANT YOU TO FIGHT,
BUT, BY JINGO, IF YOU DO,
WE SHALL PROBABLY ISSUE A JOINT MEMORANDUM
SUGGESTING A MILD DISAPPROVAL OF YOU."

From *Punch*, 1935, alluding to Anglo-French inaction over the Italian invasion of Abyssinia.
Source: C. C. Bayne Jardine, *Mussolini and Italy* (Longman, 1966) p. 59.

appointed to command; Addis Ababa fell in May 1936. The significance of the affair was considerable:

1   *The failure of collective security* was fully revealed. In July 1936, the League formally dropped its sanctions and *acquiesced* in the Italian occupation.
2   *The encouragement of fascist aggression.* The Stresa Front was in shreds, and in October 1936 Italy and Germany in the *'Pact of Steel'* agreed to coordinate their foreign policy. A year later this was followed by the extension of a German–Japanese *Anti-Comintern Pact* against Russia to include Italy; Austria

was now left in a very vulnerable position. One British civil servant saw the Italian action and events of 1935–6 as the source of the Second World War: 'we lost Abyssinia, we lost Austria, we formed the Axis. We made certain of Germany's next war'.

24.11 Conclusion

The lessons were clear enough. The League of Nations was powerless and Britain and France were not prepared to support their belief in collective security and resistance to aggression. The smaller states of eastern Europe responded by an increasing sub-servience to Germany, and in 1936 Belgium actually reverted to neutrality.

Questions

1 Describe the organisation of the League of Nations. Why did it fail to maintain international peace?
[OC]
2 What was 'collective security'? Why did it fail? [OC]
3 How well did the peace settlement of 1919–20 work in practice? [OC, adapted]
4 Describe the aims and organisation of the League of Nations. How successful was the League in dealing with international problems between 1920 and 1933? [OX]
5 How successful was the League of Nations as an instrument of collective security? [JMB, adapted]
6 Why despite the creation of the League of Nations, was there no effective disarmament in western Europe before 1934? [NEAB]
7 Study Sources A and B and then answer the questions which follow.

Source A: The sanctions of the League of Nations.

16. Should any Member of the League resort to war in disregard of its covenants under Articles 12, 13 or 15, it shall *ipso facto* be deemed to have committed an act of war against all other Members of the League, which hereby undertake immediately to subject it to the severance of all trade or financial relations, the prohibition of all intercourse between their nationals and the nationals of the covenant-breaking State, and the prevention of all financial, commercial and personal intercourse between the nationals of the covenant-breaking State and the nationals of any other State, whether a Member of the League or not.

It shall be the duty of the Council in such case to recommend to the several Governments concerned what effective military, naval or air force the Members of the League shall severally contribute to the armed forces to be used to protect the covenants of the League.

The Members of the League agree, further, that they will mutually support one another in the financial and economic measures which are taken under this Article, in order to minimize the loss and inconvenience resulting from the above measures, and that they will mutually support one another in resisting any special measures aimed at one of their number by the covenant-breaking State, and that they will take the necessary steps to afford passage through their territory to the forces of any of the Members of the League which are co-operating to protect the covenants of the League.

(a) Why were the military sanctions available to the League so limited (lines 9–12)? What alternatives might have been considered? Why were they unacceptable as well?
(b) What other sanctions were available for use in cases of aggression (lines 13–14)?
(c) What was the point of the 'loss and inconvenience' clause (line 15)?
(d) What were the fundamental weaknesses of the League of Nations?
Source: Part of Article 16 of the Covenant of the League Nations in the *Treaty of Peace between the Allied and Associated Powers and Germany*, Cmd 153 (HMSO, 1919).

Source B: The Manchurian incident.

According to the Japanese version Lieutenant Kawamoto, with six men under his command, was on patrol duty on the night of 18 September, practising defence exercises along the track of the South Manchuria Railway north of Mukden. They were proceeding southwards in the direction of Mukden. The night was dark but clear and the field of vision was not wide. When they reached a point at which a small road crosses the line, they heard the noise of a loud explosion a little way behind them. They turned and ran back, and after going about 200 yards they discovered that a portion of one of the rails on the down track had been blown out. The explosion took place at the junction of two rails; the ends of each rail had been cleanly severed, creating a gap in the line of 31 inches. On arrival at the site of the explosion, the patrol was fired upon from the fields on the east side of the line. Lieutenant Kawamoto immediately ordered his men to deploy and return the fire. The attacking body, estimated at five or six, then stopped firing and retreated northwards. The Japanese patrol at once started in pursuit and, having gone about 200 yards, were again fired upon by a larger body, estimated at between three and four hundred ...

At this moment the south-bound train from Changchun was heard approaching. Fearing that the train might be wrecked when it reached the damaged line, the Japanese patrol interrupted their engagement and placed detonators on the line in the hope of warning the train in time. The train, however, proceeded at full speed. When it reached the site of the explosion it was seen to sway and heel over to one side, but it recovered and passed on without stopping ...

Lieutenant Kawamoto's patrol ... was still sustaining the fire of the Chinese troops concealed in the tall grass, when two companies arrived from Mukden. Although his force was then only 500, and he believed the Chinese army in the North Barracks numbered 10,000, Lieutenant-Colonel Shinamoto at once ordered an attack on the Barracks ... When the Japanese reached the Barracks, which were described as glittering with electric light, an attack was made by the Third Company, which succeed in occupying a corner of the left wing. The attack was vigorously contested by Chinese troops, and there was fierce fighting for some hours ... By six o'clock a.m. the entire barracks was captured at the cost of two Japanese privates killed and twenty-two wounded ...

According to the Chinese version the Japanese attack on the Barracks ... was entirely unprovoked and came as a complete surprise. On the night of 18 September, all the soldiers of the 7th Brigade, numbering about 10,000, were in the North Barracks. As instructions had been received from Marshal Chiang Hsueh-liang on 6 September that special care was to be taken to avoid any clash with Japanese troops in the tense state of feeling existing at the time, the sentries at the walls of the Barracks were armed only with dummy rifles. For the same reason the west gate in the mud wall surrounding the camp which gave access to the railway had been closed ... At 10 p.m. on the 18th the sound of loud explosions was heard, immediately followed by rifle fire. This was reported over the telephone to the Commanding Officer ... While the Chief of Staff was still on the telephone, news was brought that the Japanese were attacking the Barracks ... As soon as the attack began, the Chief of Staff ... again reported to General Wang I-cheh by telephone. The latter replied that no resistance was to be offered ...

The Commission has come to the following conclusions:

The Chinese ... had no plan of attacking Japanese troops, or of endangering the lives or property of Japanese nationals at this time or place. They made no concerted or authorized attack on Japanese forces and were surprised by the Japanese attack. An explosion undoubtedly occurred on or near the railroad between 10 and 10.30 p.m. on 18 September, but the damage, if any, to the railroad did not prevent the punctual arrival of the south-bound train from Changchun, and was not in itself sufficient to justify military action. The military operations of the Japanese during this night ... cannot be regarded as measures of legitimate self-defence.

(a) Summarise the differences between the two accounts of the incident which are presented in this extract.

(b) Why did it matter whether the barracks were 'glittering with electric light' as the Japanese claimed?

Source: From the *Report of the Commission of Enquiry of the League of Nations in Mukden* (The Lytton Commission) 1931–2. Quoted in E. G. Rayner *The Great Dictators* (Hodder and Stoughton, 1992).

25 Soviet Russia 1917–40

Introduction

The events of the First World War had enabled a Marxist revolution in an overwhelmingly rural society with only 'islands' of urban and industrial development. In addition, in the absence of the anticipated European tide of revolution Bolshevik Russia was the isolated object of hostility and distrust. The combination of these internal and external circumstances produced dramatic changes in the pattern of government and economic management.

25.1 Consolidation of power (November 1917–mid-1918)

With only 200,000 committed Bolshevik supporters the urgent priority was to tighten the grip on power. The Congress of Soviets elected an All-Russian Central Executive Committee, which included 61 Bolsheviks in its 101 members, and a Soviet of People's Commissars with Lenin as chairman, Trotsky as Commissar for Foreign Affairs and Stalin responsible for the Nationalities.

(a) *Revolution by decree*

Negotiations with Germany were commenced in November and concluded with the Treaty of Brest-Litovsk (see Section 23.3(d)). In addition, the peasants' seizure of estates was condoned in the decree on land which nationalised all private estates and church lands and provided for an egalitarian redistribution. Other rather utopian decrees between October–December 1917 included the institution of an eight-hour working day, a declaration of universal free education, establishment of workers' control in factories, the abolition of all ranks and titles and the introduction of civil marriage as the only recognised form.

(b) *The elimination of the opposition*

1   *The dispersal of the Constituent Assembly* (see Section 13.3(c)). Elections had started on 15 November; of the 707 delegates in January 380 were SRs, only 175 were Bolsheviks. Rejection of a motion that power should reside with the soviets led to a walkout by the Bolsheviks, who then used sailors to disperse the

Assembly. Some days later the Congress of Soviets was declared to be the highest organ of power in the 'republic of Soviets'.

2   *The establishment of Cheka.* In December 1917 a secret police organisation was established under Felix Dzerzhinsky to root out potential counter-revolution and spearheaded the 'Red Terror' which led Maxim Gorky to describe this as 'starting bloody despotism all over again'.

25.2 War Communism (mid-1918–March 1921)

From mid-1918 onwards, however, there was a pronounced swing towards extreme state intervention. This hastily improvised policy was a result of three factors:

1   *The collapse of the economy.* Foreign intervention, civil war, the terms of Brest-Litovsk and peasant seizures of land accounted for the fall in output of heavy industry by 1920 to 13 per cent of the pre-war total, and by 1921 the gross crop yield was down to 50 per cent. Bolshevik actions such as the institution of 'worker control' had only worsened matters. Anarchy and confusion prevailed.

2   *The need for the restoration of the armed forces.* The old tsarist army had collapsed or defected. Trotsky needed resources to create the new Workers' and Peasants' Red Army, and a Red Fleet.

3   *'Making a virtue out of necessity'.* In particular, Lenin and other Bolshevik leaders tended to argue that War Communism was a short cut in the drive towards egalitarianism.

(a)   *War Communism in practice*

1   *Nationalisation.* There were two attitudes to industrial management.

– The left-wing 'Workers Opposition' Group advocated workers' control with equal shares in management and profits.
– Lenin saw state control as the route out of the prevailing anarchy in the factories. The nationalisation decree of June 1918 was intended originally to apply to key factories and installations, but by August 1920 there were 37,000 firms involved, 5000 employed only one worker, and many were windmills. Lenin also supported the restoration of inegalitarian material incentives and piecework bonuses, as well as the employment of former bourgeois specialists to restore proper commercial management.

2   *The 'crusade for bread'.* The need to obtain food supplies for the urban centres and armed forces which the peasants were not prepared to provide at official prices led the Bolsheviks to resort to 'foodstuffs sub-allocation':

– *Forcible seizure* of food from the villages by Cheka units and urban workers (see Illus. 25.1).
– The formation of 'committees of the poor' in the villages to turn the poorer peasants against the wealthier 'kulaks'. who would be made to bear the brunt of the requisitions.

Natural peasant responses were to resort to black marketeering through the 'sackmen' (by January 1919 only 19 per cent of food going to the larger towns went by official routes), to resistance by organised defence forces known as 'Greens', and to cutting production and slaughtering stock.

Source: A magazine illustration from the 1920s.

The peasant is surrounded by the kulak, the priest and the boot-legger, as he tries to protect his harvest.

(b)   *The end of War Communism*

1   *Economic necessity.* The loss of incentives to agricultural and industrial output and the virtual collapse of the currency in addition to the natural catastrophes of drought, famine and epidemic in 1920–2, which may have killed up to 10 million people, forced a reconsideration of economic policy.

2   *The growth of opposition.* The SRs had turned again to terrorism, assassinating the German ambassador Count Mirbach and making an attempt on Lenin's life in August 1918. By early 1920 Trotsky and the Mensheviks were urging greater

freedom of trade and abandonment of food requisitioning. Lenin's initial response was to advocate 'absolute ruthlessness', but the mutiny of sailors of the Baltic Fleet at Kronstadt in February 1921 made it clear that the rule of the Communist Party (renamed in March 1918) was seriously threatened.

3   *The decline of the military threat.* By the spring of 1921 the threat to Soviet Russia from the foreign invaders and White counter revolutionary forces was dying away. The result was that in March 1921 Lenin abandoned War Communism in 'a retreat – for a new attack'.

25.3 The New Economic Policy (NEP) (March 1921–8)

The new policy was a form of mixed economy, part state control and part private enterprise.

(a)   *Economic reforms*

1   *A free market in foodstuffs.* A 10 per cent tax on peasant produce replaced requisitions; surpluses could be sold freely.
2   *Denationalisation.* By the decree of *May 1921* the state was left with only the *'commanding heights'* of banking, foreign trade and large-scale industry. The rest of the economy reverted to *private ownership*.
3   *Currency reform.* During the height of War Communism there had even been talk of the abolition of money; in July 1922, a new monetary system backed by gold was created, and a state bank was established.

(b)   *The Soviet Constitution (1923)*

Associated with the moderation in economic policy was the adoption of a new constitution for the new Union of Soviet Socialist Republics which was, in theory, a federal system of the four republics of Russia, Ukraine, Belorussia and Transcaucasia. In reality, Russia was much the more dominant member, and the right to secede was simply a form of 'window dressing'. The key powers were held by the central Union government with the Congress of Soviets as the highest organ of state elected by universal suffrage, although it took only 25,000 urban voters to elect a deputy as opposed to 125,000 peasants. Above all, nothing was said about the Communist Party, which dominated political power since 1921–2 when the SRs and Mensheviks were virtually eliminated. The Party permeated every level of government and public service; in addition, even within the Communist Party power was increasingly concentrated into the hands of smaller groups and especially the policy-making Politburo and the Secretariat which provided the bureaucracy.

25.4 The struggle for power

The NEP measures did assist the recovery of pre-war production levels by 1929. However, there was growing dissent within the Communist Party over policy.

(a) *Economic imbalance*

NEP involved particularly a *rapid increase in agricultural output*, which had two implications:

1 *The 'scissors crisis'*. Lagging industrial development meant that food prices were falling well below the prices of manufactured goods and that peasant demand was reduced as a result. To cut industrial prices – as in 1924 – cut down the amount of capital available for industrial expansion, and so continued the problem. Foreign investment was not readily obtainable because the Bolsheviks had cancelled all of the tsarist debts. By 1926–7 only 20 per cent of the capital funds available was allocated to new industrial expansion, the rest had to go on repair, maintenance and enlargement of existing plant.
2 *'Peasant stratification'*. The class of rich peasants, the kulaks, was steadily developing. About 4 per cent of the total, they represented a form of bourgeois capitalism. Yet to seek to reduce this group would be to damage the most efficient sector of agricultural production, and cut supplies of grain to the towns and the industrial workers.

By 1927, the peasant withholding of foodstuffs from sale in the towns because of inadequate prices signalled the failure of the NEP.

(b) *'Capitalist encirclement'*

The early 1920s saw the re-establishment of diplomatic relations with Germany by the Treaty of Rapallo (see Section 27.5(b)) and with other European states. On the other hand the USSR was regarded with considerable suspicion, largely because of the activities of the *Comintern* which sought to generate international subversion and revolution. Incidents such as the publication of the infamous forged *'Zinoviev Letter'* in 1924 – an apparent encouragement to subversive activities in Britain – and the discovery of suspicious documents during a raid on the offices of the Soviet trade organisation in 1927 led Britain to break off diplomatic relations again. By 1927 the isolation of the USSR was keenly felt. Full and effective rearmament required intensive industrial development.

(c) *Personal ambition*

From March 1922 Joseph Stalin, the Georgian 'man of steel', was General Secretary of the Party. Before 1917 his role in the Bolshevik organisation had been largely that of terrorist organiser and 'hatchet man' for Lenin. From 1917 he had concentrated on rather mundane administrative duties, but by 1922 was the only Communist leader to be a member of the Central Committee, the Politburo and the Secretariat. Lenin became increasingly distrustful of his ruthless ambition and in his remarks on his Politburo colleague in his last *Testament* of 1923 expressed fears about Stalin's concentration of power and suggested that he be replaced as General Secretary. In January 1924 Lenin died, and Stalin held on to his position. In 1924 he became involved in a power struggle with his greatest rivals. His strength in that struggle came from three sources:

1 *The opportunity to insert supporters* into the Secretariat and control personnel appointments. However, at this stage, and afterwards, the level of autonomy at the lower levels should not be underestimated. Stalin had to create alliances to defeat his opponents, but his control over staffing was an important tool in doing so.
2 *The ability to destroy the organisational power bases of his opponents*. So, for example, Zinoviev's seemingly impregnable stronghold in Leningrad was

demolished in weeks as his supporters were replaced by those of Stalin.

3 *Espousal of popular policy positions.* Stalin identified himself with the cult of Lenin and adopted policies which appealed to the new members of the party who were not ideologically well developed. The membership grew from 24,000 in 1917 to 1,677,910 in 1930. The basic straightforward models offered by Stalin were attractive to them. So there was considerable backing for 'Socialism in one country' as opposed to Trotsky's alternative of 'Permanent Revolution'.

(d) *'Socialism in one country'*

There were two prevailing views about the future economic and social development of the USSR:

1 *The 'left opposition'.* As opposed to Lenin and Stalin, Trotsky believed that the emphasis should be on planned industrial development rather than the need for a prosperous peasantry. In addition, he argued in favour of active promotion of world revolution to enable the survival of the USSR. Stalin opposed these ideas,

Illus. 25.2a/b   Two photographs of Lenin addressing a workers' meeting shortly after the Revolution

Source: F. Wyndham and D. King, *Trotsky* (Penguin, 1972) p. 151. Illus. 25.2a from Popperfoto and Illus. 25.2b from Novosti Press Agency.

and his emphasis upon the possibility of achieving *'Socialism in one country'* was attractive to Russian nationalists and moderates. From 1924 onwards, by astute political management and his ability to pack Party committees with his supporters as General Secretary, he was able to strip Trotsky of power (see Illus. 25.2a and 25.2b). In 1924, Trotsky lost control of the Red Army, then in 1926–7 Trotsky, his allies Zinoviev and Kamenev and some 70 'Trotskyists' were ousted first from their party offices and then from the Communist Party itself. In 1928 Trotsky went into exile, and was eventually murdered by a Soviet agent in Mexico in 1940.

2   *The 'right opposition'.* Stalin had allied with a group which advocated industrial development on the basis of a higher peasant income level – as Bukharin described it, 'riding into Socialism on a peasant's nag'. Now he turned against his allies and in December 1927 the same Party Congress which expelled Trotsky adopted resolutions to increase taxation of the *kulaks* and prepare a Five-Year Plan for industrial development. This latter was approved in 1929 and the members of the 'right opposition' – Tomsky, Bukharin and Rykov – suffered the loss of their posts.

25.5 The four faces of Stalinism

There was little direct evidence of Stalinism in 1927. The USSR had an essentially market economy and a vigorous cultural and political life which was not obsessed with class struggle. The NEP had seen the beginning of the re-emergence of social stratification. Elitist politics had not become the pattern, and opposition still existed albeit within a limited oligarchic group. Fully fledged Stalinism reversed all of this. It had four faces.

1   An economic *'Third Revolution'* which involved a drive towards industrialisation and agricultural collectivisation.
2   Cultural and ideological conformity and the development of the *cult of Stalin*.
3   *Social mobility* on a massive scale.
4   A political revolution in the form of the *purges* which effectively destroyed politics.

25.6 The 'Third Revolution'

Stalin rejected the Trotskyist emphasis on 'permanent revolution' internationally, but did embrace his plan for intensive industrialisation (see Fig. 25.1a). The result was a massive revolution in the USSR between 1928 and 1936, in terms of economic growth and personal freedom.

(a)   *Collectivisation* (see Fig. 25.1b)

The key to the Five-Year Plans (see Illus. 25.3) was the collectivisation of peasant holdings, and the reduction of the status of peasants to that of paid *'kolkhoz'* workers. The objects were:

1   *Easier mechanisation of agriculture*, based upon the state-owned machine tractor stations established to provide machinery to the surrounding *kolkhozy*.
2   *Regularisation of the supply of foodstuffs to the growing towns*. In what became virtually a civil war in the countryside as the peasants resisted the changes, Stalin sought support by emphasising the rivalry of the richer and poorer peasantry. The

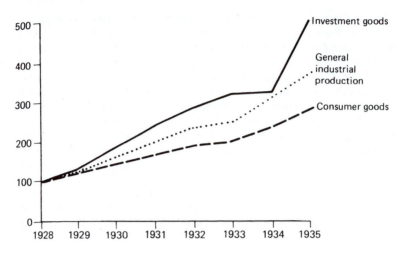

Fig. 25.1a Economic activity in the USSR (1928–35)

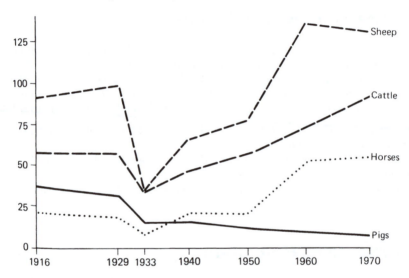

Fig. 25.1b Livestock numbers in the USSR (1916–70)

'liquidation of the kulaks' involved expropriation, enforced destitution, deportation and death of up to 10 million people.

By 1932, it was claimed that 60 per cent of agriculture had been collectivised and 2446 stations provided 150,000 tractors as opposed to the 35,000 tractors in the whole of the USSR in 1929. By 1940 the collectivisation of 97 per cent of the peasant households into 250,000 *kolkhozy* was claimed.

(b) The 'Great Leap Forward'

Initially, a massive increase in investment up to twelve times as much in the first Five-Year Plan as in 1923–8 was planned. The rate was actually increased, and in 1933–7 was

Illus. 25.3 'The Five-Year Plan (Completed in Four Years)'

A 1933 poster

Q What do you think is meant to be represented by the sneering man in the silk top hat?

increased again by 250 per cent. In real terms, the Plans involved the construction of large factories producing all sorts of industrial machinery and vehicles, enormous metallurgical and mineral plants in the Urals and Don basin and vast schemes of communications development and electrification. Lenin once remarked that 'communism equals Soviet power plus the electrification of the whole country'. By 1940, the volume of heavy industrial production was twelve times greater than 1913 and machinery construction was 35 times greater. Over 80 per cent of the national output came from plant built since 1928. Associated with this was a doubling of the urban dwelling population to 32 per cent in 1940, as opposed to 16 per cent in 1920.

(c) *Assessment of the 'Third Revolution'*

But these achievements must be qualified:

1 *Underfulfilment.* Some of the targets were hopelessly unrealistic, and were not met. In the later 1930s official statistics disguised the fact that there was a general fall in the rate of growth due to the purges and the transfer of resources to arms production. Capital goods output in 1938–41 was only 25 per cent of the objective.
2 *Limited gains in agriculture.*

   – Productivity and yields did not match the rate of expansion of cultivation.
   – From 1935 onwards, output could be raised only by actually allowing *kolkhoz* workers to have private allotments and livestock.
   – The efficiency of the *kolkhozy* varied tremendously, according to a range of local circumstances.

3 *Wastefulness.* The achievements were also won at some cost. In the struggle to collectivise, the number of cattle fell from 60 million in 1928 to 33 million in 1933, and the slaughtering of horses was in the same proportion. In industry, the wastefulness took the form of losses due to incompetence, bureaucracy, corruption and inadequate training.
4 *A reduced standard of living.* There were food shortages due to collectivisation and the need to export grain for currency; food rationing remained unchanged until 1935. Real wages fell by 39 per cent from 1928–37. There was a persistent shortage of all types of consumer goods, and also of housing. In 1935, 40 per cent of all families in Moscow lived in single rooms.
5 *Inegalitarianism.* Socialism was in the process of reinterpretation so that new élites with privileges and preferential treatment were emerging. Society was reforming into a series of ranks ranging from factory managers and doctors to *kolkhoz* workers. This inequality was reinforced by the privileges according to party members.
6 *Reduction of personal liberty.* On the one hand output was encouraged with patriotic appeals, prizes, medals and the leading of competition by 'shock brigades' and star (*Stakhanovite*) workers. On the other, the discipline of the labour force was very harsh with food rationing, internal passports and 'workbooks', penalties for the infringement of factory regulation and severe punishment for absenteeism. Ultimately there were the sanctions of arrest, imprisonment and deportation to labour camps as 'enemies of the people'.

25.7 Stalinist culture

According to Marxist theory culture and social values always reflect the interests of the dominant class. In Stalinist Russia culture was employed as another tool to achieve the economic objectives.

(a) *Socialist realism*

Literature, art and all other aspects of learning adopted radical proletarian values since culture had to contribute to the construction of socialism. However, there was an increasing change in emphasis away from the ordinary worker, toiling peasant and small man to the expert, the manager and the office holder. Egalitarianism was supplanted by hierarchy and authority. This was reflected also in public morality with the emphasis on motherhood and the traditional family structure.

(b) *Russian nationalism*

All forms of non-Russian nationalism were rejected and cultural diversity was played down. On the other hand, the great state-builders of Great Russian history such as Alexander Nevsky, Peter the Great and Ivan the Terrible were restored to favour. History was rewritten when necessary to serve the interests of Russian nationalism which served as an emotive focus for Russian workers.

(c) *The cult of Stalin*

The Cult of Lenin was officially inaugurated in 1924 with the erection of the Lenin mausoleum in Red Square and the renaming of Petrograd as Leningrad. However, Stalin had far more power than Lenin ever had. He became the source of all ideological orthodoxy from 1929. He tamed the Party so much that he could bypass the Politburo and work through the NKVD. Through an elaborate propaganda machine he could represent himself as 'leader, teacher and friend' of the people. He could even have history books rewritten to emphasise his role in the story of the Revolution and obliterate the memory of his former enemies (see Illus. 25.1).

25.8 A social revolution

On the other hand, there was considerable social mobility in this period. In the longer term between 1924 and 1959 the number of blue collar workers rose from 10.4 per cent of the total workforce to 50.2 per cent. The proportion of white collar workers grew from 4.4 per cent to 18.1 per cent. The proportion of peasants fell from 76.7 to 31.7 per cent. The bulk of this change was during the Stalinist period. It arose from:

(a) *The demands of economic development*

There was, for instance, a great increase in the need for officials to run the collectivisation programme. Peasants moved into the towns to take up factory employment and enjoy the greater opportunities offered by the city. Between 1926–39 the proportion of the population living in the urban areas grew from 18 per cent to 33 per cent.

(b) The expansion of education

There was a vast expansion of educational provision to obtain the necessary specialists and technicians to replace the bourgeois specialists. In 1926–7 there were 1,834,260 students in secondary school; by 1933–4 there were 5,940,569; by 1938–9 there were 12,088,772. The number of students in higher education grew from 159,800 in 1927–8 to 469,800 in 1932–3; the proportion with working class backgrounds grew from 25.8 per cent to 50.3 per cent. From 1930 onwards a system of universal compulsory education for all children over 8 years of age was being installed, with a strong emphasis on discipline and on basic skills.

(c) The impact of the purges

One of the positive aspects of the purges was the promotion opportunities which were created. The result was that the ranks of the Soviet élite were filled with young working-class people.

25.9 A political revolution

The political face of Stalinism did not appear in its fullest form until the late 1930s, and especially the *Great Terror* of 1936–8. There had been purges of the Party and political show trials before when the SRs and Mensheviks were eliminated, and throughout the 1920s when Party size was increased and reduced according to views as to its role. The purges of the 1930s were far more extensive and severe (see Illus. 25.4).

(a) Motives

The 'terrorist' assassination of Kirov, the popular secretary of the Leningrad Party in December 1934, was just an excuse. Stalin had him killed because he had been alerted to a plot to replace himself with Kirov. In fact the purges were the result of several converging factors:

1 *The search for enemies.* The mounting international threat and the general insecurity of the period were bound to increase tension and paranoia in the USSR. In 1928–34 this had been focused on the trials of specialists and technical experts. In the later 1930s the trawl was considerably extended.
2 *The need to improve and streamline the party.* Following Stalin's 'Dizzy with Success' article in 1930 the enemies were within the party ranks more and more. This was the start of a series of party purges.
3 *To eliminate potential opponents of Stalin.* It is wrong to exaggerate the strength of Stalin's position. In 1929 he was still only one member of an oligarchy. He did have to face opposition groups such as the Riutin Platform which opposed collectivisation. Even in 1934 270 delegates (22 per cent of the total) voted against Stalin for election to the Central Committee. The purges were particularly directed against the 'Old Bolsheviks'. Isaac Deutscher says that the purges were designed 'to destroy the men who represented the potentiality of alternative governments, perhaps not of one but of several alternative governments'.
4 *The momentum of terror.* To some extent once it started the Great Terror had its own dynamics. In particular there was

    – *The NKVD target mentality.* Arrests had to be achieved because not to do so opened the police to accusations themselves. The NKVD sought to make a case for

From a 1937 cartoon by Seppla (Josef Plank), showing anti-Stalinist sentiment in Germany before the brief peace pact.
Source: A. Rhodes and V. Margolin, *Propaganda* (Angus & Robertson, 1976) p. 55.

its own indispensability, and some writers have seen this as one of the triggers of the purges.
– *The process of denunciation.* The hope of achieving lenient treatment or to protect members of the family led people to denounce others to the police. So the circle widened continuously.

Since Stalin did not dare to slacken his rule to seek popularity he turned to the alternative. In so doing he destroyed politics in the USSR because once terror became an instrument of government the stake of opposition was raised to death.

(b) *The pattern*

The purges can be considered as a series of *waves*:

1   *The elimination of the 'Old Bolsheviks' (1934–6).* Given vastly extended power, the NKVD (successor to the Cheka) tried and shot thousands of Party members accused of 'Trotskyism' and 'terrorism'.
2   *The Yezhovshchina (1936–8).* Yezhov, the new Commissar for Internal Affairs, broadened the scope of the purges to draw in millions of people who were forced to confess to ludicrous charges then shot or sent to NKVD labour camps. The most notable feature of this period were the great *show trials* of prominent Communists such as Bukharin and Rykov who seemed to confess readily to ridiculous charges of treason and conspiracy. This readiness to give way is partly explained by long-term indoctrination in the infallibility of the Party; as Trotsky remarked: 'I know one cannot be right against the Party.'
3   *The army* (1937–8). In 1937 the great Marshal Tukhachevsky and other high-ranking officers were tried and shot. Between then and 1938 half of the officer corps and nine in ten of the generals were purged, with serious effects on the command structure.
4   *The NKVD (1938).* The last stage was the replacement and shooting of Yezhov and his cronies and the appointment of Beria, a trusted henchman of Stalin.

Altogether, some 20 million people may have been shot or sent to labour camps or forced labour; the Party itself had been purged of some 850,000 members. However, the effects on economic growth and the quality of military and administrative leadership were terrible.

25.10 The roots of Stalinism

The issue of the origin of Stalinism is an important one, not only because of the need to understand the nature of the Russian Revolution but also to be able to assess the viability of Marxism in general. There are three theories:

(a) *Contextualist*

A popular view is that Stalinist centralism developed from the backwardness of Russia and the inadequacy of the entrepreneurial middle class and the working class in a society where the revolution had come too soon and from above. There are two dimensions to this:

1   *The Trotsky bureaucratic thesis* that the bureaucracy came to exercise excessive power in a Russia with a low level of socio-economic development and an isolated Bolshevik ruling élite, which could exercise only limited political control. Stalin emerged on the back of this.
2   *The industrialist thesis* of Isaac Deutscher who saw the Bolsheviks as modernisers seeking to industrialise an underdeveloped country under pressure and as soon as possible, and forced to use coercion and dictatorial power.

The problem with these theories is that they are too deterministic, and leave insufficient scope for the role of the individual or other variable factors. There were always policy options available and there was no inevitable logic leading to Stalinism.

(b) Essentialist

The so-called 'continuity thesis' sees Stalinism as a natural development from Leninism. There is no doubt that Lenin did close down political activity and opposition, and that he pursued the creation of a one-party state. So the emphasis on social unanimity laid the ground for Stalinism. However, this is a selective view. Leninism had a very strong democratic strand. In any case, the development to Stalinism rather than any other outcome was not inevitable. It was direct intervention by political actors which was necessary to realise Stalinism.

(c) Personalist

The alternative is to regard Stalin as personally responsible; unprincipled and thirsting after dictatorial power and showing signs of mental illness. On the other hand:

1 *Other factors worked in the same direction* to produce policy changes, such as economic changes and the international situation.
2 *Stalinism enjoyed considerable support* from the beginning. Many members favoured economic direction and Stalin just responded to this to some extent.
3 *Selfish interests stood to gain.* The NKVD especially benefited from the Terror and the demand for its services. There is even a view that the murder of Kirov was organised by the NKVD to demonstrate its own indispensability.
4 *Stalin's ability to control events at all political levels is exaggerated.* His control over the party apparatus is easy to overestimate. In fact there was a good deal of freedom for local leaders and managers.

Even so, it is undeniable that it was Stalin who made the key decisions and that he was in a position to stop the worst excesses if he wished. He must be seen as having at least condoned the system. Stalinism was a result of the three factors, but it also reflected the values and preferences of the new socially mobile urban middle class which had a vested interest in it.

25.11 Conclusion

Stalin's reversal of Marxist theory to equip the USSR with an industrial base after the Revolution and to establish a personal dictatorship instead of the rule of the proletariat had paradoxical repercussions. In 1941 the initial collapses of the Soviet army when faced with the German onslaught were due very largely to the effects of the purges and lack of commitment to the Stalinist régime. On the other hand, the great industrialisation programmes of the 1920s–30s enabled the USSR to survive, and then to win. Nevertheless the route to Socialism had been lost; as early as December 1919, a disillusioned Lenin said: 'We know we cannot establish a Socialist system now, God grant that it may be established in our children's time or perhaps our grandchildren's time.'

Questions

1 What did Lenin achieve after November 1917?   [OC]
2 What were the aims of Stalin's Five-Year Plans? How much did they achieve?   [OC]
3 How far did the achievements of communism in Russia between the two world wars fulfil the aims and hopes of those who made the Bolshevik revolution in 1917?   [OX]
4 How was Russia affected after 1917 by: (a) War Communism; (b) the New Economic Policy; (c) industrialisation under the Five-Year Plans; (d) collectivisation?   [NEAB]

5 Assess Stalin's contribution to the development of the Soviet state in the period from 1928 to 1939.

[NEAB, adapted]

6 With what justification can Lenin be called 'the creator of the Soviet state' in the period 1917 to 1924? [NEAB]

7 Why was the Bolshevik régime able to survive the dangers which it faced between November 1917 and the death of Lenin in 1924?

8 Explain Stalin's success in gaining and then retaining power in the USSR from 1924 to 1939.[CAM]

9 Study Sources A and B below and then answer the questions which follow.

Source A: As long as it is necessary.

Stalin is extravagantly ruthless. It is stupid or silly to deny this. The Russian terror was a wholesale punitive assault on a class. Soviet Russia differed from other dictatorships in that it assumed from the beginning the necessity of destruction of class enemies. In Soviet Russia force is applied directly, and with social aims in view which are intended to benefit not only one hundred and sixty-five million Russians, but the whole human race. The end justifies the means, in the Soviet view. Stalin is perfectly frank about this. Lady Astor asked him, 'How long are you going to go on killing people?' Stalin replied, 'As long as it is necessary'.

His tactics have always been to use Lenin as a stick to beat opponents with. In his long struggle with Trotsky, Stalin pretended never to put himself forward for his own sake, but only as the 'instrument of Lenin'.

Above and beyond their personal conflict was divergence in political views of extreme importance. The passion of each came to embody cardinally opposed theories of the operation of the Soviet Union. Trotsky's 'Left Opposition' arose out of the doctrine of 'permanent revolution'. He did not believe as Stalin did, that socialism could succeed in a single state.

Stalin was, of course, right. The very considerable success of the first Five Year Plan proved that. It is easy to be wise after the event. Seven years ago, before Trotsky was expelled from Russia, before the Five Year Plan got under way, no one could have foreseen the outcome so surely. Great credit to Stalin for his prescience, his 'long view'.

(a) Whom did Stalin regard as 'class enemies' (line 3)? How and when were they destroyed?

(b) Give an account of Stalin's 'long struggle with Trotsky' (lines 9–10). What was its outcome?

(c) What was 'the first Five Year Plan' (line 17)? Was the author correct in believing that it enjoyed 'very considerable success' (line 17)?

(d) What do you understand by the doctrine of 'permanent revolution' (line 15)?

(e) Comment upon the view that Stalin was 'extravagantly ruthless' (line 1).

Source: John Gunther, *Inside Europe* (Hamish Hamilton, 1936).

Source B: Stalin's psychology.

[Stalin mused] ... Yes, the history of mankind was the history of class struggle, but the leader emerged as the expression of class, and therefore the history of mankind was the history of its leaders and its rulers. Idealism did not come into it. The spirit of an epoch was determined by the man who made the epoch himself ... all opponents, past, present, and future, had to be liquidated and would be liquidated. The sole socialist country in the world could survive only if it were unshakeably stable, and this would also be seen as a sign of its stability by the outside world. The state must be strong in case of war; the state must be mighty if it wants peace. It must be feared.

In order to turn a peasant society into an industrialised country, countless material and human sacrifices were necessary. The people must accept this. But it would not be achieved by enthusiasm alone. The people would have to be forced to accept the sacrifices, and for this a powerful authority was needed, an authority that inspired fear ... the theory of undying class war provided for all such possibilities. If a few million people had to perish in the process, history would forgive Comrade Stalin ... All the great rulers had been harsh ... sending Trotsky into exile out of the country had been a humane act, and therefore it had been a mistaken one: Trotsky was at large and still active. He would not send Zinoviev and Kamenev into exile abroad: they were going to serve as the first foundation stone of the bastion of fear he must build in order to defend the nation and the country. And they would be followed by their allies. Bukharin was one of their allies.

(a) How would you argue against Stalin's line of reasoning that fear and the Terror were the only keys to state stability and strength?
(b) What truth is there in the comment that 'the history of mankind was the history of its leaders'?
(c) How could all 'past' opponents be liquidated? What do you think Stalin had in mind when he said this?

Source: A. Rybakov, *Children of the Arbat*. Published in Britain in 1988 after suppression in the USSR for twenty years.

10 From Illus. 25.2a and 25.2b (p. 330).
   (a) How do these two pictures demonstrate a deliberate attempt to falsify history?
   (b) What differences between Lenin (and later Stalin) and Trotsky caused this rewriting to occur?

26 Mussolini and Italy 1918–36

Introduction

It was in Italy that the first of the post-war fascist dictatorships was established. The strains on the economy and society produced by the First World War and post-war economic fluctuations created tensions and reactions which the political and constitutional systems were ill-adapted to respond to, leaving scope for 'direct' action justified by the restoration of order and national pride. In Italy, the roots of anti-parliamentarianism were well established before 1914.

26.1 The vulnerability of Italy

The war had provided an immense psychological shock for Italy. Unprepared for war with Austria, and with an army weakened by the Libyan adventure, nevertheless the Italian army held the line at the River Isonzo until the panic rout of 700,000 men at Caporetto in 1917 which reinforced the rising tide of defeatism and social division. The dramatic victory at Vittorio-Veneto and collapse of the Dual Monarchy produced a counter-surge of hysterical nationalism. Against this background, the problems of post-war Italy were far more exaggerated.

(a) *Nationalist resentment*

By the terms of the Treaty of London, Italy had been led to expect Dalmatia in addition to the other territories she gained (see Section 23.8(a)). President Wilson resisted the claim as unjustified in terms of nationality. In 1920, a group of moderates – recognising good relations with Yugoslavia as more significant – dropped the claim to Dalmatia in the Treaty of Rapallo. The outcome was the resentment of extreme nationalists and *irredentists* directed not only against Yugoslavia and Wilson but also against the 'renouncers' and the political system. A reflection of this was the comic 'Fiume or Death!' adventure of 1919–20, when the eccentric poet Gabriele D'Annunzio occupied the Yugoslav port of *Fiume* with a band of blackshirted ex-servicemen, romantic idealists and rogues. The most disturbing feature was the support that was given to this extra-legal violence by public opinion, by army officers and some political leaders.

(b) Social tensions

The war further emphasised the weakness of the Italian economy. By 1918–19 state expenditure was three times the size of income. By 1918, the value of imports which had almost quintupled was three times greater than that of exports. Above all, inflation swept ahead of wages. According to one price index prices rose by 250 per cent between 1914–18, and then nearly doubled again between 1918 and 1922. The result was a wave of strikes by industrial workers especially in 1919–20, reaching a climax in September with 500,000 northern workers organised under self-constituted soviets. In the countryside there were agricultural strikes exploiting the labour shortage and peasant seizures of land. Altogether it was a disturbing display of lawlessness and violence.

26.2 The weakness of the political system

It is not entirely true that the old liberal régime of Italy 'committed suicide' in 1920–1. The problem was the interaction of two factors.

(a) The complacency of the Liberals

Liberal leaders like Nitti and Giolitti had too much faith in the flexibility of the political system:

1 *Neutrality in the face of disorder.* As before 1914, Giolitti believed that state intervention only exacerbated the divisions between workers and employers, peasants and big landowners. His policy of leaving movements to die of their own accord had worked before (see Section 17.7(a)).
2 *Transformism to absorb new political extremes.* In the days of a limited electorate and relatively small differences in principle between political groups it had not been easy to govern by means of reshuffling conditions. Now that the franchise was so much more extended, new mass parties had emerged which were less likely to become involved in the old personal dealing. A new voting system introduced in 1919 tended to fragment the groupings in the Chamber even more, and so worsen the chances of effective government.

In addition to this, the Liberals alienated themselves from the army by granting an amnesty to wartime deserters and by publishing a report on Caporetto which blamed officers and men for the disaster.

(b) The emergence of mass parties

New mass parties appeared which could not be 'captured' by the political system:

1 *The Christian Democrats*, or *'popolari'*. Established in 1919 and supported largely by agricultural workers, this new party was near-Socialist on its left wing but very Catholic and conservative on the right. It was led by the Sicilian priest Don Sturzo; in 1920 it had 100 seats in the Chamber. However, the 'popolari' were not prepared to make a long-term alliance with the anti-clerical liberals, although they would ally with Fascism against them.
2 *The Socialists.* By 1920 the Socialists had a membership of over 200,000, 156 seats in the Chamber and control of 2000 municipalities and 26 provinces. They were especially strong in the northern industrial cities and old radical Romagna. The problem was that their leaders' talk of revolution conjured up the 'red menace'

and, together with their anti-militarism, this alienated the army, but they were not prepared to bid for power themselves or ally with the Liberals.

3   *The Fascists.* In the absence of any alternative allies the Liberals were driven eventually to see this new phenomenon as a possible ally in the restoration of stability.

26.3 Mussolini and the Fascist Party

The son of a socialist blacksmith, but qualified as an elementary schoolmaster, Benito Mussolini could pass as an intellectual amongst the socialists before 1914. His stand against the Libyan War, editorship of *Avanti!* and the divisions of the party enabled him to become a prominent leader. Inconsistently – and probably because of French bribes – he supported the war in 1914 in *Il Popolo d'Italia* and was expelled from the Socialist Party as a result. After the war, in which he served, he became involved with a Milanese group of idealists and malcontents supporting a mixture of socialist and nationalist policies. Their programme was never very clear but by 1919–20 Mussolini's main objective was power for its own sake, and the very vagueness of the Fascist Party was its great quality.

(a)   *A broad spectrum of support*

The Party was a very loose structure under local leaders called *'ras'* (after Abyssinian tribal chiefs) who were diverse in their backgrounds – including republicans, monarchists, socialists, Catholics and anti-clericals – although very few pretended to be intellectuals. The main support for the organisation came from:

1   *Nationalists.* The sort of groups who had followed and supported D'Annunzio found the same sort of emotional appeal in Mussolini's oratory.
2   *Unsettled soldiers.* The old excitement and brotherhood of the war could be recreated in membership of the blackshirted *'squadristi'*.
3   *Landowners.* Lawlessness in areas like the Romagna and Tuscany had already led landowners to start organising their own gangs against the local socialists and against striking labourers. Landlord support was considerably encouraged by a law passed in June 1922 which was to break up the large estates.
4   *Industrialists.* The old socialist Mussolini said in June 1921 'The history of capitalism is only just beginning'. Fear of bolshevism and the prospect of a revival of markets by means of militarist expansion led industrialists to back the Party financially, as did bankers seeking to protect their investments.

By 1921, the membership had risen to 152,000, of whom 62,000 were working class and the rest were professional people and small tradesmen.

(b)   *Flexibility of methods*

In 1919–21 the blackshirted 'shock troops' (see Illus. 26.1) were active with their castor oil doses and blackjack truncheons against strikers, socialists and agricultural labourer 'squatters'. The rise of Mussolini to political power was also, however, the result of more subtle factors:

1   *An electoral alliance.* In 1921, thinking that he could use the new force against socialism, Giolitti actually made an electoral pact with the Fascists. With the

Illus. 26.1 Black jerseys and blackshirts (The Mansell Collection)

PUNCH, OR THE LONDON CHARIVARI.—November 26, 1924.

BLACK JERSEYS AND BLACK SHIRTS.

Signor Mussolini. "I SOMETIMES WISH MY 'ALL BLACKS' WERE ONLY FOOTBALLERS!"

CONTINUED TRIUMPH OF THE "ALL BLACKS" IN ENGLAND

From *Punch*, 26 November 1924, alluding to the increasing power of the Fascist Blackshirts.
Source: C. Leeds, *Italy Under Mussolini* (Wayland Publishers, 1972) p. 8.

backing of government influence, they got 35 deputies. Nevertheless, Giolitti did
not achieve a majority and resigned. Throughout 1921–2 Fascist violence
continued to mount with the apparent connivance of the stop-gap governments
and the army. The result was that the Fascists seized control of many country
districts and municipal councils.

2   *Socialist miscalculation.* In September, the party had split and the communists
broke away. However the socialists continued to appear a threat to law and order,
especially when they called a general strike in August 1922. The Fascists were able

to stand even more as the guardians of order, and between 2 and 4 August virtually invaded many of the major cities including Milan, ejecting socialist councils with official blessing.

3   *Royal invitation.* By October 1922 Mussolini's followers already controlled extensive areas and Fascism had considerable public support. In late October Mussolini began to threaten a revolutionary 'March on Rome'. Victor Emmanuel, influenced by Fascist-inclined members of the royal family, by the fear that he might be deposed if he resisted, and by the uncertain reliability of the army, invited Mussolini to form a government. Like most of the political leaders the King believed that Mussolini could be 'tamed' and converted, as Garibaldi had been. Only on 30 October, the day after he attended the palace, were trainloads of Mussolini's followers allowed to mount public demonstrations to lend an air of reality to the myth of the 'March on Rome'.

26.4 The establishment of dictatorship (1922–5)

Although he was prime minister, Mussolini's following in the Chamber was only 7 per cent of the total membership. His cabinet was made up mainly of non-Fascists. His early actions were all within constitutional law; the abolition of the elected municipal council of Rome, the conversion of the shock-troop squads into a state paid militia and the filling of official posts with Fascists were all justified by the emergency powers voted by the Chamber and Senate. Even the ultimate achievement of dictatorial power was legal.

(a)   *The Acerbo Law (1923)*

With the support not only of the Fascist deputies but also the majority of non-Fascists – the latter only partly influenced by the intimidating presence of lounging blackshirts – a law was passed giving the party which gained the largest number of votes two-thirds of the seats in the Chamber. In the subsequent 'election sports' a combination of genuine popular support, electoral violence and a divided opposition gave the Fascists 65 per cent of the total vote and 374 seats.

(b)   *The 'Aventine Secession' (June 1924)*

Overconfidence led to some rather careless use of violence, including the murder of the respected and outspoken socialist Giacomo Matteotti. There was a considerable outcry which threatened Mussolini, despite his blaming of overenthusiastic supporters going beyond instructions. In fact, he still had a majority in the Chamber and was still seen by the King and leading liberals as the only alternative to social revolution. The withdrawal of most of the opposition deputies to demonstrate the fall of parliamentary government was not a strong enough reaction, however much it echoed a very famous incident in the history of ancient Rome. In fact, Mussolini concluded the affair by publicly assuming responsibility for the murder – 'Italy wants peace and quiet, and to get on with its work. I shall give it all these, if possible in love but if necessary by force'.

(c)   *The abolition of the party system*

Mussolini turned the incident to his advantage, because the deputies who had seceded were declared to have forfeited their seats. From January 1925 the other independent parties were outlawed, communists were imprisoned and press censorship was instituted in the progressive establishment of a constitutional dictatorship.

26.5 The Fascist State (see Illus. 26.2)

From 1925 onwards Mussolini embarked upon the concentration of power and elimination of potential opposition beyond the party system.

(a) *Removal of constitutional checks*

Still employing legal means Mussolini removed constitutional checks upon his use of power:

1   *Restriction of the powers of the monarchy.* The King lost his ability to appoint and dismiss ministers to the Grand Council of Fascism. In 1925, the prime minister was made head of state. Only by abdication could the King protest his rejection of the new régime, and this he never did.

Illus. 26.2   The *Ballilla* (Keystone Press Agency)

From a photograph of Fascist children's units in January 1939. A welcome parade was being drilled for a visit by Neville Chamberlain and Lord Halifax, the British Foreign Minister.
Source: C. Leeds, *Italy Under Mussolini* (Wayland Publishers, 1972) pp. 58–9.

Q   What sort of image was this meant to convey to foreign visitors? Why was so much effort expended on involving young children actively in the Fascist (and Nazi) movements in this way? Does this differ from movements such as the Scouts or the Boy's Brigade?

2   *Rule by decree.* In 1926 the need for parliamentary approval of legislation was removed.
3   *Removal of the 'test by election'.* From 1928 onwards, the electorate was able only to accept or reject candidates selected by the Grand Council of Fascism.

(b)   *The Corporative system*

The old trade unions were abolished, but all workers and members of the professional and commercial classes were required to join one of the 22 official corporations. In 1930, a Council of Corporations was established as a sort of workers' parliament, and in 1939 the parliamentary system was officially replaced by the Chamber of Fasces and Corporations. All of the officials of the corporations were appointed by the Fascist party.

(c)   *Fusion of the state and party*

At various levels, the Fascist party actually paralleled the institutions of state. Blackshirt officers enjoyed equal rank to army officers, and party membership became an important qualification for promotion. The courts were matched by special Fascist tribunals; the prefects were at the same level as party secretaries. At the peak of the system, the head of the government and of state was the *Duce*. The party itself was kept under tight control by Mussolini; in 1926, election of the Grand Council was replaced by nomination. Potential rivals were deprived of their posts, or even killed; the popular Italo Balbo, for instance, was shot down by Italian anti-aircraft guns in 1940 in a rather unlikely 'mistake'. Apart from such discipline the loyalty of members was sustained by the thousands of paid jobs available and the variety of appointments for perquisites and corruption.

(d)   *The Concordat*

The Roman Catholic Church could not be controlled in the same way. In his rise to power Mussolini had enjoyed the favour of the Church and a friendly policy throughout the 1920s culminated in 1929 in the reconciliation of church and state:

1   The Papacy recognised the existence of Italy and the status of Rome as its capital.
2   The Vatican City was recognised in return as a totally independent state within a state.
3   Roman Catholicism was recognised as the official state religion.
4   As compensation a large sum of money was paid to the Church in the form of state bonds, and it was given a range of fiscal and legal privileges.

The Pope declared, 'We have given back God to Italy and Italy to God.' The effect was that the Church had become a pillar of Mussolini's power.

26.6 Manipulation of public opinion

A vital aspect of totalitarianism is the control of the minds of the people. The Fascist party did not, in fact, represent a very defined policy. Mussolini once remarked that 'one *squadristi* is worth two philosophers'. However, the emphasis was firmly on order, nationalism and the dominance of the party and Mussolini.

(a) *Propaganda*

Censorship was applied, not only to the press but also to the radio and film industry. In schools, the curriculum and text books were structured to emphasise the importance of Italy in world history, and of Mussolini in the development of the state. Children were also influenced through their compulsory membership of youth movements from the 'sons of the she wolf' at the age of four up to the Avanguardisti at the age of 14. In general there was a considerable emphasis on the glorious past of Italy and Rome, and also order, discipline and power as represented in well-arranged and filmed parades and processions. Mussolini was well aware of the need to play to the crowds, he remarked 'The crowd loves strong men. The crowd is like a woman'. The fact that he wore spectacles, went to bed early and fell off horses regularly was not the image that he sought to present.

(b) *Persecution*

The volume of violence in Fascist Italy was relatively small compared to Hitler's employment of force and terror. On the other hand, there was nothing in principle against the use of violence as an official aspect of state control. In 1926, a special political police force – the OVRA – was established to deal with anti-Fascists. The meaningless name was chosen by Mussolini because it sounded sinister!

26.7 The economy (see Illus. 26.3)

Great play was made with the Italian economy as a measure of the success of Fascist planning. The fivefold increase in electricity supply, the 'battle for grain' and the doubling of wheat production and the conspicuous improvements in road and rail communications made excellent propaganda material. In fact, Mussolini knew little about economics and had no consistent 'plan'. The economic recovery started in the early 1920s when private capitalism was given a fairly free rein, indeed the slump started in Italy even sooner than the economic crisis in the USA. In reality, Fascist policies did more damage to the economy than good.

(a) *The high cost of protection*

From the mid-1920s there was a growing emphasis upon the virtues of *self-sufficiency*. In 1925, import duties were increased markedly to protect home industries against competition. The result was that the incentive to cut costs and improve efficiency was lost. State subsidies to steel producers and wheat farmers had a similar effect by bolstering up inefficiency and prices. The cost of Italian wheat, for example, was 50 per cent higher than that of American wheat. In addition, the maintenance of the value of the lira at a level which made it too expensive in terms of other currencies had very adverse effects on exports and tourism.

(b) *The 'battle for births'*

Italy suffered from over-population and a shortage of land in the countryside. The situation was worsened by the restrictions on immigration imposed by the USA in the early 1920s. Mussolini pursued policies which exaggerated the problem:

From a photograph of Mussolini standing on a tractor which has been ploughing land reclaimed from the Pontine Marshes near Rome.
Source: D. M. Smith, *Mussolini* (Weidenfeld & Nicolson, 1981) p. 274.

1   *Resistance to the movement of population to the towns.* The desire of landowners to keep wages low and Mussolini's view that industrial labour was less easy to control led him to discourage the movement off the land. On the other hand, apart from the well-publicised land reclamation schemes there was no serious attempt to relieve the rural pressures since the landowners would not accept the idea of division of the large estates.

2   *Increase in family size was positively encouraged.* Financial incentives, a tax on bachelors and other official policies were aimed at an increase in the birth rate; typically, despite these efforts, it fell.

(c) *Incompetence*

The Fascist state was riddled with inefficiency. The bureaucracy was far too large and complex; Mussolini himself took on far too much and the resultant overconcentration of power meant that decisions were put off and there was marked inconsistency in policies. Many of the decrees issued were silly and unenforceable – as with the order not to shake hands! At all levels of society from the Fascist officials who received large bribes to the humble tax evader, corruption was regarded as ritual. Not surprisingly, Mussolini once described himself as 'the most disobeyed man in history'.

(d) *The failure of planning*

By the mid-1930s, the Italian economy had deteriorated according to virtually every standard. The wages were the lowest in Europe; the average hours worked had increased. A million people were out of work. In southern Italy, there were still people living in caves. In 1936 a devaluation of the lira increased the cost of living by 20 per cent and Mussolini was obliged to pretend that he intended that the Italian people would be toughened as a result – 'We are probably moving towards a period when humanity will exist in a lower standard of living.'

26.8 Conclusion

As with his predecessors who had sought to distract the Italians with foreign adventures, Mussolini saw an aggressive imperial policy and forceful diplomacy as the way out of Italy's growing internal problems. The appeal to nationalism was an alternative to genuine reforms and efficient government. The danger was that the Italian economy was far too weak to take the strain of war, and that Mussolini would become the victim of his own boast that 'Mussolini is always right'.

Questions

1 Describe the circumstances in which Mussolini came to power. What did he achieve in Italy between 1922 and 1935? [OC]
2 How firm a basis for his régime had Mussolini laid before 1940? [OC]
3 Was Mussolini more than merely an ambitious opportunist? [OC, adapted]
4 What circumstances in post-war Italy led to the appointment of Mussolini as prime minister in 1922? What were the main features of his domestic rule before 1939? [OX]
5 Why did Mussolini become the prime minister of Italy in 1922 in spite of limited parliamentary support? How far did his domestic policies fulfil the hopes of his supporters? [LON]
6 Account for the popularity of Mussolini's domestic policies. [NEAB]
7 To what extent did Italians have cause for satisfaction with Mussolini's régime during the period 1922 to 1940? [NEAB]
8 How did Mussolini seek to consolidate his power after 1922? [NEAB]
9 Describe the achievements of Mussolini at home and abroad between 1922 and 1936. Why did Italy become the ally of Germany in 1936? [CAM]
10 Study Source A below and then answer the questions which follow.

Source A: Columns of fire.

28 July–Ravenna
This night the columns proceeded to the destruction of the vast headquarters of the provincial group of the socialist Cooperatives. There was no other possible reply to be made to the attempt made yesterday on the life of Meriano and the assassination of Clearco

Montanari. As usual, the action taken by the fascists took people by surprise. The old palace ... which was the stronghold of the red leagues was totally destroyed. Fascists only undertake operations of this kind for reasons of absolute political necessity. Unfortunately the civil struggle does not employ half measures. We risk our lives every day. No personal interest spurs us on. The final aim is the salvation of our country. We undertook this task in the same spirit was when we demolished the enemy's stores in war-time. The flames from the great burning building rose ominously into the night. The whole town was illuminated by the glare. We had to strike terror into the heart of our enemies ...

30 July–Ravenna
I announced to [the chief of police] that I would burn down and destroy the houses of all socialists in Ravenna, if he did not give me within half an hour the means required for sending the fascists elsewhere. It was a dramatic moment. I demanded a whole fleet of lorries. The police officers completely lost their heads, but after half an hour they told me where I could find lorries already supplied with petrol. Some of them actually belonged to the police station. My pretended reason was that I wanted to get the exasperated fascists out of the town. In reality I was organising a 'column of fire' ... to extend our reprisals throughout the province ... This journey began yesterday morning, the 29th, at eleven a.m., and finished on the morning of the 30th. Almost 24 hours of continuous travelling, during which no-one had a moment's rest nor touched a bite of food. We went through Rimini, Sant' Arcangelo, Savignano, Cesena, Bertinoro, all the towns and centres in the provinces of Forli and Ravenna, and destroyed and burnt all the red buildings, the headquarters of the socialist and communist organisations. It was a terrible night. Our passage was marked by high columns of fire and smoke. The whole plain of the Romagna as far as the hills was given over to the reprisals of the outraged fascists, determined to break for ever the red terror.

(a) What were the general objectives of the Fascists during these activities from 28–30 July?
(b) Are there any suggestions that there were links between the Fascists and the war-time experience of Italian troops (lines 8–12)?
(c) According to this account, what was the response of the local police to these activities (lines 12–17)?
(d) What is meant by the 'red terror' (line 27)? What part was played by the activities of the other political parties in Mussolini's rise to power?

Source: I. Balbo, *Diaro 1922* (Milan, 1932)

27 The Weimar Republic and the rise of Hitler 1919–39

Introduction

As with the rise of Mussolini to power in Italy the failure of the Weimar Republic and the triumph of totalitarianism was due to the interaction of the potential weaknesses of the German constitutional and political structure and social and economic circumstances, which bred extremist attitudes. The man who represented these extremist forces and the bitter resentment of German nationalism, and who harnessed them towards his achievement of power, was Adolf Hitler.

27.1 The Weimar régime

The constitution adopted in August 1919 was an extremely democratic one, devised very much with the failings of the constitution of the Second Reich in mind (see Section 18.2).

(a) *Democratic control of the executive*

1   *A very representative legislature.* The lower house, the Reichstag, was elected on the basis of universal suffrage. A complex *proportional voting system* was designed to reflect accurately the minority groups (in contrast to the British system, which tends to exaggerate the strength of the major parties).
2   *Ministerial responsibility.* The president appointed a chancellor who formed a government which could be interrogated by the Reichstag, and be overthrown by means of a vote of no-confidence.
3   *A directly elected president.* The head of state was directly elected for a term of seven years. He had considerable powers; he could dissolve the Reichstag, and he selected the chancellor. He was the commander-in-chief of the armed forces. Under *Article 48* he could govern for a time by emergency decrees.
4   *Direct democracy.* There was provision also for a referendum on any issue, which allowed the citizen to take a direct role in policy-making. The presidential legislative veto could also be overriden by a referendum.

(b) *Stronger central government control*

The states continued, albeit renamed *Länder* or regions. Prussia still made up two-thirds of the total. On the other hand:

1   Länder governments were obliged to adopt democratic forms of government.
2   The central government had full control of taxation and played a greater role in such matters as education.
3   Decisions of the Reichstat which represented the Länder could be overridden by the Reichstag.

(c)   A guarantee of the rights of the citizen

A bill of rights guaranteed not only freedom of speech, legal equality and religious freedom, but also the right to a minimum provision of *social services*. However, the success of this guarantee depended upon the will of the German people themselves.

27.2 Perception of the Weimar Republic

In 1919, Freidrich Ebert, the Social Democrat and one-time saddler, was elected to the presidency. Throughout the 1920s the major partner in the coalitions which governed Germany was the Social Democratic Party, usually in co-operation with centre or right of centre groups because of a permanent feud with the communists. However the popular image of the Republic was very much affected by three adverse influences.

(a)   The myth of the 'Dolchstoss'

To many Germans, the true cause of the defeat of 1918 and the loss of 13 per cent of the land and population of Germany was not the failure of the army but revolution and political betrayal – the 'stab in the back' *(Dolchstoss)*. Ebert himself welcomed back the troops in December 1918 as 'unvanquished in the field of battle'. The felony of the politicians was compounded by the humiliating peace terms and the confession of war guilt.

(b)   The collapse of the mark

In 1913, the rate of exchange had been 20 marks per pound; by 1920 it had risen to 250 marks per pound. Then the combination of the international loss of confidence in the mark as a result of the post-war economic problems and the very weak financial policy of the government resulted in the collapse of the mark. By 1922 it had spiralled to 35,000 marks to the pound sterling and in 1923 a crazy 30 million to the pound. People were affected in different ways:

1   *Financiers, industrialists and landowners.* The financiers could escape by investing in foreign currencies. Landowners and businessmen could increase their rents and prices while paying off debts in valueless marks and were cushioned to some extent by the rising value of their property.
2   *Fixed-income groups.* Wage earners were paid in depreciating currency.
    Particularly badly hit were the people on fixed salaries and pensions, such as the middle-class professional and clerical groups, army veterans and small investors dependent upon the interest on stocks and shares. Weimar and financial ruin were too closely identified for these elements in society.

(c)   Leniency towards right-wing nationalism

Lacking any support from the communists, and reliant upon moderate and right-wing support, the Social Democrats were never able to follow policies of industrial and land nationalisation. In addition, the agreement with the army (see Section 23.6(b)) meant that public order was more conspicuously maintained against *left-wing groups* than against right-wing nationalist upheavals:

1 *The Spartacist revolt (January 1919)* (see Section 23.6(b)). Regular troops led by General von Luttwitz and the volunteer *Frei Korps* (Free Corps) of ex-soldiers had crushed the rebellion by German communists with extreme savagery, and killed its leaders Karl Liebknecht and Rosa Luxembourg.

2 *The Bavarian Soviet Republic (March–May 1919).* Again a communist takeover in Munich and a 'soviet republic' was suppressed with enthusiasm by regular troops and Free Corps units.

3 *The Kapp putsch* (March 1920). On the other hand, a right-wing attempt to overthrow the Weimar government was actually supported by von Luttwitz, while General von Seeckt rejected an appeal to protect Berlin. In fact the incompetence of its civil servant leader Kapp, and a general strike by trade union leaders, enabled the régime established in Berlin to endure for only four days.

(d) A narrow political base

The overall result was that the new republic was in a very precarious position. It was regarded by nationalists as unpatriotic and by right-wing groups and small property owners as a threat to private property. By the extreme left it was seen as a façade for a capitalist–militarist clique which really governed Germany. An abortive *putsch* in Munich led by Adolf Hitler seemed to confirm this latter view.

27.3 The background of Adolf Hitler

There were three important formative periods in Hitler's life.

(a) Austrian origins (1889–1913)

The son of a minor Austrian customs official of Braunau on the Bohemian border, Hitler was brought up in an atmosphere of bitter rivalry between Slavs and Germans (see Section 21.6(d)). A failed education and the death of his mother in 1908 left him without any income. From 1908–13 he lived the life of a near tramp in Vienna, doing odd jobs, selling poor sketches of the city and consoling his sense of inferiority with an exaggerated German nationalism and resentment against Slavs and Jews.

(b) The First World War

On the outbreak of war Hitler was in Munich and joined a Bavarian regiment, although he was not technically a German citizen until 1931. He found in the war a degree of companionship which he had not before enjoyed and an outlet for his nationalist senti-ments – 'I sank down on my knees and thanked Heaven out of the fullness of my heart for the favour of having been permitted to live at such a time'. He had a good military record, was wounded twice, awarded the Iron Cross First Class and was in hospital as a gas victim when the 'betrayal' of November 1918 took place.

(c) Munich (1919–24)

In 1919 he was posted to Munich as an army education officer. While he was there he made a reputation as a mob orator attacking Weimar and democracy, the threat of communism and the Jews as scapegoats for the problems of Germany. He emphasised the idea of the racial and biological unity of *'das Volk'* and the great destiny of a purified Germany. It was in these years that the basic structure of the Nazi movement was developed.

1 *The National Socialist German Workers' Party (1922).* Hitler built up an existing group with similar views and launched it as the Nazi party in 1922 along with associates such as Joseph Goebbels (an unsuccessful writer), Hermann Goering (a famous fighter pilot), and Rudolf Hess (an economics student). The original group had a membership of 50. By 1922 it had 6000 members.

2 *The Stürmabteilung (SA).* Early meetings were protected by a private army which also broke up the meetings of opponents. In 1921 this became the basis of the brown-shirted, para-military SA, the stormtroopers of the élite.

3 *Propaganda.* Considerable use was made of symbolism – such as the party flag, the swastika – and impressive processions and rallies. Above all Hitler relied upon his unrestrained oratory:

> The receptive powers of the masses are very restricted and their understanding is feeble. On the other hand they quickly forget. All effective propaganda must be confined to a few bare necessities and then expressed in a few simple phrases. Only by constantly repeating will you succeed in imprinting an idea onto the memory of a crowd ... When you lie, tell big lies. That is what the Jews do. The big cheeky lie always leaves traces behind it.

4 *Backing from the army and manufacturers.* The money for the private army and newspaper came not only from personal friends like Goering's wife but also industrialists and businessmen attracted by Hitler's anti-communist stance. He was also supported by the army, and in 1923 gained the invaluable personal support of old General Ludendorff.

27.4 The 'March on Berlin' (November 1923)

Stresemann's cessation of German resistance against the French occupation of the Ruhr (see Section 24.3(c)) provoked nationalist resentment against the régime, and an abortive coup in Berlin. In Bavaria, the situation was complex.

(a) *The Bürgerbräukellar putsch*

Opposition to a Bavarian separatist movement which also sought to restore the Wittelsbach dynasty provoked Hitler into an ill-prepared putsch. He marched at the head of a procession through Munich alongside Ludendorff in the start of what was supposed to become a 'March on Berlin'. The police broke it up, and the leaders were arrested. Hitler used his trial as a public relations exercise attacking the government and appealing to the Reichswehr 'one day the hour will come when the Reichswehr will stand at our side, officers and men'. He got away with a mild sentence of five years in Landsberg fortress and was released after six months.

(b) Mein Kampf *and the ideology of National Socialism*

While in prison and enjoying the obvious sympathy of many Germans Hitler completed the autobiographical political manifesto *Mein Kampf* (*My Struggle*), which contains the clearest expression of the basic objectives of the National Socialists. While many of these grew from his own background and prejudices, he presented a clear programme of ambitions which appealed to the hopes and fears of many ordinary Germans and which were rooted in long-term trends in German nationalism and history – otherwise he would never have achieved power through the ballot box and constitutional means in the way that he now set out to do.

1 *'Ein Reich'*. Like many inadequate people, Hitler found comfort in illusions of national superiority, and (as with many fellow old soldiers) he regarded the Treaty of Versailles as a betrayal of the Fatherland by the 'November Criminals', the Social Democrats. He advocated rearmament and the reversal of the treaty, so that all Germans would be united in a Greater Germany. This would require:

   – Recovery of the German minorities in Poland, France and Czechoslovakia.
   – Union of Germany with Austria.
   – Recovery of full sovereign control over the Rhineland.

2 *'Ein Volk'*. Hitler believed that the Aryan or nordic peoples were naturally superior in physique and intellect, and that the Germans were a 'master race' threatened with corruption by inferior races:

   – As a youth he had lived in the midst of the bitter rivalry between Germans and Slavs in Bohemia (see Section 21.6(d)) which had developed into full-scale race hatred.
   – Later in his life he had been powerfully affected by the anti-Semitism in Vienna, which was based partly upon jealousy of the wealth of Jewish businessmen.

   Thus he sought the subordination of these *'untermenschen'* (or 'sub-humans') by the prevention of intermarriage with Aryans and deprivation of legal and political rights. In fact the logical outcome of these views was that, as with people like the incurably insane, Jews and Slavs should be exterminated.

3 *'Lebensraum'* (living space). Regarding Germany as deficient in land and supplies of food and industrial raw materials, Hitler advocated the creation of an eastern central European empire, taken from Poland and Russia, and the enslavement of the native populations. This eastward-looking German expansionism had a long history dating back as far as the Middle Ages, and had been an obvious factor in German ambitions in the First World War.

4 *Socialism*. Originally Hitler also advocated reforms such as the nationalisation of the biggest industries and stores and of tracts of land, confiscation of excessive war profits and abolition of unearned incomes. These proposals were attractive to working men and the lower middle class from which Hitler came. In later years, this social revolutionary aspect would become somewhat of an embarrassment as the Nazis began to attract the financial backing of industrialists and landowners.

In the breadth of these promises Hitler had the basis of a great mass party, and the achievement of immense personal power. Immediately, he tightened his control over the party through the creation of the black-shirted *Schützstaffel* (the SS), an élite body-guard bound by oath to Hitler personally.

27.5 Weimar (1924–9)

There were really two sides to the Weimar régime before 1929 – an outer face and an inner reality.

(a) The 'German economic miracle'

Prosperity and stability returned after 1924. From August 1923 political affairs were dominated by Gustav Stresemann, a conservative monarchist but a believer in the need for a stable republic which would enable Germany to be more acceptable to the international community. Agreements were reached over reparations (see Section 24.3(d)) and over the German frontiers (see Section 24.6(a)). By 1928 there had been a 120 per cent increase in the output of coal and steel over the level for 1913. By the late 1920s, 300,000 houses and flats were being built each year; health insurance was extended to cover 20 million people. Altogether it seemed a great success story.

(b) Evasion of the Treaty of Versailles

Secretly, with Stresemann's knowledge, the Reichswehr was being restored by General von Seeckt, in defiance of Versailles:

1 *Extension of military training.* The army of 96,000 was in fact a training ground for NCOs who would be the future holders of higher office in an expanded army. In addition 'covers' like gliding clubs and the Prussian police force were used to train men for military service. The Treaty of Rapallo of 1922 (see Section 24.6) enabled the establishment of tank and flying schools in Russia where not only Russians but also Germans could train.

2 *The connivance of industrialists in the provision of equipment.* The equipment needed for the new *'blitzkrieg'* war by concentrated tanks and pre-emptive air strikes was built up by secret agreements in a number of countries, but also in Germany itself. In 1922, Krupps, the steel and armaments manufacturers, actually made an agreement with the Ministry of Defence which blatantly broke the terms of Versailles.

27.6 The Nazi achievement of power (1929–33)

The Wall Street Crash and the economic crisis in Europe produced a wave of extremism. In Germany, unemployment rose from 1.3 million in September 1929 to 4 million in 1931. However Hitler's rise to power was not based solely on these social pressures.

(a) Conspiracy or popular acclaim?

There are two views as to the causes of Hitler's success. The 'national character' view is that the German people, inexperienced in democracy, naturally opted for a 'strong man' again. On the other hand, there is the conspiracy theory that Hitler was the creation of a narrow clique of officers, civil servants and industrialists, as typified by the *Harzburg Front* of 1930 which brought together Hitler, right-wing politicians and industrialists like Fritz Thyssen and Dr Schacht of the Reichsbank. But Hitler would not prove to be so easily controlled:

1 *A mass following.* Hitler's objectives were rather vague and contradictory, but there was no doubt about the emphasis on dynamism and energy. He could appeal to all shades of opinion: the unemployed were promised work; the army anticipated rearmament and expansion; businessmen were promised large orders and the crushing of communism; the middle classes were stirred against the Jews

and 'money barons'. This broad movement would become indispensable support for any Nazi government.

2 *The mask of legality and constitutionalism.* Since 1925 Hitler had worked by the theory that power would be more easily achieved by using the system against itself; this is in fact how he did succeed.

(b) *The growing reliance on Article 48*

The failure of the Catholic Centre Chancellor Brüning to obtain a programme of budget cuts led him to rely on President Hindenberg – elected in 1925 – to rule by presidential decrees to enforce his budget. In fact to many politicians including Brüning, and army leaders like General Kurt von Schleicher, there were positive advantages in using the crisis to seek the restoration of the monarchy or permanent, army-backed, presidential rule. Constitutionalism was becoming a very thin veneer.

(c) *Mounting electoral support for the Nazis*

With 6 million unemployed by 1932 and fears of a communist revolution Hitler became increasingly attractive to industrialists, army officers and right wingers, and arrangements were made which were kept secret from the radical social-revolutionary wing of the party. Von Papen, the right-winger believed, 'We have bought him and he is working for us.' In 1930, the Nazis won 6.5 million votes and 107 Reichstag seats. In July 1932 they became the biggest party with 230 seats. In March 1932 Hitler narrowly missed defeating Hindenberg in the presidential elections, and the Prussian Diet elections gave the Nazis a clear majority.

(d) *A power auction*

Rivalry between political leaders hoping to use the Nazis in the end gave Hitler power:

1 *The influence of von Schleicher.* Brüning fell over an attempt to introduce land reforms in East Prussia. Under von Schleicher's influence Hindenberg tried to make a deal with Hitler through von Papen, the new Chancellor. The arrangement failed, von Papen fell and von Schleicher took over.

2 *The Hitler–von Papen agreement.* In January 1933 von Schleicher resigned when he failed to arrange a coalition with the Nazis. Von Papen did succeed, at the cost of the Chancellorship for Hitler but only two other cabinet seats, the rest were to go to Conservatives. On 30 January 1933 Hitler became Chancellor.

(e) *A product of the system*

In a way it could be argued that the Germans got the leader they deserved. Overwhelmed by economic crises and neurotically nationalist, ordinary Germans – by no means all brown-shirted thugs – had given enough support to a man much like themselves in his fears and prejudices to enable him to achieve power not by revolution but by constitutional means. He had also been backed by the great industrial and military interest groups which had never been curbed by Weimar. From 1930 onwards the Nazi Party was being financially backed by businessmen like Dr Schacht (head of the Reichsbank), and Fritz Thyssen (president of the largest steel combine in Europe). On the other hand although Hitler's assumption of power was not illegal, he was never to win a full majority in a free election.

Now using legal power, Hitler was able to eliminate political opposition.

(a) The Enabling Law (March 1933)

Hitler fought a new election on the basis of the need to suspend parliamentary government for four years and restore stability in Germany. He could now rely on the police to stand by and not intervene in the electioneering activities of the SA and SS. The

Illus. 27.1a   Hitler in power

From a poster of 1933 showing Hindenberg and Hitler – 'the Field-Marshal and the Lance-corporal' – allied to fight for peace and equal rights (27.1a) and a photograph of the Hitler Youth marching through the streets in Breslau during the 1938 Sports Festival (27.1b).

Sources: A. Rhodes and V. Margolin, *Propaganda* (Angus & Robertson, 1976) p. 16 (27.1a).
R. Grunberger, *A Social History of the Third Reich* (Weidenfeld & Nicolson, 1971) pp. 136–7 (27.1b).

burning down of the Reichstag building on 27 February by a demented Dutchman
called van der Lubbe was easily blamed on the communists, and was an excellent
excuse to suspend the bill of rights which rather cramped the style of the SA thugs.
Even so, the Nazis still only won 288 seats and had to rely on the support of the
Nationalist Party and Catholic Centre to pass a bill suspending the constitution.

(b)   *The abolition of opposition parties*

Most of the communists were soon in prison after van der Lubbe's action. Then in July
1933 all political parties except the Nazis were banned, and the Nazis were declared to
be the sole official party. In December 1933 a law established the unity of party and
state.

27.8 The *Gleichschaltung* (see Fig. 27.1)

'Coordination' (*Gleichschaltung*) was a polite term for subjugation.

(a) The elimination of potential sources of opposition:

1 *Centralisation of government.* The Länder assemblies and local authorities were brought under Nazi control, and Nazi governors were established. The state police came under Nazi orders and Heinrich Himmler became the chief of police as well as the SS. In January 1934, the central government in Berlin took over all power from the local assemblies. The legal profession was also purged and new Nazi 'people's courts' were established.

2 *Control of the trade unions.* In May 1933 most of the trade union leaders were rounded up and a new Nazi-led 'Labour Front' replaced trade unions. Strikes were banned and labour 'work books' were introduced.

3 *The 'Night of the Long Knives' (June 1934).* The jealousy of the Reichswehr of the SA and Hitler's need for army support meant that the only genuinely revolutionary section of the party had to be purged. Under Ernst Röhm it had come to expect a 'Second Revolution' of loot and jobs, but this would lose the support of the very groups upon whom Hitler had depended for his invitation to assume power. On 29 June 1934, following an arrangement with the army, Hitler used the SS to crush the leadership of the SA, and to remove all sorts of other embarrassing people such as von Schleicher. At least 400 people were killed in an incident for which Hitler assumed total responsibility: 'In those twenty four hours the Supreme Court of the German People was I!'

4 *The subordination of the army.* In August 1934, by agreement with the army, the death of Hindenberg was followed by Hitler assuming the presidency as well. The army took an oath of loyalty to Hitler personally. Then in 1937 the army leaders Generals Blomberg and Fritsch were ousted.

(b) Intellectual conformity

1 *Censorship.* The teaching profession was purged to remove the members who were not prepared to teach Nazi doctrine. A strict censorship was introduced symbolised by the 'burning of the books' of May 1933, while history was rewritten to emphasise the use of Hitler as the culmination of German history.

2 *Youth movements.* From June 1933 all youth organisations were taken over and a number of specifically Nazi youth movements were established for physical instruction and Nazi indoctrination. The Hitler Youth and the League of German Maidens were the most significant organisations.

3 *Control of religion.* In July 1933 a *Concordat* was concluded with the Pope. Even so, especially in the later 1930s, the various Church communities began to face persecution. Catholic youth movements were broken up and churches taken over, both Catholic and Protestant clergy were arrested and imprisoned.

(c) Racial persecution (see Illus. 27.2a and 27.2b)

Almost immediately on reaching power Hitler began to institute his racial policies. Between 1933 and 1938 legislation excluded Jews from public office, from the professions, from the stock exchange, from marriage to Aryans and from German citizenship. Jewish property was destroyed, shops were burnt and customers were forcefully dis-

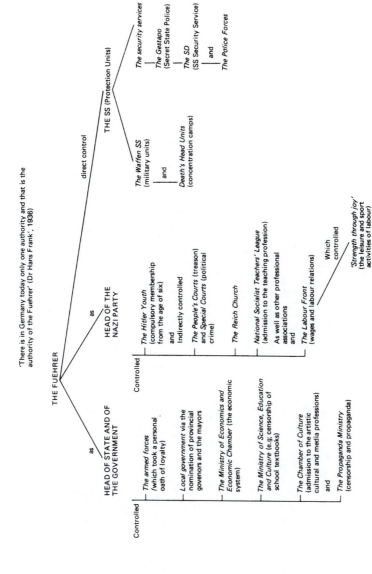

Fig. 27.1 The structure of the Nazi state

There is in Germany today only one authority and that is the authority of the Fuehrer' (Dr Hans Frank', 1936)

couraged by SA men. In November 1938 in the 'Week of Broken Glass' resulting from the murder of a German embassy official in Paris by a Jew, 7000 shops were looted and 20,000 Jews arrested. As stateless persons and largely deprived of any sort of income the Jewish community of 500,000 was very vulnerable and protected to some extent only by international opinion. The outbreak of war would remove that sanction, and the concentration camps as at Dachau, Buchenwald and Sachsenhausen would be employed for much more ambitious purposes than the 're-education' of political prisoners, unionists, gypsies and homosexuals.

Illus. 27.2a   *Anti-Semitism (Ullstein Bildendienst (27.2a/b))*

From a photograph showing the 'unofficial' 'Jews keep out' signs that appeared on swimming pools, theatres and (as here) allotments outside Berlin: most restaurants also displayed a 'Dogs and Jews not admitted' sign (27.2a); and of a German street in 1933 (in the *Archiv Gerstenberg*): a Jew without shoes or trousers, escorted by policemen, carries a sandwich-board stating: 'I'll not bother the police anymore' (27.2b).

Illus. 27.2b

Source: R. Grunberger, *A Social History of the Third Reich* (Weidenfeld & Nicolson, 1971) pp. 136–7.

Q What makes this scene doubly disturbing is that the Jew is actually being escorted by armed policemen. Why should this be seen as important?

27.9 Conclusion

The achievements of the Nazis were very public. By 1936, 5 million new jobs had been created and by 1939 there was a shortage of labour due to rearmament, the construction of public buildings and roads and the great mass of bureaucratic posts proliferated by the Nazi party. Also obvious was the return of national confidence to Germany, which fed as much as anything on Hitler's astonishing diplomatic successes.

Questions

1 What were the principal problems facing Germany between 1919 and 1933? [OC]
2 Why was the Weimar Republic unable to resist the rise of Nazism? [OC]
3 What were the main features of Nazi rule in Germany between 1933 and 1939? [OX]
4 'The problems of the Weimar Republic stemmed from the Treaty of Versailles.' Comment on this view of the failures of the Weimar Republic. [NEAB]
5 How did Hitler control Germany from 1933? [NEAB]
6 How successful was the Weimar Republic? [NEAB]
7 Outline the life and career of Hitler until the end of 1933. Why was Hitler appointed German Chancellor in January 1933? [CAM]
8 Why did Hitler's bid to seize power fail in 1923, but succeed in 1933? [CAM]
9 To what extent was the failure of the Weimar Republic due to the Versailles Settlement?
10 Study Sources A and B and then answer the questions which follow.

Source A: Hitler comes to power.

I arrived in Berlin in January. My friends in the American Embassy, my friends in the Soviet Embassy, American journalists, German journalists, everybody said, 'Hitler is through'. But on January 30, Hitler was Chancellor.

Things had happened behind the scenes. On January 4, Hitler held a secret rendezvous with Papen in the Rhineland. Papen then took him to a meeting of industrialists in Dusseldorf. From one of the participants I have an eye-witness account. Hitler was not in brown shirt but in full evening dress and white tie. Hitler told the industrialists that Schleicher was dangerous; 'But I am a friend of the German economy'. He ranted and beat his stiff white shirt. Seeing this hysterical mediocrity, the shrewd businessmen – and bad politicians – thought he would be easy to manage. It now remained to convince Hindenburg that Chancellor Schleicher was wilful and ambitious whereas Hitler was legal, patriotic and ready to talk terms. A rumour was circulated (or was it true?) that Schleicher held the Reichswehr garrison at Potsdam in readiness to stage a *coup d'état* against the government. Papen manoeuvred indefatigably for Hitler. On January 30, Hindenburg summoned the Austrian corporal and made him head of the government. That is how German democracy died.

Hitler was the raucous voice of German discontent. His millions of supporters were neither working men nor rich men, but middle class people afraid of social and economic demotion. The German middle class wanted a strong state that would save it. German big business wanted a strong state that could help it. The Republic was too chaotic and disunited to be of much use to either.

(a) State the year of Fischer's visit to Germany.
(b) Who was Papen (line 5)? Explain how he had 'manoeuvred indefatigably for Hitler' (line 14).
(c) Who was Hindenburg (line 10)?
(d) Comment upon the statement that Hitler's supporters were 'middle class people afraid of social and economic demotion' (lines 18–19). Why were they afraid?
(e) What other factors, not mentioned in the passage, helped to bring Hitler to power? Does the author present a fair account of Hitler's rise?   [OC, adapted]

Source: A visitor to Germany: cited in Louis Fischer, *Men and Politics*.

Source B: A devotional hour of the Movement.

We have witnessed many great march-pasts and ceremonies. But none of them was more thrilling, and at the same time more inspiring, than yesterday's roll call of the 140,000 political wardens, who were addressed by the Führer at night, on the Zeppelin Meadow which floodlights had made bright as day. It is hardly possible to let words describe the mood and strength of this hour ...

A distant roar becomes stronger and comes even closer. The Führer is there! Reich Organisational Leader, Dr Ley, gives him the report on the men who are standing in parade formation. And then, a great surprise, one among many. As Adolf Hitler is entering the Zeppelin Field, 150 floodlights of the air force blaze up. They are distributed around the entire square, and cut into the night, erecting a canopy of light in the midst of darkness ... The wide field resembles a powerful Gothic cathedral made of light. Bluish-violet shine the floodlights, and between their cone of light hangs the dark cloth of night ... Twenty-five thousand flags, that means 25,000 local, district, and factory groups all over the nation who are gathered around this flag. Every one of these flag bearers is ready to give his life in the defence of every one of these pieces of cloth. There is no one among them to whom this flag is not the final command and the highest obligation ... A devotional hour of the Movement is being held here, is protected by a sea of light against the darkness outside.

The men's arms are lifted in salute, which at this moment goes out to the dead of the Movement and of the War. Then the flags are raised again.

Dr Ley speaks: 'We believe in a Lord God, who directs us and guides us, and who has sent to us you, my Führer.' These are the final words of the Reich Organisational leader;

they are underlined by the applause that rises from the 150,000 spectators and that lasts for minutes.

(a) Identify the phrases and words in this extract which suggest a parallel between a propaganda rally and a religious occasion.
(b) Judging from this description what do you think are the main factors contributing to an effective propaganda rally?
(c) What allegorical meaning do you detect in the recurrent use of the contrast of light and darkness in this description?

Source: A description of the roll-call of the Political Wardens (Heads of local Party groups) at the Nuremberg Rally of 1936 as reported in the *Niederelbisches Tageblatt*, 12 December 1936.

The road to war 1936–9

Introduction

A. J. P. Taylor in his *The Origins of the Second World War* remarks that 'Wars are very much like road accidents. They have a general cause and particular causes at the same time'. From 1936 onwards the atmosphere in Europe was one of an increasing polarisation of attitudes into extremisms, which left little scope for compromise. At the same time, collective security through the League of Nations had broken down, and Britain and France in particular were reluctant to assume a very positive stance until it was too late. The result was that Hitler was able to *exploit opportunities* as they arose, until he finally miscalculated.

28.1 The polarisation of political views

The later 1930s saw European opinion increasingly split ideologically by the contrasting extremes of fascism and communism. Two episodes in the period are especially revealing.

(a) *The Spanish Civil War, 1936–9*

The effect of an election in Spain in 1936 was to give the greatest number of seats in the Cortes to a *Popular Front* coalition of republicans and all of the socialist groups, but a majority of votes to a right-wing party, the *Falange Espanõle* backed by the Catholic Church, the army, industrialists, and landowners and monarchists. To the latter, the new republic established only in December 1931 was identified with unacceptable policies of land reform, anti-clericalism, state intervention in industry and provincial devolution of power, and the freak electoral result simply confirmed the bias of the constitution. In July 1936 an army revolt started in *Morocco* led by General Franco, and this developed into a full rebellion in Spain in November. From then until April 1939 the country was the scene of a brutal civil war which had serious implications for European relations:

1   *The final discrediting of collective security.* Despite attempts to achieve non-intervention agreements men, arms and equipment were supplied to both sides by interested states. The *Nationalists* received considerable German and Italian help. Germany had up to 10,000 men in Spain and Italy at one stage up to 50,000. From

October 1937 the USSR was openly committed to sending help to the *Republicans*, although this was never anything like the volume received by their opponents.

2 *A dress rehearsal.* To some extent, Hitler and Mussolini saw the war as an opportunity to test their war machines. In the bloody civil war and the employment of the new tactics and technology with such atrocities as the killing of 1600 civilians in the bombing of the Basque city of Guernica, Europe had a full preview of the horrors of modern warfare.

3 *The growth of extremism.* The civil war was the result of far more than a struggle between fascism and communism, but the lining up of the various groups to intervene on either side could be seen as support for one or other of the extremes.

(b) The French Popular Front (1936–8)

Professor Roberts says of inter-war France, 'If . . . history is the story of significant change France has little history between the wars.' French politics in the 1930s continued to echo the well-established division between the right and left wings. This was exacerbated by the economic crisis which affected France later than other states, producing 1.4 million unemployed by mid–1932 and a mounting financial crisis. Between 1932 and 1934 there were recurrent ministerial crises and the emergence of anti-parliamentary right-wing organisations like the *Croix de Feu* and the revived *Action Française* which confronted the republicans and their socialist allies over three issues in particular:

1 *The Stavisky scandal (1933).* The 'suiciding' by the police of a financial adventurer at the centre of a web of political corruption was the trigger for a wave of demonstrations and riots by the right wing and counter-demonstrations by the left wingers.

2 *The popular front (1936–8).* The electoral success of an alliance of Radicals, moderate socialists and communists committed to a programme of 'Bread, Peace and liberty' and its social reforms led right wingers to see the prospect of a *social revolution*, which was reinforced by a wave of strikes.

3 *The Spanish Civil War.* The lines between the right wingers (increasingly using the language of fascism and anti-Semitism) and the Popular Front (led by the Jewish Leon Blum) were hardened by arguments over French intervention or non-intervention in the Civil War. The left wingers, traditionally pacifist, were in favour of war against fascists in Spain and Abyssinia. The right wingers, traditionally militarist and *'revanchist'*, opposed war because of the refusal to ally with the USSR and because it might lead to a social revolution. The result was that until 1940 and the final 'catastrophe' French diplomacy was weakened by a powerful 'defeatist' group.

28.2 Appeasement

The idea of *'appeasement'* suggests weakness and surrender to force. In practice in the inter-war period it did lead to ever increasing demands by the dictators, and it became a word of shame and political discredit. However, it was a well-established tradition in British foreign policy from the mid-nineteenth century onwards and was, in many respects, a natural policy for a small island state waning in strength and influence in world affairs.

(a) *The model of 'appeasement'*

Paul Kennedy defines appeasement as 'the policy of settling international ... quarrels by admitting and satisfying grievances through rational negotiation and compromise, thereby avoiding the resort to armed conflict, a policy based upon the positive optimistic assumption of human reasonableness and the negative fear of conflict' ('Appeasement in British Foreign Policy, 1865–1939' in *Strategy and Diplomacy 1870–1945*, pub. 1983). He argues that the policy originated in the 1860s and was based upon four factors:

1 *The concepts of justice and morality.* The application of morality to politics derived from the time of the evangelical movement and to the free traders' vision of the world as a harmonious community which emphasised international arbitration and the rejection of war as an instrument of national policy, except in cases of self-defence. The moral tones of the post–1919 period were very much in the Gladstonian tradition, and reinforced by the views of Woodrow Wilson. The 'war to end wars' was too recent a memory to allow Britain to accept easily the need to send a large conscript army to the Continent again. The concept of national self-determination justified the German territorial claims until March 1939 in well-established Gladstonian terms. Above all the League of Nations idea was the very epitome of nineteenth-century internationalism.

2 *Economic necessity.* Given the British dependence upon international trade the preservation of peace was vital to her. By the inter-war years the traditional Victorian economy had, as Eric Hobsbawm describes it, 'crashed into ruins between the two world wars'. Inevitably there was even greater pressure to cut defence spending. The British government after 1935 had the options of heavy rearmament and economic ruin or a more moderate programme and great military vulnerability. In fact rearmament started in 1936 but there were considerable gaps to cover. British air defence had been allowed to fall to six squadrons of modern fighters, there were no modern anti-aircraft guns, a 60 per cent shortage of searchlights and the new-fangled radar system only covered the Thames estuary. The deficiencies were often exaggerated. British intelligence in May 1937 overestimated the German supply of heavy bombers at 800 as opposed to Britain's 48. Whatever the realities, as late as 1938 Neville Chamberlain was being advised by his chief of imperial general staff General Ironside that 'our deficiencies are so bad that we should go to any lengths to put off the struggle'.

3 *Global obligations and diplomatic realities.* British resources were already massively overstretched by her imperial and world commitments but she was now confronted by the rise of simultaneous threats from Japan, Italy and Germany at a time when the USA was isolationist, many of the Dominions would readily follow suit and Russia was a new and unpredictable factor. Anglo-French options in Europe were circumscribed. The desire not to drive Italy into the arms of Germany partly explains their policy over Abyssinia. The small states of eastern central Europe were very vulnerable because of their territorial situation, and their own rivalries and distrust of Russia inhibited the achievement of the only link which might guarantee the states to the east of Germany.

4 *The influence of public opinion.* The steady extension of the British franchise from 1867 worked against expenditure on foreign wars and belligerent foreign policies (unless the public could be excited on a point of moral right or national honour) and in favour of social and economic reforms. Governments had to cut defence expenditure in the inter-war period or lose power. Only moral arguments were likely to sway public opinion, and they always had to be balanced against expense.

(b) The 'balance of risks'

Britain rejected the idea of alliance entanglements in Europe and would not give any sort of military commitment to France until 1939. Both countries were wary of each other anyhow, and their relationship was not especially close until the mid–1930s. In this situation, with vast global responsibilities and limited resources available to maintain them, Britain was obliged to pursue a policy of adjustment and the accommodation of conflicting interests to try to balance the risks of conflict. The Defence Requirements Committee stressed in 1935:

> It is a cardinal requirement of our national and imperial security that our foreign policy should be so conducted as to avoid the possible development of a situation in which we might be confronted simultaneously with the hostility of Japan in the Far East, Germany in the West and any power on the main line of communications between the two.

However, while the policy of balancing risks depended upon compromise and accommodation it also implied that there were limits beyond which other powers must not be allowed to go in case they threatened fundamental British interests. In the case of Germany it had been readily recognised that her grievances about the Versailles Settlement were justified; and the ending of reparations payments, starting of limited rearmament and occupation of the Rhineland were not seen as threatening British interests. Until 1939 the prevalent view was that Germany could be brought back into the great power system without destroying it and that her ambitions were limited. Only then did Hitler exceed the framework of the diplomatic game.

(c) The weakness of the model

There were three significant problems associated with appeasement as a diplomatic tool:

1   *It needed to operate on the basis of strength.* In fact in the early 1930s neither Britain nor France was well enough armed to do other than play for time, and appeasement became all the more associated with weakness.
2   *Pacifist pressure* to avoid war at all costs, underlined by the obsessive fear of aerial bombing, tied the hands of western diplomats and politicians. In fact the technical limitations of air offensives were not so readily appreciated.
2   *Ideological divisions* limited options. By the mid–1930s Britain and France were more afraid of communism than fascism. Sir Maurice Hankey, cabinet secretary, warned in 1936: 'In the present state of Europe with France and Spain menaced by Bolshevism, it is not inconceivable that before long it might pay us to throw in our lot with Germany and Italy.'

(d) The breaking of the model

Numerous advisers reinforced Chamberlain's naive idea that Hitler was 'a man whose word can be trusted'. In 1932 the British ambassador in Berlin laughed him off as a 'revivalist preacher with the appearance of a greengrocer', and in 1935 Lord Lothian was 'convinced that Hitler does not want war'. However, the emphasis on the idea of the 'Cliveden Set' of intellectuals influencing British diplomacy towards appeasement has been exaggerated. There is evidence that Chamberlain came to distrust Hitler and thought him unbalanced; on the other hand, he could hardly have behaved in public as if Hitler was an insane incendiarist! By the late 1930s, and especially in 1938, the model began to break down:

1   *The insatiable demands* of Japanese, Italian and especially German policy
    undermined its basis because they constantly flouted international guarantees,
    territorial boundaries, civil liberties and democratic rights. Appeasement came to
    be seen as supporting dictatorships.
2   *Right-wing and left-wing elements* in British politics found a common cause in
    opposing continued appeasement, whereas in the past they had tended to balance
    each other in their arguments that there was too much or too little of it. A new
    group of Conservative MPs around Anthony Eden began to oppose a policy which
    was more and more discredited as the ideal of internationalism was betrayed by
    aggressive nationalism and militarism. At the same time, Socialists and Liberals
    came to see the need, in certain circumstances, to use force to protect people
    threatened by aggression.

Realists and idealists came together in an unusual alliance in the late 1930s as events
unfolded in Europe especially, and in September 1939 the model supported by the
'middle ground' of British politics for three-quarters of a century was broken.

28.3 The arms race

Disarmament continued into the early 1930s but from 1932–33 this was reversed.
Rearmament was not confined to Germany and the western powers. World military
expenditure grew from $3500 million in 1925 to $5000 million in 1934. The arms trade
grew from $34 million in 1932 to $60 million in 1937. The result of the experience of the
First World War was that the next war was expected to be total, prolonged and requir-
ing complete economic mobilisation. The pace and direction of preparation was
affected by the availability of domestic resources, intelligence about the preparations of
other countries, rapid changes in technology and estimates as to who the potential enemies would be.

(a)   *The German* Wehrwirtschaft

Germany had learnt well the need for a totally mobilised defence economy. There were
two phases:

1   *'Armament in depth'*. Rearmament had started before 1933. The emphasis was on
    infrastructure and training. Until 1937 50 per cent of aircraft produced were
    trainers and much of the pre–1939 expenditure was on buildings. There was a lot of
    effort devoted to setting up planning for the co-ordination of production and
    resources. In fact this restricted the availability of resources for actual military
    development, and there was considerable opposition to greater armaments
    expenditure by the civilian ministries.
2   *The Four-Year Plan.* With the appointment of Goering to head the Four-Year Plan
    in 1936 there was a marked surge in armaments expenditure. In 1938–39 it rose by
    70 per cent above the level of the previous two years. With Hitler's commitment to
    a war of great proportions there came a great plan for the production of synthetic
    materials, the start of a great naval building programme, orders for the quintupling
    of air force strength and the laying of the foundations of an army with a large
    mechanised core.

However, there was no Schlieffen-type plan, and army strength was by no means as
great as was believed by Britain and France.

(b) France and the 'Maginot mentality'

France expected a long war, and planned for a war in two stages:

1 *A defensive first stage* intended to prevent the enemy from reaching French soil.
   The Maginot Line developed in the 1920s was the essence of this stage.
2 *An offensive second stage* which called for the employment of overwhelming strike
   power. In fact political divisions and deteriorating economic conditions meant that
   by 1937 French aircraft production was only a third of that of Britain and an eighth
   of Germany's. General military expenditure stagnated between 1932 and 1936.

Even so it is too easy to underestimate French strength. She was recognised as the foremost military power in Europe until the mid–1930s, and her military expenditure
increased sixfold between 1936 and 1939.

(c) Britain and deterrence

The pace of rearmament in Britain was faster. Her strategic priorities differed from
those of France because of greater imperial defence needs and reluctance to undertake
continental commitments. The emphasis was on deterrence and the threat of a strategic
blockade and attrition by sea and air power. The result was that the four-year plan
started in 1936 gave priority initially to the navy and air force. Defence expenditure
rose from £185 million in 1936 to £719 million in 1939.

By 1939 Britain was more prepared for a large war than most critics would sup-
pose.

28.4 Isolationism

Both the USA and USSR withheld themselves from European diplomacy until 1939.
The foreign policy of the USA was summed up by Roosevelt's Secretary of State
Cordell Hull as 'Keeping this country out of war'. Isolationism was underpinned by:

1 *The trauma of the First World War.* Although late to intervene the USA was
   deeply affected by the experience.
2 *Economic recession* considerably strengthened American withdrawal from
   European affairs; the emphasis was upon recovery. There was also a general view
   that world economic recovery was the key to world peace. Hull claimed, 'The truth
   is universally recognised that trade between nations is the greatest peacemaker
   and civiliser within human experience'.
3 *Distrust of Britain and France* who were seen as motivated by selfish imperial
   ambitions. It seemed to the USA that her interests would benefit more from the
   loosening of imperial ties.

The passing of the permanent Neutrality Act of 1937 represented the highest point of
isolationism. Not until 1939 would the USA move to underpin western strategy. In the
Far East there was no attempt to take any action against Japan even though American
vessels were attacked by Japanese aircraft in that year.

The attitude of the USSR was similar to that of the USA. She sought to avoid
binding commitments, was preoccupied with internal problems and had little confidence in the League of Nations. Stalinist propaganda portrayed Britain, a former paymaster of White counter-revolution, as a major enemy of the USSR, Germany did not
expect to go to war as early as 1939. However, British and French policy in 1939 was

certainly influenced by evidence that they were temporarily in a position not only to deter but also to fight with a chance of success, albeit at a high level of risk. In all three countries there was the danger that excessive expenditure on armaments would produce financial crisis and generate internal social problems; but Hitler purged political opposition in 1938 and relied on repression and economic controls while Britain and France had to work within the framework of the free market and democracy, and by 1939 had reached the conclusion that it would be better to go to war sooner rather than later.

28.5 The *Anschluss* (March 1938) (see Map 28.1)

Until 1938, none of Hitler's actions had actually overridden the territorial frontiers established in 1919. From March 1938 the policy changed. However, the absorption of Austria with its 7 million people was more accidental than by design.

(a) *The failure of the Austrian Nazi Party (July 1934)*

An earlier attempt by the Fascist *Heimwehr* got as far as murdering the chancellor Dr Dollfuss and seizing the Vienna radio station. Mussolini's hostility prevented Hitler from taking advantage of this attempt, but by January 1938 the Austrian police had unearthed plans for another Heimwehr *coup d'état*.

(b) *The threat of a plebiscite*

The Austrian Chancellor von Schnuschnigg went to see Hitler about the situation and was faced with demands that the Heimwehr be given virtual control of the state. When the Austrian Chancellor retaliated by planning to hold a plebiscite on the subject of union which would probably result in a negative response Hitler mobilised forces on the frontier and obtained a pledge of support from Mussolini who in any case had 350,000 men occupied in Spain and Abyssinia. The demands that the plebiscite be called off and that Seyss-Inquart (the Heimwehr leader) should be made chancellor were accepted, but this was too late.

(c) *Operation Otto (12 March 1938)*

German troops crossed the frontier and joined up with Heimwehr groups who had taken over local administration. Union was formally declared on 13 March, Hitler, in the 'proudest hour of my life', made a triumphal entry to Vienna. A plebiscite of 99.75 per cent votes in favour was easily constructed. There was no reaction from other states – France was occupied with a government crisis, Britain saw the union as a natural development and anyway did not have the power to intervene. Chamberlain remarked: 'In the absence of a powerful ally and until our armaments are prepared we must adjust our foreign policy to our circumstances and even bear with patience and good humour actions which we should like to treat in very different fashion.'

28.6 The Sudetenland Crisis (August–September 1938)

The classic illustration of appeasement was provided by the next crisis, over Czechoslovakia. The expectations of the 3.25 million Germans in the Sudetenland

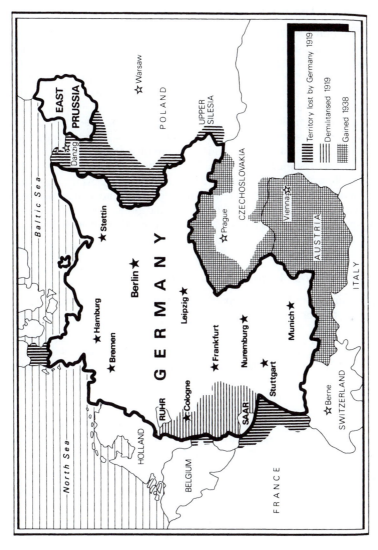

Map 28.1 The expansion of Germany (1919–38)

Legend:
- Territory lost by Germany 1919
- Demilitarised 1919
- Gained 1938

fringe were considerably increased by the Anschluss and the agitation of the Sudeten Fascist party led by *Konrad Henlein*. Henlein's demands for autonomy for the Sudeten-Germans – the 'eight points' – were accepted in September by President Beneš largely because it was clear that Britain and France would not guarantee Czechoslovakia against German intervention.

(a) The Munich Agreement (29 September 1938)

This concession only led Hitler to increase his vitriolic attacks against the Czech President, and his threats of German action. On 13 September Chamberlain took the unprecedented step of meeting Hitler at *Berchtesgaden*, where Hitler demanded the cession of the whole of the Sudetenland. Britain and France persuaded the Czechs to agree to cede all territories where the population was over 50 per cent German. However at another meeting on 22 September Hitler increased his demands to include immediate German occupation of the whole of Sudetenland, and concessions to the Poles and Hungarians as well. Chamberlain rejected this, France called up 600,000 reservists and the Czechs had already started to mobilise their 35 well-armed divisions. Then at Munich on 29 September (as a result of proposed amendments by the French and the intervention of Mussolini) an agreement was reached which gave Hitler virtually all of his demands. Czechoslovakia was obliged to surrender the Sudetenland along with a million Czechs and her main frontier fortifications. At the same time, Poland seized the Teschen district and Hungary extended its northern frontier.

(b) Assessment of the Munich Agreement

Chamberlain claimed that the agreement represented 'peace for our time'. Winston Churchill, the arch-opponent of appeasement, believed it was 'a total and unmitigated defeat':

1 *A diplomatic collapse.* France had actually betrayed her alliance with Czechoslovakia; Britain had been even more responsible, because she refused to back France firmly against Germany and to countenance any sort of agreement with the USSR. Naturally the latter regarded Munich as a plot to leave her isolated against Germany.
2 *The absence of alternatives.* Given the belief that Britain and France were still not strong enough to take on Germany, it is difficult to see what else could have been done because:

   – Hitler was probably not bluffing. A partial mobilisation was ordered on 27 September, and this together with a public commitment to 'smash Czechoslovakia' meant that Hitler could not afford to back down.
   – The idea that a *coup d'état* by generals and politicians was imminent is not proven. Plans did exist, but there was no agreement and no attempt was made until July 1944.
   – The Czechs were not strong enough without the military support of France or the USSR, and Poland and Hungary would probably have joined in with Germany to overwhelm Czechoslovakia.

The crisis had a marked effect on *British rearmament*. Aircraft production rose from 240 per month to 660 per month by September 1938. In February 1939 the commitment to raise an army of 32 divisions was undertaken.

28.7 The destruction of Czechoslovakia (March 1939)

So far, Chamberlain had enjoyed public support but now there was a dramatic change in attitude.

(a) The occupation of Prague (16 March 1939)

Czechoslovakia had been converted into a federal state with virtual autonomy for Slovakia and Ruthenia. This led to recurrent clashes, and in March 1939 President Hocha dismissed the Slovene and Ruthene prime ministers. An appeal to Hitler by the Slovak prime minister led to Hocha being summoned to Berlin and intimidated into surrendering the whole country to German protection. The result was that Bohemia and Moravia were annexed by Germany, Ruthenia was handed over to Hungary and Slovakia became a German protectorate.

(b) A diplomatic revolution

This latest move was sheer expansionism. The British ambassador in Berlin, Sir Neville Henderson, said: 'By the occupation of Prague Hitler put himself unquestionably in the wrong and destroyed the entire arguable validity of the German case as regards the Treaty of Versailles.' On 17 March, Chamberlain asked his Birmingham audience 'Is this, in fact, a step in the direction of an attempt to dominate the world by force?' This new mood was reflected in:

1 Anglo-French announcements of resistance to any German aggression against *Holland, Belgium and Switzerland.*
2 An announcement in late March by Chamberlain that Britain and France would support *Poland* in her dispute with Hitler over Danzig and the Polish corridor.
3 Guarantees of support to *Greece and Rumania* followed the Italian invasion of Albania in April 1939 as a show of strength.
4 The introduction of *universal peacetime conscription* in Britain in April 1939.

28.8 The outbreak of war (September 1939)

Hitler gave no indication of appreciating this change in tone, and turned his attentions to *Poland*.

(a) The Danzig issue

In early April the German General Staff was ordered to prepare for war against Poland. In late April, Hitler demanded the return of Danzig and denounced the German–Polish non-aggression pact of 1934 (see Section 24.8(b)); he also denounced the Anglo-German naval agreement of 1935 (see Section 24.8(c)). On 22 May, the terms of the *Pact of Steel* were published for additional intimidation. However to a meeting of senior army officers Hitler announced: 'We cannot expect a repetition of the Czech affair. There will be war. Our task is to isolate Poland'.

(b) The Molotov–Ribbentrop Pact (August 1939)

It was the Russo-German agreement in August which produced this isolation. This agreement resulted from two factors:

1 *The longstanding Anglo-French distrust of the USSR.* Distrust of Soviet ambitions by Britain, France and the states of eastern central Europe prevented any defensive alliance. In March 1939 Chamberlain said:

> I must confess to the most profound distrust of Russia, I have no belief whatever in her ability to maintain an effective offensive even if she wanted to. And I distrust her motives, which seem to me to have little connection with our ideas of liberty and to be concerned only with setting everyone else by the ears.

On 16 April, the USSR proposed a defensive alliance to include Poland; it was rejected. Then in August another attempt failed when Poland refused to countenance any Russian military bases on her territory.

2 *Common interests between Germany and the USSR.* A relationship between the two states was not as unusual as it might seem:

– There was a long tradition of 'easterners' in German military and diplomatic circles who supported the Russo-German link.
– Both states had interests in establishing spheres of influence in eastern central Europe.
– Germany sought to avoid a war on two fronts while the USSR sought to turn Germany westwards to keep her occupied. The outcome was an agreement between the German and Soviet foreign ministers which established a line for the *partition of Poland.*

In fact, the USSR seriously underestimated German strength, and the result was the disaster of 1941.

(c) *The outbreak of war*

Britain continued to back Poland. On the 25 August an Anglo-Polish treaty was announced. She still sought to achieve a negotiated settlement. However, following a series of contrived frontier incidents and especially the Gleiwitz incident, when German criminals dressed in Polish uniforms were displayed dead after a supposed attack on a German radio station, Hitler ordered the invasion of Poland on 31 August. When German troops crossed the frontier on 1 September Chamberlain, with the support of France, presented an ultimatum which expired on 3 September. France declared war on the same day.

It was Britain and France who declared war rather than Germany. War had clearly been on the cards since spring 1938. It could be argued that the change in public opinion was encouraged to support policy and give a moral gloss to a decision about to be taken for other reasons as well as anti-Fascist idealism. The key to the declaration in summer 1939 was that the time seemed ripe, and that the alternative was for France and Britain to back down as great powers.

1 *Britain and France were militarily far stronger* by summer 1939. Chamberlain had been assured that parity would be achieved with Germany by mid-1939. By 1939 French and British tank and aircraft production was greater than that of Germany. The western allies were committed to a military timetable.
2 *The USA was drawing closer to the western allies.* Roosevelt had accepted large orders for military equipment even though that involved the danger of confrontation with Congress. In the Far East the USA was assuming a more positive role so it seemed likely that the threat from Japan would be countered for the time being.

3   *Intelligence from Italy and Germany* suggested the likelihood of economic crisis.
    There was also the possibility that Germany would be able to avoid this and gather
    strength by building upon eastern European resources very soon.
4   *Internal social and economic problems* were likely to escalate from autumn 1939 as
    French and British gold and currency reserves were exhausted and inflation
    developed.

For his part Hitler had not grasped that the allies had reached the limit, and was badly
advised that they would not fight. There was consternation when his bluff was called.
Goering telephoned Ribbentrop to tell him, 'Now you have your damned war!'

28.9 Conclusion

The debate about the origins of the First World War is paralleled by one about the
Second World War, which raises similar issues. There are three major theories.

(a) *Fanaticism*

This view takes very seriously the frequent assertions of *ambition* by Hitler and his
view of himself as a *man of destiny* – 'I go the way that Providence dictates with the
assurance of a sleepwalker.' The key was the drive towards *Lebensraum* and Hitler
was, in this respect, simply the heir to William II. War with Russia was inevitable
because the objective was a *colony for settlement* rather than one for capitalist exploitation – 'The goal of the *Ostpolitik* is to open up an area of settlement for a hundred million Germans.' Advocates of this line of argument support it with claims that Hitler
was clearly preparing for war from 1933:

1   *Rearmament.* In the six years following 1933 Germany devoted 50 per cent more
    resources to armaments as Britain and France put together, and steel production
    was in 1938 25 per cent as much as that of Britain and France combined.
2   *Self-sufficiency.* Independence in supplies of vital materials such as rubber was
    essential for a state anticipating war. The production of synthetic rubber spiralled
    from next to nothing in 1936 to 22,000 tone in 1939.

The intention behind the Nuremberg trials after the war was to prove conclusively the
guilt of the Nazi leaders. The main piece of evidence quoted was the *Hossbach
Protocol* of 5 November 1937 which was a record of a conference between Hitler and
senior staff officers at which Hitler outlined plans for a war of expansion.

(b) *Opportunism*

In his *The Origins of the Second World War* (1961) A. J. P. Taylor argues that Hitler's
conduct of foreign policy was purely opportunist, and that his ranting and grand plans
were just part of a repertoire of techniques to achieve much more limited objectives.
Taylor says: 'Germany fought specifically in the second war to reverse the verdict of
the first and to destroy the settlement which followed it.' According to this theory,
Hitler's objectives were *rational* and *justifiable* and appeasement was a sensible
response; Hitler calculated on the unwillingness of Britain and France to take action,
and risked Soviet expansion in the resultant conflict.

However, Hitler gambled once too often and war broke out, although 'Far from
wanting war a general war was the last thing he wanted.' There are two vital supports
for this theory:

1   *Rejection of the idea of a plan.* Taylor claims that the Hossbach Protocol was just a record of a deliberately exaggerated expression of ambition which was being used to urge a policy of greater rearmament upon the leaders of the services and the economy.
2   *The assertion that serious rearmament did not start until very late.* Taylor remarks that: 'The state of German rearmament in 1939 gives the decisive proof that Hitler was not contemplating general war, and probably not contemplating war at all.' Even so, it was Hitler who took the initiative and insisted that 'we must accept the risk with reckless resolution'.

(c)   An inner crisis of National Socialism

The third possibility is that National Socialist Germany needed war to restore impetus to its development, and to justify the continuance of totalitarian rule. The economy was in a state of full employment and there was the danger of a revival of inflation. There had been a massive increase in state expenditure – fourfold in the 1930s – and the national debt increased by some 250 per cent. With an economy already at breaking point, further expansion was possible only as a result of war. *Blitzkrieg* was the answer because it promised rapid victories at relatively low cost; so internal pressures dictated the need for war.

Questions

1   Account for the outbreak of civil war in Spain in 1936. What were its international consequences?   [OC]
2   Why did war break out over Poland in 1939, but not over Czechoslovakia in 1938?   [OC]
3   Explain the objective of Hitler's foreign policy from 1933 to 1939, as illustrated by his relations with: (a) Austria, (b) Czechoslovakia and (c) Poland.   [OX]
4   How did Hitler's policies between 1933 and 1939 contribute to the outbreak of the Second World War?   [NEAB]
5   To what extent was Hitler's foreign policy governed by his determination to revise the Versailles Settlement?   [NEAB]
6   To what extent had Hitler achieved the objectives of his foreign policy by December 1941? [CAM]
7   To what extent had Hitler carried out his promises to the German people by 1939?   [CAM]
8   Study Sources A, B and C, and then answer the questions which follow.

Source A: Anschluss by telephone.

> *Keppler:* I would like to report what has happened. President Miklas has refused to do anything whatsoever. The Cabinet has ceased to function all the same. I talked to Schuschnigg and he told me they had all laid down their posts . . . Seyss spoke on the radio and announced that in his capacity as Minister of the Interior he would carry on the business of government. The old cabinet has given orders to the army not to resist in any shape or form. So there won't be any shooting.
>
> *Göring:* Ah well, that doesn't make any difference anyway. Now listen here: The main thing is that Seyss-Inquart takes charge of all the functions of the government now, that he secures the broadcasting facilities et cetera. And listen – Seyss is to send the following telegram to us. Take it down. 'The provisional Austrian government, which after the resignation of the Schuschnigg cabinet sees its duty in the re-establishment of law and order in Austria, urgently asks the German Government to assist them in this task and to help them avoid bloodshed. It therefore asks the German Government to send German troops into Austria as quickly as possible.'
>
> *Keppler:* Well, the SA and the SS are on the streets here, but everything is quiet and orderly. Everything has collapsed with the professional [groups]
>
> *Göring:* Oh, yes, and another thing: Seyss is to occupy the borders at once so that they won't smuggle the money out of the country.

Keppler: Yes, sir.

Göring: And above all he is to take over Foreign Affairs now ... Seyss will take over, and he will call in a couple of men to help him. He is to take those we suggest. He is to form a provisional government. It is quite unimportant now what the President feels about it.

Keppler: Yes, sir.

Göring: Form a provisional government as he had planned and inform the other countries.

Keppler: Yes, sir.

Göring: He is the only one who has any power in Austria now. Well, our troops will be across the border tonight.

Keppler: Yes, sir.

Göring: All right. And he is to send the telegram as soon as possible. He doesn't really even have to send the telegram. He only has to say he has. You get me? All right, then. Call me about this either at the Führer's or at my place. Now get going! Heil Hitler!

(a) Who was the Seyss-Inquart referred to frequently during this conversation?
(b) What was to be the justification for the German occupation of Austria (lines 9–14)?
(c) This is taken from the written transcript of a telephone conversation which has been recorded. What sort of factors affect the value of this sort of material as evidence for historians?
(d) What was the sequence of events in the occupation of Austria which was being required by Göring.

Source: Transcript of a telephone call from Wilhelm Keppler, Göring's agent in Vienna, to Göring, 11 March 1938 at 8.48 pm.

Source B: Hitler addresses a secret military conference.

It was clear to me from the first moment that I could not be satisfied with the Sudeten-German territory. That was only a partial solution. The decision to march into Bohemia was made. Then followed the establishment of the protectorate and with that the basis for the conquest of Poland was laid, but I was not clear at the time whether I should start first against the East and then against the West, or vice versa. By the pressure of events it came first to the fight against Poland.

The increasing number of [German] people required a larger *Lebensraum*. The fight must start here. No nation can evade the solution of this problem. Otherwise it must yield and gradually go down. For the first time in sixty-seven years we do not have a two-front war to wage. But no one can know how long that will remain so. Basically I did not organise the armed forces in order not to strike. The decision to strike was always in me.

Russia is at present not dangerous. It is weakened by many internal conditions. Moreover, we have the treaty with Russia. Treaties, however, are kept only as long as they serve a purpose. Russia will keep it only as long as Russia herself considers it to be to her benefit. Russia still has far-reaching goals, above all the strengthening of her position in the Baltic. We can oppose Russia only when we are free in the West.

My decision is unchangeable. I shall attack France and England at the most favourable and earliest moment. Breach of the neutrality of Belgium and Holland is of no importance. No one will question that when we have won. We shall not justify the breach of neutrality as idiotically as in 1914.

(a) What was 'the Sudeten-German territory' (lines 2–3)? Trace the steps by which it fell into Hitler's hands.
(b) Explain the references to the 'the decision to march into Bohemia' and the 'establishment of the protectorate' (lines 2–3). What were the consequences of these actions?
(c) When and why did Hitler decide upon the 'conquest of Poland' (line 4)?
(d) What do you understand by '*Lebensraum*' (line 7)?
(e) Explain: 'For the first time in sixty-seven years we do not have a two-front war to wage' (lines 9–10). What brought this situation to an end?

Source: From a retrospective view of his pre-war diplomacy by Hitler, 23 November 1939.

Source C: Stalin's viewpoint.

To what are we to attribute the system of concessions made by the non-aggressive States? It might be attributed, for example, to the fear that a revolution might break out, if these States were to go to war and the war were to assume world-wide proportions ...
But this is not the sole or even the chief reason. The chief reason is that the majority of the non-aggressive countries, particularly England and France, have rejected the policy of collective security, the policy of collective resistance to the aggressor, and have taken up a position of non-intervention, of neutrality ...

The policy of non-intervention reveals an eagerness not to hinder the aggressors in their nefarious work ... not to hinder Germany, say, from enmeshing herself in European affairs, from embroiling herself in a war with the Soviet Union; to allow all the belligerents to sink deeply into the mire of war, to encourage them surreptitiously in this; to allow them to weaken and exhaust one another; and when they have become weak enough ... to dictate conditions to the enfeebled belligerents.

Take Germany for instance. They let her have Austria despite the undertaking to defend her independence; they let her have the Sudeten region; they abandoned Czechoslovakia to her fate, thereby violating their obligations; they then began to lie vociferously in the press about the 'weakness of the Russian army' and the 'demoralization of the Russian air force' ... egging the Germans on to march further east, promising them easy pickings and prompting them: 'Just start a war on the Bolsheviks and everything will be all right'. This looks very much like egging on and encouraging the aggressor.

(a)   According to Stalin, why had England and France adopted the policy of appeasement?
(b)   This speech was made in March 1939. How would you argue on behalf of a more responsive policy by the USSR towards Britain and France, and against Stalin's perception?
Source: Speech by Joseph Stalin at the Eighteenth Congress of the CPSU, 10 March 1939.

29 The Second World War 1939–45

Introduction

The Second World War was a far more fluid war than the First. It was also a 'world war' far more, in the sense of being fought on a global scale on a wide variety of fronts. The direct impact upon the civilian population in terms of death, destruction and displacement also made it a 'total' war in a far more horrific way than the war of 1914–18.

29.1 The *Blitzkrieg* (September 1939–June 1940)

In 1935, Hitler said, 'If I were going to attack an opponent ... I should suddenly, like a flash of lightning in the night, hurl myself upon the enemy.' Unlike their British and French opposite numbers, the German General Staff had learnt from the mistakes of the First World War and the writings of British and German military theorists. The new style of war comprised pre-dawn attacks by aircraft to destroy enemy planes on the ground and to disrupt communications, 'pincer' movements by armoured divisions trapping enemy units in 'pockets' and airborne troops to seize key installations ahead of the rapid advance.

(a) *The dismemberment of Poland (September 1939)*

Within a month, Poland ceased to exist. Outnumbered two to one and technologically backward the Polish army was overwhelmed in a classic illustration of the *blitzkrieg*; by 20 September it was defeated. Meanwhile by 19 September, Russian forces had occupied eastern Poland and established bases in Estonia, Latvia and Lithuania. On 30 November the Russian army also invaded Finland to seize Karelia and the port of Hango. The effects of the purges on the officer corps and the astonishing resistance of the Finnish army under Marshal Mannerheim meant that not until March 1940 were these objectives won.

(b) *The invasion of Norway (April 1940)*

On 9 April Denmark was occupied without resistance – indeed, some Copenhagen bystanders thought a film was being made – and Norway was invaded. The purpose of this latter move was to guarantee supplies of iron ore from Sweden. It had the effect though of bringing about the downfall of Neville Chamberlain, attacked by the press for 'creeping paralysis' and the mismanagement of a British intervention to help Norway. On 10 May a coalition government was established under *Winston Churchill*.

(c) The 'Catastrophe' (May–June 1940)

On the same day, the 'phoney war', a period of inactivity, ended with a German invasion of the Low Countries which bypassed the Maginot Line then threatened to encircle the Anglo-French forces in northern France. Then a brief halt by the Panzer columns (largely because 40 per cent of the tanks were out of action) allowed Lord Gort, the commander of the British Expeditionary Force, to fall back to Dunkirk. A nine-day evacuation, the *'miracle of Dunkirk'*, rescued 340,000 British and Allied troops. Meanwhile, the pressure in France mounted. On 10 June, Italy declared war. By 12 June, the Germans were on the Seine and Paris was declared an open city. Despite attempts by Churchill to keep France in the war, advocacy of an armistice grew:

1 *The French army had been mortally injured.* 40 French divisions had been trapped in the German advance. By the end of Dunkirk the French army had lost 40 per cent of its effective manpower and 80 per cent of its equipment. It was also subject to demoralising communist propaganda.
2 *The strength of defeatism.* A new government under the stronger Paul Reynaud did not silence soon enough the anti-British defeatist elements led by *Pierre Laval*. On 17 June, a new government under Marshal Pétain sought an armistice, and despite an unauthorised broadcast by the junior minister General de Gaulle to urge the French to continue resistance on 22 June, it was signed in the historic railway carriage at *Compiègne*. All except south-eastern France was occupied and demilitarised, and the French colonies in North Africa were to be demilitarised.

On 10 July the 'revenge of the anti-Dreyfusards' was completed when the Third Republic was legally abolished. All effective power was assumed by Marshal Pétain as 'Head of the French State', with a near-fascist government based in the town of *Vichy*. The only official political party was the Legion of ex-Servicemen. The motto of the new Vichy régime was *'Travail, Famille, Patrie'* ('Work, Family, Nation').

29.2 British resistance (June 1940–June 1941)

Isolated, with threatened sea routes and a much weakened army, Britain was the only remaining obstacle to the consolidation of Nazi rule in Europe. Under Churchill, however, the will to resist was firmly displayed in the mobilisation of manpower and resources and in the disabling of the French warships in the north African ports before they were seized by the Germans.

(a) War in the air

In July, German troops and equipment were being assembled in the French and Belgian ports for *'Operation Sea Lion'*, the invasion of Britain. However throughout August and September the technical superiority of the British aircraft and the value of the comprehensive radar system were revealed in the failure of the *Luftwaffe* to win control of the air. In October, the invasion was finally called off, but the Luftwaffe turned to bombing the cities. London was bombed for 76 nights on end, then sporadically for another six months. On 14 November the centre of Coventry was totally destroyed.

(b) The war in North Africa

Meanwhile Italian forces had gone onto the offensive in North Africa against Egypt and British Somaliland. By March 1941 General Wavell had repulsed the attacks on Egypt; by May 1941 British troops had occupied Eritrea and restored the Emperor Haile Selassie to his throne. However, parts of Wavell's forces were diverted to Greece (see Section 29.2(d)) and powerful German reinforcements arrived under General Rommel to stiffen the Italian resistance. Wavell was obliged to withdraw to Egypt.

(c) The war at sea

The struggle to keep open the flow of supplies by sea was vital. In 1940 alone German U-boats sank 4 million tons of shipping. The spring of 1941 also saw the desperate surface campaign against the German heavy battleship *Bismarck*. On the other hand, President Roosevelt stretched the neutrality of the USA to its utmost with:

1   *The policy of 'cash and carry'* in late 1940, when Britain was given 50 American destroyers in return for leases on Caribbean islands.
2   *'Lend-lease' from early 1941*, which involved the 'lending' of equipment to Britain which was supplied in US ships.

(d) The war in the Balkans

In June 1940 Russia forced Rumania to surrender Bessarabia and the northern Bukovina. In August 1940, Germany forced her to surrender the southern Dobrudja to Bulgaria and most of Transylvania to Hungary. Then in April 1941, an anti-German coup in Belgrade led to an invasion of Greece and Yugoslavia by German forces, then the capture of Crete by airborne forces. British and Commonwealth forces were forced to evacuate the Balkans.

29.3 The onset of global war (June 1941–July 1942)
(see Map 29.1)

Two events dramatically changed the face of the war.

(a) Operation Barbarossa (June 1941)

On 23 June 1941, against the advice of his generals, Hitler launched 3 million troops, 10,000 tanks and 3000 aircraft into the USSR on a 1000-mile front. So sudden was the move that Russian trains were still carrying supplies into Germany. A rapid knock-out victory was vital. Hitler argued: 'We have only to kick in the door and the whole rotten structure will come crashing down.' Indeed the Russian forces initially collapsed and lost 3 million prisoners in 1941. The USSR was deprived of 63 per cent of its coal production and 68 per cent of its pig iron. However, the Russian resistance was far greater than expected. Several factors accounted for this:

1   *A pact of mutual assistance in July 1941* led to supplies from Britain, then (from September) the USA by Arctic convoys to Archangel and Murmansk.
2   *The transfer of Russian industrial plant to the Urals and Siberia*. The coal production of the Urals fields rose from 12 million tons in 1940 to 257 million tons by 1945.

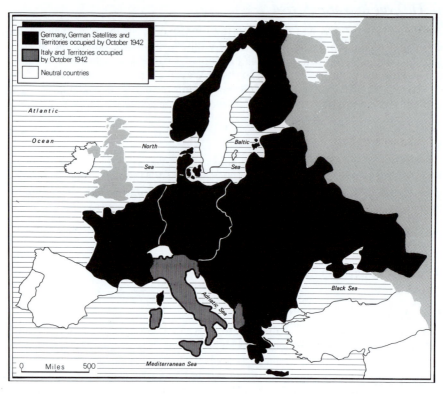

Map 29.1 Europe in October 1942

3   *An appeal to Russian nationalism.* The old religious and national persecution and
    discrimination ceased. Party membership was widened. A vigorous appeal was
    made to Russian patriotism which took in even the tsarist achievements.
4   *Winter conditions broke* when the Germans were still well east of the Crimea, 30
    miles from Moscow and besieging Leningrad.

In early 1942, the Russians were able to mount a counter-offensive.

(b)   *Pearl Harbor (December 1941)*

The Anglo-American relationship had developed such that in August 1941 Roosevelt
met Churchill in mid-Atlantic to devise the *Atlantic Charter* to guarantee the freedom
of nations and prevent territorial adjustments without the 'freely expressed wishes of
the peoples concerned'. However, the successful surprise attack by Japanese aircraft on
the battleships of the US Pacific Fleet on 7 December 1941 resulted in the USA declaring war on Japan and her European Axis allies. Immediately, the Japanese overran
East Asia – Hong Kong fell on Christmas Day 1941, Guam and Wake Island and the
Dutch East Indies were overrun in January 1942, 60,000 British and Commonwealth
troops surrendered at Singapore on 15 February 1942 and in May the Philippines were
captured. Only the victories by the US aircraft carriers at *Midway Island* and in the
Battle of the Coral Sea saved Australia.

29.4 The Nazi New Order

The German rule of the conquered territories was characterised by two features:

(a) *Racial persecution*

The Nazi racial and population policy extended beyond the Jews. The origin of the *Final Solution* programme cannot be divorced from the euthanasia campaign designed to create rule by a racially purified and revitalised 'biocracy'. There was also an eastern European population policy which sought to exclude non-Germans from Reich territory and involved deportation and killing on a vast scale of Poles, Russians, Ukrainians and other groups. However, what was distinctive about the *Holocaust* was that it was a deliberate attempt to exterminate an entire people. This had no historical precedent. Even the Turkish persecution of the Armenians between the 1890s and 1915 was incomplete and left about 10 per cent of the Turkish American population still living in Turkey, and it was not a policy based upon any sort of ideology or bureaucratic system. There are several aspects of the Nazi Final Solution which continue to provoke considerable discussion.

1   *The scale of the killing.* Of course, there are many examples of killing on a very large scale. Possibly some 14.5 million Soviet peasants died as a result of Stalin's agricultural policy in the 1930s. The most reliable estimates suggest that the Nazis killed between 5 and 6 million Jews, two-thirds of the European Jews and a third of the entire Jewish people. This should be compared against the total death roll of about 55 million in total in the Second World War, which included 20 million Soviet citizens and 15 million Chinese. However, a third of all European civilian deaths were of Jews, and the German target following the Wannsee Conference of January 1942 was to destroy all Jews in Europe, even down to the smallest communities such as the 200 Jews living in Albania.

2   *The extent to which Hitler was personally responsible.* Some historians, and especially David Irving, right-wing apologist for Hitler, have argued that he could not be held responsible because there were never any written orders from him to which the Holocaust could be traced, and that it was the result of the activity of over zealous subordinates acting out of control. Nevertheless, Hitler's philosophy regarding the Jews was always very clear from the 1920s. He saw them as an especial danger in producing the degeneration of Germany, as the inventors of Bolshevism and as a challenge to nationalism, the Führer principle and militarism because they represented internationalism, democracy and pacifism. He saw the annihilation of the Jews as a necessary step in restoring the purpose to historical development. There is no doubt that he hated the Jews intensely, whatever the philosophical or psychological reasons, and that he was the main driver of anti-Semitism in the Nazi movement.

3   *When and how the Final Solution emerged.* There had been an intensification of persecution within the Reich from 1938 onwards, but the term 'Final Solution' in use in 1940 related to proposals to deport all of the Jews to Poland or Madagascar. From July 1941 to the *Wannsee Conference* in January 1942 it began to take a different form. There are two general theories about the emergence of the programme.

   – *Intentionalism.* According to this view Hitler was responsible from the beginning and murder was on the agenda from the invasion of Poland in September 1939, although it was with the invasion of Russia that the policy of extermination really emerged, based upon the activities of SS units in murdering about 2 million Soviet Jews.

– *Functionalism.* The alternative view is that it was a decision which evolved bit by bit; starting with local initiatives in Russia on the basis of vague statements by Hitler, developing into the murder of Jews deported from Germany using improvised methods when the space to resettle them ran out, and finally moving into a much more systematic phase which was then carried forward on the basis of sheer bureaucratic and impersonal momentum by ordinary people doing a job as part of the 'machinery of destruction'.

4   *The extent of collaboration.* From 1942 extermination was a co-ordinated project on a Europe-wide scale concentrating systematically upon the Polish Jews and eastern Europe, then turning towards western Europe and then, in 1944, to Hungary. It continued right up to the last stages of the war, a massive programme absorbing much needed resources, manpower and rail-freight space. It is inconceivable that so much could have been achieved without the complicity of local bureaucrats, policemen and political leaders. In Poland and eastern Europe the Germans were able to control the process themselves. In the satellite states such as Hungary, Slovakia, Croatia, Rumania and Bulgaria the situation varied and collaboration diminished as the Nazi fortunes waned but there was considerable local involvement led by Fascist groups such as the Croat *Ustasha* and the *Arrow Cross* movement in Hungary. In western Europe there were different factors at work because the Jews tended to be more integrated into the population and German policy was more public, but the situations ranged from resistance to deportation to the camps by Denmark and Italy to substantial and enthusiastic involvement by French policemen and officials of the anti-Semitic Vichy régime where systematic policies of persecution and harassment were in place well before 1942, and French Jews were interned in camps such as that at Drancy in the suburbs of Paris in the midst of a large urban community.

5   *Why so little was done to try to stop it.* In Germany itself there is little evidence that anti-Semitism had been a particularly significant vote-winner for the Nazis. The Nazi government deliberately tried to curtain off the extermination in the east from the German people. Beyond sheer ignorance it seems that indifference and fear were to blame for inactivity. The whole point of political terror is that individuals, however well meaning, are intimidated into accepting atrocities and passing them by. In the case of the Allies and neutral states there is no doubt that information about the extermination policy was reaching them from a fairly early stage but that there was a good deal of scepticism and disbelief, a tendency to regard Japan as the great criminal power in the case of the USA, concern about the relationship with Arab states as far as the British government was concerned when confronted with pressure to accept Jewish refugees into Palestine, and a Vatican policy of maintaining political neutrality to avoid the possibility of schisms and safeguard church institutional interests. In some cases, though, considerable contributions were made by states as Spain which accepted a large influx of refugees and by the activities of individuals such as the Czech businessman Oskar Schindler and the Swedish diplomat Raoul Wallenberg in arranging protection for thousands of Jews.

(b) *Exploitation*

Germany sustained the war largely on the basis of *plundering the resources* of the defeated states. France, for instance, had to pay 'occupation costs' which amounted to 10.9 per cent of her national income in 1940 and 36.6 per cent of it by 1943. Germany also removed resources and equipment as well as people. From France alone she took

776,000 forced workers, 100,000 political prisoners and 220,000 Jews. Altogether by May 1943 there were 6.25 million foreign workers in Germany. The economies of the occupied countries were inevitably damaged; French agricultural production fell to 25 per cent of the 1939 total, and industrial production was down 50 per cent by 1944.

29.5 Turning points (October 1942–January 1943)

Almost simultaneously, the tide of the war turned in North Africa and Russia.

(a) El Alamein (October 1942)

From August 1942 General Montgomery was the commander of the Eighth Army. Reinforced by large numbers of American Sherman tanks and against German forces losing up to 75 per cent of their supply ships he won a decisive victory over Rommel at *El Alamein*. When American troops under General Eisenhower landed in Morocco and Algeria in early November in Operation Torch, Rommel was caught between two forces. Another defeat at Mareth in March 1943 and further heavy fighting led to the capturing of 250,000 Axis troops.

(b) Stalingrad (November 1942–January 1943)

On the eastern front, the Ninth Army of General von Paulus was trapped in *Stalingrad*, and after weeks of savage street fighting 93,000 Germans surrendered on 31 January 1943. The Russian offensive only narrowly missed capturing the German army in the Caucasus in a trap, and Leningrad was finally relieved. Only in March 1943 did the Germans manage to stem the onslaught and mount a counter-offensive. In 1943, the Russians resumed their advance and from then on the German front was under pressure continuously. By then the Mediterranean front was also draining resources, but one of the great problems of the German commanders was Hitler's refusal to countenance a strategic withdrawal.

29.6 The counter-invasion of Europe (January 1943–December 1944) (see Illus. 29.1)

The Allied counter-invasion of Europe was launched from two directions.

(a) The invasion of Italy (July–September 1943)

An Anglo-American conference at *Casablanca* in January 1943 favoured the concentration on Italy to drain off Axis forces and take away the threat to the Suez Canal. In July–August 1943 Sicily was overrun and a coup by Italian generals and Fascist leaders overthrew Mussolini. On 3 September, in what Hitler described as a 'a gigantic example of swinishness', Marshal Badoglio's government signed an armistice. However, German resistance seriously slowed the Anglo-American advance in Italy, and a 'leap frog' landing at Anzio was not successful. Not until 4 June was Rome finally entered.

From a German poster of 1944 prepared for the occupied Dutch territories: US 'liberation' will bring with it Jewish money, decadent dances like the 'jitterbug' and racist Ku Klux Klan sentiments; the caption reads: 'The USA will save European culture from its downfall'.
Source: A. Rhodes and V. Margolin, *Propaganda* (Angus & Robertson 1976) p. 201.

Q   This is an effective poster. On the other hand, do you see anything ironical or paradoxical in the attack which it is making against the USA when you consider the directions which had been taken by Germany under Hitler's leadership?

(b)   *D-Day (6 June 1944)*

While there had been bombing of German cities by British and American aircraft, so far there had been no fighting on German soil. The winning by 1944 of the battle against the U-boats also made thoughts of a second front in Europe more credible. On 6 June 1944, 4000 landing craft supported by 700 warships landed British, American and Canadian troops on beachheads on the *Normandy coast*. In July, American forces managed to trap much of Rommel's army in the 'Falaise Pocket'; in August, another landing in the south of France completed French liberation. By September, some 250,000 prisoners had been taken; meanwhile, the Russians were advancing along the Baltic and into Poland, and 55 divisions were held down on the Mediterranean front.

German use of terror weapons like the V1 and V2 rockets was too late to have enough effect on the 'last fling'. The 'Battle of the Bulge' in the Ardennes in December 1944 was the last attempt to block the Allied advance.

On *20 July 1944*, a group of German officers did at last attempt unsuccessfully to assassinate Hitler, with the result that most of the active opposition in Germany was eliminated.

29.7 The diplomacy of the war

By December 1944, Russian troops were well into Rumania and Bulgaria. On 12 February 1945, against considerable resistance, they captured Budapest. In Yugoslavia, the Germans had actually been defeated quite independently by the partisans led by the communist Marshal Tito; the obvious danger was of Russian political penetration in the Balkans and eastern Europe. There were two possible counters to this threat.

(a)   *The southern thrust*

In November–December 1943 at the *Teheran Conference* Churchill urged an Allied advance in the Balkans through Austria and Hungary to join up with the Russians. In effect, this would head off the challenge. Roosevelt, however, distrusted Britain and wanted a Russian alliance against Japan. Nor was he very interested in post-war Europe. Stalin, on the other hand, avoided alienating Roosevelt by supporting the idea of a United Nations Organisation, by failing to help the Greek communist insurgents, and by persuading the Italian communists to be less anti-monarchist. He supported a second front on the Atlantic coast, and a landing in southern France to drain resources from the Italian venture. At the same meeting, the break up of post-war Germany was discussed, as was the extension of the Polish frontier to the line of the Oder–Neisse rivers in the west.

(b)   *The race for Berlin* (see Illus. 29.2)

The alternative to some such compromise with the USSR was to end the war by autumn 1944, while the Russians were still in the east. However there was a strategic difference of opinion between two groups:

1   *A narrow concentrated thrust* through Holland was proposed by General Montgomery; the result was the spectacular but unsuccessful *Arnhem venture* in September.
2   *The more cautious advance on a broad front* was slower, but imposed fewer supply and communications problems; Eisenhower favoured this view.

The result was that the Russians reached Poland in February 1945. At the *Yalta Conference* in that month Churchill was clearly dependent on Roosevelt, who was himself a sick man. The principles of German dismemberment and reparations were accepted, as was the principle that France should share in any future German arrangements. The USSR pledged itself to enter the war against Japan. On the other hand, it was agreed that the USSR should keep the territories up to the old *Curzon Line* (see Section 23.7(d)), while Poland was extended in compensation to the Oder–Neisse. There was a vague pledge of assistance for the liberated countries, and support for the establishment of democratic governments with free elections. In fact, by April 1945, when Roosevelt died, Soviet intentions in Poland, Bulgaria and Rumania were already very suspect.

Illus. 29.2 *Les menteurs de Berlin* (Chelsea House Publications)

LES MENTEURS DE BERLIN

From an Allied poster of 1945.
Source: A. Rhodes and V. Margolin, *Propaganda* (Angus & Robertson 1976) p. 220.

Q What sort of weapon is being employed against the aircraft, and by whom? Why is the caption in French?

(c) *The last days*

In its final phase, the war was a huge pincer movement by Russian troops entering eastern Germany in early 1945 and western Allied troops crossing the Rhine in March 1945. British forces liberated Denmark; the Americans advanced to the Czech frontier and stopped to allow the Russians to take Prague as agreed. In Italy by April, resistance was virtually ended; Mussolini had been hanged by partisans. By 25 April, Berlin was surrounded by Russian troops, and on 30 April Hitler committed suicide in his underground bunker; on 7 May Germany surrendered unconditionally to the representatives of Britain, the USA, the USSR and France.

(d)   The Potsdam Conference (July 1945)

It was agreed at Potsdam that:

1   A Council of Foreign Ministers of the 'Big Five' (Britain, the USA, the USSR, France and China) would negotiate settlements with the Axis satellites first and then Germany.
2   Germany would be disarmed, demilitarised and denazified, and would have no central government.
3   The transfer of part of East Prussia to the USSR should be confirmed, as was the Polish administration of territories to the east of the Oder–Neisse line.

29.8 The end of the war with Japan

With the defeat of Germany, the full weight of the Allied effort was turned against Japan. A huge *'island-hopping'* movement was already under way with repeated seaborne assaults on Japanese-held islands. In mid-1944 the Philippines were opened up to the Americans by the victory at Leyte Gulf; Manila finally fell in February 1945. On 1 April American marines landed on Okinawa only 320 miles from Japan, and within bombing distance. Meanwhile, the 'forgotten' Fourteenth Army advanced through Burma taking Mandalay in March and Rangoon in May. An invasion of Malaya was imminent. Then following the Japanese rejection of an ultimatum on 26 July, the first *atomic bomb* was dropped on Hiroshima on 6 August, killing 78,000 people. The USSR hurriedly declared war on Japan as a gesture, on 8 August, the day before the Japanese town of Nagasaki was obliterated. Japan then surrendered unconditionally. Ever since the bombing of Hiroshima, the need to employ atomic bombs has been the subject of a vigorous debate. There were two main motives:

1   *A humanitarian 'short cut'*. The standard view is that the resort to nuclear bombs was necessitated to avoid the unacceptably high casualty rate which would be unavoidably incurred when the Japanese mainland was invaded.
2   *A pre-emptive strike against the USSR*. Since a Soviet declaration of war on Japan was expected, and Soviet territorial gains in the Far East were feared, it was vital that the war should be brought to a speedy conclusion.

29.9 The costs of the war

The impact of the war upon the European civilian populations and economies was immense.

(a)   Death and displacement

Altogether, the total deaths on all fronts probably amounted to 30–40 million. Germany may have lost up to 7 million people although the more moderate estimate is 3.5 million servicemen and 600,000 civilians. Some 20 million Russians died as a result of the war, a million of whom died of starvation in *Leningrad* between 1941 and 1944. Aerial bombardments killed large numbers. In Britain a total of 50,000 died in air-raids but Hamburg, in one week in 1943, lost 243,000 out of a population of 1.5 million while a million fled to the countryside. The brutal and possibly unnecessary fire bombing of

Dresden in February 1945 killed up to 140,000 people. The war also involved a vast movement of people for various reasons; up to 10 million people were 'displaced persons'.

(b) *Physical destruction*

There had been a massive destruction of resources. Especially serious in the post-war years was the damage done to communications. The USSR, for instance, lost 65,000 miles of track, 16,000 locomotives and 430,000 wagons. Germany, however, proved to be remarkably resilient. Because of the work of Albert Speer who had virtual dictatorial control of the economy after the spring of 1942, German armaments production actually tripled despite the bombing. By 1946 the value of fixed German industrial plant was still 14 per cent greater than in 1936. This was the basis of the post-war *'economic miracle'* of Chancellor Adenauer which saw the German Gross National Product (GNP) 125 per cent up on that of 1938.

29.10 Conclusion

The Second World War exhibited none of the 'war to end wars' idealism of the First. The diplomatic dealings of the last months and the growing suspicion between the USSR and her allies suggested that the war would be followed by a difficult period of coexistence in the face of ideological differences, far more evident now that common enemies had been defeated.

Questions

1 Explain the reasons for Germany's defeat in the Second World War.   [OC]
2 Why did the European War of 1939 become the World War of 1941?   [OC]
3 Why was Germany able to defeat so many countries so rapidly between September 1939 and the end of June 1940?   [OX]
4 Why was there no repetition of the 1914–18 prolonged trench warfare during the Second World War?   [OX]
5 Explain the significance of the main developments in warfare in *either* the First World War *or* the Second World War.   [NEAB]
6 'Germany lost the Second World War because she needlessly attacked Russia.' Discuss this statement.   [NEAB]
7 Why did the Second World War in Europe continue so long after the defeat of France in 1940?   [NEAB]
8 Give an account of the German campaigns from April 1940 to the capitulation of France on June 1940. Why was the Vichy government set up in France?   [CAM]
9 Study Sources A and B and then answer the questions which follow.

Source A: Gas practice.

The one thing we were certain of was that the Germans would use poison gas. Babies had gasmasks; horses had gasmasks; both were the same size, except the whole baby went inside, but only the horse's head. The baby's mother had to pump air into it, through a concertina-thing on the side.
Young children had gay blue-and-red ones that looked like Mickey Mouse. Soldiers had very grand hideous ones, with round eyepieces and a long trunk like an elephant. Wardens' were similar, but without the trunk. Ours had a short trunk, and a large window for our eyes. The moment you put it on, the window misted up, blinding you. Our Mums were told to rub soap on the inside of the window to prevent this. It made it harder to see

than ever, and you got soap in your eyes.

There was a rubber washer under your chin, that flipped up and hit you, every time you breathed in. You breathed out with a farting noise round your ears. If you blew really hard, you could make a very loud farting noise indeed. (You got caned for doing that during gas practices.) The bottom of the mask soon filled up with spit, and your face got so hot and sweaty you could have *screamed*.

Once we had our masks tested; we were led through an air-raid shelter that the wardens had filled with tear-gas. Most of us noticed nothing, but Charlie Blower's mask didn't work. He just sat in class all morning with tears streaming down his face, then the teacher sent him home.

The cardboard boxes that gasmasks came in fell apart inside a week. Our dads bought us long metal cylinders like the German soldiers carried their gasmasks in. We used to carry them round on dog-leads across our shoulders. We used gasmasks in fights, whirling them round our heads, swinging them like swords; they could cut your head open, if you didn't dodge. The guy with the most dented gasmask was the hero. We used to carry bottles of ink and sweets and secret treasures inside. When you had a sudden gas practice, this could be very embarrassing.

(a) What sort of factors affect the value of oral records for historians?
(b) Why do you think that there was such an obsession with the use of poison gas as a weapon for use against civilians?
(c) How effective do you think that the precautions outlined here were likely to prove in practice?
Source: From the transcript of a tape recording of a Tyneside man who was aged 10 years at the time of this gas mask drill story. This account is taken from R. Westall, *Children of the Blitz* (Penguin, 1985).

Source B: Operation Barbarossa.

On June 23, 1941, when Hitler drove his armies into Russia, it was twelve months to the day since the signing of the French armistice. In that year he had extended his power to the Black Sea and the Mediterranean and had tightened his grip on Western and Northern Europe, but he had failed in his most important purpose; he had failed to subdue Britain. She had spurned his offer of peace; she had withstood his bombardment and blockade; she had thwarted his plan to unite all Europe under Nazi leadership; she had foiled his efforts to exclude her from the Mediterranean; she had dared to set foot again on the Continent at a time and place most awkward for him; and she had driven him at last into the desperate and hazardous expedient of attacking Russia as the only means of freeing or securing the military and economic resources necessary for him to wage effective war against her. When he attacked in the West in 1940, he had been able to guard his eastern frontier with a Non-Aggression Pact and seven divisions, when he attacked in the East in 1941, he felt obliged to guard the Atlantic coastline against British intervention with 49 divisions.

(a) Trace the steps by which Hitler had extended his power 'to the Black Sea and the Mediterranean' (lines 2–3) during the year preceding his invasion of Russia.
(b) Why had Hitler failed to 'subdue Britain' (line 4)?
(c) With reference to the German campaigns in Russia, comment upon the extent to which the invasion proved a 'desperate and hazardous expedient' (lines 8–9).
(d) Would you agree that Britain's resistance had 'driven' (lines 8–9) Hitler to invade Russia? Did Hitler have another reason?   [OC]
Source: Chester Wilmot, *The Struggle for Europe* (Collins, 1952).

30 Post-war Europe and the Cold War 1945–53

Introduction

The post-war problems of *reconstruction* and of achieving satisfactory settlements with the defeated states were confused by the growing divisions between the Allies. The defeat and overthrow of the fascist dictatorships by no means meant that democracy was triumphant. However, there is a difference of opinion between historians over the causes and nature of the growing rift between the USSR and USA. On the one hand, there is the view that the so-called 'Cold War', a war carried on by all methods short of outright fighting, arose out of the conflict of new twentieth-century ideologies. On the other hand, there is the argument that this was just yet another episode in the long-standing pattern of distrust between Russia and the West, with the USA now playing the anti-Russian role.

30.1 The preliminary government of Germany and Austria

By the time the arrangements made at *Yalta* and *Potsdam* (see Sections 29.7(b) and 29.7 (d)) came to be applied, Roosevelt was dead and Churchill was out of office.

(a) *The occupation of Germany*

Germany was divided into four zones of occupation, governed by the power which had effective military control in the area. The Russian zone extended from the new western frontier to a line through the centre of Germany. A French zone was carved out of the British and American zones. In each zone the governing authority was the commander-in-chief. A central Control Council in Berlin could deal with matters of common concern. The arrangements for Berlin itself, physically in the zone of the USSR were a microcosm of those arrangements, with four sectors of occupation and with a central four-power *Kommandantura*.

(b) *The principles of the occupation*

The main objectives had been established at Potsdam:

1   *Demilitarisation.* Germany was completely disarmed. It was also accepted that

there should be some deindustrialisation, and the USSR in particular dismantled factories and industrial equipment and removed them.

2   *Denazification.* All Nazi organisations were dissolved and thousands of suspects interrogated and imprisoned. The major Nazi leaders were tried at Nuremburg in *1946*, although Goering, Goebbels and Himmler all committed suicide. The sick, 92-year-old Hess died in Spandau Prison in 1987, his release blocked to the end by the USSR.

3   *Democratisation.* The zones were divided into *Länder*, each with an elected and responsible system of government. From January 1947 the British and American zones were reintegrated for economic purposes, and given a *Joint Economic Council.* However, France – and especially the USSR – opposed any idea of a central government because of their fears of a revitalised Germany.

Immediately, the situation was chaotic. Cities, trade and industry were in ruins and confusion. There was a very real danger of starvation and a critical shortage of medical supplies. The situation was vastly worsened by the burden of 12 million displaced persons, mostly foreign workers and Sudetenland refugees. The currency system had utterly collapsed, and for a time cigarettes were the main medium of exchange.

(c)   *The settlement with Austria*

A Russian attempt to establish a provisional government with some communists in key positions was rejected in April 1945. Instead, a Central Council and a Joint *Kommandantura* were established, as in Germany. However, free elections were held in late 1945 and a new government under Dr Figl, a graduate of Dachau, was recognised by all of the Allies. It was given a reasonably free hand in reconstruction, but not until 1955 did a formal peace treaty establish full independence and the boundaries of 1938, but with a ban on union with Germany.

30.2 The post-war settlements

The Council of Foreign Ministers drafted settlements with all of the other states at the Peace Conference of Paris in July–October 1946, and at a session of the United Nations. The treaties were signed in February 1947. The main principle was ostensibly national self-determination, but a vital factor was the interests of the occupying power.

(a)   *Italy*

Italy was under Anglo-American occupation. She was subjected to considerable disarmament and demilitarisation. Her colonies were passed to the UN, and given independence. Albania was also restored to full independence. The Dodecanese islands were ceded to Greece, and some Alpine territory to France. There was, however, a conflict of interests between Italy and Yugoslavia over Trieste and Istria, and not until 1954 did this reach a solution with the port of Trieste going to Yugoslavia and the peninsula of Istria to Italy.

(b)   *Eastern central Europe*

1   *The territorial settlement.* Russia's main interest was the establishment of a chain of dependent buffer states. Czechoslovakia, Poland and the three Baltic States were

re-established. There were also a series of transfers of territory:

– *Rumania* lost Bessarabia and Bukovina to Russia and the southern Dobrudja to Bulgaria.
– *Hungary* lost Transylvania back to Rumania, but Ruthenia was ceded to Russia rather than returned to Czechoslovakia, so leaving Russia with a common frontier with Hungary.
– *Poland* was confirmed in her possession of East Prussia up to the Oder–Neisse line, which included the Silesian industrial complex. By this rearrangement she gained from Germany about a fifth of her pre-war territory. This transfer involved the expulsion or flight of 9 million Germans from the region.
– *Russia* retained the rest of East Prussia and Polish territories up the old Curzon Line. The price paid by Poland for her German gains was about a half of her pre-war territory and a third of the population.

In addition, Russia took the Karelia peninsula from Finland as well as northern territories which excluded Finland from the Arctic and gave Russia a common frontier with Norway.

3   The *Danube Control Commission*. The vital issue of control of the Danube was entrusted by the Council of Foreign Ministers to a conference of the interested states. The effect was that the waterway fell under Russian influence, since all of the states meeting at Belgrade in June 1948 were within the Soviet sphere.

(c)   *Assessment of the settlement*

In many ways, the settlements compared favourably to those after the First World War, but there were three vital differences:

1   *A much greater symmetry was achieved between states and ethnic divisions.* Of course by 1945 the authors of the settlement were considerably helped by the large-scale movement of German refugees from Poland and Czechoslovakia.
2   *Direct punishment was minimised.* There was no war guilt clause, although armed forces were limited and there was provision for some relatively mild reparation.
3   *The states of eastern central Europe enjoyed only the fiction of democratic government.* Where the Bolsheviks had failed in the post-revolutionary period, Stalin had succeeded through the Red Army because eastern central Europe was now under Soviet domination.

30.3 The United Nations (see Fig. 30.1)

As in 1918, war provoked attempts to establish a much more ordered world. The United Nations Organisation (UN) was the outcome.

(a)   *The origins of the United Nations*

There were two specific influences towards international co-operation:

1   *The experience of the League of Nations.* Whatever its failures, the League was seen to have been based on sound principles. Even in 1938 Churchill described it as 'the wisest, the most noble, the most sane and the most practical path' towards the avoidance of war.
2   *Allied co-operation.* The conduct of the war stimulated hopes of post-war

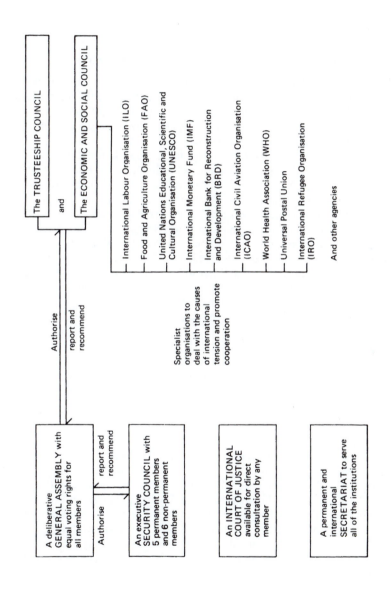

The TRUSTEESHIP COUNCIL

and

The ECONOMIC AND SOCIAL COUNCIL

Authorise

report and recommend

A deliberative GENERAL ASSEMBLY with equal voting rights for all members

Authorise

report and recommend

An executive SECURITY COUNCIL with 5 permanent members and 6 non-permanent members

An INTERNATIONAL COURT OF JUSTICE available for direct consultation by any member

A permanent and international SECRETARIAT to serve all of the institutions

Specialist organisations to deal with the causes of international tension and promote cooperation

International Labour Organisation (ILO)

Food and Agriculture Organisation (FAO)

United Nations Educational, Scientific and Cultural Organisation (UNESCO)

International Monetary Fund (IMF)

International Bank for Reconstruction and Development (BRD)

International Civil Aviation Organisation (ICAO)

World Health Association (WHO)

Universal Postal Union

International Refugee Organisation (IRO)

And other agencies

Fig. 30.1 The structure of the United Nations

co-operation. The Atlantic Charter of 1941 implied some sort of organisation, and in 1942 26 states adhered to the Charter. A scheme was worked out at Dumbarton Oaks in Washington in 1944; then in April–June 1945 a general conference of the UN at San Francisco with 51 members present drew up the UN Charter which was deliberately separated from the post-war settlement. The international headquarters were established in New York.

(b) *The structure of the UN*

The principal organs of the UN were very similar to those of the League:

1 *The General Assembly.* The Assembly is a consultative body meeting annually. It elects the non-permanent members of the Security Council and the members of its major sub-organisations. It also decides on the admission of new members. Originally, membership was limited to those who had declared war against Germany, but other members could be elected.
2 *The Security Council.* The Security Council functions continuously. It has eleven members. The USA, USSR, France, Britain and China are permanent members, and another six are elected by the General Assembly. Each of the five permanent members has the power to *veto* any issue.
3 *The specialist organisations.* The UN is served by its own bureaucracy, the Secretariat, a multinational organisation which supplies personnel to serve it and its specialist sub-organisations. These include particularly the International Court of Justice (dealing with legal disputes over treaties and aspects of international law), the Trusteeship Council (with responsibility for mandated territories) and the Economic and Social Council (which was established to promote international co-operation on a wide spread of issues). This latter has associated with it a very wide range of agencies concerned with finance, health, labour organisation, agriculture and food and refugees.

(c) *Evaluation of the UN*

In fact, many of the weaknesses of the League were carried over to the UN:

1 *The absence of an independent sanction.* Churchill demanded that 'we ... arm our world organisation', but in fact the UN relies upon contributions of contingents of troops by its members and is as limited in its exercise of economic sanctions as the League.
2 *The veto.* The veto was supposed to be a medium for the protection of national sovereignty. In fact, it has been used for very different reasons by both the USA and the USSR especially. In 1950, the provision for the veto was amended so that it could be overriden by a vote of two-thirds of the Assembly if aggression was involved.
3 *A wide membership.* The admission of new members became a matter of rivalry between the USA and USSR after the war. In addition, the process of *decolonisation* produced a doubling of the original 51 members by 1961 and the problem that many of the new members saw the UN as a forum in which to play off the two superpowers against each other.

30.4 The onset of the Cold War

The lines between the western democracies and the USSR were already being drawn in the later years of the war. However between the end of the Second World War and the

Korean War of 1950–3, these divisions became more and more fundamental and apparent. This is due to:

1 Changed circumstances in Europe itself which made it more vulnerable to ideological splits.
2 The ideological and security ambitions of the USSR which arose from the war.
3 The assumption by the USA of a much more interventionist role in European affairs.

30.5 Post-war Europe

Two factors especially made Europe vulnerable to ideological extremism:

(a) *Economic dislocation*

Europe was economically shattered by the war, and suffering from a large adverse balance of trade while seeking to re-equip for production. The danger was that this situation would lead to violence and extremism. Financial help was vital to 'jump the gap' and maintain stability.

(b) *A changed balance of power*

There was a pronounced imbalance of power on the continent after 1945:

1 *The weakening of the western democracies.* France was considerably weakened by the occupation and the war, but the cost of victory had been too great for Britain who was no longer in reality the equal of the USA and the USSR. The 'big Germany' which had dominated central Europe no longer existed. In addition, the influence of popular opinion could not be ignored, and this led to a lack of consistency in policy as governments changed. One result was the over rapid demobilisation of western forces to 'bring the boys back'. In France and Italy the *communists* enjoyed considerable electoral support, and so they could be seen as vulnerable democracies.
2 *The ambitions of the USSR.* Russian motives were twofold:

– The strengthening of national security to prevent a recurrence of the trauma which had just been endured. This involved the building up of a barrier of satellite states and annexed territories, and the retarding of German recovery.
– The renewal of the support for international revolution signalled by the establishment of the Cominform in 1947 to replace the old Comintern which had been symbolically abolished in 1943.

Through her military occupation of eastern central Europe and her ability to manipulate internal communist groups, the USSR could pursue both objectives at the same time.

30.6 Soviet expansionism (see Illus. 30.1)

Russian activities took different forms, according to the circumstances.

SEE FOR YOURSELF. IS IT NOT OBVIOUS THAT THEY ARE "DEMOCRATIC GOVERNMENTS WHICH ENJOY THE CONFIDENCE OF THE OVERWHELMING MAJORITY OF THE PEOPLE OF THESE COUNTRIES"?

From a cartoon 'Behind the Curtain', in the *Evening Standard*, 1948: Molotov is trying to persuade Bevin and Byrnes that Russia's treatment of eastern Europe was not contrary to the promises made in the wartime agreements and post-war treaties.
Source: P. Lane, *Europe Since 1945* (Batsford, 1985) p. 43.

(a) *'Integration'*

In the states where the Russian army was in military control, puppet régimes were established and democratic opposition was eliminated. This was achieved without any pretence at free elections in Poland, Bulgaria and Rumania. Only in Hungary and Czechoslovakia were free elections held, and the most the communists won was 38 per cent of the vote in the latter country. In both countries, democratically chosen governments were ousted in favour of communist-dominated ministries.

The typical approach to dealing with non-communist oppositions was the so-called 'salami technique', as displayed by Rakosi in Hungary. The secret of success was to whittle away the alternative political groups and gradually assume control of the various institutions of power. The Kings of Bulgaria and Rumania were retained for some time to preserve a façade of normality. Violence was necessary only on special occasions, as in February 1948 when Jan Masaryk's unlikely fall from a window (somewhat of a political tradition in Bohemia) removed a likely leader of resistance to the establishment of dictatorship in Czechoslovakia. Even so, there was a difference in attitude between local 'home-grown' communists like Gomulka (in Poland), Kádár (in Hungary) and Tito (in Yugoslavia) and hard-line Stalinists returning with the Red Army, as were Dimitrov (of Bulgaria), Rákosi (of Hungary) and Ulbricht (of East Germany).

(b) *Subversion*

Where Russian forces were not in full control, other methods were resorted to:

1   *Yugoslavia.* The liberation of Belgrade had been very much the achievement of the partisan forces led by Marshal Tito. Crude attempts by the Russians to establish control contributed to a growing rift between Tito and the USSR from the spring of 1948. One effect was a tightening of the grasp of Russia over the rest of eastern Europe because of the danger of 'infection' by the very independent variety of Titoist communism (see Section 32.1(a)).

2   *Iran.* From August 1941 both Britain and the USSR had forces in Iran, whose oil was vital to the war effort. At the end of the war the Russians persistently refused to evacuate and encouraged an internal separatist revolt by the communist *Tudeh* in Azerbaijan in August 1945. Not until March 1946 did the USSR withdraw her forces, when the full control of the central government of Iran was finally restored.

3   *Greece.* Athens had been liberated by the British who suppressed a communist revolt then held free elections in March 1946 which resulted in a monarchist victory. A civil war followed in which the Greek communists were supported by the USSR, Yugoslavia and Bulgaria. The presence of British forces staved off the establishment of communist control, but in early 1947 the British government announced that it could no longer maintain the burden of the defence of Greece alone. Britain's withdrawal from Greece would leave a power vacuum in the eastern Mediterranean, and this was made even more glaring by the Soviet threat to Turkey. As early as March 1946, Stalin had made it clear to the US ambassador:

> Turkey is weak and the Soviet Union is very conscious of the danger of foreign control of the Straits which Turkey is not strong enough to protect. The Turkish government is unfriendly to us. That is why the Soviet government has demanded a base in the Dardanelles. It is a matter of our own security.

30.7 The USA and 'containment'

President Truman was far more prepared to utilise American power to protect Europe against the communist threat which was apparent not only there but also in China and South East Asia. American influence was very much based upon her vast technological superiority in the sphere of atomic weapons. In fact, in 1946 (by the Baruch Plan) the USA had proposed to surrender her monopoly to a UN International Atomic Development Authority, but the scheme was rejected by the USSR. In April 1947, in response to the British announcement (see Section 30.6(b)) Truman obtained from Congress a sum of $4 million to assist Greece and Turkey against communism.

In March 1947, he had declared: 'I believe it must be the policy of the United States to support free peoples who are resisting subjugation by armed minorities or by outside pressures. I believe that we must assist free peoples to work out their own destinies in their own ways.'

(a) *The Marshall Plan (June 1947)*

The *'Truman Doctrine'* was the justification for considerable injections of American money into European economic recovery to counteract the development of social and political unrest. In June 1947, the American Secretary of State General Marshall launched a plan which involved a total of £1300 million in the first year alone. European countries in receipt of *Marshall Aid* matched it with their own funds for economic recovery. In 1948, the Organisation for European Economic Co-operation (OEEC) was established to achieve the maximum benefit from the finance. The response of the USSR was, however, unfavourable:

1   *The economic recovery of Germany and Austria was unattractive.* Even before the Marshall Plan the USA had been assisting the German recovery in the western zones.
2   *The scheme was suspected of imperialist intentions.* It was very easy to see the aid as being a method of binding the recipients politically to the USA. The economic development of Europe also served American business interests well, by initiating an inflation of the European market for US goods. The result was that the USSR rejected the offer of aid which was also open to her and her satellite states. Instead, she established her own Council for Mutual Economic Aid (COMECON) in 1949.

30.8 The German Question

The positions of the two sides hardened over the issue of Germany. Britain wanted German reunification from the start in the interests of economic recovery, and initially the USSR had supported this because of the possibility of electoral success for the German communists. France had opposed a strong central government because of her fear of a restored Germany. From late 1945, when it was clear that the appeal of communism had been exaggerated, the USSR pursued instead a policy of resistance to reunification and retardation of economic recovery. The result was the progressive breakdown of the four-power co-operation over the control of Germany.

(a)   *The Berlin Airlift (June 1948–May 1949)*

In a step towards the re-establishment of a German government Britain, France and the USA created a new German currency, but the Russians insisted that only the Russian-printed East marks would be acceptable in Berlin. The western Allies would accept the East mark only alongside their own *Deutschmark* in the western zones of Berlin. The Russians responded by closing the Berlin *Kommandatur* and trying to isolate Berlin. The western Allies responded with a huge airlift to call the bluff of USSR; for 318 days a regular air ferry service carried a total of 1.5 million tons of supplies up to a maximum of 12,000 tons a day. Finally the USSR gave way, and allowed communications to be reopened.

The blockade led to a considerable hardening of attitudes. On 11 June 1948, it was Senator Arthur Vandenberg, a one-time leading isolationist, who proposed in the US Senate a resolution calling for the US government to act within Article 51 of the UN Charter and employ force where necessary to maintain US national security.

(b)   *The partition of Germany (1949)*

In April 1949 the three western Allies agreed to the creation of a German State from their zones with a federal system of eleven *Länder*. Elections were held in August and Chancellor *Konrad Adenauer* formed a government in September. The Russian response was to establish an independent republic in the Soviet zone in October 1949. The result was that while Germany was being reintegrated into Europe it was as a divided country. In *1955* the *German Federal Republic* and the *German Democratic Republic* were recognised as sovereign states by their respective sponsors.

(c) German rearmament

In 1954, as part of the movement towards an integrated European defence system (see Section 30.9(b)), West Germany was freed from occupation, and she was permitted to raise a force of twelve divisions, an air force of 75,000 men and a small coastal naval force. The USSR condemned this final restoration of West Germany to the European community, but responded by rearming East Germany as part of the Warsaw Pact (see Section 30.9(b)).

30.9 Regional Defence Organisations

Not only was the defence of western Europe against communism an aspect of economic development and European economic integration (see Section 31.7), it was more positively promoted by military agreements which reflected a degree of lack of faith in the capacity of the UN.

(a) The North Atlantic Treaty Organisation (April 1949)

The *Atlantic Pact* of April 1949 established a defensive alliance between Britain, France, Belgium, Holland, Luxembourg, Norway, Denmark, Ireland, Portugal, Italy, the USA and Canada. In 1952, Greece and Turkey were admitted, and West Germany in 1955. NATO was seen as a specific guarantee against the expansion of Russian power in Europe. Backed by American nuclear power and conventional resources, the Supreme Commander has always been an American; there is similar provision for naval coordination of the various contingents. The formation of NATO also affirmed the dissolution of the old wartime alliance. By 1950 NATO had fourteen divisions and 1000 aircraft against the 175 communist divisions and 20,000 aircraft. However, behind this 'shield' was the 'sword' of US atomic power.

(b) The Western European Union (1954)

In May 1948, Britain, France, Belgium, Holland and Luxembourg had created the *Western European Union* (WEU) to provide for economic and military co-operation. Between 1950 and 1954 there were moves towards the establishment of a unified European army. However French resistance to the loss of sovereignty involved led to the rejection of the treaty which would have established a European Defence Community in August 1954. The alternative route was followed instead, with the extension of the European Union in 1954 to include Germany and Italy. In the following year the USSR responded with the *Warsaw Pact*, a military alliance between it and its satellites including East Germany.

30.10 The Korean War (1950–3)

By 1949 the Chinese Communist Party led by *Mao Tse-Tung* had established the *People's Republic of China* with Soviet backing. In 1948, *Korea* had been divided into an American supported republic to the south of the 38th parallel and the People's Republic to the north backed by the USSR and the Chinese Communists. Following the withdrawal of American forces the North Korean army invaded South Korea. With the USSR boycotting the Security Council over a separate issue, it could not veto a proposal for intervention by a UN force. The result was a war between largely American forces and North Korea which involved a counter-attack which carried across the Chinese frontier. China intervened openly and the USA considered a resort to nuclear weapons. In fact the frontier stabilised again at the original line and a settlement was finally achieved in July 1953, although a formal peace was never signed.

30.11 Conclusion

The Cold War had developed into an open confrontation. However the next few years were to see a thawing into a period of 'peaceful coexistence'. This was partly a result of the achievement of a nuclear balance; in November 1952 the USA exploded the first hydrogen bomb, to be followed by the USSR nine months later. It was also in part a result of a positive change in personnel and policies with the death of Stalin in 1953 and the greater preoccupation of the USSR with its own internal problems and control of its satellites while from 1952 with the election of General Eisenhower to the presidency the Republican administration was less positive in its policy of containment. The relaxation of tension in Europe was partly also a result of the transfer of the ideological struggle into the areas of the world where the painful process of decolonisation was developing.

Questions

1 Explain the aims of Soviet policy in eastern Europe between 1945 and 1955? How far were they achieved? [OC]
2 Account for the rapid spread of communism in eastern Europe after the Second World War. [OC]
3 How have East–West relations been affected: (a) by the conferences at Yalta and Potsdam; (b) the Truman Doctrine and the Marshall Plan; (c) the Berlin blockade; (d) NATO and the Warsaw Pact? [NEAB]
4 Why was Berlin partitioned in 1945 and blockaded in 1948? [NEAB]
5 Describe the contribution of the USSR from 1942 to 1945 to the defeat of Germany and her allies. Why were communist governments set up in so many eastern European countries in 1945–8? [CAM]
6 Outline the arrangements made by the Allies to rule Germany after 1945, and describe how these were changed to allow the emergence of East Germany and West Germany by 1950. [CAM]
7 Why did the 'Grand Alliance' against the Axis powers break up so quickly after the Second World War? [CAM]
8 Describe and account for the development of the Cold War.
9 Study the Sources A and B and then answer the questions which follow.

Source A: The Cold War.

I have always worked for friendship with Russia, but, like you, I feel deep anxiety because of their misinterpretation of the Yalta decisions, their attitudes towards Poland, their overwhelming influence in the Balkans, excepting Greece, the difficulties they make about Vienna, the combination of Russian power and the territories under their control or occupied, coupled with the Communist technique in so many other countries, and above all their power to maintain very large armies in the field for a long time. What will be the position in a year or two, when the British and American Armies have melted, and when Russia may choose to keep two or three hundred divisions on active service?

An iron curtain is drawn upon their front. We do not know what is going on behind. There seems little doubt that the whole of the regions east of the line Lubeck–Trieste–Corfu will soon be completely in their hands.

Meanwhile the attention of our peoples will be occupied in inflicting severities upon Germany, which is ruined and prostrate, and it would be open to the Russians in a very short time to advance if they chose to the waters of the North Sea and the Atlantic.

(a) What was the Russian 'misinterpretation of the Yalta decision' (line 2)? Why was Churchill anxious?

(b) How had Russia achieved an 'overwhelming influence in the Balkans' (lines 2–3)? What were 'the difficulties they make about Vienna' (lines 3–4)?

(c) Explain the reference to 'the Communist technique in so many other countries' (line 5).

(d) What measures were taken between 1945 and 1949 to prevent a Russian advance 'to the waters of the North Sea and the Atlantic' (lines 13–14)? [OC]

Source: A telegram from Winston Churchill to Harry Truman, 12 May 1945.

Source B: Peaceful aspirations or expansionist tendencies?

Mr. Churchill now takes the stand of the warmongers, and in this Mr. Churchill is not alone. He has friends not only in Britain but in the United States of America as well.

A point to be noted is that in this respect Mr. Churchill and his friends bear a striking resemblance to Hitler and his friends ... Mr. Churchill sets out to unleash war with a race theory, asserting that only English-speaking nations are superior nations, who are called upon to decide the destinies of the entire world ...

The following circumstances should not be forgotten. The Germans made their invasion of the USSR through Finland, Poland, Rumania, Bulgaria and Hungary. The Germans were able to make their invasion through these countries because at the time, governments hostile to the Soviet Union existed in these countries. As a result of the German invasion, in the fighting and through the deportation of Soviet citizens to German servitude, the Soviet Union has lost a total of about seven million people. In other words, the Soviet Union's loss of life has been several times greater than that of Britain and the United States of America put together. Possibly in some quarters an inclination is felt to forget about these colossal sacrifices of the Soviet people which secured the liberation of Europe from the Hitlerite yoke. But the Soviet Union cannot forget about them. And so what is surprising about the fact that the Soviet Union, anxious for its future safety, is trying to ensure that governments loyal in their attitude to the Soviet Union should exist in these countries? How can anyone, who has not taken leave of his senses, describe these peaceful aspirations of the Soviet Union as expansionist tendencies on the part of our state?

(a) To what extent would you agree with Stalin's view that Churchill was, like Hitler, motivated by a racial theory?

(b) What other circumstances increased the effectiveness of the German invasion of the USSR?

(c) How would you seek to discredit Stalin's concern about loss of life and the 'colossal sacrifices of the Soviet people'?

Source: From a speech by Stalin in response to the 'Iron Curtain' speech by Winston Churchill.

31 | European Decolonisation

Introduction

The word 'decolonisation' seems to date back only to the 1950s. However, the process started before 1939. The Treaty of Versailles marked the territorial zenith of European imperialism. When the reverse process started it gathered a momentum which culminated in a scramble as great as in the creation of empire in the late nineteenth century. As with that development it is important to think as much in terms of the changing status and internal politics of the metropolitan countries as the peripheral pressures in the colonies. Essentially what was happening was that the equilibrium established in imperial relationships began to fail. Decolonisation was by no means a regular and progressive development. There were delays, setbacks and occasional imperial revivals, and the pace and pattern varied between the different imperial systems. No two situations were ever alike.

31.1 Colonialism in a changing world (1918–39)

The Great War and post-war economic circumstances certainly obliged European imperial powers to reconsider their relationship with their colonies. Equilibrium was being disturbed and adjustments were needed. However, the imperial relationship was not necessarily doomed. Four factors especially threatened the balance:

(a) *Population growth*

Demographic expansion was the most prevalent feature of colonial societies in this period. In India, for example, the population grew from 294.4 million in 1901 to 352.8 million in 1931. The two main causes were:

1 *An improved infrastructure* in terms of transport systems and political stability which undermined the cyclical pattern of shortage and famine and evened out supply.
2 *The application of western medicine* reduced the death rate while the birth rate continued to grow.

However, the colonial authorities were too deeply involved in a balance with the established native élites to reform the agrarian and landowning systems to match this population growth.

(b) Emergence of a colonial bourgeoisie

Colonial nationalism was based on the aspirations of ambitious native middle classes rather than on worker or peasant mass movements. In particular there were two groups:

1   *Westernised bureaucrats* or 'native clerks' appeared in large numbers especially in Asia from the 1880s. By the 1920s their frustrated ambitions made them a major force in the growth of the Indian *National Congress*.
2   *Large scale native capitalists* were encouraged by the conditions of the First World War. These entrepreneurial 'family houses' were often opposed to government policies.

These were marginal and vulnerable groups in colonial society. They had rising expectations but could easily be thrust back into destitution. They were westernised and did not, as yet, conceive of the possibility of the rejection of European control.

(c) A religious revival

Native faiths, and especially Islam, were increasingly assertive and anti-western. In Burma and the Dutch East Indies, for instance, this took the form of established religious faiths, Buddhism and Islam, resisting the encroachment of other faiths and threats to religious purity; and they merged easily with national revival.

(d) The failure of economic complementarity

The economic recession of the inter-war years exaggerated these problems. As industrial and agricultural prices diverged the interaction between western capitalism and the satellite economies began to threaten rather than heighten individual expectations. For instance:

1   *Direct industrial competition* from producers who established facilities in colonies to avoid protectionist duties stimulated the growth of urban proletariats and challenged the native producers.
2   *Commodity price declines* and competition with European plantations forced peasants into mere subsistence production and shocked their material expectations, as in Malaya and the Dutch East Indies.

31.2 Models of imperial reform

The British took the lead in experimenting with alternative models of imperial relationship.

(a) Rule by proxy

The Anglo-Egyptian Settlement of 1922, stimulated by the anti-European riots of 1919 resulting from the impact of wartime controls, was a good example of indirect rule through the medium of a preferred élite. In this case it was the landed class of Egypt and the Wafd nationalist party. The alternative was the expense of force, and the danger of driving the peasants and notables together. The protectorate was ended but Britain retained control of foreign policy and other key issues, and the right of occupation was guaranteed.

(b) Divide and rule

India was the critical base for British power in Asia. By the 1920s and 1930s the consensus rule established with the main social groups was being challenged by Gandhi's Congress nationalism and the Muslim Khilafat movement. The legislation of 1935 was the culmination of a series of constitutional reforms. It established the all-India Federation and promised self government. On the other hand, the identification of separate communal electorates was readily seen as an attempt to exploit the differences. Despite Congress electoral successes in 1937 it refused to cooperate, and the British turned to direct rule by the provincial governors.

(c) Symbolism and economic benefits

The Statute of Westminster (1931) was a successful attempt to blunt the anti-imperial sentiment in the white Dominions by:

1 *Stressing unifying symbols* such as the Monarchy whilst granting full parliamentary autonomy.
2 *Strengthening the economic benefits* of Commonwealth membership, at a time when American isolationism removed the possibility of an alternative focus.

(d) Indirect rule and trusteeship

It was fear of the effects of segregationism in South Africa on the relationship with the black African subjects of British colonies which led to the curious combination of a cautious opposition to economic development and the policies of:

1 *Indirect rule* through legitimate traditional native authorities whilst employing the prestige, symbols and sanctions of imperial power. This approach, modelled on the concept outlined by Lord Lugard in *The Dual Mandate in British Tropical Africa* (1922), was employed particularly in West Africa.
2 *'Trusteeship'* was more prevalent in East Africa where there were substantial groups of white settlers and some form of compromise was necessary. 'Native paramountcy' was based on the Devonshire Declaration of 1923 and was a guarantee against demands for settler control.

31.3 The impact of the Second World War

The war demonstrated the sort of massive efforts which imperial co-ordination could produce, but also substantially reduced the chance of the survival of empires.

(a) The Japanese Revolution

The astonishing Japanese victories and the occupation had irreversible consequences:

1 *European colonialism seriously 'lost face'* as a result of episodes like the fall of Singapore and the humiliating occupation of French Indo-China.
2 *The organisation of nationalist groups* was encouraged both by the Japanese, as with the sponsorship of Sukarno and of militarist youth organisations in Indonesia, and in reaction against them, as in Malaya.
3 *A model of successful jungle warfare* was set, and reinforced the views of revolutionaries such as Ho Chi Minh and Mao Tse-Tung.

4   *The experience of local freedom* from control would make the re-establishment of imperial power so much more difficult. In Indo-China the Viet Minh were left to establish their rural strongholds while the French were distracted.

The new nationalism was most obvious in Indo-China where in the 1945 August Revolution the Viet Minh occupied Hanoi as the French began to return in force.

(b)   *The impact of imperial mobilisation*

The British Empire fought on on the basis of mobilised colonial resources, and with two consequences for its future:

1   *A stimulus to colonial economic growth* involving the encouragement of cash crops in Africa, the move towards the production of capital goods by Indian industrialists and the transformation of the infrastructure of Egypt.
2   *Inflationary pressures* benefited the urban and rural élites who opposed attempts to install price controls, increased the grievances of the urban middle classes who were vulnerable to grain speculation and deprived the peasantry of the light consumer goods which they had started to enjoy before the war.

(c)   *The Anglo-American alliance*

There were two motives present in the policy of Roosevelt towards the imperial regions:

1   *The pursuit of a world role.* The war allowed the USA to break monopolistic positions held by Britain as in Saudi Arabia and China by matching US interests with anti-colonial nationalism. Hence Roosevelt's support for Chiang Kai-shek.
2   *Belief in a world of universal democracy.* There was a lot of American antagonism towards Britain, and the Atlantic Charter of 1941 was a means of converting American public opinion to support for what had been seen as an imperial war.

By 1945 the USA was beginning to see the merit of empire in terms of maintaining stability in the face of the threat of communism. This transition was carried through to its awful, logical conclusion in the war in Vietnam.

31.4 Decolonisation in Asia (1945–54)

The withdrawal of Britain, France and Holland from their Asian colonies must be seen in the context of the growing successes of Chinese communism against the American backed nationalists. Their Asian colonies were the main imperial bases of their diplomatic and military power.

(a)   *Independence and partition in India*

By 1945 pressure of defence commitments, the failing morale of the Indian administration and a Labour electoral victory in Britain meant that some form of decolonisation was virtually inevitable. The key features of the process were:

1   *Political manoeuvring* by Congress and Muslim leaders to maximise their power after independence. The former expected that an independent Pakistan would not survive, so accepted it as a short term necessity. The latter talked the British into desperation.

2   *Increasing communal violence*, partly encouraged to force the British to recognise communal rights and partly resulting from the British insistence on a quick withdrawal.
3   *The deadline* of August 1947 was set by the last Viceroy Lord Mountbatten for a total withdrawal rather than the staged withdrawal with adequate, but expensive military security, proposed by his predecessor Lord Wavell.

The new states of Pakistan and India were born in the midst of violence and confusion, with up to 500,000 deaths and 12 million people made homeless. A number of serious problems were also bequeathed, especially the status of the Punjab and Kashmir. The latter was to be the cause of wars between the two states and the former was the cause of terrorism within India.

(b)   *The Dutch East Indies*

Dutch attempts to hold their position by means of a combination of military 'pacification' and an attempt to buy the support of moderate nationalists with the promise of a federation and local rule failed because:

1   *The prospect of a Dutch 'sell out'* meant that the moderates were always uncertain allies.
2   *The USA put pressure on Holland* to concentrate on reconstruction in Europe, and regarded the Sukarno-led republicans as a potential bulwark against communism.

The granting of independence to the new state of Indonesia had a bitter after taste because Sukarno was to turn to military adventurism in the area in the 1950s and 1960s to distract the population from internal problems.

(c)   *Indo China*

Initially, the French negotiated with the Viet Minh but in November 1946 bombarded Haiphong and in 1947 occupied Hanoi in the belief that that would shock the Viet Minh leadership into making concessions. In fact a prolonged war resulted.

1   *France was committed to restoration* as one means of re-establishing national self respect and strengthening the French voice in the post-war world.
2   *The nature and strength of the Viet Minh had been misjudged.* They controlled much of the countryside, especially in Tonkin, and were backed by a broad social coalition which included all elements, but especially the classes in the making. They enjoyed genuine support, but were equally prepared to use intimidation and cynical alliances with the established social élites.
3   *The absence of any alternative* because the so-called 'Bao Dai solution' which involved a coalition of moderate nationalists headed by the former emperor of Vietnam was not endorsed by the French.
4   *The Chinese communist victory* in 1949 meant that the French would attract American support for what could now be seen as a war for democracy and not just colonialism. At the same time the anti-communist factions would co-operate all the more enthusiastically because of the threat that faced them if the French were defeated.

By 1953 there were 230,000 French troops in Indo China. Their failure to contain a mobile guerrilla war, interspersed with the defeat of isolated French garrisons, culminated in the great defeat at Dien Bien Phu on 7 May 1954 by General Nguyen Giap. At Geneva in 1954 the partition of Indo China was agreed, but by then the USA had become heavily involved in the area. From 1964 their commitment of forces expanded considerably in a war which was to continue until 1973 when the US troops were withdrawn from a conflict in which 55,000 of them had died. The Republic of South Vietnam finally fell in 1975.

(d) The war of the Running Dogs

British attempts to establish a Malayan Union which would give equal rights to the Chinese and Indian elements were thwarted by the conservative Malay community, and the Malayan Federation which replaced it blocked the aspirations of youthful Chinese. The importance of Malaya to the British was as a key strategic location and as an area rich in natural resources which could make a vital contribution to British monetary stability. The result was the undertaking of a counter insurgency campaign against the Chinese Malayan Communist Party terrorists. The classic campaign co-ordinated by General Gerald Templar, who combined both military and civil power, involved the resettlement of Chinese squatters, the use of air strikes and patrols to break supply routes, and 're-education'. The campaign reached its peak in 1950–2 and by 1954 the Emergency was virtually over although it was not revoked until 1957. The independent *Federation of Malaya* which was established was underpinned by Malay conservatives and Chinese business classes. This textbook victory misled the Americans. In Malaya the guerrillas were the enemies of the rural peasantry, and were not absorbed into the village communities as readily as in Vietnam.

31.5 East of Suez

There seemed a strong possibility that Britain would retain her position in the Middle East. By 1956 she was eliminated as a power in the region and forced to reconsider her status as a world power. Nationalism, American influence and inherent British weaknesses all worked in the same direction.

(a) The end of the Palestine Mandate

In 1947 Britain totally reversed policy and abandoned Palestine to the certainty of partition between Jews and Arabs. This was due to:

1   *The strengthening of Zionism* as a result of the Holocaust. The Jewish lobby in the USA was especially influential. Britain played into its hands by turning back refugee ships from Europe in 1946 at Haifa in the full glare of world publicity.
2   *A Jewish state* was seen as potentially a very important US ally in a strategically sensitive area. Britain was especially vulnerable to US pressure exerted through the world currency market and this was a significant factor in 1947.
3   *British calculations* as to US readiness to assume security burdens which it gave up. The Truman government wanted Britain to remain and maintain order while partition was established. The *Bevin Declaration* threw the onus on the USA.

The UN voted for partition in November 1947. The US supplied Jewish forces were successful in the Arab–Jewish War which followed in 1948–49, and seized half of the territory allocated to the Arabs as well. The cost was the wholesale eviction of thousands of Arab refugees and the humiliation and alienation of the Arab political culture.

(b) The Iranian crisis (1951)

The nationalisation of the Anglo-Iranian Oil Company by a nationalist régime led by Mossadeq resulted in a British refusal to intervene at a time of pressure on her military capacity (the Korean War) and forced the USA to take the initiative again. The prospect was that Iran would otherwise fall into the hands of the Communist Tudeh Party. A CIA coup established a more compliant régime.

(c) The Suez invasion (1956)

In 1952 the Neguib–Nasser coup replaced the discredited monarchy and Wafd. The nationalisation of the Suez Canal in 1956 came as the culmination of a deliberate policy by Nasser to identify himself as the leader of an aggressive Arab nationalism throughout the Near East. Britain was provoked to try to reassert her independence from the USA and to invade Egypt in conjunction with France and Israel and overthrow Nasser. The USA reacted by threatening the value of the pound in currency markets and forced a humiliating withdrawal, effectively a change in leadership in Britain and the final recognition by Britain that she no longer could act as a free agent in the Middle East or world diplomatic affairs.

(d) Cyprus

The granting of self government to Cyprus in August 1960 under the presidency of Archbishop Makarios was really an epilogue to Suez. A terrorist campaign by the Greek Cypriot monarchist–fascist group EOKA in support of *Enosis*, union with Greece, started in 1955. Cyprus was seen by Britain as the alternative base to Suez, and there was also the problem of a large and threatened Turkish minority fearful of Greek Cypriot rule. However, in 1959 an agreement was reached over the status of the Turkish Cypriots and British sovereignty over military bases.

31.6 The 'wind of change' (see Map. 31.1)

Until Suez, British colonial policy was shaped by a desire to maintain the Commonwealth and the Sterling Area as a cushion against economic competition, and the alternative to absorption into a western European grouping. Thus the commitment of substantial resources to overseas development and to counter insurgency campaigns. The result of Suez was that Britain recognised that its foreign policy would have to be much more adapted to NATO objectives as defined by the USA. There would have to be much more emphasis on anti-communism and less on colonial priorities. The rapid dismantling of the residue of the British empire after 1960 was related to:

(a) The expense of nuclear deterrence

The cost of membership of the 'nuclear club' and the start of the 'independent' British Polaris programme after the Anglo-American Nassau Conference in 1962 meant that there had to be far less emphasis on conventional defence spending.

(b) Structural changes in trade patterns

By the late 1950s the benefits of involvement in big industrial blocs like the EEC were

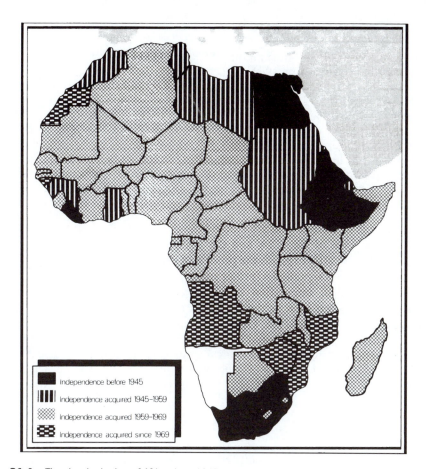

Map. 31.1 The decolonisation of Africa since 1945

Legend (within map):
- Independence before 1945
- Independence acquired 1945–1959
- Independence acquired 1959–1969
- Independence acquired since 1969

obvious. British productivity was falling behind that of her continental competitors. On the other hand, the real economic benefits of colonialism were increasingly questioned. De Gaulle was led by these circumstance to scale down French colonial commitments and to concentrate on the position of France in Europe.

(c) *The power of the floating voter*

In both Britain and France politicians were forced to look more and more to the new affluent middle classes which were increasingly resentful at the diversion of resources into colonial purposes, which seemed more associated with another age. The 'Condition of Africa' question was no longer a vote winner.

The tone was set by the speech made by Harold Macmillan at Accra, then Cape Town, in 1960: 'The wind of change is blowing through this continent, and whether we like it or not this growth of national consciousness is a political fact. We must all accept it as a fact, and our national policies must take account of it.' In the following year South Africa withdrew from the Commonwealth and an intensification of *Apartheid* began to stimulate racial unrest throughout the continent.

31.7 'Fancy footwork'

British decolonisation in Africa and the Mediterranean was a frenetic process which reached a climax in the early 1960s. According to B. R. Tomlinson, talking about the withdrawal from India, decolonisation was really an optical illusion. It was simply a change to a new form of exploitation based on surrogate imperial groupings like the Commonwealth and the proliferation of multinational companies exploiting resources in former colonies. It was a reversion to informal imperialism. The main objective was to leave behind a relatively stable political structure as a base for continued links. The paradox was that this often involved supporting westernised nationalists who had formerly agitated against or fought against the British or French because they were most likely to establish the required stability. However, the reality did not always match the theory and the path was not a very smooth one.

(a) *The unsuitability of the Westminster model*

While Ghana (1957) was held up as a model of stable self government it developed into a one-party state under Kwame Nkrumah, and this was the pattern which was followed in Zambia (formerly Northern Rhodesia, 1960), Uganda (1962), Malawi (formerly Nyasaland, 1962), Kenya (1963), and the new state of Tanzania created from Tanganyika and Zanzibar (1964). In some cases the army played a major role in providing an alternative focus to the political system, so there were recurrent coups in Ghana and Nigeria and the bloody military dictatorship of Idi Amin in Uganda from 1966 to 1979.

(b) *Tribal divisions*

The failure of constitutionalism was partly because of the need for a greater emphasis on political unity in the face of the massive problems of underdevelopment. However, it was also because of the tribal divisions which had never disappeared, and even been sustained to some extent, under British rule. So the terrible civil war in Nigeria in 1967–70 was essentially a tribal conflict triggered by the secession of Biafra and an army where opportunity for promotion was a matter of tribal affinity. This factor was present in most post-colonial situations.

(c) *White settler resistance*

The existence of Apartheid South Africa as an alternative focus aggravated the problem of achieving compromise between black and white populations, especially where the latter was substantial as in Southern Rhodesia. In 1965 Southern Rhodesia made a Unilateral Declaration of Independence to preserve white settler dominance in the face of the threat of black majority rule, which had already been recognised in its two former associate states in the Central African Federation, Nyasaland and Northern Rhodesia. This was followed by an escalating war against the ZANU and ZAPU nationalist insurgents with Southern Rhodesia heavily dependant upon South African backing. Not until 1979 was an agreement reached at Lusaka under pressure from the Conservative government of Margaret Thatcher, and very much as a result of the ending of access to the sea through the former Portuguese colony of Mozambique.

31.8 Order and chaos

It was only in the 1950s that French and Belgian colonialism became vulnerable to the pressures which had faced the British Empire for so long. The destabilisation of the Portuguese colonies was not noticeable until after 1970. There was never a pattern to timing or sequence and the scenarios varied from tight and orderly transition to bloody anarchy. In two cases the impact of colonial wars on metropolitan political stability was as significant as the decolonisation itself. There are four case studies:

1 French West Africa.
2 Algeria.
3 The Belgian Congo.
4 Portuguese Africa.

31.9 Community and cash

The situation of the French colonies in West Africa was different. This was partly a result of outlook and partly a result of variations in local circumstances.

(a) *Assimilation*

The colonies had been grouped as a federation before the war. At the Brazzaville Conference of 1944 the emphasis was on assimilation rather than independence, with a recognition of equal metropolitan rights for all those who met educational require-ments. Circumstances were different in French West Africa. There was no significant nationalist agitation for independence:

1 *A very small bourgeois group* with western education was largely restricted to the French civil service for personal advancement.
2 *Marked sectional differences* between the coastal and interior regions severely restricted the possibility of any form of national integration.
3 *Considerable French investment* through the overseas development agency FIDES, especially into infrastructural capital projects, meant that sectional differences were increased and that the interests of the French and the local élites were bound closely together.

(b) *The French Community*

In 1956, nevertheless, France undertook substantial decentralisation of power from Paris to local elected and responsible governments. By then the stability of the colonies and their adherence to France seemed guaranteed by their economic dependence and the emergence of Francophile leaders like Houphouet Boigny of the Ivory Coast. However, there was also a need to win some international credit in the face of the mounting problems in Algeria. This was probably the main reason for the flamboyant gesture of De Gaulle in 1958 in creating the federalised Community and giving the states the option of full independence with immediate cessation of economic assistance, or membership and the continuance of aid. All except Guinea accepted the latter. De Gaulle was left free to deal with Algeria.

31.10 The Algerian revolution

The situation in Algeria could not have been more different.

(a) Algérie Française

Algeria held a special status in French eyes:

1 *It was a Department of France* which had been a colony since 1830 and was very close geographically.
2 The *'pieds noirs'* white settlers numbered over a million. Most of them were working-class people who had little alternative to life in Algeria, and everything to lose.
3 *The strength of the 'colon' lobby* in fragmented French coalition politics under the Fourth Constitution meant that change and reform were easily blocked.
4 *The French civil servants* in Algeria were closely identified with local *colon* interests.
5 *The French army* saw Algeria as the last line between military honour and political weakness. Many of the men who fought there had been involved in the *Débâcle* of 1940, the defeat at Dien Bien Phu and the withdrawal from Suez, and felt betrayed all the way by corrupt politicians. Also Algeria was the origin and base for many of the finest regiments.

(b) Algerian independence

Nevertheless, in 1962 it was General De Gaulle himself, very much in power as a result of the support of the army, who achieved the *Evian Agreement* which gave Algeria her independence. The route to this outcome was a tortuous one:

1 *The Front de Libération Nationale* fought a guerrilla war in the countryside from 1954, then a terrorist campaign in Algiers itself in 1956–57 designed to provoke a racial explosion. In fact by 1961 the French army had relatively contained the threat, although at awful expense and by resorting to near counter-terrorism.
2 *The new technocrat and managerial French classes* were disenchanted with imperialism which was seen as largely irrelevant, and very expensive to sustain.
3 *The imminent prospect of a military coup* by the 'paras' in May 1958 as the likelihood of a settlement forced by world opinion grew and there was another ministerial crisis. The army did actually seize Corsica. The parliamentary factions turned to De Gaulle as the only man who could save the Fourth Republic and he was endorsed by colons and soldiers as the man who would not surrender Algeria.

In fact De Gaulle presided over the establishment of the Fifth Republic with a reformed constitution, and, following a referendum on the issue in 1961, negotiated Algerian independence. The *'pieds noirs'* flooded out of Algeria. Between 1961–2 a terrorist campaign was fought by the ex-army and *colon* extremists of the *Organisation Armée Secrète* (OAS) which was defeated.

31.11 The Belgian Congo

As late as 1955 the Belgian Congo was described as 'the most prosperous and tranquil of colonies'. However, the outbreak of riots in Leopoldville in 1959, together with plummeting copper prices, led to an abrupt withdrawal by the Belgians and a swift degeneration into anarchy as the *Force Publique* mutinied, civil authority collapsed and the copper rich state of Katanga seceded. Anarchy and civil war continued until 1964. The significance of these events was:

(a) *A stimulus to decolonisation*

The uprising in the Congo was a shock to European opinion. Decolonisation was obviously not always as manageable as was planned. The British and French movement towards decolonisation was accelerated as a result; the settlers of Southern Rhodesia were stimulated into the opposite direction.

(b) *The intersection with global ideological division*

Decolonisation had not hitherto been a focus of western–Soviet rivalry. However, the Congo did mark the emergence of an aspect of that rivalry which involved bypassing nuclear stalemate by building up coalitions in the underdeveloped world. The Russians were thus involved in backing Patrice Lumumba and the secessionist Stanleyville 'pocket' against President Joseph Kasavubu and the federal government.

31.12 The overseas provinces of Portugal

While other states decolonised Portugal became increasingly committed to her colonies in Africa. By 1974 a quarter of Portuguese adult males were in the forces, and most of those were in Africa. This was partly because of economic factors, but was also the result of the need of an authoritarian régime to find distractions and of the USA and the western powers for a regional guarantee in southern Africa. It was bound to end:

(a) *Pressure on Portuguese resources*

From 1970 the war against nationalist groups such as the MPLA in Angola and FRE-LIMO in Mozambique seriously escalated as the support of Russia, Cuba and East Germany grew. The Portuguese army was overstretched by 1974–5 and a section of it sought to break the deadlock by restoring democracy in Portugal through the *Armed Forces Movement*.

(b) *The need for EEC integration*

To the Portuguese business and bureaucratic classes the emphasis was seen to be more on economic development and membership of the EEC, which was not compatible with a draining and pointless conflict in Africa.

The coup of 1974 was the result. General de Spinola assumed transitional power. This was followed by withdrawals from Guiné, Angola and Mozambique. In the case of the two latter this was just the start of a new stage of civil war between rival African factions backed by Russia, Cuba and East Germany on the one side and by the USA and South Africa on the other.

31.13 Conclusion

With the end of the Portuguese Empire in 1975 the story of decolonisation was virtually complete. All that remained were small pockets like Hong Kong and barren dependencies like the Falkland Islands. Once the process started it had become almost as much of a scramble as had been the development of empire. However, the nature and speed of the process, and the context of changing world circumstances in the subsequent years, were to be associated with a range of legacies which considerably offset many of the benefits of independence.

Questions

1 What do you understand by the term 'decolonisation'? Why is it ambiguous?
2 What would you say was the most significant factor in the inter-war period in challenging the basis of the imperial relationship?
3 In the progress towards independence in India, what were the factors working towards partition?
4 What were the reasons for the emergence of the British concept of 'trusteeship'?
5 What was the contribution of the Japanese conquest and occupation of former western colonies to their acquisition of independence?
6 How and why did the attitude of the USA towards western imperialism change in the 1940s?
7 In what respects would you say that the effectiveness of the British response to the insurgency in Malaya contrasted to that of the USA in Vietnam?
8 Why was the Suez invasion in 1956 such a significant landmark in the story of decolonisation?
9 What would you say were the most significant factors contributing to the rapid dismantling of the western colonial structure in sub-Saharan Africa in the 1960s?
10 Why was the Algerian struggle for independence so significant in the history of France herself in the 1960s?
11 Would you say that the process and achievement of decolonisation was of benefit to the people of the former colonies or not?

32 Western Europe 1953–85

Introduction

The status of Europe was affected by the devastation of the war and the emergence of the USA and the USSR as the two great super-powers. This partly explains the process of decolonisation in the 1950s and 1960s, which signalled a further reduction in European power. On the other hand, integration of European economic and security systems has been seen as the route towards the creation of a third power bloc to match the USA and USSR. However, this latter movement has been inhibited by the persistence of national rivalries and conflicts of interest.

32.1 Strains within the western alliance

The western alliance was subject to a series of strains and tensions resulting from four sources:

1 The assumption by de Gaulle between 1958–69 of a strongly nationalist stance.
2 A dispute over the degree of European participation in control of the nuclear deterrent in the early 1960s.
3 The difference of opinion between the USA and her European allies over the scope of the interests and responsibilities of the NATO alliance.
4 Conflicts between members of NATO over matters of local interest.

32.2 De Gaulle and the French revival

In 1958 de Gaulle came to power as the first president of the French Fifth Republic, the inevitable 'strong man' following the instability, colonial failures and near civil war of the short-lived Fourth Republic. In a period when Britain was stagnating under a series of Conservative governments and there was a rising tide of Anti-Americanism in Europe resentful at US economic penetration and military dominance, de Gaulle exercised a disproportionate influence upon European affairs.

(a) *The Gaullist perception of Europe*

De Gaulle saw France as potentially a major power and a leader of European affairs. He supported the idea of a European union but not at the expense of national sovereignty and not on an equal basis. He saw the EEC (see Section 32.6) as led by a directorate of France and Germany and NATO by the USA, Britain and France. Central to his vision was French attainment of a nuclear capability.

(b) The Franco-German treaty (January 1963)

One aspect of this new nationalist policy was the creation of a sort of French–German 'Axis'. By the late 1950s relations between the USA and Germany were poor, because of Eisenhower's attempts to establish a closer accord with the USSR. Anglo-German relations were also poor because of Macmillan's attempt in 1959 to reach a European settlement with the USSR without consulting Germany.

As a result, meetings in 1960 and 1962 between de Gaulle and Adenauer resulted in a treaty designed to act as a brake on NATO, the EEC, the Anglo-American partnership or any potential American–Russian rapprochement. In fact, Adenauer was near the end of his political career and his successors were less ready to risk the American alliance.

32.3 Control of the nuclear deterrent

In 1959 the USA started to install Intermediate Range Ballistic Missiles (IRBMs) in Europe under a 'two-key' system of *dual control*. There was a growing debate in Europe about ways of increasing the degree of European participation in nuclear control; there were two views:

(a) Multilateralism

The USA and West Germany, with other states, supported the idea of a mixed-national European force. In March 1963 a scheme was proposed by the USA; it failed because of the opposition of the USSR to German involvement and because of European opposition.

(b) Multinationalism

De Gaulle proposed national sovereign control over the nuclear weapons in their states and greater participation in strategic planning; Britain supported a modified form of this as well. In the end the USA conceded only a greater share in planning; as a result, in 1966, France withdrew from NATO and pressed ahead with the development of her own nuclear deterrent with a series of tests in the Pacific.

In 1968, a wave of student demonstrations and workers' strikes convulsed Paris. This political reaction against the over-paternalist Gaullist régime was worsened by the overzealous response by the riot police (the CRS). De Gaulle weathered the storm and won a presidential election a month later in June; however he resigned as a result of the failure of a referendum to abolish the Senate, and in 1969 he died.

32.4 The purposes of NATO

In 1974 Valéry Giscard d'Estaing's achievement of the French presidency marked a new Franco-American relationship, even to the extent of involvement in NATO exercises.

However, by then there were new strains.

(a) Relative financial contributions

By the 1970s the European allies contributed 90 per cent of the land forces but the US financial contribution was a vast £1000 million a year when the USA was experiencing financial problems and the trauma of Vietnam. On the other hand, the European economies had recovered and their financial contribution seemed disproportionately small. Throughout the 1970s the situation was complicated by industrial recession and rising oil prices. In 1977, it was agreed that all members would raise their contribution by 3 per cent a year to 1983, but most of the European states failed to live up to this.

(b) The jurisdiction of NATO

On the whole, the European attitude was that NATO was a regional defensive pact. The USA, however, was involved in Vietnam, in assisting Israel and from 1979 in opposing the invasion of Afghanistan by Soviet forces backing a puppet régime. The American leadership tended to expect European support; in fact, there was mounting criticism of the war in Vietnam, resistance to attempts at US action in the Near East which would threaten the source of 80 per cent of European oil imports, and a tendency to see efforts to free Afghanistan as futile. In addition, the quality of presidential leadership in the late 1960s–70s was questionable, and simply reinforced latent anti-Americanism.

32.5 'Family conflicts'

Inevitably, there were internal disputes between the allies, which sometimes threatened the NATO installations.

(a) Turkish invasion of Cyprus (1974)

After the bitter terrorist war of EOKA in the 1950s, Cyprus gained independence in 1960. However, Greek interference and the Greek Cypriot discrimination against the Turkish minority led in 1974 to the Turkish army occupying the northern half of the island. This had two effects on NATO:

1 *A Greek boycott.* Greece withdrew from NATO operations because of its failure to take a strong stand with Turkey.
2 *Turkish brinksmanship.* In December 1974 the USA cut aid to Turkey, who responded by seizing NATO military installations and making a treaty of friendship with the USSR who gave her a large loan.

(b) The Cod Wars

The first half of the 1970s saw recurrent clashes between Britain and Iceland when the latter extended her fishing limits to 50 miles in 1972, then 200 miles in 1975. This led to some niggling violence as Icelandic gunboats risked ramming by British escorts to drive away or destroy the gear of British trawlers. In the end Britain gave up her very reasonable claims because of the importance of NATO installations on Iceland.

(c) American 'gunboat diplomacy'

The revival of US nationalism in the 1980s saw a series of unilateral military actions which disturbed the NATO relationship. the overthrowing of a left-wing government on Grenada in 1984 without due notice being given to Britain of this move against a member of the Commonwealth led to a rather prickly tone in Anglo-American relations for some time. More seriously, the American attack on Libya in April 1986 appeared as a blatant affront to her NATO allies, especially in view of the strategic and economic sensitiveness of the region.

32.6 The European Economic Community (EEC) (see Illus. 32.1)

With the admission of Spain and Portugal to the EEC in January 1986, NATO became virtually synonymous with the EEC (with a few exceptions like Ireland who is not a NATO member, and Norway who is not a member of the EEC). With its 12 members an expanded EEC included a population of some 320 million. It had been devised originally as a means to aid European economic recovery and development, to strengthen military security and – ultimately – to lead to the creation of a third major world power bloc.

(a) The European Coal and Steel Community (ECSC)

As early as 1948 a broad *Council of Europe* had been created by the non-communist states of western Europe and Turkey but with the exception of neutral Switzerland and Francoist Spain. This was not the start of European unity because its role was vague and its power negligible. Far more fundamental was the *European Coal and Steel*

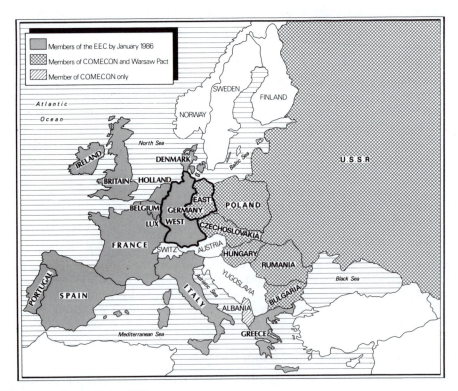

Map 32.1 Europe in the 1980s

Illus. 32.1 *Non!*

From a cartoon in the *Daily Express*, January 1963.
Source: P. Lane, *Europe Since 1945* (Batsford, 1985) p. 234.

Q To whom is General de Gaulle saying *'Non!'*? What does this cartoon suggest to you about the relationship between Britain and the USA?

Community (ECSC) created in 1951 by France, Germany, Holland, Belgium, Luxembourg and Italy, designed to coordinate production and investment and with genuine supranational authorities and a form of parliamentary control.

(b) *The Rome Treaties (March 1957)*

Sir Anthony Eden proposed in 1952 that the Council of Europe, the ECSC and the planned EDC (see Section 30.9(b)) should combine. This would have had considerable implications in terms of a wide membership and extensive powers if it had materialised. In fact, the EDC failed. On the other hand, the ECSC states did go ahead with the creation of a general unified market in the new *European Economic Community (EEC)*.

1 *The objectives.* The ostensible purposes of the EEC were *economic*.

   – The ultimate establishment of free trade within the community and a unified external tariff.
   – The removal of all factors distorting the movement of trade such as quotas, subsidies and monopolistic practises.

There was a vague agreement to coordinate economic and commercial policies, but no commitment to political unity as a goal in itself. Naturally, though, the latter had many supporters who saw the EEC as the first major step.

2   *Machinery.* The organs of the Common Market included:

– *A Council of Ministers* with voting based upon a national economic weighting.
– *A Commission* of nine members in Brussels which reached decisions by a simple majority.
– *An elected assembly* for the EEC and ECSC, and for the *Euratom* organisation which was established to oversee the use of nuclear energy for peaceful purposes.

(c) 'Sixes and Sevens'

Britain initially stood aloof of the new developments, because of:

1   *Traditional isolationism.* This seemed reaffirmed by the war and by victory.
2   *Post-war reconstruction.* The Labour government after 1945 was too preoccupied with its domestic reforms, and in any case the USA shouldered the old British policy of maintaining a balance of power.
3   *The Commonwealth illusion.* The Commonwealth relationship was argued to be a compensation for lost imperial power. In fact the Commonwealth was expensive in terms of development capital and troublesome in terms of the racial conflicts in South Africa and Rhodesia.

Initially, Britain responded to the EEC by helping to create in 1959 a *European Free Trade Association* (EFTA) of herself, Norway, Sweden, Denmark, Austria, Switzerland and Portugal.

(d) *British entry to the EEC (1973)*

There were several attempts to achieve EEC entry:

1   *The Macmillan government (1961–3).* After 1953 French production rose by 75 per cent and that of Germany by 90 per cent; Britain's production grew by only 30 per cent. With the obvious limitations of EFTA and a favourable attitude of de Gaulle seeking to establish a Europe independent of the USA, the time seemed more suitable for an approach in 1961. It was half-hearted on Britain's part, and in January 1963 de Gaulle blocked British entry when Britain accepted the offer from President Kennedy of American Polaris submarine missiles.
2   *The Wilson government (1966–70).* By the 1960s Britain was in danger of being caught in the middle of a tariff war between the USA and the EEC. France was very concerned about proposals to introduce majority voting to the Council of Ministers and the abolition of vetoes and de Gaulle anticipated British support for his resistance. The new prime minister, Harold Wilson, a convert to the idea of the EEC, urged British membership strongly in terms of the economic benefits to be gained.
3   *The Heath government (1970–4).* In June 1970, Wilson was replaced by the strongly pro-Europe Edward Heath with a Conservative government. The heads of the governments of the EEC had already agreed in December 1969 to seek British membership; in January 1972 treaties were signed and in 1973 Britain (together with Denmark and Eire) became a full member.
4   *Renegotiation.* Plans were established for a popular referendum on Britain's accession; however, Heath lost office in 1974 at a time when the British economy was moving into serious difficulties. In the election, Wilson had warned that Labour would seek to renegotiate the terms of entry; this he did after a second and

far more positive electoral victory in October 1974. Having achieved concessions over the British contribution to the community budget, Wilson could claim a successful conclusion of the issue. In June 1975 the referendum approved membership by two to one.

This was by no means the end of the story. However, because Mrs Margaret Thatcher, who won the leadership of the Conservative Party from Edward Heath then became prime minister in 1979, was committed to another renegotiation of the British terms of entry in view of the adverse economic developments of the 1970s. The basic problem was that Britain (as the largest importer in the EEC) paid a high proportion to the Community Fund; however, she gained relatively little back since British farming is comparatively small and it is the *Common Agricultural Policy* (CAP) which takes over two-thirds of the total Fund in the form of subsidies and the costs for the storage of surpluses. In 1980, and again in 1984, Mrs Thatcher did negotiate amendments to the British contribution, although this was, to some extent, at the expense of reducing British opposition to the Common Agricultural Policy.

(e) *The weaknesses of the EEC*

Despite recurrent crises, the EEC survived, and was in fact extended to take in Greece in 1981 then Spain and Portugal in 1986. These additions gave it a total population of 320 million, equal to that of the USA and Japan together. This left only 9 per cent of the Western European population not in the EEC. Assessment of its success or otherwise is not easy, because it is seen by different groups of people from the point of view of different expectations, and within very different social and economic situations:

1   *The failure to achieve political unity.* The intentions behind the EEC were originally economic, but true Europeans looked further towards the creation of a European bloc. By this standard it has failed, because of the jealous resistance of member states to the loss of their sovereignty. Only Italy appears to be an enthusiastic advocate of a real European parliament.
2   *The problems of economic harmonisation.* The fundamental problem is the harnessing of economies of considerably different specialisms and degrees of growth:

    – There are recurrent arguments about the size of the contributions which are assessed on the basis of imports from outside the EEC. This explains why in 1980 Britain contributed £1209 million as opposed to the £13 million of France.
    – A Common Agricultural Policy largely designed to protect the smaller and less efficient farmers of France, Italy and Germany has tended to encourage overproduction of foodstuffs. The 'wine lake', the 'butter mountain' and other enormities attract considerable criticism. Inefficient farmers are harboured by protection and, given the proportion of very small farmers in many of the European states, an sudden and significant change is very difficult.
    – External relationships with bodies like the Commonwealth have been affected by the protective tariff against foodstuff imports.

3   *Bureaucracy.* With 12 members and a civil service which must reflect all of them the result was a not inconsiderable bureaucracy which had to be reshuffled each time a new member joined. In the absence of a true sense of Europeanism and affected by the multitude of regulations of a largely faceless body of bureaucrats and parliamentarians of limited power, there has been a tendency to resent the EEC.

The admission of the relatively poor Spain and Portugal considerably strengthened the 'Mediterranean' dimension of the EEC, but added weight to the problems, with their low national incomes, relatively inefficient agriculture and many small industrial firms.

(f) Three steps forward

The *'Europessimism'* of the early 1980s reached a climax in 1984 and was then succeeded by a period when more hopeful views as to the prospects for the revitalisation
of the EEC prevailed. The result was three significant steps forward, or backward
depending upon the viewpoint of the observer.

The *Single European Act* passed in 1986 and operative from July 1987 resulted
from the report produced in 1985 by the European Commission under the chairman-
ship of Jacques Delors. The three key features were:

1   *A Single European Market.* The argument that the 'cost of non-Europe' was
    significant economic growth and 5 million new jobs produced agreement as to the
    urgency of proceeding to the truly single market. The implications of this were:

    – The removal of all physical, technical, administrative and legal barriers to the
    free movement of goods, services, capital and people.
    – The reduction of fiscal disparities and the convergence of VAT rates to bring
    them into line to equalise national competitiveness.
    – The removal of protective and discriminatory national public supply and
    procurement policies.

    A deadline of the end of 1992 was set for the achievement of the single market.

2   *European Political Co-operation* was given formal recognition, and from 1987 the
    member states were under a treaty obligation to 'endeavour jointly to formulate
    and implement a European foreign policy.'
3   *European Monetary Union (EMU)* in the form of a single European currency and
    central banking system was accepted in principle by all member states, except
    Britain, following the Delors Report of 1989, which proposed a three-staged
    approach to a single currency by the end of the century. Since 1979 currency
    exchange rates had been controlled by means of the Exchange Rate Mechanism
    which operated to maintain stability in the European currency market.

32.7 Conclusion

In a very short period Europe lost one role and started to move uncertainly towards
another. On the other hand, in European history it is internationalism and the idea of
'Christendom' which has had a far longer span; the narrowly bounded, intensely
nationalist state is a product only of the late eighteenth and nineteenth centuries.
However, the 'European idea' is a very fragile thing; the survival of the EEC, for
instance, has been achieved only by means of recurrent surrenders to national interests,
as urged by de Gaulle in 1965, then Mrs Thatcher in 1984.

Questions

1   What forces brought about the signing of the Treaty of Rome in 1957?   [OC, adapted]
2   What economic developments led to the establishment of the Common Market?   [OC]
3   What was Charles de Gaulle's contribution to France's post-war development?   [OC, adapted]
4   How successfully had 'European Unity' been promoted by 1963?   [NEAB, adapted]
5   Describe and account for the creation and development of the EEC.
6   Why was British entry to the Common Market delayed until 1973?
7   What were the greatest threats to the unity of the North Atlantic Treaty Organisation (NATO)
    between 1953 and 1985?

The Communist bloc 1945–85

Introduction

Churchill's 'invisible iron curtain' divided Europe into two distinct spheres of influence, the western democratic sector and the USSR dominated satellite bloc. Germany was divided into two states. However, the western democracies by no means spoke or acted in unison despite their economic and military integration, while the Soviet bloc was troubled by recurrent strains and problems of increasing seriousness. Ultimately, after 1985, the removal of the threat of Soviet tanks would reveal the real depth of division and discontent in the eastern bloc.

33.1 Post-war USSR under Stalin

The Stalinist system had triumphed in the struggle against Germany, but at the immense cost of 20 million soldiers and civilians dead or incapacitated, and the devastation of the towns and cities of the western USSR. It must also be held responsible for early setbacks in the war. After the war Stalinism retained its four faces, which had been substantially strengthened by the struggle, but its conservative aspect had triumphed over its radical–revolutionary persona.

(a) *Economic restoration*

Restoration had to be achieved largely by means of the use of domestic resources. There was only a limited foreign input in the form of industrial plant and material imported from the satellite countries of eastern Europe. The centralised and directed nature of the economy was reinforced, and pre-war policies persisted.

1 *Industrial development.* Targets and goals were set. Their achievement was, as always, limited by considerable local autonomy. Consumer goods were given a low priority. Between 1945–50 only 12.1 per cent of industrial investment was directed to light industry and the production of consumer goods. Industry was rapidly rebuilt. For instance, the 1940 levels of coal, metallurgical and electricity output of the Ukraine were achieved by 1950.
2 *Agricultural collectivisation and control.* Control over private peasant plots had been relaxed in wartime. These were now enforced and strengthened. The effect of control, inappropriate crop policies and the lack of material and financial

incentives for producers delayed recovery. By 1952 the 1940 levels of grain, potatoes and cattle had still not been reached.

(b) Reduced social mobility

There was no shortage of labour. The war had seen a considerable influx of women into the labour force, and soldiers were now returning to civilian work. There was a much lower level of social mobility than there had been before the war. Indeed women were forced into poorer jobs. The enthusiasm which had been a factor in the pre-war Stalinist years was replaced by exhaustion and loss of energy as a result of the war.

(c) Cultural conservatism

This aspect was especially marked:

1   *Russian nationalism became even more chauvinistic* and intolerant of other national cultures and values. Of course, the war had exaggerated a dimension of Stalinism which had been present before the war. Anti-semitism and attacks on 'cosmopolitanism' were features of this period.
2   *Women's rights were curbed and reduced.* There was a strong emphasis on their family responsibilities. Abortion and divorce were virtually out of the question. To encourage the birth-rate men were no longer legally responsible for children born out of wedlock.
3   *Status, hierarchy and differentiation were emphasised.* Formal titles and ranks were restored for workers in 1946.
4   *Intellectual life was stifled* by the insistence on valuation of art, literature, music and film in terms of their contribution to the construction of socialism. Experimentation was denounced. Cultural ties with the outside world were virtually cut. All spheres of education and learning were obliged to focus on the Party and its values.
5   *The cult of Stalin* meant that ideology was reduced to meaningless formulae.

(d) Political centralisation

The trends which existed before the war were reinforced after it:

1   *The subordination of state and party organs* to the will of Stalin. Decision-making rested with groups of leaders summoned by Stalin, and whose role was informal and purely advisory. Politics was no more than the rivalries between his lieutenants.
2   *The prevalence of terror* as an instrument of government. There were mass deportations of citizens from newly incorporated territories. Soviet soldiers who had been prisoners of war were sent to labour camps. There was a series of purge trials as various groups of potential enemies of the paranoiac Stalin were identified, e.g. the 'Leningrad Affair' (1945–50), the Mingrelian case (1951–2), the Crimean case (1952) and the 'Doctors' Plot' (1952–3).

33.2 The satellite empire (1945–53)

Stalin rejected the idea of a sort of 'Soviet Commonwealth' with the full incorporation of large areas of eastern central Europe. Such a step would have been too provocative, while fully-absorbed areas would have been far less valuable as buffer zones. In addition, some of the new satellite states had previously enjoyed a far better standard of living and administration than had the USSR, and the 'shock' of annexation could be very dangerous. The result was that the satellite states were much more in the position of colonies held together by unequal economic treaties, the Communist Party apparatus, police rule and – in the last resort – the sheer military power of the USSR.

(a) The Titoist threat

By means of a combination of electoral manipulation and sheer intimidation Soviet-dominated People's Democracies were established in 1947–8 in Poland, Bulgaria, Czechoslovakia, Hungary and Rumania. However, the situation in Yugoslavia developed along very different lines. Between March and May 1948, mounting disagreements led to the expulsion of Yugoslavia from the communist bloc:

1   *Titoist revisionism.* The key issue was whether communist doctrine could be varied, or whether it was unchangeable. The line followed by Marshal Tito was to seek links with both western states and the non-aligned states and to accept economic aid from the USA. In addition, however, his independent stance towards the USSR was influenced by:

    – The strength of a Yugoslav nationalism, which had been reinforced by the experience of the war and was resentful towards overpaid and arrogant Russian officials and experts who behaved as if they were in a colony.
    – The behaviour of the USSR in 1939 towards fascist Germany and the cynical partition of Poland.

2   *Miscalculation by Stalin.* Yugoslavia had been liberated very much by the efforts of the partisans, and so the USSR could not exert the sort of pressure which it did within other states. Tito also would rely on a tremendous personal following. In addition, Yugoslavia had no direct frontier with the USSR, and was therefore not so vulnerable to military threat.

(b) The impact of the Yugoslav 'deviation'

Stalin did not anticipate that Yugoslavia would receive the western aid she did; the result was that short of obvious military intervention the USSR could not remove the awkward precedent of a communist state which was not subservient to Moscow. The expulsion–secession of Yugoslavia had other effects:

1   *Defeat of the communist rebellion in Greece* (see Section 30.6(b)). Yugoslav aid to the Greek insurgents was withdrawn and in fact Yugoslavia moved towards a normal relationship with Greece.

2   *A purge of satellite communist rulers.* Between 1949–51 a number of Hungarian, Bulgarian and Czechoslovak communists were purged because of their sympathies with the Titoist arguments. Dimitrov of Bulgaria died conveniently in Moscow where he was receiving medical treatment. Gomulka of Poland was imprisoned from 1951–5. In Hungary, Janos Kádár was arrested, tortured and imprisoned from 1951 to 1954. In Czechoslovakia in November 1952 there was a show trial of fourteen (mainly Jewish) party officials accused of being 'Trotskyist, Titoist, Zionist, bourgeois nationalist traitors'. In fact, this was just the tip of the iceberg. It has been estimated that in Czechoslovakia alone in this period 2000 people were executed and 300,000 imprisoned.

3   *Closer integration of the Soviet bloc.* The American policy of 'containment' and

economic aid and the failure of the Berlin blockade, together with the emergence of the internal threat from within the satellites themselves, led Stalin to attempt to establish an even tighter hold on them.

(c) Communist integration

The tightening of Soviet control took two forms:

1 *The Council for Mutual Economic Assistance* (1949). The members of COMECON eventually included the USSR, Poland, Czechoslovakia, Hungary, Rumania, Bulgaria, Albania and East Germany. There were two purposes to it:

   – It was an anti-American gesture and a propaganda device to set against the *Marshall Plan*.
   – The satellite economies could be more fully coordinated to fit the needs of the USSR. Centralised long-term plans were imposed which aimed at the development of heavy industries suited to the needs of the USSR.

   The result was that from the point of view of the satellites, the effects were very modest until the mid 1950s.

2 *The Warsaw Pact* (May 1955). USSR military control was already established through the use of military advisers and the training of local officers in Soviet academies. In 1952 a military coordinating committee was set up with a combined general staff under a Russian general. The satellites contributed a total of 1.5 million men and finances based upon an assessment by the USSR. The Warsaw Pact was a much more definite mutual commitment; however, it was still a means of control:

   – Russian troops remained in Hungary and Rumania although by the treaty with Austria they should have been withdrawn.
   – The new 'round table' co-operation could equally well be used against members of the bloc.

33.3 Life after Stalin (see Illus. 33.1)

Stalin's death in March 1953 was followed by a three-year struggle for power within the leadership of the USSR. In particular there was a rivalry between Malenkov and Beria on one side, backed by the immensely powerful police apparatus, and Nikita Krushchev on the other, who dominated the party bureaucracy and enjoyed the favour of the military leaders. By 1954, Malenkov had been defeated and replaced as head of the government by Bulganin, although he did make an unsuccessful counter-attack in 1957. Then in 1958 Krushchev became prime minister, as well as first secretary and was firmly in the saddle until October 1964. Already in 1956 the process of destalinisation had started with the public condemnation of Stalin's policies and personality; the positive side of this was the adoption of a more flexible diplomatic position (see Section 35.1) and a revision of the relationship with the satellite states.

(a) Lessening of doctrinal rigidity

The liquidation of Beria (possibly at a Politburo meeting) and the reduction of police rule set a pattern for similar trends in Hungary and elsewhere. The reintroduction of

Illus. 33.1 'Now they've bloomed, next year we shall have fruit'

From a cartoon in *Pravda*, 1980, mocking the inefficient Russian railway system.
Source: P. Lane, *Europe Since 1945* (Batsford, 1985) p. 126.

worker management in industry and the abandonment of collectivisation were similarly signals to the satellites. This was emphasised in 1956 when Khruschev denounced Stalinism and abolished the Cominform. The implication was that there could be some flexibility in the routes to socialism.

(b) Rehabilitation of Yugoslavia

An official visit to Belgrade in 1955 repaired the dangerous rift. Tito lived on in control of Yugoslavia until 1980; however, he had problems to contend with:

1 *Nationalist divisions.* The rivalries between the Croat and Serb leaders threatened the Yugoslav ideal. In 1971 Tito acted forcefully and ousted the more extreme groups. However, the problem still remained.
2 *The balance between central and provincial government.* Associated with the nationalist rivalries were demands for separation on the one hand and support for even stronger central government on the other. In the 1950s, Tito introduced a form of federal system and in 1958 the party was actually renamed the League of Communists.
3 *Economic development.* There was a marked move away from the tight control of the economy with the emphasis on decentralisation and self-management, the introduction of workers' control in 1950 and 1961 and a relaxation of price fixing and credit availability. This was very much a result of:

– The failure of the first Five-Year Plan, with its emphasis on nationalisation and collectivisation.
– The need to attract funds from the USA and then the UN and International Monetary Fund.

These reforms were not enough to put the Yugoslav economy on a safe and sure footing. New oil price increases in 1979 and the onset of the world wide depression fuelled a notable deterioration in the economic situation. By 1983–4 inflation was up to 55 per cent, and there was 14 per cent unemployment. Politically this was reflected in a wave of repression in April 1984 which involved the arrest of most of the leading intellectuals of the country. Tito's successors were not prepared to take the ultimate step and liberalise the political system to match and strengthen the economic development which Titoism had achieved. By June 1986, inflation was at 90 per cent, there were 1.2 million unemployed and threats of mass unrest from ethnic minority groups in two of the eight republics and provinces. President Zarkovič was driven to urge near-Thatcherite economics: 'An end must be put as soon as possible to the habit of spending more than we earn, inflation must be checked and steps must be taken to receive the economy of the vast burden of social administration expenses.' Indeed Zarkovič insisted loudly that: 'It is the duty of Communists to struggle against . . . egalitarianism in incomes.'

33.4 Tensions within the Soviet bloc

The USSR had been too heavy-handed in its approach, was too identified with Russian dominance, and had obstructed regional associations between satellites to foster economic growth. Nationalist sentiments had not disappeared simply as a result of the Soviet shadow. Discontent focused on two issues:

(a) The Warsaw Pact

The Pact was the counter to NATO. However, it had other implications:

1 *It was a Russian instrument.* Forces were commanded by a Russian; the HQ was an office of the high command of the USSR. It could be seen as just an extension of Russian military power.
2 *State sovereignty was compromised.* Warsaw Pact forces were used against the satellites themselves – as in Czechoslovakia in 1968 (see Section 33.10). Even if Russian dominance was accepted there was still a resentment at the loss of state sovereignty, so Rumania persistently refused to take part in Warsaw Pact activities.

(b) COMECON

From 1962 COMECON embarked upon a series of plans intended to develop and harmonise the economies of the member states. There were two problems associated with this:

1 *The subordination of the economic interests of the satellites.* Although the satellites were allowed a far greater say through an executive appointed in 1962, the result was still that the non-Russian states had to concentrate on one or two agreed economic activities and trade within the group for Russian primary produce, especially oil. This meant that the satellite economies could be subjected to some exploitation by the USSR through high prices and that they were even more clearly subordinated to Russian rule.
2 *Economic relations with the West*

– Some states could expand faster by trade with the western bloc outside the COMECON restrictions. From the early 1970s there was indeed some relaxation, and the USSR itself even made a trade agreement with the USA which enabled trade to treble by 1975.
– The East–West price differential. The converse problem was that as prices rose in the West in the 1970s, largely as a result of oil price increases, the Soviet satellite states could either cut back trade or 'import inflation', having to export more and more to pay for imports.

33.5 Discontents and challenges

From 1953 onwards the USSR was confronted by challenges from its satellite states:

1 The East German workers' revolt (1953).
2 Polish disturbances (1956).
3 The Hungarian revolution (1956).
4 Rumanian deviationism.
5 The Czechoslovak Action Programme (1968).
6 The Polish Solidarity crisis (1977–81).

33.6 The workers' revolt (1953)

From 1945 the politics of the German Democratic Republic were dominated by long-time communist Walter Ulbricht who was, like Stalin, an excellent party manager and bureaucrat. Under him the GDR was characterised by two trends:

(a) Repression

Despite the constitution of 1949 the full apparatus of a police state was installed. Elections were manipulated and political parties were forced into a compulsory coalition, the National Front, dominated by the Socialist Unity Party (SED). All forms of media and aspects of art and culture were subject to censorship. The churches were harassed and dissidents were coerced by the Stasi secret police. On the other hand, the members of the SED enjoyed extensive privileges and perks.

(b) Socialisation

By 1952 the private industrial sector had been reduced to one quarter of the total industrial employment, and in that year a drive to agricultural collectivisation started. There was in fact a considerable increase in industrial production. During the Five-Year Plan period of 1951–5 it grew by 190 per cent alone. However, this was largely at the expense of consumption, with the supply of consumer goods still lower than pre-war levels in 1953. The supply of food was also a constant problem. This was aggravated by an inefficient distribution system and by the low quality of the consumer goods which were available.

The poor standard of living and political repression were not adequately compensated for by guaranteed employment, subsidised housing costs and comprehensive social welfare measures. The result was a drain of people to West Germany, with an exodus of nearly 330,000 in 1953 alone (or 2 per cent of the total population). Then in June 1953 increased factory quotas and reductions in worker incomes stimulated strikes by construction workers in Berlin which spread into other parts of the GDR and developed into demands for political reform, associated with some violence in East Berlin especially. However, the revolt was unco-ordinated and was disintegrating before Russian tanks and troops appeared on the scene.

Ulbricht remained in power and the so-called *New Course* allowed some temporary relaxation in control and repression and a greater emphasis on consumer goods. In fact this did not last for long.

33.7 Polish disturbances (1956)

Poland was a traditional enemy of Russia, and the events of *1939* were never forgotten, even more in view of the revelation in April 1943 that 4000 Polish officers had been murdered at *Katyn* by the Russian invaders. Then in August 1944 the advancing Soviet forces deliberately stood by while the Germans crushed a revolt by the Polish Home Army in Warsaw so that Polish nationalism would be decimated.

In March 1945, Stalin had tricked sixteen of the leaders of the Home Army into visiting Moscow, where they were seized, tried and imprisoned. From July 1945, a Stalinist régime was in power in Poland.

(a) Gomulka's rise to power (1956)

The main surviving representative of a nationalist but communist Polish ideal was the moderate Gomulka who had been dismissed as a Titoist. A wave of strikes and demonstrations in Poznan in June 1956 brought together workers, intellectuals and the Roman Catholic activists. The Polish Politburo responded by appointing Gomulka as First Secretary. The Russians had the choice of accepting this, or actually using Russian troops overtly to overturn it; they took the former view. In December, however, the new Gomulka régime was obliged to agree to a treaty which would allow the Russians to keep troops in Poland.

(b) The fall of Gomulka

Once he reached power, Gomulka proved to be more of a 'Stalinist' than a 'liberal' and although there were economic reforms including privatisation in agriculture there was no relaxation of censorship and police controls. By 1970 this, together with the falling off in the rate of economic growth and food shortages, led to strikes and riots triggered off by attempts to increase prices. Troops had to be called out to suppress the disturbances and Gomulka was replaced by Edward Gierek.

33.8 The Hungarian revolution (1956)

In Hungary the moderate Imre Nagy was also seen as a danger by the Russians, but attempts to displace him in 1956 just made him the hero of intellectual and nationalist opposition. The 1956 revolution took place in two obvious phases.

(a) Initial success (October 1956)

Russian troops were on the verge of action in October but Nagy was caught on a wave of popular enthusiasm developing from a series of demonstrations in favour of higher wages and greater liberty. He would probably have tried to become a 'Gomulka' in Hungary; however non-communists were appointed to government posts, one-party rule was abolished and the evacuation of Russian forces was demanded. On 31 October it was announced that Hungary would leave the Warsaw Pact.

(b) Counter-revolution (November 1956)

The Russians sent in troops and established an alternative government under Janos Kádár. The revolution was bloodily suppressed at the cost of the death of some 25,000 Hungarians and 7000 Russians. The western powers were preoccupied with the Suez affair and the USSR vetoed UN action. Even so, there were important repercussions:

1   The image of Russian communism abroad had received a vital blow.
2   Kadar himself was driven towards a cautious liberalisation of the economy with a greater emphasis on consumer goods and foreign imports. By the 1980s Hungary was still enjoying a standard of living which was relatively favourable.

Between 1956 and 1963, real income rose by 36 per cent. By 1984 over half of Hungary's foreign trade was with the West and much of the domestic investment was funded by western credits.

33.9 'Twenty years of Enlightenment' (1965–85)

Until 1962 the Rumanian Workers' Party was led by the old communist Gheorghiu-Dej. In 1965 the mantle of dictatorship was assumed by the one-time shoemaker Nicolae Ceauşescu who embarked upon a policy of nationalist assertiveness designed to mask and distract from repression and a worsening economic situation.

(a) An independent diplomacy

Ceauşescu set about acquiring the image of a communist maverick, exploiting the Sino-Soviet split and the western interest in splitting the Soviet bloc. Milestones in this policy were the restoration of diplomatic relations with West Germany in 1967, the refusal to break off diplomatic ties with Israel after the Israeli–Egyptian Six Day War and the condemning of the invasion of Czechoslovakia in 1968. There was even talk of leaving the Warsaw Pact. Ceauşescu hoodwinked western leaders. The US ambassador once described his foreign policy as 'throwing dust in the eyes' of those who would otherwise see his dictatorship for what it was.

(b) Industrialisation

Actually Ceauşescu never went so far as to bring down the forces of the Kremlin upon him, and never diverged from Marxist orthodoxy. However, he needed to employ these diplomatic diversions to try to distract the population from a worsening economic situation. Rumania had been seen by the Soviet Union as a supplier of raw materials, but Ceauşescu pursued a policy of industrial development towards economic independence. Extravagant expenditure on the petrochemical industry and ventures such as the Danube–Black Sea canal in fact exacerbated the problems of the economy:

1 *A spiralling foreign debt.* By 1982 Rumania had a western debt of £6000 million, and was in partial default.
2 *Shortages of consumer goods and food.* Petrol and electricity were rationed; there were considerable numbers of deaths due to hypothermia in the winter. A chronic food shortage existed because over £750 million worth of food was exported annually to pay bills abroad.
3 *Overdependence on the USSR.* Ironically Ceauşescu was obliged to rely more and more on Russian oil, coal, gas and iron ore and upon the obvious presence of Russian and Warsaw Pact forces frequently on exercises.

To make matters worse Ceauşescu developed a Mussolini-like obsession with population growth, and from 1972 began to resort to police controls to combat illegal contraception and abortion.

(c) Repression

In fact in the early years Ceauşescu began to move towards a dictatorship in very familiar guise. The process, presided over by a sort of Ceauşescu family co-operative, had several aspects.

1 *'Divide and rule'* by playing off groups against each other, e.g. workers, peasants and intelligentsia; army and police; Rumanians and the Magyar and Gypsy minorities; state and national apparatuses.
2 The *'rotation of cadres'* within the Party meant that it was difficult to mobilise an effective opposition.
3 *Police intimidation* was practised on a wide scale by the *Securitate* who suppressed strikes and crushed opposition movements.
4 A *'Nero-like'* imagery was cultivated by the self-styled 'genius of the Carpathians', 'the shepherd and saviour' of his nation and the 'conscience of the world', applauded by carefully marshalled demonstrations when appropriate.

However, the strains were more and more obvious in the early 1980s. In 1983 there were widespread strikes, especially by the miners, and troops had to be called in to restore order. The mask was starting to crack.

33.10 The Czechoslovak Action Programme (1968)

The situation in Czechoslovakia was radically different.

(a) The Prague Spring

There were a complex of factors at work here:

1 *Slovak discontent.* The harsh régime of *Antonin Novotný* from 1953–68 was Czech-dominated and anti-Slovak. In January–March 1968 a 'palace *coup*' within the party led to his replacement by the Slovak *Alexander Dubček* as First Secretary and General Jan Svoboda became president.
2 *Economic centralisation.* The industrial sector was over-centralised and incompetently managed. From the mid-1950s there were demands for decentralisation of management to restore productivity and greater trade links with the West.
3 *Discontent with the political system.* Talk of freedom in the economic sector encouraged intellectual support for the ending of censorship and for political democratisation. Dubček assisted this with vague hints as to reforms.

In April 1968, the *Action Programme* was produced. It included the maintenance of communist control but allowed for the reorganisation of the party and government, revival of parliament, some freedom for minor parties and an improved status for Slovakia.

(b) The Soviet invasion (August 1968)

Simple 'cosmetic' changes would have been acceptable. The Action Programme, though, welcomed by Tito and Ceauşescu, might have been infectious. At first, the Russians tried more persuasive methods but Dubček was caught on a tide of intellectual liberalism and could not back down. On 20 August Czechoslovakia was finally invaded by Russian, East German, Polish, Hungarian and Bulgarian forces. There was little resistance; however, there was no obvious collaborator to deal with. The result was that in October the Russians signed a treaty with Dubček allowing Russian troops to stay. Only gradually was he ousted and replaced by the moderate, but more malleable, Dr Gustav Husák. Even so, it had been made clear that if necessary Warsaw Pact forces would be used within the Soviet bloc.

33.11 The Polish Solidarity movement (1977–85)

In Poland the situation was very complex, and became markedly more dangerous.

(a) Economic crisis

Throughout the 1970s half of Poland's trade was with the West; the result was mounting import bills and foreign debts. Increased wages or farm prices led to the import of more consumer goods and mounting inflation. By 1977–80 Poland could either pay its foreign debts or feed itself, but not both. Meat production would not enable enough foreign currency to be raised and the home demand to be met based on recent wage increases. A bad harvest also produced rising bills for grain and feeding stuffs for stock, but they could only obtain credits from the USSR.

(b) The Gdansk Strike (1980)

There had been violent outbreaks against the government in the past. In 1970, 45 strikers had been killed and 100 injured when police fired on a riot produced by rising food prices. A similar situation arose in 1976, although in that year the Committee for the Defence of the Workers (KOR) was formed by politically able intellectuals to assist the workers. In 1980, the Gdansk shipyard workers, led from August by the unemployed shipyard worker Lech Walesa, went on strike, advised by KOR. The movement accepted the leading role of the communist party, Poland's socialist system and membership of the Warsaw Pact; however its demands were not only economic, they were political as well. Above all, there was widespread support from working people, not just a limited band of intellectual dissidents as in Czechoslovakia.

(c) The dilemma of the government

Polish governments had fallen in the past because of workers' demonstrations. Edward Gierek the First Secretary had replaced Gomulka in 1956 as a result of continued troubles arising from the economic situation. By 1979–80 Gierek was caught in the same trap, and faced with the prospect of increasing prices to cut consumption. However the situation was complicated by:

1   *The influence of the Roman Catholic Church.* Poland was unusual in the status of the Church; over 80 per cent of the population are practising Catholics. The new movement, as with its predecessors, enjoyed Church support and the active involvement of several of the lower clergy. In 1979 the Pole *Cardinal Wojtyla* was elected Pope. His emotive visit to Poland in 1979 made the situation even more tense.
2   *Russian inhibitions.* Gierek (and his successor Stanislaw Konia in 1980) were dependent upon the availability of Russian aid. The withholding of aid was likely only to worsen the situation and produce demonstrations. The USSR could have sent troops into Poland, but there was the prospect of resistance even from the Polish army, the draining involvement in Afghanistan and then the problem of finding someone able to head a puppet régime and face the internal economic problem.

(d) Solidarity (August 1980–December 1981)

In August 1980 the strikers won recognition of the right to strike and to form free trade unions – the first in the Soviet bloc. They also won promises of political and governmental reforms, improved pensions, wages, working conditions and holidays and regular broadcasts by the Roman Catholic Church. The Gdansk shipyard workers were now in alliance with a wide range of workers in other industries and the settlement was a national settlement with the Solidarity federation of free trade unions. However, by the summer of 1981 its demands were becoming unacceptable to the USSR. The USSR's solution was to use reliable elements of the Polish army to seize control of the government in December 1981, arrest the leaders of Solidarity and install as prime minister the respected General Jaruzielski. Although Solidarity claimed a membership of 10 million, the *coup* was relatively peaceful and only 60 people were killed by the security forces. Walesa by then had become an international hero. A deeply religious man, he had refused to push the 'revolution' too far lest it became violent; he was arrested and confined for eleven months.

(c) Poland after 1981

The situation did not change greatly. The economic problems persisted; by 1985 Poland had foreign debts of $26,000 million dollars and was virtually a Third World economy. After a period of imprisonment the immensely popular Walesa was released and, to the confusion of his enemies, won a Nobel Peace Prize. The Solidarity movement continued, albeit underground, with a membership of perhaps 1.2 million activists and led by the ex-trade union organiser Zbigniew Bujak. The strong support of the Church was a vital factor, as was the existence of a considerable underground press. The Jaruzielski régime was obliged to behave with considerable caution.

1   *The Roman Catholic connection.* The murder of the popular young curate *Father Jerzy Popieluszko* in October 1984 by a squad of secret policemen simply provided a martyr for the cause of Solidarity and hardened the link between it and the Church. A number of subordinate officers were actually tried and imprisoned to try and defuse a feared national uprising. The affair boosted Church membership and sparked off an upsurge in underground Solidarity activity.
2   *The need to restore international financial credibility.* In December 1981 the USA imposed economic sanctions upon Poland in response to the military takeover, and these did have a considerable effect. In February 1987 the sanctions were removed. By then there were notable developments in the sphere of East–West relations.

33.12 Conclusion

The problems of the states of eastern central Europe were still the traditional ones of economic underdevelopment, national and ethnic rivalries and misgovernment. The superimposition of Communist rule had merely changed the flavour and added a new Soviet dimension. The possession of the satellite empire was by no means an unmixed blessing for the USSR. It was the startling events in Poland above all which revealed the inadequacies of the Soviet brand of informal imperialism.

Questions

1   How far did Krushchev change Stalin's policies in Russia and eastern Europe?   [OC]
2   What do you understand by 'destalinisation'? How far did it affect Krushchev's policies in the USSR and eastern Europe?   [OC]
3   Give an account of the events in: (a) Hungary in 1956, and (b) Czechoslovakia in 1968. Why did the USSR intervene in these countries?   [CAM]
4   Outline the main events which took place in: (a) Hungary in 1956 and (b) Czechoslovakia in 1968. What did these risings achieve?   [CAM]
5   To what extent did Krushchev's domestic policies represent a 'revolt against Stalinism'?   [CAM]
6   What caused the rift between Tito's Yugoslavia and the Soviet bloc?
7   Describe the ways in which the following demonstrated their opposition to the Soviet Union in their own countries: Tito in Yugoslavia; Nagy in Hungary; Dubček in Czechoslovakia.
8   Study source A and then answer the questions which follow.

Source A: The '30 October Declaration' (1956).

> It is well known that, under the Warsaw Pact and under agreements between the governments, Soviet troops are stationed in the republics of Hungary and Romania. In the republic of Poland, Soviet troops are stationed under the terms of the Potsdam Agreement with the other great powers, as well as under the terms of the Warsaw Pact. There are no Soviet troops in the other people's democracies.

In order to insure the mutual security of the socialist countries, the Soviet Government is prepared to review with the other socialist countries signing the Warsaw Pact the question of Soviet troops stationed on the territory of the above-mentioned countries.

In doing so, the Soviet Government proceeds from the principle that the stationing of troops of one member state of the Warsaw Pact on the territory of another state shall be by agreement of all the member states and only with the consent of the state on the territory of which, and on the demand of which, these troops are to be stationed.

The Soviet Government believes it is essential to make a declaration regarding the recent events in Hungary. Their achieving great progress on the basis of the people's democratic order, justifiably raised the questions of the need for eliminating the serious inadequacies of the economic system, of the need for further improving the material well-being of the people, and of the need for furthering the battle against bureaucratic excesses in the state apparatus. However, the forces of reaction and of counter-revolution have quickly joined in this just and progressive movement of the workers, with the aim of using the discontent of the workers to undermine the foundations of the people's democratic system in Hungary and to restore to power the landlords and the capitalists.

(a) What were the 'recent events in Hungary' (line 15) which prompted this Soviet declaration?
(b) According to this what were the justifications for the stationing of Soviet troops in other states outside the USSR?
(c) What do you think was likely to be the real motive behind this declaration?
(d) Why did the western powers not attempt to go to the help of Hungary despite the pleas of its lawfully established government?

Source: N. Krushchev, '30 October Declaration 1956' in N. Barber, *Seven Days of Freedom* (Macmillan, 1974).

Communist Europe 1985–91

Introduction

The 'six years that shook the world' opened with the coming to power of the relatively youthful Mikhail Gorbachev and concluded with his resignation from the post of General Secretary of the Communist Party of the Soviet Union following an attempted right-wing coup in August 1991. By then the USSR had virtually disintegrated, and its components were in a state of political and economic crisis. In addition, by process of 'chain reaction', the Soviet empire in eastern and central Europe had undergone a series of revolutions and the establishment of democratic régimes which was associated with the collapse of the old communist military alliance, and the end of the Cold War. The key to these startling events was the Gorbachev policies of *perestroika* and *glasnost*, although that should be regarded as a catalyst which triggered underlying forces in the USSR and eastern Europe.

34.1 The pre-crisis

Gorbachev and the other reformers believed by 1985 that a 'pre-crisis' situation had been reached in the USSR. Despite her status as a global superpower the domestic economy could not meet the needs of the population. An unresponsive political system and inefficient planning led to crime, corruption and a black economy. Gorbachev remarked in 1985, 'Try to get a flat repaired: you will definitely have to find a moonlighter to do the job for you – and he will have to steal the materials from a building site!'

The result by the 1980s was cynicism and alienation amongst the populace, and this was reflected in high levels of alcoholism and poor labour discipline. The basic cause was the paradox of the 'administrative command system' which had two inherent contradictions.

(a) *The planning system was increasingly chaotic*

There were two fundamental problems:

1   *The sheer scale of operations.* With the activities of 25 million administrators and the production and distribution of 20 million products, it was inevitable that the theory of the system would not be matched in reality.

2   *The vested interest in providing misinformation.* To be effective, the command
    system depended upon accurate information from below. However, the fear of the
    consequences of giving bad news and failure to achieve planning targets and the
    desire to seek easier, achievable targets encouraged those below to generate
    misinformation.

The result was that a system which had more or less worked under the compulsion of
the Stalinist Terror had deteriorated into a semi-stagnant pattern of informal relationships based on the rule 'do what you have always done, but a bit more of it'. The
defence industry was more efficient and innovative but drained resources from the
domestic economy, especially as the size and cost of the Soviet fleet escalated and after
Reagan came to power in the USA.

(b)   *The all-powerful CPSU was increasingly powerless*

Party membership permeated the whole system and economy. The status and privileges
associated with membership of the *nomenklatura* depended upon apparent success,
while censorship and coercion ensured that any real criticism was stifled. The language
of revolution and change was matched with the reality of stasis and stagnation.
However, it was party links and relationships which held the whole system together.

34.2 Perestroika

When he became General Secretary at the age of 54 Gorbachev was the youngest
Politburo member, and was in good health as opposed to his two predecessors
Andropov and Chernenko (hence the question 'What support does Gorbachev have in
the Kremlin?' Answer 'None. He walks unaided'). He was a lawyer and, like his attractive and fashion conscious wife Raisa, a member of the intelligentsia. His policy of perestroika ('reconstruction') was not so much a plan as the general objective of achieving
'democratic socialism' by 'activating the human factor'. He did assume that there was a
consensus about the benefits of socialism and that the people were fundamentally loyal
to the CPSU and its ideals. However, as he adapted his strategy to achieve his goal he
unleashed forces of centrifugalism and disharmony which he could not control. There
were essentially four phases in the story of his failure.

(a)   *Uskoreniye ('acceleration') (1985–6)*

The initial view that a good dose of discipline would regain the course lost by Breznhev
was superficial.

1   *Higher plan targets were no more achievable* than previous ones because the
    planning apparatus did not work.
2   *Campaigns* against alcoholism, 'unearned incomes' and to promote quality were
    often counter-productive (see Illus. 34.1). The reduction in alcohol consumption,
    for instance, worsened the state deficit and stimulated inflation.
3   *The anti-corruption 'clean-up' was not pushed hard enough.* Boris Yeltsin's
    attempts in Moscow from December 1985 resulted in his forced resignation in 1987
    as a result of right-wing opposition.

Economic growth fell, shortages worsened, the budget deficit rose from 3 per cent in
1985 to 14 per cent in 1989 and inflation increased. Gorbachev lost credibility.

Illus. 34.1 'The male way of life'

A poster of the 1980s

Q   In fact like many of Gorbachev's 'campaigns' the attempt to cut down alcoholism had many
unanticipated and undesirable effects. Can you suggest some of these?

(b) *Revolution from above (1987–9)*

The need for more fundamental reform to increase popular commitment to the system
was recognised. The idea was that by removing Stalinist–Breznhevite repression and
control the system could be preserved. In fact it was bureaucratic and party interference which held the whole thing together.

1   *A legal and constitutional revolution* laid the foundations of the rule of law,
instituted new electoral laws at local and national level, and established executive

responsibility to a Supreme Soviet elected by a directly elected Congress of Peoples Deputies.

2   *A political revolution* in which the CPSU itself was democratised but also began to disintegrate as it lost its focus and public divisions emerged.

3   *A cultural revolution ('glasnost'* or 'openness') as censorship was removed, history was written honestly and political prisoners were released. These latter included the prominent Soviet physicist Andrei Sakharov in late 1986, Anatole Koriagen who had led the protest against the use of psychiatric methods upon political dissidents, and the leading Jewish dissident Josef Begun. At the same time, it was agreed that the case of the 10,000 Jews seeking to leave the USSR for Israel (the 'refuseniks') would be reconsidered.

4   *An economic revolution* with the Law on State Enterprises (1987) and the Law on Co-operatives (1988) which legalised small and medium-sized enterprises. There were only 193,100 by January 1990.

The attempt to restore 'people power', however, simply opened the floodgates to opposition groups of all sorts and antagonised radicals and conservatives equally because it had gone too far or had not gone far enough (see Illus. 34.2).

(c)   *Revolution from below (1989–February 1990)*

Until March 1990 the CPSU still held a monopoly of political power officially but in that month it surrendered its 'leading role' in the constitution. There were two general causes.

1   *A spiralling economic crisis.* The 'administrative command system' was being replaced not by a free market economy but by chaos. Disorganisation led to shortages and hoarding, mounting inflation and further falls in productivity. By 1989 40 million people were living below the official poverty level of 75 roubles a month.

2   *Growing political awareness.* From May 1989 when the newly elected Congress met the televised debates and open denunciations of government policy had a revolutionary effect. Anatoly Sobchak, a radical who later became mayor of Leningrad, said, 'The political awareness of people changed more in three weeks than in the preceding 50 years' (see Illus. 34.3).

In March 1990 the CPSU agreed to transfer power to the legislatures of the republics, and its own disintegration was accelerated as a result.

(d)   *Crisis management (1990–1)*

From then until August 1991 Gorbachev manoeuvred between the conservative and radical wings but without a long-term policy. His position worsened because of:

1   *Economic collapse.* By 1991 inflation was up to 22 per cent. In the first six months the GNP fell by 10 per cent, exports by 23.4 per cent and imports by 50 per cent. In summer 1990 Gorbachev failed to force through his *Shatalin Plan* for a 500 day drive towards a market economy against right-wing opposition.

2   *The 'war of laws'.* The fifteen republics all elected legitimate governments and they, and some of the federal territories, declared themselves independent or autonomous. Their resistance to central demands just aggravated the economic problem. In late 1990–early 1991 Gorbachev turned to the right, and there were attempts to restore censorship and curb strikes and demonstrations. However, the use of tanks in Lithuania in January 1991 and the deaths of eleven people in

„ПЕРЕСТРОИЛИСЬ"

A poster of 1987

The shields read: 'red tape', 'careerism', 'incompetence', 'bureaucratism', 'show', 'conformism'. The bureaucratic opponents of Perestroika form for the attack.

Vilnius merely worsened the centre–republican struggle.

3   *Deterioration in authority and legitimacy.* Gorbachev assumed considerable executive powers in March 1990 but there was still not a new constitution, and his failure to stand for election and give up the post of CPSU General Secretary

Source: A poster of January 1989.

Under Gorbachev, reform threatened to reach even the classroom.

undermined his popularity and authority. On the other hand, Boris Yeltsin had been elected president of the RSFSR in June 1991 and was the leader of the radical reformers.

In April 1991 Gorbachev turned to an alliance with Yeltsin and eight other republics to achieve genuine decentralisation, but this was the trigger for the abortive August coup.

34.3 Disintegration of the USSR

The twin, related process was the revelation that the nationalities policy of the CPSU had not been as successful as it appeared. There were three negative factors at work:

(a) *Inherent national and ethnic divisions*

1   *The ill definition of USSR internal borders.* There were 15 Union republics and 38 autonomous republics, regions and areas. Only 30 per cent of the boundaries were legally defined.
2   *Ethnic fragmentation.* Although every ethnic group had a territory 60 million people actually lived outside their own republics with great potential for discord between majority and minority groups.
3   *Latent hostility.* Antagonism was often deep rooted and historical. The Armenian–Azeri conflict over Nagorno Karabakh dates back to the last century in its origins. The Baltic republics had been independent until 1940.

(b) *Russification*

In pursuing cultural integration the CPSU had given a clearly preferential position to Russia and Russians. The result was that Russia was identified with unpopular central policies and this caused resentment not only amongst non-Russians but also Russians.

(c) *Centralism and economic complementarity*

The central authorities depended heavily on Russian wealth for their power. On a wider scale, the economy of the USSR had been developed in such a way that there was massive interdependence and that the drive towards a market economy required the involvement of the republics.

From 1988–9, and most obviously in the Baltic republics, there were moves towards democracy and sovereignty. The refusal of Gorbachev to concede local control over resources or fixed assets, or to negotiate a new Union treaty together with the election of nationalist Popular Fronts in the republics in 1989–90, resulted in declarations of sovereignty and mounting resistance to military drafts, price increases and central budgetary contributions. Gorbachev failed to produce a new treaty when he was allied with Yeltsin (summer 1990), then moved towards the right with his first draft (November 1990), but failing to obtain sufficient support for it in a referendum he turned back to Yeltsin and finally produced a treaty which would grant autonomy (April 1991) but triggered the August coup. Significantly, the new *Confederation of Independent States* (CIS) was the result of an agreement between Russia, Ukraine and Belarus which bypassed Gorbachev and the central authorities. He resigned on Christmas Day.

34.4 The August Coup

The detention of Gorbachev and his family on 18 August by a group of right-wing plotters was followed by attempts to re-establish censorship and mobilise military forces to 'restore order'. The plotters believed that the economic crisis and proposed Union Treaty would produce anarchy and the disintegration of the USSR, and expected to have considerable public support because of disenchantment with Gorbachev. It failed because of a combination of:

(a) *Indecisiveness*

Plans had been established but the 'Gang of Eight' was divided and not ruthless enough to implement real coercion. There were no mass arrests, the tanks in Moscow were simply told to 'enter and stay put' and control of communications was never complete.

(b) *Illegitimacy*

The claim that it was a legal assumption of presidential power because of Gorbachev's illness merely emphasised its self doubt. In fact there was a good deal of popular support according to public opinion polls.

(c) *Resistance*

Yeltsin's counter decrees led and symbolised the resistance to the coup, but since they were in the name of Russia rather than the USSR they were a sort of hidden coup. Also the waves of strikes, some mass demonstrations and refusal by many young army and KGB officers to take part in the coup were more effective.

There is a theory that Gorbachev was actually a party to the coup plan which was an attempt to rally support and restore order by means of a legitimate presidential declaration of a state of emergency. However, in the event he resigned as General Secretary, the process of dismantling the power and symbols of the CPSU and USSR began and the republics declared their independence.

34.5 East European end games

The developments in the USSR were bound to affect the stability of its satellite states but Gorbachev signalled the start of the process of democratisation on the July 1989 when he spoke at the Council of Europe and openly rejected the so-called 'Brezhnev Doctrine' of 1968, which justified the invasion of Czechoslovakia and opened the way to the separate development of the satellite states. Throughout the next 18 months the communist régimes were all replaced with popularly elected governments in a process which was inevitably linked not only by the removal of the external threat of Soviet tanks but also by the examples displayed in the press and on television screens, and also, occasionally, by the helping hand of the KGB.

The way in which the changes occurred varied according to local circumstances but it is possible to categorise them into three:

1 The East German 'bloodless revolution'.
2 A northern pattern in Poland, Czechoslovakia and Hungary where communism had been externally imposed from the start.
3 A Balkan pattern in Albania, Bulgaria, Rumania and Yugoslavia where communism was more deeply rooted and entwined with ethnic nationalisms.

34.6 The East German 'Bloodless Revolution'

The GDR had always been a purely artificial state with a régime which was only positively supported by a minority élite. The bulk of East Germans were indifferent to it. There were three key stages in the fall of the régime:

(a) *The fall of Erich Honecker (October 1989)*

1 *The growth of dissidence.* By the late 1980s the basis of the régime was already weakening because of the greater contact of the GDR citizens with the West and because it had clearly failed to achieve the goal of a classless society (having merely created, it was said, the upper classless, the middle classless and the lower classless). Dissent developed from two directions:

– The peace movement was originally government sponsored and designed to attribute belligerent motives to the West, but it became independent and more

outspoken under the leadership of Protestant clergymen.
– An active environmentalist movement which dated from the 1980s.

Dissidence was stimulated by the success of Solidarity and by Gorbachev's policies and was very obvious in the demonstrations in January 1988, which coincided with the annual march to commemorate the deaths of Karl Liebknecht and Rosa Luxembourg, and in 1989 at the time of the local elections.

2   *The acceleration of migration.* Travel restrictions had been relaxed throughout the 1980s. In 1987 1.2 million East Germans visited the West alone. However, there was mounting pressure for greater freedom and this was unexpectedly stimulated when Hungary opened its Austrian border and refused to stop the movement of East Germans across it (10 September 1989). Attempts to plug that gap simply turned the flood towards Poland and Czechoslovakia and provoked greater dissidence in the form of protest meetings, the formation of independent civic organisations and the appearance of a Social Democratic Party.

3   *Political inflexibility.* Erich Honecker applauded the bloody Chinese suppression of dissidence and claimed, in January 1989, that the Berlin Wall would last for another century. However, in October 1989, at the celebration of the fortieth anniversary of the GDR, Gorbachev made it clear that the days of the Soviet bloc were over and made his sympathy with the reformers very clear. This was the trigger for huge popular demonstrations in Leipzig, and when the local authorities held back from police suppression of the march on 9 October, other cities began to follow suit. When Honecker finally fell in October 1989 it was the result of an internal party coup led by Egon Krenz and others who had a slightly more moderate image.

(b)   *The opening of the Berlin Wall*

Opposition was focused upon the right to travel, and the most dramatic symbol of the fall of the régime was the accidental total opening of the checkpoints on 9 November. This resulted from a misleading impression given in a press conference which led to floods of excited citizens converging on the exits where the guards were confused by the reports and made no attempt to close them.

(c)   *National elections (March 1990)*

Continued demonstrations, internal party dissension and revelations of the privileges and corruption of the party élite led to the resignation of Krenz and his replacement by Hans Modrow, whose régime was increasingly influenced by a *Round Table* group of dissident leaders and moderate communists. When it forced the dissolution of the *Stasi* in January 1990 it had virtually obtained a veto. It forced the pace to free elections in March 1990 in which the Christian Democratic Union won 41 per cent of the total turnout of 93 per cent and formed a coalition government under Lothar de Maizière.

The next stage was the reunification of Germany (see Section 36.5).

34.7 The Northern pattern

As in East Germany the conversion of Poland, Hungary and Czechoslovakia was relatively bloodless.

(a) Poland

Stalemate between Solidarity, whose impetus was dwindling, and a party which ranged in attitude from ultra-right old guard Stalinists to advocates of a 'marketeering pluralism' was broken by Gorbachev urging Jaruzielski towards political reform:

1   *The repudiation of the Party* by the electorate in June 1989 was stimulated by social unrest amongst blue collar workers and the recognition of the truth about the Katyn Forest massacre. Despite an agreement with Solidarity and 65 per cent reserved places for the party it was massively rejected.
2   *Divisions within Solidarity* began to emerge as the Communist Party began to break up. It was the leader of a coalition government which benefited from an economic recovery but a rift between the intelligentsia and the Walesa led blue collar group began to appear.
3   *Walesa was elected as president* in November 1990 when Jaruzielski resigned. However, an alarming aspect was the strength of support for the politically unknown expatriate businessman Stanislaw Tyminski.

(b) Czechoslovakia: the 'velvet revolution'

The downfall of the repressive Husák–Jákes régime arose from the coalescence of three groups:

1   *The dissident groups* VONS and Charter 77 which were reformist socialists of the 1968 style, students and intellectuals.
2   *The Catholic Church*, inspired by the election of the Slavic pope John Paul II and led by Cardinal Tomasek. Its opposition was based on the human rights issues, and focused upon a struggle to obtain the filling of vacant sees which was finally agreed upon in 1989.
3   *Spontaneous demonstrations* by young people in Prague, in 1989, stimulated by the events in East Germany, the counter-productive effects of police brutality and the missionary influence of Polish and Hungarian dissidents. These were anti-socialist. There is a theory that they were deliberately fanned by secret police and KGB units acting under instructions from moderates in Czechoslovakia in alliance with Gorbachev, intending to achieve the replacement of the régime but maintain a socialist system, but they lost control of events. The death knell of the régime was when there was swelling blue collar support for the demonstrations, since they had been effectively courted by the régime.

The dissident dramatist Vaclav Havel brought these elements together into Civic Forum and on 10 December Gustav Husák resigned following massive demonstrations of *c.* 750,000 people in Prague and a symbolic general strike. On 29 December 1989 Havel was elected as president.

(c) Hungary

There were several factors at work in this rather more confused and fragmented situation:

1   *The impact of the 'second economy'* of Kádár's New Economic Mechanism which benefited peasants and entrepreneurs although not the factory blue collar workers. It began losing its appeal in the 1980s because of the dependence on low quality East European imports and its cost in worker stress.
2   *The proximity of Austria* constantly held up the lure of western goods and tastes,

especially in the conditions of the late 1980s when there was a marked deterioration in health and social conditions.

3   *The power of history* and the symbolic decision in June 1989 to rebury Imre Nagy and the other heroes of 1956 in a grave of honour.

In fact Karoly Grosz who replaced Kádár in 1988 as a result of an internal party coup just slipped into greater concessions as the dissidence grew and his policy of buying off opposition with economic reforms failed. Strikes were legalised in July 1989, the general move to a market economy was accepted in August, the borders with Austria were opened in September and in October 1989 the Communist Party renamed itself the Socialist Party. In April 1990 it was voted out of power and replaced by the *Democratic Forum* which formed a coalition.

34.8 The Balkan pattern

Where communism had not been simply imposed from outside and where nationalist divisions and values were more significant, the course of events was more painful and the effects were not so clear cut.

(a)   *Rumania: the confiscated revolution*

Ceauşescu had effectively mobilised Rumanian nationalism to support his brand of communism, and survived by playing off groups within Rumania as well as exploiting divisions between the USSR, China and the West. However, his sudden fall from power in December 1989 resulted from:

1   *General social and economic failure.* By 1989 he had lost all popular support because the price of his régime was economic chaos, low quality goods, food shortages, pollution, malnutrition and rising mortality.
2   *Magyar resistance* to the removal of a popular reformist priest from Timisoara. What started as a Magyar response to ethnic persecution became a broad transethnic political rebellion.
3   *Personal miscalculation* by Ceauşescu. The 'conscience of the world' misread the situation and a demonstration marshalled at Bucharest was allowed to get out of hand on 21 December 1989. He and his wife were shot on Christmas Day after attempting to flee the country.
4   *Internal manipulation* by Communist Party apparatchiks who connived with Securitate and army elements to concert and steal the revolution under the guise of the *National Salvation Front*, which had existed for at least six months beforehand and was largely the creation of General Militaru who had been plotting against the régime since 1984. It is also likely that the Russian KGB was actively involved in this attempt to dispose of a serious embarrassment in the drive towards a new Europe.

The death of Ceauşescu was followed by a period of fighting between civilians, soldiers and Securitate, following which the NSF won the elections of May 1990 and the presidential office was taken by Ion Iliescu. However, the change had not been so dramatic. The new régime used a mob of miners in June 1990 to attack dissident students and intellectuals, and even established a bogus Leninist Party as a sham opposition. The old culture of 'divide and rule', alienation and nationalist persecution persisted.

(c) Bulgaria: a palace coup

The régime of Todor Zhivkov had been based upon a very close adherence to the USSR and a nationalist stance against the 'historic foes' of Greece and Turkey. However:

1 *The reduction of Soviet oil supplies* and other subsidies from summer 1985 put the economy under pressure and eventual attempts to embrace a form of perestroika in 1989 seriously damaged Zhivkov's credibility within the party.
2 *From 1988 a human rights group* and other dissident organisations were in existence.
3 *Persecution of ethnic minorities was counter-productive.* The mass emigration of Turkish Muslims produced chaotic labour shortages.
4 *Preference of Vladimir Zhivkov* by his father for ministerial office may have been the eventual trigger since he was very unpopular.

In November 1989 Zhivkov was ejected by a Politburo vote. The Communist Party changed its name to Socialist and committed itself to develop a new market economy. In fact it actually won the national elections in June 1990. Only over the next couple of years did the new opposition groups begin to assume greater importance.

(c) Albania

Here the Communist Party had even greater legitimacy as a 'native' growth and the country had been managed by a combination of self sufficiency and the opening of relationships with virtually all states except the USSR and USA. With the death of Enver Hoxha in 1985 the new régime responded to more vociferous opposition from students and dissident groups and recurrent embarrassing emigration of shiploads of dissidents to Italy in the full glare of the world media:

1 *Nationalist assertion* against the Serb repression of Albanians in Kosovo, but also as a tool to harness support for the régime.
2 *Elimination of internal party ultra Stalinist opponents* won Ramiz Alia the image of a moderate, quite unreasonably.
3 *A steady stream of political concessions* to try to forestall opposition by means of 'firebreaks' culminated in free elections in March 1991 which the Communists actually won, installing Alia as president.

(d) Yugoslavia: the 'Serbian Corollary'

The key to understanding the Yugoslav tragedy is the strength of Serb nationalism based on deep-rooted historical tradition, the belief that 'Only solidarity saves the Serbs', the vested interest of Serb political and industrialist élites, and the confusing fragmentation of Serb minorities throughout Yugoslavia, which was acceptable only while it was a single state. There were two aspects to the developments from 1987.

1 *Increasing nationalist aggressiveness* of the Serb extremists represented especially by Slobodan Milosevič, the leader of the Serb Socialist Party, who became president of Yugoslavia and the League of Communists in 1987 by process of ethnic rotation.
2 *The movement towards republican independence* partly in reaction against the danger that the Serbs would seek to withdraw autonomy in the way that they had in 1989 with the Albanians in Kosovo. So in April–May 1990 democratic elections in Croatia and Slovenia returned nationalist governments which declared

independence in June 1991 after the breakdown of discussions about a remodelling of the Yugoslav confederation.

The result was a brief and ineffective intervention by the Serb-led federal army in Slovenia where the Serb minority was negligible, then a far more serious conflict with Croatia in 1991 where the minorities were much greater and wartime antagonisms were still easily revived, and then in Bosnia Herzegovina where there were substantial Serb minorities in a largely Muslim republic. In the process the emphasis on 'ethnic cleansing' grew, as did the greater local control of hostilities by guerrilla and militia groups.

34.9 Conclusion: the speed of the tiger

The underlying cause of these developments was the failure to stimulate enough growth and prosperity to ensure the legitimacy and acceptability of the communist régimes. Gorbachev lost control and ended up 'riding the tiger' whose speed became his best insurance until he fell. In eastern Europe his reforms were only a trigger to change but Gorbachev lost control there as well as economic problems began to force the pace. In the post-USSR era the most prevalent feature is the revival of a virulent nationalism with potential flashpoints associated with irredentas, border anomalies and historical claims. The most obvious of these are in the Baltic ethnic maelstrom, and especially Macedonia, but also in Moldavia and Transylvania where the Balkan instability threatens to spill into eastern central Europe. As alarming is the possibility of the intervention of Turkey to support fellow Muslims, stimulated by its own nationalist revival based on economic growth.

Questions

1 What was meant by the term 'pre-crisis'?
2 By what means had the post-war planning system of the USSR actually degenerated into a block to economic development?
3 Summarise the sequence of events by which Gorbachev's reforms culminated in the overthrow of the very socialist system which he was seeking to maintain?
4 What was the significance of the so-called 'war of laws'?
5 Why did the August Coup of 1991 fail?
6 To what extent was the East German Revolution a product of events beyond the borders of the state?
7 Why were there different patterns to the decline and fall of communist authoritarian régimes in the various states of eastern central Europe and the Balkans? Did the revolutions have anything in common?
8 What was meant by the 'Serbian Corollary' to the dissolution of Yugoslavia?
9 Study source A and then answer the questions which follow.

Source A: The Gorbachev analysis.

> We act according to Lenin ... which means to study how the future grows out of the present-day reality and to map out our plans accordingly ... The renewal of developing socialism is a process which goes beyond the turn of the century ... Of everlasting importance is the fact that Marxism, developing the ideas of socialism, represented socialism as the natural product of the progress of civilisation ...
>
> As we delve deeper into the essence of our own history, it becomes increasingly clear that the October Revolution was not an error – and not only because a realistic alternative to it was by no means a bourgeois democratic republic, as some people now try to make us believe – but an anarchic mutiny, a bloody dictatorship of the military and the establishment of a reactionary anti-popular régime ...

At the present complex stage, the interests of the consolidation of society and the concentration of all its sound forces on the difficult tasks of perestroika prompt the advisability of keeping the one-party system ... The socialism to which we advance during perestroika means a society based on an effective economy, on the highest achievements of science, technology, and culture, and on the humanised social structures.

(a) What is the essential theme of Gorbachev's remarks?
(b) Why did he justify the keeping of the one-party system? Why could this be seen as in contradiction to the need to develop socialism in the USSR?
(c) Why did Gorbachev emphasise the fact that the October Revolution was the result of a deliberate act by anti-democratic elements?

Source: M. Gorbachev reported in *Pravda*, 26 November 1989.

Introduction

The years of the Cold War tempered and hardened the communist and anti-communist blocs. Encouraged by the process of decolonisation this division was becoming *global* from the 1950s, and extending into the regions of the 'Third World'. One effect of this has been that whereas European affairs had been at the heart of world history in the nineteenth century, Europe has now become just one of the theatres – albeit a major one – dominated by the rivalry of the two great superpowers. Since the 1950s there have been distinct fluctuations in the relationship between the two blocs, associated with changes in personalities and internal political structures, weapons technology and colonial and post-colonial developments.

35.1 The 'Thaw'

The death of Stalin in March 1953 and the inauguration of Eisenhower as US president in January the same year marked the start of a new phase in the relationship between the USA and USSR, although Secretary of State Dulles called for communism to be 'rolled back' as Truman had done.

(a) The 'Geneva Spirit'

The new current was reflected by a series of international discussions and arrangements:

1 *The Geneva Agreements (July 1954).* In May 1954, the French army was decisively defeated by the Vietnamese guerrilla forces led by General Giap at the siege of Dien Bien Phu. Although the USA was prepared to intervene on a large scale to counteract the triumphant *Viet Minh* forces, she was dissuaded from any exercise in brinksmanship by the British foreign secretary Anthony Eden and the French prime minister Pierre Mendès-France. At Geneva, it was agreed with China and the USSR that Vietnam should be divided into two states by the 17th degree of latitude, with Laos and Cambodia to be given their independence to form Eden's 'Protective pad' around them.

2 *The Austrian State Treaty (May 1955).* One result of an attempt by Eden to obtain a demilitarised zone in central Europe was the agreement that the occupation forces should be withdrawn from Austria which was pledged to perpetual

neutrality. This was a significant concession by the USSR, but the day after the treaty was signed the Warsaw Pact came into existence officially.

3   *The Geneva Conference (July 1955).* For the first time in ten years the leaders of the USA and USSR came together at the conference table, along with the representatives of France and Britain to arrange a treaty for Germany similar to that for Austria. In fact, it was unsuccessful.

(b)   The Paris Summit (May 1960)

The USA remained committed to its policy of *'containment'* while Khrushchev made it perfectly clear that *'coexistence'* was only a tactic, announcing to western diplomats in November 1956: 'we will bury you'. In the late 1950s, the problem of nuclear weapons entered a new phase when the USSR launched *Sputnik 1* in October 1957 and the USA followed with its first satellite, *Vanguard 1*, in March 1958. Largely as a result of the efforts of the British prime minister Harold Macmillan, arrangements were made for a summit conference in May 1960 to discuss the problems of the future of Germany, and of disarmament.

35.2 Challenges to 'peaceful coexistence'

The process of destalinisation encouraged revolts in Poland and in Hungary (see Section 33.5). In the latter case, the Hungarian government actually appealed (see Section 33.8) for help to the outside world. The western powers were at that moment distracted and divided by the Suez crisis and the USSR could veto any action by the UN. Even so, Soviet intentions were seriously discredited by the event. However, the end of the thaw in relations was reflected in a series of events in 1960–1.

(a)   The U2 'spy plane' crisis (May 1960)

By 1960 Khrushchev was committed to a long-term economic plan, with greater emphasis on the production of consumer goods, and so was more favourable towards some sort of restoration of relations and even submitted a sweeping plan for disarmament to the UN General Assembly. However, in May 1960 Khrushchev employed the incident of the shooting down of an American reconnaissance aircraft and capturing of its pilot Gary Powers to discredit the USA and destroy the Paris summit. Such flights had been going on for some time and were well known to the Russians; Khrushchev's apparent inconsistency of attitude was probably due to the development of opposition within the Soviet bloc from two sources:

1   The 'China lobby' within the USSR was bitterly opposed to any rapprochement with the USA, and the effect this would have on Russo-Chinese relations.
2   Military and non-military groups were increasingly alarmed by Khrushchev's defence policy of cutting conventional forces and relying more on nuclear missiles.

(b)   The Berlin Wall (August 1961)

By August 1961 the flight of refugees from East to West Germany had reached the alarming rate of over 1000 a day. Between 1949 and 1961 some 3 million people had escaped. This drain could have alarming economic and psychological consequences. The result was the extreme action of the German Democratic Republic in physically dividing Berlin to stem the flood. This was a very provocative act as far as the USA was concerned, and was a gauntlet which was taken up by President John F. Kennedy in his famous *'Ich bin ein Berliner'* speech (1963).

(c) The Cuban missiles crisis (October 1961)

In the aftermath of the disastrous failure of the Bay of Pigs invasion of Cuba in April 1961 by CIA-backed Cuban émigrés seeking to overthrow the newly established communist régime of Fidel Castro, Khrushchev began to enhance armaments supplies to Cuba. The threat to the USA posed by the siting of nuclear bombers and missiles in the Caribbean led President Kennedy to institute a blockade and warn the USSR to cease further deliveries. Khrushchev backed down, recalled a convoy approaching Cuba and agreed to cease the offending construction work on the island. This victory by Kennedy was considerably helped by a recent sharp deterioration in Russo-Chinese relations, and by the American achievement of a missile superiority of some 500 intercontinental ballistic missiles against the 75 of the USSR. But the confrontation had other consequences:

1   It was a stark revelation that the fate of the world and of Europe was in the hands of two superpowers, who were liable to act without consultation with even their allies.
2   The danger of such an incident leading to a nuclear war was reduced by the installation of a 'hot line' telephone link between the White House and the Kremlin.
3   In general the narrowness of the escape from catastrophe was a stimulus to disarmament discussions and to avoidance of direct confrontation.

35.3 The emergence of détente

From the 1960s the USA and USSR were involved in a wide range of indirect and proxy wars in Vietnam and in various parts of Africa in which success seemed primarily to favour the USSR. By the late 1960s, however, a number of factors contributed to a change in the pattern of relations between the superpowers.

(a) The internal problems of the USSR

From 1964–82, power in the USSR was concentrated in the hands of Leonid Brezhnev. Initially there was little change in policy; throughout the period though it became increasingly apparent that the Soviet economy was in difficulties – general economic growth fell from 8 per cent in the 1950s to 3.7 per cent in 1980. Within this context, there were two particular problems:

1   *The inadequate supply and quality of consumer goods.* The Russian people were offered little incentive in the form of consumer goods; the influence of the military – Khrushchev's 'metal eaters' – and the heavy industry bureaucracy ensured that this situation prevailed, because the share of heavy industry in total output rose from 68 per cent in 1953 to 74 per cent by 1979.
2   *Inefficient agriculture.* Under Khrushchev the heavy investment in agriculture and the 'Virgin Lands' scheme failed to expand output sufficiently. In 1972 the combination of the weaknesses of the agricultural system and bad weather meant that the grain crop was 18 million tons less than in 1970. In 1975 weather

conditions triggered a major agricultural failure, with a shortfall of 65 million tons. Not until 1977 did Brezhnev manage to introduce an element of private enterprise into the collectivised system as had already been done in Hungary and the other satellites.

The result was that the USSR was dependent upon imports of 'capitalist grain' – largely from the USA – and needed substantial technical aid and capital investment from the West. Between 1972–6 the USSR borrowed 11 billion dollars from the West; by 1980 this had doubled.

(b) The 'web of interests'

On the other hand, US policy towards the USSR in the early 1970s was biased towards increasing trade links. There were two particular influences in this direction:

1   *US economic problems.* The economic advisers of President Nixon, beset by the problems of a trade deficit and depreciating dollar, saw the USSR as a potential market.
2   *The theory of international peace based upon interdependence.* Secretary of State Henry Kissinger argued that by assisting economic development in the USSR and stimulating rising living standards, the West could expect the rising expectations of the Russian people to lead them eventually to support internal reforms in the political and administrative systems.

The result was the growth of all sorts of cultural and scientific exchanges, and of trade. In 1972, the two superpowers established a commercial commission and produced a trade agreement which was the basis of a considerable build-up of commerce.

(c) The 'China option'

The diplomatic situation of the USSR was considerably complicated in the 1960s by the sharp deterioration in her relationship with China over ideological and territorial differences. In 1969, this disagreement actually flared up into prolonged and bloody clashes on the frontier of the two states. A startling result of this growing alienation was the readiness of China under more moderate leaders to establish links with the West. In November 1968, China announced her readiness to live in peaceful coexistence with the USA. In 1971, the USA lifted all trade and travel restrictions. Then, in May 1972, President Nixon visited China and signalled a major diplomatic revolution in so doing. It was also notable that this, as with the unilateral releasing of the dollar from a fixed rate of exchange for gold (1971), was done quite independently of any consultation with the allies of the USA.

35.4 Détente

Apart from the growing commercial links and the disarmament discussions (see Section 35.5) the period was characterised by two particular developments.

(a) Ostpolitik *(1969–74)*

Even in 1966–9 a Christian Democrat–Social Democrat coalition had started to abandon Konrad Adenauer's policy of rejection of relations with eastern Europe. The failure to reach agreement with the Soviet bloc was also due to the fear of Polish leaders that relaxing the anti-West Germany stance would weaken the justification for firm communist rule in Poland and Russian reluctance to appear to be weakening in support for East Germany. The invasion of Czechoslovakia (see Section 33.9) was, to some extent, the result of Russian fears of any sort of *'Ostpolitik'* softening the lines of division between East and West. As far as Willy Brandt was concerned, the clear message from this invasion was that West Germany must accept the *status quo*. As Chancellor between 1969 and 1974, and leader of a coalition of Social Democrats and Free Democrats, he followed a concerted policy of reducing the areas of difference between West Germany and the Soviet bloc. This involved a series of agreements:

1 *A non-aggression pact with the USSR in August 1970*, which involved an acknowledgement of the existing European frontiers, including that between the two Germanies.
2 *Restoration of diplomatic relations with Poland in November 1970*, and the recognition of the Oder–Niesse frontier.
3 *A series of agreements between 1971–3*, resolving differences between the two Germanies, involved mutual recognition of their membership of NATO and the Warsaw Pact and culminated in the admission of both states to membership of the UN in 1973.

These agreements and the opening of diplomatic relations with Czechoslovakia, Hungary and Bulgaria resolved many of the problems left since 1945. But Berlin was still divided, and Brandt's *Ostpolitik* was very unpopular with many Germans. A growing decline in electoral support was crowned by the revelation that a very close aide had been a long-term Soviet spy and Brandt resigned to be succeeded by Helmut Schmidt.

(b) *The Helsinki Agreements (1975)*

A western European desire for security and the more relaxed attitude of the USSR in the 1970s led to the European Conference on Security and Co-operation in Helsinki between 1972 and 1975 which was also attended by the USA and Canada. The USSR was seeking a general endorsement of the post-1945 European frontiers and a discussion of security. In fact, she was manoeuvred into accepting considerably more:

1 *The Final Act.* A total of 35 states signed the complex of agreements about governmental and non-governmental contacts for social, economic and technical co-operation and a general recognition of European frontiers. In addition, the famous 'Basket Three' included a series of general principles in which also figured guarantees of human rights.
2 *Periodic reviews.* A number of Helsinki Watch committees were also set up in many of the participant countries, including the USSR, and there were general meetings to review progress in Belgrade in 1977 and Madrid in 1980–1. By then, however, the USSR had invaded Afghanistan and members of the Watch committee of the USSR were being persecuted. Even so, the hopes excited by Helsinki probably contributed to the growing ferment in central Europe, and especially in Poland.

35.5 Disarmament and arms control

The history of disarmament discussions has reflected not only changes in political will and popular enthusiasm but also the changing nature of nuclear technology itself. There were several stages.

(a) The failure of the Baruch Plan

In 1946, the USA proposed complete international ownership and control of nuclear energy with American stocks to be transferred to an international body. This was aborted by two factors:

1   The objection of the USSR to international ownership and insistence that all US stocks be destroyed.
2   A marked decline in interest resulting from the explosion in 1949 of the first Russian nuclear weapon and the preoccupation of the USA with events in China and Korea.

A revived attempt in 1951 also failed, but by the early 1950s there was growing concern about the effects of radioactive fallout.

(b) Phased disarmament proposals (1954–5)

Anglo-French and Russian plans envisaged a phased process involving reductions in conventional forces, reductions in nuclear stocks, the removal of bases on foreign soil, cut-offs in nuclear production and bans on the use of nuclear weapons. However, these proposals were blocked by:

1   Continued difficulty over the idea of an international control organisation.
2   A reluctance on the part of the western powers to drop the rearmament of West Germany.
3   The insistence of the USSR on the abandonment of the US bases in western Europe which were so vital to its defence.

Even so in 1957 there was a cessation of nuclear tests by tacit agreement – very much because enough knowledge had been acquired for the time being.

(c) The era of 'peaceful coexistence' (1958–63)

Several plans were proposed by the two superpowers and by a ten-nation disarmament conference at Geneva in 1960. There were significant results:

1   *The McCloy–Zorin recommendations (1960).* The Geneva Conference was short, but did consider a series of principles to govern future disarmament negotiations. In particular there was the problem of inspection and verification.
2   *Nuclear test ban agreements (1961–3).* The launching of the Campaign for Nuclear Disarmament (CND) in Britain in 1958 reinforced Harold Macmillan's pursuit of the goal of a nuclear test ban, and he acted as a vital intermediary between the USA and USSR. In July 1963 a UN sponsored conference produced agreement on a treaty to ban nuclear tests in the atmosphere, outer space and under water for an unlimited period. Apart from Britain, the USA and USSR (amongst other states) signed the agreement, but China and France did not.

(d) The Nuclear Non-Proliferation Treaty (1968)

Although the 1960s saw a surrogate war between the USA and USSR through their protégés in Vietnam, there was nevertheless a considerable degree of tolerance as far as nuclear war was concerned. The development of new methods of defending missile sites by means of hardened silos or by launching from submarines reduced the danger of preemptive surprise attacks because a 'second strike' retaliation was an effective deterrent. A significant agreement was achieved in 1968 between Britain, the USA and the USSR to seek to exclude other states from acquiring nuclear weapons. By 1980 this treaty had been signed by 114 states; notable exceptions were France, China, South Africa and Israel, who all had a nuclear capability.

(e) *SALT I*

By the late 1960s the balance was being affected by the development of MIRVs (multiple independently targeted re-entry vehicles) which could deliver a number of nuclear warheads, and of ABMs (anti-ballistic missiles) which could reduce the deterrent stability of balanced second strikes. In addition, the new missiles were capable of accuracy of a matter of yards. The Strategic Arms Limitation Talks (SALT), which started in 1969, had resulted in a variety of agreements by 1972:

Illus. 35.1   'America – 1983'

Source: A USSR poster.

1   The Sea-Bed Treaty banned the placing of nuclear weapons on the sea floor.
2   The Treaty on the Limitation of Defensive Anti-Ballistic Missiles restricted the two superpowers to two ABM sites each.
3   The Interim Agreement on Certain Measures with Respect to the Limitation of Strategic Arms which was to last until October 1977 fixed the level of missiles at the level of July 1972, and banned further construction of fixed land-based missile launchers.

(f) *SALT II*

Already SALT I was being bypassed in various ways. New secret MIRVs, the Backfire nuclear bomber and the SS-20 mobile launcher did not fit into the SALT I limited categories. On the US side there was the B-1 bomber and the new 'cruise' missiles which could bomb with pinpoint accuracy (see Illus. 35.1). New negotiations were started as early as November 1974. President Nixon had resigned over the Watergate issue, and it was President Ford who kept an appointment with Brezhnev to start work towards SALT II, albeit in a context of growing US distrust of the USSR resulting from the violation of the Helsinki agreements. In January 1977, Jimmy Carter became president. In June 1979, he signed a new SALT treaty to define each power's weaponry until 1985. Carter called it 'the most detailed, far-reaching comprehensive treaty in the history of arms control'.

35.6 Conclusion

Despite this fanfare, the US Senate refused to ratify Carter's treaty, and it was adhered to only voluntarily by the USA and USSR until May 1986 when President Ronald Reagan announced that in view of Soviet breaches, the USA would no longer observe the terms. Amidst a wave of American nationalism fanned by the Iranian holding of the American hostages at Teheran following the invasion of the US embassy, the support of the USSR for the Vietnamese invasion of Kampuchea, and the Russian invasion of Afghanistan in December 1979, the Republicans won the presidential election and Reagan was inaugurated in 1981.

Questions

1   To what extent, and for what reasons, was there détente between East and West in the period between 1953 and 1964?   [CAM]
2   How far was the Conference on Security and Co-operation in Europe (1972–5) able to overcome the forces dividing East and West?
3   Describe the development from Cold War to coexistence in the mid-1950s and 1960s, and to détente in the 1970s.
4   To what extent was the death of Stalin followed by a 'thaw' in international relations?
5   What were the main challenges to 'peaceful coexistence' in the early 1960s?
6   How successful were the various nuclear disarmament plans, proposals and agreements made between 1946 and 1979?

36 European unity and discord

Introduction

The sending of Soviet troops into Afghanistan in December 1979 to prop up a shaky communist régime was a dangerous start to the decade, and the continued fighting in Afghanistan cast a constant shadow over international relations until the mid-1980s. However, the remarkable events in the USSR and eastern Europe brought about by the policies of Gorbachev have signalled the possibility of profound changes in the relationship between western Europe and the successor states of the USSR and its former satellites. At the same time these developments, together with changes in American domestic politics, have affected the relationships of the western alliance.

36.1 New perspectives

The invasion of Afghanistan was the signal for the start of a new period of East–West relations. There were two factors contributing to the changing attitude of the West.

(a) *A revived fear of Soviet expansionism*

Soviet intervention, direct or indirect, had continued in Africa and was now extending to Afghanistan and Nicaragua. Throughout the 1970s the USSR had embarked upon a considerable expansion of her naval power, which implied a new policy of adventurism on the seas and escape from confinement to the continent. From the European standpoint there was a growing fear that the western European states were far more vulnerable to an onslaught by the overwhelming conventional forces of the USSR, since no American president would resort to nuclear weapons with the vast cost to the world and the USA which that would imply. The shooting down in September 1983 of a Korean commercial aircraft with a death toll of 260 because it had strayed over a military zone of the USSR did much to harden attitudes.

(b) *The Reaganite stance*

In May 1979 the election of Margaret Thatcher as the British prime minister reinforced a trend towards a more hard-line policy towards the USSR. This earned her the sobriquet 'Iron Lady' (frequently confused in the press with the 'Iron Maiden' which was a medieval instrument of torture). Then in 1981 the inauguration of Ronald Reagan as president marked a new departure in US foreign policy. Nuclear disarmament negotiations were renewed. In June 1982 the *Strategic Arms Reduction Talks* (START) round of negotiations commenced but this was in the context of a clear movement away from Kissinger's 'web of interests':

1 *The introduction of sanctions.* The USA was far more prepared to resort to sanctions on trade to strengthen its diplomatic initiatives and responses. In particular this applied to the export of advanced technology to the USSR. An aspect of this was the argument of the USA with her allies in Europe over the building of a gas pipeline from the Siberian gasfields to supply gas to Germany and France as well as the USSR.

2 *Increased armaments expenditure.* The development of the neutron bomb which could kill without causing significant damage to buildings was abandoned by Carter to underline his good intentions, but it was renewed by Reagan. Similarly, work on the manufacture of B-1 bombers was recommenced. In Europe the deployment of cruise missiles went ahead despite considerable anti-nuclear and environmentalist campaigns. Above all the USA embarked upon the *'Star Wars'* initiative (the Strategic Defence Initiative or SDI) which would carry warfare beyond the nuclear stage by employing new space technology such as laser power. However, this latter was seriously retarded by the destruction of the American space shuttle 'Challenger' in January 1986, which set back the SDI programme by at least three years.

3 *Ending of the SALT truce.* In May 1986 President Reagan announced that in view of Soviet breaches of the unratified SALT 2 treaty of 1979 (see Section 35.5(f)) the USA would no longer abide by the agreement. The USSR had actually added 8000 nuclear warheads to its arsenal since SALT 1. Both of the SALT treaties had actually allowed expansion in some areas, and made very little provision for verification.

36.2 The Gorbachev gambit

Gorbachev was very imaginative in his approach to foreign policy. He recognised that the Cold War was crippling the USSR and his policy was motivated by the need to reduce the burden of the arms race on the domestic economy. By 1987 the USSR was spending some 15–17 per cent of its GNP on defence as opposed to the 6 per cent of the USA. Gorbachev was also seeking to reduce the high cost of overseas military aid to pro-Soviet Third World countries and eastern Europe, while enhancing chances of improving exports to western Europe and importing high technology and negotiating aid from the West. In general a more stable international environment would give him the time he needed to proceed with internal domestic reform.

(a) Arms limitation and reduction

Gorbachev discarded all of the old Stalinist concepts and embraced a new radical military approach based on the idea of *'asymmetrical reductions'*, the USSR should cut deeper where it had a preponderance over the USA and seize the initiative. He took a series of steps:

1 *A unilateral ban on nuclear weapons testing* was introduced in 1985 and in 1986 he committed himself and the USSR to work towards the ridding of nuclear weapons from the world by 2000.

2   *The Reykjavik disarmament talks* in 1986 were followed by the reaching of an agreement with the USA, based on a proposal made by Gorbachev in March 1987, to eliminate all medium-range nuclear missiles from Europe and to eliminate strategic missiles over a ten-year period. This agreement was the basis of the *International Nuclear Forces Treaty* of 1987 which resulted in the USSR cutting 1836 missiles with 3136 warheads as opposed to 859 single warheaded US missiles. This was the first nuclear disarmament or limitation treaty which actually involved the destruction of a significant proportion of nuclear missiles, although it only covered 4 per cent of the nuclear arsenals of the two countries.

3   *A programme of unilateral cuts* in Soviet forces which started in December 1988 and aimed at a reduction by 500,000.

(b)   Withdrawal of Soviet troops

From 1986 Soviet troops were being withdrawn from Afghanistan until by 1989 the USSR had disengaged from a disastrous conflict in which it had lost 14,000 men. The various Afghan factions who had united against the invader turned against each other in a civil war. In late 1986 Gorbachev made it clear to eastern European party leaders that they would no longer have Soviet military intervention to rely upon. This was followed in 1987 with discussions about reductions in Soviet troops based in satellite states.

36.3 Strains in the western alliance

The process of arms limitation was helped by, and added complications to, strains which were appearing in the western alliance. At the same time, the deteriorating image of President Reagan within the USA made it all the more urgent that he should seek triumphs in the sphere of foreign policy.

(a)   US gunboat diplomacy

In the nineteenth century it was Britain who was accused of the arrogant use of power against small states. In the 1980s a revival of US nationalism was associated with a number of unilateral military actions which disturbed the relationship with NATO. These included the overthrowing of a left wing régime in Grenada in 1984 and retaliatory bomber raids on Libya in 1986 (see Section 32.5(c)).

(b)   The 'zero option' and the 'flexible response'

At Reykjavik the US proposal that the USA would eliminate all of its intermediate nuclear weapons in Europe if the USSR did the same, and which was similar to offers which had been made and rejected in 1981 and 1983, angered her NATO allies who had not been consulted first. This was seen as threatening to withdraw a 'rung' from the 'ladder' of escalation which was the alternative to massive retaliation. The intermediate missiles were also a very physical symbol of US commitment to European security. The fear was that Europe could be exposed to a sort of blackmail because it would remove the option of threatening Soviet targets, leaving the western European states dependant upon shorter range battlefield nuclear weapons or the long range American intercontinental systems to counter the very pronounced imbalance in conventional forces. In Europe at the time the Warsaw Pact had three times as many tanks, three times as many guns and twice as many tactical aircraft as NATO. Instead of the general weaponry agreement which would have been preferred by the Europeans, the USA and USSR signed the INF Treaty which was the sort of coup desired by both Reagan and Gorbachev to try to offset their internal domestic problems. As if to confirm the divorce of interests in late February 1987, President Reagan dismissed the NATO supreme commander General Bernard Rogers when his advisers, disturbed by his use of the term 'we Europeans', argued that Rogers had 'gone native'.

(c) The 'Irangate' scandal

The relationship between the USA and her NATO allies was not helped by the revelation that the Reagan administration had traded arms with Iran in order to secure the release of American hostages, using the proceeds to provide weapons for the right-wing 'contra' rebels in Nicaragua. By 1987 a victory by Iran in the Iran–Iraq War seemed likely, a result which was regarded by the western allies of the USA as being the worse of two evils. The report of the Tower Commission on the affair in February 1987 condemned many members of the Reagan staff for their involvement in unauthorised activities, and presented the image of a president who was losing control and could not remember whether or not he had authorised the arms sales in the first place.

36.4 From 'Cold War' to 'Cold Peace'?

The dissolution of the Soviet empire at the end of the decade and the change in the status of Russia as a result of the Gorbachev reforms have presented the states of western Europe with a range of new threats and problems, as well as opportunities to pursue stabilisation and achieve some sort of 'peace dividend'. There are three related issues especially:

1 *The impact of a reunited Germany* on the European balance of power.
2 *The status of Russia* and its relationship with the CIS, its so-called *'near abroad'*.
3 *The adaptability of the European security structures* and the need to develop a new set of institutions appropriate to the new European pattern.

36.5 The reunification of Germany

(a) The process of unification

There were three stages in the move towards unification.

1 *The failing legitimacy of the GDR.* Once the borders were opened the flood of emigrants started. By the end of 1989 this had swollen to 344,000, mostly young people and many of them key workers in industry and the state service. Consumer demand fell with the prospect of access to western goods. COMECON was faltering and western demand for GDR goods fell as the future of GDR state enterprises became doubtful. By summer 1990 there was 20 per cent unemployment and there were strikes and demonstrations in support of rapid unification.
2 *The election of a CDU dominated government.* Chancellor Kohl had initially advocated a moderate plan for unification in gradual stages, but was increasingly

driven to support a much more rapid and complete plan which was advocated by the East German CDU. A decisive step was Kohl's promise that no one would be worse off as a result of unification. In March 1990 with a 93 per cent turn-out the CDU won 41 per cent of the vote and formed a coalition under Lothar de Maizière with a majority sufficient to change the constitution. The target of 1 July 1990 was agreed for economic union and significant steps were taken in the establishment of a 1:1 exchange rate between the deutschmark and the ostmark and the extension of social legislation to eastern Germany.

3   *The 'Two plus Four Treaty'.* On the basis of an agreement made in February 1990 the two German states presented proposals for unification to the four occupying powers, for signature in September 1990. Key features were the guaranteed permanence of the Polish border, the freedom for Germany to join any alliance, the renunciation of biological, chemical and nuclear weapons, and the limitation of army strength to 37,000. By separate treaty with the USSR a schedule for Soviet withdrawal was agreed, together with substantial German trade credits.

On 3 October 1990 reunification took place. On 2 December the first all-German elections resulted in the victory for a Christian Democratic Union and Christian Socialist Union led coalition and the re-election of Helmut Kohl as Chancellor.

(b)   *The implications of unification*

Kurt-Georg Kiesinger once remarked that 'Germany has either been too strong or too weak for the peace of Europe'. Certainly there are aspects of the new Germany which raise the question as to a possible challenge to European security.

1   *It stands in the context of a fragmented Europe* which is once again vulnerable to ethnic and nationalist centrifugalism, and with eastern Europe likely to be an arena for German–Russian rivalry which is especially serious where they sponsor rival groups as in Yugoslavia with the Serbs and Croats.
2   *The sheer size and strength of the new Germany.* It is the second most populous state in Europe and the leading economy in the EU with 31 per cent of the GDP. However, the demographic trend is falling, and the economy is handicapped by the problems and costs of reunification.
3   *An increase in nationalist sentiment* is the inevitable corollary of reunification and the incorporation of East Germany, where the problems of unemployment and fall living standards are creating ethnic and social tensions and political unrest.
4   *It has the potential to be less restrained* because of the removal of strategic dependence and vulnerability and restraints on sovereignty, and the decline of 'national guilt'.

On the other hand, it is more likely that it will pursue its interests through exploitation of economic opportunities in eastern Europe and is also restrained by its membership of multinational institutions and procedures.

36.6 Russia, the CIS and 'near abroad'

The Confederation of Independent States (CIS) which replaced the USSR is a very fragile structure which exists only because of the integrated nature of the economy, which had been created and which could not operate without some form of understanding. Fear of a possible conservative reaction towards Soviet centralism and suspicion of Russian power meant that the loose association with periodic meetings of heads of state was the most that was acceptable, and even then the three Baltic states and, initially, Georgia withheld themselves from it. The suspicion of Russia was strengthened especially by the nationalist and right-wing successes in the 1993 elections, and particularly the rise of Vladimir Zhirinovsky, and comments by Yeltsin's ministers about the unification of the former USSR republics with the exception of the three Baltic republics. In Georgia the government of Edouard Shevardnadze was forced to enter the CIS following a successful 'rebellion' sponsored by the Russian army.

Stability in the area is threatened by a complex of factors.

(a) Ethnic relations and nationalism

A number of factors fan continued centrifugalism:

1 *The infectiousness* of the success of the larger republics and ethnic groups which set an agenda easily followed by others.
2 *The prevalence of weapons* resulting from the disintegration of the Soviet army and its withdrawal from eastern Europe. By July 1992 it was estimated that there were about 30 million firearms in private hands in the lands of the old USSR.
3 *The interlinked relationships* between ethnic groups and states. So, for example, the treatment of Uzbeks in Tadjikistan influences the treatment of Tadjiks in Uzbekistan.
4 *The vested interest of ethnic élites* in protecting their positions by resisting the greater concentration of authority necessary to try to counteract the divisions caused by economic disintegration.
5 *Aggravation over the division of former Soviet assets* as with rival Ukrainian and Russian claims to the Black Sea fleet.

(b) Economic crisis and the market economy

The transition to a market economy is hampered by:

1 *The social consequences* of the withdrawal of subsidies and social spending. So, for instance, the 'shock therapy' programme in Russia, in November 1991 to mid-1992, was stopped at the end of 1991 when 60 per cent of the population of Moscow was living beneath the poverty line and accelerating inflation and falling growth persisted.
2 *The technical problems of privatisation* which requires intricate legislation and challenges established interests.
3 *The prevalence of corruption* and the development of 'anarcho-capitalism' in the 'mafia superpower'.

(c) Authoritarianism and the 'nationalist card'

The unstable political situation in most of the new CIS states has encouraged the move towards authoritarian nationalist régimes which are often founded on the old communist party structures and personnel, as with, for example, the Kravchuck régime in the Ukraine. In Russia itself there has been a parallel development albeit associated also with the trauma of the loss of imperial status. Under Yeltsin there has been a return to the old CPSU centralist model, and even the revival of the KGB as the Ministry of Security. However, world concern as to the fragility of this new régime was displayed quite clearly when the failing health of Yeltsin in late 1995 produced shudders in stock markets fearful at the prospect of an ultra right-wing take-over.

One prospect is that the CIS could easily disintegrate and bequeath all of the problems of economic failure, responsibility for the huge USSR debt of 70 billion dollars, international agreements, and the control of nuclear power installations. The area is also full of potential flashpoints, and Russia's assumption of a responsibility for its 'near abroad' has involved the use of Russian forces in both open and covert operations.

(d) The invasion of Chechnya

The most serious challenge to the Yeltsin régime thus far has come from the break-away Caucasus region of Chechnya, a republic of the Russian Federation itself which straddles the key oil pipeline from the Caspian Sea to the Black Sea and has a long tradition of hostility towards Russia. It had, under its elected president Dzhokar Dudayev, declared independence in 1991. This excited considerable apprehension amongst Russians because the Chechen are a fierce people blamed very much for organised crime in Russia. Following the failure of covert attempts to destabilise the régime as in Georgia, in December 1994, Russian forces were finally sent into the republic amidst fears that this would be the start of another Afghanistan (see Illus. 36.1).

36.7 A new European security architecture

European diplomacy in the 1990s is very much dominated by the implications of the collapse of Soviet dominated eastern Europe. The testing ground for the European institutions in responding to these so far has been, above all, the Bosnian crisis in Yugoslavia, where there have been three sets of circumstances to take into account:

Illus. 36.1   Boris Yeltsin's shot backfires

Source: *The Observer*, 8 January 1995.

The invasion of the Republic of Chechnya in December 1994 resulted in embarrassing setbacks for the Russian army which failed in its initial attempts to storm the capital, Grozny. There were fears that another Afghanistan would result. The political survival of Yeltsin seemed to be in doubt as he fell more and more under the influence of 'hawks'.

Illus. 36.2 The spectre of death uncaged

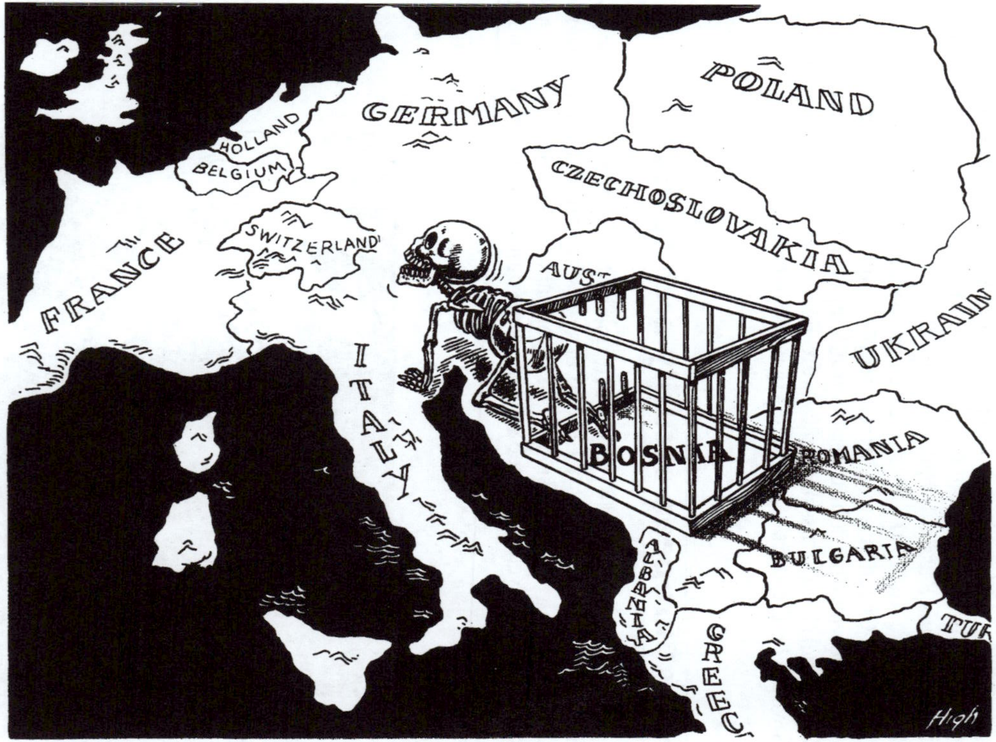

Source: *The Scotsman*, 3 May 1995.

A Croat offensive against the secessionist Serb-held region of Krajina resulted in a Serb rocket attack on Zagreb. This brought the end of a fragile truce, and produced fears that the war would spread beyond the borders of former Yugoslavia.

a What factors would be likely to assist the spread of ethnic and nationalist conflict into other regions of Europe in the 1990s?

1   The nature of the Bosnian crisis.
2   The differing perspectives of the USA, its western allies and Russia.
3   The adaptability and flexibility of the existing pan European institutions.

36.8 The Bosnian crisis

As Serb forces pursued the objective of the 'ethnic cleansing' of Bosnia and as repeated peace initiatives failed to hold the war in Bosnia began to display a number of alarming dimensions.

(a)   Civil and international war

The break-up of Yugoslavia was recognised by outside powers as was the independence of Slovenia, Croatia and Bosnia. The result was that it could be argued that the Serb aggression was a challenge to international order. In fact the real danger is that the war in Bosnia could easily spill into neighbouring countries (see Illus. 36.2). The USA regarded the conflict as an international one while its allies preferred to interpret it otherwise.

(b)   A new holocaust

From 1992 onwards when the first pictures of Serb internment camps were published and stories of Serb atrocities against Muslims began to circulate, the fighting began to assume a moral tone which had not been so marked previously. The American media especially found its public very receptive to the view that the arms embargo enforced by NATO should be lifted to enable the Muslims to defend themselves more effectively. It was this view which also began to erode the relationship between the USA and her western allies and led to NATO air strikes against Serb forces in 1994 as they repeatedly flouted UN attempts to guarantee 'safe areas', held UN soldiers hostage and blocked relief columns of lorries carrying food and medical supplies for civilians, and generally gave credibility to the US view that it was not enough to try to keep the peace where no peace existed in the first place.

(c)   Darker forces in the wings

An international embargo on fuel supplies to Serbia and other sanctions were slow to take effect; Belgrade traffic jams persisted remarkably. However, with a currency falling in value, a generally weakened economy and inflation, the Serb leaders attempted to restrain, then broke with the Bosnian Serb leaders and Britain, France and Russia began to press for the lifting of sanctions against the opposition of the USA. The situation was complicated by the awareness that there were even more extremist elements in both Serbia and Bosnia plotting against Milosevič and Radovan Karadzič the Bosnian Serb leader.

36.9 Russia and the USA

As the Bosnian crisis unfolded the perspectives of the USA and Russia were such as to abort any attempt at concerted direct European intervention (see Illus. 36.3).

Illus. 36.3 The mugging of Bosnia

Source: Chappatte, *La Tribune de Genève*. Reproduced in the *Daily Telegraph* in 1994.

Confronted with mindless thuggery by the Bosnian Serbs, the United Nations, NATO, the European Union and the USA are at a loss as to what should be done and who shall do it.

(a) *'America First!'*

The trend towards isolationism which was apparent in the late 1980s was strongly reflected in and reinforced by the election in 1994 of a right-wing Republican majority in Congress with the power to dictate foreign policy to President Clinton, including the unilateral ending of the monitoring of the NATO arms embargo which was a sharp shock to the alliance. At the same time, Britain and France were accused in the American press of appeasement. Other factors worked towards US isolationism:

1 *A relative inexperience of war and casualty levels.* During the whole trauma of the war in Vietnam only 47,000 Americans died. In the Second World War only 292,000 Americans died as compared to over 400,000 British service personnel and civilians and to the 13.6 million Russian and 3.25 million German service personnel alone. Protected by geography from the full horror of war the US perspective is bound to differ.
2 *The exaggerated effectiveness of modern technology.* The American preference for air strikes is the corollary of their unwillingness to commit ground forces although in fact they have proved to be largely ineffective against small mobile targets. For instance, in the Gulf War against Iraq US pilots claimed to have destroyed 90 Scud missile launchers, but in fact none was destroyed.
3 *The end of the Soviet threat* and the promise of a 'peace dividend'. In fact all that has happened is that the threat has become more complicated, many sided and less predictable.

(b) *Greater Russian assertiveness*

From 1989 Russia adopted a subordinate, supplicant and often humble posture towards the West from which economic support was needed. However, from the mid-1990s what is still the second largest nuclear and military power in the world began to be more assertive. This change occurred because of:

1 *The growing strength of Russian nationalism* feeding on the continuing failure to reform and destabilise the economy and the historical tendency for Russian rulers to focus discontent against foreigners.
2 *The revealed political weakness* of the western alliance, especially over the Bosnian crisis.

This manifested itself not only in military intervention in Chechnya and the rejection of proposals for CSCE sponsored peacekeeping operations in the Nagorno-Karabakh area, but also in unambiguous support for the Serbs and remarks by Yeltsin about the prospect of a 'Cold Peace' and 'You can't expect to rule the world from a single capital . . .'

36.10 The European security structure

The increasing insecurity in eastern Europe and the associated threat to general European peace has raised serious questions about the continued relevance of existing peacekeeping organisations:

(a) *North Atlantic Treaty Organisation*

The enlargement of NATO to include the states of eastern Europe is one option, and the preferred option for its main European members and especially Germany. However, there are three problems:

1 *The scope of the extended membership.* Avoidance of the creation of an unwieldy and diluted security structure means that there must be some selection, and the extension of security commitments to eastern Europe implies a preparedness to use force to guarantee security, with a nuclear shield for the new members but a nuclear threat to the countries on their borders. It involves drawing another line across Europe.
2 *Russian opposition to the idea of NATO expansion* which could conflict with its views as to its legitimate spheres of influence and the possibility of 'peace keeping' intervention in areas in its 'near abroad', within the CIS area. An extended NATO could be seen as merely an alliance against Russia.
3 *The USA is unwilling to commit ground forces* to respond to crises in Europe. However, the USA has the military resources and access to costly satellite surveillance systems which its European partners do not, while the latter expect to benefit from a 'peace dividend' to stimulate their economies.

(b) *The Western European Union*

The WEU has been in existence since 1954 and is the European pillar of NATO, the proposed defence body of the EU and with forces assigned to it albeit largely toothless. However, it was the EU which took the lead in intervening in Bosnia in 1991. There are conflicting views as to the future of the WEU:

1 France argues on behalf of the EU having its own military identity.
2 The British view is that the hasty creation of a European structure could drive the USA further into isolationism.

Germany sees merit in both views. An attempted compromise has been the concept of the Combined Joint Task Forces (CJTF) with the idea that NATO (or US) equipment could be made available to the WEU if necessary to respond to conflicts significant enough to warrant European but not American intervention. This failed in Yugoslavia when it was clear that the USA would not divorce itself entirely from European concerns.

(c) Conference on Security and Co-operation in Europe (CSCE)

This pan-European body of 53 members has existed since 1975 when it was established to monitor the Helsinki Final Act and to ease East–West tensions (see Section 35.4(b)). It is distinctive in that it includes the whole of Europe (including Russia) and the USA. Russia sees the CSCE as a more acceptable forum for European security negotiations, and the USA has sympathised with this proposal as a means of encouraging Russia to accept the enlargement of NATO. On the other hand, the fear is that either the CSCE will continue to be meaningless, or else it would just be a means of giving Russia a veto over NATO action while allowing it to act only as an observer of crises largely created by Russia itself.

36.11 The European Union

In the 1990s the story of the European Union is one of the move towards greater integration whilst confronted by a series of challenges.

(a) The Maastricht Agreement

In December 1991 at Maastricht the European Council agreed a treaty which would carry the Community towards eventual union.

1   *The powers of the European Parliament* were extended so that it would be less of a talking shop and had powers of co-decision with the European Council in a range of sectors and could also halt the legislative process if an absolute majority of MEPs agreed.
2   *A protocol on social policy*, the so-called *Social Charter*, was adopted by all members except Britain. This sets out the rights to be enjoyed by workers throughout the EU in matters such as fair pay, equal opportunities, health and safety, freedom of association, and collective bargaining and better working conditions.
3   *An irreversible commitment to a single currency.* A schedule and mechanism was established to provide for the achievement of Stage III by 1999. Britain reserved the right to opt out, and Denmark reserved the right to hold a referendum on the matter.
4   *A new European Union* 'founded on the European Communities supplemented by the policies and forms of co-operation established by this treaty' was established. Procedures were established for agreement and implementation of joint action in foreign policy.

(b) Nationalist tensions and popular cynicism

From 1987 onwards Turkey, Austria, Cyprus, Malta, Sweden, Norway, Finland and

Switzerland all applied to join the European Community. From October 1990 the new reunited Germany was a member, and Rumania, Bulgaria, Poland, the Czech Republic, Slovakia and Hungary have also expressed a desire for eventual membership. On the other hand, Denmark rejected the Maastricht Treaty in its initial referendum in June 1992, and only narrowly approved it in a second. In Britain the treaty passed through the House of Commons by only two votes. Finland, Austria and Sweden voted for membership in popular referenda but against considerable popular opposition, 47 per cent against in the case of Sweden. In Norway, where membership of the EEC had been rejected in 1972, membership of the EU was rejected in November 1994 by a 52.2 per cent majority. According to a poll in *Der Spiegel* and the *Financial Times*, in December 1994, only 24 per cent of Germans and 33 per cent of Britons want a single currency and it was remarked that 'a certain amount of passive support for Europe was unfortunately crumbling'.

Several factors contribute to the image problem of the EU:

1   *Concern about the impact on national sovereignty* and singularity. This is most obvious in Britain, but exists to varying degrees in all of the member states. The fear is that centuries of history, political sovereignty and national characteristics will be swept away and submerged beneath the paperwork of faceless bureaucracy.

2   *The scandals of the 'gravy train'.* A report by the Court of Auditors in 1995 claimed that there were so many serious and substantial errors in transactions underlying the budget that the legality of the EU accounts could not be guaranteed. Of a total budget of £56 billion in 1994 it was estimated that 4 per cent had not been properly accounted for and had probably been handed out in error. Beyond that was a further 14 per cent which could not be verified because proper accounting procedures had not been adhered to. Equally well publicised are the high salaries and perks of European MEPs and officials whose lifestyle contrasts very favourably with that of the average worker.

(c)   *Making the CAP fit*

A ready source of stories of waste and corruption and the greatest burden on the EU budget is the CAP. The Court of Auditors reckoned that about 5 or 6 billion pounds, or 10 per cent of the EU budget, was wasted each year and especially in the effect of 'lakes' and 'mountains' of surplus wine, butter and beef. Typical of these was the expenditure of £900 million per annum in supporting wine production which had produced a wine lake of 19 billion bottles, or four cases for every European! There have been several responses to this problem which have attracted just as much bad publicity.

1   *The sale of surpluses* at low prices or for alternative uses to markets outside the EU. So Brazilian cars have run on fuel produced from wine, and New Zealand women have daubed their lips with a derivative of EU surplus butter. Butter has been sold cheaply in the USSR (even then German businessmen profiteered by overcharging) and given away to people on state benefits.

2   *Methods designed to curb supply* by, for instance, 'set-aside' payments to farmers to divert land into alternative uses or out of production entirely, or to use production quotas as for dairy produce.

3   *Price reductions* are no longer beyond negotiation but the problem is that the issue of agricultural prices and farmers' income involves considerably more than the EU. Any overall reduction requires involvement in negotiations of all other major agricultural producers and needs to be related to the issue of world monetary and financial reform to stabilise exchange rates.

The real solution is to change the European agricultural structure, and this is occurring as the number of farmers falls and the levels of productivity rise. However, the incorporation of new, more backward economies could threaten this.

On the other hand, the solution could be brought about by natural forces, and especially by heat and drought. By the end of 1995 the world's worst food crisis for 20 years meant that stocks of grain had fallen dramatically and prices were rising to record heights. For the first time in 20 years the EU had stopped subsidising exports and started to tax them instead, and the proportion of land to be set aside by farmers was cut. The grain mountain had fallen from 33 million tons to 5.5 million tons in two years. The result was that pressure to reform the CAP had weakened.

(f) *Expansion into eastern Europe*

The entry of six central European states, the three Baltic republics and Slovenia as well as Cyprus and Malta would produce a union of 27 states with a population of 480 million. However, this has several fundamental implications for the EU.

1   *A massive increase in the CAP* and other regional and structural funds. Already 85 per cent of the EU budget is devoted to these purposes, and this would double. The high CAP prices could provoke a massive expansion of eastern European production which would not be compatible with the EU commitment to the General Agreement on Trade and Tariffs (GATT) of 1994. Since the richer member states will not pay for this the alternatives are to reform or abandon these policies which would produce all sorts of tensions and conflicts of interest between members.
2   *A major constitutional reconsideration* would be necessary and this would impel the EU towards political integration. The trigger would be the need to revise the voting weight of the larger countries. However, the smaller states will require more majority voting and more powers for the European Parliament in exchange, and this debate will produce a confrontation between the majority who want a more tightly integrated union and the minority, led by Britain, who want a looser union, the so-called 'fast track' and 'slow track'.

36.13 Conclusion: the ECU curtain

The problem of the EU and the security apparatus of Europe is the reaching of some sort of accommodation about the grey area between the states of western Europe and Russia, the countries looking towards the West but trapped by geography, politics and history. The old Iron Curtain of Churchill's speech in 1946 is gone but a new frontier is emerging. It is the function of the EU, NATO and the CSCE to manage the relationship between the countries of the East and the West. However, there are wide variations in economic development and political stability, with potential 'fast track' and 'slow track' candidates. The result is that a new line is emerging. Nor do the European powers and the USA have much time. The construction of a revised set of 'interlocking institutions' which will provide for the needs of the states of Europe and yet be acceptable to the sensibilities of the USA and Russia would take time anyhow, but time is limited and there are many possible flashpoints throughout eastern Europe which can test the strength of 'interlocking institutions' to breaking strain, as in Bosnia, and frustrate attempts to produce a co-ordinated response.

Question

1 Study source A and then answer the questions which follow.

Source A: Intervention in Afghanistan.

> Developments forced us to make a choice: we had either to bring in troops or let the Afghan revolution be defeated and the country turned into a kind of Shah's Iran. We decided to bring in the troops. It was not a simple decision to take. We weighed the pros and cons before taking it. We knew that the victory of counter-revolution and of religious zealots and revenge-seeking feudal lords would result in a bloodbath before which even the crimes of the Chilean junta would pale. We knew that the victory of counter-revolution would pave the way for massive American military presence in a country which borders on the Soviet Union and that this was a challenge to our country's security. We knew that the decision to bring in troops would not be popular in the modern world even if it was absolutely legal. But we also knew that we would have ceased to be a great power if we refrained from carrying the burden of taking unpopular but necessary decisions, extraordinary decisions prompted by extraordinary circumstances ... There are situations when non-intervention is a disgrace and a betrayal. Such a situation developed in Afghanistan. And when I hear the voices of protest from people who claim to be democrats, humanists and even revolutionaries, saying they are outraged by Soviet 'intervention' I tell them this: it is logic that prompted us. If you are against Soviet military aid to Afghanistan, then you are for the victory of counter-revolution. There is no third way.

(a) What was meant by the remark that Afghanistan could turn into 'a kind of Shah's Iran'?
(b) Why is this sort of journalism effective in swaying its readers?
(c) Do you think there was a 'third way'? Could the USSR have acted differently?
Source: A. Bavin, *Izvestia*, April 1980

Further reading

General

The best general introduction to the whole period is: Thomson, D., *Europe since Napoleon* (Penguin, 1966). There are also a number of good series available such as the Fontana *History of Europe* and Longman's *A General History of Europe*. The relevant volumes in these series are as follows:

Rudé, G., *Revolutionary Europe, 1783–1815* (Fontana, 1964).
Droz, J., *Europe between Revolutions, 1815–1848* (Fontana, 1967).
Grenville, J.A.S., *Europe Reshaped, 1848–1878* (Fontana, 1976).
Stone, N., *Europe Transformed, 1878–1919* (Fontana, 1983).
Wiskemann, E., *Europe of the Dictators, 1919–1945* (Fontana, 1966).

Ford, F.L., *Europe, 1780–1830* (Longman, 1967).
Hearder, H., *Europe in the Nineteenth Century, 1830–1880* (Longman, 1966).
Roberts, J., *Europe, 1880–1945* (Longman, 1967).

For more specialist subjects there are various contributions by expert authorities included in:
The *New Cambridge Modern History*, vols. IX–XII (Cambridge, 1957).
Cipolla, C.M. (ed.), *Fontana Economic History of Europe* (Fontana, 1963).

Other useful books of a general nature include:
Hinsley, F.H., *Power and the Pursuit of Peace* (Cambridge University Press, 1963).
Kennedy, P., *Strategy and Diplomacy 1870–1945* (Allen & Unwin, 1983).
Seaman, L.C.B., *From Vienna to Versailles* (Methuen, 1955).
Seton-Watson, H., *Nations and States* (Methuen, 1977).

Books of documentary extracts include:
Brooks, S., *Nineteenth Century Europe* (Macmillan, 1983).
Brown, R. and Daniels, C., *Twentieth Century Europe* (Macmillan, 1981).
Welch, D., *Modern European History, 1871–1975* (Heinemann, 1994).
The Longman *Seminar Studies in History* series provides excellent introductions to debates and documentary extracts on a wide variety of subjects.

Chapter 1

For French history in general the best source is:
Cobban, A., *A History of Modern France* (Penguin, 1965–6), 3 vols.

For the French Revolution a useful selection would be:
Blanning, T.C.W., *The French Revolutionary Wars* (Hodder & Stoughton, 1995).
Blanning, T.C.W., *The French Revolution: Aristocrats versus Bourgeois?* (Macmillan, 1987).
Goodwin, A., *The French Revolution* (Hutchinson, 1953).

Hampson, N., *A Social History of the French Revolution* (Routledge, 1963).
Price, R., *A Concise History of France* (Cambridge, 1992).
Rayner, E.G. and Stapley, R.F., *The French Revolution* (Hodder & Stoughton, 1995).
Rudé, G., *The Crowd in the French Revolution* (Oxford, 1959).
Rudé, G., *Interpretations of the French Revolution* (Historical Association pamphlet, 1961).
Shennan, J.H., *France before the Revolution* (Routledge, Lancaster Pamphlets, 1995).
Temple, N., *The Road to 1789: From Reform to Revolution in France* (University of Wales, 1992).
Thompson, J.M., *The French Revolution* (Blackwell, 1943).
Townson, D., *France in Revolution* (Hodder & Stoughton, 1990).
Wright, D.G., *Revolution and Terror in France, 1789–1795* (Longman, 1974).

Chapter 2

Barnett, D., *Bonaparte* (Allen & Unwin, 1978).
Best, G., *War and Society in Revolutionary Europe* (Fontana, 1982).
Ellis, G., *The Napoleonic Empire* (Macmillan, 1991).
Geyl, P., *Napoleon: For and Against* (Cape, 1949).
Markham, F.M.H., *Napoleon and the Awakening of Europe* (Weidenfeld & Nicolson, 1954).
Stiles, A., *Napoleon, France and Europe* (Hodder & Stoughton, 1993).
Thompson, J.M., *Napoleon Bonaparte: His Rise and Fall* (Blackwell, 1952).
Woolf, S., *Napoleon's Integration of Europe* (Routledge, 1991).
Wright, D.G., *Napoleon and Europe* (Longman, 1954).

Chapter 3

Hobsbawm, E.J., *The Age of Revolution: Europe 1789–1848* (Weidenfeld & Nicolson, 1962).
Kissinger, H., *A World Restored* (Gollancz, 1973).
Sked, A. (ed.), *Europe's Balance of Power, 1815–1848* (Macmillan, 1979).
Walker, M. (ed.), *Metternich's Europe* (Macmillan, 1948).
Webster, C.K., *The Congress of Vienna, 1814–1815* (Bell, 1919).

Chapter 4

Gildea, R., *Barricades and Borders* (Oxford, 1987).
Hobsbawm, E.J., *The Age of Revolution, Europe 1789–1848* (Weidenfeld & Nicolson, 1962).
Jones, P., *The 1848 Revolutions* (Longman, 1981).
Kohn, H., *Nationalism: its Meaning and History* (Anvil Books, 1955).
Schenk, R.G., *The Mind of the European Romantics* (Constable, 1966).
Stearns, P.N., *The Revolutions of 1848* (Weidenfeld & Nicolson, 1974).
Talmon, J.L., *Romanticism and Revolt, Europe 1815–48* (Thames & Hudson, 1967).

Chapter 5

Bury, J.P.T., *France, 1814–1940* (Methuen, 1954).
Lough, J., *An Introduction to Nineteenth Century France* (Longman, 1978).
Randell, K., *France: Monarchy, Republic and Empire* (Hodder & Stoughton, 1991).
Magraw, R., *France 1815–1914: The Bourgeois Century* (Fontana, 1983).
Woodward, E.L., *French Revolutions* (Oxford 1934).

Chapter 6

There are several general histories of Italy. These include:
Carrie, R.A., *Italy from Napoleon to Mussolini* (Columbia, 1950).
Duggan, C., *A Concise History of Italy* (Cambridge, 1994).
Mack Smith, D., *The Making of Italy, 1796–1866* (Macmillan, 1968).

Woolf, S., *A History of Italy, 1700–1860* (Methuen, 1979).

On the 'idealistic' period of the Risorgimento there are not so many books in English. There are several on Mazzini, including:

Griffith, G.O., *Mazzini: Prophet of Modern Europe* (Hodder & Stoughton, 1932).
Hales, E.E.Y., *Mazzini and the Secret Societies: The Making of a Myth* (Eyre & Spottiswoode, 1956).
Riall, L., *The Italian Risorgimento* (Routledge, 1994).

Chapter 7

There are numerous general histories of Germany. These include:

Fulbrook, M., *A Concise History of Germany* (Cambridge, 1991).
Mann, G., *The History of Germany since 1789* (Chatto & Windus, 1968).
Martel, G., *Modern Germany Reconsidered, 1870–1945* (Routledge, 1992).
Ramm, A., *Germany 1789–1918* (Methuen, 1967).
Sagarra, E., *An Introduction to Nineteenth Century Germany* (Longman, 1980).
Taylor, A.J.P., *The Course of German History* (Methuen, 1969).

A selection should also include:

Hamerow, T.S., *Restoration, Revolution, Reaction: Economics and Politics in Germany, 1815–1871* (Princeton, 1958).
Henderson, W.O., *The Zollverein* (Cambridge, 1939).
Kohn, H., *The Mind of Germany* (Macmillan, 1965).

Chapter 8

There is a handful of general histories readily available. These include:

Bridge, F.R., *The Habsburg Monarchy among the Great Powers, 1815–1918* (Berg, 1991).
Macartney, C.A., *The Habsburg Monarchy, 1809–1918* (Hamish Hamilton, 1941).

In addition Hungarian nationalism is covered by:

Barany, G., *Stephen Szecheny and the Awakening of Hungarian Nationalism, 1791–1841* (Princeton, 1968).
Macartney, G.A., *Hungary: A Short History* (Edinburgh, 1962).

Chapter 9

Deak, I., *The Lawful Revolution* (Columbia, 1979).
Fetjo, F. (ed.), *The Opening of an Era: 1848, An Historical Symposium* (Wingate, 1948).
Kranzberg, M., *1848: A Turning Point?* (Heath, 1959).
Namier, L., *The Revolution of the Intellectuals* (Oxford, 1948).
Price, R., *The Revolutions of 1848* (Macmillan, 1988).
Robertson, P., *Revolutions of 1848: A Social Study* (Harper & Row, 1952).
Sperber, J., *The European Revolutions, 1848–1851* (Cambridge, 1994).
Stearns, P.N., *The Revolutions of 1848* (Weidenfeld & Nicolson, 1974).

Chapter 10

The general histories of Russia include the following:

Freeborn, R., *A Short History of Modern Russia* (Hodder & Stoughton, 1966).
Kochan, L., *The Making of Modern Russia* (Pelican, 1963).
Sherman, R., *Russia, 1815–81* (Hodder & Stoughton, 1991).
Summer, B.H., *Survey of Russian History* (Methuen, 1961).
Westwood, J.N., *Endurance and Endeavour: Russian History 1812–1971* (Oxford, 1973).

The reforms of Alexander II are dealt with by:

Mosse, W.E., *Alexander II and the Modernisation of Russia* (English Universities Press, 1958).

Chapter 11

Anderson, M.S., *The Eastern Question, 1774–1923* (Macmillan, 1966).
Crawley, M., *Greek Independence, 1823–1833* (Cambridge, 1955).
Gooch, B.D., *The Origins of the Crimean War* (Heath, 1969).
Hibbert, C., *The Destruction of Lord Raglan* (Longman, 1961).

Chapter 12

Bury, J.P.T., *Napoleon III and the Second Empire* (English Universities Press, 1964).
Gooch, G.P., *The Second Empire* (Longman, 1960).
McMillan, J.E., *Napoleon III* (Longman, 1991).
Simpson, F.A., *Louis Napoleon and the Recovery of France* (Longman, 1965).
Smith, W.H.C., *Second Empire and Commune: France, 1848–1871* (Longman, 1985).
Zeldin, T., *The Political System of Napoleon III* (Macmillan, 1958).
Zeldin, T., *Emile Ollivier and the Liberal Empire of Napoleon III* (Oxford, 1963).

Chapter 13

Beales, D., *The Risorgimento and the Unification of Italy* (Allen & Unwin, 1971).
Coppa, F.J., *Origins of the Italian Wars of Independence* (Longman, 1992).
Gooch, J., *The Unification of Italy* (Routledge, Lancaster Pamphlets, 1986).
Hearder, H., *Cavour* (Basil Blackwell, Historical Association Pamphlets, 1972).
Mack Smith, D., *Cavour and Garibaldi 1860* (Cambridge, 1954).
Mack Smith, D., *Victor Emmanuel, Cavour and the Risorgimento* (Oxford, 1971).
Ramm, A., *The Risorgimento* (Historical Association, 1972).
Riall, L., *The Italian Risorgimento* (Routledge, 1994).
Ridley, J., *Garibaldi* (Constable, 1974).
Stiles, A., *The Unification of Italy* (Hodder & Stoughton, 1989).

Chapter 14

Abrams, L., *Bismarck and the German Empire, 1871–1918* (Routledge, Lancaster Pamphlets Series, 1995).
Eyck, E., *Bismarck and the German Empire* (Allen & Unwin, 1950).
Medlicott, W.N., *Bismarck and Modern Germany* (Athlone Press, 1965).
Pflanze, O., *Bismarck and the Development of Germany* (Princeton, 1963).
Stiles, A., *The Unification of Germany, 1815–1890* (Hodder & Stoughton, 1989).
Taylor, A.J.P., *Bismarck: The Man and the Statesman* (Hamish Hamilton, 1955).
Waller, B., *Bismarck and Germany, 1862–1890* (Longman, 1986).

Chapter 15

Betts, R., *The False Dawn: European Imperialism in the Nineteenth Century* (Oxford 1976).
Fieldhouse, D.K., *The Colonial Empires: A Comparative Survey from the Eighteenth Century* (London, 1966).
Fieldhouse, D.K., *The Theory of Capitalist Imperialism* (Longman, 1967).
Fieldhouse, D.K., *Economics and Empire* (Weidenfeld & Nicolson, 1973).
Fieldhouse, D.K., *Colonialism 1870–1945* (London, 1981).
Gallacher, J.A. and Robinson, R.E., *Africa and the Victorians* (Macmillan, 1961).
Hobsbawm, E.J., *The Age of Empire, 1870–1914* (London, 1987).
Kiernan, V., *European Empires from Conquest to Collapse* (Fontana, 1984).
Louis, W.R., *Imperialism: The Robinson and Gallagher Controversy* (New York, 1976).
Mackenzie, J., *The Partition of Africa* (Routledge, Lancaster Pamphlets, 1983).
Owen, R. and Sutcliffe, R., *Studies in the Theory of Imperialism* (Longman, 1972).
Porter, B., *The Lion's Share: A Short History of British Imperialsim, 1850–1970* (Longman, 1984).

Porter, B., *European Imperialism, 1860–1945* (Macmillan, 1994).
Wehler, H., *The German Empire, 1871–1918* (Berg, 1984).

Chapter 16

Langer, W.L., *European Alliances and Alignments* (American Book Supply Co., 1943).
Medlicott, W.N., *The Congress of Berlin and After* (Methuen, 1938).
Taylor, A.J.P., *The Struggle for Mastery in Europe, 1848–1918* (Oxford, 1954).
Waller, B., *Bismarck at the Crossroads* (Athlone Press, 1974).

Chapter 17

Mack Smith, D., *Italy: A Modern History* (Ann Arbor, 1959).
Salamone, A.W., *Italy from the Risorgimento to Fascism* (David & Charles, 1970).
Seton-Watson, C., *Italy from Liberalism to Fascism* (Methuen, 1976).

Chapter 18

The biographies of Bismarck can be supplemented with:
Balfour, M., *The Kaiser and His Times* (Penguin, 1975).
Berghahn, V.R., *Germany and the Approach of War in 1914* (Macmillan, 1993).
Craig, G., *Germany, 1866–1945* (Oxford, 1978).
Evans, R.J. (ed.), *Society and Politics in Wilhelmine Germany* (Croom Helm, 1978).
Kohut, T., *Wilhelm II and the Germans* (Oxford, 1991).

Chapter 19

Bury, J.P.T., *France, 1814–1940* (Methuen, 1954).
Bury, J.P.T., *Gambetta and the Making of the Third Republic* (Harvard University Press, 1967).
Chapman, G., *The Third Republic of France, 1871–1894* (Longman, 1962), Vol. 1.
Johnson, D., *The Dreyfus Affair* (Blandford, 1966).
Randell, K., *The Third Republic, 1870–1914* (Hodder & Stoughton, 1991)

Chapter 20

Kochan, L., *The Making of Modern Russia* (Jonathan Cape, 1962).
Lynch, M., *Reaction and Revolutions: Russia, 1881–1924* (Hodder & Stoughton, 1992).
Seton-Watson, H., *The Decline of Imperial Russia* (Methuen, 1952).
Shub, D., *Lenin* (Pelican, 1966).
Wolfe, B.D., *Three who made a Revolution* (Penguin, 1956).

Chapter 21

Crankshaw, E., *The Fall of the House of Hapsburg* (Longman, 1963).
Jenks, W.A., *Austria under the Iron Ring, 1879–1893* (Virginia, 1965).
May, A.J., *The Habsburg Monarchy, 1867–1914* (Harvard University Press, 1965).
Mason, J.W., *The Dissolution of the Austro-Hungarian Empire, 1867–1918* (Longman, 1985).
Pelling, N., *The Habsburg Empire* (Hodder & Stoughton, 1995).

Chapter 22

Evans, R.J.W. and Strandmann, H.P. von (eds), *The Coming of the First World War* (Oxford, 1988).
Henig, R., *The Origins of the First World War* (Routledge, Lancaster Pamphlets, 1993).
Remak, J., *The Origins of World War 1, 1871–1914* (Holt, Rinehardt & Winston, 1967).
Schmidt, B.E., *The Origins of the First World War* (Historical Association, 1958).

Turner, L.C.F., *The Coming of the First World War* (Warne, 1968).

Chapter 23

The First World War:
Ferro, M., *The Great War* (Routledge & Kegan Paul, 1987).
Taylor, A.J.P., *The First World War* (Hamish Hamilton, 1963).
Turner L.C.F., *The First World War* (Warne, 1967).

The impact of the war:
Carsten, F.L., *Revolution in Central Europe* (Temple Smith, 1972).
Ferro, M., *The Russian Revolution of February 1917* (Routledge, 1972).
Ferro, M., *October 1917* (Routledge, 1979).
Hill, C.E., *Lenin and the Russian Revolution* (English Universities Press, 1947).
Laver, J., *Russia, 1914–41* (Hodder & Stoughton, 1991).
Marwick, A. (ed.), *Total War and Social Change* (Macmillan, 1988).
Nicolson, H., *Peacemaking, 1919* (Methuen, 1964).
Pares, B., *The Fall of the Russian Monarchy* (Vintage Books, 1961).
Sharp, A., *The Versailles Settlement: Peacemaking in Paris, 1919* (Macmillan, 1991).
White, J.D., *The Russian Revolution, 1917–1921* (Hodder & Stoughton, 1994).
Wood, A., *The Russian Revolution* (Longman, 1978).
Wood, A., *The Origins of the Russian Revolution* (Routledge, Lancaster Pamphlets, 1993).
Zerman, Z.A.B., *The Break-Up of the Habsburg Empire, 1914–1918* (Oxford, 1944).

Chapter 24

Dexter, B., *The Years of Opportunity* (Viking, 1967).
Gathorne-Hardy, G.M., *A Short History of International Affairs, 1920–1939* (Oxford, 1950).
Gilbert, M., *Britain and Germany between the Wars* (Longman, 1964).
Henig, R., *Versailles and After, 1919–1933* (Routledge, 1984).
Northedge, F.S., *The League of Nations* (Leicester, 1988).
Walters, F.P., *History of the League of Nations* (Royal Institute of International Affairs, 1951), 2 vols.

Chapter 25

Carr, H., *A History of Soviet Russia* (Penguin, 1950–64), 7 vols.
Conquest, R., *The Great Purge* (Macmillan, 1969).
Deutscher, I., *Stalin* (Oxford, 1949).
Deutscher, I., *Trotsky* (Oxford, 1954–63), 3 vols.
Gill, G., *Stalinism* (Macmillan, 1990).
Ward, C., *Stalin's Russia* (Routledge, 1993).

Chapter 26

Bayne-Jardine, C.C., *Mussolini and Italy* (Longman, 1966).
Blinkhorn, M., *Mussolini and Fascist Italy* (Routledge, Lancaster Pamphlets Series, 1994).
Fermi, L., *Mussolini* (Chicago, 1961).
Hibbert, C., *Benito Mussolini* (Longman, 1962).
Morgan, P., *Italian Fascism, 1919–1945* (Macmillan, 1995).

Chapter 27

Bullock, A., *Hitler: A Study in Tyranny* (Odhams, 1952).
Carsten, F.O., *The Rise of Fascism* (Batsford, 1967).
Elliott, B.J., *Hitler and Germany* (Longman, 1966).
Eyck, E., *The Weimar Republic* (Harvard, 1962–4).

Fest, J., *The Face of the Third Reich* (Weidenfeld & Nicolson, 1970).
Geary, R., *Hitler and Nazism* (Routledge, Lancaster Pamphlets Series, 1993).
Hiden, J.W., *The Weimar Republic* (Longman, 1974).
Kershaw, I., *The Nazi Dictatorship* (Edward Arnold, 1985).
Laver, J., *Nazi Germany, 1933–45* (Hodder & Stoughton, 1991).
Laver, J., *Hitler* (Hodder & Stoughton, 1995).
Nicholls, A.J., *Weimar and the Rise of Hitler* (Macmillan, 1991).
Shirer, W.L., *The Rise and Fall of the Third Reich* (Secker, 1960).
Williamson, D.G., *The Third Reich* (Longman, 1982).

Chapter 28

Gelber, H.G., *The Coming of the Second World War* (Warne, 1967).
Gilbert, M., *The Roots of Appeasement* (Weidenfeld & Nicolson, 1966).
Henig, R., *The Origins of the Second World War, 1933–39* (Routledge, Lancaster Pamphlets Series, 1985).
Hiden, J.W., *Germany and Europe, 1919–1939* (Longman, 1977).
Rayner, E.G., *The Great Dictators* (Hodder & Stoughton, 1992).
Robbins, K., *Appeasement* (Basil Blackwell, Historical Association Pamphlets, 1988).
Taylor, A.J.P., *The Origins of the Second World War* (Hamish Hamilton, 1961).
Thomas, H., *The Spanish Civil War* (Penguin, 1961).
Wheeler-Bennett, J.W., *Munich* (Macmillan, 1948).
Wiskemann, E., *Europe of the Dictators, 1919–1945* (Fontana, 1966).

Chapter 29

Calvacoressi, P. and Wint, J., *Total War: Causes and Course of the Second World War* (Pelican, 1968).
Churchill, W.S., *The Second World War* (Cassell, 1948–54).
Falls, C., *The Second World War: A Short History* (Methuen, 1948).
Shirer, W.L., *The Collapse of the Third Republic* (Heinemann, 1970).
Werth, A., *Russia at War* (Barrie & Rockliff, 1963).
Wilmot, C., *The Struggle in Europe* (Fontana, 1959).
Wright, G., *The Ordeal of Total War, 1939–45* (Harper & Row, 1968).

Chapter 30

Ball, S., *The Cold War* (Hodder & Stoughton, 1995).
Fleming, D.F., *The Cold War and its Origins* (Allen & Unwin, 1961), 2 vols.
Lane, P., *Europe since 1945* (Batsford, 1985).
Laver, J., *Joseph Stalin* (Hodder & Stoughton, 1993).
Leffler, M.P. and Painter, D.S., *The Origins of the Cold War* (Routledge, 1994).
McCauley, M., *Communist Power in Europe, 1944–1949* (Macmillan, 1979).
McCauley, M., *The Origins of the Cold War* (Longman, 1983).
McInnis, E., Hiscocks, R. and Spencer, R., *The Shaping of Post-War Germany* (Dent, 1960).
Rayner, E.G., *The Cold War* (Hodder & Stoughton, 1992).
Wood, A., *Stalin and Stalinism* (Routledge, Lancaster Pamphlets Series, 1990).
Yergin, D., *Shattered Peace: The Origins of the Cold War and the National Security State* (Penguin, 1990).

Chapter 31

Betts, R., *France and Decolonisation* (Macmillan, 1991).
Chamberlain, M.E., *Decolonisation: The Fall of European Empires* (Basil Blackwell, Historical Association Pamphlets, 1985).
Darwin, J., *Britain and Decolonisation: The Retreat from Empire in the Post-War World* (Macmillan, 1988).

Hargreaves, J.D., *Decolonisation in Africa* (Longman, 1988).
Holland, R.F., *European Decolonisation, 1918–1981* (Macmillan, 1985).
Wilson, H.S., *African Decolonisation* (Edward Arnold, 1994).

Chapter 32

Balfour, M., *West Germany* (Croom Helm, 1982).
Daltrop, A., *Politics and the European Community* (Longman, 1982).
Grosser, A., *The Western Alliance* (Macmillan, 1980).
Mowat, R.C., *Creating the European Community* (Blandford, 1973).
Urwin, W., *Western Europe since 1945* (Longman, 1968).
Werth, A., *De Gaulle* (Penguin, 1965).

Chapter 33

Ash, T.G., *Polish Revolution* (Cape, 1983).
Bialev, S., *Stalin's Successors* (Cambridge, 1980).
Brown, J.F., *The New Eastern Europe* (Praeger, 1966).
Childs, D., *The GDR: Moscow's German Ally* (Allen & Unwin, 1983).
Cohen, S.F., Rabinowitch, A. and Sharlet, R., *The Soviet Union since Stalin* (Macmillan, 1980).
Lewis, P.G., *Central Europe since 1945* (Longman, 1994).
Lomax, B., *Hungary, 1956* (Alison & Busby, 1976).
Remington, R.A., *The Warsaw Pact* (Massachusetts Institute of Technology, 1971).
Silber, L. and Little, A., *The Death of Yugoslavia* (Penguin, 1995).
Wilson, D., *Tito's Yugoslavia* (Cambridge, 1979).

Chapter 34

Armstrong, D. and Goldstein E. (eds), *The End of the Cold War* (Frank Cass, 1990).
Daniels, R.V., *The End of the Communist Revolution* (Routledge, 1993).
Hosking, G., *The Awakening of the Soviet Union* (Heinemann, 1990).
James, H. and Stone, M., *When the Wall Came Down* (Routledge, 1993).
Rothschild, J., *Return to Diversity* (Oxford, 1993).
Swain, G. and Swain, N., *Eastern Europe since 1945* (Macmillan, 1993).
Turner, H.A., *Germany from Partition to Reunification* (Yale, 1992).
Walker, R., *Six Years that Shook the World* (Manchester University Press, 1993).

Chapter 35

Johnstone, D., *The Politics of Euromissiles* (Verso, 1984).
Nash, H.T., *Nuclear Weapons and International Behaviour* (Sidjhoff-Leyden, 1975).
Newhouse, J., *Cold Dawn* (Holt, Rinehart & Winston, 1973).
Sheehan, M., *The Arms Race* (Martin Robertson, 1983).

Chapter 36

Feld, W., *The European Community in World Affairs* (Westview Press, 1976).
Fitzmaurice, J., *The European Parliament* (Penguin, 1979).
Herman, V. and Lodge, J., *The European Parliament and the European Community* (Macmillan, 1978).
Nelson, B., Roberts, D. and Veit, W. (eds), *The European Community in the 1990s* (Berg, 1992).
Pinder, J., *European Community: The Building of a Union* (Oxford, 1991).
Silber, L. and Little, A., *The Death of Yugoslavia* (Penguin, 1995).
Urwin, D. and Paterson, W., *Politics in Western Europe Today* (Longman, 1990).

Index